AFRO / POLIS

CITY
MEDIA
ART

AFRO / POLIS

CITY
MEDIA
ART

edited by
Kerstin Pinther
Larissa Förster
Christian Hanussek

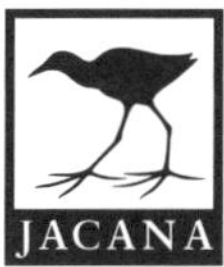
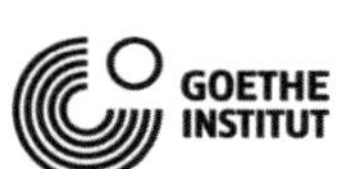
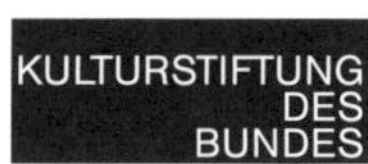
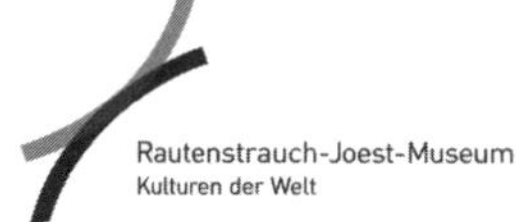

Cairo

Lagos

Nairobi

Kinshasa

Johannesburg

ARTISTS/PROJECTS

ARTISTS/PROJECTS

ARTISTS/PROJECTS

Preface

In this catalogue, we learn from the field studies of the Kenyan scholar Dr Mbugua wa Mungai that *matatu,* the generic name for the hundreds of thousands of Toyota minibuses careering at full speed through the streets of Nairobi, is derived from the local word for "thirty cents". In the 1950s when suburban commuter traffic in *matatu* minibuses took off, that was the price of a trip between downtown Nairobi and its suburbs. Today, without the daily, affordable urban mobility provided by the privately run *matatu* minibuses, local passenger traffic in Kenya's capital would grind to a halt. Yet the *matatus* are much more than just that. They are colourful marvels of design, whose monikers as "Joker", "Matrix" or "Marlboro" provide multi-faceted references to global popular culture; they are booming sound boxes for local underground rappers, the meeting point for young men and women on the way to work and school, a distribution hub for stories of life in an African metro-polis – in brief, the *matatus* are the cultural manifestations of a progressive urbani-sation influencing the reality of everyday urbanite life in such African metropolises as Nairobi.

Over recent years, the theory of megacities has experienced an important shift of emphasis. Aside from the accepted statistic-based analyses of urban infrastruc-ture, the focus is increasingly on informal urban processes. This shift is connected with a change in research perspective. We know from United Nations reports that since 2007, for the first time in human history over half the world's population, at present 6,5 billion, live in cities. We also know that, as a result of Africa's demo-graphics, these epochal urbanisation processes are especially marked in the metropolises there. But to understand the concomitant transformation processes better, the *Afropolis* project leaves the macro-political level of statistics and devel-opment scenarios to explore the level of social networks and cultural relations shaping life in African megacities.

The project focuses on five cities: Cairo, Lagos, Nairobi, Kinshasa and Johannes-burg. Scholars and artists set out on a process of cultural fieldwork and research in these five cities, meeting local cultural practitioners, carrying out interviews, compiling photo and film documentation, selecting and in some cases initiating artistic works voicing the very particular qualities of each *Afropolis* from, for example, *matatu* mobility and Slum-TV in Nairobi to soundscapes and a library of contemporary cultural theory in Lagos, or futuristic urban views in Kinshasa, a building's changing biography and the symbolic appropriation of the World Cup 2010 in Johannesburg, and young design and the struggle over public space in Cairo.

The histories of *Afropolis* cannot be shaped into a linear narrative. They deal with different things than the figures on population development and the growth of poverty. They have little in common with the usual negative clichés of the African continent. As one contributor to the catalogue confidently notes: "In other words, instead of regarding the urban poor and excluded urbanites as the problem, we can recognise the energies and ingenuity that they marshal to retain a foothold in the city despite the odds" (S.35). And what does that recognition involve? It entails grasping the role of urbanites as the self-willed producers of urban life; developing a better understanding of the significance of social networks and informal processes in cities; gaining a vivid picture of African cities based on both artistic as well as on scholarly views; and not least contrasting current urban development in Germany and Europe – in particular the experience of shrinking cities and migration – with the wealth of urban strategies in the growing African metropolises.

In its 'Art and the City' programme, the Kulturstiftung des Bundes (German Federal Cultural Foundation) engaged intensively with the meaning of urban transformation for modern societies. It focused on the phenomenon of "shrinking cities" in Western industrial countries just as much as on the informal structures in urban development, looking at Caracas in detail as an example. The *Afropolis* project will have a leading place in the group of research projects developed around this topic. We are very glad to provide funding for this project and would like to thank Prof. Dr Klaus Schneider as the Director of the Rautenstrauch-Joest-Museum – Cultures of the World, the RJM's Curator of the African Department Dr Clara Himmelheber, and in particular the curatorial team for successfully realising this project – Prof. Dr Kerstin Pinther, Dr Larissa Förster and Christian Hanussek, as well as the Iwalewa House in Bayreuth, the Goethe-Institutes in Nairobi and Johannesburg and all the scholars and artists involved. It is our sincere hope that the Afro-European cooperation developed in the course of this project will continue to bear fruit in future.

Kulturstiftung   Hortensia Völckers   Alexander Farenholtz
des Bundes   Executive Board/Artistic Director   Executive Board/Administrative Director

Translation from German by Andrew Boreham

Foreword

Since the 1990s, the exhibition programme developed by the Rautenstrauch-Joest-Museum – Cultures of the World has firmly included positions of contemporary art from Africa, either as solo shows for individual artists (e.g. Soly Cissé, Senegal, 1999; Amouzou Glipka, Togo, 2000) or as themed exhibitions such as *Sexuality and Death – Aids in contemporary African art* (2004), which showcased twenty artists from eleven African countries. With the opening of our new museum in October 2010, we are continuing this series by dedicating our first project to the diverse art scenes in major African cities. Over the last twenty years, each of these cities has developed a quite specific and exceptionally dynamic art scene, often with a particular emphasis on the theme of the city and urbanity.

We are often asked why contemporary art from Africa is shown in an ethnological museum which, by definition, focuses on cultural history. As in other parts of the world, artists in Africa and the Diaspora are exploring pressing questions about life today. Through their artistic works, they can reflect on these concerns in a way that is sometimes freer and more critical than is possible, for example, in scholarly work. The new Rautenstrauch-Joest-Museum seeks to connect historical and current issues, for example, by contextualising the historical holdings of its collection to create contemporary references to today's globalised world. The idea for and conceptual design of *Afropolis. City, Media, Art* was developed by Kerstin Pinther, who teaches African art and visual culture at the Department of Art History at the Freie Universität Berlin. Supported by the RJM's Curator of the African DepartmentClara Himmelheber, the exhibition design was expanded to create the first special exhibition for the RJM's new building. The Afropolis exhibition was curated by Kerstin Pinther, cultural anthropologist Larissa Förster from Cologne, and Christian Hanussek, an artist and curator from Berlin. I would like to thank all three curators – as well as project assistant Annabelle Springer and the curatorial assistants Clara Giacalone and Ulrike Nestler – for their exceptional level of commitment. Such a comprehensive project as this lives from the enthusiasm of all those involved!

Close cooperation with the artists, curators and scholars from the participating cities was one major and defining feature of both the exhibition and the project. Without their keen support, the exhibition and catalogue could not have been realised in this innovative form. The original catalogue may well become a standard work on this topic in Germany, not least because of the key scholarly essays on African cities it contains which, through the translations from English, have become accessible to a German-speaking audience for the first time. Similarly, the

English translation of the catalogue also makes German scholarly work on the topic available to a broader readership.

The exhibition and German version of the catalogue were made possible by the generous funding of the German Federal Cultural Foundation. Here, I would especially like to thank Hortensia Völckers and Alexander Fahrenholtz of the Executive Board of the German Federal Cultural Foundation for their valuable support. In spring 2010, the Goethe-Institut in Nairobi presented a preview of this exhibition topic, and I would also like to particularly thank Johannes Hossfeld, Institute Director, for his commitment and financial support. My thanks also go to the Goethe-Institut in Johannesburg, in particular Director Katharina von Ruckteschell-Katte and Peter Anders, then Head of the Cultural Programmes, for their financial assistance, above all in developing some of the new artistic works. The German Federal Foreign Office (AA) also supported the Rautenstrauch-Joest-Museum as part of its 'Action Africa' programme. From the start, the Iwalewa House in Bayreuth was a partner for a planned further venue for the exhibition, and our thanks go to Tobias Wendl and his successor Ulf Vierke for their support. Finally, I would like to thank the Franke | Steinert office and the graphic artist Katrin Erl for the exhibition and catalogue design, the Walther König publishing house for the production of the original German version of the catalogue, and Jacana Media, and in particular Russell Clarke, for the production of the English version. The English version of the catalogue was made possible by the generous funding of the Goethe-Institut in Johannesburg and the enthusiasm of its Director Katharina von Ruckteschell-Katte and its current Head of Programmes Lien Heidenreich.

Prof. Dr Klaus Schneider
RJM Director

Translation from German by Andrew Boreham

Words of Welcome

1 AbdouMaliq Simone 2004, People as Infrastructure: Intersecting Fragments in Johannesburg, *Public Culture* 16/3 Johannesburg – The Elusive Metropolis, edited by Achille Mbembe and Sarah Nuttall, p. 407–429, here p. 407; reprinted in this catalogue, see p. 38

"African cities are characterised by incessantly flexible, mobile and provisional intersections of residents that operate without clearly delineated notions of how the city is to be inhabited and used."[1]

Metropolises often evoke images of flashy high-rise buildings, permanent background noise, backed-up cars and people moving quickly in all directions in their masses. New York, Tokyo, London, Peking, São Paulo. But what about Cairo? Lagos? Nairobi? Kinshasa? Johannesburg? How are African metropolises perceived? It was indeed an interesting undertaking for the curators of the *Afropolis* exhibition and the editors of this publication to examine Africa's major cities under a microscope. The image of these cities that emerged could hardly be more diverse or multifaceted. Now dubbed *Afropolis,* it is clear that African metropolises are entirely different from their counterparts in the north. Their state of constant flux and shifting occupancy, the new definition of urban spaces is a feature of all of them. In short: *Afropolises* are places that, in the context of the new age of globalisation, are blending their postcolonial structures with postmodern influences and ultimately also supplanting them. The result is new ideas, new realms of imagination, new hopes and new cultural spaces that defy comparison with others the world has to offer. The African major city, the African metropolis per se, does not exist, however. Each city, individual to the core, gives birth to new structures, new architectural and sociocultural forms that make Lagos, Lagos and Nairobi, Nairobi.

The Goethe-Institut is interested in these metamorphoses, in what these spaces generate from a cultural and artistic perspective because it is precisely in this generation that the Institute wishes to participate, to start projects in these spaces where innovation and cultural dialogue arise. The new definitions of public spaces, of new architectonic forms, and of innovative designs that develop from these encounters are fields to which and in which the Goethe-Institut wants to contribute and jointly create projects. The new is born from the exchange of African requirements and finds expression in the diversity of ways in which spaces are used differently, in how cultural traditions are reshaped into something new, or in how new formats of exchange, of artistic expression or even new audiences originate.

Afropolis, represented here, is already history, yet, the selected artists and their works point towards the future, herald change and anticipate the constant reshaping. In this context we cannot refer to development in the 'Western' sense; rather, this has more to do with changes that might even give direction to global development. No one knows for sure, but the possibility exists.

Afropolis – the African major city – is therefore of interest to us all. These *Afropolises* will give rise to the future: economic potential, social change, artistic innovation. The Goethe-Institut's projects in sub-Saharan Africa in the domain of the city and public space – including, for example, the production of a short-film series on African metropolises – will carry this study on *Afropolis* forward. And even these short films will only be able to show snapshots of cities that change with every second that passes. The people in these cities are constantly on the move and move the city along with them.

Afropolis – the exhibition and this publication – are also only snapshots in time and reveal a moment that represents enormous cultural potential, innovative developments and above all, a hopeful future.

The Goethe-Institut has had the publication *Afropolis* translated into English because this makes an important contribution to the discussion around African metropolises – particularly around their artistic developments – and, in this way, is made accessible to a wider readership.

I would like to seize this opportunity to thank the editors and Jacana Media for the wonderful partnership that has made this publication possible.

Katharina von Ruckteschell
Goethe-Institut Regional Director for sub-Sahara Africa

In Afropolis

KERSTIN PINTHER, LARISSA FÖRSTER
AND CHRISTIAN HANUSSEK

How do you curate an exhibition on African megacities? What sort of approach do you use? Whether in exhibitions, films or essays, representations of Africa are often viewed with mistrust; there are questions about the image of the continent they depict and whether the authors have any right to represent Africa at all. Such reservations come from a long history of often transgressive and ideological definitions on how and what Africa is that stem from both outside and inside the continent. For the colonial powers, disseminating a particular image of Africa was not merely a means to justify their actions. Instead, their picture of Africa as a continent which, by European standards, needed to be 'developed' was a vital plank in their political and economic identity as modern states. The diverse concepts of Pan-Africanism, Afrocentrism and the African Renaissance, especially as developed by the African diaspora in European and US cities, drew a picture of the continent reflecting their own particular ideologies. In common with the images of Africa forged in Europe, they defined the continent as solely rural, with static art forms rooted in traditional life. The 'one tribe-one style' paradigm[1], where style supposedly corresponds to ethnicity, grew out of the notion of Africans as representatives of rural ethnic communities. It was not until after a paradigm shift in the late 1990s that non-Western metropolises in general, and African cities in particular, ceased to be described in terms of shortcomings. Now, they were perceived as possible role models for the development of future cities.[2] At the same time, the demographics and prognoses of global urbanisation processes similarly shifted the focus to *Afropolis* – cities in Africa.

Nowadays, over half the world's population live in cities. But while in some regions, cities are shrinking, above all in Europe and in certain parts of America, the countries of the Global South are undergoing rapid urbanisation. There are around 30 megacities in the world. The Western industrialised countries only account for four of them – London, Paris, New York and Los Angeles. All of the others are located in Latin America, Asia and Africa. The urban populations on the African continent are growing by over four per cent each year – the highest global rates of urbanisation, occurring especially in medium-sized cities. In this context, specific urban topographies and cultures have evolved that are notably different from European-American models of urban development. According to Rem Koolhaas[3], an all-over urbanisation has completely changed the concepts and ideas of what defines urbanity. In a phase where the future of Western cities is uncertain, attention turns to possible alternative city models and this ultimately leads to the question of how to think about, describe and present African cities – urban centres whose spectrum stretches from such small conurbations as Tamale or Lubumbashi to million cities like Ouagadougou and Kampala to such megalopolises as Lagos or Cairo. But it is not only the diversity of the cities that makes it difficult to find suitable modes of representation and theorisation. In many respects, the urban practices and topographies of the cities, which are – at least from the perspective of European-American models of urban development – unusual and innovative, can themselves hardly be subsumed under traditional urban research notions and parameters. How should one approach a city like Kinshasa which, despite its vast size, has almost no scheduled flights and whose airport now resembles nothing short of a local train station? How can you locate the Kibera neighbourhood in Nairobi if it is not even marked on the official city maps? How should you conceptualise Lagos, a city with fifteen million inhabitants that sinks into near-total darkness at night and where – in the absence of a functioning electricity network – the hum of generators is an integral part of the daily soundscape?

Questions about the history and future of cities have been discussed for several years on a number of different levels, and are also in debate in exhibitions. While individual shows have been dedicated to the Asian megalopolises and their art production – for example, *Cities on the Move* (1997) and *Polypolis* (2001),[4] or the global networking of European cities[5] – there is still a notable lack of exhibitions extensively concentrating on the topic of African cities.[6] Despite the discussion triggered by Documenta 11's Platform 4 in Lagos,[7] African cities are rarely placed in relation to other metropolises or even to one another.

Thinking *Afropolis*

Against a purely urbanist perspective where demographic and infrastructure developments are taken as the starting point of the analysis, *Afropolis* wants to set a concept of urbanity with a far broader understanding of the phenomenon of the city. In our

1   The paradigm was introduced in 1965 by British art historian William Fagg, see Sidney L. Kasfir 1984, One Tribe, One Style: Paradigms in the Historiography of African Art, *History in Africa* 11: 163–193.

2   For a discussion of various aspects of cities in the Global South see the individual volumes in the metroZones series, e.g., Neue Gesellschaft für Bildende Kunst (ed.) 2003, *Learning from * Städte von Welt, Phantasmen der Zivilgesellschaft, informelle Organisation,* Berlin (= metroZones 2)

3   Rem Koolhaas 1999, Stadtkultur an der Jahrtausendwende, in: Stefan Bollmann (ed.), *Kursbuch Stadt. Stadtleben und Stadtkultur an der Jahrtausendwende,* Stuttgart, p. 7–13, here p. 8

4   Hans Ulrich Obrist, Hou Hanrou 1997, *Cities on the Move,* Ostfildern-Ruit, Ludwig Seyfarth (ed.) 2001, *Polypolis. Kunst aus den Megastädten Asiens,* Freiburg

5   See Wolfgang Scheppe 2009, *Migropolis. Venice Atlas of a Global Situation,* Stuttgart

6   Other exhibitions concerned with megacities only deal with cities in Africa marginally, if at all. For example, *Century City* looked at eight metropolises – including three cities in the Global South, Bombay/Mumbai, Lagos and Ibadan – as locations creating new social and artistic movements, see Ilona Blazwick (ed.) 2001 *Century City: Art and Culture in the Modern Metropolis.* London. A show in London's Tate Modern on *Global Cities* included Cairo and Johannesburg (2007).

7   Okwui Enwezor et al. (ed.) 2002, *Under Siege: Four African Cities: Freetown, Johannesburg, Kinshasa, Lagos* (= Documenta 11_Platform 4), Stuttgart

sense, urbanity embraces a multiplicity of urban practices, urban (sub-)cultures and urban lifestyles through which city residents first create the city as such. Moreover, this is not only meant in a material sense, but also in a non-material and, above all, social sense. Hence, *Afropolis* is also located within more recent, actor-centred approaches in urban research on Africa. A series of recently published studies by AbdouMaliq Simone,[8] Filip De Boeck[9], Achille Mbembe and Sarah Nuttall,[10] Dominique Malaquais, Edgar Pieterse and Jennifer Robinson[11] represent a reconstituted discourse on postcolonial cities in Africa. Although they also regard urban centres as 'fragile systems', they are nonetheless focused on the creative dynamism enabling urban residents to create new forms of urban life – often beyond state control and planning. In *People as Infrastructure: Intersecting Fragments in Johannesburg* which, as a key text in African urban research, was translated into German for *Afropolis*, sociologist AbdouMaliq Simone emphasises the importance of social networks for everyday life and survival in cities such as Johannesburg. According to Simone, the particular dynamism of African cities not only results from the permanent intertwining and overlapping of social networks, urban visions, and economic interests and activities, but also from the high degree of flexibility of these networks. The anthropologist Filip De Boeck also underscores the significance of the immaterial, speaking of Kinshasa as an "invisible city". At the same time, he references the practice of imagining and the core importance of imagination in constituting the urban. In his catalogue contribution *Death Matters: Intimacy, Violence and the Production of Social Knowledge by Urban Youth,* he focuses – as does Charles Didier Gondola's *Tropical Cowboys* – on generation gaps and the role of the youth in Kinshasa. Here, he addresses another particularity of African cities: with over half the urban populations under 25, they are considered to be extremely 'young'.

These newer approaches all seek to revise the concepts and assumptions emerging from normative urban research, urban development and structural adjustment programmes. In *Alternative City Futures*, Edgar Pieterse argues for urban policies informed by participative structures and forms of negotiation rather than normative control processes, and policies building on small, reversible steps and the empowerment of poor urban residents rather than large-scale development programmes. Significantly, this catalogue contribution too, in common with all the authors above, underlines the part that research into African cities in particular is capable of playing with respect to urban cultural theory in general.

This is further highlighted by Sarah Nuttall and Achille Mbembe in their much-acclaimed collection *Johannesburg – The Elusive Metropolis.* In their introduction, they characterise Johannesburg as the exemplary African metropolis, conceptualising it, too, as *Afropolis.*[12] They introduce the concept of Afropolitanism to strengthen a re-reading of African metropolises beyond known urbanist approaches and such meta-narratives as urbanisation, modernisation and crisis, and 'write' them into cultural theory. In this way, Nuttall and Mbembe develop an independent "African cosmopolitism", arguing that the cosmopolitan aspects and transnational networking of African cities have to be understood differently and in a more context-specific way than allowed for by the Global City concept. For the *Afropolis* exhibition and catalogue too, a thorough and detailed examination of the history and specific dynamics in African cities were constitutive, as was the aim of making the insights gained in this process productive for the discussion on non-African cities as well.

The City as the Location and Topos of African Art and Cultural Production

Against the background of a concept of urbanity that, in common with Henri Lefebvre[13] and Michel de Certeau[14], does not view urban space as a 'given' but investigates the act of its creation in everyday life, *Afropolis* focuses on areas of urban production and interaction often only treated as 'decorative trimmings' in mainstream discussions on cities – the sectors of cultural production in general and artistic approaches and positions in particular.

At the latest since the 1950s, African cities have not only become a prime location for modern art production but also a theme in itself, which is explored in the fine arts – though, admittedly, initially only in individual cases. The South African artists Georges Pemba (1912–2001) and Gerard Sekoto (1913–1993) were among the first to take urbanity as their subject. In the 1930s and '40s, Sekoto, described by art historian Marylin Martin as the "pioneer of black modernism", created a series of paintings narrating everyday life in the townships of Sophiatown (Johannesburg) and District Six (Cape Town) in powerful, expressive colours. After the Group Areas Act came into force in 1950, such "hotspots" of black art and culture, to use writer Don Mattera's terms, were torn down. Thus, Sekoto's paintings not only represent how the urban can be portrayed but, at the same time, have acquired an archival status.

In fact, Pemba and Sekoto only found individual 'imitators' much later in the 1960s and '70s, and sometimes even after that – for example, Muhummad Abla in Cairo, and Adebisi Fabunmi and Uzo Egonu in Nigeria. In focusing on urban motifs, they were preoccupied with subjects transcending the category of 'authentic African art' as propounded by the protagonists of the Workshop movement[15] as well as the heads of the first art colleges. The promotion of art by the state, established in the 1960s in Senegal and Egypt, also ignored artists who took urban scenes

8 AbdouMaliq Simone 2004, *For the City Yet to Come: Changing African Life in Four Cities,* Durham, London
9 Filip De Boeck, Marie-Françoise Plissart 2004, *Kinshasa: Tales of the Invisible City.* Ghent-Amsterdam
10 Achille Mbembe, Sarah Nuttall (eds) 2004, *Johannesburg – The Elusive Metropolis. Public Culture* 16(3)
11 Jennifer Robinson 2005, *Ordinary Cities. Between Modernity and Development,* London
12 Sarah Nuttall and Achille Mbembe 2008, Introduction: Afropolis, in: idem. (eds) *Johannesburg – The Elusive Metropolis,* Johannesburg, p. 1–34

13 Henri Lefebvre 1996, *Writings on Cities,* Oxford
14 Michel de Certeau 1988, *Kunst des Handelns,* Berlin
15 Art classes or art schools started by Europeans in various countries in Africa were called Workshops. The Workshop *Le Hangar* founded by Pierre Romain-Desfossés in 1944 in the Belgian Congo and the Poto-Poto School started by Pierre Lods in 1951 in Brazzaville are examples here. In their lessons, they tried to release the sense of rhythm and aesthetics allegedly 'natural' to Africans.

as their theme. In Senegal, for example, raising Négritude to the level of a national aesthetic set the standard of only creating works that referenced 'traditional' art or pan-African motifs. In Egypt, on the other hand, the official frame of reference was 'Pharaonic art' that had a clear policy of depicting pastoral scenes and portraying the farmers as 'noble, prototypical Egyptians'. However, while in some works by Sekoto and his 'imitators' everyday life in the city or township appears just as picturesque as everyday life in the countryside, later artists adopted a considerably more political approach to the subject of the city. In the 1980s and '90s, such artists as the South African Sam Nhlengethwa depicted the cities in all their ambivalence. Nhlengethwa, who became well known for *The Death of Steve Biko* (1990), his homage to civil rights activist Steve Biko, no longer showed the streets of Johannesburg's townships in peaceful everyday scenes but as contested locations, places of violence and counter-violence expressed in resistance against the apartheid regime.[16]

In the 1950s and '60s, against the background of particular cultural policy debates, the process of critically engaging with urban reality primarily took place in popular culture and in other areas of cultural production – in studio photography, film, literature and journalism. The background settings of photographers especially reflect an experience of cities rooted in the rapid urbanisation of the 1960s. Here, for example, the street lamp became the first leitmotif and a central icon symbolising the electrified city, while the tower blocks, banks, dual carriageways and junctions expanded the range of motifs. The first futuristic city views were created in the 1980s. The settings can exemplarily indicate how the urban at this time acquired an iconicity in many artistic and popular cultural genres. This applies equally to African *auteur* filmmakers who, since the 1960s, have taken the city as their subject. For this reason, in her contribution, film theorist Marie-Hélène Gutberlet explores the connection between *The City and Film in Africa.* Matthias Krings' essay focuses on the photo novel, which was distributed in several African cities and, in terms of popularity, can be considered the forerunner of today's video films. In his *Sketches of Postcolonial Kenyan Literature,* literary scholar Tom Odhiambo describes the development of the urban novel in Nairobi, which represents a paradigm shift in the image of the city and cultural production in the 1970s.

The critical artistic engagement with urbanity took a decisive turn in the 1990s. At that time, with the credibility of the propagated idealised traits of African art and culture having already been widely discounted, increasing numbers of artists turned to the concrete reality around them. Crucially, they also turned away from the traditional cultural institutions and created their own platforms, usually by going directly out into urban public space and occupying it with new images, objects and art practices.

As a result, even today questions about the histories and futures of African cities are not only asked by urban planners, economists and politicians, but equally by artists and cultural producers. For this reason, *Afropolis* brings together cultural (historical, urbanist, etc.) studies and artistic positions and perspectives on African cities and relates them to one another.

Curating *Afropolis*

By adopting this approach, *Afropolis* is also breaking new ground in its choice of exhibition format, which is neither the classic 'urban/cultural history' exhibition nor an 'art exhibition'. In an interlocking perspective, cultural science as well as artistic analyses and reflections are related to their own specific forms of knowledge production and to each other in a productive exchange. In this process, cultural science and art meet in the question of how reality can be reflected and depicted, and they benefit from each other's different approaches and possibilities. What may sometimes be hard to grasp in scholarly discourse can be dealt with in a graphic and metaphorical way in the arts and made experiential.[17]

From the outset, then, a certain concept of curatorial practice was central to *Afropolis*. Hence, researching into and selecting main thematic areas and artworks from and about African cities neither resulted in being solely guided by urban theory debates on African cities nor in accessing the different locations exclusively through the networks, media and discourses of a global art scene. Instead, it involved primarily establishing networks with diverse local cultural scenes to make the local constellation of discussions, genres and formats the starting point of reflection. As a result, many of the works (and core themes) presented in *Afropolis* are based on geographically and historically specific productions and conceptual reflections. However, at the same time they seek to approach urban theoretical discussions on a global level from these local perspectives. While the images commonly shown of African cities tend to be one-sided, either scandalising or prettifying, the selected works here investigate the ambivalences of urban everyday life – a strenuous, exhausting life, influenced as much by a fundamental solidarity, high productivity and energy as, not least, moments of happiness and contentment. The contributions by artists, activists and scholars that have been chosen or produced for *Afropolis* confront these ambivalences, taking them as the basis for and the content of their work. As varied as their subjects, approaches and media may be the contributors all reflect the city analytically or metaphorically so that they highlight everyday life and practices. This is connected with a focus on artists (collectives) and cultural

---

16 See John Peffer 2009, *Art and the End of Apartheid,* Minneapolis

17 Such an approach is thus also distinct from such exhibitions as *Africas. The Artist and the City.* The show curated by Pep Subiros, which read the cities and megacities of the African continent as a location of art and cultural production, did not regard the artworks themselves as a medium through which the city could be thought about and analysed. Nonetheless, the exhibition and eponymous catalogue were an important source of inspiration for *Afropolis* – above all, in its transnational orientation, evident in the way Subiros also included cities with main diasporas, such as Paris and London.

producers, who take a research-driven approach, often working at the interface between art and politics and who, for their part, are also networked with scholarly and activist positions. Here, the work of urban geographer Ismail Farouk from Johannesburg and Cape Town is a prime example. On the basis of scholarly research, Farouk employs artistic strategies, media and formats to ask questions about economic change and social participation in the city – and to call for it especially for marginalised groups, such as immigrants. Just as Ismail Farouk's approach shows how scholarly, activist and artistic strategies can be interlinked, works by Cairo-based artist Lara Baladi highlight a different strategy for dissolving boundaries. Baladi not only firmly locates her work within the store of images from popular culture and media, but also works with advertising images or, in the case of her *Borg el amal (Tower of Hope)* taken as the basis for her *Amal (Hope)* on show in *Afropolis,* she realises her project with workers from the informal construction industry. While Baladi draws her inspiration from the visuality of the city, Rana El Nemr adds documentary material to her video installation.

The dual perspective adopted by *Afropolis* as a whole is reflected in these works, as it is in many others as well. This also indicates one of the premises underlying *Afropolis:* the term of dissolution, understood as removing or blurring boundaries, does not solely apply to the works of art and cultural production selected for this exhibition. Instead, it addresses some of the key characteristics of African cities. In contrast to the idea reinforced by the older Africa images cited above, African cities have been connected by transnational (trade) networks for hundreds of years and still are. In this process, urban centres had always developed, in Africa as well, at points where the trading routes met and crossed – for example, at such precolonial Sahel cities as Kumbi Saleh or Timbuktu, established at the terminus of trans-Saharan trade routes, or through the intercontinental trade between Africa and Asia across the Indian Ocean which gave birth to the urban Swahili culture of the coastal towns.[18]

Consequently, *Afropolis* does not think of African cities as closed entities, but systematically reads them within their manifold networks. Through the lenses of postcolonial architectural theory, which recalls the entangled history of European and African cities, Regina Göckede examines the powerful cartography of colonisation. Taking the example of plans drafted by German architect Ernst May for Kampala, Uganda, in the 1940s, she highlights how the colonial planning paradigms have shaped African cities. During the time that Ernst May, city planner and former head of municipal planning in Frankfurt am Main, rose to become a leading reformer, theorist and practitioner of the modernist *Neues Bauen* movement in Germany, the British colonial government commissioned him to draft a master plan for Kampala. As in other colonial cities, here too town planning was used as a means to secure military control, limit activities, separate individual parts of the population and establish a particular aesthetic and political structure based on Cartesian standards.[19] Rather than presenting May's urbanist work as an 'autonomous practice' in organising space, Göckede shows the complex socio-political conditions of colonisation.

The close links between urban and rural space, as Filip De Boeck has described in the case of Kinshasa, are another aspect of dissolution. "There is simply no urban alternative to the rural place," Lindsay Bremner wrote, "but rather complex configurations of lived space, neither rural nor urbane."[20] At present, Africa's urban centres are also connected via migration networks and they make African cities into permanent places of departure. As Dominique Malaquais has pointed out, mobility is not so much unusual as normal.[21] Here, Johannesburg is an especially striking example. From the 1950s at the latest, Hillbrow, a residential neighbourhood on the northeastern edge of the inner city, was a popular 'white' quarter for immigration; today, it is a pan-African district where Zimbabwean, Mozambican and Nigerian social and economic networks, and those of many other diasporas, overlap and interlace. Hillbrow's cosmopolitan character not only illustrates the transnational connections of African metropolises, but also their character as transitional spaces, as temporary and dynamic social structures that burst open national state borders and, indeed, the borders of the continent itself. In this sense, African metropolises are hubs in South-South networks, migration and mobility.

For the *Afropolis* curators, investigating these networks and making them visible meant not only inviting artists living in the African cities to take part but also artists from Europe. As a result, Laura Horelli, a Finnish artist based in Berlin, developed a video installation on the expat lifestyle in Nairobi, starting from her own biographical experience, while in *Architekturen des Eigensinns,* Berlin photographer Karola Schlegelmilch, who has been working for several years in West Africa, examines everyday architecture.

Afropolis: Selecting the Cities

Afropolis presents five cities – Cairo, Lagos, Nairobi, Kinshasa and Johannesburg – to discuss issues around urbanity and cultural production, using the examples of these specific local contexts. Even if the spectrum of cities in the exhibition stretches across Africa from north to south and east to west, we are naturally not claiming that this gives a comprehensive geographical picture of the continent. Instead, our aim is to draw attention to cities where certain issues emerge with particular clarity or to cities where the key discussions on new forms of urbanity were and are being conducted *in* them and *about* them. In these cities,

18 Here, it is only possible to mention urban histories very briefly. There are several works providing an overview: Catherine Coquery-Vidrovitch 1993, *Histoire des villes d'Afrique noire. Des origines à la colonisation,* Paris, David Anderson, Richard Rathbone (eds) 2000, *Africa's Urban Past,* Oxford, Bill Freund 2007, *The African City. A History,* Cambridge.

19 See Gwendolyn Wright 1991, *The Politics of Design in French Colonial Urbanism,* Chicago, London, Çelik Zeynep 1997, *Urban Forms and Colonial Confrontations: Algiers under French Rule,* Berkeley. See also the documentation on the exhibition *In der Wüste der Moderne* (2008), curated by Marion von Osten and others for the Haus der Kulturen der Welt, retrieved on 25 September 2010 from http://www.hkw.de/de/programm/2008/wueste_der_moderne/_wueste_der_moderne/ projekt-detail_wueste.php

20 Lindsay Bremner 2004, *Johannesburg. One City Colliding Worlds,* Johannesburg, p. 23–24

21 Dominique Malaquais 2005–2006, Villes fluxes. Imaginaires de l'urbain en Afrique aujourd'hui, *Politique Africaine* 100 (Dossier Cosmopolis: *de la ville, de l'Afrique et du monde*): 17–37

urban practices, styles and strategies are especially apparent. Moreover, the way artists and cultural practitioners articulate them is accessible in our choice of exhibition format. The resulting heterogeneity of our selection also deliberately testifies to the impossibility of simply categorising cities into different 'types' or various 'development models'. Instead, they all develop a degree of contingency and their own energy, forming social, discursive and creative networks that are highly specific (geographically, historically, socially and culturally). Precisely so that these specific conditions and dynamics can be explored, each of the five cities chosen for the exhibition has a different main focus.

Cairo: Public Space and Art Production

With a population of nearly 16 million, Cairo is one of Africa's megacities. Not least due to its geographical location, it is closely connected to cities in the Arab world. Located on the River Nile and surrounded by desert, Cairo is also one of the most densely populated cities in the world. In historical terms, Cairo's multilayered past stretching back over several thousand years allows *Afropolis* to examine the *longue durée* of urban development and history. At the same time, the exhibition investigates the images circulating of and in the city. These range from the orientalising depictions of the 'Islamic' Cairo since the late 19th century to the unconventional and, at times, eccentric studio photography by Van Leo, a member of the Armenian minority in the cosmopolitan Cairo of the 1950s, to the current articulations of the megacity by artists and cultural producers – whether in such large-scale installations as Hala Elkoussy's *We're by the Sea now,* Rana El Nemr's research-based work *The Olympic Garden,* Mandy Gehrt's investigation of cultural policies, or Magdy El Shafee's graphic novel *Metro.*[22] Moreover, Cairo is the production site of one of the largest film industries and thus a place where popular urban images are also created and disseminated. Viola Shafik's contribution to *Afropolis* explores the representation and negotiation of the informal settlements in film.

The 21st century Cairo appears to be a city constantly absorbing other conurbations, both in successive and parallel processes. These are cities, from informal settlements to planned desert cities, which stretch far into the outskirts. Some of their residents move along the Rind Road from one peripheral location to another, without ever seeing or getting to know Cairo's inner city. At the same time, Cairo exemplifies the extensive growth of informal settlements, a development that also shapes the character of other African cities. In his contribution, Hany Darwish, a cultural journalist from Cairo, not only explores the histories of informal settlements but, using the example of his own family, underlines the 'normality' and widespread prevalence of this form of settlement. The origins of Cairo's informal city districts stretch right back into the first decades of the 20th century. They are always rooted in the need to create residential space in a city where the population has grown six times larger over the last 60 years. The periphery is also addressed by cultural producers as a topic, both in its geographical form and as a metaphor for social, political or other forms of marginalisation; in *Afropolis,* this approach is evident, above all, in Lara Baladi's work *Hope.*

Doing Lagos: Self-Organisation and Urban Theory

The Nigerian megacity of Lagos has an estimated population of 15 million people. The city stretches far into the mainland over a number of islands and peninsulas, including Lagos Island, Ikoyi and Victoria Island. As early as the 15th century, some of the land bordering the lagoon around today's Lagos was settled by Yoruba-speaking groups who developed their own urban identity. Two hundred years later, the first court for the Oba, the traditional Yoruba king, was established on Eko Island. Today, Lagos is ranked among the world's fastest growing cities. In terms of urban space, it is spreading like a rhizome, with new areas of the swamps constantly being drained.[23] The debates among urban researchers are not solely fuelled by examples of rapidly growing cities such as Lagos or Kinshasa, a city where the provision of the most basic services such as electricity or water is not guaranteed, but they are particularly relevant to them. How do residents organise their everyday life? What role do informal types of organisations, regional and transnational networks play?

For many years, Lagos has been the topic of urban history research and urban and artistic debates.[24] Nearly five years ago, the *Harvard Project on the City,* run by Dutch architect and urban theorist Rem Koolhaas, found itself in the media spotlight. In *Mutations* he developed his provocative hypothesis that "to write about the African city is to write about the terminal condition of Chicago, London or Los Angeles".[25] Lagos had become a laboratory of urban development. Matthew Gandy, a British geographer, was not alone in criticising the apolitical, euphemistic "eulogy of a society's self-organisation" as the aesthetic ennoblement of the city.[26] Even in Lagos itself, Koolhaas's hypothesis and his accompanying set of images provoked a reaction. For *Afropolis,* taking the urban icon of *Oshodi,* Peter Probst traces that discourse, one where photography also played a major role. Lagos also has a long history of photography connected with such names as J.D. Okhai Ojeikere, Don Barber, Tam Fiofori and Jide Adeniyi-Jones. In his photographic works, Berlin and Lagos-based Akinbode Akinbiyi has been exploring this city for nearly 20 years. In *Lagos. All Roads,* he now continues this process for *Afropolis.* Similarly to photography collectives such as DOF and

22 The artworks mentioned and a detailed discussion on cultural policy can be found in the essay *Going Places* in this volume.

23 On the history of Lagos see Sandra Barnes 1986, *Patrons and Power. Creating a Political Community in Metropolitan Lagos,* Manchester; Andreas Eckert 2006, Lagos im 20. Jahrhundert. Informalität als urbanes Prinzip, in: Wolfgang Schwentker (ed.), *Megastädte im 20. Jahrhundert,* Göttingen, p. 238–256; Kristin Mann 2007, *Slavery and the Birth of an African City: Lagos, 1760–1900,* Bloomington. Also see *Stadtbauwelt* 164: The Lagos Experience from 2004, edited by Dagmar Hoetzel and the exhibition catalogue *Lagos. STADTanSICHTen* (2004) published by the Institut für Auslandsbeziehungen; the exhibition was curated by David Aradeon, Akinbode Akinbiyi and Simone Scholten.

24 See above all Kunle Akinsemoyin and Alan Vaughan-Richards 1976, *Building Lagos,* and *Glendora Review* 1997, 2/1, and *Glendora Review* 2001, 3/2 which were dedicated to Lagos and the West African cities. *Lagos. A City at Work* from 2005, edited by Olakunle Tejuoso and Weyinmi Atigbi as graphic designer, includes contributions by Akin Mabogunje, David Aradeon, Onookome Okome and photography by artists living in Lagos.

25 Rem Koolhaas, *Harvard Project on the City* 2000, Lagos, in: Rem Koolhaas et al. (ed.), *Mutations,* Barcelona, p. 652–720, here p. 653

26 Matthew Gandy 2004, Lagos trotz Koolhaas, *Stadtbauwelt* 48: 20–30

Black Box, Akinbiyi is also interested in the informal arrangements and structures that seem to constitute such cities as Lagos. The photos by Uche Okpa-Iroha from his *Under Bridge Life* series show how the infrastructure programmes implemented in the 1960s and '70s, such as bridges and elevated roads, play a crucial role, even today, in providing space for new kinds of informal use.

A monument from the 1970s is also at the centre of *State-Theatre [1]: Lagos* by Constanze Fischbeck and Daniel Kötter – in this case, the Lagos National Arts Theatre built for the FESTAC '77 (Second World Black and African Festival of Arts). Along with other buildings such as the Musée Dynamique that opened in Dakar in 1966 for the first Pan-African festival, the National Arts Theatre testifies to the desire to showcase a national culture.[27] Today, though, it stands for a cultural policy of large-scale empty gestures that have no sustainability. In his article on the FESTAC, Denis Ekpo interprets the continent's culturalisation connected with such projects as a political instrument intended, first and foremost, to draw attention away from economic and social problems and conceal them.

Although individual artists and intellectuals had always distanced themselves from this state cultural policy, it was not until the 1990s that initiatives emerged in Africa's cities that critically attacked the antiquated official policy standards and opened up alternative (art) spaces.[28] Such initiatives, which started independently from one another, were often founded by artists themselves. The Centre for Contemporary Art (CCA), Lagos, founded by curator Bisi Silva, provides just such an arts space. She not only established the first specialist library for visual arts resources but, through CCA, also provides a platform for contemporary art practices opening up forms of political activism, media culture and theoretical reflection. This is also the context for the participative project *Lagos Open,* curated by Emeka Udemba, which experimentally connects public space and art works.

Kainebi Osahenye's current works are also informed by an experimental approach. In *Casualties,* he has arranged hundreds of squashed cans to create a cascade-like installation. His approach of 'recuperation', based on reusing and converting items found in the artist's environments, reflects the informality and scarcity of materials in a city such as Lagos. This aesthetic practice seems to be particularly inspired by the city, its specific logic of production and particular visuality. The relevance of urban centres in producing the aesthetics in contemporary art is also evident in the work of another artist shown at *Afropolis.* Using auditory media, Emeka Ogboh explores the specific soundscape of Lagos, focusing on the noises in and around the *danfo* buses. As the urban means of transport in Lagos, these cadmium-yellow VW minibuses foster a unique style of communication, creating their own landscape of sound.

Nairobi: Island Urbanism

Through its regular lecture series, the Goethe-Institut Nairobi is well established as a centre for discussion.[29] As such, it was the ideal location for us to join in a debate on the current phenomena of the city and related issues with historian George Gona, literary scholars Mbugua wa Mungai and Tom Odhiambo, architects and city planners Paul Mpungu and Alfred Omenya and, last but not least, the writers Charles Matathia and Tony 'Smitta' Mochama. Other contacts facilitated by the Goethe-Institut and, above all, Sam Hopkins as local curator, led us to artists and activists across the most diverse city districts and in the slums of Kibera and Mathare. On this journey too, the idea was to understand the city from inside out to allow us to integrate its dynamic into *Afropolis* and make it visible in the exhibition. The Kenyan capital city has become an exceptionally dynamic commercial and banking centre. This is not only due to its transnational links but, in particular, to the Indian business community, which has played a central role in Nairobi since it was founded just over 100 years ago. The de facto dissolution of Somalia in the 1990s has led to a recent major influx of Somali immigrants. As Manuel Herz describes in *Somali Refugees in Eastleigh,* a Nairobi city district has now become a kind of extra-territorial capital of the neighbouring state. As a hub for many international organisations, including one of the United Nations headquarters, Nairobi has a political importance for all East Africa and beyond. It may thus seem rather paradoxical that the city also contains vast slum areas, often directly bordering prosperous districts. The exhibition's documentary module presents the historical development of the colonial city planning which laid the foundations for these urban island structures. Our view of Nairobi, though, is directed primarily to the links between these intertwined yet extremely different quarters which, through their polarities, drive the city forwards.

The dynamism of Nairobi is also evident in its forms of mobility. The local identity of residents is often linked to the different lines of elaborately pimped minibus taxis called *matatus* that ferry them every day to the inner city and back. Nairobi has developed its own *matatu* culture with these elaborately designed and highly conspicuous taxis; each line has its own character and specific aesthetic appeal. Through its names, music and images, the *matatu* embodies a contested social identity that is constantly being renegotiated and developed. In his contribution, Mbugua wa Mungai deals with the generation gaps and gender conflicts portrayed and expressed in *matatu* culture. The *matatus* are moving social interaction platforms. They are not only places where urban myths are created, but also can become urban myths themselves, as in the *matatu* rumours circulating around the city which Sam Hopkins has collected for his *Roomah* installation.

27 On the FESTAC and its political and economic context, see Andrew Apter 2005, *The Pan-African Nation: Oil and the Spectacle of Culture in Nigeria,* Chicago.

28 For an overview, see Christian Hanussek's project "Gleichzeitig in Afrika …", which from 2004 to 2006 presented independent artists' groups, art initiatives and art journals from Africa in Nuremberg, Bayreuth, Potsdam and Berlin.

29 An event series at the Goethe-Institut in 2008/2009 is documented in: Mbugua wa Mungai and Georg Gona (eds) 2010, *(RE)MEMBERING KENYA, Vol 1, Identity Culture and Freedom,* Nairobi.

Nairobi's slums are not self-contained units. They are closely connected with other city districts – and also, not least, an important resource for international state organisations engaged in highly remunerative slum-upgrading projects. Slum-TV is a grass-roots initiative founded in Mathare, Nairobi, primarily dedicated to producing documentary video clips. The documentarians developed the idea of acting out some scenes in the story of a slum-upgrading programme. The result is *Upgradasion,* an installation of video fragments in a style somewhere between a TV soap and a comic. This work offers an insight into the power relations playing a role in the slum in the intended upgrading process. The catalogue contribution by sociologist Deyssi Rodriguez-Torres describes a genuine slum-upgrading project in the 1990s, analysing how irreconcilable interests led to the project's failure.

In *Hurlingham Shopping Centre,* Laura Horelli, a Berlin-based video artist, presents what could be considered the opposite side to Slum-TV. She looks at the foreign specialists in the many organisations based in Nairobi trying to improve the conditions of the impoverished population, asking them about how they see their own role and showing how and where they live and work.

Kinshasa: Utopia/Dystopia

Soon expected to have a population of 9 million, Kinshasa, the capital of the Democratic Republic of the Congo, is ranked as Africa's third largest urban conurbation after Lagos and Cairo. Soon after it was founded in 1881 as a trading post, the growing city was named Léopoldville after Léopold II, the Belgian king at that time. By the mid-1950s, Léopoldville already had 250,000 residents – many of them Europeans living in their own districts, such as today's Gombe and Kintambo, then separated from the African quarters. After independence in 1960, Kinshasa grew rapidly, attracting young people in particular.

For the Belgian colonial administration, photographs of the colony and its capital city played "an active and constitutive role in the colonial efforts to bring an alleged 'salvation' and 'civilisation' to the Congolese people."[30] In the 1950s, the *Centre d'information et de documentation du Congo Belge et du Ruanda-Urundi (CID)* was founded, which had masses of photos and films produced. This propaganda image in impeccable neatness of the colonial project's civilising mission is still reproduced today, for example, in Jan Raymaker's 2009 bestseller *Congo – De schoonste tijd van mijn leven.* The authoritarian postcolonial regime also continued the tradition of making its negative side invisible in the media by repressively censoring anything not a 'positive image'. That only makes all the more shocking the pictures circulating in the media today of poverty, crises and a violence that violates human dignity, especially that of the victims.

In today's Kinshasa, photography is forbidden – which is understandable since it is impossible not to see the piles of garbage lying around, the blocked and overflowing sewers and the general decay. J.B. Mpiana sings about Kinshasa: *"Oooh gai namiyokeli mawa a eeh namiyokeli mawa!"* – "It makes me ill and I feel sorry for myself!"[31] In his night photos, Cédrick Nzolo, a young designer and photographer from Kinshasa, depicts the scandal of the living conditions in his home town. His approach, though, is lyrical, taking as a metaphor the homemade paraffin lamps, which he calls *Les divas de la honte.* They shroud the night market stalls in a flickering yellow light, lending them a particular atmosphere. He sees qualities in them going far beyond a talent for improvisation or a stopgap solution, since the lamps are given names and these provide an insight into the lives of the residents, as humorous as it is intimate.

Combining a scholarly and artistic approach, the University of Gent working group under Johan Lagae and artist Méga Mingiedi are engaged in the mapping as well as the historical and political archaeology of a city originally founded as a strategic trading centre, which then developed into an industrial and administrative centre and finally, during the decades under Mobutu Sese Seko, plunged into a series of ever-worsening economic crises. Today, the surviving remains of the once *Kin la belle* are haunted by the ghosts of the Belgian colonial regime and Mobutu's reign of terror. The essays on the youth culture of the 1950s and '60s (Didier Gondola), the *Rumble in Kinshasa* (Dominique Malaquais) and the history of popular music (Gary Stewart) examine this cultural and political legacy that led to the fall of the city into a doubly traumatised dystopia.

For many decades, Kinshasa was the centre of Africa's music production and its records were distributed across the entire continent and even beyond its borders. In the exhibition's documentary section, *Afropolis* narrates the history of Kinshasa through these songs. They emerged in nightclubs where an urban culture of liberality opposed the colonial restrictions. They reflect both the euphoria of independence and the era of dictatorship under Mobutu, who also knew how to use music for his own propaganda. When Mobutu fell, the entire economy collapsed, and the music industry fell with it. In the 1980s, the exodus of musicians to Brussels and Paris had already started – along with anyone else able to afford it. While the Belgians once imagined Léopoldville as a mirror image of Brussels[32], now the Kinshasans dreamt of Paris and Brussels as exaggerated, mythical locations, as *mikili* (in Lingala: worlds). The borders of reality and imagination, here and elsewhere are blurred: *Mikili* can be anywhere and suddenly turn from a utopia into a dystopia, from a dream to a nightmare. The multidisciplinary collective Mowoso has constructed *mikili* as an Afro-futurist machine; their *GROUND OVERGROUND UNDERGROUND* multimedia installation opens

---

30 Fassil Demissie 2007, Visual Fragments of Kinshasa, *African Identities* 5/2: 291–302, here p. 293

31 J.B. Mpiana: *Kinshasa on the album TH,* 2000

32 Johan Lagae 2007, Léopoldville, Bruxelles: villes miroires? L'architecture et l'urbanisme d'une capitale coloniale et métropole africaine, *Cahiers Africains* 73: 67–99

a vertical space where the linearity of time has dissolved and Kinshasa is connected to coordinates at once real and imaginary. Kinshasa was and still is a place where people dream of models of an ideal city. At present, the dream is of the *Cité du fleuve*[33], a massive real estate project *à la* Dubai, recalling the many never-realised colonial plans for a new Kinshasa, for example, Georges Ricquier's 1948 *Le Grand Léo*. Bylex's *Cité touristique* is the artistic model of such a utopian city, designed to offer tourists all possible comforts and amities while guaranteeing them the best security possible. The *dome royale,* the central domed building, has a spiritual function – as a museum, it is intended to encourage meditation and support reflections on morality.

The artists' collective SADI explored the opposite of the utopian city in the Kindele district, which was being destroyed by soil erosion. In this decaying landscape of ruins nothing is certain any more and no one knows whose house the next rains will wash away. For the artists, this is a starting point to investigate the life of the people who lived here before they became the victims of the mudslides. In this process, SADI investigates the objects left behind and reconstructs their stories.

Johannesburg: Contested City

With a population close to four million, Johannesburg is far smaller than the African megacities. Nevertheless, it is regarded as a main business hub in Africa and as a political, economic and cultural interface between African, South-South and global networks. Initially a colonial city that also copied European architectural fashions, over the last decades Johannesburg has developed into a cosmopolitan African city, but one that is also fragmented and, in part, fiercely contested. The social and political upheavals since the end of apartheid in 1994 have radically changed the cityscape, made it negotiable and turned the urban topography 'upside down'.

Since the discovery of underground gold deposits in 1886, the 'City of Gold' has come to epitomise the immigrant destination par excellence. It not only embodies the dream of economic success but is also the African springboard to other cosmopolitan cities around the world and is regarded, in a certain sense, as symbolising African modernity. It is no coincidence that the cultural and social science work on Johannesburg has generated key ideas in the theories of African megacities, from Abdou-Maliq Simone's notion of "people as infrastructure" to Sarah Nuttall and Achille Mbembe's concept of Afropolitanism.[34] Over the last 15 years, either alone or with other South African cities, Johannesburg has repeatedly been taken as the theme of exhibitions, collections of essays in cultural studies and special editions of journals.[35]

Recently, Johannesburg's cosmopolitan and de-boundaried dimensions, already present in its history as a mining and immigrant town, are often related to the example of its inner city. Over the last 30 years, this has been transformed from a 'white district' into an African, even a Pan-African, quarter. In *Afropolis,* cultural scientists Naomi Roux and Hannah le Roux as well as the artist duo Deadheat have each developed a project on this topic. The *Biography of a Building,* a research work, and *Passage,* an artistic intervention, both focus on a modern 1950s building which for some years has been the centre of the Ethiopian diaspora's economic network in Johannesburg. While these two projects are clearly research-based, Minnette Vári's video installation *The Calling,* which is set high over the rooftops of the downtown area, takes a metaphorical look at the city. This work focuses on Johannesburg's utopian and dystopian aspects, presenting it as a metaphor for a "broken metropolis".

Despite the manifold new impulses over the recent years, Johannesburg remains marked by a segregation policy that, under the apartheid regime, was implemented in its most extreme form on the African continent. For this reason, numerous urban practices and social debates today revolve as a whole around the renegotiation of spaces, their use and significance – and ultimately, this led to the main theme explored in the exhibition and catalogue sections where the focus is primarily on Johannesburg as a contested city. The historian Noor Nieftagodien provides a basis for such a reading in his essay, narrating the history of Johannesburg from the perspective of Alexandra, a township in the north of the city. Here, the significance of urban strategies of resistance already becomes apparent. In his contribution, anthropologist Thomas G. Kirsch takes the example of electricity theft in Soweto to illustrate the practices of resistance with which Soweto activists and residents have both been demanding their rights to the city.

(Former) segregated spaces and social boundaries were and are constantly being renegotiated in popular discourses, as well as in political and academic ones. This can also be traced, for instance, in the culture of Johannesburg magazines – from the legendary *Drum* Magazine to *Staffrider* and the newer titles on the teenage magazine market. The exhibition's documentary section deals with this aspect in detail. In this context, Sarah Nuttall's cultural analysis entitled *Stylising the Self* has proved to be groundbreaking. Taking the example of youth trends in music, clothing and advertising, Nuttall shows how urban identities, spatial and racial attributions are constantly deconstructed and reconstituted in visual culture. *Itchy City,* a spoken word recitation by Kgafela oa Magogodi, also represents the very new crossover genre of music and literature. In the film version by Jyoti Mistry, the work is included both in the catalogue and the exhibition.

Numerous artists from Johannesburg have also taken contested spaces and locations as their theme. Sam Nhlengethwa, men-

---

33 http://www.lacitedufleuve.com, retrieved on 16 May 2010.

34 Sarah Nuttall and Achille Mbembe (2008). This contains a highly informative research review of the cultural and social science studies on Johannesburg.

35 See exhibition catalogue and conference volumes: Leora Farber (ed.) 2008, *Representations & Spatial Practices in Urban South Africa,* Johannesburg; Hilton Judin and Ivan Vladislavić (eds) 1998, *Blank – Architecture, Apartheid and After,* Rotterdam; Dagmar Hoetzel (ed.) 2005, *Fast Forward Johannesburg,* Berlin; Stadtbauwelt (1997), Nr 133. In addition, the historiographical literature on Johannesburg is so extensive, it can not be detailed here. See though, e.g., footnote 34.

tioned earlier, belongs to the generation of artists who were already tracing and reflecting the social debates and transformations in the 1970s and 1980s. This also indicates the historical depth of various art discourses in South Africa. Johannesburg probably has the best established art scene in any of the five cities presented here, with numerous galleries and an arts fair, as well as various art magazines and publishers. Artistic positions have constantly returned to the question of what constitutes public space, how artists can read urban spaces 'against the grain' and work with residents to change the city together, or how the city and its history can be visually represented.[36] In *Hauntology of Johannesburg,* artist and art theorist Leora Farber discusses exemplarily and in general the works of 10 performance, video and media artists who deal with these and similar questions. The catalogue concludes with a work by photographer Sabelo Mlangeni developed in the shadow of the most recent global representation of Johannesburg – the World Cup images circulating in the media. To a certain extent, the work presents a local counterview of this major event.

The *Afropolis* exhibition and catalogue were only possible due to the enthusiasm for the idea shown by so many project partners and participants. Clara Himmelheber from the Rautenstrauch-Joest-Museum (RJM) brought *Afropolis* to Cologne. RJM's director Klaus Schneider took over the project management and integrated the project as the first special exhibition at the new RJM. Annabelle Springer enabled the exhibition to be realised as perfectly as we had hoped. Clara Giacalone assisted the curatorial team with organisational and substantive issues, while Ulrike Nestler took on the main coordination of the accompanying programme of events. The project's external partners were also crucial in ensuring the project's survival. During our on-site research, we were able to benefit from the valuable help provided by co-curators Sam Hopkins and Akinbode Akinbiyi, as well as numerous other dialogue partners. We would also like to thank Johannes Hossfeld, head of the Goethe-Institut in Nairobi, and our local project partners. Dominique Malaquais provided input as well as concrete advice and contacts to support the selection of topics and artists in the exhibition section on Kinshasa. Our thanks also go to everyone, above all the artists and authors, for their hard work and fruitful and inspiring cooperation. The English version of the catalogue was made possible by the generous funding of the Goethe-Institut in Johannesburg and the enthusiasm of its Director Katharina von Ruckteschell-Katte. Our thanks also go to the translator Andrew Boreham and the editor Jennifer Gallagher. Our project assistant for the English catalogue Hanna Prenzel has done a wonderful job!

Translation from German by Andrew Boreham

36 On this, see also Peter Anders and Matthew Krouse (eds) 2010, *Zeitgenössische Künstler aus Südafrika,* Göttingen, which does not only present the visual arts but also literature, caricatures, theatre, dance and even work in museums.

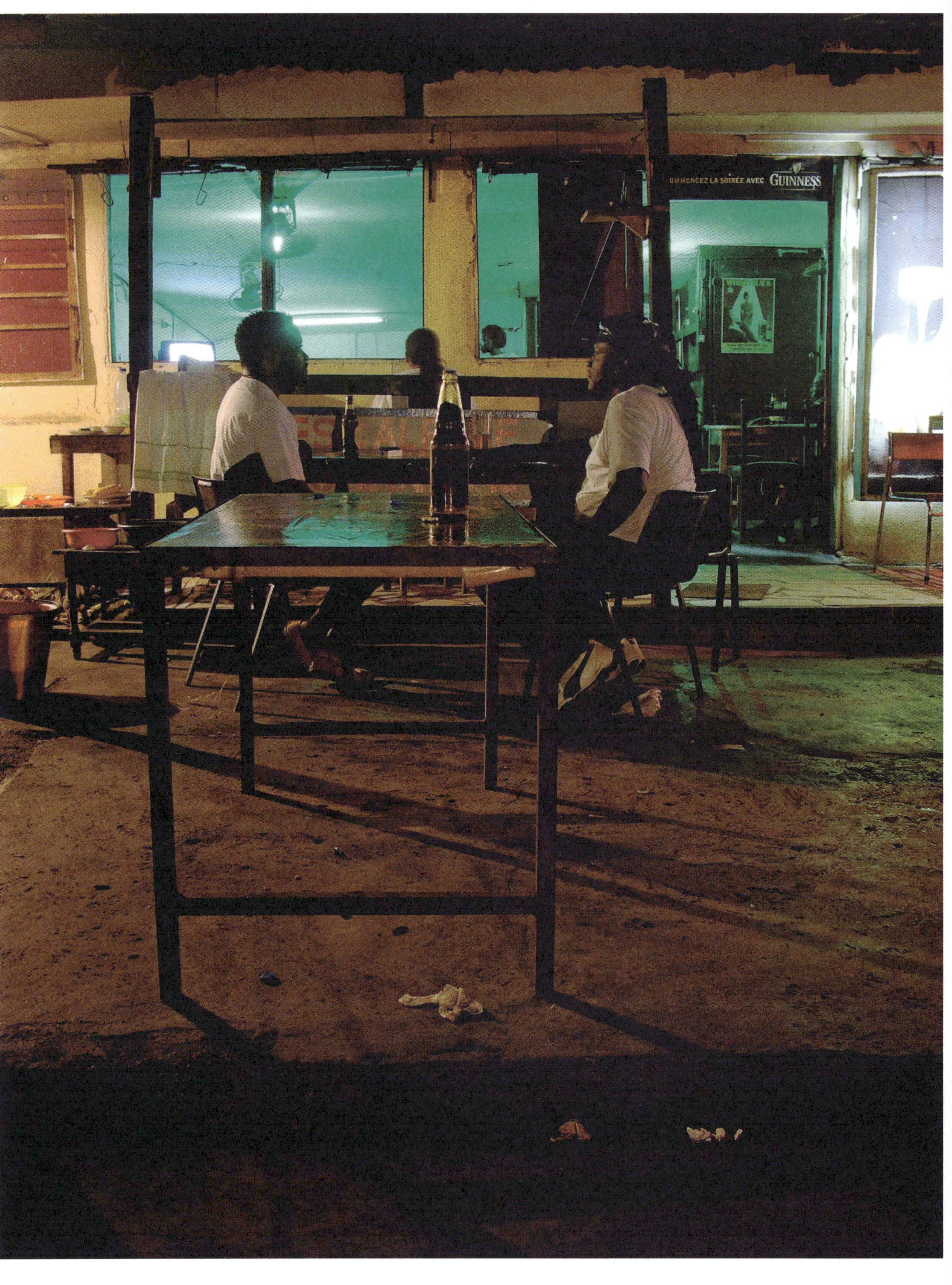

MMENCEZ LA SOIREE AVEC GUINNESS

Quel est l'endroit idéal?

CHRISTIAN HANUSSEK
AND SALIFOU LINDOU

Douala may not be the ideal African city for religious redemption or happy-clappy born-again-Christians speaking in tongues, but if your idea of salvation after the hardships of daily life is a refreshing beer, then this is the place to be. *Les Brasseries du Cameroun* is the country's largest industry and dedicated to guaranteeing a steady flow of liquid amber to the vast proliferation of bars, restaurants, nightclubs and other unidentified nightspots – some still in Maquis-style hiding – that have mushroomed all over the city. But how do you make your night? What is it that attracts you to one place and not another? Our survey has no claims to be anything but personal preferences – but that still won't deter us from analysing our criteria of choice, from interior design and architecture to how the venues are anchored in the life of the city in today's urban space. Admittedly, we aren't drawn to expensive furniture and upmarket decorations in that hallmark ambience irresistible to wannabe snobs. In our quest for real style, we have to leave our options open. Even after a great time at one venue on one evening we still have to confront that fundamental question the morning after: But what is the ideal place?

The city's long-standing bar-strip is a 200-metre stretch of beer-fuelled raucousness in the Bali quarter; if you want simultaneous music from several competing sound systems above the yelling of the crowd but still enjoy your drink and retain control of your basic motor functions, *Nuit Blanche* is the place of our choice and the perfect spot to observe the action. Its white walls and furniture reflect the current penchant for snowy hues. The divinely unpretentious Monoblock A chairs are the most comfortable bar seating in all Douala and the atmosphere swings between garishly lit and sultry and well, garishly sultry and lit. The beer on offer is brewed in accordance with the German purity law of 1516. It's a nice venue, immaculately clean and very spruce – a place where even the German purity law could feel at home. Here, we meet local artists Hervé Yamguen and Hervé Youmbi and over a beer or two we get all the latest gossip about the Douala art scene.

"C'est bon, mais c'est trop fort," ("It's good, but it's too hot") says Dou Kaya, putting even more pepper sauce on his grilled fish. Dou – multitalented Egyptologist and musician – lives in an impressive mansion, a signature building of German colonial architecture right across the street from *L'Escale de Bonantone.* This restaurant/bar heads our list for its excellent seafood and the sophisticated atmosphere of the mixed but distinguished Deido quarter crowd. The high-concept design of intersecting patios and terraces with soothing purple and green spots blurs the boundaries between indoors and outdoors, design and function, seeing and being seen. We can comfortably watch the constant flow of passers-by or a selection of international video productions on multiple screens that include stunning surprises even for the new media connoisseur. The interior has plenty of wow: a shell of a building with exposed raw concrete beams and walls in a teasingly unfinished state skilfully set off against a corrugated-steel ceiling. The toilets are also deliberately designed to perplex alcohol-addled minds: the doors are hinged in the opposite direction to the way they look and there's no light switch … the door snaps shut behind you and – ta-da! – total darkness and no sense of orientation. What a lark.

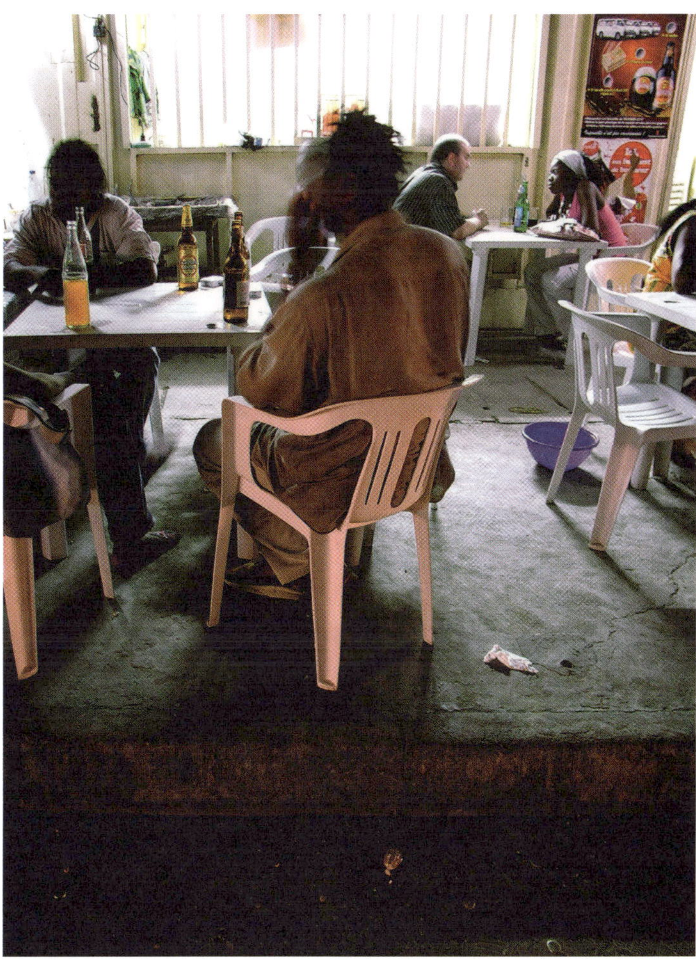

The pleasure-themed *Alt. Délices du Wouri* guarantees the ultimate in relaxation. The well-equipped shelves behind the bars
provide the input for heavenly dreams and the sheer enjoyment
of the good vibes of the company around. In the early evening,
this is the preferred meeting point for amorous couples and
later – after they have left for the more serious part of the date
– the artists and intellectuals take over. We were honoured to
share the night with painter Koko Komegne, the good spirit and
heart of the Douala art scene. He always finds the right words
to express the most profound thoughts with lightness and humour. But why do we discover the highest level of aesthetic consciousness here? It must be the bar's understated, minimalist
design and soft flow of fluorescent light that gives this venue its
unique atmosphere – which is just pinch-me-I'm-dreaming
magical.

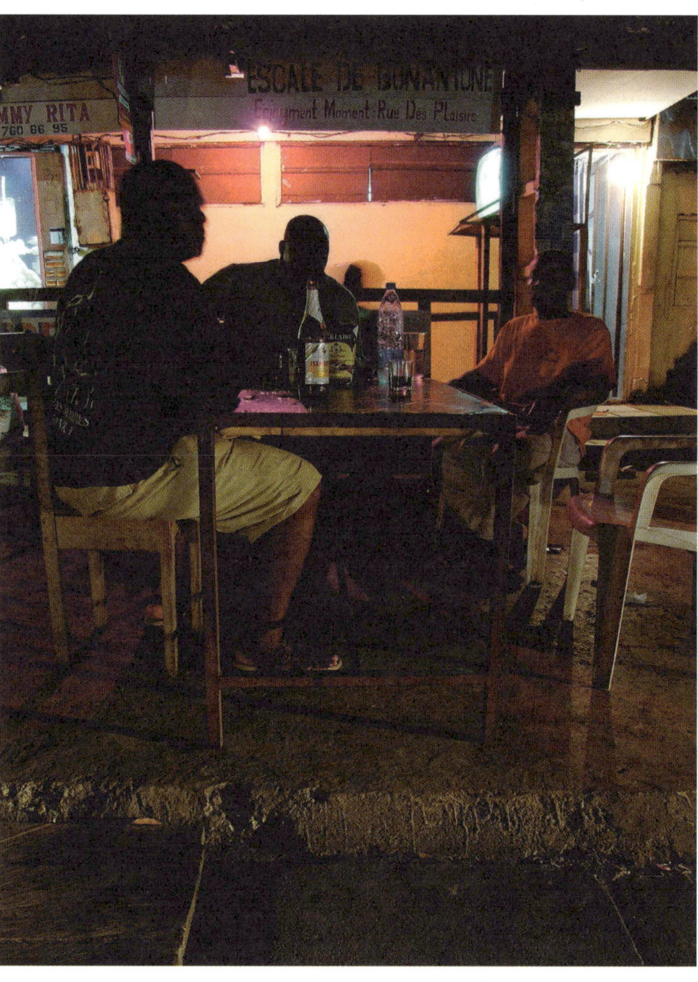

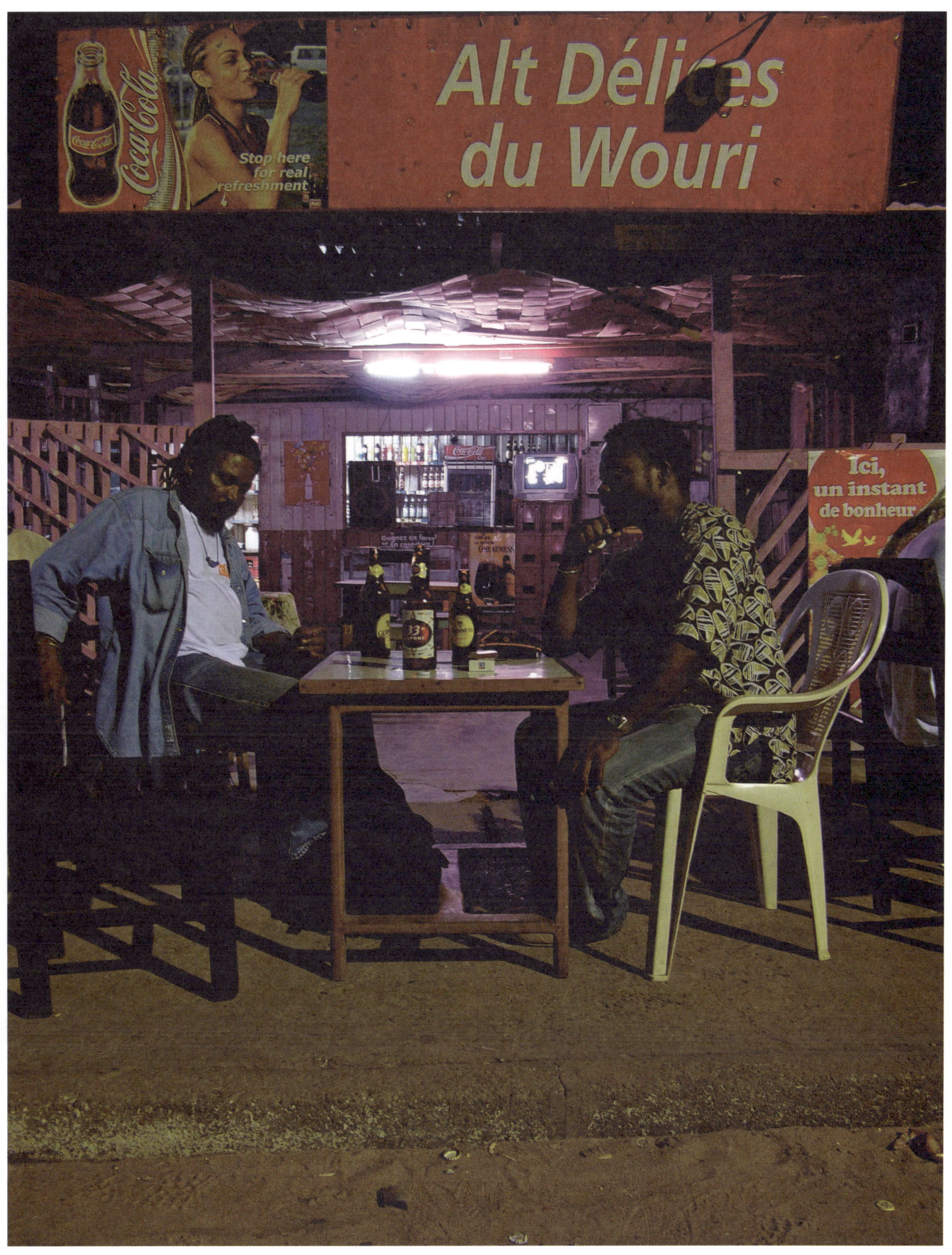

All photos: HANUSSEK & LINDOU, **ALT. DÉLICES DU WOURI**, 133 × 100 CM, 2007

Alternative City Futures[1]

EDGAR PIETERSE

The substantive objectives of the fifth session of the WUF (World Urban Forum) are to take stock of where the world stands with respect to the 'right to the city', to analyse who is getting the benefits of the urbanisation process and who is left out. The Forum also aims to share perspectives and viewpoints on the contemporary relevance of this right, to identify what is needed to bridge the urban divide, and to facilitate a prompt and sustainable transition from a city that is partially inclusive to one that is fully inclusive.[2]

We live in an era when the ideals of human rights have moved to the centre stage both politically and ethically. A great deal of energy is expended in promoting their significance for the construction of a better world. But for the most part the concepts circulating do not fundamentally challenge hegemonic liberal and neoliberal market logics, or the dominant modes of legality and state action.[3]

It is noteworthy that the recently completed global stage for urban policy debate, the World Urban Forum, was convened under the banner "Right to the City – Bridging the Urban Divide". It was a qualitatively different tenor to the previous forum where the headline message was "harmonisation". Significantly, the 2010 World Urban Forum was hosted by Brazil, which has gone further to enshrine the right to the city in law through the Statute on Cities.[4] The advancement of a more robust rights discourse, close on the heels of the global financial crisis and recession, the failed climate change negotiations in Copenhagen in December 2010 and the ongoing breakdown of the Doha trade negotiations are significant and suggest that there may be a fresh appetite to look more rigorously at the driving forces of structural poverty, inequality and urban exclusion in most cities of the world, no least in Africa. In this context, one could be inclined to concur with David Harvey that we are not seeing any fundamental realignment of power or control over resources that determine the fate of cities, but rather a feeble attempt to say the 'right' things from political and policy platforms without altering the status quo.

At the end of the World Urban Forum the Executive Director of UN-Habitat, Anna Tibaijuka, unveiled the World Urban Campaign. It came with a logo, YouTube-clips and a number of corporate partners – for instance Siemens, Veolia, ARCADIS – and a powerful invocation of: partnerships! And that seemed to be it! In her explanation, Tibaijuka pointed out that the campaign seeks to give effect to the Habitat Agenda adopted in Istanbul in 1996. But this is where communication about the substantive content of this new campaign ended. Presumably, it will continue or extend the two precursor campaigns on *Shelter for All* and *Good Urban Governance,* which have been trumpeted by UN-Habitat since the early 2000s, but not even this is clear.

Nevertheless, there can be little dispute that the urban question has arrived for good on public policy platforms as evidenced in the most recent World Bank Development report 2009,[5] OECD studies on climate change and cities[6], and most significantly, private sector policy perspectives.[7] Most recently, the African Development Bank embarked on a policy development process to produce an Urbanisation Strategy for Africa. By the end of 2010 this policy will be unveiled. On the other end of the spectrum, cities are also becoming increasingly the primary bases for the expression of political dissatisfaction through various forms of contestation and protest, raising the political relevance of urban settlements across diverse African contexts.

In this entire landscape one is left unsure about the nature, direction and possible outcomes of various urban interventions across Africa. In this essay I will explore the sounding mainstream policy approaches of UN-Habitat and associated agencies with regard to the recent campaigns to promote greater urban inclusion through the Shelter for All and Good Urban Governance campaigns. On the back of a critical review of these efforts, I will

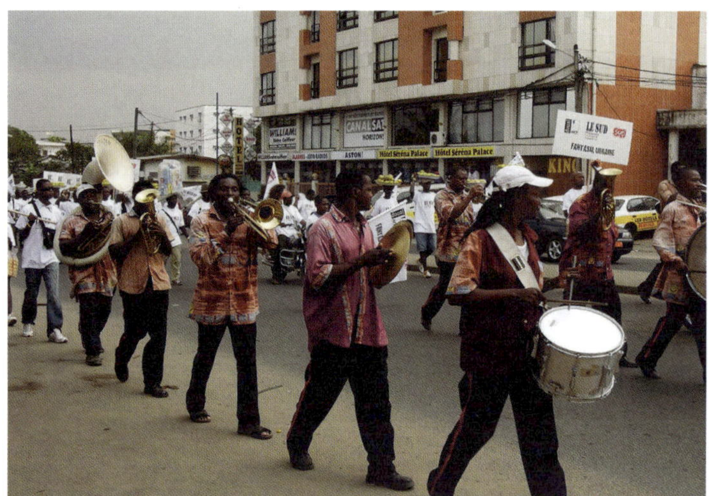

1   Parts of this essay are drawn with some modifications from Edgar Pieterse 2008, *City Futures: Confronting the Crisis of Urban Development,* London.

2   UN-Habitat 2010, *WORLD URBAN FORUM V: The Right to the City: Bridging the Urban Divide, Background Document* (unpublished report circulated to speakers at the WUF, author's personal copy)

3   David Harvey 2008, The Right to the City, *New Left Review* 53 (September–October): 23–40, here p. 23

4   Edesio Fernandes 2010, Participatory Budgeting Processes in Brazil – Fifteen Years Later, in: Caroline Wanjiku Kihato, Mejgan Massoumi, Blaire A. Ruble, Pep Subirós, Allison. M. Garland (eds), *Urban Diversity. Space, Culture, and Inclusive Pluralism in Cities Worldwide,* Baltimore

5   World Bank 2009, *World Development Report 2009: Reshaping Economic Geography,* Washington, DC

6   Lamia Kamal-Chaoui, Alexis Robert (eds) 2009, *Competitive Cities and Climate Change,* Paris

7   Monitor Group 2009, *Africa from the Bottom Up. Cities, Economic Growth, and Prosperity in Sub-Saharan Africa,* Johannesburg

move to a more propositional register and first set out some theoretical entry points about how to imagine alternatives before concluding with a fairly pragmatic agenda for what can be done if we are serious about intervening in the complex, shape-changing dynamics of African cities.

Navigating Progressive-Sounding Urban Discourses

There are two primary legs to the mainstream urban development agenda of development agencies during the past decade: a focus on securing tenure for all urban dwellers and a push for the adoption and deployment of participatory governance systems and practices, both within a broader institutional agenda of decentralisation. At face value these are all progressive ambitions that have important resonance just about everywhere in the Global South including Africa. If implemented successfully, these policy drives can indeed dramatically improve the living conditions and opportunity structure for urban majorities in African cities. It is therefore important to embrace these policy agendas but also remain vigilant about whether they are rigorous enough to attend to systemic drivers of urban poverty and inequality. In what follows, I will briefly explore both the *Shelter for All* agenda and then the Good Urban Governance campaign.

Shelter for All

The right to adequate housing was heavily contested at *The Habitat II Conference* in Istanbul in June 1996, primarily because the United States was vehemently opposed to it. This is one battle it lost, not least because newcomer on the global scene, South Africa, took a very strong position on the issue. Correctly, progressives in the urban development field celebrated the endorsement of a rights-based approach to housing, shelter and, by extension, land, as a momentous victory. However, by 2004, UN-Habitat admitted that "since the City Summit in Istanbul, it has become all too apparent that the conditions of the world's poor have not been improved, but have continued to deteriorate".[8] Thus, on the heels of the authoritative *The Challenge of Slums:* Global Report on Human Settlements 2003,[9] UN-Habitat unveiled a refined agenda to drive the Global Campaign for Secure Tenure (GCST). It became the central plank to advance the commitments member states made in the Habitat Agenda to providing "adequate shelter for all". The GCST, at the highest conceptual level, focused on preventative and adaptive strategies. The former focuses on a perspective and response that moves away from trying to stop migration from rural to urban areas, but rather to focus on how such patterns can be slowed down and managed more effectively to realise a more dispersed pattern of urban settlements, more amenable to economic and social management. Adaptive strategies are defined on the basis that developing countries need to come to terms with the enduring reality of large-scale informal settlements. Once acceptance occurs, substantial policy scaffolding needs to be developed and instituted. The adaptive focus provides guidance on what these policies are and how best to institutionalise them in various contexts. The absolute starting point of adaptation is an unambiguous move to ensure security of tenure. Thereafter, an array of policy considerations came into play.

In practical terms, adaptive strategies are cost-effective programmes and projects aimed at providing, in a sustainable manner: decent housing or house improvement schemes, including micro-credit for low-cost housing; a range of affordable tenure options that give tenure security to the poor; water and sanitation; disaster preparedness and prevention; community-led safer cities initiatives; solid waste management services; transport infrastructure and services; attracting investment through appropriate regulatory framework and increased productivity; environmentally sound urban policies; promoting inclusion, gender awareness and participatory decision-making; and building local capacities through decentralisation, legislative and institutional change and strengthening local governments.[10]

Furthermore, the GCST advocacy framework explicitly identifies it as a major problem and weakness in the overall shelter effort that the right to housing is largely ignored and frequently violated. In response, the GCST seeks to draw attention to the legal obligations on states to take it seriously and it has enrolled the Office of the United Nations High Commissioner for Human Rights, which in turn has appointed a Special Rapporteur on adequate housing. Interestingly, in 2007 the Special Rapporteur carried out a review of South Africa's housing policies and programmes. In one of his recommendations he points out the imperative for South Africa "to consider intervention in the market to regulate the current high and unaffordable prices, and to check against land and property speculation".[11] This is fascinating because it is of course the dominance of property rights, particularly private property rights (enshrined in the Constitution), that play a big part in the inability of South Africa to give effect to the progressive realisation of housing rights. Unfortunately, the tension between private property rights and housing rights are left hanging in the GCST, which weakens the transformative potential of the document. This is a curious oversight since the document itself recognises the causal role of unregulated, speculative land markets in perpetuating slums.

This silence also intimates a number of other problems in the GCST. A core message of the GCST is that "all forms of secure tenure can only be effective when they operate within an enabling legal framework, and they are supported by good governance

8   UN-Habitat 2004, *Global Campaign for Secure Tenure. A Tool for Advocating the Provision of Adequate Shelter for the Urban Poor. Concept Paper. 2nd edition.* Nairobi, p. 14

9   UN-Habitat 2003, *The Challenge of Slums. Global Report on Human Settlements 2003,* London

10   UN-Habitat 2004, p. 25

11   Press release: "United Nations Expert on Adequate Housing concludes visit to South Africa", retrieved on 13 February 2012 from http://www.unhchr.ch/huricane/huricane.nsf/view01/677CD0B04A46B831C12572D400412717?opendocument

and an administrative capacity."[12] The question this immediately raises is: To what extent are these preconditions likely to exist? Moreover, what are the factors that militate against their existence? For example, if informalised and back-street deal-making is the norm, how does one really engage and root out patronage-based politics? In most developing countries, especially in Africa, with relatively young or fragile democracies, political parties are embedded in the broader context of limited economic opportunities and a desperate need for access to scarce public resources. In these contexts, clientelist and patronage politics are a way of life.[13] Can weak local states be "fixed" in a short period of time? In any case, are there any firm indicators or evidence that national political-cultural factors that undermine substantive and funded decentralisation of functions are likely to change in the immediate future given trend patterns over the past decade? It is important to contextualise these lines of questioning by reference to the aftermath of devastating structural adjustment policies that have eroded national power, authority and capability. None of these central governance questions are satisfactorily addressed or even flagged in the campaign materials.

Furthermore, market pressures and trends are under-estimated in the document. Part of why effective regulation of land and property markets is difficult is because developing countries are typically highly dependent on a relatively small tax-paying class that sustain the coffers of the state, and often, also the individual interests of senior politicians in the ruling party and the state. Considering the impact of the globalisation of property markets, and increasingly, real estate and developer companies, it is apparent that the regulatory power of states with regard to developers and investors are limited. And as the GCST recognises, without strong regulatory intervention in land markets through appropriate tenure systems and land-use instruments, advancing the approach advocated for by the GCST will be very difficult. In this context, it is a serious omission that there is not a more explicit and detailed argument about specific regulations and regulating systems to structure and steer land-use patterns more effectively. It seems to me that an emphasis on particular kinds of tenure that are most optimal for the urban poor cannot be divorced from a larger framework of urban management instruments that needs to be in place to impact decisively and effectively on urban land markets.

This gap in the approach to tenure security as a pathway to adequate shelter, throws up the question, what are the elements of the bigger picture? Clearly, the first aspect is access to basic services within a framework that guarantees access for those who are too poor to pay. Also, tenure regularisation must unfold in tandem with a "locality-within-a-region" approach to the extension of basic services. In other words, infrastructure investments and maintenance systems for a particular informal settlement must be designed and planned with explicit reference to a larger urban regional approach. In part, because how services are extended and maintained offer crucial opportunities to deal with unemployment and informal service providers who can be enrolled into more regularised and context sensitive models of delivery. In another sense, a regional approach is crucial because the infrastructural response must be consistent with regional-level objectives to achieve a more environmentally sustainable urban form and system, for example a system that progressively reduces unsustainable patterns of consumption and production and facilitates more equitable spatial patterns and relations.

Participatory Urban Governance

The second leg of the mainstream urban development agenda is governance, which found expression in *The Global Campaign on Urban Governance* (GCUG). The GCUG is striking for its bold discourse evidenced in the explicit poverty-reduction focus underpinned by the principles of equity, urban justice and urban citizenship. These are of course potentially powerful principles that are suggestive of radical reform. Flowing from these principles, the campaign sets its sights on the policy ideal of realising an inclusive city, "because inclusive decision-making is at the heart of good urban governance"[14]. According to the concept paper, local contexts in cities and towns are always marked by "the messy reality of competing interests and priorities" and it is therefore essential that the institutions charged with balancing and reconciling competing interests are as inclusive as possible because inclusivity guarantees "the greatest likelihood for sustainability".[15] There are a number of conceptual leaps made here which require a closer look.

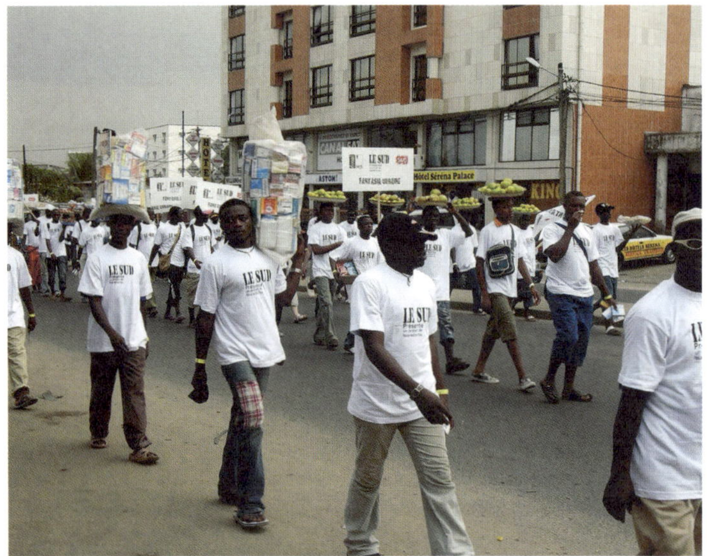

---

12 UN-Habitat 2004, p. 41

13 For a fascinating and counter-intuitive exploration of these issues and their implications for economic development, see Solomon Benjamin 2004, Urban Land Transformation for Pro-Poor Economies, *Geoforum 35/2:* 177–187, for the African context, see Patrick Chabal 2009, *Africa: The Politics of Suffering and Smiling,* London.

14 UN-Habitat 2002, *The Global Campaign on Urban Governance. Concept Paper. Revised edition,* Nairobi

15 UN-Habitat 2002, p. 15

Conceptually, the position paper then moves on to define a range of norms that substantiate what good urban governance means and these are: sustainability, subsidiarity, equity, efficiency, transparency and accountability, civic engagement, and citizenships and security, which are all defined as interdependent and mutually reinforcing. The bulk of the concept paper is then devoted to unpacking each of these principles in terms of objectives and practical actions that can be embarked upon to give effect to each of the principles. In this regard, the objectives are mostly incontestable and the practical measures suggested are indeed far-reaching. Furthermore, a wide array of "cutting-edge" urban management reforms are endorsed and promoted by the document. For example, participatory budgeting, full information transparency on the part of governments, quotas for women in local councils because of their systematic disempowerment in most societies, full inheritance rights for women, and so on. Indeed it is hard to quibble with most of the proposed objectives and practical measures.

In particular I want to lift out three of the policy positions which provide an important set of reference points for a radical urban agenda. Firstly, the foregrounding of the urban poor is an important step forward. In most cities in the world, not least in Africa, the urban poor remain largely voiceless, excluded from decision-making, and usually the biggest sufferers of painful urban reforms whether reforms are in the economy, environment or the built environment. Also, where local democratisation processes are underway, it often continues to effectively exclude the poor as elites – who straddle political and economic domains – quickly achieve dominance over nominally democratic systems for cultural, historical and economic reasons.[16] Secondly, the strong emphasis on a comprehensive rights-based approach to development is important because it leads one to a set of political claims that can expose the unequal distribution of resources more clearly, which in turn could serve as a basis for multi-pronged mobilisation strategies that include litigation. Thirdly, the focus on the indivisibility of the various areas of reform is very significant and important to reinforce. Often reluctant states tend to window-dress their democratisation efforts with one or two symbolic measures and leave the larger functioning of their economies unreformed. The approach of the policy paper makes it clear that such attempts at policy sophistry are wrong and unacceptable.

Despite these important advances in thinking and prescription, the policy paper also suffers from a number of serious weaknesses, which may be unavoidable due to the fact that it is a UN document and must by definition find a language and minimalism, or rather, sophisticated implicitness, which is accommodating of the diverse interests of member countries. Nevertheless, given the influence and mandate of the UN, it is equally important to point out the consequences of issues left unsaid or glossed over. The biggest problem with the paper is that it leaves power unexplained and therefore unexposed. There is no explicit line drawn between the conditions the document seeks to remedy and the causal drivers of those conditions. In particular, there is no explanation of why urban exclusion, inequality and systematic dispossession is by and large the norm in most African cities, and more importantly, how these conditions persist, often get worse, despite public policies that are nominally pro-poor. This is particularly important because modern forms of rule by post-colonial states rely on justifications (or public discourses) for their actions that may be progressive at the level of formal rhetoric but deeply unjust in terms of the systematic exploitation of the urban poor that it tolerates and effectively facilitates by failing to regulate elite and private sector actions effectively, while maintaining an impression that the state is pro-poor. This insidious form of modern rule[17] is one of the most important aspects of urban governance that requires direct engagement if we are to advance the principles promoted by the UN-Habitat concept paper on urban governance.

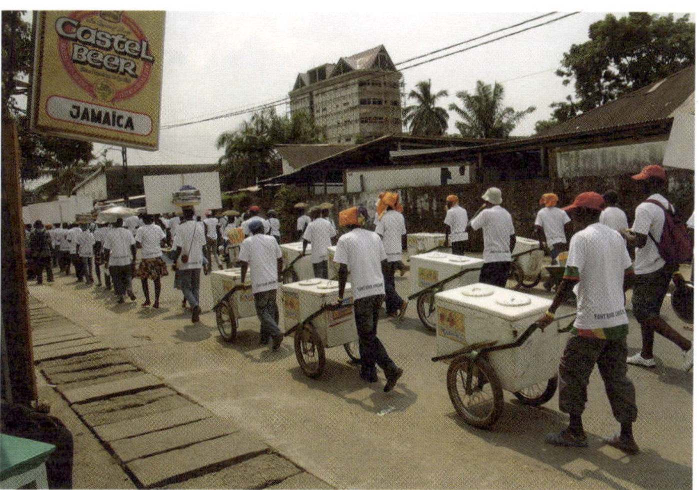

Another major problem with the concept paper is that it projects a too homogenous and uncomplicated view of the urban poor as if they are a single category. For instance, when the document argues that "the ability of the urban poor to influence local decision-making greatly determines the 'pro-poorness' of local strategic planning"[18] it obscures the fact that if one does not disaggregate the urban poor in terms of locality, economic positioning, religious and ethnic identity, generation, political sympathies, and so forth, one can design and propagate very bad participatory processes and institutions. In most cities of the Global South social life and identities comprise a myriad of complex fissure lines and ever changing moods. Also, poor sectors are marked by a variety of hierarchies and lines of internal exclusion and

---

16 James Manor 2004, Democratisation with Inclusion: Political Reforms and the People's Empowerment at the Grassroots, *Journal of Human Development, 5/1:* 5–29

17 For more explicit elaborations of this phenomenon, see Andrea Cornwall 2004, Spaces for Transformation? Reflections on Issues of Power and Difference in Participation in Development, in: Samuel Hickey, Giles Mohan (eds), *Participation: From Tyranny to Transformation. Exploring New Approaches to Participation in Development,* London: p.75–91; and Faranak Miraftab 2004, Making Neo-liberal Governance: The Disempowering Work of Empowerment, *International Planning Studies,* 9/4: 239–259; for a more nuanced articulation of this argument, see Glyn Williams 2004, Evaluating Participatory Development: Tyranny, Power and (Re)Politicisation, *Third World Quarterly, 25/3:* 557–578.

18 UN-Habitat 2002, p. 11

domination, which can produce "winners" and "losers", and "insiders" and "outsiders" amongst the poor. Effective governance processes aimed at transforming unequal power relations must be highly sensitive to these dynamics and refrain from the constructing of the large numbers of urban poor as in any way homogenous or singular.

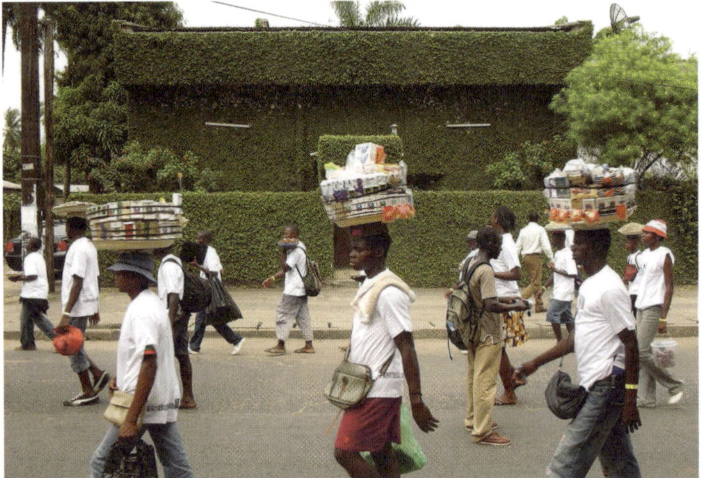

My last major problem with the concept paper is that it relies heavily on a consensus-based model of urban politics. This is explicitly asserted in the idea that stakeholder forums that bring together the various actors in the city are best placed to "agree on a broad-based, mission statement and long-term vision for the city, using tools such as strategic planning". The assumption is that deliberative democratic[19] forums are most likely to facilitate an explicit process of surfacing differences in the city, and through carefully guided processes arrive at agreements on how best to move forward. As I have demonstrated elsewhere this kind of over-confidence in the necessary outcomes of stakeholder-based deliberative democracy is simply misplaced because urban conflict and the irresolvability of many urban questions are an integral part of vibrant urban politics and need to be accepted and recognised as such.[20] On this note, I will move to the second half of the essay that sets out some broad theoretical markers for how best to think about alternatives before exploring implications for Africa.

Alternative Urban Approaches

In thinking through the prospects of alternatives, it is crucial to appreciate the constitutive nature of power and complexity in the city. Any analysis of urban conditions and future prospects must come to terms with the dimensions of complexity and the ways in which it is sutured by various dynamics of power. This opens the door, conceptually, to two central ideas: radical incrementalism[21] and recursive[22] political empowerment. But first a few comments of clarification on the intertwined ideas of complexity and power and particularly the tension wire that runs between these dynamics and which animates much in the contemporary city.

Following the broader turn in the social sciences to ideas about complexity, the pervasive reality of contingency is widely recognised. Contingency reminds us that incessant uncertainties and surprises are commonplace in most development contexts. Of course such uncertainties coexist with structural factors that reproduce uneven spatial development patterns but such factors do not explain or predetermine the fate of development ambitions and interventions. According to Emery Roe, development issues are fundamentally "highly uncertain and complex [because] many, if not most, parties to these issues, including the experts, are in the grip of many unknowns, frequent surprise, and little agreement, where few involved know what really is in their best long-run interests, and where almost everyone is playing it by ear – and this includes the so-called power brokers."[23] In more recent times, complexity theory as a philosophical stream has also been deployed to capture the interactions of various physical, social, economic, political, ecological and cultural systems in urban spaces, producing an infinite number of unpredictable dynamics. Thus, for urbanist David Byrne the city must be approached and explored as a fundamentally emergent and therefore open-ended reality: Cities are plainly dissipative complex systems with emergent properties and evolutionary history. The identification of cities as dissipative systems matters a great deal because it describes the relationship between urban places, the "unnatural" location of contemporary life within a "built" environment and the natural systems of this planet. Cities are indeed complex systems that are themselves embedded within both the complex system of global economic and cultural relations, and the complex systems which compose the natural world.[24] What this dense formulation suggests is that there are always so many variables at play in how cities function, unfold and incessantly become something different. It is important to assume a constitutive complexity, heightened by the rapidity of change in a globalised world, as central to the rebus character of cities. On the other hand it is also fair to say that even if we are to appreciate the significance of complexity, uncertainty, surprise and therefore open-ended futures, or at least malleable futures, we cannot deny that power is at the heart of city development because governance boils down to questions of control over decision-making about how resources are used in a sea of competing and different interests. Fortunately our thinking about power has evolved beyond mere notions of "Who benefits?", "Who is getting exploited?", "How badly are they exploited?" to understanding the dynamic, capillary and decentred nature of circuits

19 The concept of deliberative democracy comes from political theory and characterises a form of democracy where the public formulation of consensus on objectives and opinions plays a major role. A deliberative democracy has a multiplicity of discourses and negotiation processes [editor's note].

20 Edgar Pieterse 2005, Transgressing the Limits of Possibility: Working Notes on a Relational Model of Urban Politics, in: AbdouMaliq Simone, Abdelghani Abouhani (eds), *Urban Africa. Changing Contours for the Survival in the City,* London: p. 138–176

21 Incrementalism describes a strategy or political style of taking a gradual, step-by-step approach to changing existing structures and processes. This facilitates a monitoring process and, if necessary, the withdrawal of the individual reforms that have been introduced [editor's note].

22 In political science, recursion describes strategies and measures where the objectives and results are continually compared with the corresponding starting conditions and their gradual change [editor's note].

23 Strictly speaking, Emery Roe distinguishes between the following dimensions of complexity: "The number of components in a system, the degree of differentiation in components, and the degree of interdependence between components [...] The most important characteristic of complexity in Demchack's words, is 'that complexity produces surprise.'" (Emery Roe 1993, Against Power: For the Politics of Complexity, *Transition*, 62: 90–104, here p. 93–94).

24 David Byrne 2001, *Understanding the Urban,* New York, p. 11

of power that are always unstable and vulnerable to resistance and transformation.[25] In response to Roe, and taking on board the insights about complexity, anthropologist Donald Moore offers a useful multifaceted approach to power: "Instead of simply mapping typologies of power [as Roe does], alternative perspectives could emphasise the practices through which power operates, the symbolic and material effects power produces, and its performance. "In feminist cultural critic Judith Butler's terms: Performativity describes this relation of being implicated in that which one opposes, this turning of power against itself to reproduce alternative modalities of power, to establish a kind of political contestation that is not a 'pure' opposition, a 'transcendence' of contemporary relations of power, but a difficult labour of forging a future from resources inevitably impure."[26]

The reason I find these two lenses – complexity and power – useful is because it allows one to respond to the existing mainstream literature and more critical conceptual approaches to cities and begin to build something akin to a bridge between them. The complexity lens allows us to address the technical, technocratic and managerialist discourses and imperatives characteristic of the various literatures in the domain of urban management. Thus, it makes it possible to not simply dismiss all mainstream evolution in policy thinking as mere expressions of neo-liberal forms of rule but rather to engage in a more differentiated way with what can be the basis for radical imaginings and interventions, and what cannot, as I have attempted to do before. This is not to lose sight of the fact that technical solutions are often oblivious to power dynamics and by default are in fact profoundly political in their effects. A danger that is ever present as progressive-sounding urban policies continue to produce or perpetuate unjust and inequitable urban outcomes.

Radical Incrementalism

The existential core of urbanism is the desire for radical change to bring all the good implied in the original utopian association of the city.[27] This radicalism impulse stands in contrast to the necessary prudence and constraints of "incremental change", which is the only way of intervening in conditions of profound complexity and entrenched power dynamics embedded in capitalist modernities.

We know that the current scale of human suffering and violence that flows from the profoundly unequal distribution of resources and opportunity is fundamentally inhumane and intolerable. Yet, we also know that we cannot wish into existence an overnight revolution that will make everything all right in the world. At the same time it seems futile to simply work away at creating the right conditions for insurrectionary revolutions that will eventually bring to life a large-scale "militant refusal" by the world's urban multitudes, as intimated by Mike Davis.[28] This leaves one with bringing change into the world through more discrete avenues: surreptitious, sometimes overt, and multiple small revolutions that at unanticipated and unexpected moments galvanise into deeper ruptures that accelerate tectonic shifts of the underlying logics of domination and what is considered possible. Radical incrementalism is a disposition and sensibility that believes in deliberate actions of social transformation but through a multiplicity of processes and imaginations, none of which assumes or asserts a primary significance over other struggles. This position may not resolve the existential struggle of urbanism, but it provides a means to confront the struggle and perpetually work one's way through it, stumbling across what works and does not. Stuart Hall captured this sensibility with great acuity: "[…] are we not all, in different ways, and through different conceptual spaces […] desperately trying to understand what making an ethical political choice and taking a political position in a necessarily open and contingent political field is like, what sort of 'politics' it adds up to?"[29] Keeping this sensibility of ethical searching in mind, I will now briefly explore recursive political empowerment.

Recursive Political Empowerment

Transformative change in cities cannot be bestowed by a (benign) state, nor can it take root simply as a consequence of good policy plus political will (whatever this over-used and under-specified notion may mean). Transformative urban change that leads to the enhancement of "capabilities" of the poor and abandoned require agency by these very same constituencies; agency, ideally inserted into a multidirectional meshwork of institutions and discourses that frame the functioning and reproduction of urban systems. However, the mobilisation of these constituencies is not at all a straightforward matter because "the poor" and "the abandoned" – as already mentioned – are never cohesive, or coherent, or homogenous in any way. Complex and shifting identities and group-based associations, embedded in dynamic cultural processes, render the urban majorities inherently fragmented and contested. Furthermore, neighbourhoods and associational circuits where the urban poor are concentrated are typically stratified by deep power differentials between those who control and channel resources in and out of these areas and those rendered dependent on such gate-keeping.

Engaging with these multilayered realities requires a degree of awareness and a (personal) decision to participate in structures and processes that can lead to an improvement in one's lot. Significantly, people's sense of possibility is closely tied to culturally shaped assessments of opportunities and threats associated with participation. Such calculations, in turn, are intertwined with a sense of being and self in relation to place and particular

25 Ash Amin, Nigel Thrift 2005, What is Left? Only the Future, *Antipode, 37/2:* 220–238, and Joanne P. Sharp et al. 2000, Entanglements of Power: Geographies of Domination/Resistance, in: Joanne P. Sharp, Paul Routledge, Chris Philo, Ronan Paddison (eds), *Entanglements of Power: Geographies of DominationRresistance,* London, p. 1–42; an interesting attempt to question the totalising tendencies of some Foucauldian interpretations of power can be explored in Clive Barnett 2005, Consolations of Neoliberalism, *Geoforum,* 36/1: 7–12.

26 Donald Moore 1994, Optics of Engagement: Power, Positionality and African Studies, *Transition* 63: 121–127, here p. 123; Judith Butler quoted after: Judith Butler 1995, *Körper von Gewicht. Die diskursiven Grenzen des Geschlechts,* Berlin, p. 318.

27 Ash Amin 2006, The Good City, *Urban Studies,* 43/(5/6): 1009–1023

28 Mike Davis 2005, *Planet of Slums.* London

29 Stuart Hall 1996, When was 'The Post-Colonial'? Thinking at the Limit, in: Iain Chambers, Lidia Curti (eds) *The Postcolonial Question. Common Skies, Divided Horizons.* London, p. 242–260, here p. 244

30 These ideas are persuasively developed in the various writings of Arjun Appadurai whose work seeks to capture the indeterminate dynamics of processes of identity formation and agency in some of the harshest urban contexts in the world; see Arjun Appadurai 2002, Deep Democracy: Urban Governmentality and the Horizon of Politics, *Public Culture,* 14/1: 21–47; Arjun Appadurai 2004, The capacity to aspire: culture and the terms of recognition, in: Vijayendra Rao, Michael Walton (eds), *Culture and Public Action,* Stanford, p. 59–84.

communities.[30] Thus, a viable notion of empowerment of the poor requires an appreciation that empowerment is fundamentally an individual process that deepens with time if individual efforts are consciously embedded in more collective forms of solidarity and mutual empowerment. The practice of Slum/Shack Dwellers International (SDI) illustrates this effectively.[31] SDI explicitly seeks to build autonomy from the state and informal power brokers, whilst socialising their members into an alternative normative framework, which in turn becomes the basis of mobilisation and legitimacy in their work. With these conceptual anchorage points in place, I will now explore in brief strokes what the drivers of urban public policy failure are in Africa and what the specific elements of alternative agenda may be.

African Urban Crisis

In many African cities and towns, slum life is the norm. As demonstrated in Mike Davis' *Planet of Slums,* this translates into a harsh, complex (because it is also interlaced with the energies and ingenuity of people living their lives) but ultimately unacceptable condition for humans making their way in the world. However, UN-Habitat instructs us in the latest *State of the World's Cities Report 2008/09* that almost all of the projected urban growth in Africa, over the next two decades, will take the form of slum growth. This is a startling assertion given that routinised exploitation, in the form of insecure tenure, evictions or threats thereof, and generalised extortion for access to any basic or economic service, dominate the lives of slum dwellers. The urban poor who eke out a livelihood in Africa's slums arguably pay the highest transaction costs even though their states and local markets systematically fail them. Of course, it goes almost without saying that this scale of abuse cannot simply reproduce indefinitely. It is already clear, as second and third generation urbanites reach adulthood in African cities, that social unrest and generalised volatility become features of everyday life, threatening not only the well being of slum dwellers but the political stability of the city and the private market interests that agglomerate there. Strikingly, even though no one can predict how long this state of affairs can continue without erupting into outright violence and social disruption, there seems to be no discernable sense of urgency or concern amongst political and business elites about this state of affairs. In fact, the dominant policy response to the deepening crises associated with urban growth and expansion is inertia.

Drivers of Public Policy Failure

There are many complex factors that underlie the failure of urban policy and development in Africa of which external ones related to Africa's general marginalisation in the global economy is not an insignificant issue. However, here I am more interested in proposing four internal factors that require deeper analysis and response. First and foremost is the prevailing governmental attitude that urbanisation is something bad or undesirable that needs to be prevented and, failing that, reversed through effective rural development policies leading to a refusal to provide for "illegal" urban dwellers. As a consequence of this official attitude poor urban dwellers are regarded with deep suspicion and loathing because they are seen as a threat to the "order" and "stability" of the (formal) city. Second, political elites in many African countries have grown up and consolidated their positions through the effective nurturing of political cultures of authoritarianism and sectarianism. Practically, what this means is that the interest of the party always trumps the interest of the state or society at large. Consequently, policy agendas, priorities and resource allocations are driven by narrow party interests (and especially those of party leaders) as opposed to a democratically negotiated consensus around public interest. In urban areas this often means that the need for control of local neighbourhoods and resources comes before the empowerment of local actors, whether they be local state institutions or autonomous civil society organisations.

Third, it is important to underscore the centrality of limited public funding for urban development programmes. Given that up to 70 per cent of urban economic economy can be informal, revenue from local taxes is simply too limited to cover the cost of essential infrastructures and intergovernmental transfers are not adequate to address these deficits. Fourth, another crucial systemic failure in the African response to the challenges of urbanisation is the weakness of civil society institutions that are compelled to function in fragile democratic political spheres, draining cities of accountability. In fact, given the scale of need, urban contexts are ripe for conflict, abuse and routinised exploitation of the destitute. This makes the emergence of democratic civil society institutions very difficult.

These factors, wanton governmental neglect of the urban question, linked to short-sighted imperatives to maintain political control of ideas and spaces, amidst very limited financial resources and ineffectual civil society voices, add up to a context with no, or very limited, political accountability. Without accountability there is simply not the requisite incentive to devise, sustain and deepen a meaningful urban policy reform agenda. Against this backdrop of long-term and intractable policy failure, I want to now turn to key aspects of alternative agenda for urban development rooted in the sensibilities of radical incrementalism and recursive empowerment.

31 Celine d'Cruz, David Satterthwaite 2005, *Building Homes, Changing Official Approaches: The Work of Urban Poor Organizations and their Federations and their Contributions to Meeting the Millennium Development Goals in Urban Areas,* Working Paper 16, London

Towards an Alternative Development Trajectory for African Cities

The first step in addressing the crises of urbanisation in Africa is to accept the need for a paradigm change in how we think about and respond to this complex and challenging phenomenon. At the heart of this new paradigm is the subversive idea that our greatest resource and opportunity to solve the African urban crises lies with the people who eke out an existence in slums. In other words, instead of regarding the urban poor and excluded urbanites as the problem, we can recognise the energies and ingenuity that they marshal to retain a foothold in the city despite the odds. Achieving this paradigm shift in minds and institutional machineries of African governments and politicians will be a gargantuan challenge but one we need to overcome through careful argument, backed by evidence and effective coalitions of interest to simultaneously advance the agenda for urban transformation on multiple fronts.

A major implication of this paradigm adjustment is that the urban poor who live in informal settlements and on occupied land must be recognised and afforded security in our cities. Once this happens, it opens up the possibility for urban consolidation, which, in turn, is a precondition for investment and asset growth. If the urban poor are secured from forced evictions and extortion by unregulated (informal) land and rent-lords, they are more likely to prioritise the education of their children, which is the only long-term solution to economic inclusion and the empowerment of whole populations. Furthermore, if the urban poor are secured against arbitrary violence and abuse, they are more likely to invest in social formations and organisations that can play a pivotal role in improving health and social wellbeing. The more the health status of the urban poor improves, the greater the likelihood of successful and growing small-scale enterprises and savings associations. The more the urban poor are enrolled in economically viable and growing concerns, the greater their aggregate contribution to the urban economy. This will generate demand for more services and finance in the economy, which in turn has the potential to grow the tax base and resource pool for city-wide infrastructure, benefiting the entire economy at a city-region and national level. But this virtuous circle begins by fundamentally changing mindsets.

In very broad outlines, we can foresee seven lines of action and research that can be pursued to advance the paradigm shift and to consolidate urban transformation once the shift is in place. The first dimension is what one can term open-source social infrastructures. The rich experiences of savings-based urban social movements such as Shack/Slum Dwellers International and Streetnet epitomise the kind of social infrastructure we have in mind. Their practice makes it possible to envisage a more democratic, horizontal, network-based "Wiki" model of urban development that takes the collective efforts of the urban poor to address their needs as a starting and inspiration point for how to design appropriate urban interventions. This model, which centres on autonomy, democratic exchange, learning and joint priority setting between the local state and the urban poor (without excluding other actors who have a bearing on the city) provides the key to the institutional framework required to address our urban crises.

Second, given the crises of un- and under-employment, it is crucial to ramp up more imaginative and effective public works programmes catering for the following categories of need: a) labour-intensive jobs to install, maintain, repair and revitalise urban infrastructure, especially in informal settlements but also along strategic transport corridor routes required to capitalise on the global demand for African commodities; b) social development services to address the home-based care needs of Aids sufferers, orphaned children, pre-school children and the elderly who have been left redundant; c) environmental services related to recycling economies and the replenishing of degraded ecosystem services that our cities and towns rely on; and d) artistic and cultural services to animate public spaces, enrich learning spaces and animate collective action. All four of these areas of public service activities can be designed and rolled out at scale, creating a mechanism to channel large numbers of youth into the formal labour market.

Third, infrastructure-led actions and urban reforms to simultaneously address economic, social and environmental challenges that coalesce in cities offer another vital avenue for action. It is clear that Africa is at the centre of the raw material inputs that is driving international growth, particularly in the emerging economies. This economic positioning must be deployed more strategically. The challenge is to recognise the need for "targeted" infrastructure investment to improve the logistical efficiency of African economies to get products to these markets and use the same investments to radically lower the economic and social reproductive costs of the urban poor. This will ensure more widespread and equitable access to urban services for local labour forces, helping to grow labour absorption and enhance productivity. There is an undeniable opportunity for synergy between addressing the fundamental needs for safe water, decent sanitation, affordable energy and transportation by urban populations (often the majorities in African cities) who live without these essentials, and the imperative of improving the logistics of getting products and services to regional and global markets.

Fourth, given the centrality of land markets to the patterning of urban growth and movement, it is imperative to pursue reforms in this domain. One of the most devastating and pernicious systems of urban exclusion in many African countries is the approach to land-use management and land rights. State and market failure with respect to investment in housing that is suitable to the needs and life-cycle conditions of the urban poor is at the heart of the slums crisis. Thus, what is required are more effective policies to achieve an approach to land-use regulation that can simultaneously address the unique needs of the urban poor who live in ill-defined legal contexts, and the formal city that depends on clear-cut regulations. One practical instrument to overcome this divide is "innovative planning zones or action plans for slum upgrading."[32] Such instruments allow municipalities to advance better urban integration, but also investment frameworks that allow for the systematic upgrading of services in informal settlements without producing a new cycle of exclusion.

Fifth, we need to build meaningful democratic systems that impact on the allocative decisions that drive urban development processes. This implies the need for effective countervailing institutions and organisations, in particular, autonomous organisations of the urban poor. We need to think of deepening the democratic agenda in Africa's cities and towns along three tracks that reinforce one another. The first and most urgent priority is to create an explicit incentive system for the urban poor to organise themselves effectively to advance their own social and economic reproductive interests. The second imperative is to deepen and widen democratic deliberative forums beyond the halls of local government and national agencies. Instead, forums for democratic deliberation that are focused on competing needs and the imperative of making choices about trade-offs for clearly defined reasons, must be established. Experiments in participatory budgeting are good examples of more potent deliberative mechanisms. However, participatory budgeting or other tools to democratically discuss and contest resource allocation priorities can fail if they are not tied to an explicit engagement with the spatial form and dynamics of the city. Thus, the third aspect of reform must recognise the inherently uneven and unequal allocation of value in urban spaces and seek a corrective for that. Another important agenda for democratic reform and embedding is, thus, the democratisation of planning in general and more recent innovations such as City Development Strategies that aim to forge a shared agenda for long-term urban investment and development.

Sixth, all of the above imply the existence and evolution of robust institutions, networks and learning as the preferred means to address knotty urban problems that manifest uniquely in different urban settings. Defining strategies, drivers and resources to develop such infrastructures must therefore be prioritised as an integral part of the urban transformation agenda.

Lastly, effective data collection and analysis to inform processes, decisions and action on an ongoing and recursive basis is a fundamental prerequisite for success of the lines of action explored here. At the most basic level we need to invest many more resources to improve the coverage and reliability of conventional survey instruments such as national surveys. However, over and above the problem of basic data, we are also confronted by an intellectual legacy in the urban field that is atheoretical, aspatial and often even ahistorical. Instead, urban research suffers from a "relevance" reflex. A number of urban scholars and activists pride themselves in the fact that they are only interested in practical policy questions that can solve real problems. The problem with this approach is that it fails to appreciate that all data must be interpreted and interpretation depends on theoretical assumptions and the more one renders those invisible, the greater the likelihood that analysis will be wrong or partial. We must come to terms with the fact that African cities are characterised by profound levels of hybridity and complexity and will remain impervious to understanding and effective policy action unless we can foster a richer, more nuanced and context-specific lexicon of African urbanism.

In Conclusion

In this essay I have sought to demonstrate that the urban development question is becoming increasingly recognised on the global policy stage. Within this landscape, the pertinence of campaigns of UN-Habitat on shelter for all and participatory urban governance both seek to advance greater urban inclusion, or in recent policy parlance, the right to the city. These are welcome discursive shifts but we need to remain vigilant about the disjuncture between these policy ideals and the material political practices on the ground in African cities. With this criticality we need to formulate alternative, more politically robust, claims for how the crisis in African cities could be understood and addressed. As *Afropolis* demonstrates, artistic and cultural interventions and reimagining have a substantive contribution to make in this regard. In all, African criticality calls forth a new kind of politics of intervention that is equal measure to science, craft and art, inevitably perched on the edge of the impossible …

Editors' notes translated by Andrew Boreham

---

32 Nicholas You 2007, Sustainable for Whom? The Urban Millennium and Challenges for Redefining the Global Development Planning Agenda, *City,* 11/2: 214–220, here p. 219

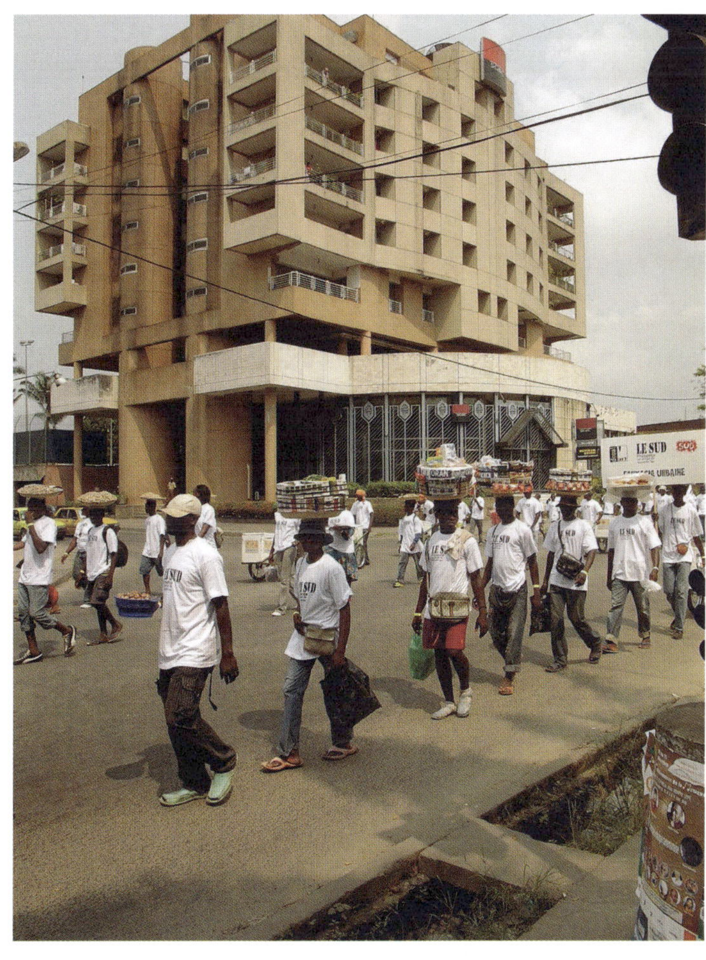

All photos: ©Christian Hanussek. The photos document *Fantasia Urbaine,*
an art project by Pascale Marthine Tayou, on the occasion of the festival
SUD (*Salon Urbaine de Douala*), 16 December 2007.

People as Infrastructure
Intersecting Fragments in Johannesburg[1]

ABDOUMALIQ SIMONE

The inner city of Johannesburg is about as far away as one can get from the popular image of the African village. Though one of Africa's most urbanized settings, it is also seen as a place of ruins – of ruined urbanization, the ruining of Africa by urbanization. But in these ruins, something else besides decay might be happening. This essay explores the possibility that these ruins not only mask but also constitute a highly urbanized social infrastructure. This infrastructure is capable of facilitating the intersection of socialities so that expanded spaces of economic and cultural operation become available to residents of limited means.

This essay is framed around the notion of people as infrastructure, which emphasizes economic collaboration among residents seemingly marginalized from and immiserated by urban life. Infrastructure is commonly understood in physical terms, as reticulated systems of highways, pipes, wires, or cables. These modes of provisioning and articulation are viewed as making the city productive, reproducing it, and positioning its residents, territories, and resources in specific ensembles where the energies of individuals can be most efficiently deployed and accounted for.

By contrast, I wish to extend the notion of infrastructure directly to people's activities in the city. African cities are characterized by incessantly flexible, mobile, and provisional intersections of residents that operate without clearly delineated notions of how the city is to be inhabited and used. These intersections, particularly in the last two decades, have depended on the ability of residents to engage complex combinations of objects, spaces, persons and practices. These conjunctions become an infra-

structure – a platform providing for and reproducing life in the city. Indeed, as I illustrate through a range of ethnographic materials on inner-city Johannesburg, an experience of regularity capable of anchoring the livelihoods of residents and their transactions with one another is consolidated precisely because the outcomes of residents' reciprocal efforts are radically open, flexible, and provisional. In other words, a specific economy of perception and collaborative practice is constituted through the capacity of individual actors to circulate across and become familiar with a broad range of spatial, residential, economic, and transactional positions. Even when actors do different things with one another in different places, each carries traces of past collaboration and an implicit willingness to interact with one another in ways that draw on multiple social positions. The critical question thus raised in this ethnography of inner-city Johannesburg is how researchers, policymakers, and urban activists can practice ways of seeing and engaging urban spaces that are characterized simultaneously by regularity and provisionality.

Urbanization conventionally denotes a thickening of fields, an assemblage of increasingly heterogeneous elements into more complicated collectives. The accelerated, extended, and intensified intersections of bodies, landscapes, objects, and technologies defer calcification of institutional ensembles or fixed territories of belonging. But does this mean that an experience of regularity and of sustained collaboration among heterogeneous actors is foreclosed? We have largely been led to believe that this is the case. Thus, various instantiations of governmentality have attempted to emplace urbanizing processes through the administration of choices and the codification of multiplicity. The potential thickness of social fields becomes the thickness of definitions and classifications engineered by various administrations of legibility and centres of decision making.[2] Once visible, the differentiated elements of society are to assume their own places and trajectories and become the vectors through which social power is enunciated.

In this view, urban spaces are imagined to be functional destinations. There are to be few surprises, few chances for unregulated encounters, as the city is turned into an object like a language.[3] Here, relations of correspondence are set up between instances of two distinct and nonparallel modes of formalization – of expression and content.[4] Particular spaces are linked to specific identities, functions, lifestyles, and properties so that the spaces of the city become legible for specific people at given places and times. These diagrams – what Henri Lefebvre calls "representations of space" – act to "pin down" inseparable connections between places, people, actions, and things.[5] At the same time, these diagrams make possible a "relation of non-relation" that opens each constituent element onto a multiplicity of relations between forces.[6] In this multiplicity of connotations, it is

1   This text is a reprint of the primary publication: AbdouMaliq Simone 2004, People as Infrastructure: Intersecting Fragments in Johannesburg, *Public Culture* 16/3 *Johannesburg – The Elusive Metropolis*, edited by Achille Mbembe and Sarah Nuttall, p. 407–429. Therefore, the spelling of the American English was maintained.

2   Henri Lefebvre 1991, *The Production of Space*, Oxford
3   Henri Lefebvre 1996, *Writings on Cities*, trans. Eleonore Kofman and Elizabeth Lebas, Cambridge, Massachusetts
4   Cary Wolfe 1998, *Critical Environments: Postmodern Theory and the Pragmatics of the Outside*, Minneapolis
5   Henri Lefebvre 1976, Reflections on the Politics of Space, trans. Michael Enders, *Antipode* 8: 30–37, here p. 33
6   Lefebvre (1976), Reflections, p. 33; Gunnar Olsson 2000, From a = b to a = a, *Environment and Planning* A 32/7: 1235–1244, here p. 1242

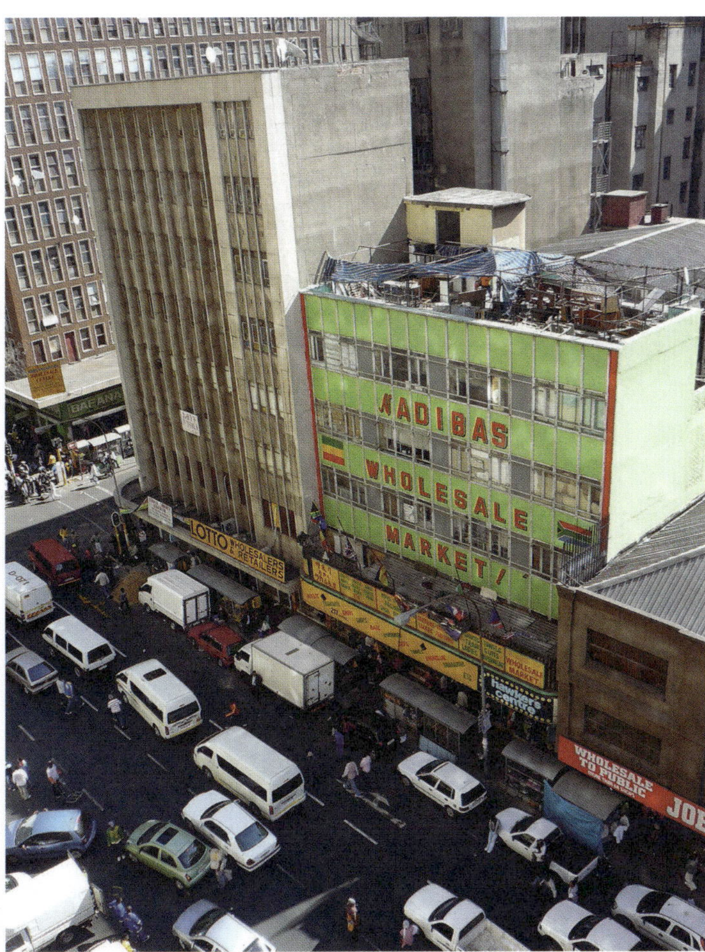

In contrast to these imaginaries, African cities survive largely through a conjunction of heterogeneous activities brought to bear on and elaborated through flexibly configured landscapes. But it is important to emphasize that these flexible configurations are pursued not in some essential contrast to non-African urban priorities or values but as specific routes to a kind of stability and regularity that non-African cities have historically attempted to realize. Consider the incomplete, truncated, or deteriorated forms and temporalities of various, seemingly incompatible institutional rationalities and modes of production – from the bureaucracies of civil administration to the workshop, the industrial unit, subsistence agriculture, private enterprise, and customary usufruct arrangements governing land use. All are deployed as a means of stabilizing a social field of interaction. In part, this is a way to continuously readapt residents' actions to engage the open-ended destinations that their very collaborations have produced.

For example, the transport depot in Abidjan is full of hundreds of young men who function as steerers, baggage loaders, ticket salespersons, hawkers, drivers, petrol pumpers, and mechanics. There are constantly shifting connections among them. Each boy who steers passengers to a particular company makes a rapid assessment of their wealth, personal characteristics, and the reason for their journey. This reading determines where the steerer will guide prospective passengers, who will sell their tickets, who will load their baggage, who will seat them, and so forth. It is as if this collaboration were assembled to maximize the efficiency of each passage, even though there are no explicit rules or formal means of payment to the steerers. Although each boy gives up control of the passenger to the next player down the line, their collaboration is based not on the boys adhering to specific rules but on their capacity to improvise.

Such a conjunction of heterogeneous activities, modes of production, and institutional forms constitutes highly mobile and provisional possibilities for how people live and make things, how they use the urban environment and collaborate with one another. The specific operations and scopes of these conjunctions are constantly negotiated and depend on the particular histories, understandings, networks, styles, and inclinations of the actors involved. Highly specialized needs arise, requiring the application of specialized skills and sensitivities that can adapt to the unpredictable range of scenarios these needs bring to life. Regularities thus ensue from a process of incessant convertibility – turning commodities, found objects, resources, and bodies into uses previously unimaginable or constrained. Producer-residents become more adept at operating within these conjunctions as they deploy a greater diversity of abilities and efforts. Again it is important to emphasize that these conjunctions become a coherent platform for social transaction and livelihood.

always possible to do something different in and with the city than is specified by these domains of power while, at the same time, acting as if one remains operative inevitably only within them.[7] This notion of tactics operating at the interstices of strategic constraints is a recurring theme in the work of Michel de Certeau.[8]

In other words, the disposition of regularities and the outcomes of collaborative work in the city can be open-ended, unpredictable, and made singular. The truncated process of economic modernization at work in African cities has never fully consolidated apparatuses of definition capable of enforcing specific and consistent territorial organizations of the city. State administrations and civil institutions have lacked the political and economic power to assign the diversity of activities taking place within the city (buying, selling, residing, etc.) to bounded spaces of deployment, codes of articulation, or the purview of designated actors.

According to conventional imaginaries of urbanization, which locate urban productivity in the social division of labour and the consolidation of individuation, African cities are incomplete.[9]

7   John Rajchman 1998, *Constructions,* Cambridge, Massachusetts

8   Michel de Certeau 1984, *The Practice of Everyday Life,* Berkeley

9   This is a common assumption about the nature of urban Africa but one with its own histories and disputes. See David M. Anderson and Richard Rathbone 2000, Urban Africa: Histories in the Making, in: David M. Anderson and Richard Rathbone (eds) *Africa's Urban Past,* Oxford, p. 1–17.

This process of conjunction, which is capable of generating social compositions across a range of singular capacities and needs (both enacted and virtual) and which attempts to derive maximal outcomes from a minimal set of elements, is what I call people as infrastructure.[10]

This concept is not meant to account for inner-city Johannesburg in its entirety. Many residents, battered by the demands of maintaining the semblance of a safe domestic environment, find few incentives to exceed the bounds of personal survival. But people as infrastructure describes a tentative and often precarious process of remaking the inner city, especially now that the policies and economies that once moored it to the surrounding city have mostly worn away. In many respects, the inner city has been "let go" and forced to reweave its connections with the larger world by making the most of its limited means. Still, the inner city is embedded in a larger urban region characterized by relative economic strength, an emerging Pan-African service economy, political transformations that have sought to attenuate the more stringent trappings of population control, and a highly fragmented urban system whose regulatory regime was never geared toward high-density residential areas. This ensemble, in turn, has given rise to a markedly heterogeneous domain of people.

Spaces of the Inner City

Under apartheid, Johannesburg was designed as a cosmopolitan, European city in Africa, but only for a small segment of its population. When this truncated cosmopolitanism could no longer be enforced by a white minority regime, whites fled to distant northern suburbs and gated communities where cosmopolitanism was precluded, thus leaving the inner city open to habitation of all kinds. Roughly ninety per cent of Johannesburg's inner-city residents were not living there ten years ago.

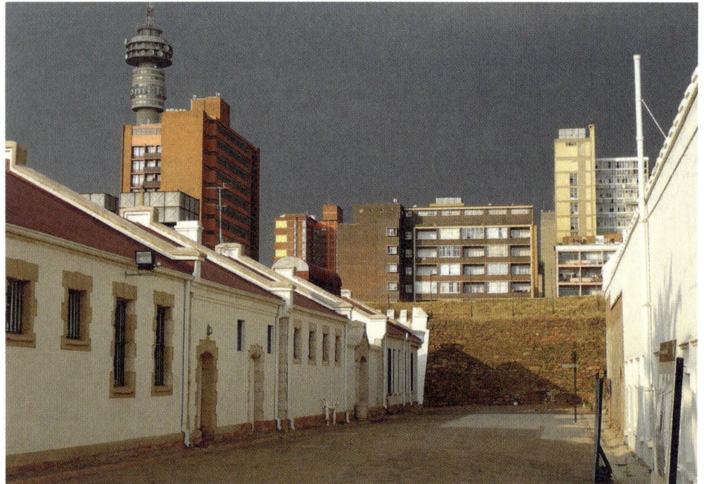

A drive around the circumference of the inner-city neighbourhoods of Hillbrow, Berea, Joubert Park, Yeoville, and Bertams takes less than twenty minutes. Yet navigation of their interior requires familiarity with many different and, on the surface, conflicting temporal trajectories through which Johannesburg has changed, with its sudden switches across ruin, repair, and redevelopment. For example, a five-minute walk along Quartz Street starting at Smit Street takes you from Death Valley, a strip of seedy prostitution hotels and clubs, to a concerted effort to resecure the tenancy of working families in a series of tightly controlled renovated buildings. In part, this minor effort at gentrification was motivated by a sense that the block north of Smit Street had become way too dangerous. From the late 1980s through the late 1990s, Death Valley functioned as "sex central" – with scores of bored prostitutes waiting at all times of day in the alcoves of its hotels.

There was little safety in numbers for participants in this sex market; the concentrated availability of bodies served only to increase the exploitation of prostitutes. As a result, whatever and whoever passed through this particular area of Smit Street acquired a large measure of expendability. The immediate area emptied out yet remains a kind of no-go zone, with the traces of the wild recent past still keeping other prospects at bay. Still, just one block away is The New Yorker, a relatively well-appointed block of studio apartments recently fixed up and with a long waiting list restricted to South Africans who can show five pay slips.

Further north there is a single block along Quartz Street where hundreds of Ibo Nigerians gather on the street, usually between two and seven p.m. They are here not so much to deal narcotics, for which they are renowned, but to display impunity and solidarity while buying daily meals from the curbside street vendors. It is, of course, always possible to buy a packet of drugs or arrange a larger quantity. The King's Den, a bar whose second-storey veranda overlooks the street, usually hosts the more prominent "middlemen", whose drivers pull up in red and black Jettas. Many of these men, now in their mid-fifties, retain the Ibo dress of *boubous* (robes) and felt skullcaps, as well as a sense of determination honed in the labour movements of Port Harcourt and Calabar, Nigeria. The block used to serve as a taxi stand for Lingala-speaking drivers waiting for calls from the airport, and a few still remain to ferry the occasional Greek, Zambian, or Congolese desperate to unload marginal contraband from Lubumbashi, Democratic Republic of the Congo, so they can shop in the wealthy suburb of Sandton.

Several young Ibo men have told me that part of the reason for this public display is to reaffirm the fact that they are in Johannesburg in large numbers. But this affirmation of common nationality does not translate into ready collaboration. They cannot forget

10 This notion attempts to extend what Lefebvre meant by social space as a practice of works – modes of organization at various and interlocking scales that link expressions, attraction and repulsion, sympathies and antipathies, changes and amalgamations that affect urban residents and their social interactions. Ways of doing and representing things become increasingly "conversant" with one another. They participate in a diversifying series of reciprocal exchanges, so that positions and identities are not fixed or even, at most times, determinable. These "urbanized" relations reflect neither the dominance of a narrative or linguistic structure nor a chaotic, primordial mix.

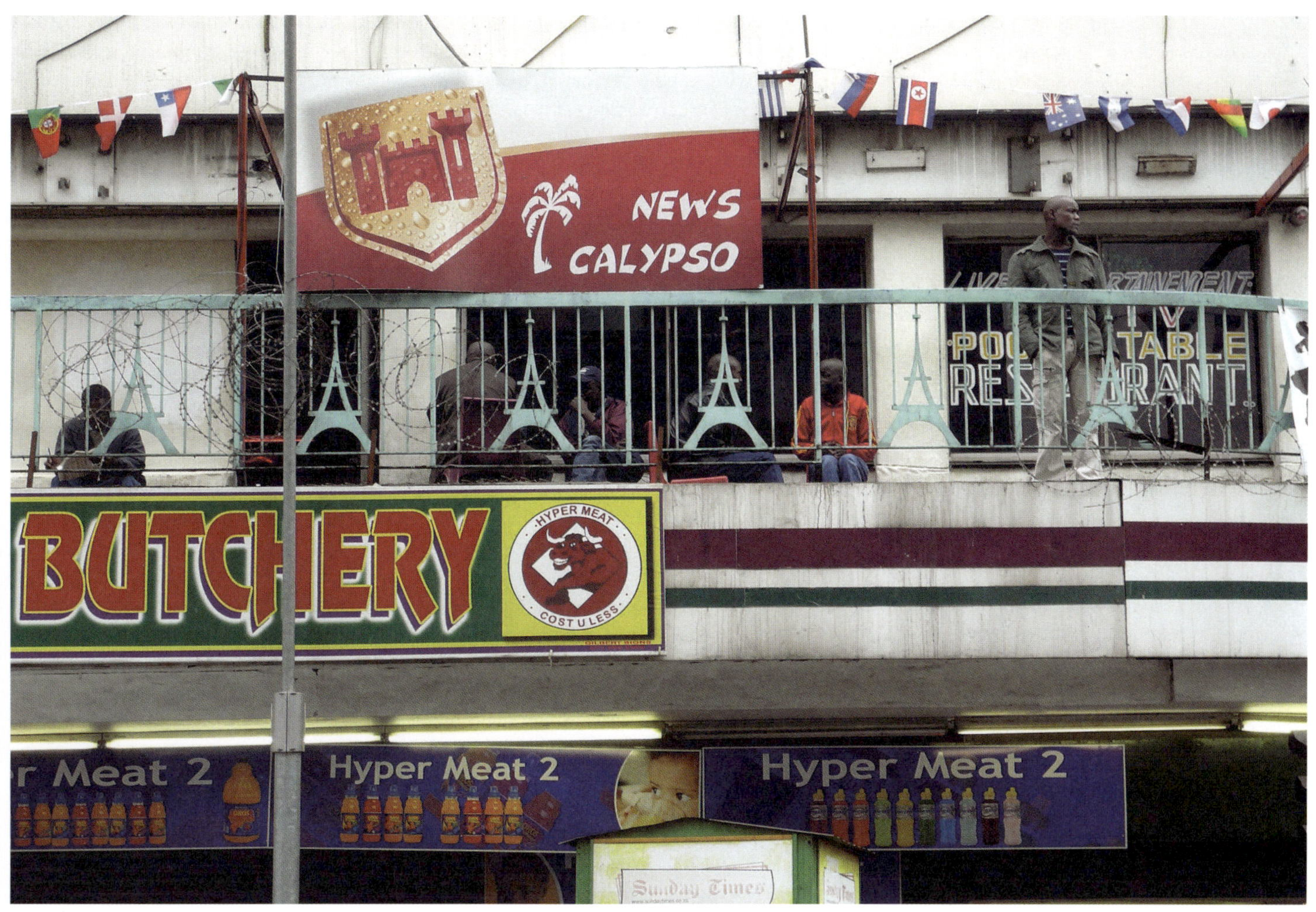

that despite whatever skills they may have — whether formal postgraduate education, vast knowledge about trade, or street smarts — there are likely to be scores of their compatriots who are more proficient in these areas. Thus, there is an incessant need to do something bold yet not rash. The older men, the ones with the real money or connections, watch to see what various individuals are capable of doing. And so the younger ones submit to being watched. A few bide their time selling cigarettes and candy; almost all engage in shifting conversations. Many wait to take their turn at the Internet café just around the corner (where one can buy five hours of computer time and get the sixth free) to engage in credit card fraud, check shipping orders, or write e-mails to mom or 419 letters.[11]

Crossing Kotze Street, Quartz Street is interrupted by the somewhat frayed Highpoint Centre — a large apartment block anchored by a supermarket and other commercial properties, many of them now abandoned. Because it is watched by security guards, the mezzanine is a popular place to withdraw money from ATMs. There is also a beauty parlour and another Internet café; but the porterhouse steak restaurant, the recreational centre, the American Express travel agency, and the health food store have long been closed. A Zambian company now manages the complex and is fairly well regarded by local residents and customers because it maintains an office on the premises and has kept the local stationery and magazine store open (where the strong educational desires of children and youths translate into purchases of vast quantities of pens and notebooks). Five years ago, the residential part of this complex — some three hundred flats — used to be the turf of coloured people, now all gone. Underneath Highpoint Centre is a cavernous parking garage. The last time I ventured there, by mistake at two in the morning some two years ago, I found hundreds of women, adherents of the Zionist Christian Church, kneeling in unison.

11 "419" refers to a type of scheme in which mass mailings are sent out, seemingly from a prominent, usually Nigerian, figure or company that needs to get large amounts of money out of the country. In return for temporary use of the recipient's bank account or other financial instruments, a significant share of these funds is promised. The letter usually requests a faxed authorization to deposit these funds, which in turn enables the "419" fraudster to withdraw money from the account. Often, "419" victims are enticed to travel to Nigeria, where they are robbed or extorted.

On the other side of Pretoria Street is a block representing an early effort by the Metropolitan Council to draw street traders into an organized market with rented stalls and shedding. A variety of fruits and vegetables is sold here, as well as clothing, shoes, and kitchen goods. But the traders must pay rent for their stalls. Although the money is used to provide a clean and safe environment, its goods are consequently more expensive than those of the hawkers who still line much of Pretoria Street and whose trade this formal market was supposed to dispel. As we continue north along Quartz Street, the formal market dissipates in a contiguous block of unregulated street hawkers and alleys where stolen goods are sold. But in the surrounding arteries there are large apartment blocks, and it is clearly an area where the South African township has moved in. The pool halls and game rooms are crowded, and the block pulses with hip-hop and *kwaito* music. Corner walls are lined with hundreds of makeshift notices offering rooms for rent. Every ten yards, it seems, there is a shop or improvised street stand with a telephone – an important service for the majority of residents who cannot afford their own phones. Ten years ago there were German pastry shops, health clubs, and tie shops on this block. On the many occasions when I have crossed this stretch between Goldreich and Caroline streets, I have always seen violent incidents: a single shot to the head, or even an *assegai,* a short spear, quickly thrust and removed. Crowds gather, mostly in silence, as calls are made to police officers who are in sight just a few blocks away, stopping cars in the cocaine zone.

The next block is inhabited by homeless squatters, whose cardboard edifices and stolen shopping carts line mounds of burnt ash from fires they use to cook and keep warm. There is an acrid smell and the incessant sounds of whistles and catcalls. Young street toughs, Congolese mechanics who use a nearby petrol station to repair and store cars, and Malawians who have long dominated the residential buildings all engage in a territorial dance for control of the block.

Finally the street ends at a major lateral artery, Louis Botha Avenue, and the Mimosa Hotel. The Mimosa is one of about ten hotels operated, if not owned, by Nigerian syndicates, where rooms are shared to keep accommodations for an army of "foot soldiers" under R10 (roughly $1.50) per night. Here, recent doctorates in designer frames mingle across street-side card tables with ex-Area boys from Lagos on the run from being framed. Some keep an eye out for everything. Others wait to unload the small quota of narcotics that will allow them to eat that night. There are those who direct old and new clients to choice rooms in the hotel in order to meet their needs; and still others are there to tell stories, often about deals, both real and made up. These are imported tricksters, whose job is to celebrate the ruthless economy that most of these young Ibo guys pursue,

provide occasional cautionary tales, but in the end get others to reveal what they are after, what their capacities are, where they have been, and how well they might fit certain jobs. The police and the city council have declared victory over Nigerians several times by shutting down the hotel. On the ground level, a passing observer might be fooled into thinking that the place is finished, but if you look up you might notice that the windows are full of freshly laundered clothes.

Reworked Intersections

This is an inner city whose density and highly circumscribed spatial parameters compel uncertain interactions and cooperation among both long-term Johannesburg residents and new arrivals, South Africans and Africans from elsewhere. There are interactions among various national and ethnic groups, between aspiring professionals and seasoned criminals, and between Aids orphans living on the streets and wealthy Senegalese merchants living in luxurious penthouses. At the same time, life in the inner city fosters intense cooperation among fellow nationals and ethnics. The coupling of these trajectories produces an intricate territorialization and a patchwork of zones of relative security. Some blocks and many buildings clearly "belong" to particular national groups, in part due to the disparate practices employed by building owners and their managing agents. These actors have their own interpretations of the relative benefits and costs of renting to South Africans or foreigners.

To what extent does this narrowing of space along ethnic or national lines enforce a ghettoization of economy or mentality? For those who are rigidly ensconced in a limited territory of relative safety and predictability, everyday familial and public relations can be quite strained, even suffocating.[12] However, such circumscribed spatial arenas are only one domain within a networked milieu of diverse locations through which residents pass, and which are actively or symbolically linked to the seemingly highly bounded inner-city territories. For many South Africans, these inner-city neighbourhoods are linked to long-standing townships or periurban settlements. Hillbrow, for example, has often served as a place of both temporary and long-term escape from problematic kinship and neighbourhood relations in Soweto. For those living in the vast squatter areas of Orange Farm, south of the city, Joubert Park serves as an anchor for small-scale trading across Johannesburg. Zimbabweans and Malawian sojourners and petty traders, coming back and forth often on two-week visas, use several large inner-city hotels as temporary bases of operation and storage. For many Africans across the region, Johannesburg is a site for the bulk purchase of various commodities. It is a locus of complex barter arrangements and transshipment, a site for laundering money, sending remittance,

12 Alan Morris 1999, Race Relations and Racism in a Racially Diverse Inner City Neighbourhood: A Case Study of Hillbrow, Johannesburg, *Journal of Southern African Studies* 25/4: 667–694

and for upscaling a variety of entrepreneurial activities through the dense intersections of actors from different countries and situations.

But a "cat and mouse" game largely prevails. Many foreign Africans cite the need for maintaining hyperawareness of their surroundings. They are constantly on the lookout for police officers, many of whom seem focused on entrapping foreigners in various shakedowns, luring them into what appear to be highly favourable apartment rentals only to then raid them and expropriate money and goods. When interviewing migrants, one notices their constant wariness about whom they can safely talk to and in what contexts. There are multiple levels of intrigue and conflict among migrants from the same region, regardless of whether they share common ancestry, politics, or commercial experience. Such infighting is typical among South African institutional personnel as well. For example, a well-known story concerns a police raid on a Senegalese mosque in Bez Valley during Ramadan, when the large Murid Senegalese community in Johannesburg was gathering contributions to be sent to the religious centre of Touba, Senegal. Apparently, a Gambian immigrant dealing in false papers had targeted a Senegalese rival, whom the police threatened to toss from the window of his nineteenth-storey apartment in Hillbrow unless he was able to "do something for himself" (i.e., come up with a large payoff) within twenty-four hours.

Despite this incident, the Senegalese community is much admired in Johannesburg for its ability to work together in highly complementary ways across geographical distance and commercial sectors. The political vicissitudes of almost all other African "feeder" nations generate a great deal of suspicion and internal conflict within national communities residing in Johannesburg, especially as political events constantly send new groups of varying political complexions into exile. With a few exceptions, common national identity provides only a limited platform for economic and social collaboration. The fact that the Senegalese are able to draw on such collaboration provides an important point of reference. Efforts are made to reconstitute such an experience across national identities, particularly where subgroupings of individuals sharing a common national identity are framed within a larger rubric of regional, religious, or professional commonality.

For example, common national identity can provide a concrete framework for support among individuals who may have very different kinds of jobs, ranging from repairing automobiles to teaching French at the Alliance Française. These articulations are used by larger corporate groupings – cutting across several national identities – that facilitate various business efforts through subcontracting arrangements. One such enterprise might draw on the professional legitimacy of teachers, use their students as potential customers or corporate informants, and incorporate the trading circuits developed by petty traders and the repair skills of mechanics.

The game can take on a simultaneously sinister and comical quality. Bakassi Boys chase after former Revolutionary United Front sobels to settle ECOWAS scores; they are aided by Gambian ex-soldiers who refused to support the Casamance rebel-backed marijuana trade that sustained Yaya Jammeh's government. Zanu-PF veterans of the liberation war rob the suburban houses of Rally for Congolese Democracy-aligned businessmen, who in turn use money earned by Lissouba-backed Zulu militias from Brazzaville to make another run at Sassou-Nguesso's Cobras.[13] The inner city boasts an array of ex-combatants, intelligence operatives, and exiled politicians all chasing one another, all running from one another, and in the process many strange bedfellows and business ventures emerge. At one time, the majority of these actors may have represented a cause, an ethnic group, or a nation. But these identities get lost in Johannesburg, and their new affiliations can be traced only by following how they move from one opaque deal to the next.

The relative absence of a systematic and formal framework for investment in the inner city means that the ideas, entrepreneurial experience, and networks that the bulk of foreign Africans bring to Johannesburg are largely underutilized. A prevailing xenophobia among many South Africans forces Africans from other countries to regulate their visibility – their dress, residential location, and the kinds of economic activities they pursue. As a result, many foreign actors have focused on taking quick profits and marshalling critical sections of the built environment to support the trade in narcotics, stolen goods, and various Internet-based fraud schemes like the infamous "419s" and credit card scams. According to my interviews with various foot soldiers and middlemen in these loosely organized, largely Ibo-based syndicates, the profits from this trade are used to import a broad range of commodities, such as industrial parts, consumer goods, electronics, and machinery, from Southeast Asia to West and Central Africa.

Inattention to the realities of the inner city by key municipal and corporate institutions has led to an intensification of the xenophobic attitudes that force foreign Africans deeper underground. Residents' efforts to secure the range of illicit and informal trades available to them by consolidating control over specific spaces, clients, and domains of inner-city life increasingly clash with the limited upgrading and redevelopment initiatives pursued by the key municipal institutions, such as the Johannesburg Development Agency, the Better Buildings Program, and the Central Johannesburg Partnership. Normative interventions centre on major building projects, such as the new Constitutional Court building just west of Hillbrow with its anticipated multiplier effects

---

13 Bakassi Boys is a network of well-organized youth gangs that controls many neighbourhoods in southern Nigerian cities and increasingly has operated as a paramilitary force for various politicians. Sobels were military personnel in the Sierra Leone Army who, in the late 1990s, joined with the opposition rebel movement, the Revolutionary United Front, to try to control the diamond trade. Yaya Jammeh is the president of Gambia; originating from a town reputed to be at the centre of the regional marijuana trade, Jammeh assumed power as a young soldier in his late twenties. Zanu-PF is the ruling party of Zimbabwe, whose military assumed control of many mineral concessions in the Democratic Republic of the Congo when Laurent Kabila, the former head of state, requested Zimbabwe's assistance in the long civil war, (in which the Rally for Congolese Democracy is one of the primary antagonists). South Africa has hosted a protracted series of negotiations among the main armed groups to try to bring an end to the conflict. Pascal Lissouba is the former head of state of the Republic of the Congo; he was replaced by Daniel Sassou-Ngueso. Both men organized private militias during their struggle for power, which largely decimated the capital city of Brazzaville during the mid-1990s.

of increased property values and the restoration of commercial zones. They also entail the demolition of residential buildings with substantial arrears and code violations, the use of existing bylaws to clear out buildings and hotels used for illicit activities, and the seizure of illegally acquired assets.[14] The complicity of some police officers and customs and immigration officials, as well as the enormous costs of continuous and targeted regulation, limit the efficacy of these interventions.

While residents of different backgrounds try to keep out of one another's way, they do form emergent interdependencies ranging from crude patron-client relations to formally constituted Pan-African entrepreneurial collaborations. The sheer proximity of Africans from diverse ethnic and national backgrounds leads many residents to explore tentative cooperation based on trust. Such relationships are risky in a climate of insecurity and incessant trickery, but also enable participants to exploit, in highly profitable ways, the common assumption that trust is not really possible. Given the various skills and networks that different immigrant groups bring to the table, the potential profits in combining trades, markets, and networks far exceed those from commercial activities compartmentalized within narrow ethnic and national groupings. Examples include the buying, selling, and repairing of cars or the domestic or international consigning of goods by individual traders using informal credit systems and flexible collateral. Other activities, usually managed by women, include the cultivation of informal restaurants and bars as safehouses for potentially volatile negotiations among those conducting illegal business. Young women of various nationalities are increasingly enrolled and partnered as foot soldiers in barter schemes – for example, gems for luxury accessories – that may take place in Brazil or Venezuela.

It is difficult to infer the existence of a collective system from even scores of individual interviews or multisite field observations. Yet it may be possible that this texture of highly fragmented social space and these emerging interdependencies complement each other in forming an infrastructure for innovative economic transactions in the inner city.

Operating Infrastructures

Such infrastructure remains largely invisible unless we reconceptualize the notion of belonging in terms other than those of a logic of group or territorial representation. People as infrastructure indicates residents' needs to generate concrete acts and contexts of social collaboration inscribed with multiple identities rather than in overseeing and enforcing modulated transactions among discrete population groups. For example, no matter how much Nigerians and South Africans express their mutual hatred, this does not really stop them from doing business with each other, sharing residences, or engaging in other interpersonal relations. The dissipation of once-relied-upon modes of solidarity, the uprooting of individuals from familiar domains, and the ghettoization of individuals within highly circumscribed identity-enclaves constitute an explosive mix of amorphous urban conflict. Residents can orient themselves in this conflict and discover profitable opportunities only through constant interactions with real and potential antagonists.

Efforts on the part of both the urban government and civil society to reconstitute viable territories of belonging and accountability through an array of decentralization and popular participation measures may have the converse effect of highlighting the failures of groups and individuals to secure themselves within any durable context. A coalition of churches, community arts programs, environmentalist NGOs, and community policy projects has attempted to transform small inner-city blocks in Joubert Park into outdoor public gathering places where local artists and theatre groups can perform or display their work. Local craft markets, beautification projects, youth workshops, peace festivals, "take back the street" campaigns, and citizen ward committees have all been initiated to facilitate a sense of community and local solidarity. But this is a "community" where the negotiations, ownership, and financial responsibilities involved in maintaining a stake in an apartment are complexly layered. This is a community where the insecurity of residence and the dangers of movement generate a home-grown industry in various forms of protection and payoffs and where a certain stability to public spaces and streets is fostered by the sense that anything could happen to anyone, that no one has an advantage over everyone else. As such, community building is often perceived by residents as a peripheral disciplinary exercise that distracts residents from developing the real skills that they need to survive. Community building projects tend to micromanage a wide range of day-to-day political and economic relationships in order to promote public safety and enterprise. But this approach is ineffective, for the inner city requires not only opportunism but precisely the ability to hide one's intentions and abilities within complex relationships of mutual dependence.

The Metropolitan Council of Johannesburg has established ward committees to try to make politics responsive to local needs and styles. But as governance is relocated to the particularities of discrete places, the responsibility of citizens to embody and display normative attitudes toward managing their individual performances as entrepreneurial agents is also entrenched. Urban politics then operates not as a locus of mediation and dialogue among differing experiences, claims, and perspectives but as a proliferation of technical standards by which every citizen's capacities are to be compared and judged. In such a politics, everyone is found wanting, and group identity is reaffirmed

14 Based on a series of interviews conducted by Bascom Guffin
    with staff of the Johannesburg Development Agency and
    the Central Johannesburg Partnership, 8–10 July 2002.

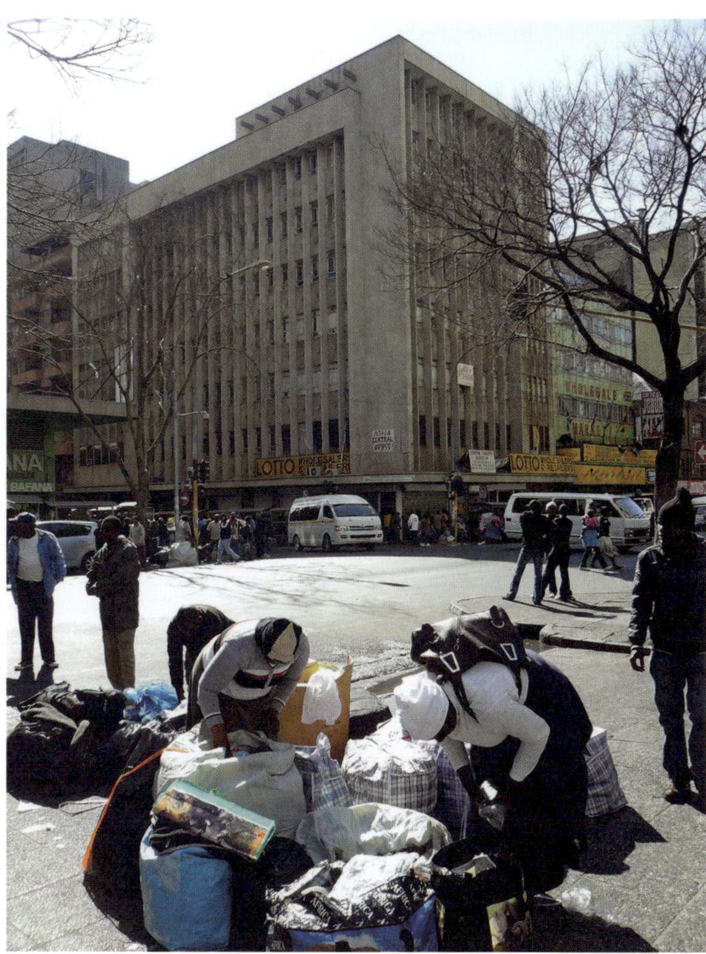

and plotting traffic routes are complementary yet highly territorialized. Usually, discrete units administer each domain so that disruptions in one do not jeopardize the trade. Nigerian syndicates have instituted an interesting governance structure, which uses the hotels in Hillbrow to accommodate a large transient population that camouflages their development of a steady clientele of drug users, including sex workers. The hotels, now largely managed by Nigerian syndicates, become discrete localities housing not only workers in the drug trade but also Nigerians working in a wide range of activities. These syndicates are largely hybrid organizations incorporating elements of pre-existing Nigerian organizations into evolving organizations specific to the Nigerian experience in Johannesburg. They dominate the governing committees that establish rules for each hotel. For example, there are often no-go areas for Nigerians; and fines, used for legal fees incurred by residents in criminal cases, are levied for various infractions, such as storing stolen goods in the building. Nigerians not directly involved in the drug economy are also counted on to provide a semblance of internal diversity, even if they are often used and manipulated for their access to cars, office machinery, or social connections. The individual operations of the drug trade must be integrated in such a way that complicity and cooperation become the prevailing practices. Within each domain, each operator has a specific place and is expected to demonstrate unquestioning loyalty. This is the case even though the illicit nature and practical realities of the trade constantly generate opportunities for participants to seek greater profits and authority outside the syndicate hierarchies.

Thus, it is apparent to most inner-city residents which hotels, residential buildings, and commercial enterprises belong to which syndicates and what their national affiliations are. Since any given narcotics enterprise handles only certain facets of the overall drug trade – and renders itself vulnerable if it attempts to dominate more functions or territory – neutral spaces must also be defined and maintained. But it is precisely within these spaces, where anything might happen, that the most vociferous claims of belonging emerge. These are often articulated through "contests" over women motivated by the impression (common among South African men) that economically better-off migrants are stealing local women.

Thus, the inner city has a complex geography that residents must navigate according to a finely tuned series of movements and assumptions. There are places where they know they must not go or be seen – but this knowledge often depends on highly variable notions about which places are safe and which are not. A South African municipal worker living in the well-run Metropolitan apartment blocks in Berea is unlikely to sit and read the newspaper in the lobbies of the Mark or Sands hotels, domains

as both compensation for and insulation from expanding fields of interaction whose implicit objective is to reproduce the compartmentalization of individuals.

The narcotics enterprises that constitute an important component of the inner-city economy are commonly seen as the purview of Ibo-dominated Nigerian networks. While this may generally be true, narcotics enterprises are by no means ethnically or nationally homogeneous. Rather, in a business that has little recourse to legal or official commercial standards, the appearance of ethnic or national homogeneity is used to convey a certain impenetrability. It deflects external scrutiny, infiltration, and competition, and thus allows the enterprise to covertly incorporate the diversity of actors it often requires in order to constantly change supply routes, markets, and so forth. In other words, such enterprises parody a national or ethnic notion of belonging.

In the commercial culture of the inner-city narcotics economy, the discrete tasks of importation, circumvention of customs regulations, repackaging, local distribution, money laundering, dealing with legal authorities, territorial control, market expansion, of Nigerian drug dealers. But even though this municipal worker would have to make his or her way along a street packed with thousands of drug dealers from noon until midnight, this would actually be safer than making a telephone call from the public stand at the nearby petrol station.

The drug economy, with its hyperactive sensibilities and codes of belonging, has been able to entrench itself in Hillbrow and Berea precisely because these dense, highly urbanized areas were being vacated both by their former residents and by financial and governmental resources. The drug operations tend to provincialize certain parts of the inner city in relation to clearly marked territories and fiefdoms. But the boundedness of organizations and territories is more a necessary performance than a description of actual operations. The more entrenched and expansive the drug economy becomes, the more it is compelled to generate ambiguous interfaces. These include interfaces between supposedly discrete groups, between illicit activity and legitimate investment, and between inner-city Johannesburg as an increasingly well-known site of the drug economy and other less visible, and often more advantageous, sites of operation.

Here the salience of belonging specifies the need for its own demise. A frequently heard rallying cry in the inner city is for blocks and neighbourhoods to be restored to their "real" owners – but who are these citizens and what would they do with these neighbourhoods? To what extent is the drug economy the most visible component of an otherwise invisible unfolding of the inner city onto the uncertainties of the metropolitan region? In a city preoccupied with questions of belonging, where movements and operations are insecure, there is a heightened need to identify spaces of safe residence. Yet the drug operations do not need the inner city either as market or base of operation. Already there is some indication that several syndicates are moving on, seeking other locales, and that associations over the past decade between specific agents and specific territories have become more arbitrary. One can even hear local nostalgia for this territorialization in claims that drug dealers stalled the demise of certain blocks, which are now vulnerable to an influx of petty criminals.

While immigrant networks depend on the constant activation of a sense of mutual cooperation and interdependency, these ties are often more apparent than real – especially as a complex mixture of dependence and autonomy is at work in relations among compatriots. For many foreign Africans in the inner city, Johannesburg is neither the preferred nor the final destination, especially at present. Because the South African economy is increasingly intertwined with other African national and regional economies, Johannesburg is more accessible to foreign migration than are European or North American destinations. The city's geographic location facilitates the petty- to medium-scale (whether conventional or unconventional) trade that characterizes a significant percentage of immigrant economies. In the official commercial and informal markets of Congo-Brazzaville, Congo-Kinshasa, Zambia, Angola, or Mozambique, a substantial percentage of commodities originates in or is imported through South Africa, often by South African-based immigrants.

Although most immigrants dream of a quick score that would enable them to return home with significantly enhanced prestige and purchasing power, this rarely happens. Instead, the norm is many years of toil in a series of low-wage jobs, with the bulk of one's savings remitted back home to support an array of family members. Additionally, there are often bribes to pay to policemen and unofficial surcharges owed to landlords. All traders run the risk of goods being seized, lost, or stolen. The perseverance of immigrants – especially in South Africa – only highlights the enormousness of the difficulties they would face at home. While fellow nationals or immigrants of various nationalities may band together to share living expenses, information, and risk, the possibilities for corporate action are limited. Individuals try their best to make ends meet and to deal with specific family, community, or political situations back home. Each is in some way a competitor, and cooperation is based on self-interest, self-protection, and camaraderie, not on a long-term investment in the cultivation of a place of operation in Johannesburg.

These dynamics take place in an urban environment that, however fleetingly, once hinted at the possibility of a more cosmopolitan urban South Africa. But the country has long repressed what the image of that cosmopolitanism might look like. Instead, it is reimagined primarily in politically vacuous, "rainbow nation" terms. The inner city has existed for what feels like a lifetime without any significant development of urban policy or programming – especially during the period between 1988 and 1994, when the residential controls of apartheid were suspended and a rapid demographic shift took place.

The inner city largely represents a process of running away, where the inside and the outside render ambiguous any definite sense of where residents are located and what their identities and interests really are. Black South Africans are fleeing the restrictive sociality of township life, a life too long situated in arbitrary, isolated places designed to prevent cultural reproduction. Foreign Africans, fleeing sometimes deadly conflicts in their native countries, are seeking whatever is possible to maintain a sense (and often just the illusion) of home. Still, an extensive transactional economy has developed from the range of tactics that residents use to deflect constraint, surveillance, and competition and from the varied forms of sociality that emerge to increase access to information, destinations, and support. It is to these transnational economies that the inner city increasingly belongs.

Infracity: Johannesburg and Urban Africa

On the surface, inner-city Johannesburg has many features in common with inner cities in the United States. Many of the economic and political mechanisms that produced American inner-city ghettos have been at work in Johannesburg, and these are only reinforced by the strong influence of US urban policy on South Africa. But large swathes of Johannesburg reflect the failures of strong regulatory systems and the economic and social informalities commonly associated with urban Africa. To this extent, inner-city Johannesburg is a kind of hybrid: part American, part African. Indeed, it is mainly Johannesburg's American features – its developed physical infrastructure, social anonymity, and extensive range of material and service consumption – that have attracted large numbers of urban Africans. It is easy to show that changes in the global economy have substantially restructured and respatialized cities everywhere, often around residual pockets of ruin. The potential significance of reflections on Johannesburg, in contrast to other global cities, rests in how the city embodies, speeds up, and sometimes brutalizes aspects of urban life common to many African cities.

One such aspect is its urban residents' constant state of preparedness. Driven by discourses of war, contestation, and experimentation, many African cities seem to force their inhabitants to constantly change gears, focus, and location. Of course, there are some quarters whose residents have grown up, raised families, and devoted themselves to the same occupation or way of life without moving. Yet even this stability is situated within a larger, more fluid arena where people must be prepared to exert themselves. There is the need to ensure oneself against a lifetime without work or the means to establish a family or household of one's own. There is the need to prepare for the possibility that even hard work will produce nothing.

There is the need to prepare for an endless process of trickery. Government officials trick citizens with countless pronouncements of progress while finding new and improved ways of shaking them down. Parents trick their children with promises of constant nurturing – if only they would sell themselves here or there, as maids, touts, whores, or guardians. And children trick their parents with promises of support into old age – if only they would sell the land, the house in exchange for fake papers, airline tickets, or a consignment of goods that just fell off the truck.

This sense of preparedness, a readiness to switch gears, has significant implications for what residents think it is possible to do in the city. Households do display considerable determination and discipline, saving money over the course of several years to send children to school, build a house, or help family members migrate. They are in a place, and they demonstrate commitment to it. At the same time, African cities are a platform for people to engage with processes and territories that bear a marked sense of exteriority. The reference of this "exterior" has commonly been other cities, both within and outside the continent. Increasingly, it includes various interiors: rural areas, borders, and frontiers. These interiors may also be symbolic or spiritual and involve geographies that are off the map, as demonstrated in popular descriptions of subterranean cities, spirit worlds, or lucrative but remote frontiers. Cities straddle not only internal and external divides and national and regional boundaries but also a wide range of terrain and geography, both real and imaginary.

In many respects, then, Johannesburg not only displays and accelerates these tendencies by providing a rich urban infrastructure on which they operate, but it also stands as a receptacle, witness, and culmination of this preparedness. The inner city is a domain that few want to belong to or establish roots in. But it keeps alive residents' hopes for stability somewhere else, even as it cultivates within them a seemingly permanent restlessness and capacity to make something out of the city. One has to canvass only a small sample of the stories of foreign migrants to see how many different places they have been within the recent past. One informant from Cameroon showed me a passport with stamps from Congo, Angola, Namibia, Zimbabwe, South Africa, Dubai, India, Malaysia, Thailand, Singapore, China, Brazil, Uruguay, Paraguay, Chile, Peru, Venezuela, Guyana, Trinidad, and Argentina – all acquired over a seven-year period. The same holds true even for residents of South Africa, Lesotho, or Swaziland who may never have left the region but whose trajectories through diverse rural towns and urban townships encompass a very wide world.

Increasing numbers of Africans are situated in what could be called half-built environments: underdeveloped, overused, fragmented, and often makeshift urban infrastructures where essential services are erratic or costly and whose inefficiencies spread and urbanize disease. The majority of Africans still do not have access to clean water and sanitation. They are malnourished and, on average, live no longer than they did twenty years ago, even though the raison d'être of built environments would suggest a continuous trajectory toward the improved welfare of their inhabitants.

The international community has made a substantial effort over the last decade to help African municipalities direct urban growth and restructuring. Here, capacity building centres on developing proficient forms of codification. Not only does the city become the objective of a plurality of coding systems, it is meant to manifest itself more clearly as a system of codes. In other words, it is to be an arena where spaces, activities, populations, flows, and structures are made visible, or more precisely, recognizable and familiar.

Once this enhanced visibility is accomplished, urban spaces and activities are more capable of being retrieved and compared for analysis and planning. The emphasis is on the ability to locate and to define the built environment, specific populations, and activities so that they can be registered. The prevailing wisdom is that, once registered, these phenomena can be better administered and their specific energies, disciplines, and resources extracted. But it is clear that much of what takes place in African cities is fairly invisible: the number of people who reside in a given compound; how household incomes that can support only one week's survival out of every month are supplemented; or how electricity is provided for ten times as many households as there are official connections.

In Johannesburg's inner city, the heightened emphasis on visible identities and the converse need of actors to hide what they are actually doing generates a highly volatile mix. But it is in this play of the visible and invisible that limited resources can be put to work in many possible ways. Throughout urban Africa, residents experience new forms of solidarity through their participation in make-shift, ephemeral ways of being social. At the same time, these makeshift formations amplify the complexity of local terrain and social relationships by engaging the dynamics of a larger world within a coherent, if temporary, sense of place. Sometimes this sense of place coincides with a specific locality; other times, and with increasing frequency, it is dispersed across or in between discernible territories. In this economy of interpenetration, notions about what is possible and impossible are upended, and urban residents are ready to take up a variety of attitudes and positions.

Take, for example, African urban markets. They are renowned for being well run and for their multitude of goods and services overflowing whatever order is imposed upon them. In these markets, cooking, reciting, selling, loading and unloading, fighting, praying, relaxing, pounding, and buying happen side by side, on stages too cramped, too deteriorated, too clogged with waste, history, energy, and sweat to sustain all of them. Entering the market, what do potential customers make of all that is going on? Whom do they deal with and buy from? People have their networks, their channels, and their rules. But there are also wide spaces for most people to insert themselves as middlemen who might provide a fortuitous, even magical, reading of the market "between the lines", between stall after stall of onions or used clothes, between the fifty cent profit of the woman selling Marlboros and five thousand freshly minted twenty-dollar bills stuffed into sisal bags with cassava and hair grease, tossed on top of a converted school bus heading somewhere into the interior. For it is these possibilities of interpretation, fixing, and navigation that enable customers to take away the most while appearing to deliver the minimum.

Throughout much of urban Africa, accidents, coercion, distinctly identified spaces, clandestine acts, and publicity are brought together in ways that trip up each of these categories. The clandestine becomes highly visible, while that which is seemingly so public disappears from view. More importantly, the apparently fragmented and disarticulated collection of quarters and spaces that make up the city are opened up to new reciprocal linkages. These linkages are sometimes the constructions of individuals who desire to master self-limitations as opposed to merely straddling divides. At other times, urban residents invent a range of practices – religious, sexual, institutional – capable of relocating individual actors within different frames of identity or recognition. This relocation enables them to understand their relationships with other actors and events in new, broader ways. Actors speak and deal with one another in ways that would otherwise be impossible. Such unanticipated interactions can be used to rehearse new ways of navigating complex urban relationships and to construct a sense of commonality that goes beyond parochial identities. Still, residents invest heavily in opportunities to become socially visible in ways that are not necessarily tied to formal associations. For example, throughout urban Africa, the proliferating neighbourhood night markets do not simply provide an opportunity for localized trade or for extending trading hours, but serve primarily as occasions to be public, to watch others and whom they deal with, and to listen to their conversations. The task is to find ways to situate oneself so one can assess what is happening – who talks to whom, who is visiting whose house, who is riding in the same car, who is trading or doing business together – without drawing attention to oneself, without constituting a threat.[15]

Inner-city Johannesburg raises the stakes on these realities and capacities. It does not use the residual features of its "American side" to either resolve or make them more manageable, palatable, or visible. With its well-developed communications systems, efficient yet pliable banks, and relatively easy access to daily comforts, Johannesburg would appear to have more sophisticated parallel (though often illegal) economies than other African cities. What the inner city provides is an intersection where different styles, schemes, sectors, and practices can make something out of and from one another. In these respects, inner-city Johannesburg is the quintessential African city. Johannesburg becomes a launching pad not only for better livelihoods within the inner city but also for excursions into a broader world, whether Dubai and Mumbai or the pool halls of Hillbrow and the white suburb of Cresta only a few kilometres away. On the other hand, the density of skills, needs, aspirations, and willingness brought to work in the inner city makes it a sometimes brutal place, where everything seems to be on the line.

15 Asef Bayat 1997, Un-Civil Society: The Politics of the 'Informal People,' *Third World Quarterly* 18/1: 53–72

Concluding Note

The intensifying immiseration of African urban populations is real and alarming. For increasing numbers of urban Africans, their cities no longer offer them the prospect of improving their livelihoods or modern ways of life. Yet the theoretical reflections that underpin an ethnographic observation of inner-city Johannesburg point to how the growing distance between how urban Africans actually live and normative trajectories of urbanization and public life can constitute new fields of economic action. In striking ways, the translocal scope and multilateral transactions displayed by these more ephemeral economic machines are similar to the operations pursued by the dominant transnational economic networks of scale. But they are just similar, not the same – for their similarity is generated precisely through the disarticulation of coherent urban space. In significant ways, both the global/regional command centres and the dispersed, provisional, quotidian economies of the popular urban quarters do not intersect.

With limited institutional anchorage and financial capital, the majority of African urban residents have to make what they can out of their bare lives. Although they bring little to the table of prospective collaboration and participate in few of the mediating structures that deter or determine how individuals interact with others, this seemingly minimalist offering – bare life – is somehow redeemed. It is allowed innumerable possibilities of combination and interchange that preclude any definitive judgment of efficacy or impossibility. By throwing their intensifying particularisms – of identity, location, destination, and livelihood – into the fray, urban residents generate a sense of unaccountable movement that might remain geographically circumscribed or travel great distances.

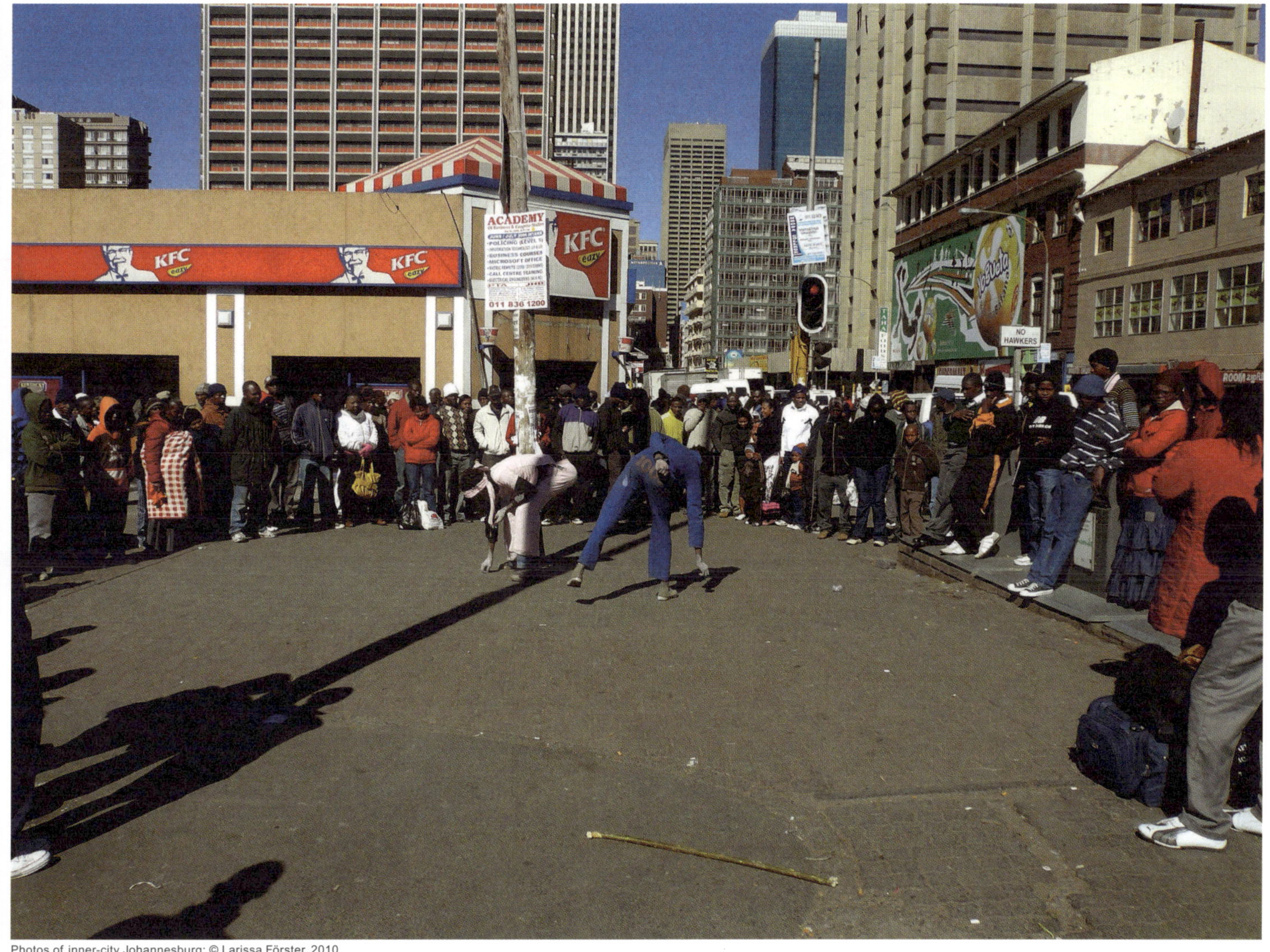

Photos of inner-city Johannesburg: © Larissa Förster, 2010

On Informal Architectures

A DISCUSSION BETWEEN
DAVID ADJAYE AND FINN WILLIAMS

British architect David Adjaye, the son of a Ghanaian diplomat, was born in Dar es Salaam, Tanzania, in 1966. Before he moved to London when he was nine years old, he had already lived with his family in Libya, Cairo, Beirut and Saudi Arabia. Motivated equally by his personal background and his keen interest in informal structures in urban space, Adjaye has spent several years on a project documenting African cities. The results of his work were shown from May to September 2010 in his exhibition *Urban Africa* (Design Museum, London). In 2007, the Berlin-based magazine *mono.kultur* interviewed him on his work as an architect.

FINN WILLIAMS: Your architecture often employs informality as a tactic, for example the way the Whitechapel Idea Store responds to the street market in front. Is informality a more productive state for you?

DAVID ADJAYE: I think informality is much underused in architecture. And so I'm very interested in it. There are tons of examples of formal architecture. The *de rigueur* mode of architecture is to always be formal in some way, and I think that we live in an age where things are incredibly fluid. I mean, we can still make structures which are formal, but I think it's more interesting to engage with the informality of how things are, and to try and manifest those as physical, concrete forms.

FINN WILLIAMS: A lot of your buildings take these informal aspects of the city, like the pavement, and give them an intensity that makes them something more specific. With, for example, Dirty House, which appropriates the materials of London's streetscape, are you in fact formalising the informal?

DAVID ADJAYE: Yeah, always. Every act is a formal act in the end. But what I'm interested in is the concretizing of an alternative perception. The problem with architecture is the minute you've made something, you've made it formal. So everything you do in architecture is formal; even a transient piece is formal. That's not something I can overcome or am worried about. What I am concerned about is the intellectual trajectory of that formalism. And if that intellectual trajectory talks about a kind of notion of civilization based on upright citizens being under a certain kind of umbrella, I'm deeply troubled, and I think the age we're in isn't about that kind of quality.

FINN WILLIAMS: Don't people also deformalise the architecture as soon as they take over the building and start using it?

DAVID ADJAYE: Totally, that's exactly the reality. This is the schizophrenia of architecture: that people are always deformalising. And what I'm saying is there's a kind of schizophrenia between what the architect thinks the thing should be and what the people are actually doing, and wouldn't it be interesting to now just give that up and see what happens when you do it the other way round?

FINN WILLIAMS: Have you ever gone back to buildings, seen how they are being used and thought, "That's not really what I had in mind …"?

DAVID ADJAYE: No, because I gave up the idea of authoring control after I hand over a building. When I did houses, people were always like, "Don't you want it to just be clean and pure?" But no, I have been commissioned to create a certain kind of condition and I've not been commissioned to make a static, frozen timepiece. So, the fact that people come in and do what they like … that's what happens in any house. The test of my architecture is whether it's robust enough to be able to handle that. It should be able to handle whatever's being thrown at it and still give quality. So for me it's not about, "It only works if the chair is here." It works because it can handle a lot of stuff. In my work, looseness is a way of being able to deal with multiplicity.

FINN WILIIAMS: You're currently in the middle of an ongoing project to visit and photograph every capital city in Africa. How has your understanding of informality been altered by these trips?

DAVID ADJAYE: It's been magnified, if anything. Even when the public realm is denied, taken away from people by modernity – modernity kills public life – there is still a kind of reclamation. Especially when the infrastructure is not there in the substantial way that it is in our Western cities, i.e. the legislation is not as rigorous as it is in Western cities. So you have these slippages, of informal economies etc… Scenarios about appropriation, which I'm not in any way endorsing, but I'm saying what they can do is talk about the way in which resistance occurs to structures and to systems, and that actually there is something to be learnt about the innate desire in people to always switch that off. They'll either do it in a digital world or they'll do it in a physical world; they'll do it if you keep trying to make these scenarios. I'm very interested in discovering a model of urbanism that is more able to articulate and script these things into the way in which they are made, so that they can happen without actually becoming a problem or a kind of degradation. I love utopia, but I'm deeply frightened of complete projects.

FINN WILLIAMS: But isn't there a need for certain structures, even as a form of security?

DAVID ADJAYE: Yeah, but I think that it's all about the image of what we think we want our societies to be. I think need is based on law, and law is based on an image of society. Where do you want it to be?

FINN WILLIAMS: You've also collected a sort of globetrotting range of influences, from writing your dissertation on the Yemeni town of Shibam to measuring 16th century tea pavilions in Japan. Why have you now decided to focus exclusively on Africa?

DAVID ADJAYE: I'm doing two things: I am being slightly political by choosing Africa, but I'm also being deeply biographical as well. My childhood was spent growing up in East Africa, West Africa and North Africa, so there's some kind of script in my head that is very lucid and not very visual. I want to complete my own programming that my parents started. But also I'm very interested in African cities, because – and I haven't been to all of them yet so I can't say – they're twentieth century cities, and there is this mythology of Africa as a place that's underdeveloped or not developed. It's ironic because the actual construct of every single capital city is based on a modernist script of what the city should be. What you had were vestiges of vernacular and colonial settlements, but always this idea of the grid or this idea of the super-efficiency of programmes, which in the West has always been about agglomerating existing conditions, and destroying and making, but in Africa it's *tabula rasa.* And this makes a very interesting condition, because it's a kind of futurism; it forces a very much land-based society to move straight into a hyper-modernism. So there's a disconnect between the image of the city and the people, but it's fascinating because at the same time they completely understand modernity. It's what they understand making the city is about and what the future is. So modernity in Africa is not even an issue; it's expected. There's been a huge leap from literally flat to vertical, so it's very fascinating to me, this incredible acceptance of modernity. It's not ignorance; it's a kind of programming that came from nationalism. But I also lastly feel that the image of the continent is predominantly war and poverty and tourism. And I find these three things exhausting and boring. I don't want to see another fucking image of Africa and an elephant. I'm interested in the idea of seeing Africa and the people who live there in the city as part of the global context, and seeing that as part of the fabric of the planet. So I said to myself, I want to make this database for myself, but also this database is potentially a way of revealing what this place is. Because nobody else is going to do it. And I couldn't do the sort of coffee table book editing of just choosing five countries that are cute. I said we have to deal with the entire plate and present it as unauthored as possible. I say this is the kind of criteria that I'm using to present each place, this is the information that I'm giving you, and here is a database. We're thinking about an institution that will have this archive eventually, but there will be a book, hopefully next year. [2008]

FINN WILLIAMS: It's interesting that you've focused on completing the unfinished programming of your childhood, when in a way that rootlessness you have from growing up in so many countries has been an advantage when dealing with complex urban places like London.

DAVID ADJAYE: Yes, but my rootlessness, or my non-specificity to place, is what I will always use as a way of questioning. Because ultimately what I think I have gained from rootlessness is not some psychobabble kind of magic wand to look at things in a different way; it's just that it forces me to take observation very seriously. I literally have to survive through critical observation, because all I have is critical observation as opposed to critical assumption. I have to always land and go, "Okay, what is all this about?" very fast.

FINN WILLIAMS: Do you think that there's a relation between the economics of a place and the type of work that then becomes possible?

DAVID ADJAYE: There's something that critical thinkers do, which is that they mine places that are delicate and don't have strong economic authoring tendencies. It's about surviving and negotiating when things are actually weak, and that makes for a lot of creative potential. Everything's so collapsed that you can't have assumptions anymore. The assumptions go out the window, which opens the space for potential. There's a lot of inspiration in that – painters can react to it. When places become extremely wealthy, things do close down. The edginess goes and everything becomes really clean. Everyone wants to spread the money like butter, everywhere.

FINN WILLIAMS: Is that something you can observe in Africa as well?

DAVID ADJAYE: It's also why I'm fascinated by Africa, because it's not been buttered yet. But it's happening, it's happening really fast and people don't realise. I can't tell you how many gated, lush communities I've visited which shock me. Money is appearing – you'd be surprised at how well you can live in Africa. There are more "McVillas" going up in certain parts of Africa than in Dallas, it's incredible. The world is changing.

FINN WILLIAMS: I heard once that only two per cent of the buildings in the world are designed by architects. In a way, through Africa, and the *favelas* of Brazil, you've been looking at the other ninety-eight per cent. How do you translate the informal qualities of these vernacular buildings, even slums, into what in some cases is quite a buttered-up context?

DAVID ADJAYE: Actually, when you think of it like that, it becomes a little bit heavy sounding. And it's not really about levelling or anything like that. It is about constantly being inspired and looking, and what I love about informality is that it is an unconscious act of aesthetics which seems like it's not meant to be aesthetics, but every act is an aesthetic act for me. Just doing that [puts his hands together] is an aesthetic act. So architecture always has to be about something made which you look at, and learn from. Every built scenario for me is interesting, and not interesting to judge as good or bad, but interesting to look at as just built fact. The fact that a *favela* might use honeypot blockwork – which is just a clay pot thing they're making on the building sites that they're working on, and that's all they could nick – but then make so many different variations out of it that nobody would have thought of, is fascinating. You would never get that chance normally because the damn thing is never seen as a product that you use in that way. So in the act of looking, you look at the pyramids, and I also want to look at the shack.

FINN WILLIAMS: And you've said to look at the shack, you've sort of reprogrammed yourself "to no longer look at these things as conditions of crises". In that sense are you not also ignoring the political and economic reasons for their existence in the first place?

DAVID ADJAYE: No, no, no, this is not about amnesia. I mean, I understand all of that, and oh my god, it's not about saying, "Hey, preserve these!" No way! A slum is a slum – there's no shifting of any issue around that. But it's to say that, "Hey, there are certain qualities in this which actually teach us something too about the human condition."

FINN WILLIAMS: You started a foundation course in art. What stopped you from becoming an artist?

DAVID ADJAYE: I think I just ultimately wasn't interested in the art that I saw as being that of an artist. I found that not interesting. I just didn't want to be a painter or sculptor – I wasn't inspired by that. I wanted to act socially, and I think maybe I wasn't aware of the incredible social movements that were happening in the sixties, as an art student … I didn't see that activism in art as part of the category of an artist, so I didn't think that it was the agency that would give me the greatest satisfaction in terms of what I wanted to do. Whereas when I saw architecture, I understood its ability to act as an agent in society, and I thought, "Yay".

FINN WILLIAMS: In what way do you think architecture can incorporate this social aspect?

DAVID ADJAYE: I think architecture is an art form, it is a built form. But it only becomes architecture if it is somehow connected to society. It's society that makes architecture. Because if it doesn't manifest society, then it's art – something on its own, a pure thing.

FINN WILLIAMS: What do you think you can actually achieve socially with architecture?

DAVID ADJAYE: Basically, the built environment is the biggest script, apart from writing, that we have for stories about who we are. At least for me, we script who we are and how we live in two ways: we write and we make things. And for me, made things are profound in the sense that they affect the psychological state of people around. Yes, the architect is not any longer in control of the programme, as in the content, of the built environment. He's in control of the manipulation of that information into built form. But that's still very powerful in that there are choices that are made which affect the way in which people perceive themselves and perceive their place in society. And I feel I want to engage in that slice.

Extract from: David Adjaye 2007,
The Failure of Formality, mono.kultur #14
(www.mono.kultur.com)

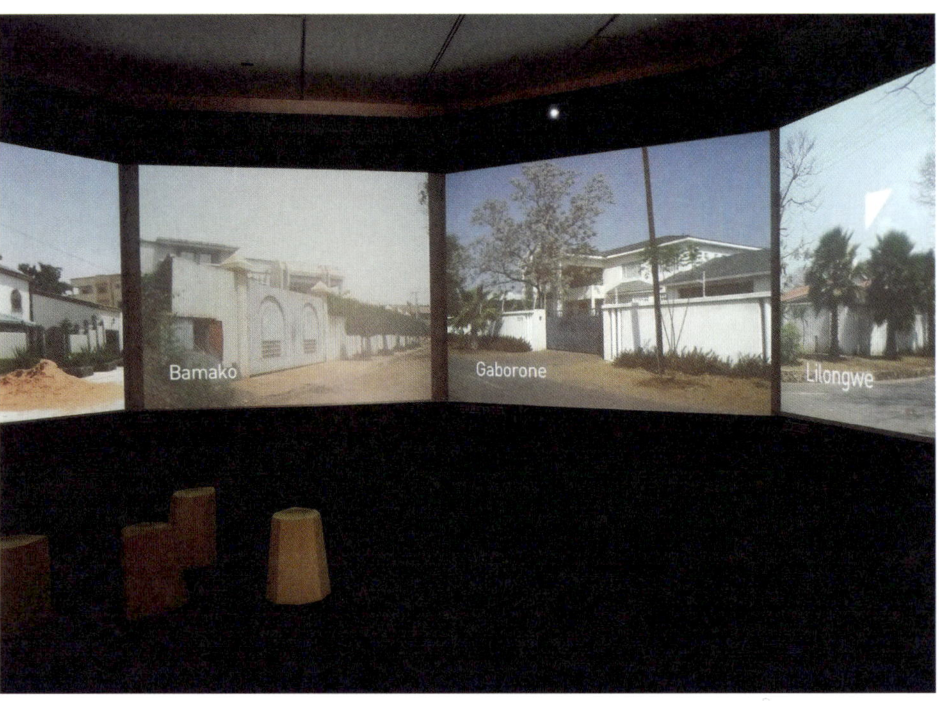

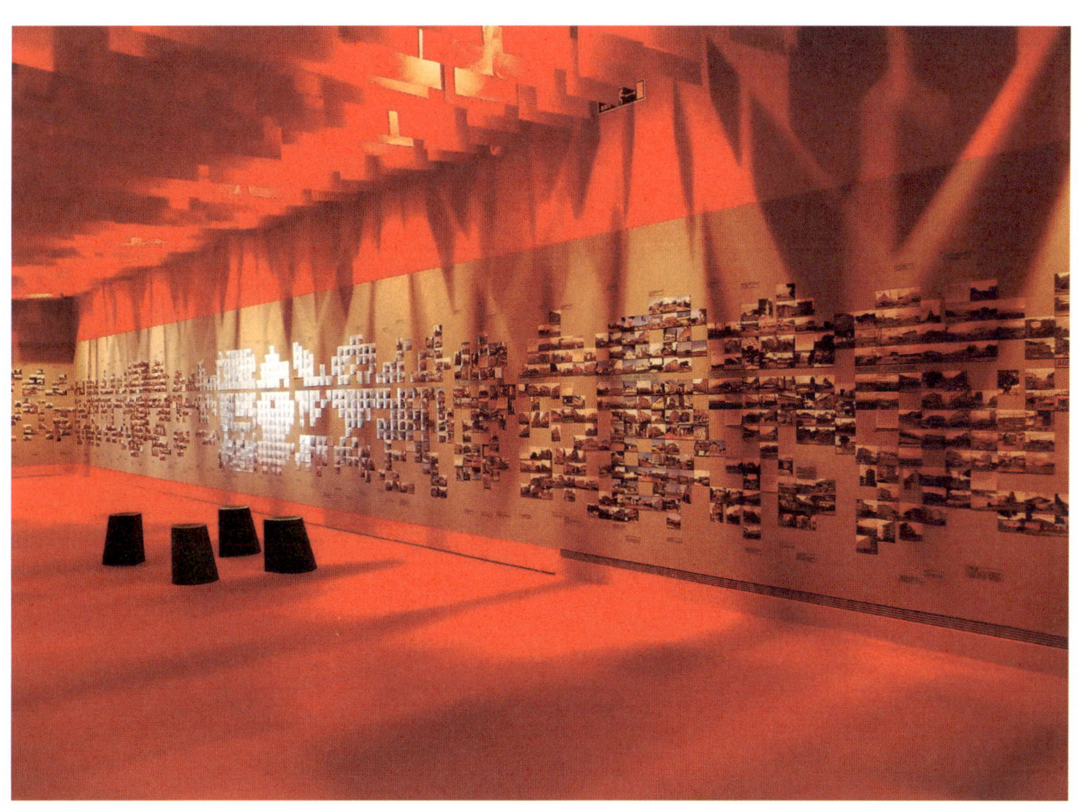

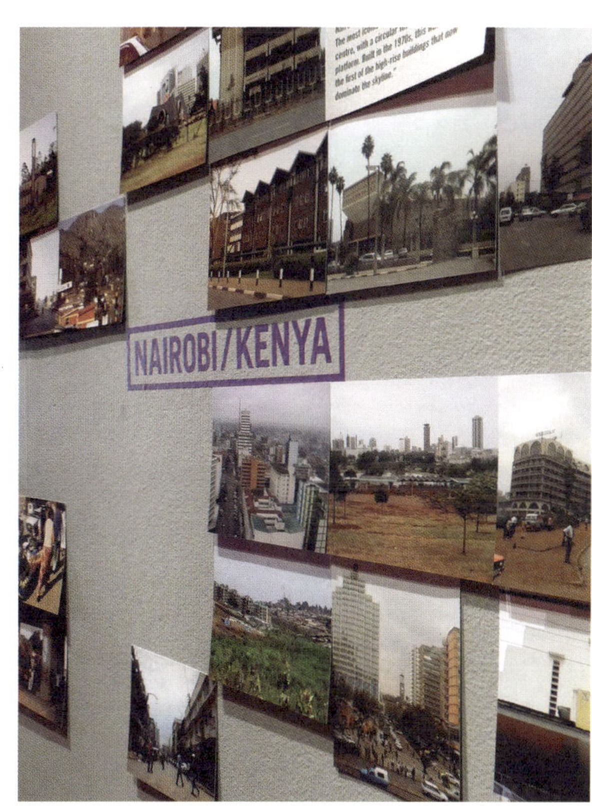

Exhibition views of *Urban Africa. David Adjaye's Photographic Survey,*
Design Museum London, April–September 2010

The Architect as a Colonial Technocrat of Dependent Modernisation
Ernst May's Plans for Kampala

REGINA GÖCKEDE

"Ernst May fought for the humane city."[1] This is how the *Hamburger Abendblatt* of 15 September 1970 summarised the life's work of the renowned German architect Ernst May, who had died a few days earlier. May was an honorary professor at the Technical University of Darmstadt and the recipient of many prizes, honorary doctorates and the Order of Merit of the Federal Republic of Germany. Regarded as the "founder of social urban planning" in the West Germany of the 1950s and 1960s,[2] he had already achieved international fame in the 1920s. In that period he was head of the city of Frankfurt's building department, initiating a programme of residential building, with large numbers of new residential complexes and housing estates, that set the standard for the whole of the Weimar Republic's social housing construction. After the Second World War, he became planning-department director for the trade-union housing corporation Neue Heimat, Hamburg, and president of the German Association of Housing Construction, Town Planning and Regional Planning, significantly influencing the course of West German planning. The *Abendblatt* obituary for this "world-famous architect"[3] and avant-gardist of architectural modernism describes his Weimar career in great detail, but devotes just a single sentence to what was by far the longest period of May's professional activity – a sentence that remains vague in both substance and geography: "In the Hitler years, May went to Africa. After the war, he was [...] called to take up a post in Hamburg."[4] The glancing reference relegates May's two decades of work for the British Empire in East Africa to the status of an irrelevant interlude.

The Globalisation of Architectural Modernism

If we follow the dominant narrative that makes the successful global export of European architectural modernism an indicator of the growing globalisation of civilised life, then this process of dissemination starts with the successful transatlantic acculturation of the German architecture of New Objectivity after 1933.[5] In this view, the new architecture only reached the countries of the Global South once modernism had already become an international emblem of technological and social progress and democratic development in the United States. Influential architectural historians such as Nikolaus Pevsner and Henry-Russell Hitchcock define the worldwide triumphal march of modern planning models and architectural forms as beginning with the decolonisation phase,[6] yet this ignores both colonial contingencies and the colonial framework that conditioned the genesis of early modernism within Europe, as well as the history of its colonial adaptations outside the continent. This applies in equal measure to the alliance of convenience, by no means always a secret one, between ethnological discourses of primitivism and the aesthetic claim to a radical breach with tradition around 1900,[7] and, again, to the global economic context of European industrialisation as the local prerequisite for the cultural dynamics of modernisation.

Among the notable proponents of modernist architecture, which was headed by Le Corbusier himself, one searches in vain for critical comments on colonialism let alone anti-colonial stances.[8] Although a clear majority of the Weimar Republic's avant-gardists – including Walter Gropius, Bruno Taut, former Berlin building commissioner Martin Wagner, or indeed Ernst May – came from an internationally oriented, socialist or social democratic environment, and have not been shown to have participated directly in the German colonialist movement, we may assume that their emancipatory self-image as cultural workers for a more equitable world was primarily directed at the geographical space of Europe. To take one example, the 1929 publication *Befreites Wohnen* (Liberated Living)[9] offers a decidedly Eurocentric utopia despite its universalist claims. The new human beings for whom architectural modernism promised to create living space were, first and foremost, the sovereign citizens of Western democracies, not the colonised majority of humanity. For the avant-garde of modernist architecture, these non-European societies and cultures represented at best a traditional form of community characterised by deficits in rationality and secularism – the

1 Ernst May kämpfte um die menschenwürdige Stadt. Zum Tode eines weltbekannten Architekten, *Hamburger Abendblatt,* 15 September 1970

2 Werner Hebebrand 1961, Ein Begründer des sozialen Städtebaues, *Die Zeit* 46: 34

3 *Hamburger Abendblatt* (1970)

4 The *Die Welt* obituary also failed to mention May's African work. See Anna Teut 1970, Vom Zeitgeist verraten. Zum Tode des Architekten Ernst May, *Die Welt,* 15 September 1970

5 Regina Göckede 2007, Weiße Götter und der Schatten ihrer Erfolgsgeschichten – Prätention und Selektion in der Historiographie des transatlantischen Architekten-Exils, in: Anke Köth, Kai Krauskopf, Andreas Schwarting (eds), *Building America – eine große Erzählung,* Dresden, p. 207–233, here p. 221 ff

6 Nikolaus Pevsner 1961, Part 1. The Larger Dominions, in: J. M. Richards, *New Buildings in the Commonwealth,* London, p. 13–16, here p. 14–15; Pevsner's discussion relates to Canada, Australia and New Zealand. See Henry-Russell Hitchcock 1977 (1958), *Architecture, Nineteenth and Twentieth Centuries,* Harmondsworth, p. 556.

7 Hilde Heynen 2005, The Intertwinement of Modernism and Colonialism: A Theoretical Perspective, in: Architects Association of Tanzania, Proceedings: Conference *"Modern architecture in East Africa around independence",* 27th–29th July 2005, Dar es Salaam, Tanzania, Utrecht, p. 91–97, here p. 93–94

8 Mark Crinson 2003, *Modern Architecture and the End of Empire,* Aldershot, p. 2

9 Sigfried Giedion 1929, *Befreites Wohnen,* Zurich

foil against which they outlined their own, superior models of rational planning, urbanity and citizenhood. But the narrative of the guiltless globalisation of architectural modernism after the end of colonialism does not stand up to scrutiny in terms of the actual history of events.[10] Rather, high modernism corresponded to the economic era that Fredric Jameson, in his study of the interplay of cultural production and economic practices, describes as the period of imperialist capitalism.[11] It was the colonial situation itself, and not the national independence of previously colonised societies, that created the crucial conditions for the worldwide dissemination of the modernist movement in urban planning and architecture. My own study here proposes that under the conditions of late colonialism, this movement turned out – counter to its own programmatic agenda – to serve not primarily as a path to social and political emancipation, but as an instrument for consolidating racist spatial hierarchies and modernising the colonial economics of exploitation.

Ernst May emigrated to East Africa in early 1934, and in summer 1937 he began to work in various architectural offices, initially on contract as a planner, and later the senior partner in a wide range of different construction and planning projects. At first, he mainly designed residential houses and villas for the privileged British colonial upper class and other European immigrants, but he later also worked on offices, commercial buildings and cultural facilities. It was only after the end of the Second World War that May was able to realise larger-scale, more ambitious projects in residential building, such as Delamere Flats in Nairobi or the Port Tudor housing estate in Mombasa. In what had previously been his core interest and activity, urban planning, he kept a very low profile. In this sense, his plans for Kampala, commissioned by the British protectorate government of Uganda in the mid-1940s, constitute an exception. As I will show, the urban extension scheme proposed by May can be regarded in multiple respects as paradigmatic of the process by which modernism was technocratically corrupted – or corrupted itself.

On the Necessity of a Postcolonial Reading

In his 1963 survey *New Architecture in Africa,*[12] Udo Kultermann describes both the modernising impulses emanating from Europeans and the purposeful recuperation of autochthonous architectural traditions. Here, May's African works are interpreted as early examples of a successful transfer of modernism: "In these works the revolutionary tradition of this architect of considerable stature, who had previously been able to realise new social concepts in architecture in Frankfurt and in Russia, has been transplanted to suit East African conditions."[13] What is remarkable in Kultermann's comment, and points the way to later portrayals, is the formulation of a transfer hypothesis in which New Objec-

tivity is imagined as a complex socio-revolutionary project while Africa appears as a space without social or architectural history, defined by nothing more than climate and topography. The first comprehensive portrayal of Ernst May's "East African period" appeared in 2001,[14] in the wake of increased interest in the transformations of New Objectivity outside the Weimar context under the conditions of emigration and acculturation.[15] The study focuses on May's biography and oeuvre as an autonomous element of a history of style. The author seeks the "common denominator in the African works",[16] and ultimately finds it in the architectural language and planning theory by means of which May made the achievements of modernism fruitful for "each location's particularities and climatic conditions".[17] Although the specific socio-political circumstances of his actions are occasionally touched upon, for the greatest part they are left without comment.[18]

Even when later studies identify the colonial dimension of May's importation of modernism, they are not prepared to deviate from the idealistic paradigm of architectural modernism as an emancipatory success story.[19] Kai K. Gutschow, the author of the most recent and hitherto most detailed analysis of the Kampala extension project, is also reluctant to abandon his general historical model of continuous progress (within the individual work and in the modernist movement) in view of the repressive colonial praxis of modernisation.[20] Gutschow recognises the cultural agenda underlying May's planning as the paternalist expression of a hierarchical model of development led by Europeans – but he, too, is considerably more interested in the progressive elements of the transformation that occurred when canonical modernism emigrated to the colonised tropics.[21] Here, modernism's symbolic articulation and urban diversification of the existing social situation is acclaimed as transcending the colonial dynamic by contributing to a "new hybrid African urban culture";[22] separation according to ethnicity is reframed as a necessary acknowledgement of cultural difference and individuality. Despite identifying the colonial patterns of segregation, Gutschow's conclusion appears, quite undaunted, to affirm the person and œuvre of Ernst May as representative of architectural modernism's universal project.[23] How should we interpret this almost fetishistic insistence on the humane character of architectural modernism, detached from the concrete political and economic culture of colonialism? What is the origin of the vehement refusal by commentators on May to interpret their subject as an integral component and expression of far-reaching cultural imperialism? And, even more importantly, where may we find points of departure for a fundamental change of perspective, for a rigorous recontextualisation of Ernst May's East African projects, and for a principled critique – and self-critique – of colonialist modernism?

10 Crinson (2003), p. XII

11 Fredric Jameson 1988, Architecture and the Critique of Ideology, in: Fredric Jameson, *The Ideologies of Theory: Essays 1971–1986,* London, p. 35–60, here p. 53

12 Udo Kultermann 1963, *New Architecture in Africa*, trans. E. Flesch, London

13 Kultermann (1963), p. 24

14 Eckhard Herrel 2001, *Ernst May. Architekt und Stadtplaner in Afrika 1934–1953,* Schriftenreihe zur Plan- und Modellsammlung des Deutschen Architektur-Museums in Frankfurt am Main (vol. 5), ed. Evelyn Hils-Brockhoff, Wolfgang Voigt, Frankfurt/Main, p. 153

15 On this, see Regina Göckede 2005, *Adolf Rading (1888–1957): Exodus des Neuen Bauens und Überschreitungen des Exils,* Berlin, p. 47 ff.

16 Herrel (2001), p. 7

17 Herrel (2001), p. 156

18 For a more detailed critique, see Göckede (2005), p. 58 ff.

19 See especially Bernd Nicolai 2002, "The docile body". Überlegungen zu Akkulturation und Kulturtransfer durch exilierte Architekten nach Ostafrika und in die Türkei, in: Viktoria Schmidt-Linsenhoff (ed.), *Kunst und Politik,* Jahrbuch der Guernica-Gesellschaft, Osnabrück, p. 63–78, here p. 66.

20 Kai K. Gutschow 2009, *Das Neue Afrika: Ernst May's 1947 Kampala Plan as Cultural Program,* p. 236–268, retrieved from www.andrew.cmu.edu/user/gutschow/materials/03e %20May.pdf on 13 February 2012.

21 Gutschow (2009), p. 240, 247

22 Gutschow (2009), p. 250

23 Gutschow (2009), p. 259

To a greater extent than the fine arts, architecture and urban planning are dependent on the parameters imposed by specific socio-political circumstances. Although these disciplines play a crucial part in shaping the spatial coordinates of life in any local society, Western historians of the globalisation of architectural modernism have woven a representational web in which Europe is the sole cultural space of reference and holds a monopoly on the sovereign subject. Unlike literary studies, architectural historiography for a long time completely ignored racism and colonialism. In the following, I will show that the colonial framework of racism and economic exploitation is a crucial dimension of May's 1947 study on the expansion of Kampala. This approach will enable us not only to identify May's racism, but also to recapitulate the historical dialectic between architectural praxis and racist inscription. In this respect, a critical historiography of architecture must reveal both specific material inscriptions and the relations of power and knowledge that are concealed by the discursive rules of its own discipline.

Numerous theoretical and methodological approaches are now available for a project of this kind. Postcolonial architectural history draws important impulses from the critical debate on space and spatial identity as an articulation of power and prestige, a debate that arose in the late 1980s with the "spatial turn". Whether in postcolonial cultural geography,[24] the transnational history of planning,[25] a world-system theory of urbanism,[26] research on "global cities" or "world cities" [27], or under the umbrella heading of postcolonial urban and architectural studies[28] — what most of these scholarly efforts share is a critique of an architectural history and urbanist spatial knowledge that masks its own involvement in the history of colonialism and imperialism.

May's Place in the Sun

Writing in 1935 to Martin Wagner, who had emigrated to Turkey, Ernst May comments on his recent experiences as a farmer in Tanganyika as follows: "Here I have worked incessantly and have [...] created a 'third Reich' for myself".[29] [→ Fig. A] May, previously head of the Frankfurt building department, worked in the Soviet Union from 1930 and was prevented from returning to Germany when the Nazis took power in January 1933; at the end of that year he decided to emigrate directly from Moscow to what was then Tanganyika. In early 1934, he purchased around 172 hectares of land in the shadow of Mount Meru, near Arusha in the mountainous north east of the region that was previously known as the "Protectorate of German East Africa" and since 1919 had been under British mandate. There, May recalled in a 1953 lecture, he very soon succeeded in "conjuring up vibrant life out of nothing."[30] Although his comment portrays an autarkic agricultural organism created by the farmer all alone, the most

important precondition for this colonial settler independence was the relationship of exploitation legally codified by the mandate administration, based on compulsory labour and underpaid contractual agreements.[31] May had the materials to build the farmhouse – which he called the "West Meru Alp" – brought from a nearby quarry.[32] Up to seventy "native hands" worked for the German settler "for little money".[33] Since 1925, the British mandate authority had been permitting former German colonialists to return to the country. May came to Tanganyika with these colonial revisionists whose declared aim was to win back their former protectorate territories.[34] The extent to which the Weimar Republic's politically organised colonial movement or highly popular colonial literature[35] actually influenced May's own decision and personal expectations would be difficult to reconstruct. There is, however, no doubt that in everyday German thinking in the early 1930s, the colonies functioned as more than idealised landscapes of memory. Irrespective of political allegiances, the conviction remained unshaken that the Germans, too, had a legitimate claim to a "place in the sun".[36]

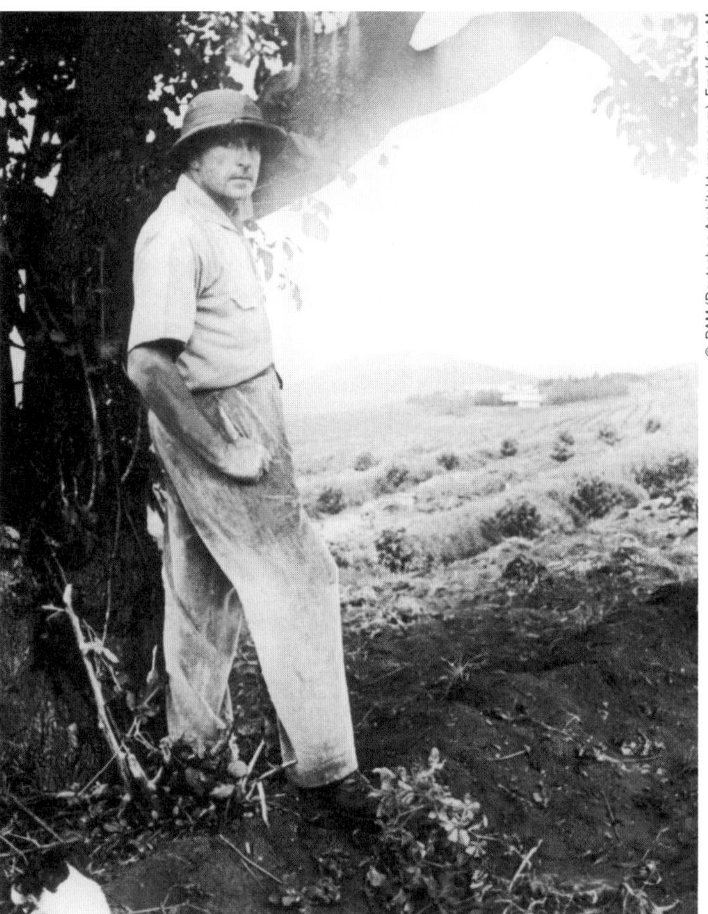

A Ernst May on his West Meru Alp Farm, ca. 1935

24 Alison Blunt and Cheryl McEwan (eds) 2002, *Postcolonial Geographies,* New York; Kay Anderson, Mona Domosh, Steve Pile and Nigel Thrift (eds) 2003, *Handbook of Cultural Geography,* London

25 Anthony D. King 2003, Writing Transnational Planning Histories, in: Joe Nasr, Mercedes Volait (eds), *Urbanism: Imported or Exported. Native Aspirations and Foreign Plans,* London, p. 1–14

26 Anthony D. King 1990, *Urbanism, Colonialism and the World-Economy: Cultural and Spatial Foundation of the World Urban System,* London

27 Neil Brenner and Roger Keil 2005, *The Global Cities Reader,* London

28 Gülsüm Baydar Nalbantoglu and Wong Chong Thai (eds) 1997, *Postcolonial Space(s),* New York; Jane M. Jacobs 1996, *Edge of Empire: Postcolonialism and the City,* London; Crinson (2003). On colonial modernity in East, West and South Africa,

see Architects Association of Tanzania, *Proceedings: Conference "Modern architecture in East Africa around independence", 27th–29th July 2005,* Dar es Salaam, Tanzania, Utrecht; Rhodri Windsor Liscombe 2006, Modernism in Late Imperial British West Africa. The Work of Maxwell Fry and Jane Drew, 1946–56, *The Journal of the Society of Architectural Historians* 65/2: 188–215; Fassil Demissie (ed.) 2008, *Postcolonial African Cities: Imperial Legacies and Postcolonial Predicament,* London. On colonial North Africa, see also Janet L. Abu-Lughod 1980, *Rabat. Urban Apartheid in Morocco,* Princeton; Paul Rabinow 1989, *French Modern. Norms and Forms of the Social Environment,* Cambridge, MA; David Prochaska 1990, *Making Algeria French. Colonialism in Bône, 1870–1920,* Cambridge; Zeynep Çelik 1997, *Urban Forms and Colonial Confrontations. Algiers under French Rule,* Berkeley.

29 Ernst May to Martin Wagner, 20 October 1935, in Nicolai (2002), p. 70

This metaphor, introduced to the German discourse by Secretary of State for Foreign Affairs Bernhard von Bülow in the late 19th century, is also to be found in May's writings. As he writes in the manuscript for his lecture titled Sunshine and Darkness in East Africa, he "first got to know that sun as a farmer in Tanganyika".[37] For European settlers like the influential Kenya-based Baron Delamere, Tanganyika was a "weak link in the chain of white settlement"[38] that needed to be strengthened by a proactive settlement policy. May was one of the 9,000 European settlers following that call.[39] When the number of Germans among them climbed again, reaching 3,000 in the mid-1930s, the mandate authority began to give special support to British plantation owners through cheap loans, enabling them to expand their property.[40] But despite these national considerations, May's early colonial socialisation probably differed very little from that of a member of the British colonial class. He lived and worked with his family on an isolated farm. His contact with his own social class was restricted largely to occasional meetings with other settlers, colonial administrators and military men. It must be assumed that his relationship with the indigenous population was similar to that described by the political scientist and economic historian E.A. Brett for a typical member of the British colonial elite: "His other world, which he came out to direct and control, consisted of peoples which, if they were not actually considered inferior, were necessarily considered immature and therefore […] not to be treated as equals and allowed a decisive say in determining the long-term future of their country."[41] Ernst May gave up his farm in 1937, soon after the introduction of the Chesham settlement scheme in which the Colonial Office in London drew a line under further colonisation of Tanganyika on the Kenyan model. He did not manage to sell the West Meru estate until the following year.[42]

Return to Architecture and Internment

Ernst May first began to take on private planning projects again in early 1936 alongside his farming activities. When he moved to Nairobi, he returned to architecture full time and soon found himself a supra-regional actor in the field. Until spring 1940, May collaborated with the English architect L.G. Jackson. Their Nairobi office had branches in Dar es Salaam and Kampala. This period saw the construction of an English school in Tanganyika, an office and commercial building in Kampala, the Kampala factory and administrative building of the East African Tobacco Company, and several prestigious villas for Europeans.
But the German emigrant's recently resumed professional career was interrupted by the outbreak of the Second World War: he was interned in April 1940, suspected by the British Secret Service of spying for the Nazis.[43] Although the accusations could not be proved, May was detained for two and a half years in various East and South African camps, and thus prevented from working. Wherever his future work was to be geographically located, he now realised for the first time – so he wrote to his wife in early 1942 – that the complex questions of architecture and urban planning could not be resolved without a clear political line.[44] This insight into the socio-political foundation of every purposeful intervention into the urban space came to May not least through Mumford's 1938 book The Culture of Cities[45]. May's letters often show him inspired by the democratic planning principles put forward by Mumford.[46] However, this German planner in the British Empire understood community, justice and democratic order in an extremely selective way, as well as bypassing Mumford's criticism of imperialism.[47] That can be seen most clearly in his plans to expand Kampala, the economic capital of the British protectorate of Uganda.

The Dual City and the Colonial Negation of Indigenous Urbanity

In August 1942, Ernst May returned to Nairobi as a free man. Now politically rehabilitated, he initially managed to scrape a living as a draughtsman and designer for a British construction company, producing studies on the use of mudbrick and on standard houses made from precast concrete components. In June 1945, he was commissioned by the Ugandan protectorate authorities to plan the expansion of the centre of Kampala, which was then experiencing rapid economic growth. In the two years that followed, May worked closely with the relevant planning officers to regulate the expansion of an urban organism whose systematic colonial planning history had begun only in the late 1920s.[48] He explicitly located his work in the direct lineage of the 1929/30 plans by A.E. Mirams, who had been the first to introduce a comprehensive traffic framework and functional zone planning structured on racist lines.[49] Yet the indigenous history of organised urban settlement in the area covered by today's Kampala reaches back considerably further than older Eurocentric narratives allowed. Whereas these all identify the beginning of Uganda's urban history as Captain Lugard's construction of the first East Africa Company military base on one of Kampala's hills in 1890, since around the mid-1990s a younger generation of scholars has tried to reconstruct the pre-colonial history of this sub-Saharan city.[50] Long before the arrival of European missionaries, traders and the military, large settlements already existed in the territory of present-day Kampala, with a considerable degree of organisational differentiation. By the mid-19th century, it was the location of the political, economic and military heart of the kingdom of Buganda, the dominant tribal power in the region around Lake Victoria.[51] Until then, the *kibuga* or royal

30 Ernst May 1953, *Sonnenschein und Finsternis in Ost Afrika. Mit Besonderer Berücksichtigung des Mau-Mau-Aufstandes,* unpublished lecture manuscript, DAM Nachlass Ernst May, no. 160-903-010
31 E.A. Brett 1973, *Colonialism and Underdevelopment in East Africa: The Politics of Economic Change, 1919–1939,* Studies in East African Society and History, New York
32 Ernst May (1953)
33 Ernst May 1968, *Afrika nach 20 Jahren,* unpublished lecture manuscript, lecture held at the Technical University Darmstadt, DAM Nachlass Ernst May, no. 160-903-012
34 Winfried Speitkamp 2005, *Deutsche Kolonialgeschichte,* Stuttgart
35 Gutschow refers to the novel *Fremde Vögel über Afrika* (1932) by the veteran pilot Ernst Udet, a book recommended to May by a mutual friend; Gutschow (2009), p. 245.
36 Speitkamp (2005), p. 36
37 Here and the following points: Ernst May (1953)
38 Quoted in Brett (1973), p. 221
39 Brett (1973), p. 225
40 Brett (1973), p. 226 ff
41 Brett (1973), p. 39
42 Herrel (2001), p. 33
43 Ernst May to Ilse May, 23 March 1942, DAM Nachlass Ernst May, no. 160-902-24. May learned of the accusations in early 1942.
44 See Ernst May to Ilse May, 11 January 1942, DAM Nachlass Ernst May, no. 160-902-24
45 Lewis Mumford 1938, *The Culture of Cities,* New York
46 See, for example, Ernst May to Ilse May, 12 February 1941, DAM Nachlass, no. 160-902-23, or Ernst May to Ilse May, 25 February 1941, DAM Nachlass, no. 160-902-23.
47 Mumford (1938), p. 371

capital of the Baganda or Ganda was peripatetic, regularly relocating on the basis of military, sanitary and agricultural or ecological considerations, but under Suna II (ca. 1830–1856) the royal residence of the *kabaka,* or king, gravitated to this area, and it was ultimately made permanent on Mengo Hill, within sight of the lake. The royal compound, divided into segments corresponding to the provinces, was also home to the *lukiiko,* a parliament organised rather similarly to that of a constitutional monarchy. The *kibuga* had its own system of streets, squares and wooden palisades, and formed a town surrounded by other settlements.[52] The size of the *kibuga's* population appears to have fluctuated significantly. Whereas in times of war up to 150,000 soldiers, along with their families, swelled the royal residence to a substantial garrison town, in peace time the *kibuga* shrank down to its political and administrative functions. Nevertheless, by the 1870s more than 10,000 people were living there, and a 1911 census recorded 32,441 inhabitants.[53] In contrast, before the First World War the residents of the neighbouring colonial settlement of Kampala numbered only a few hundred Europeans, around 800 Asian (mainly Indian) merchants and around 3,000 Africans.[54] It is thus far from the case that indigenous townspeople were only a marginal presence when the British arrived.

In 1929, A.E. Mirams, urban planning adviser to the mandate government, began warning of the dangers arising from Kampala's uncontrolled growth and the unregulated civilisation of the African population. He anticipated a chaos generated by slums and illegal building activity, and proposed countering it with a strictly controlled system of planning zones separated by economic function and race.[55] However, Mirams' plan focused primarily on improving the Europeans' living conditions and optimising trading and transportation routes.[56]

The Colonial City and the World Market

When Ernst May was commissioned by the mandate government to work out plans for the expansion of Kampala in 1945, the African population of the region's urban centres was growing rapidly. While Entebbe, on Lake Victoria, had become established as the administrative seat of the protectorate government, Kampala was Uganda's economic hub. It was from here that raw materials were transported to the British Isles. Despite the dismal wages and living conditions in the city, migration from the countryside constantly increased.[57] At the same time, the long-term consequences of the Great Depression, and above all the disastrous economic impact of the Second World War, was forcing Britain to change its political and economic strategy. Because of the transformation of global trade and London's financial frailty, the colonial economies needed to be integrated more efficiently into the British trade system. This would have to

involve more than a one-sided and costly exploitation of East Africa's agricultural raw materials. Instead, the Colonial Office aimed to create local colonial export economies that were independent of financial subsidy, but nevertheless followed the mother country's rules of trade.[58] To this end, local elites were to be offered participation in the profits, and the mass of the colonised to be more effectively trained for productive labour. London had already been propagating the idea of a pan-colonial community during the phase of war-time mobilisation, and the Colonial Development and Welfare Act of 1940 brought recognition of indigenous people's rights, along with promises of social reform and increased political participation. However, these measures served first and foremost to consolidate relations of exploitation and thus to safeguard British hegemony.[59] The promised progress changed the perceived role of people in the colonies from producers of raw materials to consumers for the international market, and simultaneously affirmed the hierarchies of the colonial division of labour. This new ideology of development refined the old, nation-based system of colonial exploitation, making it a far more efficient model of transnational commercial colonisation and thereby paving the way for new global relations of economic dependence after Independence that, in view of their continuity, can justly be described as neocolonial.[60] May's farsighted modernisation of Kampala's urban space mirrors this often contradictory ideology of dependent development in the sector of urban planning and architecture.

Social Hygiene and Urban Apartheid

In the introduction to his 1947 report, May wastes no time in highlighting the innovative dimension of his proposal: "The Kololo-Naguru scheme maintains the emphasis on new settlement areas for Europeans and Asians, but at the same time lays considerable stress on developing the organized civic life of the African so that he may graduate to full citizenship."[61] If May here cites the paternalist pedagogical objective of catch-up development for the African majority population, he accords no significance to either their specific experiences of urban life or the pre-colonial urban history of Kampala.

Although the seat of the Buganda government on Mengo Hill had long been the centre of the city's largest African residential area, and Africans made up a clear majority of Kampala's residents,[62] May imagines the African population as inhabitants of a traditional village. He plans the eastwards expansion of Uganda's commercial capital with a view to the viability of the larger organism of "Greater Kampala".[63] Starting from the city's specific topographical and climatic conditions, he develops his argument along the predicted development in the sectors of industry, trade and transport. But the most important basis of his planning

48 On the planning practices of cities in the British colonial empire, see Robert K. Home 1997, *Of Planting and Planning: The Making of British Colonial Cities,* Studies in History, Planning and the Environment 20, London.

49 Ernst May 1947, *Report on the Kampala Extension Scheme, Kololo-Naguru,* Nairobi

50 See Andrew Burton (ed.) 2002, *The Urban Experience in Eastern Africa, c. 1750–2000,* Nairobi, p. 36–37.

51 Peter C.W. Gutkind 1963, *The Royal Capital of Buganda: A Study of Internal Conflict and External Ambiguity,* The Hague

52 See Richard Reid 2002, Warfare and Urbanisation: The Relationship between Town and Conflict in Pre-Colonial Eastern Africa, in: Andrew Burton (ed.), *The Urban Experience in Eastern Africa, ca. 1750–2000,* Nairobi, p. 46–62, here p. 54 ff.; Deborah Fahy Bryceson 2008, *Creole and Tribal Designs: Dar es Salaam and Kampala as Ethnic Cities in Coalescing Nation States,* Crisis States Working Papers Series 2, London, p. 3–4; Barnabas Nawangwe 2009, *The Evolution of the Kibuga into Kampala's City Centre – Analysis of the Transformation of an African City,* retrieved from http://web.up.ac.za/sitefiles/file/44/1068/3229/9086/African%20Perspectives/PDF/Papers/NWANGWE.pdf on 13 February 2012.

53 Gutkind (1963), p. 13–14

54 Gutkind (1963), p. 14

is Kampala's social composition.

In the mid-1940s, the body of the city was spread across seven hills, and was segregated in line with colonial urban planning. Fort Hill, the former British military base, had become a residential district mainly inhabited by Indians. A large African quarter had arisen around the *kibuga* on Mengo Hill, which by this point had become part of expanding Kampala, as had the Christian missions on Rubaga Hill and Namirembe Hill, along with the educational and health facilities on Makerere Hill and Mulago Hill [→ Fig. B]. May's planned new business centre is positioned on the southern slopes of Nakasero Hill, an area mainly inhabited by Europeans. To the south east of this is an area earmarked for industry.

May proposes the addition of two further residential hills to the seven existing ones: Kololo and Naguru in the east. His analysis of the proposal's social preconditions does not go beyond a recursive affirmation of racial difference. It is upon this basis that the functionalist planner explains the organisation of his proposed changes in the field of living, working, leisure and transport. Although the coexistence of Europeans, Asians and Africans

provides what he calls "a more colourful and variegated background",[64] the growing presence of Africans poses a serious problem for the development of a viable urban community: "Civic development is, however, more difficult where wide sections among the population have seldom done much thinking of their own, let alone been prepared to think and act co-operatively."[65] Because, May's argument runs, the African residents do not have the resources for equal participation in a modern urban community due to their civilisational backwardness, it is up to the urban planner to awaken these primitive members of society from their self-imposed lethargy and educate them to become equal and responsible members of the community of nations.[66] At the same time, the self-appointed urbanist aid worker considers it impossible for Europeans to understand the mentality of the African. As a result, he argues, one cannot predict how much time the African will require to close the civilisational gap between himself and his more advanced fellow citizens. And until he succeeds in this task, a strict separation between the population groups is imperative.[67] This circular argument equates everything African with intrinsic backwardness and elevates race to the categorising principle of a segregated social urban planning. May's proposal follows the fundamental rules of modern town planning by starting from the family as the smallest social unit. However, he does not assume the needs of an abstract or universal family, but rather those of various types of families, which are categorically distinguished by their membership of different races.

May's extension plan aims to create housing for a total of 30,000 people. But whereas the generously dimensioned Kololo district is designed for up to 11,000 residents, mainly of European origin, Naguru Hill is to house 16,000, all Africans.[68] May places the Indians on the outermost slopes of Kololo Hill. A distinct residential area for migrants from the countryside is to be built on the south eastern edge of the city, between the road leading out to Jinja and the industrial area. This will provide temporary accommodation for the indigenous migrant labourers who have hitherto mostly lived in illegally constructed slums along the rail line to Mombasa.

The two new residential zones of Kololo and Naguru are clearly separated by the extensive green space of the Lugogo valley. [→ Fig. C] May makes use of the natural topography, featuring hills and valleys, to reinforce his zone planning of racist segregation. Although he argues primarily in terms of the educational, health and aesthetic benefits of systematically planned green areas, these strips of green evidently have a further function that goes far beyond the English garden-city model. They delimit the social frontiers of the urban space and simultaneously ensure the long-term maintenance of those frontiers: "[T]he town planner's job is to see to it that social units are laid out

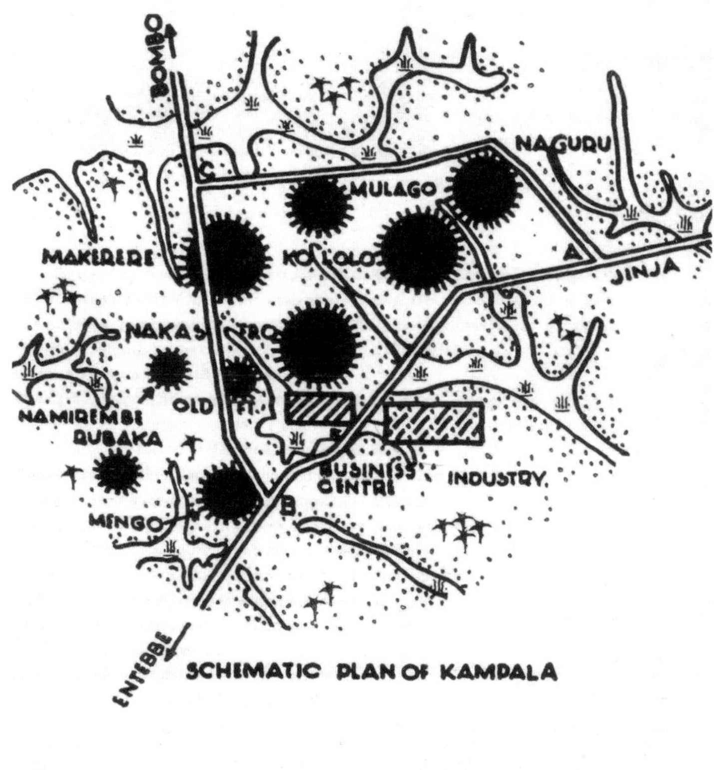

B Schematic plan of Kampala (Ernst May 1947, *Report on the Kampala Extension Scheme, Kololo-Naguru*, Nairobi, p. 2)

55 In the following, the term "race" will not be used in a biologistic, pseudoscientific sense but above all as a discursive citation. By the mid-20th century, the word had come to cover a complex semantic field: depending on the context of its use, it could refer to ethnicity, culture, nation or skin colour. From here on, I will not set the term off with quotation marks, because the notion of race is a political category, historically shaped by unequal constructions of power and identity and, especially in the colonial context, the source of very tangible effects on individual and specific bodies.

56 Henry Kendall 1955, *Town Planning in Uganda: a Brief Description of the Efforts Made by Government to Control Development of Urban Areas from 1915 to 1955*, London, p. 22

57 Burton (2003), p. 19–20

58 Brett (1973), p. 54–55

59 Liscombe (2006), p. 192–193

60 Arturo Escobar 1995, *Encountering Development: The Making and Unmaking of the Third World*, Princeton

61 May (1947), p. 2

62 May (1947), p. 6

63 May (1947), p. 2

64 May (1947), p. 5

65 May (1947), p. 5

66 May (1947), p. 5–6

67 May (1947), p. 6

68 May (1947), p. 22

clearly demarcated as such […], and kept apart by permanent open spaces".[69]

If May repeatedly stresses that the green areas directly or indirectly serve to protect the health of the urban population, his discourse of tropical medicine and hygiene, regarding Africans as carriers of disease, has a conspicuously colonialist and racist dimension.[70] Like the *cordons sanitaires* of French colonial urbanistics, the Lugogo green areas function as a means to divide the European city from the indigenous one in a way that is clearly visible and easily controlled by administration and police – as a means to generate and consolidate urban apartheid.[71] The unbuilt space not only delineates the political, administrative and economic segments of Kampala, but also prevents any overlap between disparate spatial identities. May's plan precludes urban spaces of uncontrolled coexistence and undesirable in-between zones of social contact. Through urban planning, the residential areas of the colonised and those of the European colonisers are staged not as complementary but as a purposefully emphasised duality. This Manichaean spatial order does not aspire to unity at a higher level.[72] As a colonial planner, May knows that the power and authority of the British rest on the assertion of their radical difference from the African population, on strategies of hierarchisation and marginalisation. His regulation of the urban space thus pays particular attention to the possible contact zones within Kampala. It upholds the binary pattern of the divided city while offering enhanced utilisation of the internal borderlands.

Parallel to the streets on the outer slopes of the two residential areas, there are ribbons of allotment gardens, once again underlining the separating function of the green areas. These plots, some laid out in rows of three, abut directly onto the residential streets of Naguru, whereas the European district remains separated from them by a further strip of green. The gardens are intended primarily for the wives of African migrant labourers. May intends the allotments to help persuade these women and their husbands, employed in Kampala's industry, to settle permanently in the city. However, the pedagogical ambitions of his planning reach significantly further – and almost without exception, they address the African population alone. It is here that the German planner, working for the British government, sees a particularly urgent need for catch-up socialisation and education.

Planning as an Instrument of "Inconspicuous" Education and Economic Assimilation

Even before May selected the green areas of Kampala's valleys as future sites of leisure and education, the city possessed numerous sports facilities, access to which was based on rigid racial separation. The golf course – an integral component of the British colonial city in Lagos and Accra as well – was located near the old district of Nakasero and reserved exclusively for Europeans. In May's proposal, the new green areas are designed not only to create space for community facilities such as primary schools, hospitals and police stations, but also to offer recreation and adult education. His plan therefore includes an extensive central park for Asians and Africans on the south east slope of Kololo, where facilities for various kinds of sports, such as hockey, cricket, football, swimming and tennis, are to be located [→ Fig. **D**]. Cafés, small shops and play areas will line a broad promenade. The park also has a cinema with a restaurant and an open-air theatre. These are intended not only for film screenings and theatrical performances, but also for lectures and assemblies. In addition, exhibition buildings of different sizes are distributed across the entire park, so that even those visitors who are initially attracted only by the sports and entertainment can also be given instruction in the areas of art, crafts, health or agriculture.[73] The author of the first monograph on Ernst May, Justus Buekschmitt, explains the idea underlying these amenities as an "inconspicuous" form of education tailored to the indigenous population's particular stage of development:[74] they will allow Kampala's African inhabitants – whom May evidently assumes to be unwilling to learn voluntarily – to be made familiar with the essentials of modern civilisation, and most importantly

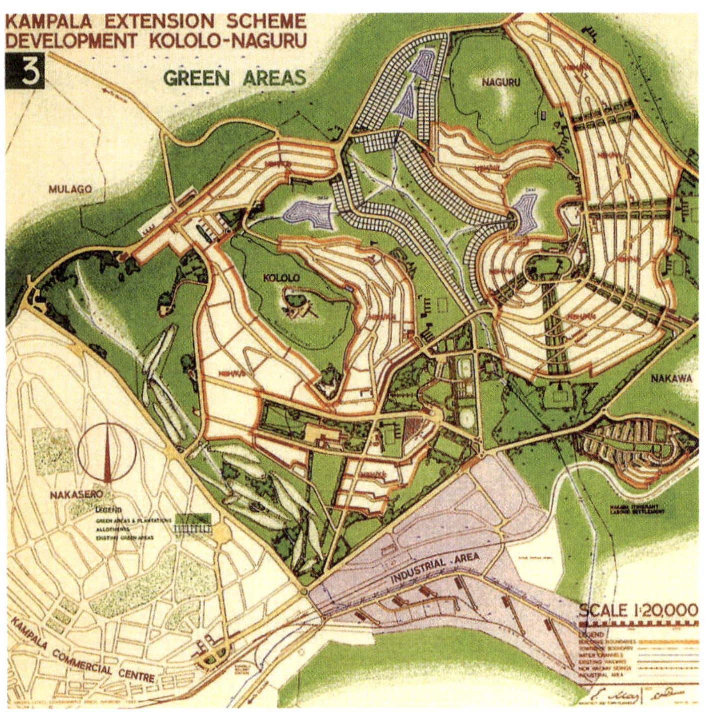

C Plan of green areas for Kololo-Naguru (Ernst May 1947, *Report on the Kampala Extension Scheme, Kololo-Naguru,* Nairobi, appendix)

69 May (1947), p. 13
70 See Maynard W. Swanson 1977, The Sanitation Syndrome: Bubonic Plague and Urban Native Policy in the Cape Colony, 1900–1909, *The Journal of African History* 18/3: 387–410. Using the example of South Africa, Swanson was one of the first to point to the interrelation of medical and hygienic measures with urban practices.
71 Abu-Lughod (1980), p. 145 ff
72 On the Manichaeanism of the colonial situation, see Frantz Fanon 2004 (1963), *The Wretched of the Earth,* trans. Richard Philcox, New York, p. 1–52.
73 For descriptions of the park, see Justus Buekschmitt 1963, *Ernst May. Bauten und Planungen* (Vol. 1), Stuttgart, p. 10–11
74 Buekschmitt (1963), p. 88. Buekschmitt is writing in German, but appears to be quoting May directly by using the English phrase.

with the state of modern technology.

Envisaging critics who might consider a pleasure and recreation park of this kind superfluous, May responds by insisting upon the economic necessity of integrating the African majority population into urban processes of commerce and industry: "[S]uch a centre of pleasure and recreation, combined with education, will form an essential contribution to the efforts made to induce the African labourer to become more stable, and to cease wandering back to his native village after a few months of work, a practice which is most detrimental to any kind of systematic trade or production".[75]

The urban integration of the indigenous population, then, is driven primarily by the objective of assimilating their labour into the colonial production process. The same motivation of controlled assimilation also guides the organisation of the Naguru residential district, with its subdivision into "neighbourhood units". These units are kept deliberately small, in order, May explains, "to reduce the alarm that the African may feel at the contrast between his traditional native village life and the life of the town"[76]. Each unit consists of numerous family groups combined into family councils. While each such council is to be allocated just one

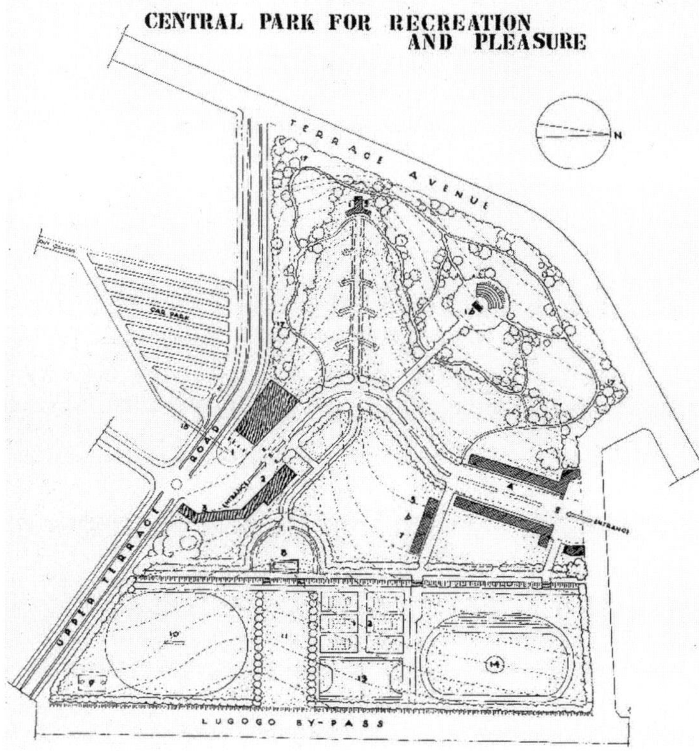

D   Plans for Central Park for Recreation and Pleasure; Legend: 1. Cinema and Lecture Hall, 2. Shops, 3. Restaurant, 4. Shops and Amusement, 5–7. Exhibition Building, 8. Swimming Pool, 9. Basket Ball, 10. Cricket, 11. Lawn, 12. Tennis, 13. Hockey, 14. Stadium, 15. Tea House (Ernst May 1947, *Report on the Kampala Extension Scheme, Kololo-Naguru*, Nairobi, p. 11)

midwife and a small medical facility, the neighbourhoods, limited to 3,000 persons, are intended to have their own primary schools and clinics. Again, in the afternoons the schools will provide adult education. The next social and administrative unit is described as a "community", with forums composed of representatives of the neighbourhood councils. It is on this level that the higher schooling for Asians and Africans is organised. The children of the Europeans, in contrast, are intended to receive their secondary education in Kenya and Britain.[77]

May's extension scheme for Kampala regards the indigenous population as a collective body of pupils. The social subdivision that underpins this conception is presented as a necessary precondition for learning key skills for life in a democratic polity, as is the "inconspicuous", but nevertheless systematic, cultural and technical instruction of adults. No mention is made of the fact that the rigorous socio-spatial separation of the colonised population serves not only the needs of administration but, in an era of resistance movements, also those of policing and military control, and that a selective colonial education often serves to legitimise the existing relations of power. Finally, it is important to note that May's democratic urban "learning laboratory" by no means aims for equal participation by the African majority; it is presented exclusively as an optional and open-ended training for citizenship, on the model of a catch-up socialisation and civilisation. The promise of cultural, technical and political development in the very long term helps to strategically conceal the practice of deliberate underdevelopment. I will now explore this point by examining the typology of dwellings that May developed for his extension plan.

Race as a Stylistic Category

"The problem before us, therefore, is, how can we achieve architectural harmony in a town composed of different racial elements? Can it be achieved at all?"[78] Ernst May appears to be convinced in general that, in view of the enormous cultural diversity of Kampala's population, the city's stylistic chaos cannot be appropriately addressed by recourse to the different historical architectural styles of the residents' places of origin. Instead, he recommends that the residential development of the two new districts should draw upon the contemporary and universal architectural language of modernity.[79] He does not specify this architectural language in any further detail, and advises against transferring European models to the tropical situation without taking account of the special constraints of local materials, protection from the sun and ventilation. Nevertheless, his most important reference point is a European architectural modernism that increasingly claims international status. At the same time, May's proposal makes race the crucial category for the design

75 May (1947), p. 10
76 May (1947), p. 6

77 May (1947), p. 7
78 May (1947), p. 18
79 May (1947), p. 18

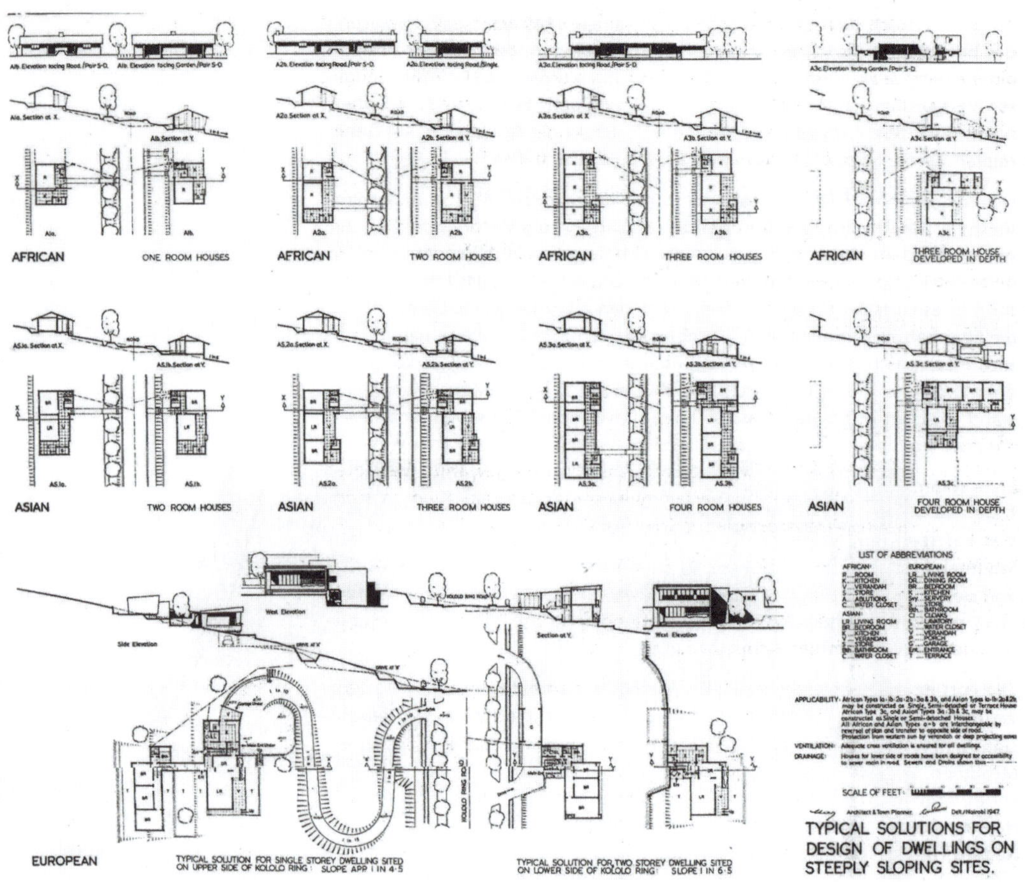

E Proposals for residential dwellings for Africans, Asians and Europeans (Ernst May 1947, *Report on the Kampala Extension Scheme, Kololo-Naguru,* Nairobi, n.p.)

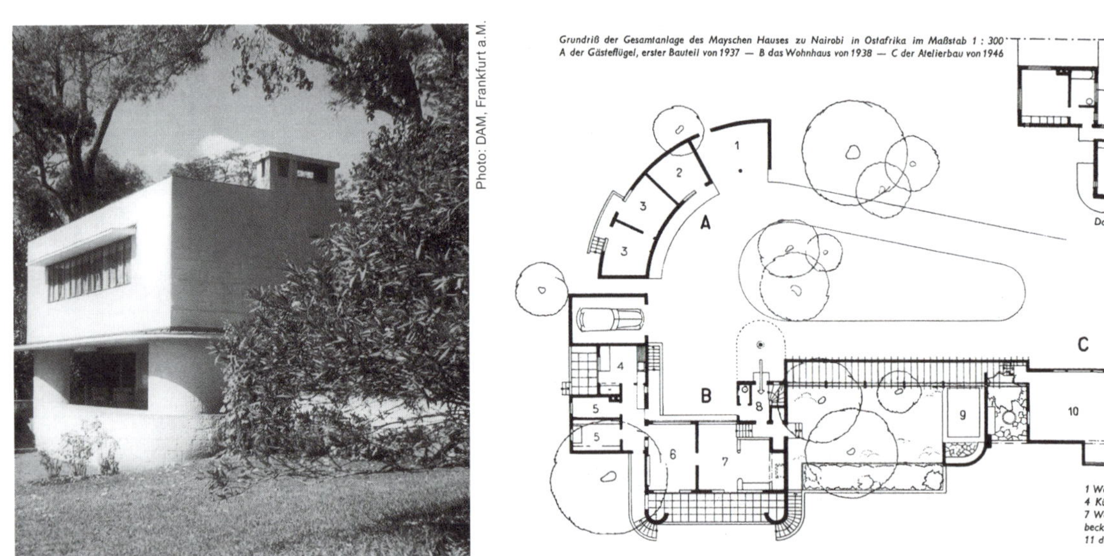

F May's home in Karen, near Nairobi, 1937/38 and 1946. View from the south west

G Ground plan of May's home (*Bauwelt* 1956, no. 6)

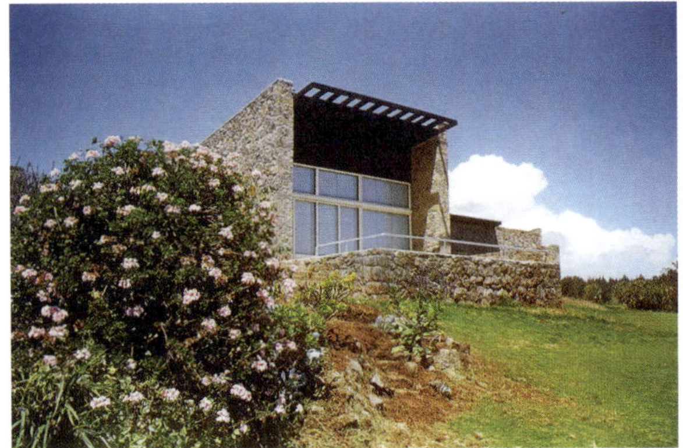

H Maison Samuel near Molo, Kenya 1950/51. View from the north

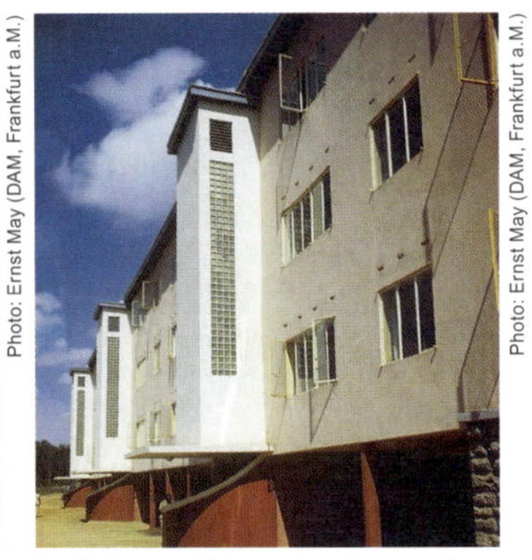

I Delamere Flats residential complex, Nairobi, built 1949–1951

of standard houses that are rigorously distinct in terms of not only their formal design but of their room allocations and materials. The colonial social order takes visible shape in the proposal for three basic types of home: May distinguishes between houses for Europeans, houses for Asians and houses for Africans. [→ Fig. E].

In fact, the architectural language of modernism is applied only in the two variants of the European house type. These in many ways recall the modernist villas that May had built in Kenya from the mid-1930s on. In both the single-storey and the two-storey dwelling, there is a consistent rejection of any historical formal language. The smooth cubes of different heights are placed additively, side by side, giving the structure a rhythm that is ruptured by asymmetrically positioned windows, some of them arranged as strips of ribbon windows. There are striking similarities here with the home built for May and his family in an elegant suburb of Nairobi, as regards both the mode of design and the elaborate floor plan (including a garage), which accords with the standards of upper-middle-class European housing at the time. [→ Fig. F, G] Even the structural response to the curved drive, laid out almost like a *cour d'honneur*, recurs in the type of houses for Kampala. Although the types proposed for the Kololo slope do not restrict themselves to classically modernist flat roofs but also have some pitched roofs, their interiors offer an almost identical functional organisation. Here, May draws formally and conceptually on his experience in the sector of private residential construction for the privileged colonial elite of East Africa. At the same time, there is a conscious rejection of the idiom of the English country house or estate, so popular in British circles. Instead, the dwellings planned for modern Kampala already anticipate the luxury bungalow projects that May would draw up in the early 1950s – such as Maison Samuel near Molo in the Kenyan highlands [→ Fig. H] or the plan for the Aga Khan's residence in Dar es Salaam. Here we see the emergence of a tropical variant of international modernism like the one that Maxwell Fry and Jane Drew planned for West African cities and introduced into the media debate.[80] Multi-storey apartment buildings, such as those built by May between 1947 and 1951 for less wealthy European immigrants in Nairobi [→ Fig. I] or planned in 1953 for the African population in Mombasa, are envisaged on just one part of Kololo Hill, but are not included in the typology of dwellings. The gable-roofed houses for the Asians and Africans, their floor plans subjected to an extreme formal minimisation, consist essentially of rooms placed side by side and faced by minimal functional areas. Whereas the Asian types have up to four rooms, with clear functional attributions, the one- to three-room African dwellings do not even have a separate bathroom. Neither is any distinction made between living and sleeping areas. May suggests an even more reduced solution for the Nakawa district in the south east of the extension area. There, accommodation for the migrant labourers working on the industrial sites is designed above all to serve the needs of economics, security policy and hygiene. Previously, provisional homes had been constructed to accommodate exclusively male temporary workers, using traditional building methods and largely on the builders' own initiative, outside the control of the protectorate authorities. The plan now is to turn the immigrants from rural areas into city dwellers in the long term. May justifies the lack of toilets and bathrooms by observing that the accommodation must necessarily be primitive.[81] Whereas communal facilities such as kitchens, dining rooms or common rooms are to be organised centrally, the latrines will be positioned outdoors and only screened by mango trees. The settlement is arranged around a large green area, in the shape of a camp managed by a European steward. At the guarded entries to the complex there are small shops, so that the industrial labourers can spend part of their meagre wages on British imports without having to leave the compound. The living quarters, designed for four inhabitants each, are to be constructed as cheaply as possible from slabs of precast concrete or fired clay.[82] May had published his "hook-on slab reinforced concrete system" in *The Architects' Journal* as early as 1946.[83] [→ Fig. J] This prefabricated modular system consists of slightly curved concrete slabs with flange-like protrusions on the inside, which are assembled on a parabolic framework to form a space that can be varied only in length. May knew very well that the African population of Kampala for the most part preferred the forms of dwelling he reserved exclusively for the Europeans. As Justus Buekschmitt remarked, describing the reactions of the people May intended to live in his prefabricated dwellings: "They want to live in houses like those of the Europeans!"[84] Clearly, the house types designed for Kampala reproduced the dominant colonial, racist hierarchies and power relationships. The assertion of a fundamental cultural and developmental rift between Africans and Europeans not only served to justify the dramatic staging of difference by means of racist dwelling typologies, but indeed formed the very *raison d'être* for Kampala's socio-spatial organisation – in other words, for May's colonial and racist zone planning.

Conclusion: Architecture, Racism and the Ambivalence of Late-Colonial Modernisation

Ernst May's plans for the expansion of the burgeoning economic metropolis in the British protectorate of Uganda, Kampala, are impossible to slot smoothly into the idealistic teleology of an ideology-free, increasingly universal rationality in the sector of architecture and urban planning. Such an interpretation is precluded by the obvious collision between the modernist postu-

80 Maxwell Fry and Jane Drew 1964, *Tropical Architecture in the Dry and Humid Zones*, London. On the work of Fry and Drew in West Africa, see Liscombe (2006).

81 May (1947), p. 19

82 May (1947), p. 19

83 Hook-on Slab: Precast Concrete Slab Construction for External Wall Covering; Designed by: E. May, *The Architects' Journal* 13 June 1946: 453–455

84 Buekschmitt (1963), p. 100

late of an as yet incomplete civilisational project of emancipation and the repressive momentum that underlay the concrete practices of planning. These contingencies do not merely affect the project's historical conditions of possibility; they form the content constitutively expressed by the *mise en scène* of residential cultures and the regulation of urban spatial hierarchies.

At the end of the 1940s, the globalisation of modernist architecture was being played out on a late-colonial stage, the most powerful actors of which, pressurised by changed global economic parameters and anti-colonial resistance, were searching for new performative techniques to fortify their political and economic hegemony. May's Kampala scheme expresses with particular clarity the contradiction between development ideology's promise of a global equality in technology and society, with democratic integration, and the strategic affirmation of race as cultural difference. To this extent, his project is a significant document of urban planning, which reveals how colonial technolo-

gies of rule were transformed before the advent of formal decolonisation. It therefore also enables us to reflect upon the continuities between the colonial situation and postcolonial practices of exploitation within dependent development.

After the Second World War, against the backdrop of movements for liberation, the strict racist segregation between black and white could no longer be ethically defended. In economic terms, however, the more or less complete exclusion of the colonised from the rapidly transnationalising global market still seemed to be a profitable strategy. In this context, the British government was anxious to use social and political reforms in the colonies to integrate a growing number of subjects into the Empire – no longer only as supplies of raw materials, but also as industrial producers and as consumers of British goods. May's task was to implement this political and administrative agenda in the sector of urban planning and architecture without undermining the European claim to rule. Working on behalf of the protectorate government, May is evidently aware of the "invisible walls"[85] that must divide the colonial city's various population groups and delineate the separate spheres. He is also conscious that ever greater parts of the indigenous population see their objective as "imitating Western lifestyles as closely as possible"[86], but evaluates the colonial imitation of Western residential, production and leisure forms as a hastily chosen and incorrect route that ignores the need for the culturally backward Africans to catch up in their development. While adopting the model of European modernism as the goal of development, May does not believe "that the advancement of the black race will proceed at a rapid pace"[87]. In his planning, the conventional racist positing of intrinsic difference is presented as the empirical result of cultural, political and technological backwardness. It is from this standpoint that May justifies the staging of an underprivileged African form of dwelling that hovers between neo-primitivism and pseudo-traditionalism. It is on this basis that he plans the gradual guiding of the majority population, conceived of as politically immature, to the idea of a participatory urban polity. And it is by this means that the maintenance of the strict segregation and unequal economic stakes of Europeans and Africans are to be vindicated.

In Kampala, Ernst May did not plan for the abstract citizen of a future independent Uganda. The starting point of his planning and architectural deliberations was not, as May later explained with respect to his post-war projects in Hamburg, "the human being" as such.[88] Neither did his ideas for Kampala conflict with the essentialist notion of an authentic African culture, because they reduced the individual to being the bearer of particular functions.[89] It seems that May was operating with a concept of humanity in which the implicit demands for freedom, equality and justice were valid for Europeans alone. He planned for human

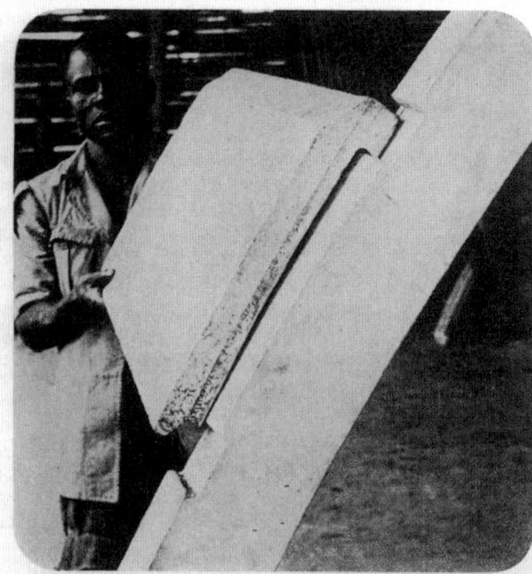

Photo: DAM, Frankfurt a. M.

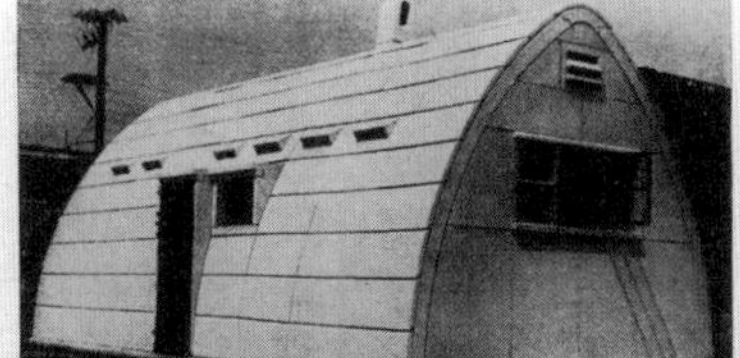

J Presentation of the hook-on slab system in *Architects' Journal,* 13 June 1946

85 Ernst May 1950, *Städtebau in Ostafrika,* Die neue Stadt 4: 60–64, here p. 60
86 May (1950), p. 60
87 May (1950), p. 60
88 Ernst May quoted in Buekschmitt (1963), p. 117
89 Jonathan Manning 2004, Racism in Three Dimensions: South African Architecture and the Ideology of White Superiority, *Social Identities* 10/4: 527–536, here p. 529 ff. Manning here refers to Steve Biko's critique of the European image of humanity in *I Write What I Like* (1996).

types divided by differences that were unbridgeable in the long term. In the Kampala plans race does not function as a quasi-scientific category, yet traditional racist ascriptions such as irrationality, backwardness or political immaturity are directly brought to bear. Race is the ultimate metaphor for the social distinctions whose regulation is May's declared goal. The Kampala extension scheme claims only to order pre-existing developmental distinctions. In fact, however, May's project inscribes the development-policy notions of racial difference into the urban body; it thus reaches beyond the immediate colonial context and is a project of underdevelopment by means of dependent development.

My aim in this essay has been to make these ascriptions visible. It is impossible to do so without simultaneously revealing the historical relations of knowledge and power that are usually obscured in architectural studies of the history of style. To this extent, my indication of the ideological concatenation of racist economic alienation with modern architecture has direct consequences for theory. Architectural history and criticism concerned with the process of architectural modernism's globalisation has hitherto accorded racism and colonialism only a very small role or none at all. Yet the postcolonial analysis of historical continuities is a necessary step if we are to formulate emancipatory visions of an alternative future. In view of this, it is unjustified to leave unquestioned the canonical colour-blind, apolitical production of meaning and interpretation in architectural history.

Translation from German by Kate Sturge

Karola Schlegelmilch
Architectures
of Particularities

PHOTOGRAPHS AND A DISCUSSION
BETWEEN KAROLA SCHLEGELMILCH
AND CHRISTIAN HANUSSEK

KAROLA SCHLEGELMILCH: That's what I meant when I mentioned the pictorial earlier. When suddenly layers are peeled away … So when I fall in love with houses, it often involves a surprise. Things come together which I hadn't anticipated, and something indeterminate is created. There's a mural or a relief covering an object, which already has its own particularity – and that creates this shift from one layer to another. This also includes the style: the stripes, colours and atmosphere or presence of the house, the physical feeling I have about it, its impact or how it oscillates between its different conspicuous features. And there's also the meaning of the elements, or ideas about their origins – for example, the stripes remind me of *brise-soleil*. Sometimes this historical aspect is fairly distinct and locates the complex perceived – similarly to the way I find myself thinking of associations with other buildings.

Then there's also the layer of time, fate and patina. And you can also see the individual style, which I mentioned before: who, or what constellation of preferences, lies behind the way it has been created as it is.

This is just one interesting aspect, but there are others as well. The delicate construction of the kiosks, for instance, which I find I suddenly associate with European art history – or that it can be abstracted, is no longer a kiosk, but is floating between a kiosk and something related to my own knowledge of images and my own mindset.

Dakar / Senegal

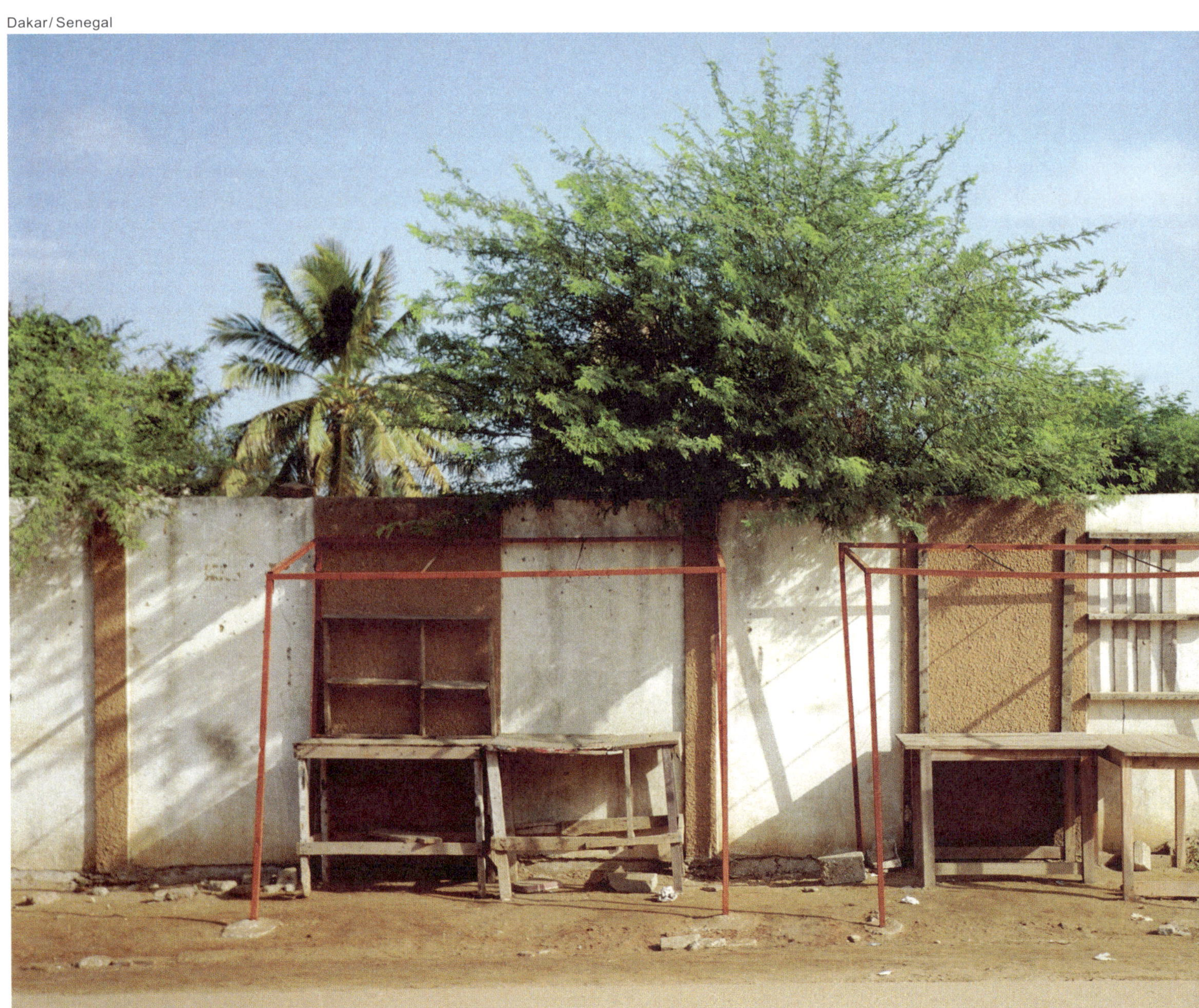

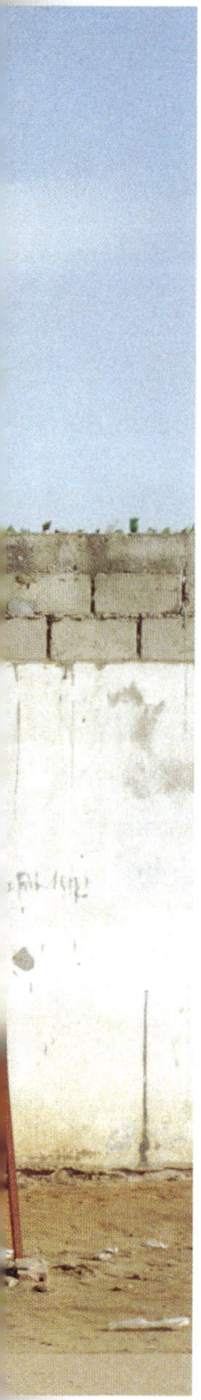

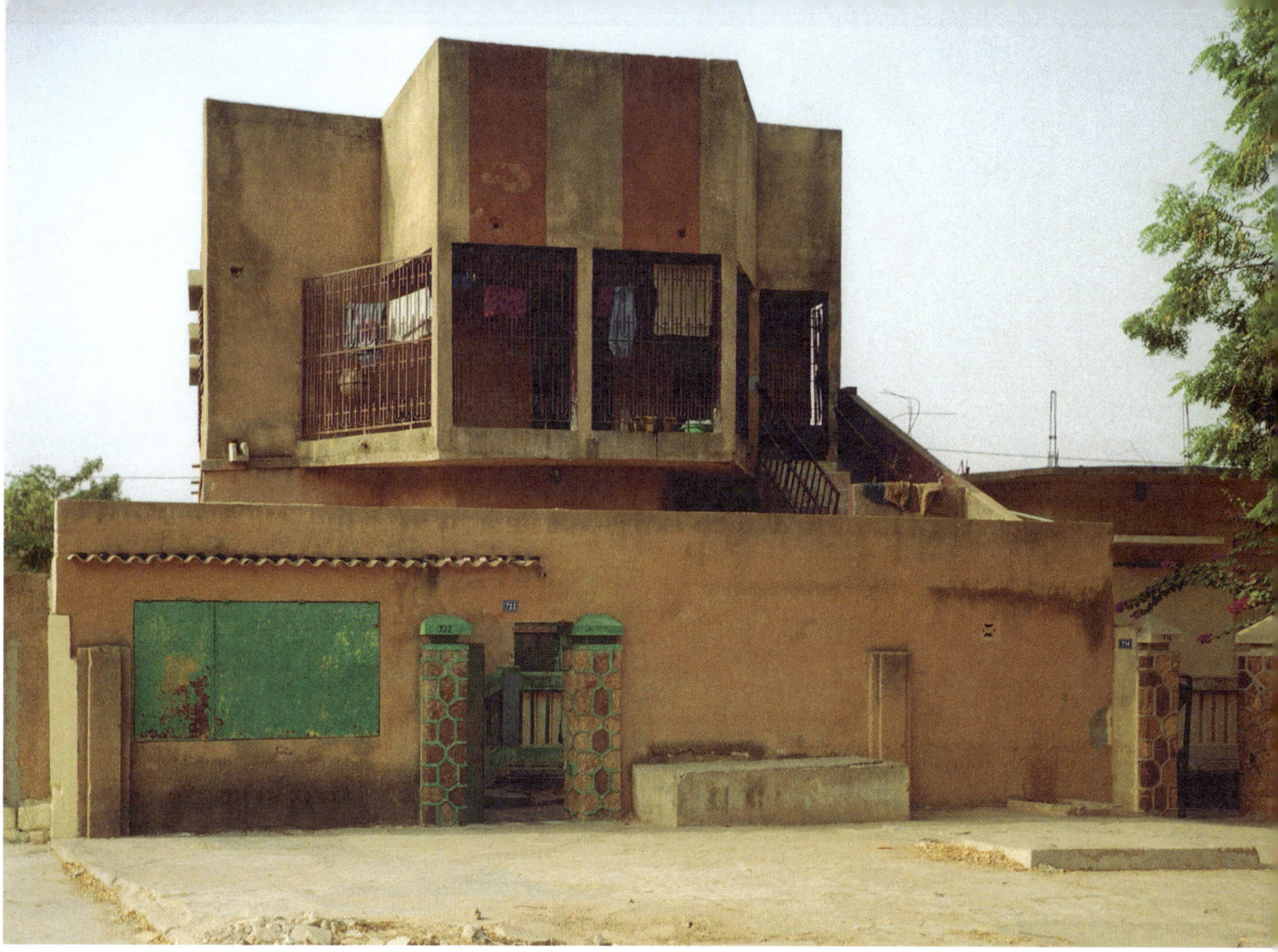

Thies / Senegal

Yoff / Cap Vert / Senegal

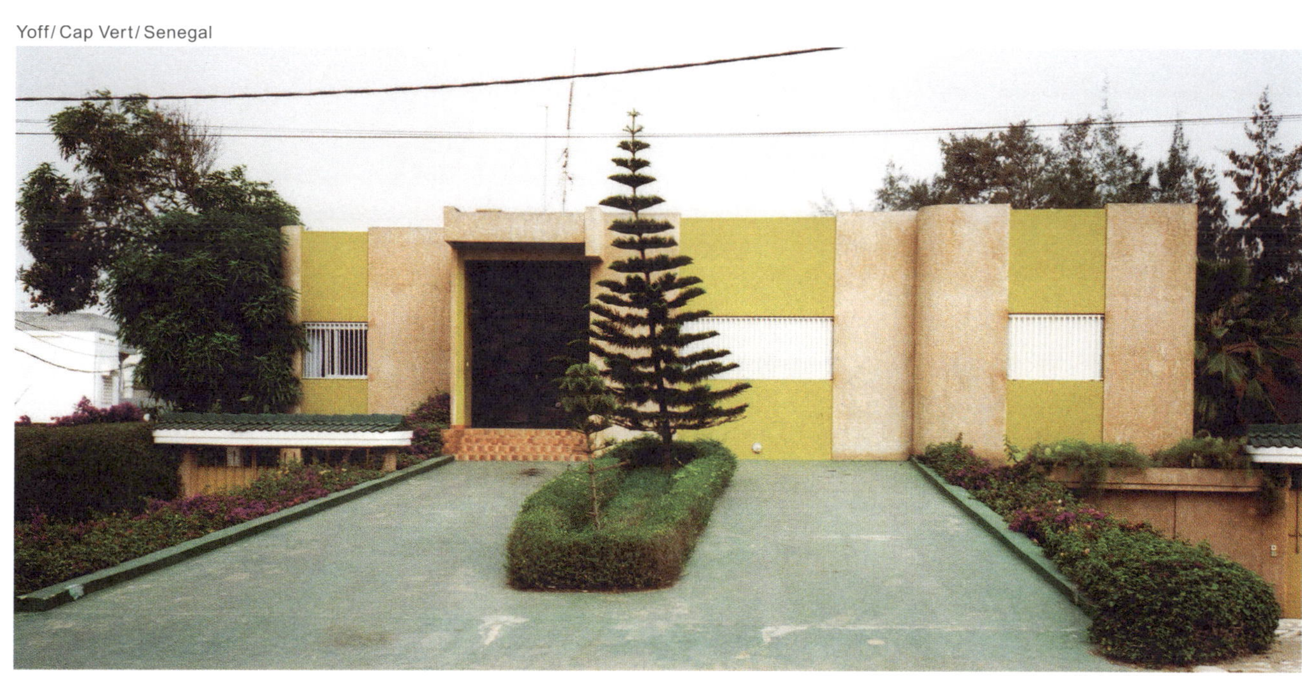

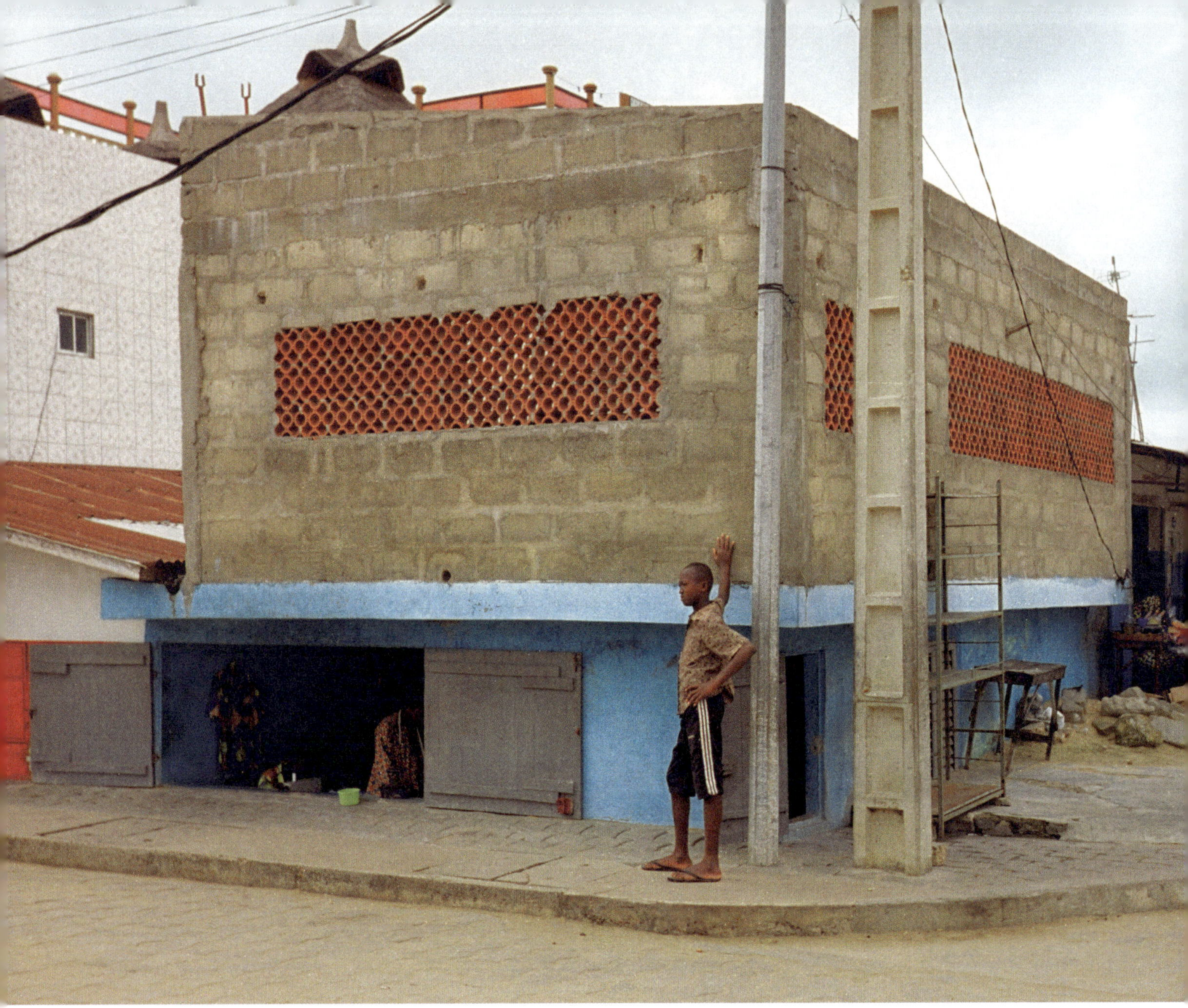

Cotonou / Benin

Parcelles Assainies / Cap Vert / Senegal

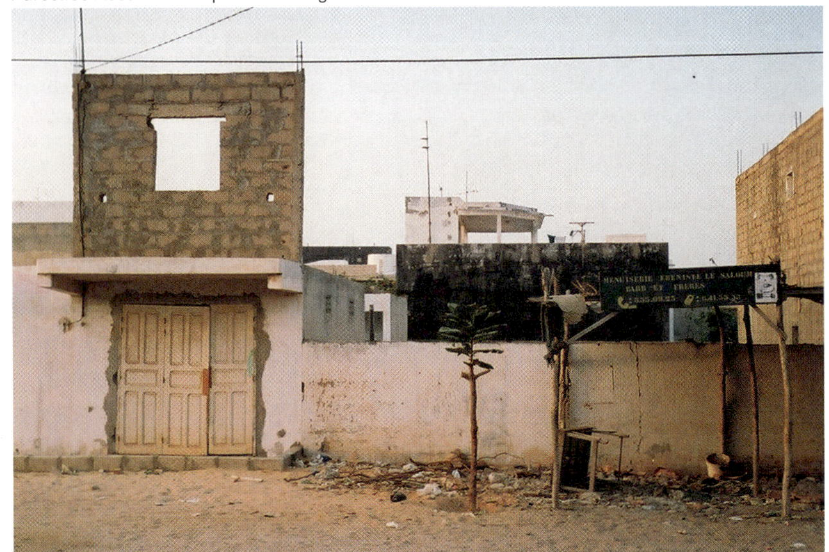

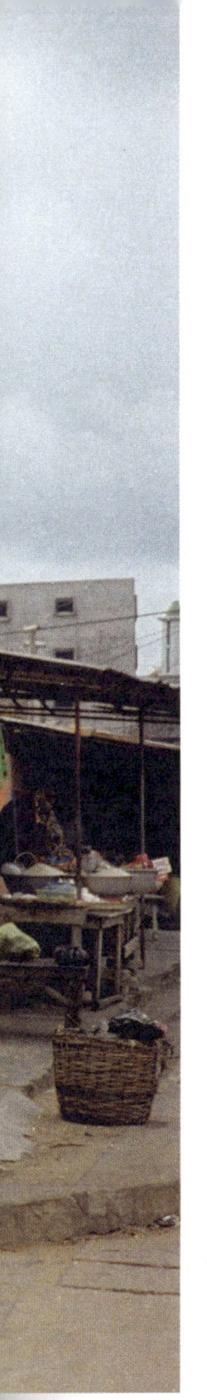

CHRISTIAN HANUSSEK: Something might have very different functions at very different locations. Or are you suggesting such phenomena as stripes always derive from a similar idea?
KAROLA SCHLEGELMILCH: I don't know if someone would have had exactly the same reasons as his immediate neighbour. It seems presumptuous to assume it. I wouldn't try to find it out by asking questions about the reasons for such decisions either. But I do see the aura of the building, its appearance, influenced by life inside, and possibly by it being a few years old.

Of course, there are facts and a kind of history that can be narrated or researched. But this kind of image is always transmitted in a complex manner able to be assimilated without words. And I think you can see a lot in the different materials. That's the great thing about houses. In the texts, I call it an "object-like presence", something that is simply there and has some unique particularity of its own that sometimes jumps out at you. Something expressive, transmitting fine nuances of preferences and histories.

Accra / Ghana

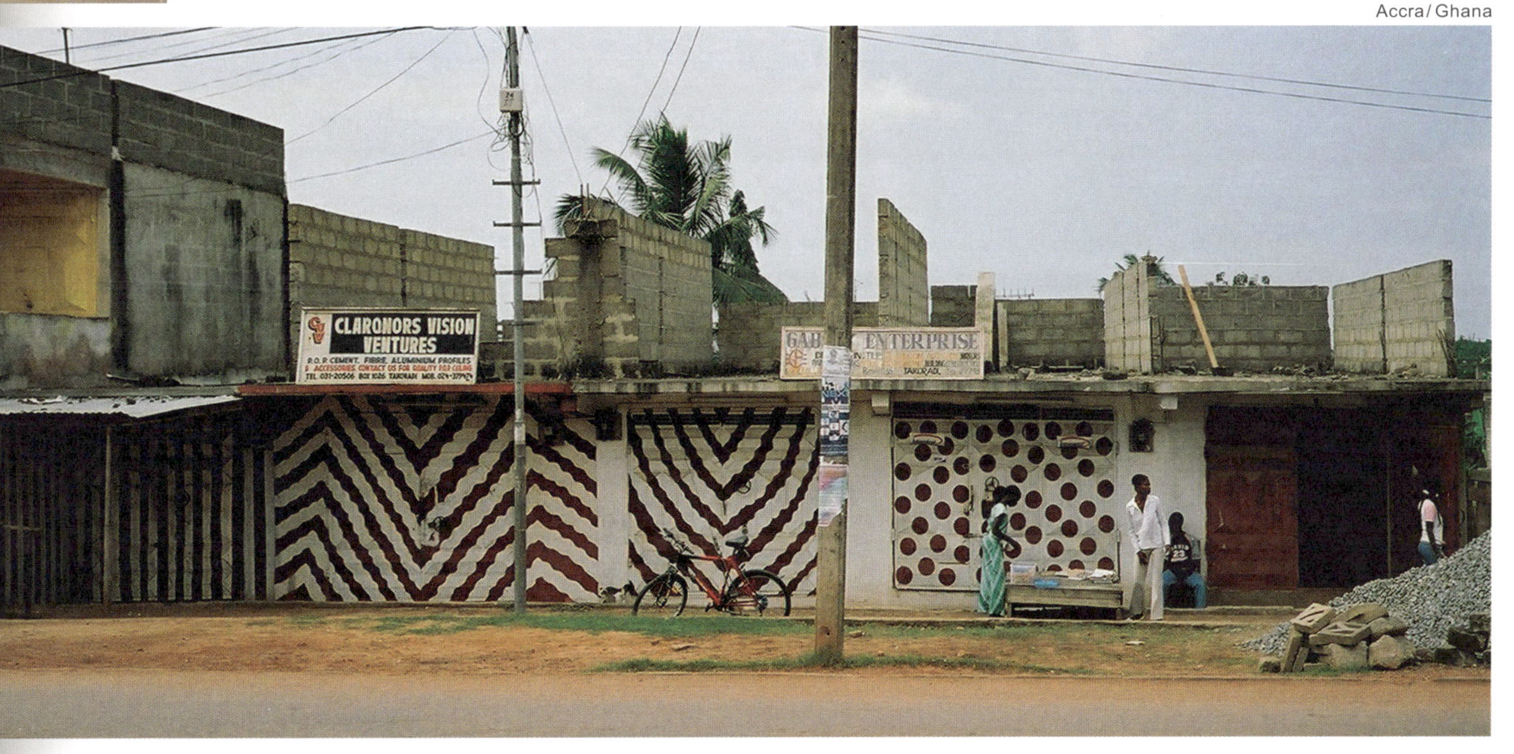

CHRISTIAN HANUSSEK: But the perspective of the entire building is here somewhere; that also shows where you stood. I find something like that fascinating. An example like this clearly illustrates the intense tension created in a photo because it actually isn't possible to photograph these buildings in a proper frontal view. They are so complex in themselves. There may well be infinite possibilities … you could move across here centimetre by centimetre and each time something new would be created.

KAROLA SCHLEGELMILCH: It's great, isn't it?
CHRISTIAN HANUSSEK: One wonders what kind of room that is – you'd like to have a look inside.
KAROLA SCHLEGELMILCH: Yes, look at the ventilation!
CHRISTIAN HANUSSEK: It doesn't have a window, only the slits.
KAROLA SCHLEGELMILCH: That's one. Mind you, it could be a wooden door. You also don't have any idea what it looks like behind it …
CHRISTIAN HANUSSEK: This door – where does it go to? That's far too narrow for a balcony.

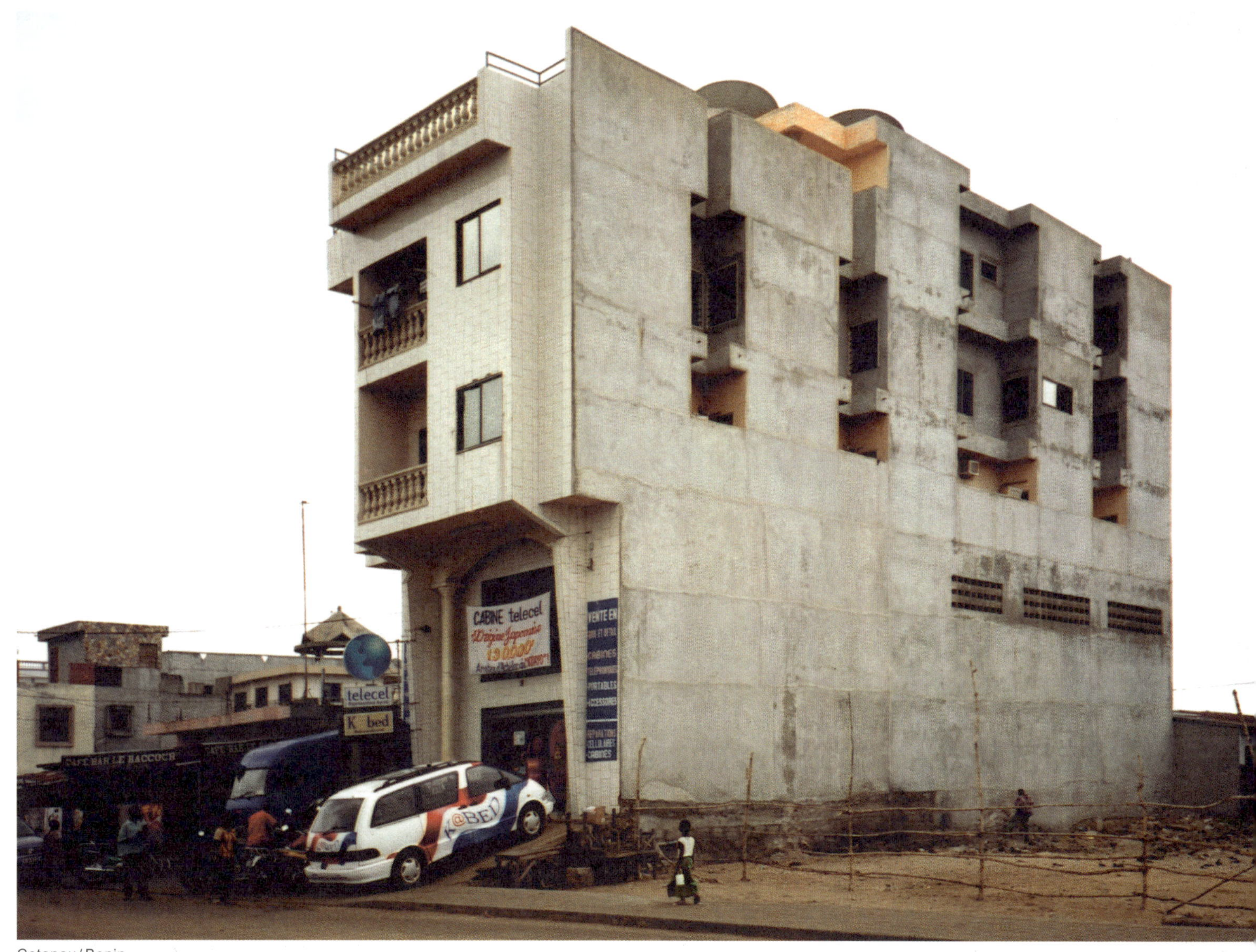

Cotonou / Benin

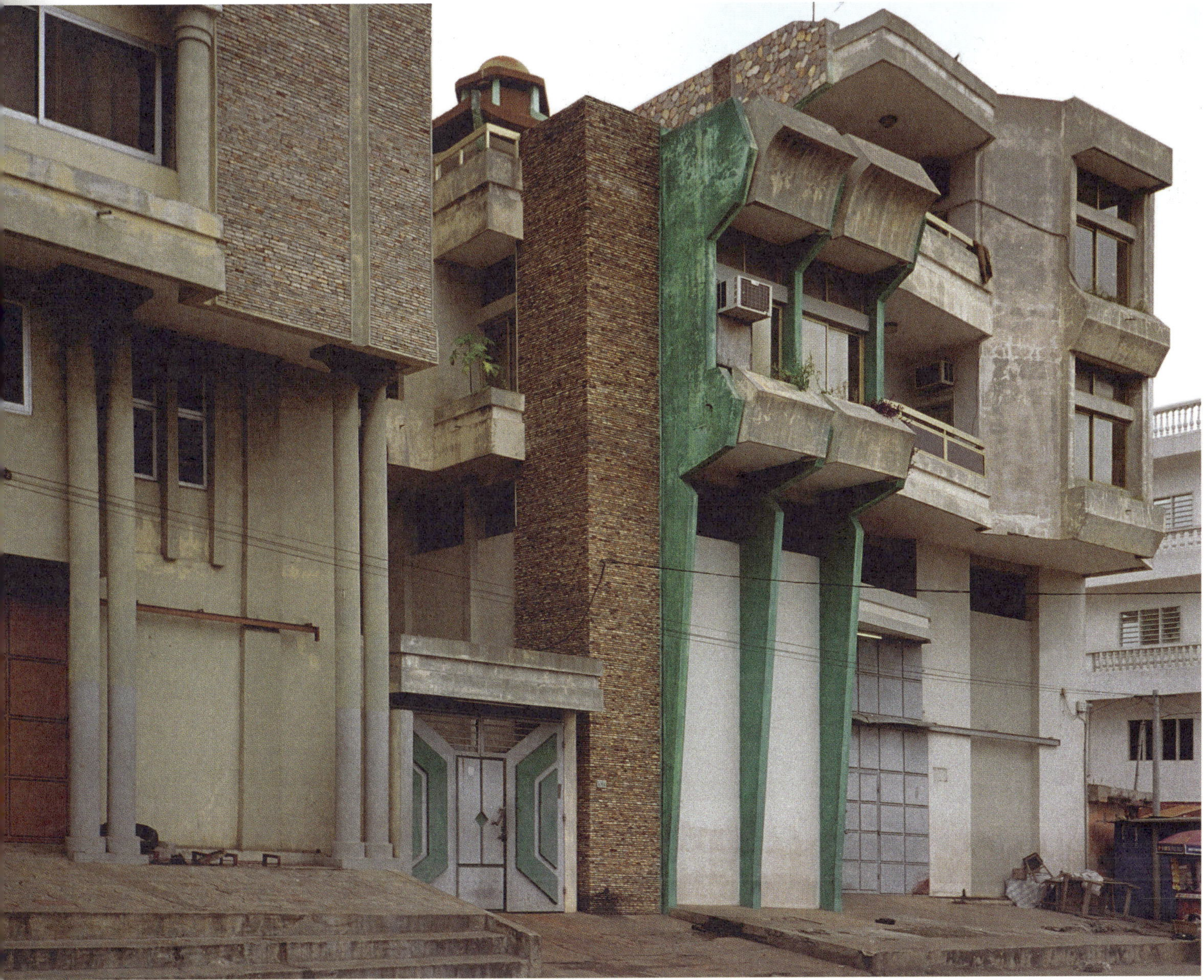

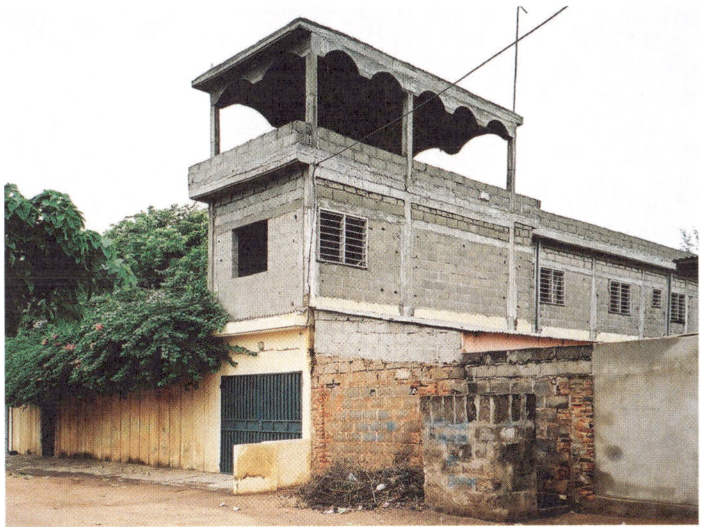

Cotonou / Benin

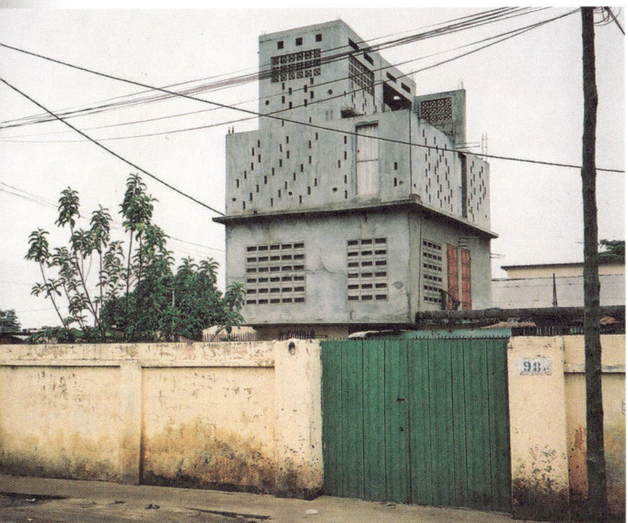

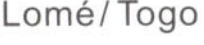

Lomé / Togo

Lomé / Togo

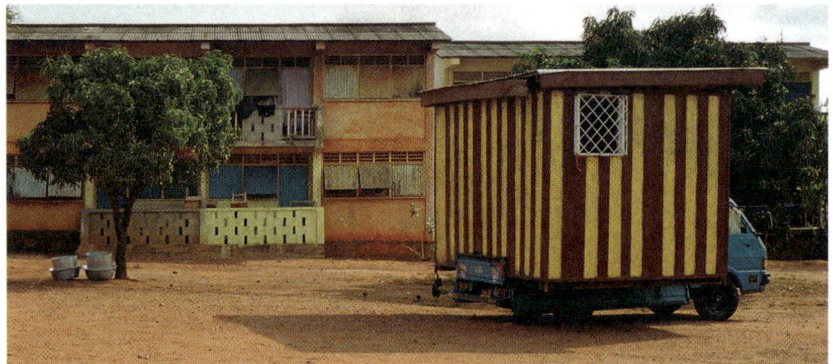

Accra Pigfarm / Ghana

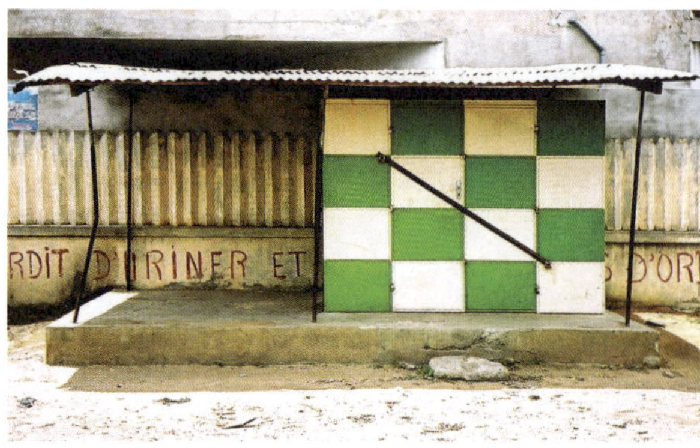

Cotonou / Benin

CHRISTIAN HANUSSEK: Is that a kiosk? There's a pub inside.
KAROLA SCHLEGELMILCH: I call it a kiosk, but it's definitely a commercial object. I like the previous picture very much too. It has something sacred about it, like an altar, because of this symmetry; or the delicacy here, the subtlety of the painting.
CHRISTIAN HANUSSEK: It's again rather reminiscent of Bodys Isek Kingelez, or one of those absurd home-made models. Like a model of a house.
Whereas I think this is rather good, with the very different architectural elements; there's a number of different stylistic elements coming together there.

…

CHRISTIAN HANUSSEK: Here, too, I find the same transitory access – it could have been photographed to look much more static. In your case, my feeling is that the photos strongly convey a sense of the process of taking in the city by walking around it.
KAROLA SCHLEGELMILCH: It's a process of hunting and gathering. I see something, am impressed in some way, and I take a photo. If I stopped to get involved in some protracted setting up of the camera, the shot would have changed a little just at that moment because, for example, the environs might have reacted to me.
I have a mass of these individual photos at home, sorted into groups by keywords.
When I exhibit them, I work on them again. I simply have a look at how the building creates the clearest effect, and then I sometimes retouch or deblur the highlights, or change the segment visible. It's rather a difficult balance. If you can notice there's been some kind of external control, that gets integrated into the image and takes something away from what I like about it. It should be clear that these are objects I've found by chance, taken from my perspective. It's not supposed to suggest some kind of documentation, which I don't believe is possible anyway. Yet at the same time, the other side, the opposite, shouldn't be lost entirely either.
CHRISTIAN HANUSSEK: It creates a quite particular aesthetic quality. It retains something everyday. These stalls are simply there, used in a totally normal way, and are not something taken by an artist and put into a very different context.

The conversation took place on 11 June 2010 in Berlin.
Karola Schlegelmilch's photographs were taken between 2001 and 2006.

Translation from German by Andrew Boreham

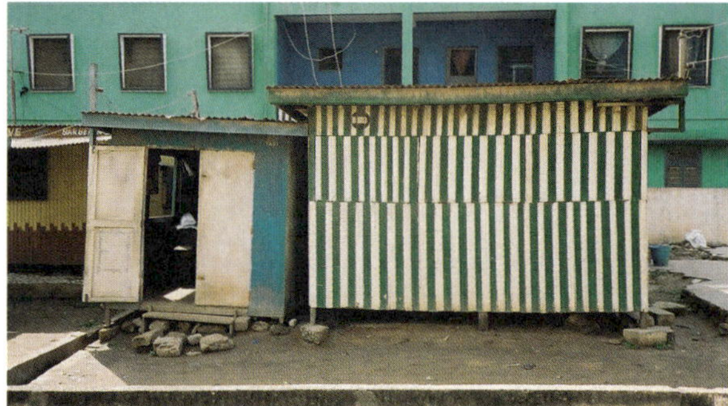

Takoradi / Ghana

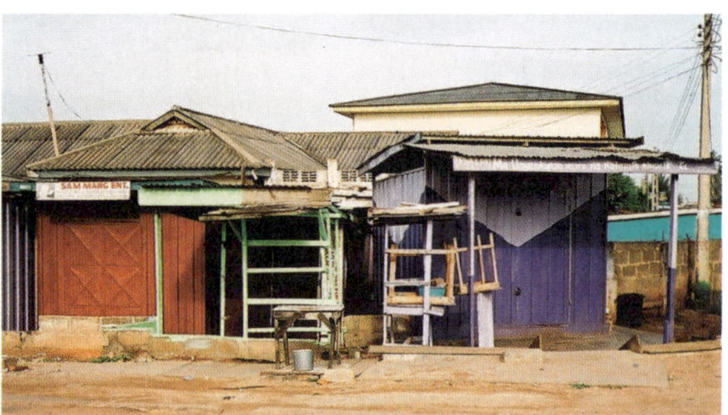

Accra New Town / Ghana

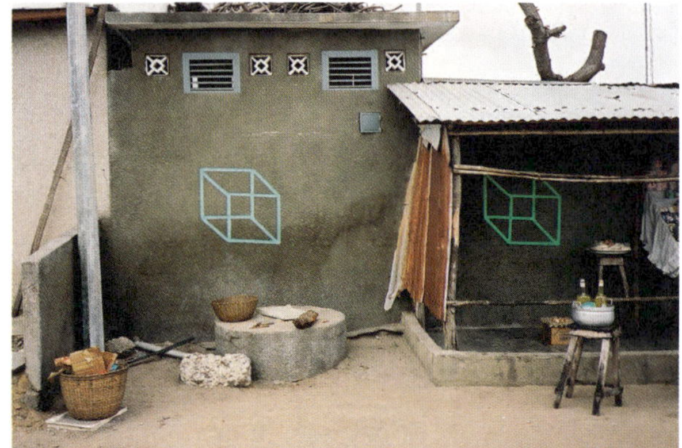

Cotonou / Benin

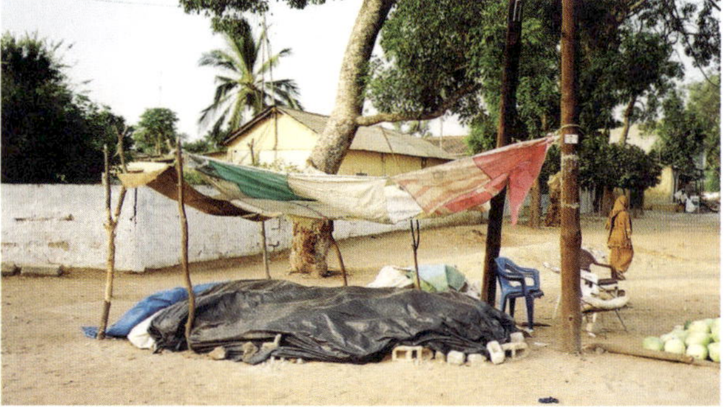

Thies / Senegal

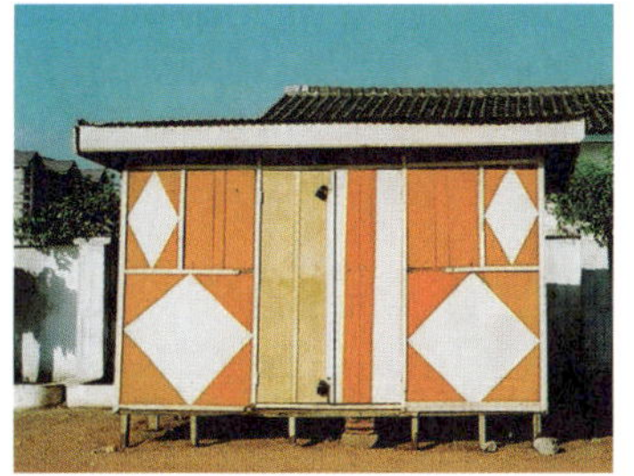

East Legon / Ghana

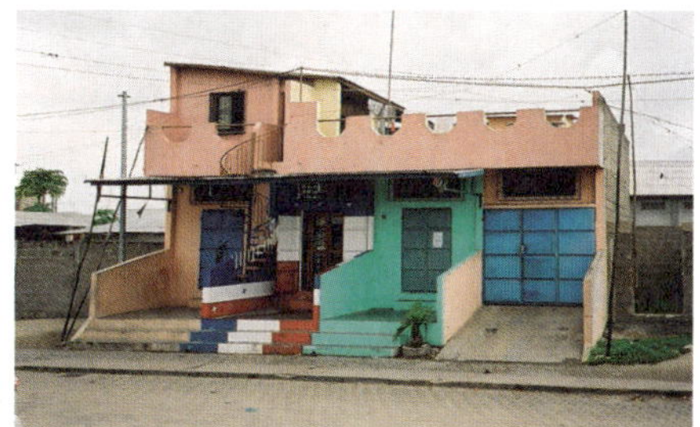

Dahomé / Benin

Ouidah / Benin

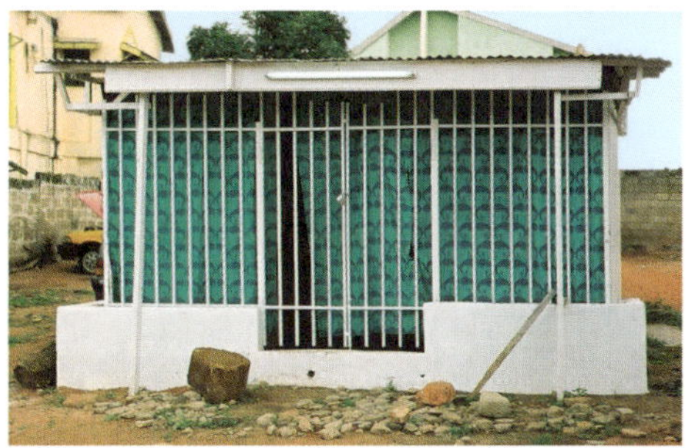

Dansoman / Ghana

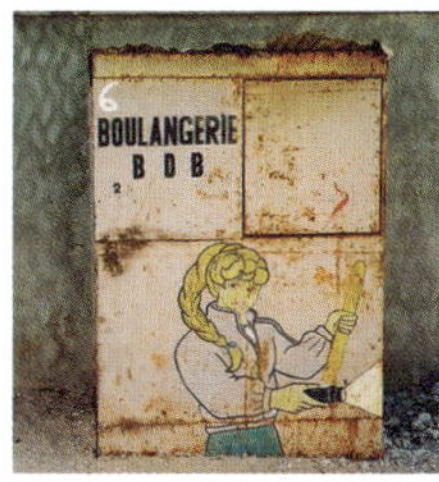

Grand Médine / Cap Vert

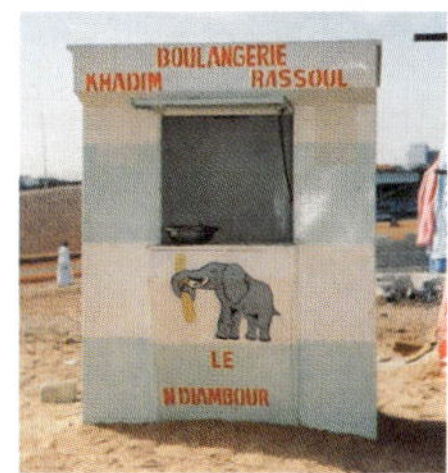

Grand Médine / Cap Vert

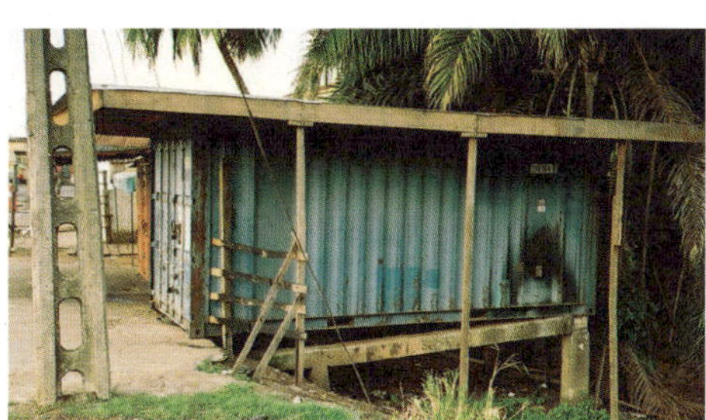

Cape Coast / Ghana

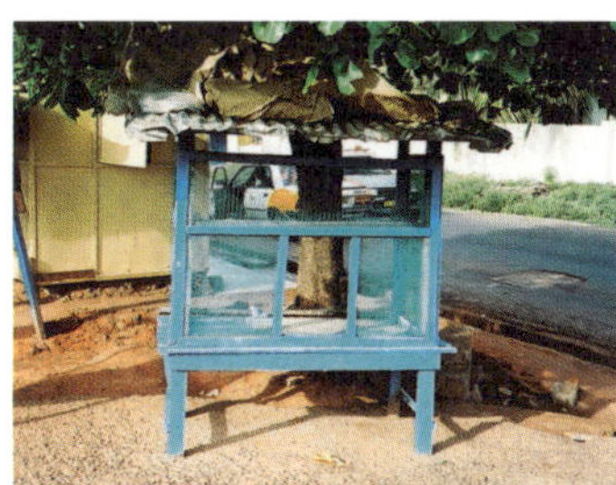

Nima / Accra / Ghana

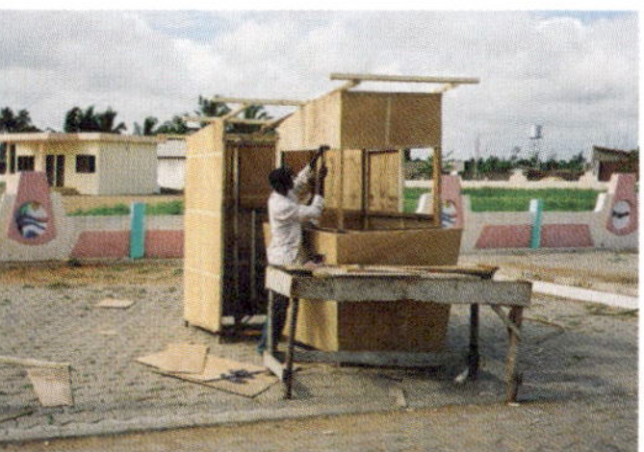

Grand Popo / Benin

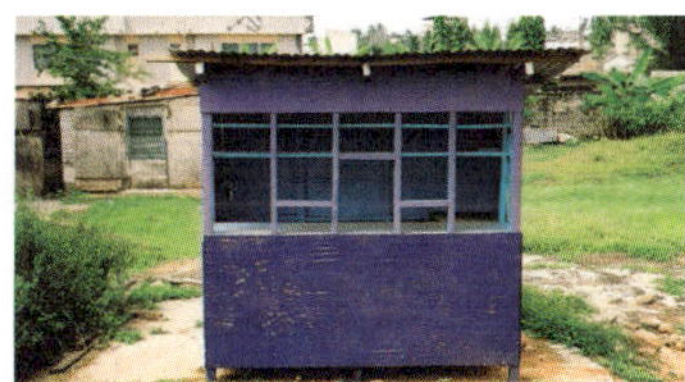

Takoradi / Ghana

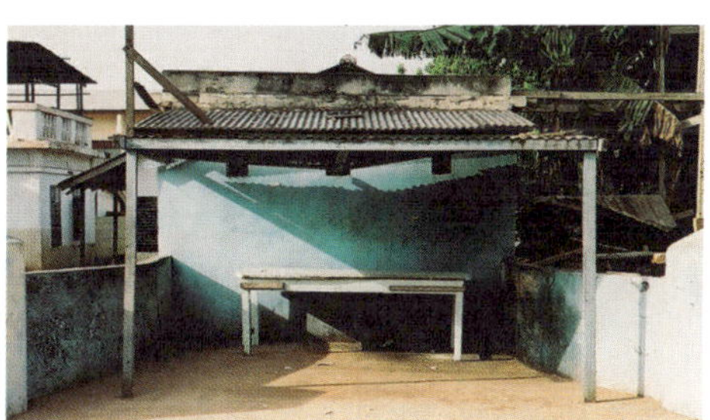

Cape Coast / Ghana

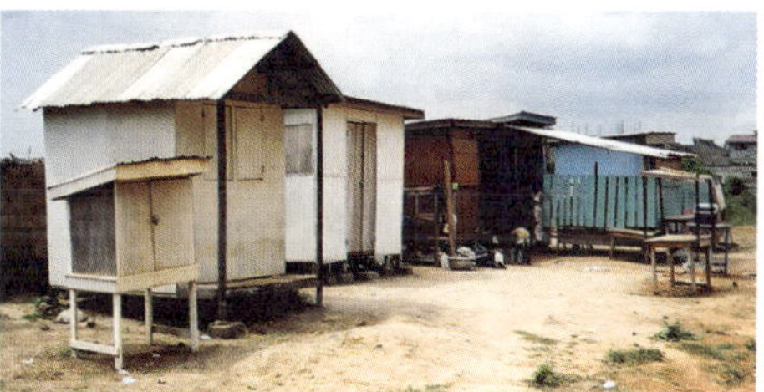

East Legon / Ghana

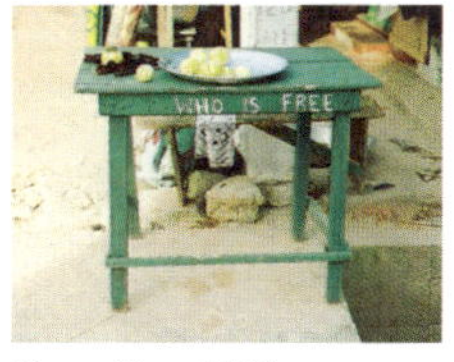

Cape Coast / Ghana

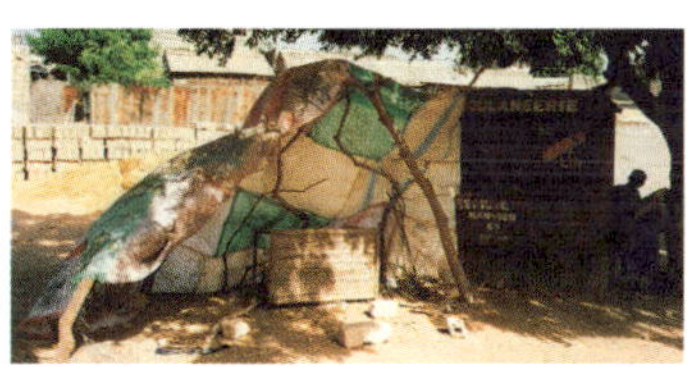

Rufisque / Senegal

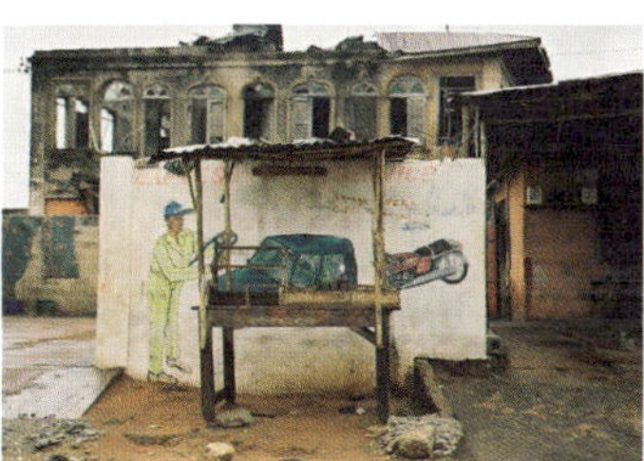

Porto Novo / Benin

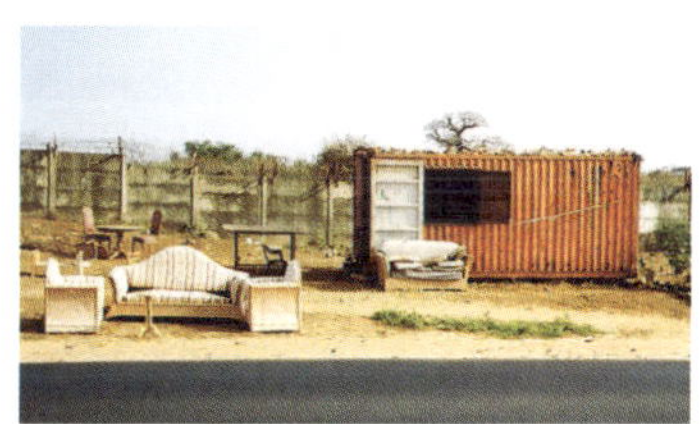

Yoff / Cap Vert / Senegal

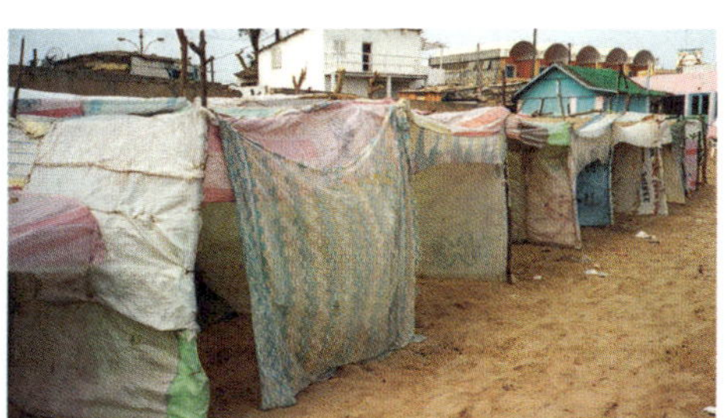

N'Gor / Cap Vert

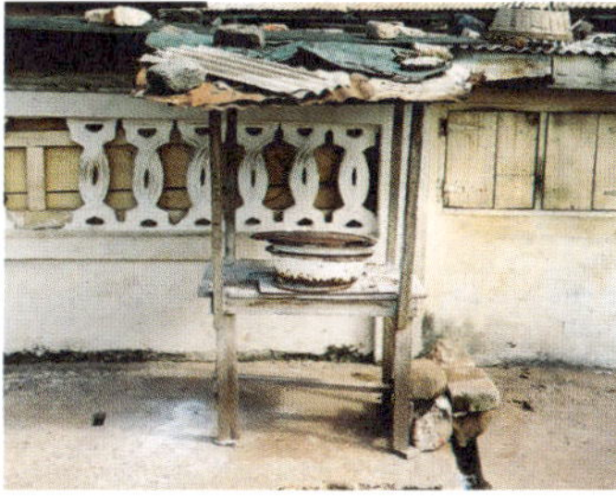

Nima / Accra / Ghana

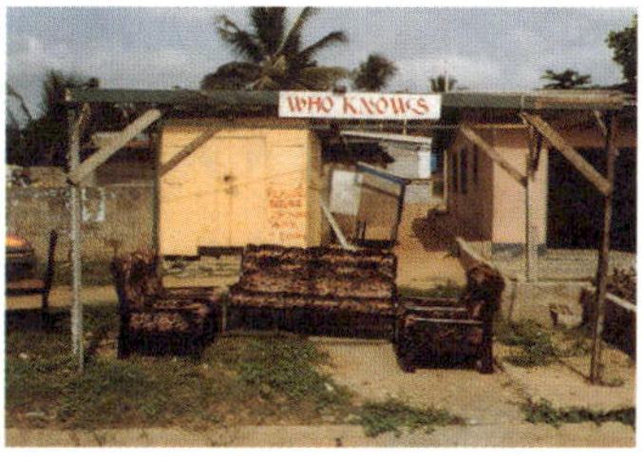

Nungua / Ghana

Cities and Cinemas
Fragments of an African History of the Urban in Cinema and of Cinema as an Urban Matter

MARIE-HÉLÈNE GUTBERLET

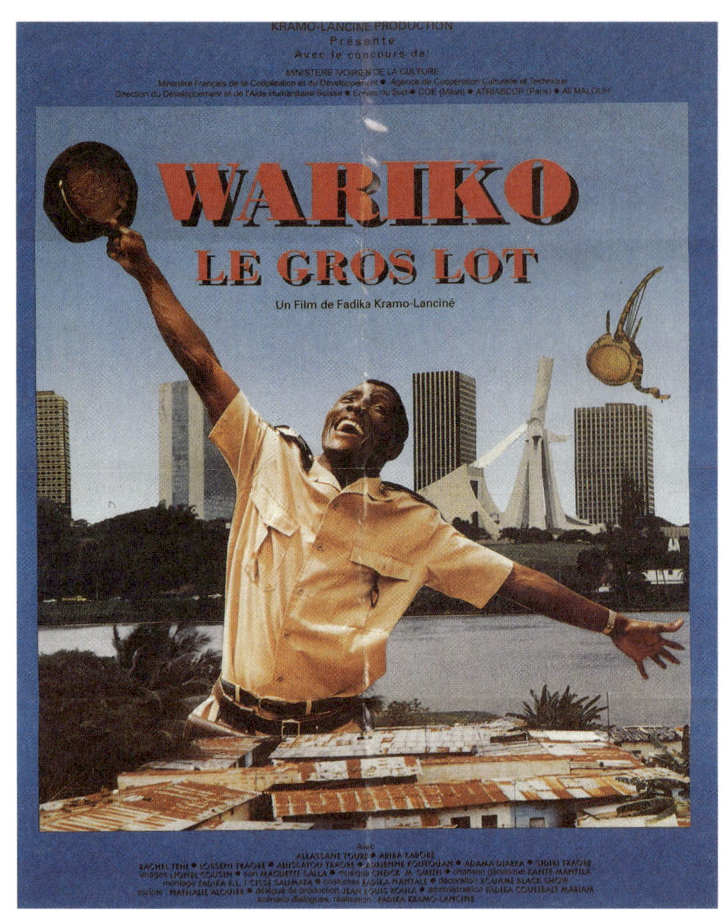

Abidjan (Côte d'Ivoire): poster for *Wariko, Le Gros Lot,* Fadika Kramo-Lanciné (1994)

"It is African filmmakers who were the first to see the African city. They did the city a great favour because, before them, nobody could say what it was."[1]

Ever since the invention of the cinematograph in 1896, there has been a close relationship between city, cinema and film. The early cinema was a paradigmatic location of urbanity in the rapidly growing metropolises of Europe and North America, a modern institution of visual curiosity. The films shown in its interior naturally also reproduced scenes of urban life, and cinema mirrored the city's changed perceptual dispositifs. Cinema and city are inextricably entwined. Serge Daney has said that cinema belongs to the city, that they share the same destiny, and that, just as there was a time before cinema, there will also be a time after cinema.[2]

But how does this connection between city and cinema take shape in the African context? Is the idea of a shared fate for city and cinema really convincing given that – as Daney proposes – we have both an actual African cinema, the village cinema,[3] and the diagnosis that there is an African cinema whose hour has not yet come?[4] Where can we identify the connection, how should we approach it? Where does it begin, and where does it end? Which cities are at issue? Which urban themes are negotiated in films, which others only gestured to?

We may note first of all that both cities and cinemas consist of built forms – they possess a certain materiality, they are to some extent 'designed', and they have something that takes place in the interior, something not so easily materialised. They are like stages, marketplaces, sites of vitality, the perception of which arises only with the moment of participation in them. The city and the cinema, then, are participatory forms. This is not to say that they are locations of social communication; it means, rather, that anybody who is not inside and taking part is excluded. Just as the bored street café patron becomes part of the city-

---

1   Pierre Haffner 1986, Les cinéastes d'Afrique noire et leurs villes, *Filméchange* 36: 39–46, p. 41

2   Serge Daney 1987, Ville-ciné et Télé-banlieue, in: *Cités-Cinés* [exhibition catalogue], Paris, p. 121–127, here p. 121

3   Daney is certainly thinking of the films by Idrissa Ouédraogo, Souleymane Cissé and Cheikh Oumar Sissoko that attracted critical and theoretical interest at international film festivals in the 1980s.

4   Daney's view accords with Gaston Kaboré's: Gaston Kaboré 1995, Avant-Propos, in: Fédération Panafricaine des Cinéastes (FEPACI) (ed.), *L'Afrique et le Centenaire du Cinéma/ Africa and the Centenary of Cinema,* Paris, p. 15–18.

5   Brian Larkin 2008, *Signal and Noise. Media, Infrastructure, and Urban Culture in Nigeria,* Durham

6   Larkin (2008), p. 3

scape even though he believes himself uninvolved, so the members of a cinema audience become part of the perceptual situation, ultimately even part of the construction of the space in which they sojourn.[5] It could therefore be said that cinema and city are form and imagination; that the city provides the external structure within which urban life unfolds, while the cinema accommodates the film in which ideas of a life in the city (and not only there) are processed and given concrete shape – just as the city itself develops particular effects and the cinema refers back to those experiences and effects. The allure is in the dynamics binding the two together. The dynamics of urban life are, figuratively speaking, that of people on the move, of traffic and the constantly changing built substance of the city with its ambient noise, smells, lights, haptic experiences. Paralleling those dynamics are the movements of the apparatus of film (and their continued technical development) as well as the movements of the senses participating in the perception of film. This shared dynamic principle not only makes cinema the ideal audiovisual chronicler of the city, but alters the concept of urbanity itself. In relation to Africa and its visual culture, it entails a different, modern technological and aesthetic image of Africa.

In this paper, I will explore the technological and aesthetic material of cinema and film and begin to cast some light upon it. Rather than offering finished ideas or hypotheses, I work with impressions and insights gathered in the course of my many years of experience of films and the places where they are shown. This will not yield an isolated line of argument, but perhaps some fragments of a history of the urban in cinema and of the cinema as an urban form in Africa, which may be further pursued elsewhere.

1. African Cities as Contact Zones with Film

Film screenings (from around 1900) and the construction of dedicated cinema buildings (probably from the late 1910s) changed the shapes and images of cities in Africa as elsewhere. As colonial society became more fully differentiated and women and children arrived to join what had initially been a male-dominated European society, the demand for leisure facilities and amusement grew in the colonial cities of Africa. The first cinemas were thus built in the colonial parts of town. At the same time, films were also shown to the indigenous population, as a medium of instruction, indoctrination and entertainment – aiming to make the spectators into "modern colonial citizens"[6]. In the countryside, this goal was pursued by means of mobile cinema vans or *cinébus,* whereas in African towns and cities, especially in the 1950s, the topography of cinema diversified. Important components in the development of the cinema as an urban institution were the open-air screens from which film, as a spectacle of

light and noise, diffused into the surrounding streets. The urban centres were also crucial to the emergence and development of African auteur cinema from the 1950s and 1960s onwards: Abidjan, Accra, Bamako, Dakar, Harare, Johannesburg, Cairo, Niamey, Ouagadougou, Tunis and Yaoundé all had cinemas where the filmmakers of the future first watched movies, but, more importantly, these cities also became sites of film production.[7] Starting from the 1960s, they also hosted festivals – such as FESPACO (Festival Panafricain du Cinéma et de la Télévision de Ouagadougou) in the then Republic of Upper Volta, now Burkina Faso, and the Festival de Carthage in Tunisia – along with promotion bodies and film bureaus,[8] later also film production and distribution companies.[9] From the 1970s until well into the 1990s, some cities even had their own cinematic chroniclers: Djibril Diop Mambety and Ousmane Sembene for Dakar, for example, or Jean-Marie Teno for Yaoundé. In its turn, the video market came to change the media scene just as cinema had done a century before. It has impacted on the technological, economic and infrastructural parameters of the city's image.[10]

Today, the production of Western or transnational movies in Africa is growing, whereas African film-making, as local production by African auteurs in Africa, is in the process of disappearing. Contemporaneously with these tendencies, a highly mobile African film-making diaspora has emerged that connects the cities of the South to the European centres. These filmmakers are at home both in the West and in Africa, acquire their finance in Europe or the United States and make their films in their countries of origin – often querying conventional views of the African city. With their knowledge of 'both sides', these transnationally oriented artists respond to the images of Africa traditionally prevalent in the West and address the interplay between identity processes, globalisation and migration. Mweeze Ngangura (*Le roi, la vache et le bananier* 1994), Jean-Marie Teno (*Vacances au pays* 2000) and Idrissou Mora Kpai (*Si-Gueriki, La reine mère* 2002), for example, explicitly engage with the theme of return after long residences in Belgium, France or Germany. Reflection upon one's own biography and upon changes in the location and society one has left also implies a proposed alternative image of African life, a picture sharply distinct from the exotic African scenarios circulating in the Western media. The cities, too, have changed, and differ substantially from the filmic models of the city set out by the first generation of African filmmakers in the 1960s and 1970s.

In addition, film and video technology is currently developing in ways that make the hitherto strict distinction between analogue and video or digital recording and reproduction technology increasingly permeable, and allows the two forms to be combined. As a result, image properties are becoming more closely aligned: the optical parameters of photography and film (depth of focus,

---

7 In the 1960s and 1970s, large numbers of private and state production companies were established. Aside from the well-funded productions in South Africa and some Maghrebian states, these auteur-based production forms were and remain dependent on Western post-production partners. Even where post-production technology is available locally, Western cooperation offers better prospects of future distribution.

8 Manthia Diawara 1992, *African Cinema, Politics and Culture,* Bloomington, p.1–11 and 51–83. Diawara here describes the "Colonial Film Units" in Nigeria and Ghana, from which the national bureaus arose.

9 See the founding of INAFEC (Institut Africain d'Education Cinématographique) in 1976 and of CIPROFILM (Consortium Interafricain de Production de Films) in 1979 and CIDC (Consortium Interafricain de Distribution Cinématographique) in 1979. Claire Andrade-Watkins 1995, Portuguese African Cinema, 1969–1993, in: Michael T. Martin (ed.), Ci-

nemas of the Black Diaspora. Diversity, Dependence, and Oppositionality, Wayne, p.181–203, here p.193

10 Since the mid-1990s, local structures have been replaced by the international funding of individual, rigorously selected film projects. The local film production infrastructure for auteur films has largely collapsed. The market for videos from Nollywood and its emulators that flourished in the 1990s is important in this context, and has been a point of reference for fifteen years. Some have regarded it as competition: see Birgit Meyer 2003, Ghanaian Popular Cinema and the Magic in and of Film, in: Birgit Meyer, Peter Pels (eds), *Magic and Modernity: Interfaces of Revelation and Concealment,* Stanford, p.200–222, others as a genuine alternative to the expensive complex of film and cinema: see Jean-Marie Teno 1993, Liberté, le Pouvoir de Dire Non, *Cinéma et Liberté (Contribution au Thème du FESPACO)*, Essais er Propos, p.13–16, here p.16.

composition using degrees of focus, lighting) can now be achieved using digital cameras, and, conversely, the effects of digital photography (blurring, colour effects in low-light photography) have been taken up by the aesthetics of film. At the same time, digital picture resolution is improving steadily, so that the image noise typical of video is gradually becoming a thing of the past. The polarity is dissolving, the rift becoming narrower between self-declared film aesthetes and those advocates of the popular video market who celebrate Nollywood as an independent trash-style African self-portrait and condemn the auteur film as work for the West on Western models. With today's technology, the distinction between popular and auteur films no longer rests solely on technical criteria. It is now possible to make all kinds of films using digital cameras and digital post-production. This changes not only the status of filmmakers, but also their gaze at the city. The city casts a different vision of light and colour, and demands new forms of creativity under these new technological conditions.[11]

2. Cinema's Participation in the Modernity of African Cities

On the African continent, cinemas are almost as old as the colonial forms of urbanisation. Films have been screened in the coastal metropolises, ports and mining towns since around 1900. The African audience – at first mainly men who had hired out their labour in the transport and mining industry – was to be entertained. Movies served as an attraction and as a technical vehicle for colonial society's claim to civilisational superiority. It seemed to be, if not a propagandistic and didactic resource, then at least a harmless alternative to the distractions offered by drinking and gambling, which the colonial administration considered corrosive to the work ethic.

Research on this colonial film practice has often either focused on contemporary film policy and the colonialist ideological motivations behind treatments of African motifs, or investigated the content of films, in other words the stories that they tell. Less attention has been paid to the specific context in which such films were produced and watched. In the 1990s, some work on African audiences' modes of perception was carried out, questioning the success of the colonial project of using film as a manipulatory medium for colonial ideology and presenting the colonial cinema as the site of a temporary counter-public sphere.[12]

The role of cinema architecture in the context of film screening, colonial prestige and perception has, however, been addressed only in the most recent studies.[13] Thus, in African cities there are many cinemas that were built in the early or mid-20th century, yet the connection between African urbanisation in the wake of colonisation post-1884 and the first use of the cinematograph, less than two decades later, has not yet been studied in the context of architecture and urban planning. To mention just a few examples that may highlight this relationship, the Cinéma Sandaga[14] in Dakar recalls the rough brickwork of simple colonial buildings; Le Normandie in N'Djamena, the setting of Mahamat-Saleh Haroun's *Bye Bye Africa* (1999), is a concrete construction with a Moorish touch; Amadou & Mariam pay homage to Dakar's Le Paris, now demolished, in their song *Senegal Fastfood*[15]. All the cinema buildings still standing are – like hotels and restaurants, stations and administrative offices – the products of colonial, and later postcolonial, architectural visions that united a modern overall impression with specific historical and local detail. Investigating cinemas, their location, architectural style and sociopolitical status has now become a pressing task, for several reasons. On one hand, it can be tied into discourses on African urbanity, urban development, modernity and architectural history – in this respect, cinemas might become visible as embodiments of urban history and sites of individual memory.[16] On the other, the cinemas are increasingly dilapidated and are at risk of vanishing completely. Visual material on cinema architecture is sparse, but the existing pictures show an extremely interesting degree of architectural diversity, as is shown by Annett Busch's photographs of Dakar. [→ Fig. **A**]

Certainly, despite the scanty information currently available on cinema architecture in Africa, the volume of construction itself was anything but small. In 1989, film scholar Pierre Haffner became one of the first to write about cinema auditoriums in Africa, publishing statistics on the number of cinemas in fifty-four African states for 1972.[17] The statistics were headed by South Africa with a total of 3,504 cinemas (buildings and open-air), followed by Egypt with 1,400; in the mid-field were Zaire (now DRC) with 267, Ghana with 157, Rwanda with 93, Senegal with 89[18] and Sudan with 75; amongst the last on the list was Burkina Faso (at the time Republic of Upper Volta), with only eight auditoriums.[19] Looking at these figures from a present-day perspective, it becomes clear that in the 1950s – just a few years after decolonisation – African cities entered a boom phase in cinema construction. Yet by the 1970s, a mere twenty years later, the cinema as the key setting for the reception of film was already facing ideological and technological challenges. Technical innovations that, in North America and Europe, were already reducing revenues in the cinema sector now began to affect the African context as well: the rise of television, video technology and then digital media. Whereas in Kinshasa, Niamey and Bamako this led to a

11 See Diawara (1992); Keyan Tomaselli 1989, *The Cinema of Apartheid. Race and Class in South African Film,* London; Peter Davis 1996, *In Darkest Hollywood. Exploring the Jungles of Cinema's South Africa,* Athens; Frank W. Ukadike 1994, *Black African Cinema,* Berkeley

12 Imruh Bakari and Mbye Cham (eds) 1996, *African Experiences of Cinema,* London; June Givanni (ed.) 2000, *Symbolic Narratives. African Cinema. Audiences, Theory, and the Moving Image,* London; Marie-Hélène Gutberlet 2004, *Auf Reisen. Afrikanisches Kino,* Frankfurt/Main, p.70 ff

13 Larkin (2008), p.123 ff

14 See the illustration at www.flickr.com/photos/pulp-o-rama/ 2276576337/ [retrieved on 13 February 2012].

15 See the video clip of the song on the album *Dimanche à Bamako* (2005), featuring Manu Chao, www.dailymotion.com/ video/x10igt_amadou-mariam-senegal-fastfood_music [retrieved on 13 February 2012].

16 Thus, for example, the ABC cinema in Colobane became known beyond Dakar when filmmaker Djibril Diop Mambéty described his own experiences associated with the locale. See Alessandra Speciale 1998, Djibril, Le Prince et le Poète du Cinéma Africain, *Écrans d'Afrique/African Screen* 24/7: 6–10, special issue *Hommage/Tribute: Djibril Diop Mambéty*

17 Pierre Haffner 1989, *Kino in Schwarzafrika,* Revue CICIM 27/28, München; statistics first published in Guy Hennebelle 1972, *Les Cinémas Africains en 1972,* Paris.

18 According to Alioune Ndiaye's recent survey on Senegal, in 2006/2007 sixteen cinemas were still in operation in Senegal and another twelve were about to be closed or rebuilt for other uses. Alioune Ndiaye 2007, *La Promotion du Cinéma Sénégalais par la Télévision,* Dakar (unpublished Masters thesis, Institut Africain du Management, 2006/2007), retrieved from www.scribd.com/doc/24707547/Promotion-du-Cinema-Senegalais-par-la-television on 13 February 2012, p.110–111.

19 In the 1980s, during the presidential term of Thomas Sankara, numerous cinemas were built across Burkina Faso. The FESPACO Festival, initiated in 1968, enjoyed a heyday in 1990s Ouagadougou – at that time, the city had thirteen working cinemas. In 2010 just two were still regularly showing films.

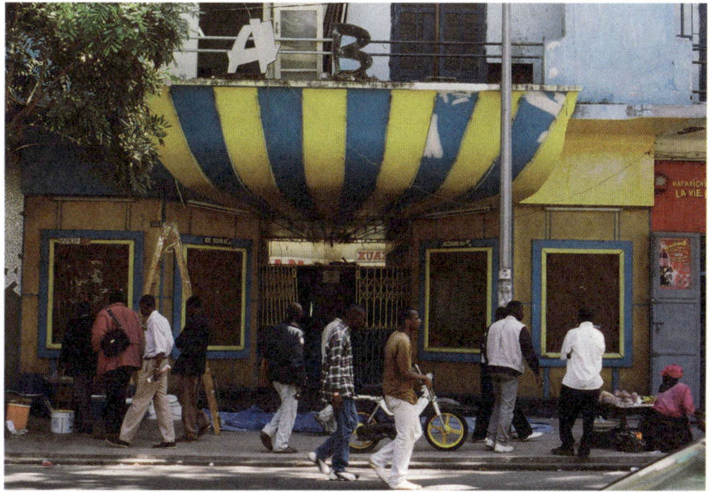

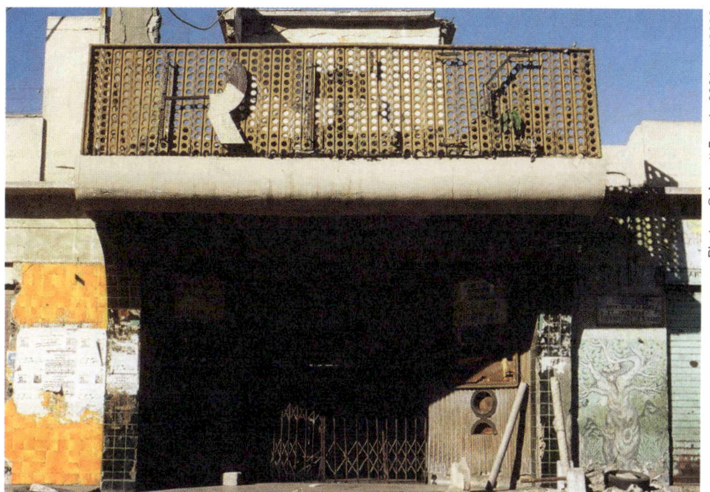

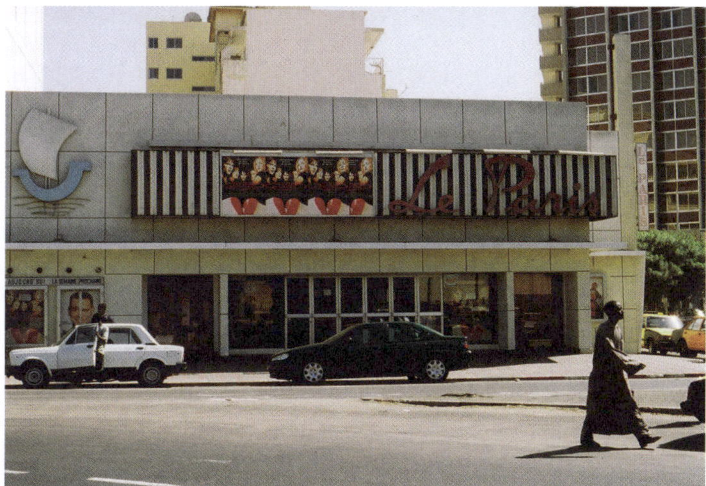

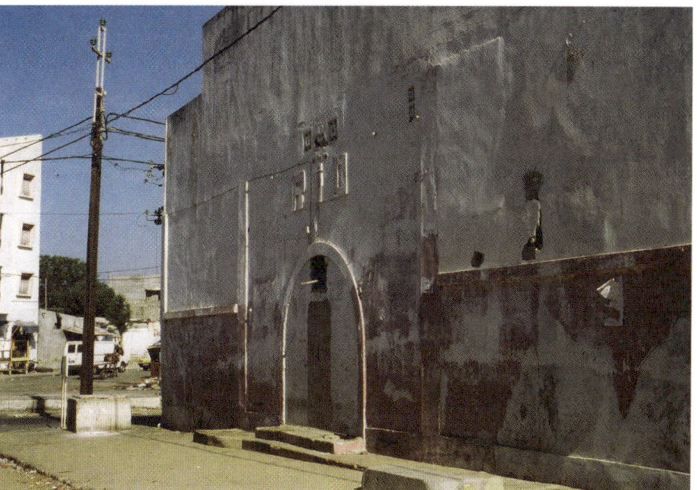

A   The "ABC" in Colobane (Dakar), renovations
The "Le Paris" in Plateau (Dakar), before demolition

The "Rex" on Avenue Faidherbe in Medina (Dakar)
The "Rio" in Gueule Tapée (Dakar)

near-disappearance of cinemas, in the 1980s and 1990s other cities, such as Ouagadougou and Dakar, experienced a boom thanks to film festivals and a policy of local film promotion.

3. The African Auteur Film and its Analysis of the City's Imagery

The collapse of most colonial regimes around 1960 brought with it the end of censorship, which had long stopped African filmmakers from realising films in their countries of origin. French censorship, for example, in the shape of the 1934 *Decret Laval* that applied in all French colonial territories, forced many African film students to make their films in Paris. The best-known of these, *Afrique sur Seine* by Paulin Soumanou Vieyra and Mamadou Star, was made in 1955 and portrays the French capital's African milieu. Many filmmakers shot their debut films in Paris, such as Désiré Ecaré with *Concerto pour un exil* (1968), Ben Diogaye Beye with *Les princes noirs de Saint-Germain-des-Prés* (1975), or Med Hondo with *Les bicots-nègres, Vos voisins* (1974) and *Soleil O* (1975). These movies are about life in the diaspora, but they also seek a visual language for the city where their directors live, Paris. Unlike the films of the French New Wave, in which the street is deliberately sought out by the characters and political discourses are brought into the public sphere there, the protagonists of African auteur films visibly find it difficult to step into the public space. Paris exerts a magnetic attraction for the young filmmakers, but at the same time it is politically, culturally and cinematically overpowering – almost a threat for the overseas students who are trying to find a place to live and make their films.

Ousmane Sembene and Djibril Diop Mambety began their work in film at nearly the same time as these films were breaking new ground by confronting the potency of *la culture française* with an analysis of the space claimed by the African protagonists. Sembene and Mambety, too, address the dominance of French culture, if in a different urban context: in Dakar, the long-time capital of the French colonial empire in West Africa and the cultural hub of colonial francophone Africa. Other renowned filmmakers, such as Moussa Sene Absa or Mansour Sora Wade, also created a large number of highly regarded film shorts, feature films and documentaries set in Dakar.

In the Dakar films of the 1960s and 1970s, we encounter a French-African contrast similar to that found in African filmmakers' images of Paris. Sembene and Mambety's Dakar is divided by a border: the border between a modern, Europeanised 'French' Dakar, with tarred roads, traffic lights, cars and the typical French white-bordered traffic islands, and the Senegalese 'native' city with its low-rise architecture, dust roads and colourful markets. As the Cameroonian director Jean-Marie Teno has said in several interviews and on panels, that which is perceived as 'modern' is always an imported European idea, a European city. Every African-seeming form of construction or settlement that cannot be derived directly from the European idea of modernity is, he notes, therefore non-modern, categorised as traditional. Mambety calls this *la ville autochtone*[20] (in *Contras' City*); the residential neighbourhoods of the indigenous population are also referred to as the *quartiers populaires*. These areas are set against the elegant and exclusive French neighbourhood, Plateau, where the Europeans live. The binary opposition between the modern section, portrayed in the films as almost extraterritorial, and the autochthonous section is referenced by every narrative in the first films to be made in Dakar. The city itself becomes the main protagonist, and the films revolve around its cartography and social surfaces.

The first film made in Dakar by an African director is Ousmane Sembene's *Borom Sarret* (1963). The cart driver in *Borom Sarret* transports goods, but is not permitted to drive his cart into modern Dakar. Needing to earn money, he does so nevertheless. For a while, he drives around the Plateau district, timidly marvelling at the skyscrapers, the broad sidewalks and the traffic lights. He pays a high price for his excursion into the forbidden zone, losing his cart and returning empty-handed to the Medina neighbourhood, his own Dakar of small homesteads and hungry children. Sembene pursues a similar line in *La noire de …* (1966) and *Mandabi* (1968), aligning his filmic images along his protagonists' movements within the urban landscape. In *Xala* (1974), too, bodies move like points along vectors on an urban matrix, allowing us to experience the economy of time and the urban structure as interlocking ideological magnitudes. Here, Sembene works with the contrast between European/modern and autochthonous/African elements in urban architecture, as well as in habits, lifestyle, actions, languages, and so on. The colonial legacy is the legacy of modernity, which may materialise in a three-piece suit and tie, in the French language, in gastronomic preferences or in hairstyles. Sembene intensifies this contrasting materiality of cinematic movements through the city into an ideological critique that aims to unmask the new, 'Westernised' ruling class. He wants to show that although the new African elite has replaced the colonial regime, it follows the same rules and puts the same attributes into play.

Mambety – the second great director of Dakar films – looks for a narrative perspective that unfolds from the corporeal time of his protagonists. Here, the protagonists' inner life is articulated by film, not by the urban dispositif of time imposed upon them. What we see is therefore not so much their psychological state as their experience of time and movement, their wishes and visions. The result is a flux and montage of images that is soaked in the performativity of urban life. When Mambety stages boys loitering (in *Badou Boy* 1968, *Contras' City* 1968, *Touki Bouki* 1973), he is not pursuing an impulse for social criticism but exploring his characters' space of action as it emerges through film. And when, in *Contras' City,* he observes churchgoers posing in their finery on the steps of the Cathédrale de Dakar, his interest is in their performance, their *mise en scène* of the self. The most renowned scene of this kind is in *Touki Bouki.* [→ Fig. **B**] Protagonists Anta and Mory are determined to get to Paris, savouring the phrases 'Champs-Elysées', 'Montmartre', 'Tour Eiffel', 'Charles de Gaulle' and imagining themselves as participants in an official parade. Mambety realises their vision using a montage of film scenes with the two characters and documentary footage of an official procession. Dakar is a stage whose surfaces, streets, neighbourhoods form the narrative substance of the film. Everything that can be captured as an impression is drawn into the film, as material with its own particular idiom. Mambety scans the city in, so to speak, and assembles it anew. The assemblage generates an extremely condensed image of urbanity. In this universe, film is a medium of documentation, but more than that it is a medium for enabling an idea to be actualised, to be made true, that in real life would be crushed by circumstances. That is the substratum upon which new images of the city and its inhabitants arise: the city is a visual puzzle, switching between real-life Dakar and the imaginary Dakar based on Paris.

Sembene and Mambety represent two fundamentally different

20 The French word *autochtones* could be translated as 'the indigenous' or, bearing in mind the provocative tone of Mambéty's cinema, 'the natives'.

approaches to the filmic interpretation of the urban. Unlike Sembene, Mambety bases his work not primarily on a polarity of African and European codes, but on hybrid forms and scope for creativity. His films have a historically analytical dimension and an artistically creative one, which attaches itself to the everyday life of ordinary people (*Le Franc* 1994 and *La petite vendeuse du soleil* 1996). Generations of filmmakers took Sembene's *œuvre* as their model for critical and political cinema, and Mambety's as a source of inspiration for a syncretic approach to form that is reflected in works such as the Dakar films of Moussa Sene Absa (*Tableau feraille* 1998 and *Madame Brouette* 2002), Mansour Sora Wade (*Picc Mi* 1992) or Alain Gomis (*Petite lumière* 2002).

Analogously to Dakar, other cities play a similarly prominent role in the work of other film auteurs, a matter that cannot be detailed here – quite apart from made-for-TV feature films, urbanthemed documentaries, sitcoms,[21] and music videos, along with the many Western productions ranging from colonial-era news reels and city portraits to tourist formats, current feature and documentary films, TV documentaries and countless amateur YouTube clips.

4. The Documentary Momentum in Contemporary Cinema

Alongside the cinema of a Mambety or a Sembene, with its analysis of urban dispositifs, there is the far more common approach of making the city the backdrop against which a particular narrative is played out. This applies especially to genre cinema, which gives rise to specific lines of tradition and, accordingly, specific images of the city.

An example of this is South African cinema, which has drawn on American film noir to develop its own lineage of reference in the gangster film, from *Jim Comes to Jo'burg* (1949), *Come Back Africa* (1959) and *Mapantsula*[22] (1988) to *Tsotsi* (2005) and *Jerusalema* (2008). [→ Fig. C] The city, especially Johannesburg, here serves as a realistic setting for plot- and character-driven stories, thus remaining unspecific, without sharp contours. Nevertheless, the locations – Soweto's shebeens or the high-rise city centre with its Hillbrow Tower – add a substantial documentary aspect to such films.

Haffner calls this manner of representing the city "décor-ville" or "la ville comme décor", the city as scenery:[23] it is the plot and not the city that governs the rhythm of the film. Here, the location portrays an actual cityscape only incidentally, allowing a series of very heterogeneous genre- or plot-related or technically motivated themes to come to the fore. I will now briefly sketch these themes. Issues of genre cannot be discussed in sufficient detail here, but I would like at least to indicate the richness, diversity and complexity of the relationship between film and city and how, starting from the films, we might retrace a path through film history and the history of the treatment of this material. Narrative patterns influence the form of these films just as, conversely, formal decisions influence their narration.

Coming to Town

Let me begin by observing that in several South African, Congolese and Ivorian productions, there is a plot pattern that takes a young man's arrival in the city as the film's starting point. He typically carries a suitcase and hopes to make his fortune.[24] *Jim Comes to Jo'burg* combines this story with the protagonist's rise to become Soweto's most respected musician. In *Come Back Africa,* the newly arrived protagonist wants to work, but faces the pass laws of the 1950s apartheid regime.[25] The young protagonist of *Mapantsula,* a petty criminal, encounters political activists during his forays through the city. In *La vie est belle* (1987) it is Papa Wemba himself who rides into Kinshasa

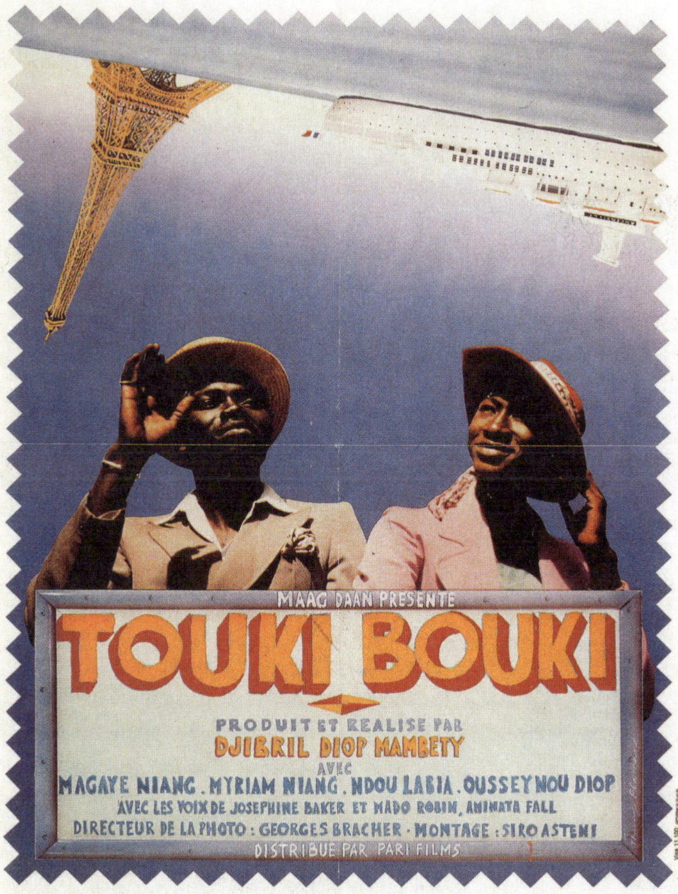

B Dakar: poster for *Touki Bouki*, Djibril Diop Mambéty (1973)

---

21 See Sophie Hoffelt 2002, *Sitcoms Africaines: une Image des Africains pour les Africains par les Africains,* retrieved from www.africultures.com/php/index.php?nav=article&no=2290 on 13 February 2012.

22 Jacqueline Maingard 1994, New South African Cinema: "Mapantsula" and "Sarafina", *Screen* 35/3: 235–243

23 Haffner (1986), p. 41

24 Manthia Diawara 1993, Flaneure, Verlorene und Gambler. Betrachtungen zur Stadt im afrikanischen Film, *Zeitschrift für Film* 11: 4–7

25 Tomaselli (1989), p. 57

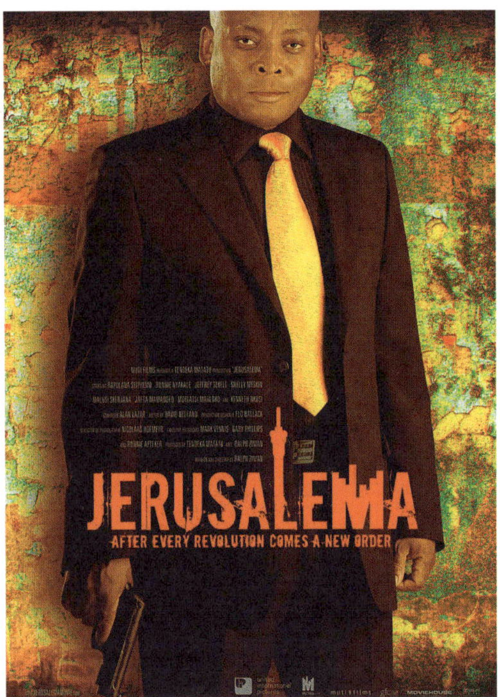

C   Johannesburg: poster for *Jerusalema*,
Ralph Ziman (2008)

heure), play football and make a nuisance of themselves (*Quartier Mozart* 1992, *Laafi, Udju azul di Yonta* 1990); here that business proceeds on a small or large scale (*Chikin Biznis … the Whole Story* 1999; *U-Carmen eKhayelitsha* 2004) and a bar around the corner beckons (*Temedy* 1996 and *I.T.* 2000, *Macadam Tribu,* etc.). Beyond the borders of the *quartier,* the city is big; it is full of people whom you don't know and neither do any of your friends.

Style

Style is cool, style helps us to find our bearings and sets signs of recognition. There are the inconspicuous styles that indicate a location (in Dakar, women dress differently from those in Cotonou or in Bamako or in Luanda). And then there are the flamboyant styles like *sape*[27] in Kinshasa, *swenka* in the Johannesburg townships or *baïfal* in Dakar (which inspired Mike Sylla's fashion designs). Describing style is no easy matter, because it is more than the sum of its specific meanings: style has a politically subversive core, but it also has a complex repertoire of articulations that encompasses music, clothing, gestures, language, attitude and religion.

"Tout pour la sape, tout pour le style", runs a line in *Tourbillons* (Alain Gomis 1996), and if in *La vie est belle* the *sape* star and fashion luminary Papa Wemba controverts his image to appear in shabby dress, he has the audience laughing on his side. Stylists and couturiers such as Oumou Sy, Chris Seydou or Lamine Kouyaté and musicians such as Papa Wemba, Youssou N'Dour or Baba Maal importantly influence set design and costumes, and thus also the mood of the films. Film is one more component in a highly eclectic pop culture, but it also responds to styles, displaying their assimilation, as in the case of American gangster style (for example in *Hijack Stories* 2000 or *Tsotsi*), setting out stylistic polarities, such as that between the boubou style and the short etui dress (*Xala*), or reflecting the deployment of political accessories like Amilcar Cabral's hat (*Tourbillons*), Lumumba's spectacles (*Macadam Tribu*) or the English wig (*Hyènes* 1992). Additionally, films can invent styles, like that of the girls in *Quartier Mozart,* the boys wearing flares and tunics in *Badou Boy,* the body-hugging camisoles in *Les saignantes* (2005) or the almost radioactively fluorescent bazin fabrics in *Picc Mi* (1992). Style is not merely the body's outer wrapping or rhythm; it provides information on an individual's state of mind, context and intellectual horizon – and, above all, it plays with the meanings of external appearances.

The Body

Cinema, of course, depends on that impact of the protagonists' external appearance, and on their physical presence – on their

like a conqueror. Many other films fit this pattern as well. The reason why they so effectively arouse the audience's empathy – whether with the young man who knows nothing of the city, or with the city dwellers he meets – is that urban and rural experiences are both articulated in the film's events. Town dwellers recognise their city in the film, while country dwellers see what it means to move to town. Once they have arrived, though, very different topics take centre stage.

Le Quartier

Many films are set in the *quartier,* or neighbourhood. African metropolises are said to be accumulations of *quartiers* and, looked at purely demographically, they are primarily a habitat of young people.[26] Characters like the omniscient kiosk owner on the corner (*Laafi* 1992 or *Macadam Tribu* 1996), the auntie with her shop across the road (*Touki Bouki*) or the little peanut-seller standing at the kerb (*Un matin de bonne heure* 2006) play an important role not only for the social network, but also for the narrative structure. These figures, who know what's happening and who relates how to whom, are the ones who are asked and interrogated. The *quartier* is home. It is here that people know each other, lend each other a hand or feud with each other; here that children grow up together (*À nous la rue* 1987; *Un matin de bonne*

26 Statistics show that more than half the urban population of Africa is younger than twenty-five and lives on less than two dollars a day. See Jean-Christophe Servant 2010, Kontinent der Slums, Dossier Stadtwelten, *Le Monde diplomatique* 4/16: 6; also *The State of the African Cities Report 2008,* retrieved from http://www.unhabitat.org/pmss/listItemDetails. aspx?publicationID=2574 on 24 February 2012.

27 Justin-Daniel Gandoulou 1989, *Dandies à Bacongo: le Culte de l'Elégance dans la Société Congolaise Contemporaine,* Paris; Paul Smith and Daniele Tamagni 2009, *Gentlemen of Bakongo. The Importance of Being Elegant. A Journey with the Sapeurs of the Bakongo District,* London

corporeality as carriers of the narrative. *Jerusalema,* for example, draws its vitality from the imposing presence of actor Rapulana Seiphemo, famous in South Africa for his soap-opera roles. Just as the presence of the camera alters the physicality of the filmed and, so to speak, transports them into a different physical state, so the city alters the body in a similar way. Bodily control and body language take on the subtlest significance where people ride squashed up with strangers in a minibus taxi (*Le Franc* 1994 or *Niiwam* 1988), work in offices and factories (*Baara* 1978, *La tête dans les nuages* 1994) and perhaps cultivate a piece of land as well, or where they are exposed to the eyes of the crowd at the market (*Macadam Tribu*) and themselves eye others (*Afrique, je te plumerai* 1994). It is meaningful how you walk down the road (*Temedy*), work on the street (*Madame Brouette*) and are watched and desired there, how your foot impacts on the road, grazes the ground, whether your flip-flops raise little clouds of dust or a tiny clacking sound. Within this logic, it is obvious that shoes have more than an economic value; they contribute, literally, to a person's footing on the urban stage. Equally significant is the tightness of the fabric wrapped around the body, the parts of the body exposed and those covered, and the self-confidence with which old and young adults and children move at home or on the street, within the *quartier* or outside it; the degree to which bodily fluids such as sweat become visible, making the skin sparkle and brightening its visual image. Things are possible in the *quartier* that would not be thinkable outside – but on the other hand, the anonymity outside the *quartier* permits a freedom of dress and movement that might be considered indecent at home.

Every film has its very own bodily logic and presence, a specific form of self-assertion, libidinous quality and physical awareness. Thus, *La vie est belle* at times seems incredibly lascivious, *Macadam Tribu* athletic. The theme of prostitution (in *Rue princesse* 1993, *Bal poussière* 1988, *Puk Nini* 1996, *Les saignantes*) could be considered the social extreme of physicality as bodily labour. Child labour (in *Picc Mi, La petite vendeuse du soleil, Roaming Around* 2007) is another of the many forms of more or less obvious physical exertion and of encroachment and assault upon the body. Others are illness, Aids, drugs and the image of physical decay. The documentaries *Hillbrow Kids* (2000), *Darwin's Nightmare* (2004) *and Roaming Around* show glue-sniffing street children who stray through the residential districts: perhaps the most dramatically concentrated image of the injured body. The fact that these three films are European productions seems to be relevant in terms of their image of Africa, very distinct from that to be found in the African auteur films – but this first impression would require closer examination with respect to notions of the body and the image, and to the intersection between them.

Transnationality

The image of the city – with its neighbourhoods, styles and the physical presence of its inhabitants – that is captured en passant in genre cinema has a modern, transethnic and transnational dimension. This becomes clear in small details like the trans-African culinary spectrum in *Le Franc,*[28] which recalls the drift to the cities and trans-African migration. People of Lebanese, Vietnamese, Chinese and European origin can be seen in these films. Some may be employed in the diplomatic or development services, others in international businesses; others again have lived in Africa for generations. Occasionally the strangers may even be extraterrestrials (*District 9* 2009[29]). Every city has its segments and quarters that are preferred, inhabited or frequented by particular groups, and one group's territory is often inaccessible to the other groups. Films break through those borders when they slip into the life of one particular district or into the communities of a particular social stratum: in *Silimandé* (1998) we invisibly visit a Lebanese family where the mother never leaves the apartment and knows Ouagadougou only through the view from her balcony; in *I. T.* we accompany young people living in a Conakry tower block; in *Moi et mon blanc* (2004) a Frenchman flees to Burkina Faso and lives with a Burkinabé acquaintance on the outskirts of Ouagadougou. The visuality of the urban with its streets, traffic and crowds, then, becomes associated with a filmic opening of domains that are otherwise closed off to both local city dwellers and faraway film audiences. Particularly spectacular in this respect are presidential residences and grand compounds with their quietly humming air-conditioning, long corridors and lush gardens, as in *Silimandé, Le damier, Papa National Oyé* (1996) or *The Last King of Scotland* (2006). Despite their local and cinematic specificity, these thematic images of the city all culminate in the representation of an African city, urban architecture and population as part of an African and cosmopolitan network.

Cities at Night

A recent phenomenon in this context is the setting of films at night. Near the equator, nights are as long as days, and cities that never sleep have a special cinematic allure. That is not only because the night generates particular musical, political and criminal milieus, but also because the city's infrastructure would not function without such non-stop activity. Obviously, films of this kind are striking first of all by being very dark. Their real-life settings lack street lighting comparable to that of Paris, Brussels or Moscow; cars with functioning headlamps, and the few sources of light give off a different kind of luminosity, captured by the camera in a very special way. This technical and aesthetic

---

28 In *Le Franc,* different dishes are associated with different population groups: "To a Serere crying, give him couscous and mbum, to a Bambara crying, give him sulux mbalax, to a Jola crying, give him nyankatang – white rice, to a Lebanese crying, give him shawarma"; see Mbye Cham 1998, Son dans le Ton des Petites Gens/Sounds in the Keys of Ordinary Folk, *Ecrans d'Afrique/African Screen* 24/7: 44–53, here p. 52, special issue *Hommage/Tribute: Djibril Diop Mambéty.*

29 Fritz Göttler 2009, Apartheid gegen Aliens. Eine Stadt, die sich selber auffrisst: "District 9" – ein kleiner Film aus Südafrika zeigt Apartheid gegen Aliens und ist der Hit des US-Kinosommers, *Süddeutsche Zeitung* 198: 11

potential was first exploited by Souleymane Cissé in his film *Yeelen* (1987), which he shot mainly in the mornings just after sunrise and the evenings just before sunset. He worked during a time window of around twenty minutes during which the light is soft and warm, before taking on a glaring brightness or vanishing completely. Cissé's knowledge of light and of the camera's possibilities enabled him to turn these brief phases to aesthetic effect.

Today's digital recording technology makes it possible to film moving images in very low light – although the pictures are often blurred and have a certain sense of somnambulist deceleration. These images first appeared a little over ten years ago in feature films such as the Berlin-set *Plus Minus Null* (1998). They made an aesthetic resource out of the shortcomings in generating an accurate image, and showed the shady sides of a city at night. Several films have made use of this altered picture resolution and quality to portray night-time Yaoundé (*Les saignantes*), Lagos (*Relentless* 2007), Luanda (*Luanda, a Fábrica da Mùsica* 2009), Bamako (*Future in Present Tense* 2007; *Balade nocturne* 2008) or Saint Louis (*Le jardin de Papa* 2004). However widely these films diverge in terms of their narrative and their treatment of nocturnal themes and motifs, they share a single technical and artistic approach. Firstly, night-for-night shots eliminate every exotically colourful cliché; in its place, digital colour effects come to the fore and generate an artificiality that is practically flaunted, leaving 'multicoloured Africa' behind and offering instead a technologically induced image of the city. This is closer to the nocturnal cities of other films (those by Eoin Moore or Wong Kar Wai, for example) and the aesthetics of the video clip than to the preceding generation of African auteur films. That rupture is significant, and heralds the rise of a new African film aesthetic. The colourful was once folklore; it is now technology. Skin colour, too, loses its relevance, and the distinction between picture surface and the objects and substances represented is levelled out.

In this way, the nocturnal setting gives rise to visions of the future. When daytime people sleep, gathering energy for tomorrow, the night-time people awake: the little boy who strolls along a Bamako road in *Balade nocturne* or the protagonists of *Future in Present Tense,* who imagine a future for themselves in a sci-fi mode. At night, events anyway follow a different logic from that of the daytime. There are accidents (*Le jardin de Papa*), murders (*Les saignantes*) and acts of revenge (*Relentless*). Objects such as televisions or neon tubes, otherwise sharply outlined, become amorphous. The cold, blue-tinged light serves less to illuminate the situation than to stage a performance on its own account as a body of light. Cities can be filmically reshaped at night, can literally be shown in a new light. The fact that this can be achieved using technical resources ultimately liberates the creator of a city image from the moral obligation to counter the clichés about African cities through naturalism. For both city and film, it opens up a new perspective onto the future.

Translation from German by Kate Sturge

FILMS: **TITLE**, DIR., YEAR [CITY IN WHICH THE FILM IS SET]

À NOUS LA RUE, MOUSTAPHA DAO, 1987 [OUAGADOUGOU]
AFRIQUE, JE TE PLUMERAI, JEAN-MARIE TENO, 1992 [YAOUNDÉ]
AFRIQUE SUR SEINE, PAULIN SOUMANOU VIEYRA/MAMADOU SARR, 1955 [PARIS]
BAARA, SOULEYMANE CISSÉ, 1978 [BAMAKO]
BADOU BOY, DJIBRIL DIOP MAMBÉTY, 1968 [DAKAR]
BAL POUSSIÈRE, HENRI DUPARC, 1988 [ABIDJAN]
BALADE NOCTURNE, TIÉCOURA N'DAOU, 2008 [BAMAKO]
BOROM SARRET, OUSMANE SEMBENE, 1963 [DAKAR]
BYE BYE AFRICA, MAHAMAT-SALEH HAROUN, 1999 [N'DJAMENA]
CHIKIN BIZNIS … THE WHOLE STORY, NTSHAVENI WA LURULI, 1999 [JOHANNESBURG]
COME BACK AFRICA, LIONEL ROGOSIN, 1959 [JOHANNESBURG]
CONCERTO POUR UN EXIL, DÉSIRÉ ECARÉS, 1968 [PARIS]
CONTRAS' CITY, DJIBRIL DIOP MAMBÉTY, 1968 [DAKAR]
LE DAMIER, PAPA NATIONAL OYÉ, BALUFU BAKUPA KANYINDA, 1996 [LIBREVILLE]
DARWIN'S NIGHTMARE, HUBERT SAUPER, 2004 [MWANSA/TANZANIA]
DISTRICT 9, NEILL BLOMKAMP, 2009 [JOHANNESBURG]
LE FRANC, DJIBRIL DIOP MAMBÉTY, 1994 [DAKAR]
FUTURE IN PRESENT TENSE, NEIL BELOUFA, 2007 [BAMAKO]
HIJACK STORIES, OLIVER SCHMITZ, 2000 [JOHANNESBURG]
HILLBROW KIDS, MICHAEL HAMMON/JACQUELIN GÖRGEN, 2000 [JOHANNESBURG]
HYÈNES, DJIBRIL DIOP MAMBÉTY, 1992 [DAKAR]
I.T., GAHITÉ FOFANA, 2000 [CONAKRY]
LE JARDIN DE PAPA, ZÉKA LAPLAINE, 2004 [SAINT LOUIS/SENEGAL]
JERUSALEMA, RALPH ZIMAN, 2008 [JOHANNESBURG]
JIM COMES TO JO'BURG, DONALD SWANSON, 1949 [JOHANNESBURG]
LAAFI, S. PIERRE YAMÉOGO, 1992 [OUAGADOUGOU]
THE LAST KING OF SCOTLAND, KEVIN MACDONALD, 2006 [KAMPALA]
LUANDA, A FÁBRICA DA MÙSICA, KILUANJE LIBERDADE/INÊS GONÇALVES, 2009 [LUANDA]
MADAME BROUETTE, MOUSSA SENE ABSA, 2002 [DAKAR]
MACADAM TRIBU, ZÉKA LAPLAINE, 1996 [BAMAKO]
MANDABI, OUSMANE SEMBENE, 1968 [DAKAR]
MAPANTSULA, OLIVER SCHMITZ/THOMAS MOGOTLANE, 1988 [JOHANNESBURG]
MOI ET MON BLANC, S. PIERRE YAMÉOGO, 2004 [OUAGADOUGOU]
NIIWAM, CLARENCE T. DELGADO, 1988 [DAKAR]
LA NOIRE DE …, OUSMANE SEMBENE, 1966 [DAKAR]
PETITE LUMIÈRE, ALAIN GOMIS, 2002 [DAKAR]
LA PETITE VENDEUSE DU SOLEIL, DJIBRIL DIOP MAMBÉTY, 1996 [DAKAR]
PICC MI, MANSOUR SORA WADE, 1992 [DAKAR]
PUK NINI, FANTA NACRO, 1996 [OUAGADOUGOU]
PLUS MINUS NULL, EOIN MOORE, 1998 [BERLIN]
LES PRINCES NOIRS DE SAINT GERMAIN, BEN DIOGAYE BEYES 1975 [PARIS]
QUARTIER MOZART, JEAN-PIERRE BEKOLO, 1992 [YAOUNDÉ]
RELENTLESS, ANDY AMADI OKOROAFOR, 2007 [LAGOS]
ROAMING AROUND, BRIGITTE BERTELE, 2007 [ACCRA]
LE ROI, LA VACHE ET LE BANANIER, MWEEZE NGANGURA, 1994
RUE PRINCESSE, HENRI DUPARC, 1993 [ABIDJAN]
LES SAIGNANTES, JEAN-PIERRE BEKOLO, 2005 [YAOUNDÉ]
SILIMANDÉ, S. PIERRE YAMÉOGO, 1998 [OUAGADOUGOU]
SI-GUERIKI, LA REINE MÈRE, IDRISSOU MORA KPAI, 2002
SOLEIL O, MED HONDO, 1975 [PARIS]
TABLEAU FERAILLE, MOUSSA SENE ABSA, 1998 [DAKAR]
TEMEDY, GAHITÉ FOFANA, 1996 [CONAKRY]
LA TÊTE DANS LES NUAGES, JEAN-MARIE TENO 1994 [YAOUNDÉ]
TOUKI BOUKI, DJIBRIL DIOP MAMBÉTY, 1973 [DAKAR]
TOURBILLONS, ALAIN GOMIS, 1996 [PARIS]
TSOTSI, GAVIN WOOD, 2005 [JOHANNESBURG]
U-CARMEN EKHAYELITSHA, MARK DORNFORD-MAY, 2004 [CAPE TOWN]
UDJU AZUL DI YONTA, FLORA GOMES, 1990 [BISSAU]
UN MATIN DE BONNE HEURE, GAHITÉ FOFANA, 2006 [CONAKRY]
VACANCES AU PAYS, JEAN-MARIE TENO, 2000
LA VIE EST BELLE, MWEEZE NGANGURA, 1987 [KINSHASA]
XALA, OUSMANE SEMBENE, 1974 [DAKAR]
YEELEN, SOULEYMANE CISSÉ, 1987

CAIRO

The Third Citizen

A CONVERSATION
WITH VAN LEO

Like many of his generation who fled to settle in the multi-ethnic society of Egypt in the early twentieth century, Van Leo's family escaped the genocide and relocated first to Alexandria, then Cairo in 1930. His practice spanned for over fifty years that crossed a major chapter in Egypt's history. He is a very special character indeed. I was struck first by his self-portraits, especially one in which he appears as a prisoner. The photograph looked very modern to me even if it was taken in 1944. When I saw him for the first time in 1998, I couldn't help but notice how we age. For the very few who had the chance to talk to Van Leo informally, it was quite common to hear him use the term "third Egyptian" to signify himself. To answer my inquiry about the meaning of this expression, Van Leo explained, in a simplified way that may sound almost naïve but still true, that the first Egyptians are the Muslim majority who own most of the privileges in the country. After that, come the second Egyptians, the Copts, then the third Egyptians, which is a category for everybody else including Armenians such as Van Leo. He was famous only within particular circles of artists and people in the entertainment industry.

Going through the political and demographic changes in Egypt during the last fifty years added to Van Leo's bitterness and sense of insecurity that caused his isolation and sense of hesitation. One of the earliest images that he recalls was of being chased by the kids in the schoolyard because he'd picked the sponge from the top of a tree.

AKRAM ZAATARI: You are renowned as a portraitist; indeed, you may be one of few photographers in Arab history to consider photography as art. How did an Armenian kid named Levon Boyadjian become Van Leo?

VAN LEO: I was born in Turkey, in 1921, a couple of years after the genocide. My father had been working for Baghdad Railways. He met a lot of people who were fleeing their villages, taking to the mountains to escape. That's how he met my mother. A friend of his convinced him to marry one of the women he met, to save her. He liked her, so they were married. There was no priest, no wedding reception – just an empty room. And that's how they got married: in an empty room, by the light of a gas lamp.

I was three years old when we moved to Egypt. We went first to Alexandria, then to Cairo, before we settled in Zagazig. My father was hired as an accountant at a tobacco company called Gamsaragan. In Zagazig, I was known to be a difficult child and had to change schools three times. I had long hair, and people used to ask whether I was a boy or a girl. [He laughs.] I've never gone back to Zagazig. But the place is carved into my memory. I can still see it now. There was a casino by the Nile, where my father used to take us on Sundays. I also remember seeing the French circus, when it came to town.

Anyway, Gamsaragan was closing down, and my father was transferred to Eastern Company, another tobacco business, just outside Cairo. So we went to Cairo – first to Faggala, and then downtown. My father worked at Eastern Company for the rest of his life.

AKRAM ZAATARI: Did you speak Armenian at home?

VAN LEO: Yes, but everybody spoke Turkish when older family members came by – most Armenians of my father's generation spoke Turkish. I was only a boy, but I understood some of what they said about the genocide. My father used to speak seven languages: German, French, English, Arabic, Greek, Turkish and Armenian. He used to speak Greek at the grocery store when we were still in Zagazig.

AKRAM ZAATARI: How did you become interested in photography?

VAN LEO: I've loved photography ever since I was a child – I used to collect magazines with photographs of Hollywood stars. I would study those images, thinking about the lighting, the costumes and the sets. In Cairo, I worked as an apprentice to Artinian, owner of Studio Venus on Qasr el Nil Street – that was one of the most highly regarded studios in the city. With Artinian, I was working for free, but I learned all the technical skills I needed. And it was one of Artinian's clients – a British guy – who convinced my father that I had talent. So my father put me to work: I photographed most of the tobacco company executives, and I also took group portraits of the accounting staff – there were about three hundred managers, and four thousand workers.

My father couldn't afford to set me up with a proper studio, so we opened up Studio Angelo – named for my brother, who also wanted to be a photographer – in two rooms of our family's apartment. That was in 1941. Cairo was still a small city then: maybe two and a half million people. There were a lot of Brits and South Africans living here. One day, a British officer who was also a theatre actor came to see me. He wanted me to take some photographs for an opera he was appearing in. I told him I'd take all the photographs they needed, free of charge, if they'd put an ad for Studio Angelo in the playbill. He agreed, and he also agreed that actors who wanted copies of their photographs would have to pay for them. And so that's how I got started. In 1947, I moved into this studio.

AKRAM ZAATARI: At the beginning of your career, you were your own most frequent subject.

VAN LEO: That's right. I took something like five hundred self-portraits between 1942 and 1946. I would look into the mirror and decide on the frame, the composition, the lighting. I was free to try anything – that's not always the case with clients! And I was young, willing to take risks, to experiment. I wanted to explore different ways of lighting the face, and I was fascinated by the way you could change its features just by lighting it differently. And with props, of course.

AKRAM ZAATARI: What was your clientele like in those days?

VAN LEO: Oh, I photographed thousands of people. Sometimes I would take a single picture, but if someone's face inspired me, I might take ten or more. Once I photographed a beggar, a guy who used to come in and offer me a flower as a way of asking for a few coins. I liked his face. I thought he was a dignified beggar, so I called his portrait *The Beggar Philosopher*. Even when I was taking pictures of people for money, there were still times when I took pictures purely for pleasure.

You know, some photographers used to run after kings or presidents – they considered it a privilege to photograph famous people like that. And they knew it would help their careers. I didn't run after anyone. I just photographed whoever came by.

AKRAM ZAATARI: How do you make a great portrait?

VAN LEO: First, I study the face. You have to light it properly, and decide on a point of view. Then comes the decisive moment, when you take the picture: the expression has to be just so. After that, there's the lab work, which has to be done flawlessly. That's why I have never allowed anyone to help me print a photograph.

AKRAM ZAATARI: Who owns the portrait?

VAN LEO: When clients pay for a portrait, they are really paying for a print. So the client owns that print, of course. And it's the photographer's right to exhibit a successful portrait in his window – with the client's permission, of course. So in some sense, a portrait belongs to both the photographer and the client. But the negative is the property of the studio, no matter what. The negative never leaves the studio – and that's written on their receipt. I never sell my negatives.

Once, a client who had brought a woman to my studio asked me for the negatives of her portrait. He was prepared to pay any price. But I refused to give them to him – they weren't for sale. He was insistent. So I fetched the negatives, and I burned them there at my desk, right in front of his eyes. That was the only possible solution. He was so relieved! He came close to me and kissed my forehead.

AKRAM ZAATARI: Why is it so important to hold on to your negatives?

VAN LEO: Listen, photographers have to make a living from their work. And keeping the negative is the only way to ensure that clients will return to the studio when they need a copy of a photograph. Sometimes they don't even have their original – they only have the date, or the number on the back of the photo. But I always keep the negatives, so I can always make a new print, even after many decades have passed.

AKRAM ZAATARI: Tell me something about retouching – is that a big part of the process?

VAN LEO: Well, it depends on the size and the quality of the print. In the past, photographers used to employ specialists, who got paid by the piece. And they got good money, too: it cost five cents to get a passport photo done, and ten cents for a postcard-size photo, but retouching a wedding photograph could cost as much as fifty cents. I do my own retouching – not to save money, really, I prefer to do it myself to insure the perfection of the work. The tools come in grades like needles; some for retouching prints, others for the negatives. We used to import them from Czechoslovakia. They're usually used to retouch white spots on the print; you select the size depending on the size of the spot.

On the other hand, some prints don't need retouching at all. When I see a print, I know immediately whether or not it needs retouching. Look at my portrait of the writer Taha Hussein – it was enlarged without any retouching at all. Nubar's profile was enlarged with no retouching at all. They say that photography is painting with light. Which means that you define the features of a face by the light that you project on it. If you do that well, you won't need to retouch it.

AKRAM ZAATARI: Many photographers of your generation were interested in nude photography. Were you ever interested in the nude?

VAN LEO: Yes. I took hundreds of nude portraits. But I don't have any of them anymore. I burned them all ten years ago, because of the fundamentalists. I knew that having those negatives around could get me in trouble.

AKRAM ZAATARI: Was it difficult to persuade clients to undress?

VAN LEO: Well, it's never easy to be naked in front of a camera. You worry about the image becoming public, you worry about blackmail. There's something personal about nude photographs; they represent very intimate moments. As a photographer, you have to know your client well before you ask her to be photographed nude. Otherwise, there's no way she'll accept. All the nudes I did were of people I knew very well. All of them except for one: there was this Egyptian woman from Heliopolis, about twenty-five years old, and she wanted me to do a series of portraits. As I was taking the photographs, she started undressing until she was totally naked. I didn't know anything about her – I didn't even know what she did for living. But she was the only one I didn't know, the only person who ever asked to be photographed in the nude.

AKRAM ZAATARI: Did you ever do nude portraits of men?

VAN LEO: No, but I often photographed male athletes, and those pictures always highlighted their bodies, and muscles.

AKRAM ZAATARI: What about yourself – did you ever do nude self-portraits?

VAN LEO: No! [indifferent] I just wasn't interested.

AKRAM ZAATARI: If you had to do it all over again, would you still become photographer?

VAN LEO: No. I mean, I love my work. But the problem is that a photographer will never become a rich man. A talented businessman can get rich in a couple of years, but it's not like that for a talented photographer. I've spent fifty years in this studio, and what do I have to show for it? Very little.

You see, photography isn't really respected in the East. Clients just drop in without making an appointment. And most of them only want small prints – six centimetres by nine centimetres. They say: "I'll enlarge it if I like it." They pay fifty cents or a pound. How can photography thrive in such conditions? Imagine if you had a client who came to you, confident of your talent, and offered you fifty or a hundred pounds in advance! If a client did that, the result would be a masterpiece, I assure you. But clients don't usually have the confidence to pay in advance. No one wants a nice, big portrait – not until someone dies. Then the whole family comes running to you, clutching a passport photograph – a stamped passport photograph, sometimes – asking for a big enlargement. [Angry] This is how people think here! If I lived in Canada, I would be a millionaire. At least people over there know the difference between fine art and a passport photo.

AKRAM ZAATARI: But I thought you said you weren't interested in running after money.

VAN LEO: Well, yes. In photography, you have to choose between money and art. And most of the work I've exhibited has been done for free, for my own satisfaction. Look at my pictures of the pyramids, for example. I used to go to the Mina House hotel every Sunday, just to photograph the pyramids. Do you think I took those photographs for money? That was purely for art. When I worked at studio Venus, owned by Artinian, he used to have a fixed set for the lights and the camera. He hardly moved them. He never worked on the shades, and lights, so his photographs were kind of uniform. I move the lights and camera for every customer, imagine!

AKRAM ZAATARI: You've lived in Cairo over seventy years – your studio on 26th of July Street was open for almost 50 years. How has the city changed in that time?

VAN LEO: You know, when I first moved here, this neighbourhood used to look like part of Europe. Jewish merchants owned the most prestigious shops, and the Armenians worked as craftsmen, jewellers or tailors. There were some rich Armenians, too. Like Nassibian, who had a monopoly on European photography equipment. He had a shop on Fouad Street and a film studio in Faggala. He lived like a king, with a Berber driver and a Cadillac. But he left Egypt long ago. In fact, most of the big businessmen left Egypt in the fifties. In 1952, the whole downtown area burned down – my studio was nearly destroyed, as well. The jewellery shop downstairs burned down, and so did a lot of other businesses. After that came the revolution, and then the Suez crisis, and all the wars with Israel. There was no such thing as normal life! I stayed in Egypt because of my studio – that was the only thing that kept me from leaving. Now, I think maybe I was wrong. The Greeks, the Italians and the Jews all sold whatever they owned and left. The Jews were the first to leave. We have an expression here: "A country without Jews is a country without wealth."

My father had managed to save some money by buying some shares in the stock market. With Nationalisation, they were all confiscated by Nasser's government. I have to admit, I'm not sure whether Nasser went to war against Israel, or against everybody, including us Egyptians.

But I love this country, and I got used to living here.

AKRAM ZAATARI: What do you think will happen to this studio?

VAN LEO: I don't really care anymore. I think I'm finished. In fact, I think I should have stopped working ten years ago. You know, a cousin of mine in Lebanon wrote me recently, inviting me to go and live there. But I didn't respond. I'd rather stay here, I suppose.

AKRAM ZAATARI: What do you think of photography today?

VAN LEO: Photography is dead, thanks to colour photography and video. Nobody goes to a studio to have his or her photo taken. It's just like tailoring: nowadays, everyone buys ready-made clothes, and hundreds of tailors are unemployed. But I believe photography is immortal. And I'm not just saying that because I'm a photographer. People love new clothes, and yet they go out of fashion, or deteriorate. A picture still looks great after seventy years. Look at this photograph of me as a seven-year-old boy – there's no way I could remember that I posed this way, or that I wore so or so, without this photograph. A photograph is evidence.

This text is a reprint of the primary publication:
Akram Zaatari 2002, The Third Citizen.
A Conversation With Van Leo, Transition 91: 106–139;
see also: Arab Image Foundation (ed.) 1999,
Portraits du Caire: Van Leo, Armand, Alban, Paris

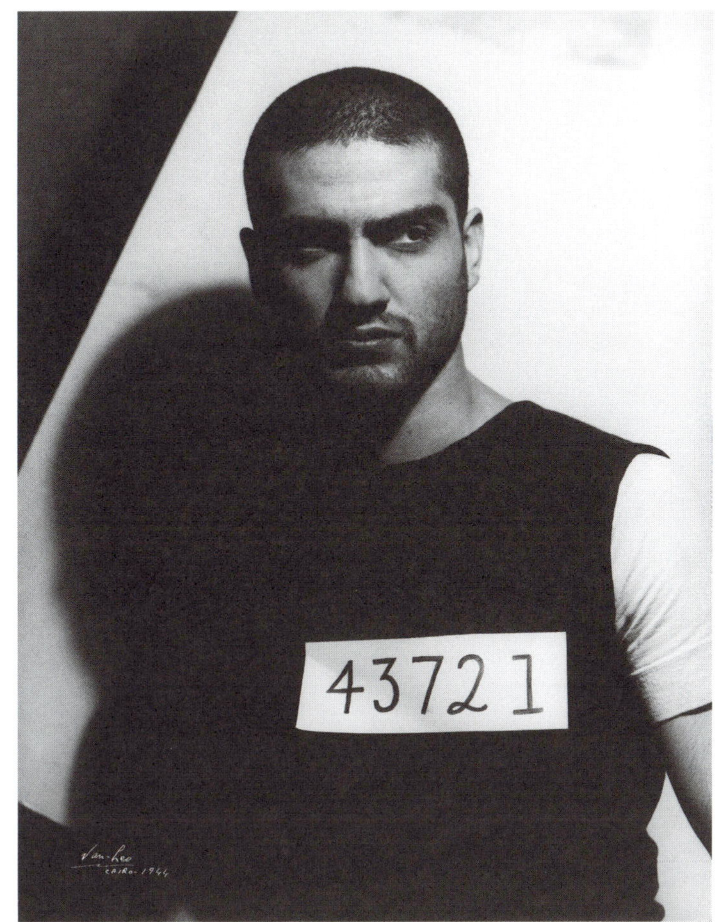

SELF-PORTRAIT, CAIRO 1944

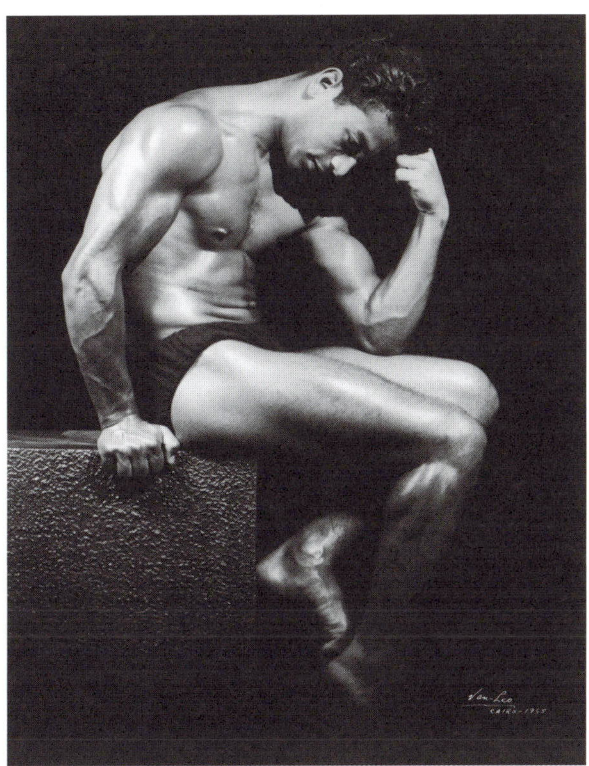

EGYPTIAN ATHLETE, CAIRO 1945

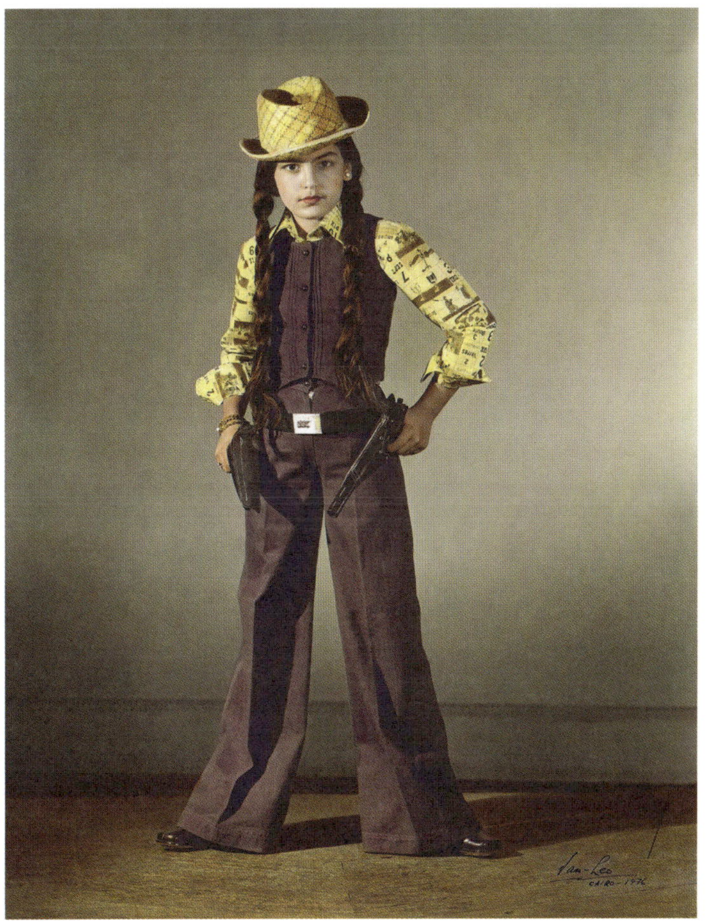

SHERIHANE, CAIRO 1976

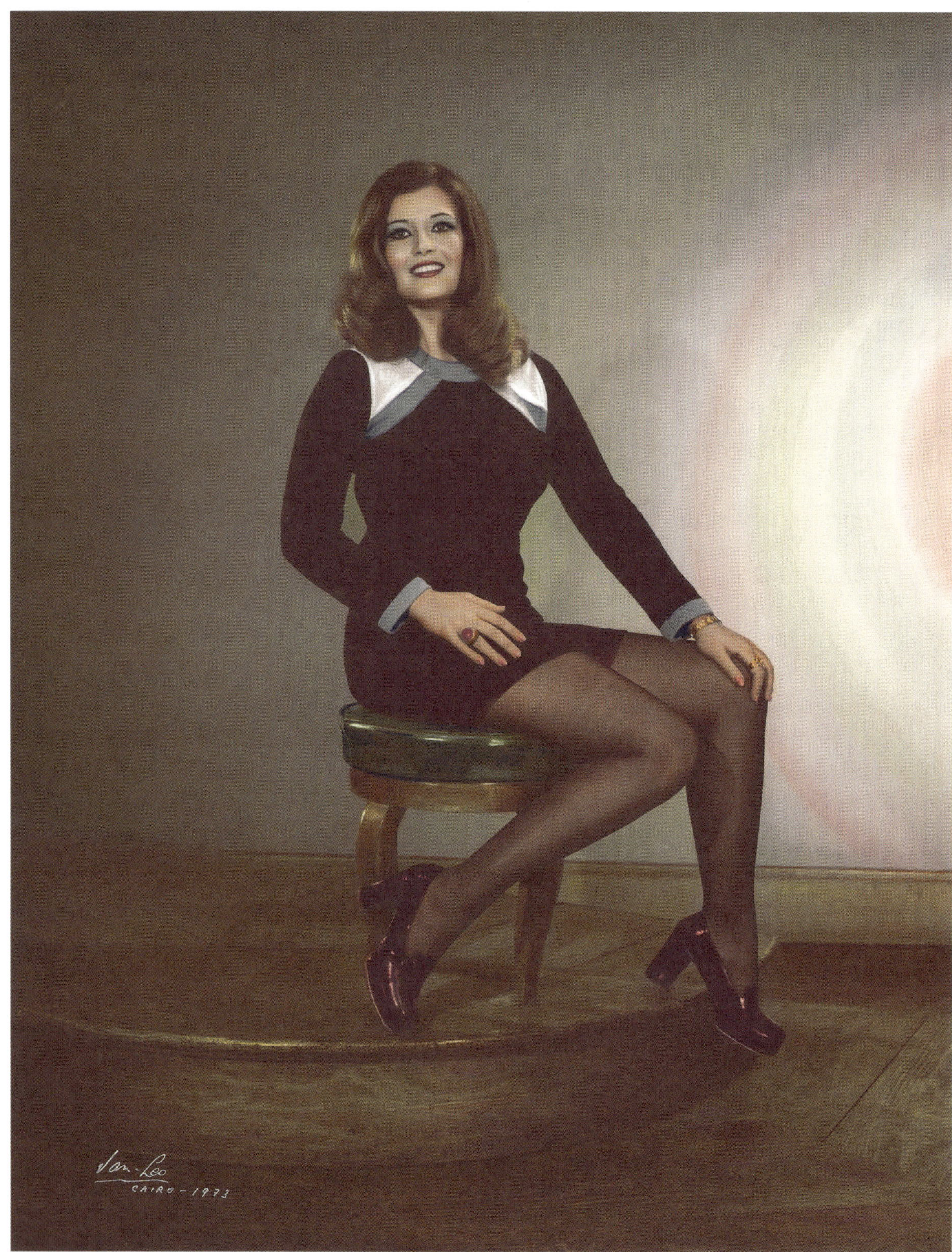

MIRVAT AMINE, ACTRESS, CAIRO 1972

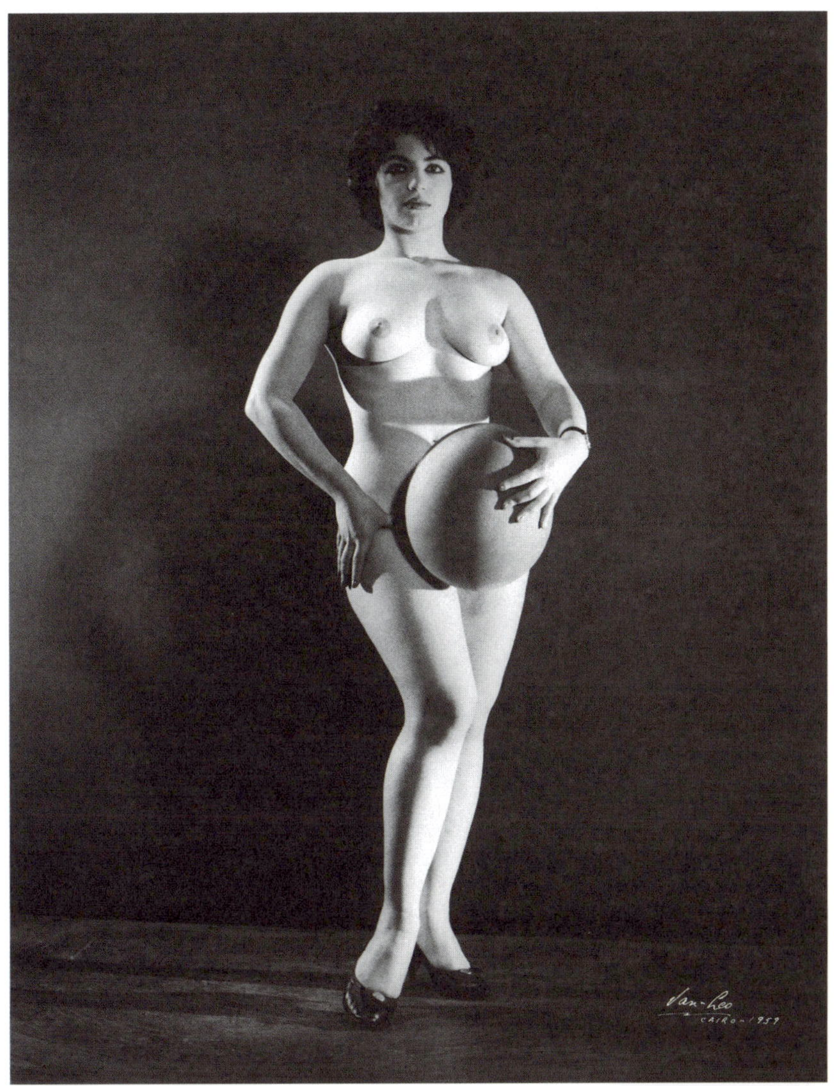

UNKNOWN, CAIRO 1959

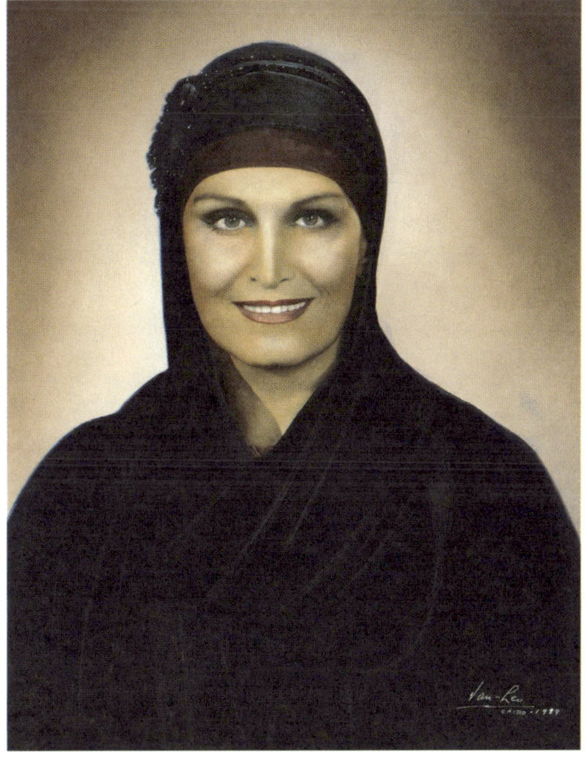

DALIDA, SINGER FROM PARIS, CAIRO 1986

From Alley to Shanty Town
Representing the Nation through Cairo's Changing City-Scape

VIOLA SHAFIK

"Go to *hina maysara/Until further Notice* to learn how to avoid this fire – the fire of the slums. You might possibly suffocate from the stench of merging bodies; it is possible that you are hardly able to bear sinful sex and drug consumption; you will possibly sense that all skin and respiratory diseases have infected your body. Endure all that and think about what Khalid Yusuf and scriptwriter Nasir `Abd al-Rahman wanted to say. It is a message of warning carried by a wonderful cinematic picture of the slums and what is going on there. Think well and pay attention! Cairo is surrounded by more than seventy-six shanty towns […] Cairo has been encircled by these areas. If the inhabitants of these areas decided to outburst, at once they would turn Cairo into hell. Their outburst might happen, for the dwellers of these areas don't own anything. This is the real danger: Those who have no possessions will not be gracious to us, if they decide to bring down the temple on top of everyone they have nothing to shed tears for, even for themselves, as they got used to selling themselves all the time."[1]

Indeed, with his film *hina maysara/Until further Notice* released in 2008, director Khalid Yusuf has created a fairly bleak image of life in Cairo's shanty towns. Densely populated with entire families cramped in one room, barely educated, hardly working in a regular profession, making ends meet day by day, this is the environment in which Yusuf's epic story unfolds. `Adil, a young mechanic, lives with his mother, Umm Ridda, in a small room in a courtyard shared with a number of other families. The mother and son are in charge of a bunch of children who are the offspring of `Adil's sister, killed by her jealous husband, and Ridda –`Adil's brother who travelled to Iraq in search of work. `Adil has neither been seen nor heard of since. The life of the family is caught in a downward spiral. While Umm Ridda holds out hope that her eldest son will come back from Iraq and shower the neighbourhood with gifts and money, `Adil gets his first prison sentence when he tries to rescue a runaway girl called Nahid from sexual harassment. When he is released from prison he finds Nahid waiting for him at his mother's. He falls for her and they manage to make love despite the place being so crowded. However, when Nahid becomes pregnant he makes a dubious promise to marry her and accept the child if he has the financial means to do so; literally he says: *"Hina maysara"*, which means "when conditions allow". As they do not, Nahid returns home to her mother, and her stepfather whose sexual overtures had been the original reason for her leaving home. She eventually gives birth to a son. Meanwhile `Adil makes up his mind and confesses to his mother about his relation with Nahid. He decides to bring Nahid and his child back. However it is too late. When he arrives, Nahid is gone, having escaped her stepfather's never-ending pursuits. In a state of desperation she dumps her child in a bus and heads for Alexandria, where she sells merchandise to visitors and sleeps on the beach until an old woman has mercy on her and takes her in.

For his part, `Adil decides to take matters into his own hands. He joins a hashish trafficking gang and fights its members until he is able to dominate the neighbourhood. At the same time he starts cooperating with the police by reporting clandestine activities of Muslim fundamentalists in the area.

Years pass, `Adil and Nahid's son, who had been sold to an affluent childless couple, gets kicked out by his foster parents the moment they are finally able to conceive a child of their own. The boy takes to the streets and joins a group of street children with whom he grows up. Not inhibited by any taboos, he makes love to one of the girls who then gives birth to a child.

Meanwhile Nahid, who is thrown back onto the streets again after the demise of the old lady, is taken in by a lesbian who runs a brothel, but Nahid is unable to cope with the place. Upon escaping she gets raped by a group of young men. Understanding the futility of her attempts to defend her body she becomes

---

1 Khalid Hifni (n.d.), *fi "hina maysara" al-`ashwa'iyat nar Khalid Yusuf al-muwqada*, retrieved on 28 July 2010 from http://www.elfagr.org/NewsDetails.aspx?nwsId=7980&secid=2317

"

a belly dancer and hostess, and assists rich businessmen in improving their deals by flirting with their clients. This career, too, ends as abruptly as it started when there is a police raid. `Adil, in turn, gets caught between the front lines of the authorities and the fundamentalists. Each side tries to make use of him until state security learns that his brother Ridda joined the ranks of the fundamentalists before his departure to Iraq. Relying on American sources, state security suspects Ridda to be an al-Qaida member. It detains his whole family including `Adil's best friend and neighbour Fathi, and his two wives. All are subjected to brutal torture, until they find out that Ridda is only a phantom created by the Americans.

Upon his release `Adil seeks to revenge his family by helping the fundamentalists to set a trap for the police. When the security forces move into the neighbourhood they find themselves surrounded and bombed by the militants. There is only one option, which is to root out the militants by moving in with bulldozers and demolishing the entire neighbourhood. As people are forced to evacuate their homes, `Adil urges his family to leave. However his mother courageously refuses, joined by her grandchildren, Fathi and his wives. `Adil and Nahid, as well as their son and his girlfriend, find themselves united without prior knowledge on the same train to Alexandria that takes them into an open future.

That is the summary of the extremely meandering and epic storyline of *hina maysara*. Yet, what does it say about the representation of the city in Egyptian film? What insights does it give us into the development of Cairo and social change in real life? In particular when one knows that in Egypt, Cairo is colloquially referred to as "Masr", which is the Arabic word for "all of Egypt". In other words, Cairo is equivalent to Egypt and vice versa.

Doubtless, the film is a matter of subjective and individual reading. I am thinking here of Hifni's earlier cited film review, which seems to be occupied in trying to justify the film's sexual preoccupation and permissiveness, while conjuring at the same time the horrors of social unrest and rebellion. As for my own first impression, *hina maysara's* depiction of the `ashwa´iyat (literally: random) or shanty towns, reminded me of Laura Mulvey's words on the representation of the nocturnal city in the genre of melodrama in the 19th century that was symptomatic of the heavy social changes that accompanied industrialisation and proletarisation of the time. It embodied "the outside to rule of order. To the individual swallowed up in the crowd, to the law in search of a criminal, to morality faced with a profusion of bars and prostitutes, the city at night epitomises chaos and uncertainty".[2]

Moreover, I was struck by the findings of Paul Amar described in his study *Cosmopolitan Brutality of Urban Security: Race/Sex Globalization and Policing in Rio de Janeiro and Cairo* when reading it on the backdrop of this film. The study focuses on the similarities between the persecution mainly of homosexuals in Brazil and Egypt, comprehending them as a feature of globalised cosmopolitan brutality and – what is more important – in the era of globalised multi-corporation economy, and mass tourism. Its author describes this persecution as an attempt to cleanse the national body from what is now considered to be sullying national culture. In both countries miscegenation and sexual libertinage have ceased to be read as a positive attribute of cosmopolitanism, but have turned into an increasingly unacceptable low-brow aspect of local culture advertising aspects of high-brow culture. To summarise, Amar states: "Sexual profiling removes its subjects from the realm of legality and declares them military targets in the paralegal realm of security."[3] In a way, this statement could be extended to the inhabitants of the slums as portrayed in Yusuf's film; their sexual profiling goes hand in hand with subjecting them to exploitation, exclusion and even extermination.

Intrigued by these arguments in the above-mentioned review with regards to social change, its stress on a morally tainted vocabulary, such as "merging bodies" and "sinful sex" while describing the slum dwellers' evidently unrestrained sexual behaviour that contrasts starkly with prevalent concepts of chastity and patriarchal sexual morals in Egyptian society today, I started wondering to what extent this film may be considered a continuation of or a departure from the often idealised depictions of lower-class environments in earlier Egyptian films. The latter quite often chose the alley or *hara* as an idealistic centre piece of narratives on the nation, a location that opened the space for debating and challenging questions of modernity and gender relations. To put it more concretely: is *hina maysara* just a new stage of the trope of the *hara* (alley) and the urban lower-class neighbourhood as an allegorical location of an authentic essence of the nation, or is it rather expressing an increasing social polarisation, distinction and exclusion that targets the poor as the real inner enemy?

Historically the cinematic trope of the alley has been linked to the anti-colonial nationalist sentiment that spread in the wake of the 1919 revolution and the subsequent strife for complete national independence. During this period the lower-class neighbourhood, particularly the traditional alley set in Cairo's old Islamic city came to represent how the nation was imagined, as opposed to the palaces of the pashas or the Turkish aristocracy of the time. Particularly after the coup in 1952, Egyptian critics started insisting on this schism even more heavily in the 1970s, describing "pre-revolutionary" cinema as marked by misguided consciousness. This was precisely because of its preference for splendid upper-class settings, those "feudal palaces" which were later replaced by "the apartments of employees and the alleys of Cairo" in more realist accounts.[4] However, the so-

2   Laura Mulvey 1989, *Visual and other Pleasures,* Bloomington, p. 70

3   Paul Amar 2004, *Cosmopolitan Brutality of Urban Security: Race/Sex Globalization and Policing in Rio de Janeiro and Cairo,* Paper at the SSRC Beirut-Conference "Public Spheres" (AUB), p. 1; An in-depth discussion of Amar's assumptions will be available in his forthcoming publication The Security Archipleago: Human-Security States, Sexuality Politics, and the End of Neoliberalism (Duke University Press, 2012).

4   Samir Farid 1973, Nahw manhaj li-kitaba `ilmiyya li-tarikhunna al-sinima'i, *al-Tali`a* 3: 149–157, here p. 150

called revolutions did not annihilate the schism. Cairo's alleys, with their cramped streets and modest, dilapidated houses and flats, or the rooms on top of elegant multi-storey buildings have remained a quite consistent feature since the first appearance of cinematic Egyptian realism in the late 1930s. However, in the years following the coup, palaces and land estates of the royalist period have been gradually eclipsed by either fashionable multi-storey buildings or the modern elegant villa with garden and swimming pool. Thus, the alley became part of nationalist ideology and a source of symbolic identification based on two iconographic antipodes, differentiating between the spatial particularities of an overtly Westernised (in fashion and furniture, not necessarily in values) upper class on one hand and a more traditional-oriented lower class on the other. In their cinematic outlook the inhabitants of the alley were not necessarily confined to the working class, but often also included so-called petit bourgeois characters, who may have had an education but lacked any corresponding influence or property. What was important, though, was their connection to traditional culture – or what one imagined was traditional culture.

For good reasons the cinematic representation of lower-class environments did not go uncontested as it seemed opposed to colonialist as well as bourgeois modernist agenda, and was suspected of leftist if not communist agitation. According to Mustafa Darwish (the head of state censorship between 1966 and 1968), royal official censorship as well as the press during the Royalist era was hostile to the representation of Egyptian villages and the working class.[5] Thus, the still relatively rare picturing of workers, like in *al-`amil/The Worker* (1942) by Ahmad Kamil Mursi, was not welcomed at the time.

A similar logic was applied to a film that made excessive use of a traditional neighbourhood and its alleys (as created in a studio) and was later considered a landmark not only of realist Egyptian cinema but also regarding its advocacy for its inhabitants as the representatives of cultural authenticity and national achievements, namely Kamal Selim's *al-`azima/Determination* (1939). Despite the importance of the alley and its inhabitants as a main protagonist, Studio Misr, the producer of the film, refused to release it under the title *The Alley* as he considered it too risky to advertise.[6] The film itself was quite conciliatory in its approach to social difference.

The film's hero, an educated young man from lower-class origins, whose father works as a hairdresser, cannot find a job until a rich pasha intervenes. At the same time he has to struggle for the heart of his beloved neighbour's daughter, who is promised to the rich but uneducated butcher. In fact, the pragmatism that was displayed in *Determination* regarding to the cooperation between prosperous aristocracy and the educated, but poor, lower-middle class did not deny its lower-class protagonists of the prospect of social ascent. It spoke in favour of the core issues of modernism, namely companionship, marriage and education, as a precondition for national progress. Moreover in the end, solidarity and loyalty among the hero's lower-class neighbours and friends initiates the happy ending and helps the hero to retrieve his beloved bride from the claws of the rich butcher. Gender played an important role in these narratives. Love stories on the one hand ran counter to the traditional concepts of gender segregation and patriarchal domination of women, but they were also pivotal in reinforcing patriarchal morality by insisting on female chastity and virginity. In other words, love stories were instrumental in reconciling so-called tradition with modernity to a certain degree. At the same time, the films also promoted a series of other traditional values, such as respect for one's parents, hospitality and the like.

After *al-`azima/Determination,* the motif of loyalty appeared often in realist films, such as in *al-futuwwa/The Thug* (1957) by Salah Abu Saif, for example. It was presented as part of a traditional moral framework which in turn seemed to guarantee national authenticity that invited positive identification. Traditional neighbourhoods, such as Harat al-Yahud (Jews' Alley) or al-Gamaliya, well known from Nagib Mahfuz's writings and the realist films based on his works produced in the 1930s to 1960s, were made to radiate authenticity (even though these neighbourhoods were, in reality, likewise subject to uncontrolled growth) by means of their ancient architecture. This authenticity could still be ascribed to more recent popular neighbourhoods (*hay sha`bi*) because of their density and crowdedness, their narrow streets and poor architecture. Al-Kitkat for example, located between the shores of the Nile and the middle-class neighbourhood Dokki, both dating back only to the post-1952 revolution era, became the subject of a very successful New Realist film by Daoud Abd El Sayed with the same title. In the film, released in 1991, the close interaction of neighbours in combination with the typical spatial signifiers of the cinematic alley (which was all rebuilt in the studio), such as narrow alleys, architectural simplicity and dilapidation, street vendors, a saint's shrine and last but not least a traditional coffee shop, safeguarded the continuation of the elements of the traditional *hara*. Moreover, the film discussed through the motif of an old house that is supposed to be torn down, issues of loyalty to home, community and tradition, double standards and loose sexual morals. Yet, unlike *hina maysara,* the location was not portrayed as a source of danger and unrest threatened by extermination; this is despite the fact that in reality al-Kitkat is known as an important hiding place for militant Islamists and where several police crackdowns were witnessed in the 1990s.

In contrast to the cinematic al-Kitkat, oriented on tradition and the past, the shanty town of *hina maysara* has moved into the

---

5   Mustafa Darwish 1989, Censure et espace, in: Marie-Claude Bénard et al. (ed.), *Le Caire et le cinéma égyptien des années 80,* Cairo, p. 65
6   Galal al-Sharqawi 1970, *risala fi tarikh al-sinima al-`arabiyya,* Cairo, p. 78

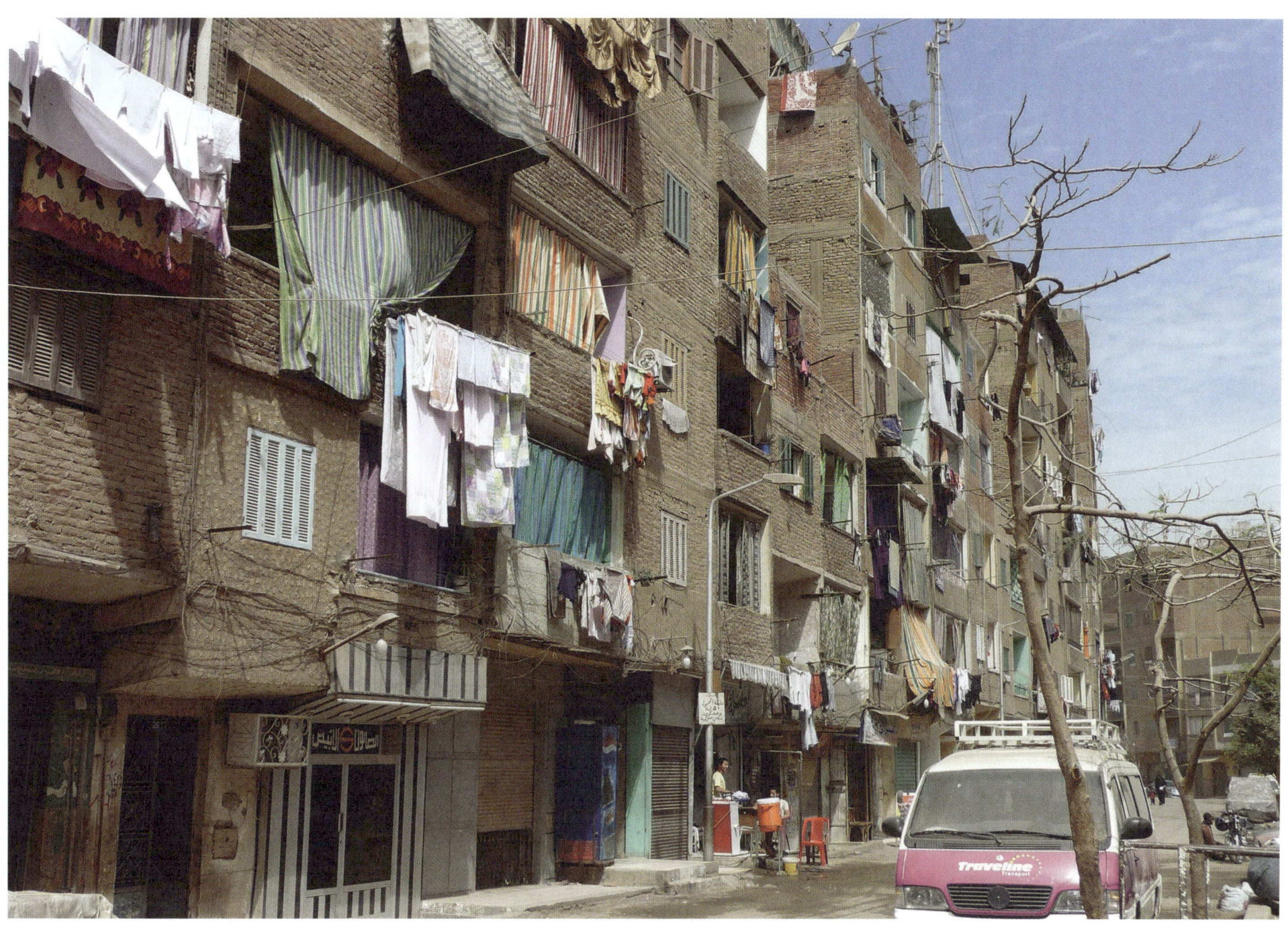

centre of national conflict: the neighbourhood in the end gets blown up and demolished as a result of the violent friction between militant Islamists and a pragmatic inhumane state power. It is a place without future, deemed to be evacuated or burying its inhabitants under the rubble (which happened in reality at al-Dawiqa in 2008, where almost 500 people lost their lives when rocks from the Muqattam mountain crushed parts of an informal settlement).

Informal housing, as such, dates back to the late 1910s when Cairo had been turned into a modern metropolis and its older neighbourhoods and cemeteries started attracting rural immigrants. However, it gained its real momentum after the Second World War when the population started exploding. It reached its peak in the mid-1980s when the government started apprehending the gravity of uncontrolled settlement, particularly on fertile farming land, and started to criminalise it.[7] By the late 1990s half of Cairo's population was estimated to be living in `ashwa´iyat or shanty towns.[8]

What is decisive about the geography of modern Cairo is its increasing social division with its "old" (meaning early 20th century) upper-class areas, such as Maadi, Heliopolis, Zamalek and Garden City; its middle-class neighbourhoods such as Shubra and Munira (meanwhile lower-middle-class); its ascendant middle to upper-middle class in Mohandessin and Nasr City, and lower-class areas such as the historic city of Cairo (Gamaliya among others), al-Matariya, `Izbat al-Nakhl and many more. Historically these spatial distinctions have usually been interrupted by the presence of doorkeepers and their families, small entrepreneurs who provide services for the wealthier neighbourhood residents as well as the presence of uneducated but prosperous merchants et cetera in the poor neighbourhoods. However, as some researchers see it, the last two decades of

7   David Sims 2003, Cairo, Egypt in: UN Habitat (ed.), *The Challenge of the Slums,* London, p.195–228 retrieved on 31 July 2010 from http://www.ucl.ac.uk/dpu-projects/Global_Report/cities/cairo.htm

8   Anouk de Koenig 2009, *Global Dreams. Class, Gender and Space in Cosmopolitan Cairo,* Cairo, p. 39

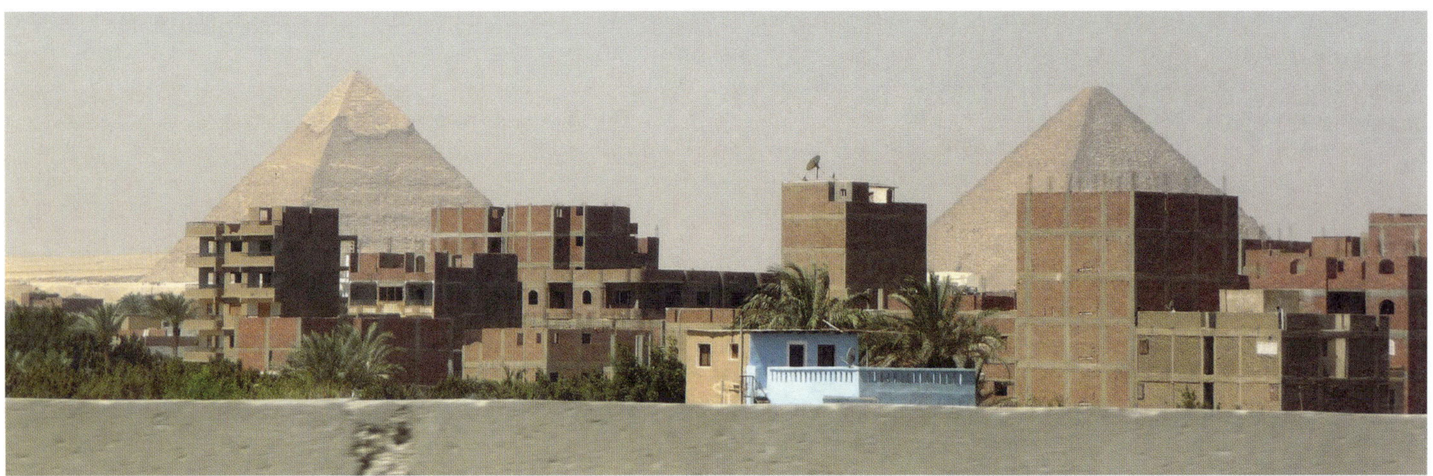

economic liberalisation and globalisation have been character-ised by an increasingly "total segregation of spaces, the fortifi-cation of the middle and upper classes and the increasing ne-glect of older public spaces along with the lower-class residents who populate them".[9] While Anouk de Koenig regards the new exclusive gated communities in the desert surrounding Cairo to be the "most conspicuous expressions of Egypt's new liberal age"[10], Asef Bayat and Eric Denis discern the current tendency toward spatial segregation in the parallel growth of gated com-munities and `ashwa´iyat on Cairo's peripheries.[11]

Indeed the ferocity of this double exclusiveness gets alluded to in the motif of violent extermination in the ending of *hina maysara*. This is despite the fact that the film is far less interested in reflecting the development of informal housing in Egypt and its social implications than in making a more political statement on economic liberalism and neo-colonialism, as it indicates the years 1990 to 2003 through its temporal framework that pic-tures the neighbourhood and its inhabitants as falling prey to intense and interrelated international and national conflicts.

Indeed, the early 1990s were very decisive years for Egypt in-ternally. First, not only did they see a number of ferocious terror-ist attacks within Egypt on civilians, Copts and tourists, there were also heavy crackdowns on Islamists by government forces and state security. This was all accompanied by deteriorating human rights conditions. Second, in the year 1990 during the First Gulf War, Western and allied Arab forces intervened and tried to reverse Iraq's invasion of neighbouring Kuwait with Op-eration Desert Storm or the four-day-bombing of Iraq in 1998, ending with the 2003 invasion and subsequent occupation of Iraq by US armed forces and its European allies. The film al-ludes to these events through news clips and by adding protag-onists who immigrate to Iraq in search of a living and whose aspirations have been thwarted by subsequent political events.

For example, like Ridda and `Adil's brother whose fate remains unknown while American allegations regarding his al-Qaida in-volvement cannot be verified. The same applies to Fathi's brother-in-law. He returns empty handed after the 2003 invasion and is just happy to be alive. The filmmaker's political statement there-fore is clear: it is Egypt's poor who pay the price.

Khalid Yusuf, who actually started his career as director's assis-tant to Egypt's late star director Youssef Chahine, is a man with a political agenda. He ran as a candidate (unsuccessfully) for the position of the head of the Arts syndicate in 2010, and is also known for his Nasserist sympathies. His political films have a rather populist stance, though, like his first film *al-`asifa / The Storm* (2001) in which he publicly expressed his indignation over the disappearance and/or unaccounted murder of hundreds of Egyptian guest workers in Iraq during the Saddam regime. As a part of his populist stance, which is also evident in *hina maysara,* he presents topical social criticism in the well-known guise of Egyptian genre film and by doing so becomes enmeshed in ana-lytical contradictions.

Portraying the lower-class neighbourhood as a realm outside the official order as such is not a completely new phenomenon. During the late 1970s and early 1980s, as cinema started to tackle the evident negative effects of Sadat's Open Door Policy or *infitah,* a few action-melodramas, such as *al-Batniya* (1980) by Husam al-Din Mustafa, which pictured the alley as being governed by a vicious capitalist-oriented monopolist who takes control of the place, displaying a Manichean battle between good and evil that could largely be resolved by the removal of the dictator. This type of narrative continues to exist until the present day and has been even transferred to the most recent `ashwa´iyat-film *Ibrahim Labyad* (2009) by Marwan Hamid, for example. Similar narratives were developed for the thug-cycle, using the recurrent schematic formula of an urban lower-class character

---

9   Petra Kuppinger 2004, Exclusive Greenery: New Gated
    Communities in Cairo, *City & Society* 16/2: 35–61, here p. 40
10 Anouk de Koenig (2009), p. 41
11 Asef Bayat, Eric Denis 2000, "Who is afraid of Ashwaiyyat?"
    Urban Change and Politics in Egypt, *Environment & Urbani-
    zation* 12/2: 185–99, here p. 199

who is, thanks to his physical capabilities including traditional stick fighting, able to positively or negatively monopolise power in the "traditional" neighbourhood. However, such a figure may also, at times, pursue either egoistic or altruistic ends. This film type experienced a peak in production during the 1980s with *futuwwat al-gabal/Mountain Thugs* (1982) by Nadir Galal; several films by Samir Saif, such as *shawari` min nar/Streets on Fire* (1984) and *al-mutarad/The Chased* (1985); as well as *futuwwat al-Salakhana/al-Salakhana Thugs* (1989) by Nasir Husain, which appeared first in the mid-1950s.

The term *futuwwa* emanated originally during the Middle Ages, signifying members of Islamic brotherhoods who were governed by chivalrous precepts. It was not until then that it acquired, in the colloquial Egyptian context, the connotation of thug, bully or racketeer. On the screen it carries the latter meaning, but has fused in its positive coding with the *ibn al-balad* character (literal meaning: son of the country). Narratives of the traditional alley usually advertise the so-called *awlad al-balad* honour codex, which is often also instrumental in working out moral dilemmas and reinstalling order. The core values of this codex are loyalty to kin and community, generosity in addition to courage, toughness and virility.

In fact, `Adil, the main character of *hina maysara,* embodies some of these features since he becomes the *futuwwa* of his neighbourhood for a time, although he also often deviates from it. Rescuing Nahid and avenging his family in an attempt to safeguard their honour puts him in line with this tradition, while also refusing to acknowledge his son and trying to steal his mother's gold bracelets. However, he also fails to meet up to this norm when, in the end, he abandons his family, forcing them to face the power of the state on their own. At one point he explains his often negative behaviour to his friend Fathi, saying that the world is pushing him, that he had been tied to a wall, and that untied he broke loose with no choice in his weapons of defence. This contradictory depiction of the hero reflects also on his neighbourhood; it is part of his moral failure. `Adil's personal flaws and the unfavourable social conditions are one and the same.

In this way, the film shifts the shanty into the heart of the national condition; it becomes an allegory of the nation. However, unlike the traditional alley it seems less capable in embodying a positive centre of the nation, a safeguard of local tradition and cultural authenticity, an advocate for its highly regarded *awlad al-balad* code of honour. This is the case not only because the slums cannot hide the fact that the informal housing phenomenon is linked to uncontrolled growth, fast urbanisation and failed government planning, which became particularly evident as a problem after Sadat's *infitah,* the open door policy of the 1970s, but also that *hina maysara,* itself, pursues a contradictory objective.

To come back to my original question whether *hina maysara* is a disruption or a continuation of a cinematic tradition, I would suggest that it is both. For here, the shanty town is a place that hosts the typical lower-class young man who has all the preconditions to become a true *ibn al-balad,* but due to the external and internal political and social situation in which he has no say, he is forced by the very place, he inhabits to abandon his true essence and to fight for his survival by all means possible. In other words, the poor neighbourhood is no longer the heart or origin of the nation. In its new outlook as `ashwa´iyat or shanty town it has rather become an entity that turns against itself, devouring, destroying and maiming itself after having lost all hopes and aspirations for a better modern life that once governed a narrative like *Determination.*

Disruption and continuation in *hina maysara* is also safeguarded by its gendered representation. If the young man who was supposed to be the nation's pride failed for reasons he cannot control, the young woman is more of a traditional victim. Her sexual vulnerability reinforces the originally melodramatic and cinematically recurrent motif of sexual exploitation as a metaphor for social injustice. In that sense her sexual involvement with `Adil gets whitewashed by their mutual love and her subsequent exploitation. Yet, this trope is paired with another far more ambiguous representation of sexuality that serves the opposed purpose of social distinction and exclusion of the poor from the bourgeois nation or, in other words, achieves "their sexual profiling".

As mentioned earlier the film indulges in the depiction of a sexually permissive shanty town, where, on the one hand, traditional (and modern bourgeois) norms of gender segregation and, on the other hand, bourgeois chastity are neglected, circumvented or violated regularly, and on purpose, not only in the case of `Adil and Nahid but also in the case of other characters like Fathi who, despite being married, chases another girl and tricks her brother into offering her to him. Of course this allows diverging interpretations depending on the standpoint of the viewer. It may be either used to blame the socio-political system for creating such moral incompatibility (in a sort of solidarity with the poor) or it may be read as a good reason for the exclusion or even extermination of the shanty town as a hotbed of vice and disorder.

Interestingly, the film review quoted in the beginning exposes the same ambiguity. It tries to whitewash the permissive cinematic representation on the one hand because of its social critique while using, on the other hand, a number of morally tainted expressions, such as "merging bodies" (as opposed to segregation) or unbearable "sinful sex" (as opposed to chastity), picturing the shanty town as a place outside bourgeois morals and order that could "bring down the temple (that is the larger nation!) on top of everyone". Thus and more importantly, *hina maysara* expresses, very clearly, the increasing social schism that has taken hold of the city of Cairo and, as a result, the new incapability of the poor neighbourhood in representing a united "authentic" nation.

Born in the
Century
of Randomness

Where Should One Be Laid to Rest?[1]

HANY DARWISH

My ambitions are going to be modest for this narrative. I must seize this stream of ideas and narrate it, out of love for my friends whose heads have ached from the great ideas that have found their limits at my ears … No, these are not ideas intended for a documentary film or a novel, but only for an article whose readers will quickly forget this tour, and who are shaking the dust from of their hands, panting behind street names and areas and lives that will never affect them, neither in place nor in time. But do follow me for a while and surrender to this stream, for you are the only ones worthy of this particular obsession.

It is not my intention to address an absent collective consciousness. That is a brazen assumption similar to the possibility of the presence of each and every individual consciousness, just as unlikely as that morning when – I could not believe my own sight in the mirror – I found myself to be the one picking his modest clothes in preparation for a trip in the city of Cairo, the itinerary of which would be akin to a giant arc.

The mission is to visit my eldest sister to congratulate her for an overdue pregnancy. She lives on the outer periphery of the Qalyubiyah Governorate (north of Cairo), at the bottom of an overpass stairway called Hassanein that is preceded by a well-known stairway named Umm Bayoumi, located before the Mostorod exit on the Ring Road. From the moment I get into the Ring Road microbus going from El Remaya Square (North Giza) to the Sayeda Umm Bayoumi exit, three governorates away – all of which the microbus will journey through – an elderly passenger is persistently inquiring about the ticket price and is imploring the driver to swear not to forget to alert him in sufficient time before reaching Umm Bayoumi.

What my modest clothing tried to conceal was given away by the coloured box of Monginis sweets that I carried with me, as an older brother who supposedly should not be entering his sister's house empty-handed. I was debunked by the bourgeoisie of the box and my concern for it, which cost me a spiteful look from the driver for my insistence on sitting in the aisle of the bus, holding onto the box tightly, and as such obstructing the passengers' paths in their quiet attempts to board and get off the bus furtively. The Ring Road, which surrounds Greater Cairo and its outskirts like a wristband, measures forty-two kilometres and spans the outer edges of three governorates that together form the Greater Cairo region, El Giza, Cairo and Qalyubiyah to its north, south, east and west boundaries respectively. Only ten years ago, these areas were purely agricultural land – the backyard of the capital, where manufacturing, trading and shabby servicing projects were running to provide for a city already squeezed. With the social and entrepreneurial displacement of the new urban generations emerged the predominance of red brick in these areas, and it was there that a sizeable mass of the workforce of this shabby city remained, settling in the areas at the bottom of the Ring Road. The sons and daughters of poor families who were living in areas like Boulaq, Shubra, Imbaba and Matareya in the 1980s and 1990s (the cluster of informal districts created by urbanisation processes in the 1970s, to borrow from urbanist Galila El-Kadi) shifted from being heirs of poverty to being the dwellers of the outer margins of agricultural land extensions. The residents of Imbaba moved to Teresa and Zoheir Faisal. The inhabitants of Matareya moved to Umm Bayoumi, Bahtim and the Shubra El-Kheima suburbs. This is how the exodus of a large chunk of the capital's population took place, taking along with it its age-old mentality, in order to function outside of the city. Entire generations do not know Downtown Cairo, and do not consider it worthy of a visit or as a place of transit. Thousands use the Ring Road daily to travel between the areas outside of the capital without ever touching the city's core spirit. Thousands travel using dashing or crawling means of public transportation on this concrete snake, which has finally connected them to the industrial and service areas on the outskirts of the city. The scenery is powerful when one sets off, without interruption, from the foot of the Pyramids to abruptly cross over the sumptuous Nile at Warraq, from the Cairo desert road onto the Fayoum desert road and the Oases desert road, passing onto the Alexandria agricultural road to the Ismaelia agricultural road, and on to the Ismaelia desert road until the Suez desert road. Inevitably, one becomes aware of the existence of a hidden

1   The article was published in Arabic on 20 January 2009 in
the Lebanese newspaper *Al-mustaqbal*.

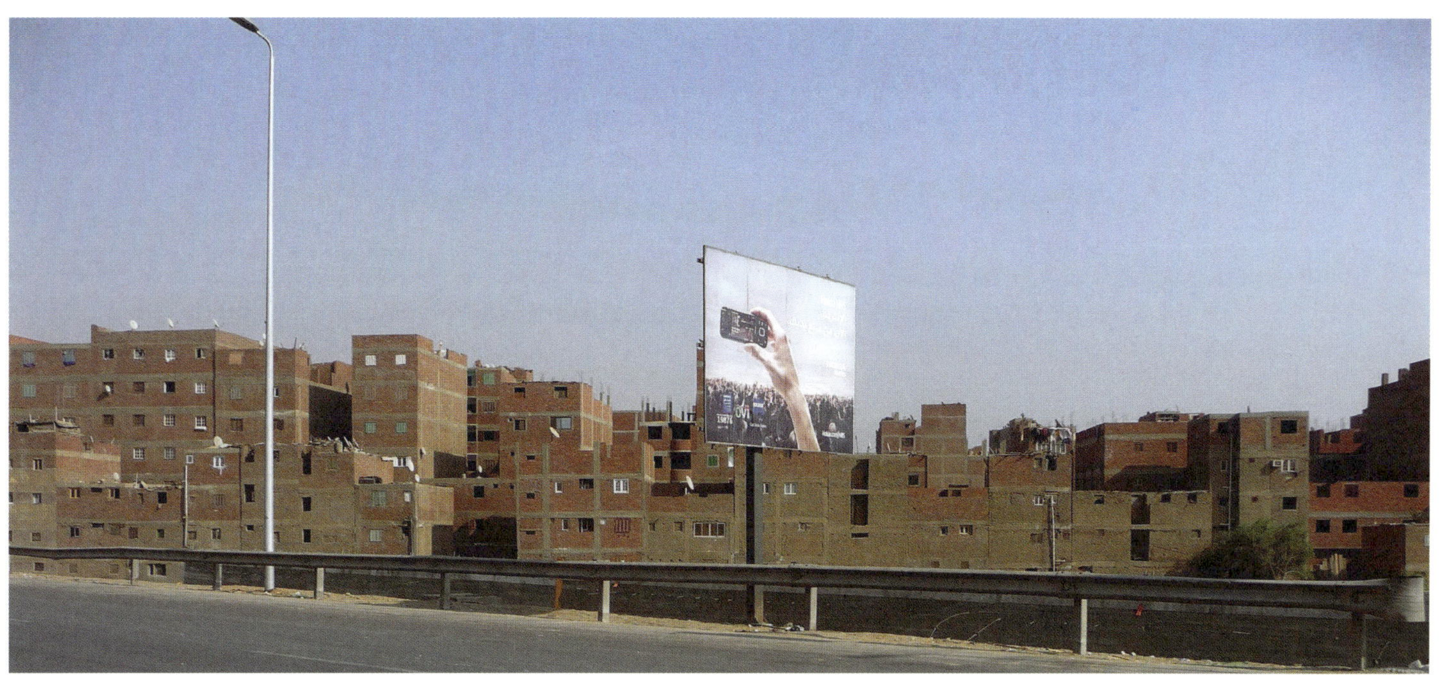

mind that shapes the lives of millions on the map. It is as though, on one night, that mind made a decision that determined the fate of imaginations, cultures and social and economic relationships with the stroke of a pencil.

My sister lives further beyond the Umm Bayoumi stairway. The microbus driver, whose stoned stare did not part from the box of delicious desserts laying on my lap, who prohibits smoking in the bus despite being addicted to hallucinating pills, and who listens to the groans of Mahmoud El Leithy, pioneer of the popular folksy song *The Brown Cigarette*, made fun of me as I fumbled with the name of the stairway exit. He let me out, delivering me to the sight of the extended and abandoned field, lying flat below the overpass. The stairway is carved into the heart of the large bridge, a purely local creation. For nearly one kilometre, I walk on a dirt lane that divides a field of rotting vegetation. I can smell the cattle manure, bringing me back to the days of rustic boyhood. I listen to *Rock the Casbah* by Rachid Taha, turning my face to the side of the brick buildings, which extend into the horizon like a cold arrowhead. Salwa lives behind the first row of these buildings. For my first and only visit to her after the wedding, I travelled by way of five different means of transportation in my insistence to reach her from the city centre, surrendering to my fate dictated by the "repressive whims of the pencil" and riding along the entire arc of the Ring Road while playfully entertained by my late discovery of my fantasies of estrangement from the city – the city as I know it from the history of my Cairene family.

I am Hany Darwish, son of a century of the city's spontaneity, as described in *L'Urbanisation Spontanée au Caire,* the book by researcher and urbanist Galila El-Kadi. Before reading the book, which was recently published by the National Centre for Translation and Dar al-Ain, I had imagined that I, along with my brothers, were the only symptoms of the randomness typical of the latest generation of an early 20th century-style emigrant family. In her wonderful book she reveals that our Cairene family (on my mother's side) lived nowhere other than in informal settlements throughout an entire century. My grandfather had moved to Cairo from his village in the centre of the Delta for my mother, and volunteered for the Royal Guard (after his father, an Egyptian-Sudanese son of a nomad, fell in love with a peasant woman, married her and settled in that village). He bought a slice of land from the land parcel in the Sidi El Tounsi area, on the periphery of the Cairo cemetery. And indeed, he had actually bought a tomb and built his family house on top of it, which resulted in the systematic development of the Tounsi neighbourhood on top of the famous Sadaka Tombs. Galila El-Kadi writes that the settlement pattern on top of tombs in the early 20th century is the actual beginning of the establishment of the informal areas of Old Cairo, and she cites the example – notice the coincidence – of the Tounsi neighbourhood, which appeared in 1917. Chance has it that my grandfather, Mohammed El-Sadiq Ibrahim, was born that same year. Galila goes on to explain that this settlement pattern coincided with another spontaneous pattern that appeared in the settlements of rural migrants who occupied large houses in the popular Khedival neighbourhoods of Cairo. There, migrant families took over large houses in the neighbourhoods of Khalifa, Sayeda Zeinab, Bab El She'reya and Gammaliya following their abandonment by merchant families at the end of the 19th century. Each family occupied a room, and shared a bathroom with the rest of the families. My grandfather's sister, Um Suleyman, lived in one of these houses in the Kharta neighbourhood in Gabal el Qala'a. She raised my orphaned mother in her room, and it was in that same room that I was born in 1974.

Before you feel lost, dear reader, and in order for you to understand my shock, you must have some patience. My mother was born in 1951. Coincidentally, Galila El-Kadi surveys the numbers and statistics of that same year, which happens to be the beginning of the second wave of informal settlements in Cairo, represented in the emergence of the Matareya district in the east of Cairo. To complete the wonderful coincidences, my migrant father, who was originally from the same village as my mother (he had migrated as a teenager of sixteen to Cairo in order to work at a public company for building and construction), married his pretty neighbour, who was living in the Kharta district near the Citadel in the 1960s. After a long engagement period, they married in the then-developing Matareya district, the old planning ground for the July revolution, in 1972. Do you remember dear reader, that I was born in 1974? And that my mother gave birth to me in my grandmother's room? Remember the date, because Galila El-Kadi surveys the third wave of informal settlement formations in Cairo in that same year (1974), and provides as examples the neighbourhoods of Ain Shams, El Marg and Ezbet El-Nakhl. The latter, namely Ezbet El-Nakhl, is where our socially deteriorating family would move to in 1987.

I am thus the son of the century of Cairo's randomness. At the age of thirty-five, and after having judged migrants of rural origins thousands of times, I discover that I was never a Cairene, neither by birth, nor by heredity, and that the city of Cairo, with its octopus-like, sprawling expansion, had changed her skin hundreds of times and stripped me of the honour of being a city person.

Let us begin the story from the middle of its first chapter, as I promised I would. My sister lives on a street that is approximately five metres wide, and is called Khalid bin El-Waleed. The street is dark, since the buildings extend to the eighth floor without even a sufficient glimpse of sky, and without an elevator. In the stairwell, each person marks their religious identity in the form of carvings and words of blessings on the doors of the apartments. The colours are garish and vary according to the degree of the degeneration of taste from the first floor to the last. Crosses and images of the Virgin opposite Qur'anic verses … Even my sister, who works in the fields of human rights and development, bustles around her apartment while three different

Qur'anic recitals blare in the background. The first emanates from the El Nas channel on television, without any spectators. The second comes from the Qur'an broadcast on the radio, which is set in the kitchen to drive out evil spirits (she leaves it on even when she is not at home). And the third is the wailing Saudi recital of the Qur'an on the cassette player.

My sister, who was given maternity leave to tend to her pregnancy, the successful completion of which is questionable (due to a birth defect), married a wonderful young man whose father used to work at the Yassin factory for glass production in Shubra Al-Kheima, another source of pride in the 1960s. Her father-in-law is a migrant from Upper Egypt who cried during the wedding of his youngest son, and her husband works at the National Authority of Military Production. Their family's transition from Upper Egypt to Shubra to the outskirts of the Ring Road occurred within a circle whose radius is only a few kilometres wide, but which is filled with wistful nostalgia due to social demise, and with gratitude and thankfulness for being allowed to wallow in the remnants of the familiar dust of the 1960s. Salwa whirls counterclockwise to her husband's commute on the Ring Road. He travels northeast to Madinet El Salam while she continues onto Helwan across the other end of the Ring Road. She and her husband do not know the fate of their child in the future legacy of the Ring Road.

I leave her neighbourhood using the old roads and I observe how the empty spaces between the different quarters have filled up, since, as a child living in Matareya, I remember the eastern area of that district used to end at the Ismailiya canal, and was a jungle of vegetation. Now, when I come from the easternmost part of the district, I traverse above the canal across neighbourhoods, all of which have their individual urban downtown areas. The Oil Companies Street (note that it was named at the time when it was still empty) has turned into a long urbanised and unified artery that connects the west bank of the Qalyubiyah district with the east bank of the easternmost district of Cairo. The long street spans residential towers more "spontaneously urbanised" – to use the term coined by Galila El-Kadi – than those on the historically agricultural neighbouring bank where my sister lives. I muse while riding the large minibus, passing through neighbourhoods that were born out of nothing, at the sunglasses shop "Magdy and Farouk", which fills the large street with advertisements every five metres. Lives, businesses, passengers and faces in the consecutive rectangles. But how did this shop come to occupy all this space on the street and what kind of sunglasses does it sell to the people living below the poverty line here? I imagine how much money was paid to the local authorities, and then I see the answer right in front of my eyes. The trail of advertisements ends in front of the shop with a giant billboard carrying the name of the shop and a picture of President Hosni

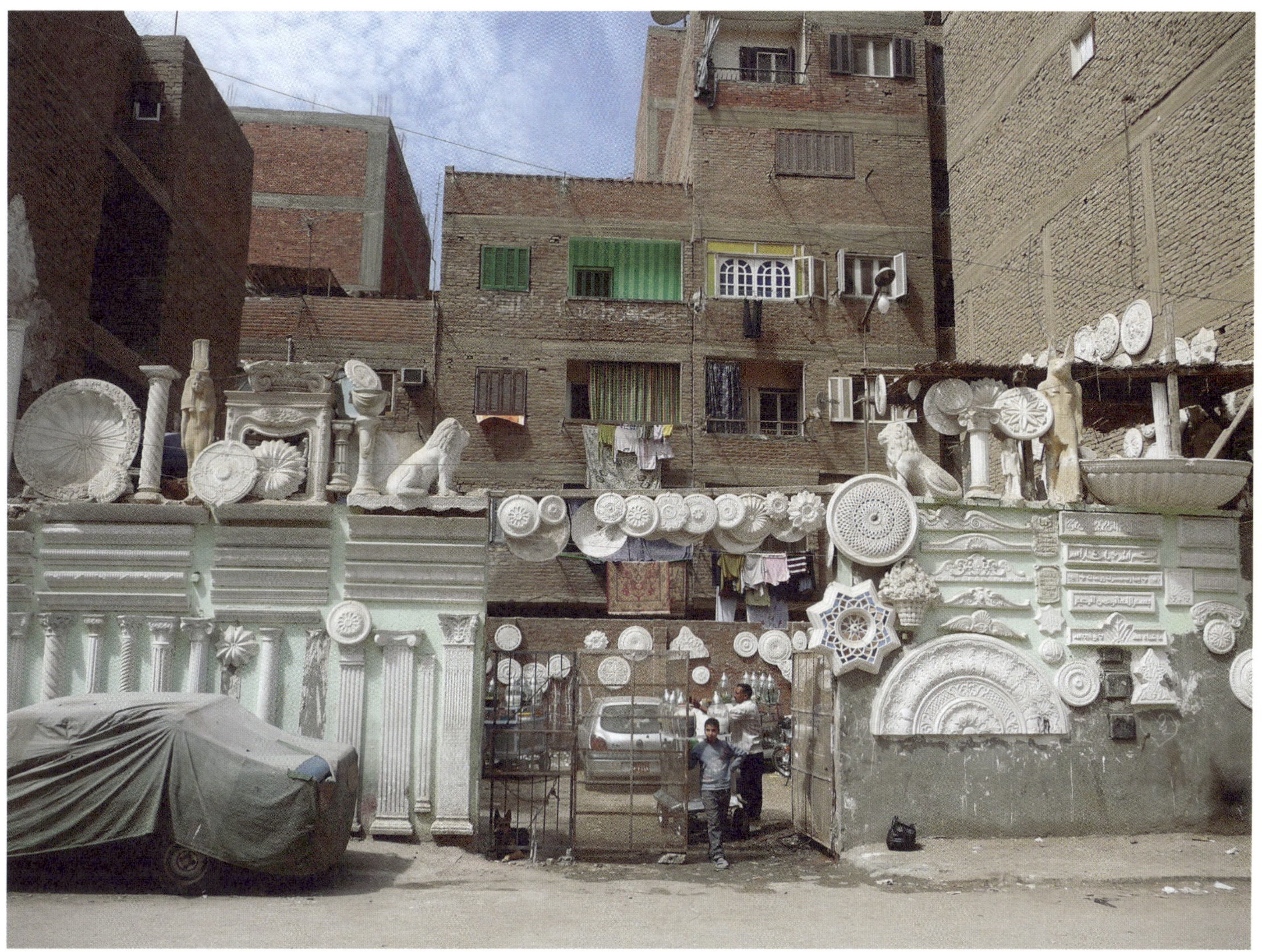

Mubarak with the words "Get Well Soon, Dear President", followed by a tribute to the governor and a list of the names of security officials.

My journey continues by means of another microbus, after which I take the metro from the Ghamra station. I could never have imagined this connectedness between neighbourhoods I only know of from the "Accidents" pages in daily newspapers. There is no public transportation, only minibuses and microbuses and *tatatik* cars (the plural of the infamous Pakistani *tok tok)*. I arrive at the heart of the capital in the original Downtown area with a headache, and climb the stairs of the famous khedival building on Emad El-Din Street. The building's history dates back nearly one and a half centuries, and houses the student club of the Greek community in Cairo. I inquire about how I could reserve the club for a private New Year's Eve party. By the way, I used to come into this building as a child because it housed a branch of my father's company, the apartments of which were sold after the company was privatised.

My father died and his body was returned to the town in the heart of the Delta. I am dizzy and tired of all this roaming, which will lead me I do not know where. My body will not be sent to the countryside, but now even Cairo, it seems, I do not know. Goddamn you Galila El-Kadi, I was satisfied with the illusion of another life. Where should I be put to rest after all this lifetime?

Translation from Arabic by Amy Arif

Metro

MAGDY EL SHAFEE

For a number of years, Cairo has been home to a rapidly growing young scene of comic, graffiti and graphic artists. The authors of this 'ninth art', as comics are often dubbed, can locate themselves in a tradition of (political) cartoons going back to the 1920s.

Metro (2008) by Magdy El Shafee is the first Cairo graphic novel in Arabic. The story focuses on the young software designer Shihab who gets caught up in the corrupt deals of a loan shark. He finds a businessman ready to help him, but then, unable to intervene, witnesses the man being murdered. Shihab decides to rob a bank to pay off his debts – and ends up with both the police and the loan shark's henchmen hot on his heels in a wild chase accompanied, thwarted and betrayed by a series of characteristic urban figures. Cairo appears as a pulsing, vibrant city, with its residents trapped by economic and social insecurities. Every chapter is introduced with the image of a different metro system, often with an accompanying political commentary.

Magdy El Shafee claims that his inspirations for this work included the novel *Being Abbas El Abd* by Ahmed Alaidy, which is written in a style informed by streetwise language and text messaging. He also cites the 'raw' and direct tone of bloggers, such as those active in Cairo during the *kefaya* movement in 2004, as another influence. Just a few months after it appeared, *Metro* was banned as supposedly "a danger to public morals". Magdy and his publisher Mohammed El-Sharqawy were sentenced to pay substantial fines.

Magdy El Shafee clearly addresses the social and political problems in his society, from corruption to arbitrary policing, sexual frustration, the lack of perspectives for young people, and the role of the media. Although this kind of social criticism is not new in Egyptian literature, it is new to find it expressed through graphic art and in the language of the youth and everyday life. In addressing these themes, Magdy El Shafee's work is totally in tune with the trend of recent Egyptian cultural production. His subject matter, though, its visualisation and direct language proved just too much for the Egyptian censors.

This extract is set in Sayyida Zeinab, a popular and heavily populated quarter. The centre of the district is dominated by the holy pilgrimage site of the mosque of the Prophet Mohammed's granddaughter Zeinab, Cairo's patron saint. The highpoint of the veneration of the saints is marked by the annual *mulid,* or *mawlid,* birthday festivities, though these are actually based on popular belief and not part of the official Islamic religious practices. With their shooting galleries, clowns, conjurers, roundabouts, puppet theatres, special sweets such as roasted chick peas, and a host of other attractions, they are more comparable to our funfairs. In contrast, though, these celebrations also include free food for the needy, Sufis performing ritual dances, live music, and wares ranging from amulets to prayer beads and incense. The fortune teller who speaks to Shihab in the final frame can be located within this setting.

Shihab, a young software engineer, on the run from a loan shark and the police, is in hiding at his aunt's in Sayyida Zeinab. There he meets up with Dina, his girlfriend. She is a journalist who supports the political opposition. Shihab is helped by Mustafa, a young friend with no job. Mustafa, who would love to be like Shihab, dreams of making a quick buck. Dina mentions a murder to Shihab, thinking she has pulled off a journalistic coup by getting an interview with the suspected murderer. Shihab knows more than he wants to admit. Dina senses something, and her discovery of the murder weapon forces Shihab to confide in her. He can't go to the police, and still owes money to the loan shark. In allusion to a well-known pro-government TV presenter, an interview is broadcast where the alleged murderer – who has quite obviously been severely maltreated – is paraded in front of the camera.

Stefan Winkler and Kerstin Pinther
Translation from German by Andrew Boreham

SAYYIDA ZAYNAB STATION

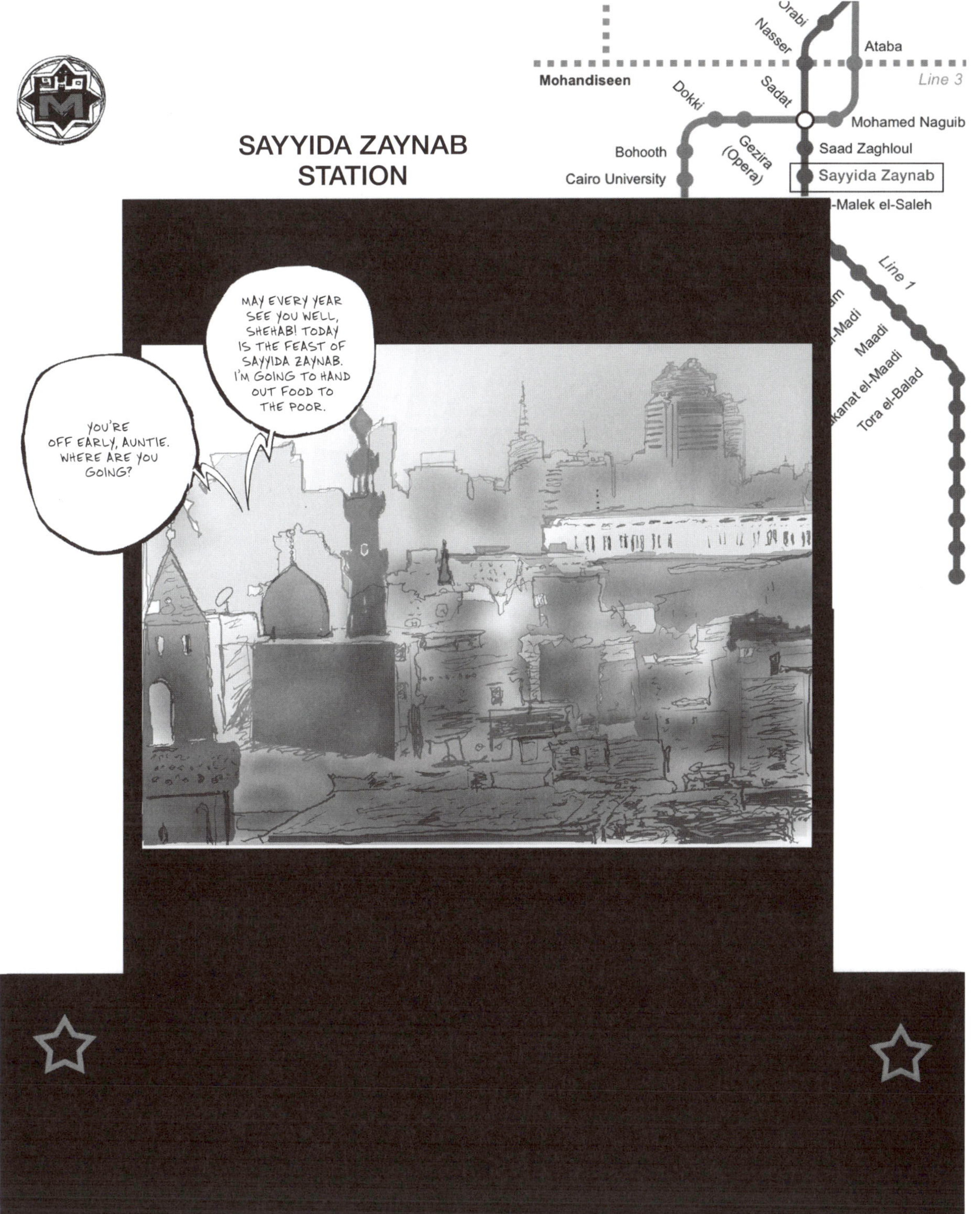

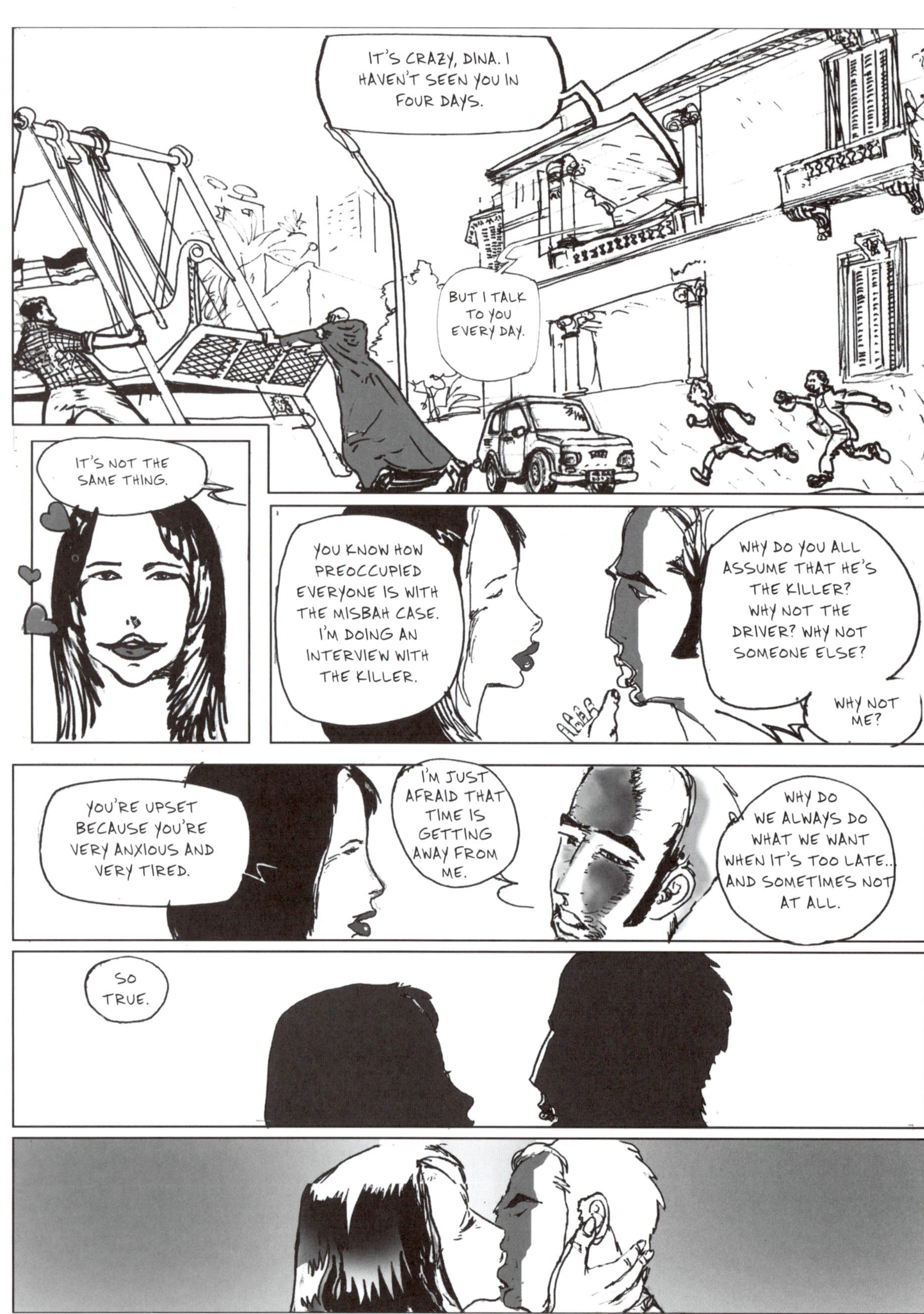

IT'S CRAZY, DINA. I HAVEN'T SEEN YOU IN FOUR DAYS.
BUT I TALK TO YOU EVERY DAY.
IT'S NOT THE SAME THING.
YOU KNOW HOW PREOCCUPIED EVERYONE IS WITH THE MISBAH CASE. I'M DOING AN INTERVIEW WITH THE KILLER.
WHY DO YOU ALL ASSUME THAT HE'S THE KILLER? WHY NOT THE DRIVER? WHY NOT SOMEONE ELSE?
WHY NOT ME?
YOU'RE UPSET BECAUSE YOU'RE VERY ANXIOUS AND VERY TIRED.
I'M JUST AFRAID THAT TIME IS GETTING AWAY FROM ME.
WHY DO WE ALWAYS DO WHAT WE WANT WHEN IT'S TOO LATE... AND SOMETIMES NOT AT ALL.
SO TRUE.

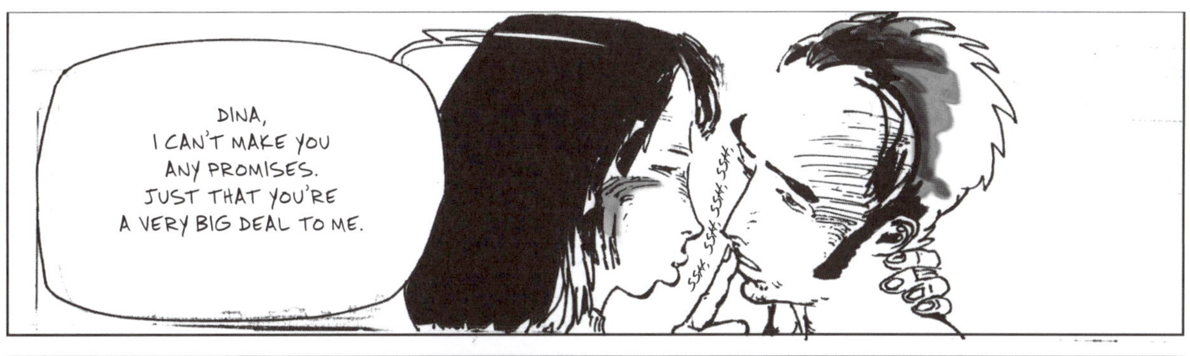

DINA,
I CAN'T MAKE YOU
ANY PROMISES.
JUST THAT YOU'RE
A VERY BIG DEAL TO ME.
SSH, SSH, SSH, SSH.

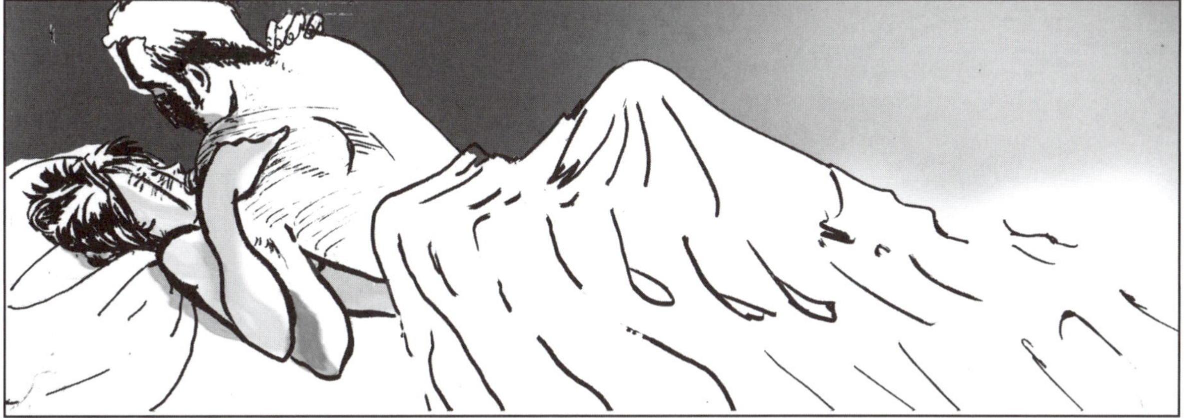

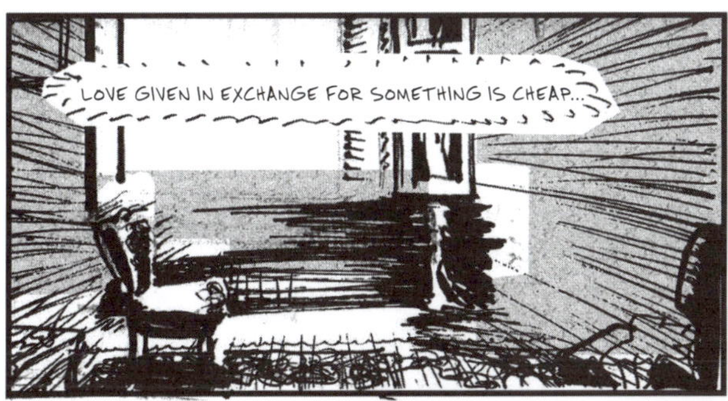

LOVE GIVEN IN EXCHANGE FOR SOMETHING IS CHEAP...

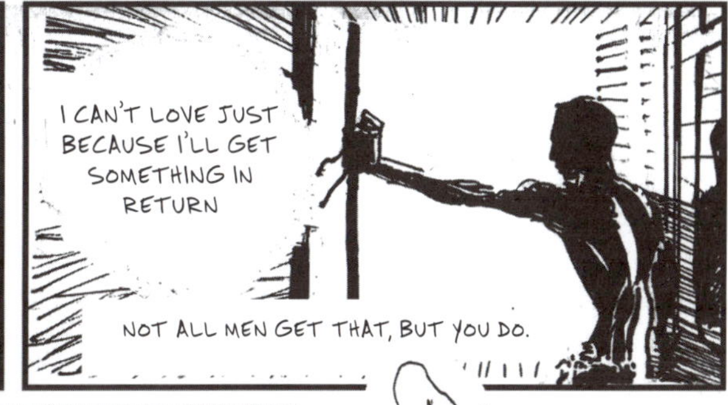

I CAN'T LOVE JUST
BECAUSE I'LL GET
SOMETHING IN
RETURN
NOT ALL MEN GET THAT, BUT YOU DO.

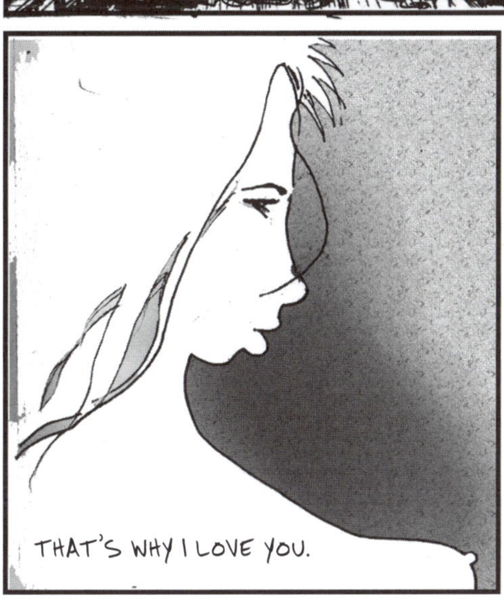

THAT'S WHY I LOVE YOU.

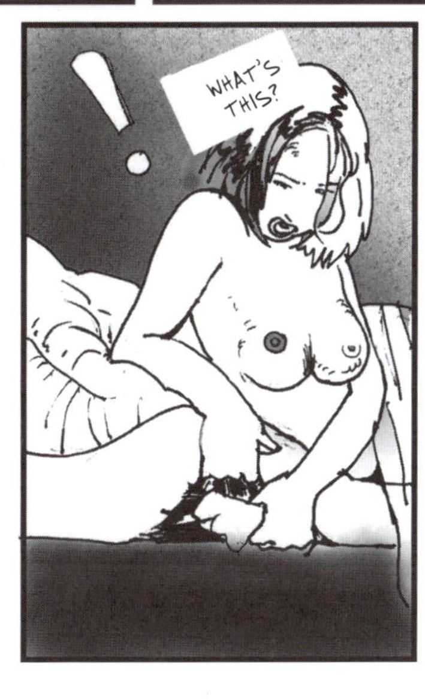

!
WHAT'S
THIS?

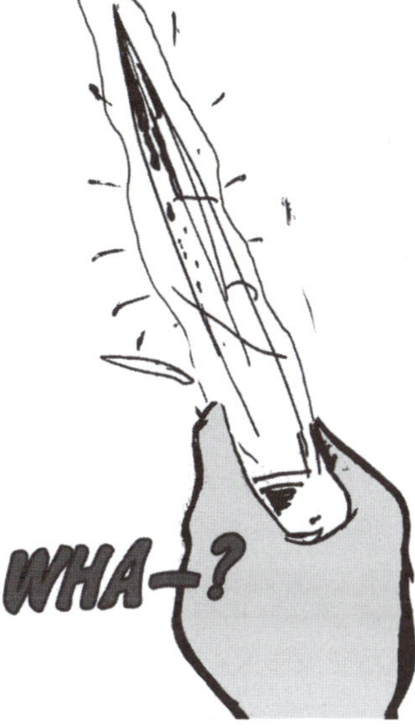

WHA—?

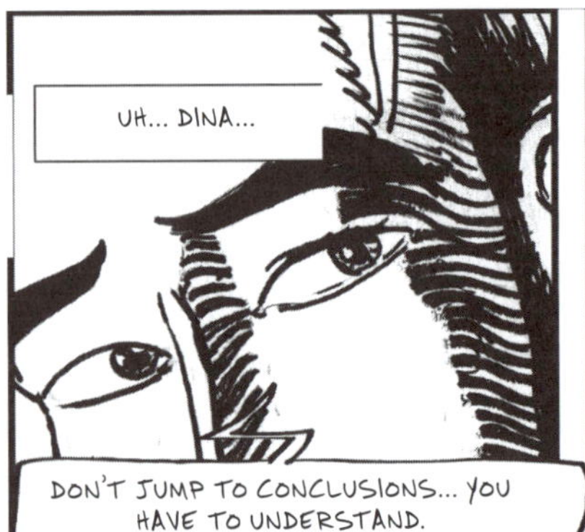

UH... DINA...
DON'T JUMP TO CONCLUSIONS... YOU HAVE TO UNDERSTAND.

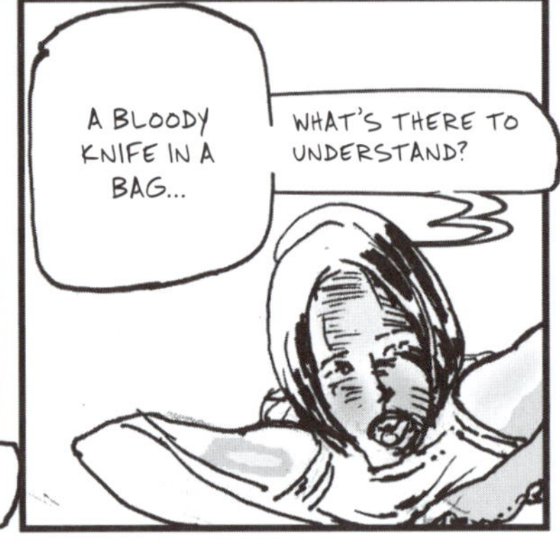

A BLOODY KNIFE IN A BAG...
WHAT'S THERE TO UNDERSTAND?

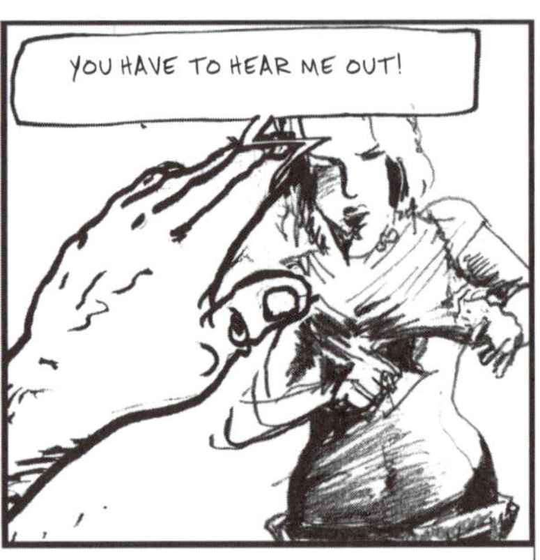

YOU HAVE TO HEAR ME OUT!

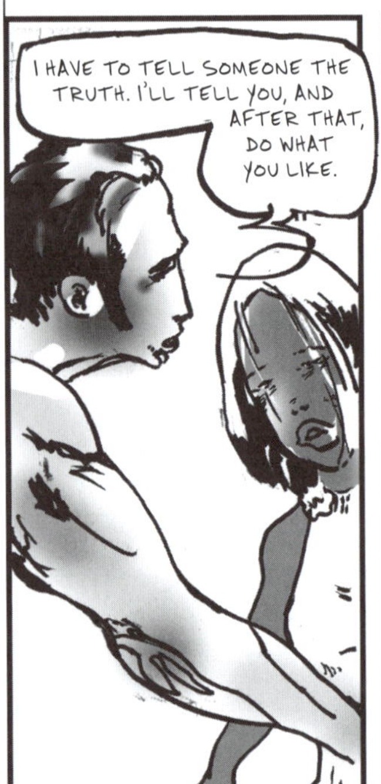

I HAVE TO TELL SOMEONE THE TRUTH. I'LL TELL YOU, AND AFTER THAT, DO WHAT YOU LIKE.

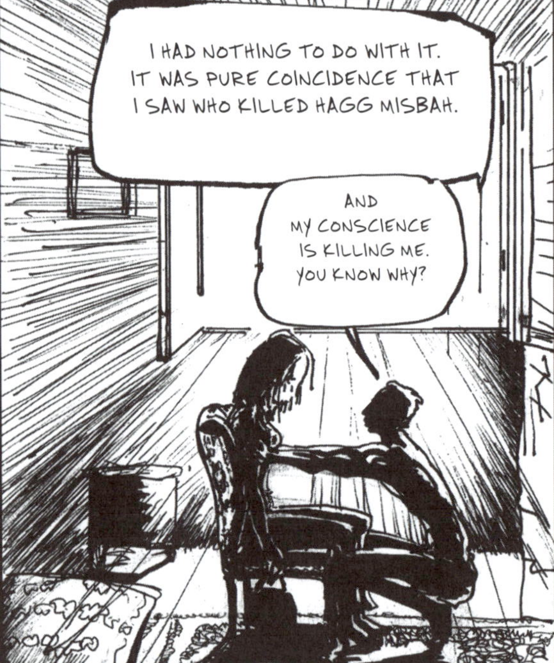

I HAD NOTHING TO DO WITH IT. IT WAS PURE COINCIDENCE THAT I SAW WHO KILLED HAGG MISBAH.
AND MY CONSCIENCE IS KILLING ME. YOU KNOW WHY?

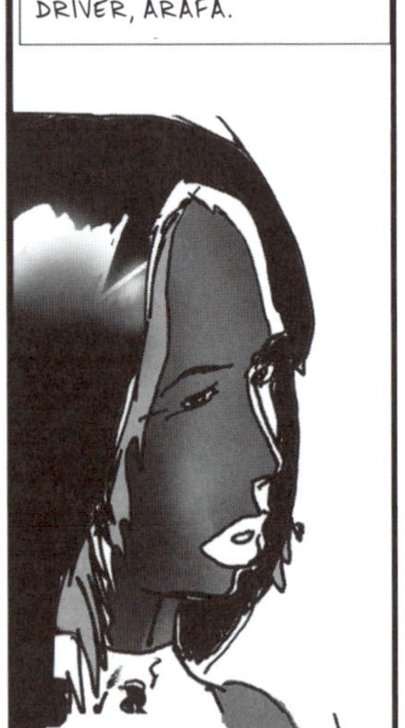

BECAUSE THE GUY YOU'VE ACCUSED IS INNOCENT... AND THE MAN WHO REALLY DID IT IS MISBAH'S DRIVER, ARAFA.

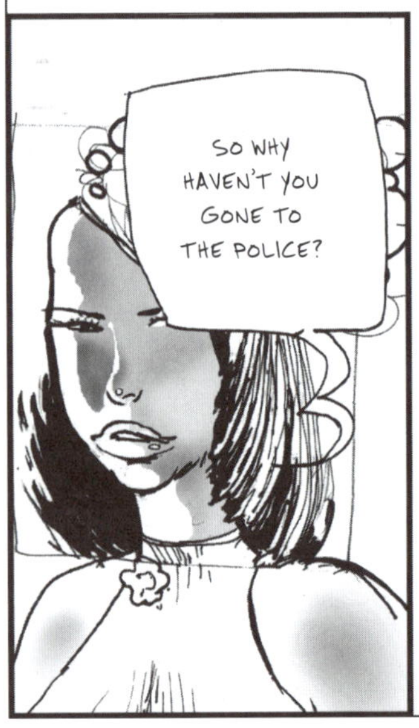

SO WHY HAVEN'T YOU GONE TO THE POLICE?

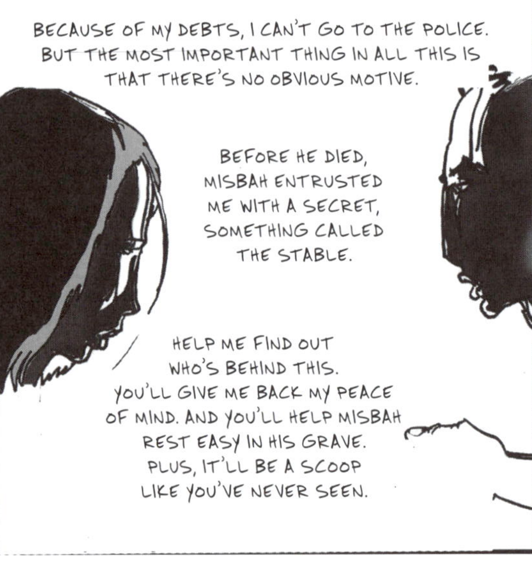

BECAUSE OF MY DEBTS, I CAN'T GO TO THE POLICE. BUT THE MOST IMPORTANT THING IN ALL THIS IS THAT THERE'S NO OBVIOUS MOTIVE.
BEFORE HE DIED, MISBAH ENTRUSTED ME WITH A SECRET, SOMETHING CALLED THE STABLE.
HELP ME FIND OUT WHO'S BEHIND THIS. YOU'LL GIVE ME BACK MY PEACE OF MIND. AND YOU'LL HELP MISBAH REST EASY IN HIS GRAVE. PLUS, IT'LL BE A SCOOP LIKE YOU'VE NEVER SEEN.

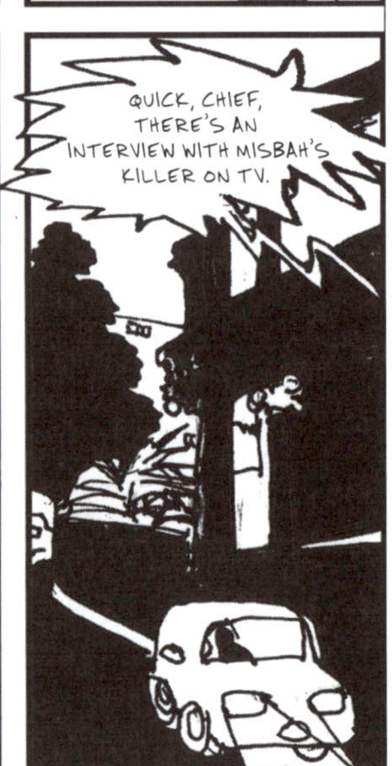

QUICK, CHIEF, THERE'S AN INTERVIEW WITH MISBAH'S KILLER ON TV.

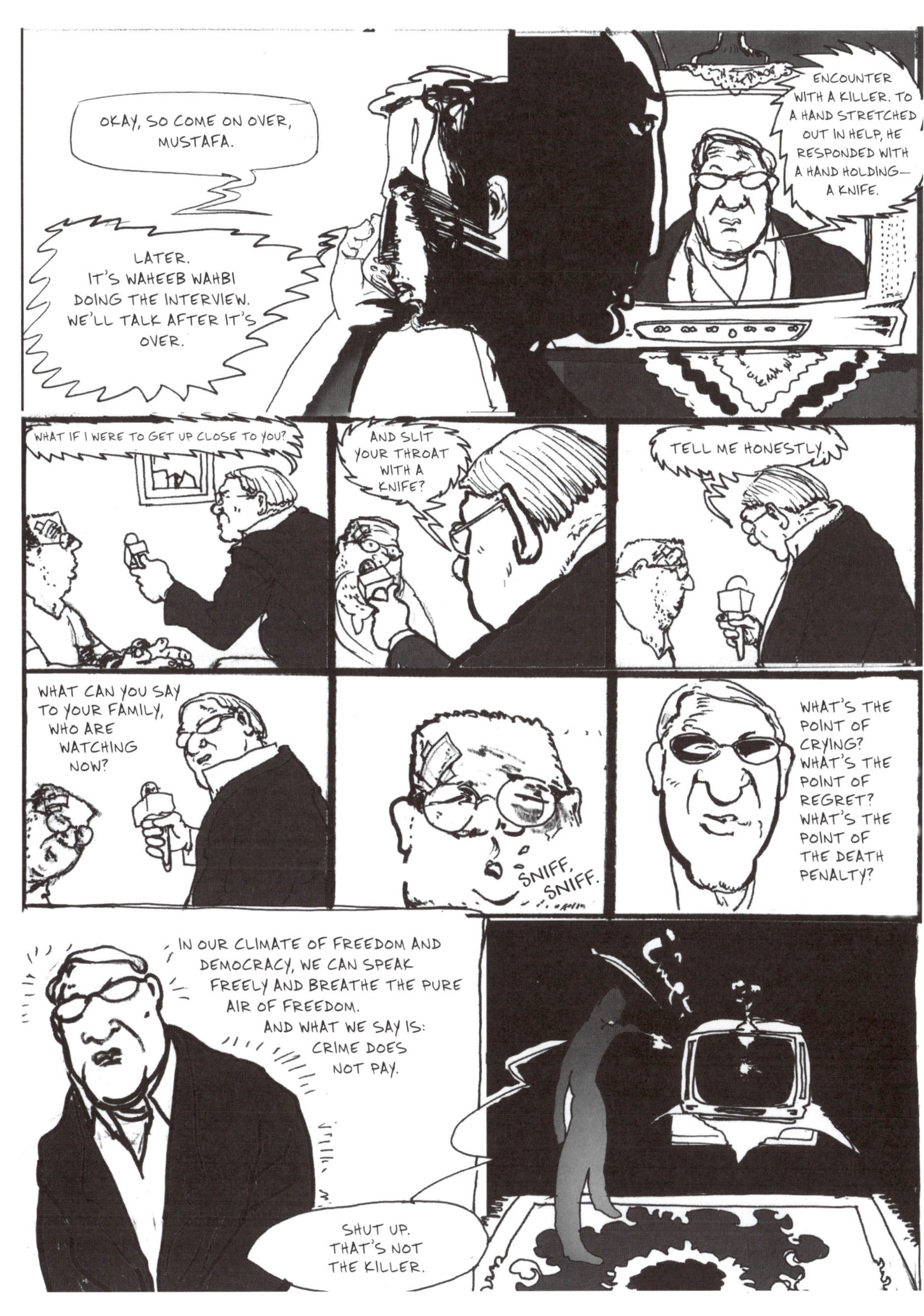

OKAY, SO COME ON OVER, MUSTAFA.
LATER. IT'S WAHEEB WAHBI DOING THE INTERVIEW. WE'LL TALK AFTER IT'S OVER.
ENCOUNTER WITH A KILLER. TO A HAND STRETCHED OUT IN HELP, HE RESPONDED WITH A HAND HOLDING— A KNIFE.
WHAT IF I WERE TO GET UP CLOSE TO YOU?
AND SLIT YOUR THROAT WITH A KNIFE?
TELL ME HONESTLY.
WHAT CAN YOU SAY TO YOUR FAMILY, WHO ARE WATCHING NOW?
SNIFF, SNIFF.
WHAT'S THE POINT OF CRYING? WHAT'S THE POINT OF REGRET? WHAT'S THE POINT OF THE DEATH PENALTY?
IN OUR CLIMATE OF FREEDOM AND DEMOCRACY, WE CAN SPEAK FREELY AND BREATHE THE PURE AIR OF FREEDOM. AND WHAT WE SAY IS: CRIME DOES NOT PAY.
SHUT UP. THAT'S NOT THE KILLER.

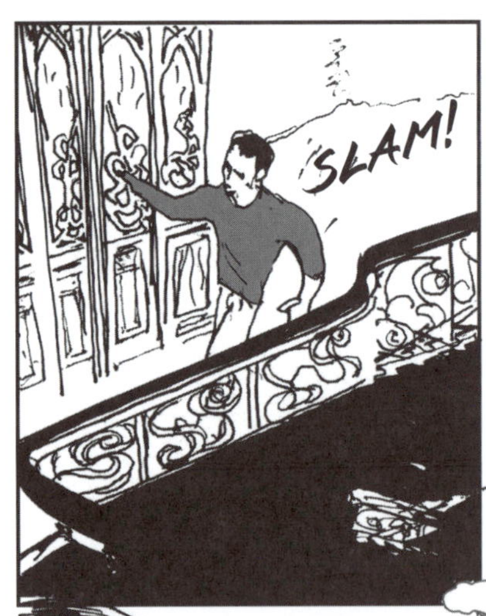

SLAM!

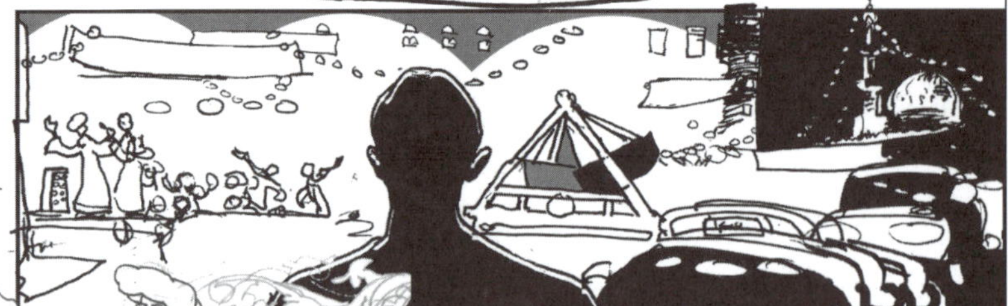

THEY NEVER SPEAK A WORD OF TRUTH. HOW IS ANYONE TO GET AWAY FROM THEM? THEY'RE EVEN IN YOUR OWN HOME.

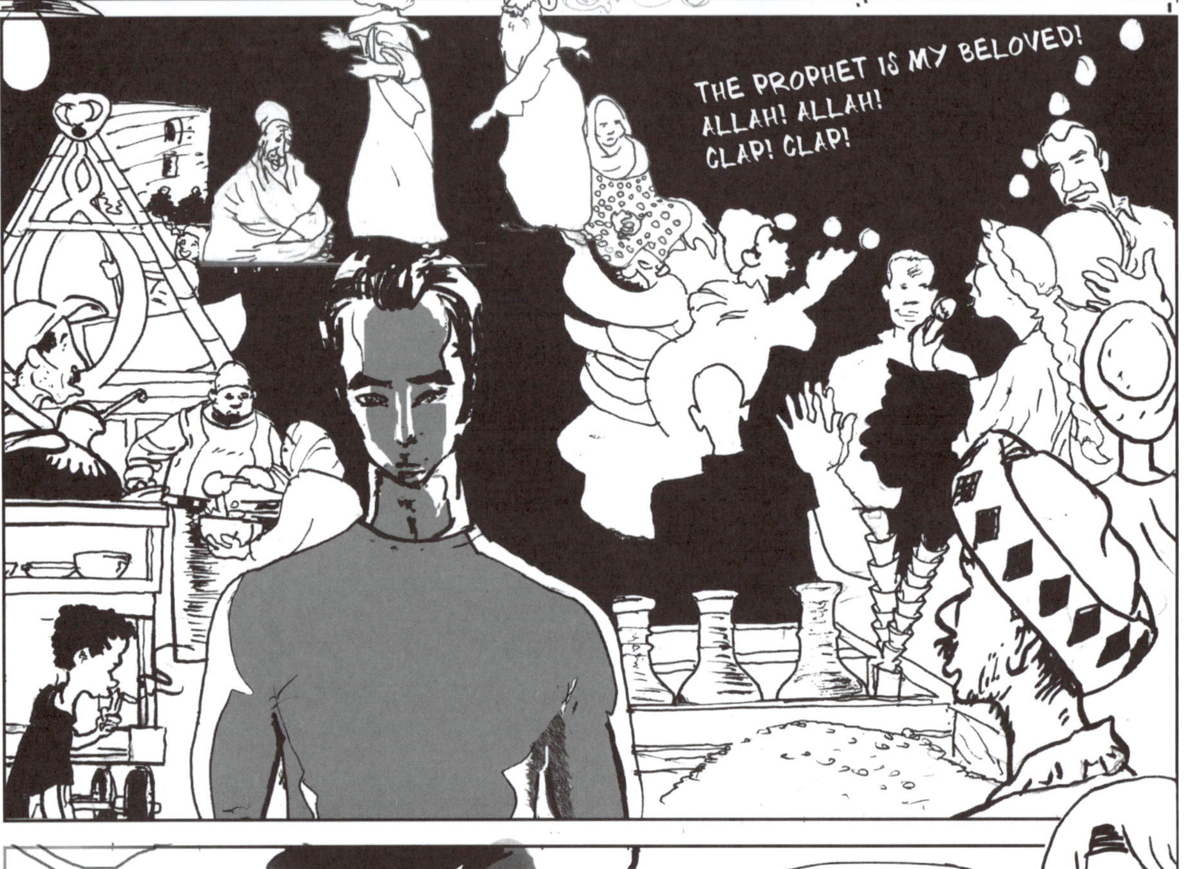

THE PROPHET IS MY BELOVED! ALLAH! ALLAH! CLAP! CLAP!

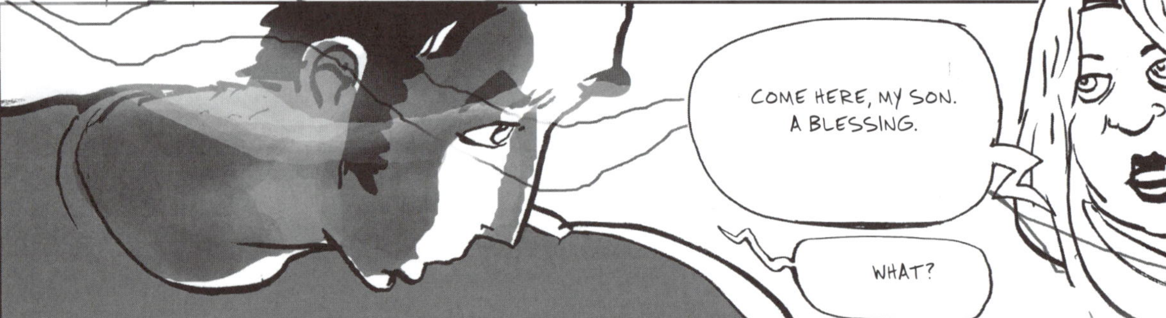

COME HERE, MY SON. A BLESSING.
WHAT?

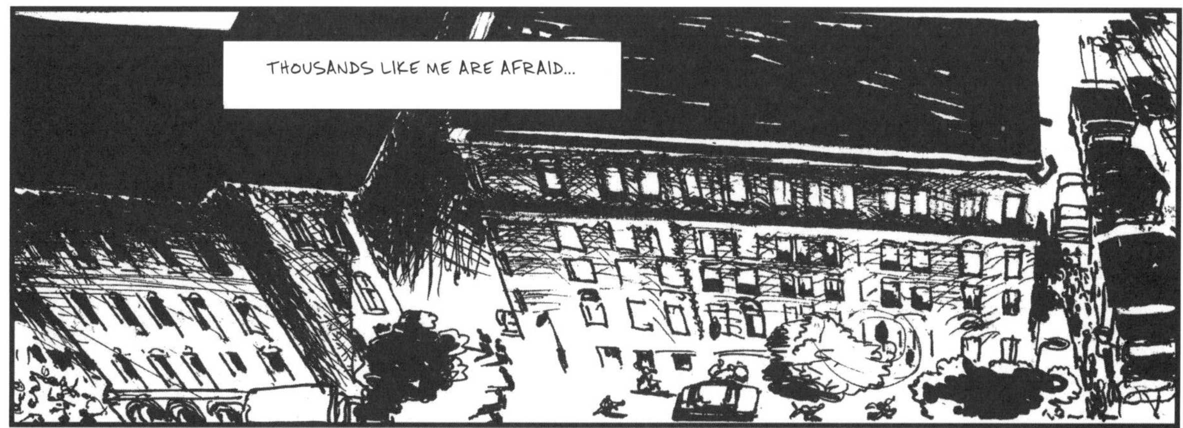

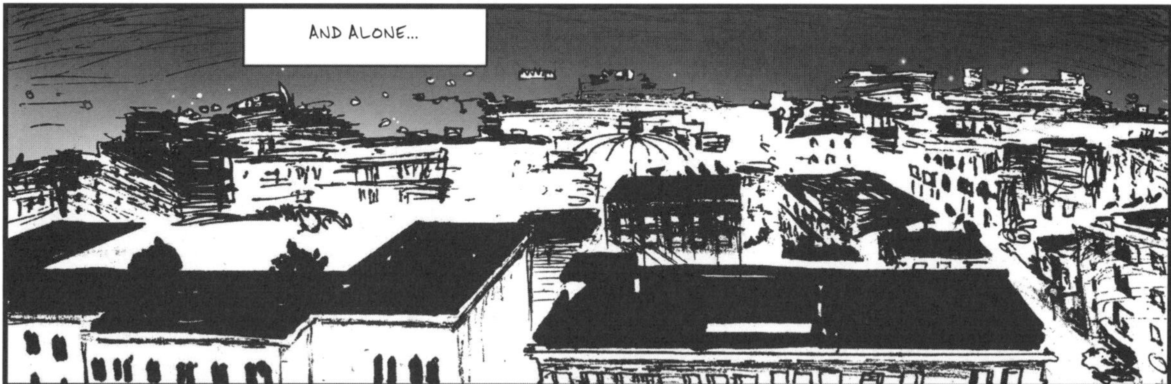

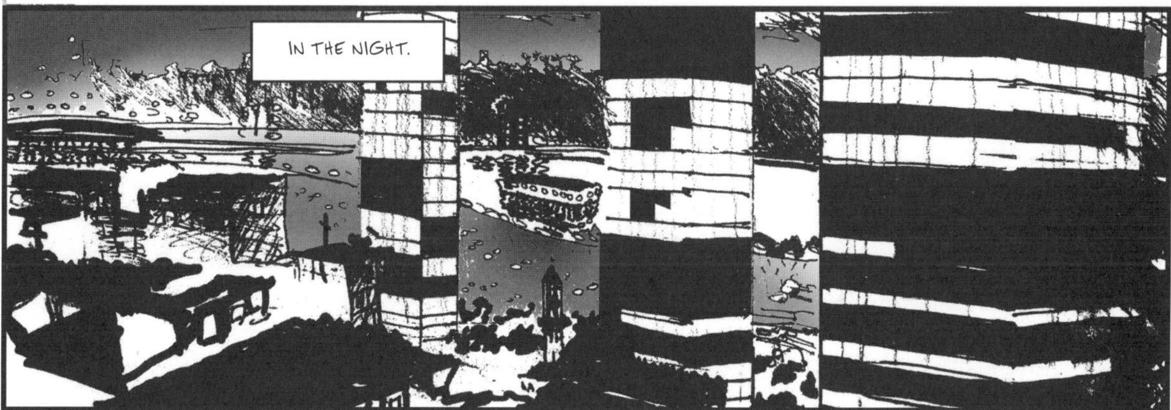

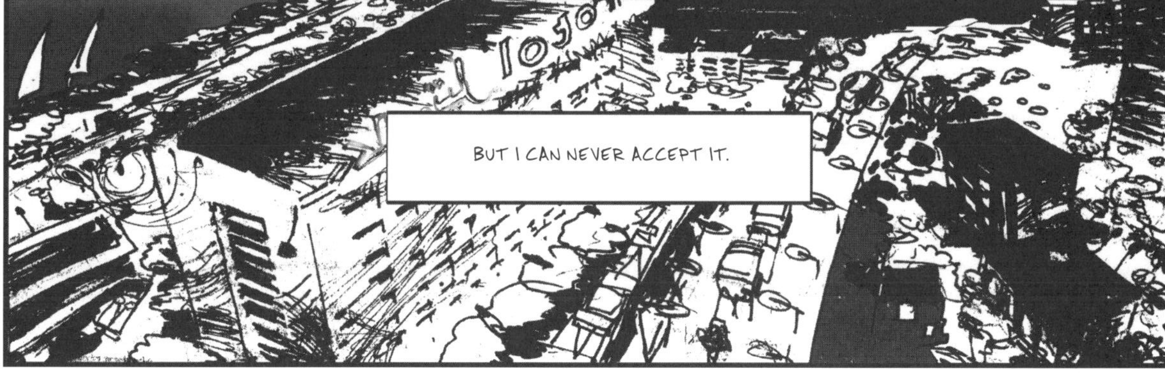

Excerpt of p. 50–56 from the book *Metro: A Story of Cairo* by Magdy El Shafee
Copyright © 2012 by Magdy El Shafee
Reprinted by permission of Henry Holt and Company, LLC.

Going Places
Image Policies, Artistic Practices, Urban Spaces

KERSTIN PINTHER

Cairo is actually a conglomerate of many different cities developing successively and in parallel; it can look back over many centuries at a very chequered history of different rulers, dynasties and occupiers.[1] Soon Cairo will have a population of seventeen million people, not only putting it alongside Lagos as one of Africa's megacities, but also making it the largest metropolis in the Arab world. As in many other postcolonial cities, over the last decades Cairo has seen a rapid construction of new spaces that are not only radically different from older ones, but usher in a change in the way they are perceived. Here, the new shopping malls [→ Fig. A] are a prime example; for instance, City Stars, with over 12,000 square metres of retail space – as are the exclusive parks and clubs, and the gated communities outside the city. This development has emerged hand in hand with the devaluation of the downtown area as a location primarily frequented by the poorer social classes. At the same time, the old town, which goes back to the Fatimid dynasty and the Mamluks, is experiencing restructuring and gentrification, with some neighbourhoods especially refurbished to attract tourists. In this context, sociologist Mona Abaza speaks of a Saudi Arabisation of society in the wake of several waves of emigration to the oil-producing countries which began under President Sadat's *infitah* 'open door' economic policy. In her view, since then the middle-class way of life has increasingly been influenced by the importing of a hard-currency lifestyle and fashion items. She also notes the widespread distinction between the 'chic malls', and the 'chic people' (*bi'a*) who go there and the *baladi,* the people from the rural village.[2] In a parallel development, the 1990s saw the state retreating from home construction, leaving it in the hands of private investors, often from the Gulf states.[3] For a number of years, a new city has been growing to the east of Cairo – New Cairo.[4] At the same time, estimates now suggest that soon sixty-five per cent of Cairo's residents will be living in informal settlements. Such settlements are by no means only housing the city's poor; the residents there are just as likely to be members of the middle classes – young married couples, students and public service employees.[5] More than five years ago, the force of the criticism of neoliberal reforms and an urban policy favouring the rich, as well as the desire for democratisation, led to massive protests which gained broad support across society. The joint slogan was *Kefaya* – Enough![6] Pictures of public demonstrations were splashed across the newspapers, something never seen before in modern Cairo where public space is strictly controlled under the emergency law currently in force.

For a long time, images of Cairo oscillated between orientalising depictions of the 'Islamic Cairo' as constructed in the 19th century – both externally and by a local elite and widely disseminated at World Fairs – and by postcards and travellers' reports,[7] and

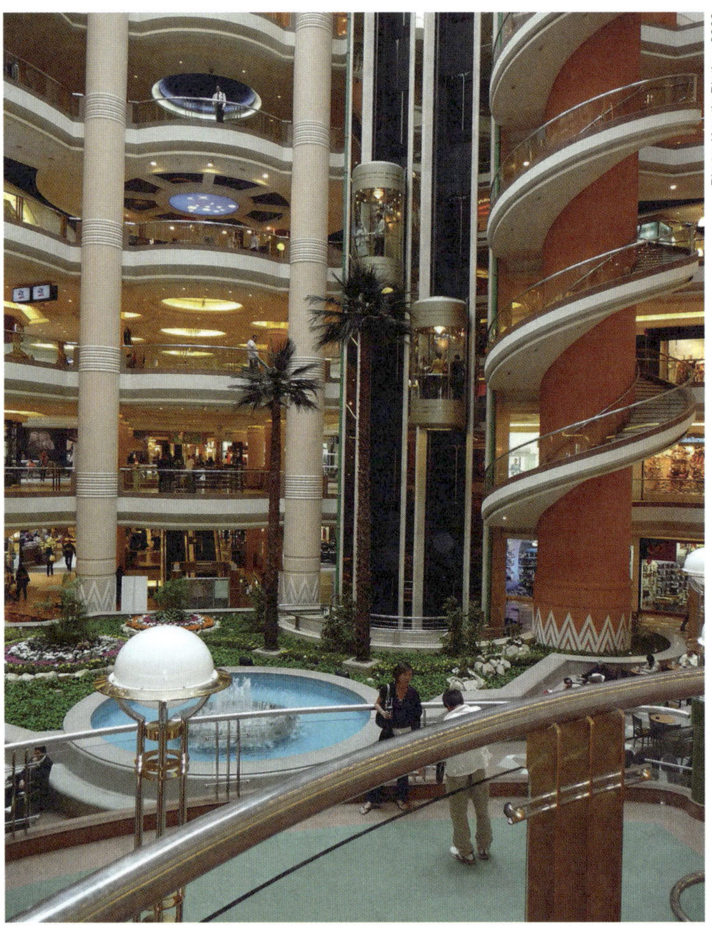

A   City Stars Shopping Mall in Heliopolis, Cairo

1   For a detailed description, see Janet Abu-Lughod 1971, *Cairo: 1001 Years of the City Victorious,* Princeton, and André Raymond 1993, *Le Caire,* Paris.

2   Mona Abaza 2006, Egyptianizing the American Dream: Nasr City's Shopping Malls, Public Order, and the Privatized Military, in: Diane Singerman, Paul Amar (eds), *Cairo Cosmopolitan. Politics, Culture, and Urban Space in the New Globalized Middle East,* Cairo, p. 193–220, p. 209 ff; some articles in this collection also trace these developments, as do some in the subsequent volume: Diane Singerman (ed.) 2009, *Cairo Contested. Governance, Urban Space, and Global Modernity,* Cairo.

3   Eric Denis 2008, Desert: From Ghost Towns to Forbidden Cities, in: Aglaia Konrad, Johan Lagae (eds), *Desert Cities,* Zurich, p. 117–125

4   See Iris Lenz (ed.) 2006, *Kairo. Bauen und Planen für Übermorgen,* Stuttgart.

5   On the informal settlements and their stigmatisation, see Asef Bayat, Eric Denis 2000, "Who is Afraid of Ashwaiyyat?" Urban Change and Politics in Egypt, *Environment & Urbanization* 12/2: 185–199.

6   See the edition of the literature journal *A Public Space* (Cairo 2010 after Kefaya), dedicated to this topic, retrieved on 23 April 2012 from http://www.apublicspace.org/focus/

7   See Nezar Alsayyad, Irene A. Bierman, Nasser Rabbat 2005, *Making Cairo Medieval,* Lanham.

8   Hala Elkoussy 2005, *Peripheral – The Art Scene in Cairo.* Lecture, given as part of the *Gleichzeitig in Afrika / Menwhile in Africa …* project curated by Christian Hanussek. online, retrieved on 23 April 2012 from: http://www.bpb.de/internationales/afrika/afrika/59164/ausstellung-gleichzeitig-in-afrika, retrieved on 23 April 2012.

9   My contribution is based on a four-week stay in Cairo. Here, I would like to thank the Goethe-Institut, which funded my

stereotypical images of Cairo as a metropolis of uncontrolled growth. Over the last ten years or more, though, a new generation of artists has become established in Cairo who are aware of, and oppose, that standardised visual culture. Aside from their critical stance towards the dominant policy on images, they share the objective of making public space a key point of reference for artistic work. For example, the art project *Going Places: A Project for Public Buses,* realised over several months in 2003–2004 at public places in Cairo, involved Iman Issa, Hassan Khan, Maha Maamoun and Bassim Magdy placing their photos on buses in the spaces usually reserved for advertising. "This project," wrote Hala Elkoussy, who as co-founder of the Contemporary Image Collective was also the initiator of the intervention, "is an entry point, an attempt to infiltrate Cairo's public space – a space monopolized by the combined institutional grip of both corporate and governmental powers. This infiltration was made possible by appropriating the tools of these authorities highlighting the irony that is a pertinent facet of urban life in this city: Access to the public realm can only be realized through privatization." [8]

Even if *Going Places,* more than many other artworks, relates directly to public space and a specific logic influenced by economic and political conditions, the question of a contemporary articulation of the megalopolis is omnipresent. In particular, those artists interested in art's political impact often both refer to the dynamics of public space *and,* at the same time, reflect local and global image policies. My article also addresses this interface of cultural policy, artistic practice and urban space.[9]

State Cultural Policy: Early Days and History

Unlike in the majority of African countries – such as Congo or Nigeria – the roots of modern art in Egypt do not go back to Western intervention and the *"protégé art"* which it so often generated.[10] In 1908, under Prince Yusuf Kamal, the first School of Fine Arts was founded. For religious reasons, the art it favoured was abstract, ornamental and non-figural. In 1927, as Cairo's College of Fine Arts, it was placed under a state ministry, laying the foundation for a system of arts promotion both organised *and* regulated by the state – a system that in the African context can only be compared, even today, with Senegal's cultural policy under Lépold Sédar Senghor. Consequently, art production was a matter of national importance and the artistic 'fads' and preferences largely reflected the political objectives of changing regimes. The declared aim of art education under the state-embedded system was, and still is, the promotion of "authentic art"[11], the training of art teachers and the "embellishment" of urban space.[12] The task of creating an art informed by ancient Egyptian forms and designs still remains a benchmark, and it

was especially prevalent in the first generation of artists in the 1930s and 1940s as is evident, for example, in works by Mahmoud Moukhtar [→ Fig. **B**] or Ragheb Ayyad. Liliane Karnouk has coined the term "neo-pharaonism" to describe this approach.[13] A second premise called for the depiction of pastoral scenes, where farmers and agricultural workers were displayed as a kind of 'noble, prototypical Egyptian'. Under the socialist rule of Gamal Abdel Nasser, there was a growing awareness of a national art, and collectives such as the Group of Art and Life sought to bridge the gap between an art movement perceived as elitist and the lives of ordinary people, and craft work.

Even today, Egypt's state cultural policy has considerable funding available and a complex structure for promoting the arts.[14] However, this support is almost exclusively designed for artists

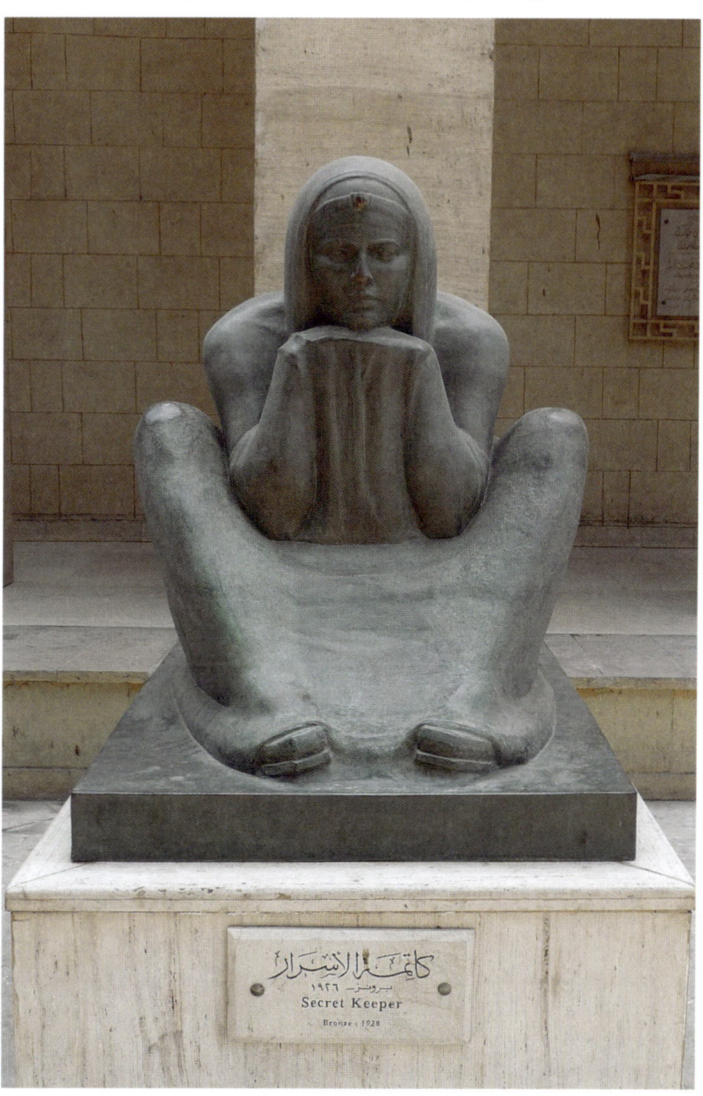

B Mahmoud Mukhtar, sculpture in front of the correspondent museum

research under its grant programme for curators. I would also personally like to thank Barbara Honrath and Friedrich Dahlhaus. In particular, I am grateful to Stefan Winkler, formerly from Goethe-Institut, Alexandria, for his valuable suggestions and advice. In Cairo, my research was assisted by Huda Lutfi, Lara Baladi, Lisa Lounis, Khaled Hafiz, Rana El Nemr and many other artists who agreed to discussions and interviews, and my thanks go to them too. For pictures of the works mentioned here, see the catalogue section on Cairo.

10 See Toma Muteba Luntumbue 2006, Verschränkte Aneignungen. Künstlerische Dialoge zwischen Afrika und dem kolonialen Europa, in: Marjorie Jongbloed (ed.), *Entangled. Annäherungen an zeitgenössische Künstler aus Afrika,* Bonn, pp. 22–61.

11 See Stefan Winkler 2010, Kulturelles Erbe – Authentizität – Tradition. Zur Genese des Ausstellungstitels *"Mustaqbal al-asala – Asala(t) al-mustaqbal"* (The Future of Authenticity – The Authenticity of the Future from contemporary Arab discourse), in: Chris Dercon, Léon Krempel, Avinoam Shalem (eds) Zukunft der *Tradition – The Future of Tradtion,* Munich, pp. 48–55

12 Jessica Winegar 2006, *Creative Reckonings. The Politics of Art and Culture in Contemporary Egypt,* Stanford, pp. 53, 57

13 Liliane Karnouk 2010, *Modern Egyptian Art 1910–2003,* Cairo

14 According to Mai Abu El Dahab, a curator from Cairo, only the Ministry of Defence is better funded than the Egyptian Ministry of Culture. See Gerhard Haupt and Pat Binder in an interview with Mai Abu El Dahab on the art scene and curators in Egypt (2005), retrieved on 23 April 2012 from http://universes-in-universe.org/eng/nafas/articles/2005/curators_in_egypt. For this reason, the current situation in Egypt can only be compared to the strategies of state art

whose subject matter, aesthetic and choice of media adhere to the official canon. This state dominance is evident in the Museum of Modern Egyptian Art, [→ Fig. C] opened in 1988, as well as in the Palace of Arts at the exclusive Opera House complex on Gezira Island in the River Nile. This policy also informs the Egyptian Pavilion at the Venice Biennial, first opened in the 1950s, the Cairo Biennial, founded in 1984, and the Salon of Youth.[15] In addition, aside from providing state financial support for art institutions and events, the Egyptian system of official curators and art experts – often also artists, such as Faruq Hosni, the incumbent Minister of Culture since 1987 – provides a direct means of influencing the development of artistic work, as well as exclusion and inclusion. Under such conditions, Cairo, its urban space or urban subjects, are not topics addressed at all, or only in a quasi (self)-orientalising way.[16] Here, the work of Muhammad Abla provides a rare exception, with the city and its residents seemingly very much present in his *mixed media images.* In the 1990s, together with others, he organised the first artistic and political intervention in Kom Ghorab, an informal settlement in the Coptic quarter of the city threatened by demolition.[17]

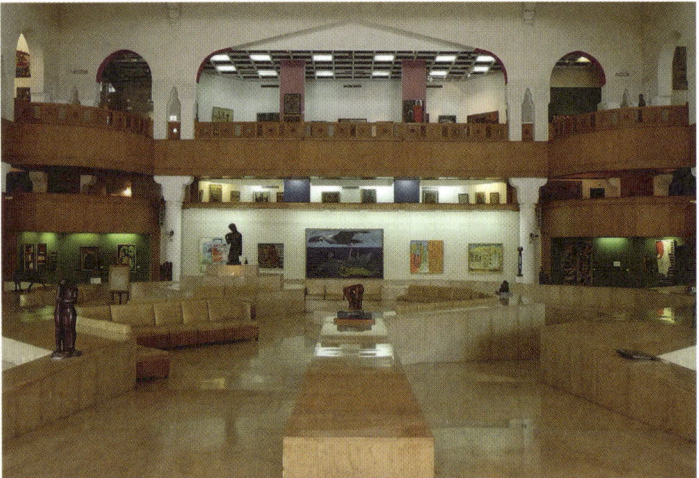

C   Museum of Egyptian Modern Art

Independent Scene(s): From the 1990s to date

Since the early 1990s, independent art scenes have become established in Cairo, as in many other African and Arab cities. In general, the protagonists are primarily young artists and cultural producers forming networks and establishing themselves outside state institutions. In Cairo, the Townhouse Gallery, founded in 1998 by Canadian William Wells, provided a first platform for this independent scene.[18] The gallery is located in a renovated townhouse in the heart of Antikhane, a popular neighbourhood in the downtown area. Even the choice of venue is significant with, for example, the participative project of Dutch artists Wouter

Osterholt and Elke Uitentuis indicating just how far the townhouse is geographically and conceptually 'worlds removed' from those state art spaces subject to government authority at the Opera House site. During their residence at the Townhouse Gallery, Wouter Osterholt and Elke Uitentuis developed their *Model Citizens* project. In this work, they focused their research on the microcosm of Antikhane. Like the entire inner-city area, this district, renowned for its repair workshops, is also threatened by massive transformation and gentrification schemes. According to the word on the street, the municipal authorities want to change Antikhane to make it more attractive to tourists. Through interviews and discussions, Osterholt and Uitentuis used a form of oral history to trace the memories of Antikhane's past. They simultaneously worked on a model of the Townhouse Gallery and the surrounding streets and buildings. However, *Model Citizens* did not stop at the model. Instead, to give a public face to the local population's hopes and aspirations, residents were invited to view the model and suggest alternative designs and structures. Working with a group of local assistants, the artists then integrated the proposed changes into the model. As Elke Uitentuis and Wouter Osterholt said: "It didn't remain a static representation of reality. Moreover people were asked again, not about their ideas of the past, but about their hopes for the future."[19]

Unusually for a gallery, though not uncommon in the African urban context, the Townhouse Gallery is managed as a non-governmental organisation and projects are largely funded with the assistance of the Ford Foundation, Pro-Helvetia and other international organisations. Over the last years, though, a network with other art institutions has become established, first and foremost in the Arab world, but also with connections to African cities – primarily to Douala, Bamako and Dakar.[20] In 2000, the founding of the Al Nitaq Festival, a cooperation between the three galleries of Karim Francis, Mashrabia and Townhouse, was another milestone in establishing an independent scene. The second festival in particular offered a kind of counter-programme to the state-run Cairo Biennial, and as such provoked a ban by the authorities. In contrast to state-funded art, which still remains mainly focused on the medium of painting, the Al Nitaq Festival exhibits predominantly multimedia installations and conceptual art. Since 2002, PhotoCairo has presented a variety of themes dedicated to photography as well as video art, both media similarly neglected in the official art discourse. PhotoCairo is organised by the Contemporary Image Collective (CIC). The CIC initiative, cofounded by artists Heba Farid and Hala Elkoussy, is devoted to promoting the visual image and fostering a contemporary visual language in Egypt and the region.[21] Their work reveals a particular interest in space and in documentary and research-based artistic work processes.

promotion under Lépold Sédar Senghor in Senegal in the 1960s. The parallels are not limited solely to the amount of funds available. In Dakar too, culture was instrumentalised by the political sphere and Négritude raised to a 'national aesthetic' connected with the task of creating works which were supposed to either take 'traditional' forms or Pan-African subjects as their point of reference. This approach produced its own independent art infrastructure with the founding of art colleges and the Musée Dynamique, now closed. See Elizabeth Harney 2004, *In Senghor's Shadow. Art, Politics, and the Avantgarde in Senegal, 1960–1995,* Durham.

15 See Omnia El Shakry 2010, Artistic Sovereignty in the Shadow of Post-Socialism: Egypt's 20th Annual Youth Salon, *e-flux.* Retrieved on 23 April 2012 from www.e-flux.com/journal/view/70.

16 See Nat Muller's quote of Hassan Khan on the "fetishising of antiquity". Nat Muller 2009, Wie sich vor dem Epischen schützen? Zeitgenössische mediale Artikulation der Megalopolis Kairo, *Springerin* Vol. 2, retrieved on 23 April 2012 from http://www.springerin.at/dyn/heft.php?id=59&pos= 1& textid=2195&lang=de.

17 See Fatimah Ismail Afifi 1997, The Kom Ghorab Project in Cairo, in: Katy Deepwell (ed.), *Art Criticism and Africa,* London, pp. 94–96. In retrospect, Mohammed Abla regarded the project less as an artistic intervention and more a political necessity. Interview with Mohammed Abla, 10 April 2008.

18 *Cairo Modern Art,* an exhibition shown in the Netherlands and organised in cooperation with William Wells sparked a debate on the right of representation between Wells and Farouk Hosni, the Minister of Culture. See Prita Meier 2003, Territorial Struggles: Cairo and Contemporary Art, *Nka. Journal of Contemporary African Art* 18: 34–39, p. 36.

19 More details at http://www.osterholtuitentuis.nl/model-citizens/model-citizens, retrieved on 23 April 2012.

Borg el Amal (Tower of Hope): Lara Baladi

Lara Baladi's *Borg el Amal (Tower of Hope)* project, created for the 2008 Cairo Biennial, can also be located within this context. Baladi, who was born in Beirut and grew up in Cairo, Paris and London, has lived in Cairo for over ten years. She trained as a photographer, and is also the co-founder of the Beirut-based Arab Image Foundation, which seeks to archive and analyse the history of images and media in the Middle East. At present, Baladi prefers to work in the medium of multimedia installations, combining painting, photography, video and audio, and often cooperates with local craft workers or (poster) painters. In earlier works, such as, for example, *Oum el Dounia* (Mother of the World, 2000) or *Sandouk el Dounia* (The World in a Box, 2001), she had already engaged specifically with Egypt and Cairo's visual culture. However, the ambivalent and contested relationship between art and politics in Cairo, official art support and autonomous artistic practice, becomes especially evident in her site-specific installation *Borg el Amal (Tower of Hope).*

This work, which Baladi herself has described as an "ephemeral construction", comprises a three-storey unfinished tower of red brick set in a concrete skeleton. The tower has no roof, but has windows offering partial views, and a series of disrupted staircases, some ending abruptly, connecting the different storeys. Inside there are galleries, a suggestion of a mosque rising into the sky, with symbols and writing in white paint on the walls. Taking a similar approach to her cooperation with poster artists on *Oum el Dounia,* Lara Baladi hired local workers from the informal building sector to construct the tower. The installation itself and *Hope,* her subsequent book project, were based on extensive research in the "Red City" on Cairo's periphery. In over 600 photos, she documents the architecture of innumerable informal settlements which house more than five million people, often without running water and electricity.

The emergence of informal city districts in old Cairo goes back to the 1920s and settlements on cemeteries. From the mid-1950s, when Nasser accelerated industrialisation, a wave of young men arrived in Cairo from the countryside. They often initially found a home in the crowded, abandoned Khedive palaces or rented a cheap place somewhere on the edge of the city. From the 1960s, it became common to build in the periphery, often illegally on former agricultural land. Today, those informal, fiercely 'contested' and debated settlements nearly form a complete ring around the city. They have diverse histories of development, and correspondingly diverse infrastructures and social organisations. With the (partial) absence of state services, many social institutions have been established by self-organisation, or through neighbourhood or religious networks. Although in Cairo, as Lara Baladi emphasises, nearly everyone has family members or friends living in the informal settlements, these settlements are spoken of in disapproving terms – an attitude that is also intensified by local media.[22]

In a literal and figurative sense, Lara Baladi's *Borg el Amal (Tower of Hope)* is not just a work designed for a particular event (the art biennial), but a site-specific installation whose significance extends beyond the art context. After all, her ephemeral construction – evoking, on one hand, the temporary character of her work and, on the other, the precarious lifestyles of those who build such red-brick and concrete frame structures – was located in the heart of the exclusive Opera House complex, guarded by the military, in front of the Palace of Arts where the biennial exhibition was held. Her installation included a musical work entitled *Donkey Symphony,* played over loudspeakers in the interior of the tower, evoking further points of reference, especially when related to the biennial's general theme of 'The Other'. The music resonated with the image stamped into a number of bricks of a donkey, the animal of the poor, pulling a cart. In a quite concrete material way, Lara Baladi brought the urban periphery into the centre of the city – and so simultaneously addressed a topic that had previously remained invisible in official art. One could claim, together with Mona Abaza, that Lara Baladi confronted and infiltrated the city's 'chic places' with the 'repressed' and marginalised: here, the periphery moved into the centre.

The Olympic Garden: Rana El Nemr

The processes involved in 'place making' are also central in the artistic practice of Rana El Nemr. Born in Germany in the early 1970s, Rana El Nemr studied at the American University in Cairo and is especially interested in the appropriation of architecture, often designing series as long-term studies. Together with Randa Shaath, who became known in particular for her documentation *Under the Same Sky, Rooftops in Cairo* (2002–2003), Rana El Nemr is one of the few photographers whose Cairo images transcend romanticised portrayals of the Orient or stereotypical visions of a megacity.

In fact, her oeuvre reveals a continuing preoccupation with Cairo – a preoccupation fuelled by knowledge of the city's methods of (self)organisation, and its residents' urban strategies and tactics. Her series *Metro* (2003) is an example of this work. [→ Fig. **D**] The first underground on the African continent went into operation in Cairo in 1987, an event that the local press proudly applauded, comparing the technical achievement of constructing the subway to the building of the pyramids. The subway was linked to high hopes of mobility and progress for the 'broad masses'. Today, as her images document, you find a subway system in a state of 'decay' not only evident in the stations themselves, but also in the hopelessness of a population disap-

---

20 Connections exist on the one hand via biennials that are held in Dakar (Dak'art) and Bamako (*Rencontres de la photographie africaine de Bamako*), and on the other through independent art spaces such as Doualart in Douala, Cameroon, where, for example, Khaled Hafez, an artist from Cairo, was artist in residence.

21 Both of these artists studied at art colleges or universities in Europe, which in a certain sense is typical of the protagonists in the independent scene. Similarly to the situation in Lagos – see the interview with Bisi Silva in this catalogue – 'returnees' and cosmopolitans played a decisive role in constituting an independent scene. The American University in Cairo (AUC) is considered to be an equally important source of training beyond the state institutions. On the Contemporary Image Collective, see www.ciccairo.com

22 See the contributions by Hany Darwish and Viola Shafik in this catalogue. The discussion with Lara Baladi took place on 16 April 2008 in Cairo.

pointed in the material aspirations that this development inspired.

In her *Balcony Series* (2003), she documented the practice of individual, often improvised, appropriation of architecture by residents of the informal districts. As a virtually semi-public area, the balconies are given particular designs – with geometrical or floral patterns, or sometimes with stucco elements, or optical illusions and playful images. Yet they always evidence the attempt of the people living there to escape homogenisation and monotony, and assert their individuality. In *Telekinesis,* Rana El Nemr used the fanfolds with the balcony photographs to create an individual architectural structure – transcending normative plans and specifications.

In *The Olympic Garden* (2008), her most recent installation, she follows events when the authorities built a wall separating the Egyptian Olympic Centre from the neighbouring informal quarter of New Maadi. In her triptych-like installation, Rana El Nemr uses photography, newspaper reports and a soundtrack of discussions between local residents and members of the ministry to document how the location has changed. Designed as a long-term project, *The Olympic Garden* illustrates the ambivalent relations between the ideas of the authorities and the way local residents use public space.

We're By The Sea Now: Hala Elkoussy

Hala Elkoussy, born in the mid-1970s in Cairo, completed an MA in Image and Communication in 2002 at Goldsmiths College in London. On returning to Cairo, she became a lecturer on photography at the American University. After two years as artist in residence at the Rijksakademie Van Beeldende Kunsten, she now lives mainly in Amsterdam, although her artistic practice has retained its strong ties to Cairo.

After *In a Furnished Flat in Cairo* and other works exploring the balance of the borders between private and public space, her installation *On Refrains, Sets and a Backdrop* (2006) focuses explicitly on Cairo's inhabitants. Also part of this installation, and similarly to the kaleidoscope of narratives, characters and scenes in *Peripheral* (2005), her video *We're By The Sea Now* is composed of a disparate flow of (fictive) narrative, anecdotes, and urban legends divided into thirteen chapters. These accounts are not suited to any kind of linear meta-narrative: As Hala Elkoussy notes[23]: "In the chapter entitled 'Well done, Bravo!', a young man sits on top of a typical Cairene roof littered with large satellite dishes. A modest bright blue sheet of paper partially blocks the background. He wears a T-shirt bearing in red the word 'BRAVO' and holds a yellow helium-filled balloon. His accoutrements stand in sharp contrast with his almost monochrome surroundings. He candidly addresses the camera and speaks of the difficulties he encounters 'down there' that push him to regularly seek refuge on the roof. The simplified world he has created for himself stands for any place he can possibly imagine. In his reverie, he travels to America, then a hotel lobby in Paris, to Italy and Pakistan … At a certain moment, he reports pointing to the blue sheet of paper: 'We're by the sea now!', his excited voice not managing to quite drown the noises of the bustling city in the background."

The title of her work, *On Refrains, Sets and a Backdrop* references the components of her installation that evoke memories of a theatre or cinema auditorium, an association further intensified by the heavy black curtains on either side of the rows of chairs. A kind of photo-wallpaper with an image of densely crowded developments with high-rises, so characteristic of Cairo, provides a backdrop on which the fragmentary narratives, mixing fact and fiction, unfold. Here Cairo is presented as a socially produced space and interpreted in Michel de Certeau's sense of juxtaposing the pedestrian's point of view located on street level with the omnipotent panoramic perspective of the god-like voyeur. The pedestrian's activity points to a different concept of

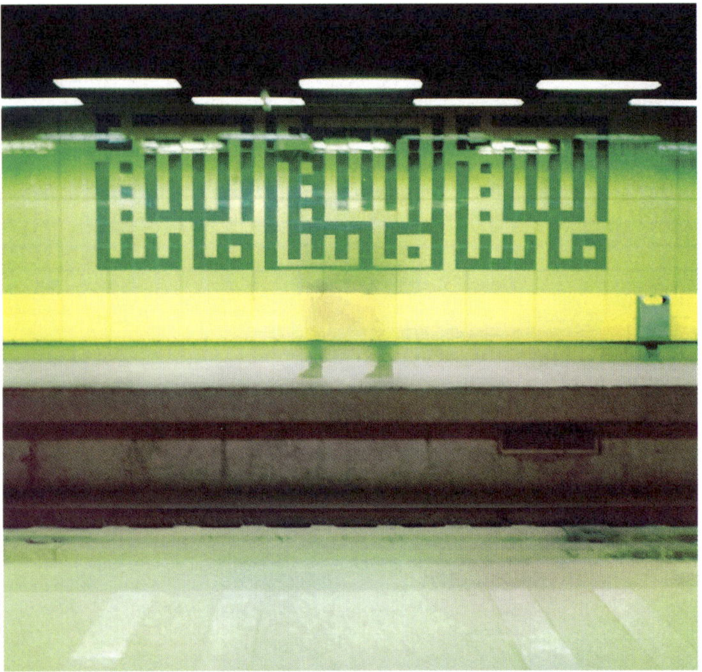

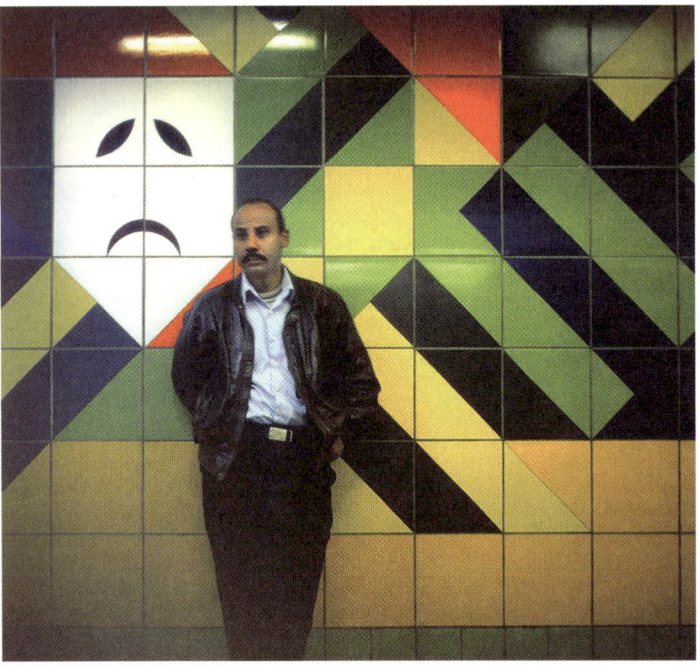

23 See Hala Elkoussy in an accompanying text on her work, retrieved on 23 April 2012 from http://halaelkoussy.com/on-refrains-sets-and-a-backdrop-2006.

24 Michel de Certeau 1984, *The Practice of Everyday Life*, transl. by Steven F. Rendall, University of California, p. 93

25 At present, there are several groups and scenes in Cairo working in a loose cooperation or parallel to each other. These are supplemented by such new initiatives as the exhibition space Darb 1718, founded by the artist Moataz Nasr, in the Coptic quarter. In addition, there is movement in the official cultural police, evident in the appointments of Bassam El-Baroni, Hassan Khan and Wael Shawky – artists and critics who are not known for their proximity to state policy – as jury members of the Salon of Youth.

D **METRO 22/23**, RANA EL NEMR, 2003

spatiality, namely an "anthropological, poetic and mythic experience of space" – an experience that corresponds to that of normal city users.[24]

Tales Around the Pavement:
Artistic Interventions

Together with many other artists, Lara Baladi, Rana El Nemr and Hala Elkoussy belong to independent scenes. These, though, are not organised into any institutionalised grouping.[25] Instead, cultural producers and artists are unified, often through their generational concerns, by a shared desire to overcome the constraints of the national state and its accompanying aesthetic and artistic prescriptions and practices, and create alternative spaces for art. This context is informed both by a critique of the hegemonic claim of an art world still dominated by the 'West' attempting to define what is 'African' or 'Arab' art, and the objective of steadily opening 'standard' art events, regarded as elitist and exclusive, to public space and fostering the greater inclusion of and appeal to a local urban audience. Sherif El Azma's *Psychogeography,*[26] video films such as Doa Aly's *Chinese Sweet Chinese Pretty* (2006) portraying Cairo as a destination of transnational migration, Maha Maamoun's *Domestic Tourism II,* which investigates the relation between the Pyramids in Egyptian films and their particular political meaning, or Ayman Ramadan's sculptures with their material drawn directly from the urban environment, are other examples of multimedia installations directly referencing Cairo.

In addition, over the last years Cairo has become home to a rapidly growing scene of comic, graffiti and graphic artists. The authors of comic books, which are often dubbed the 'ninth art', can locate themselves in a tradition of (political) cartoons going back to the 1920s. Graphic designers not only find their sources of inspiration in calligraphies in general and Arabic script in particular, which is considered extremely open for typographic elements, but also in Cairo's visual landscape with its flood of images, Arabic and Western scripts, billboards, (hand-painted) posters, pictograms and graffiti – to say nothing of the images in global circulation.[27] Some graffiti and comic producers, including Ganzeer, Kareem Lotfy or Marwan Fayed, have been directly involved in art projects in public space. In their efforts to create autonomous spheres of action and networks beyond state regulation, their temporary interventions can be located in the context of critical reflection on Cairo's new spaces, which are state controlled and influenced by a neo-liberal policy.

For *Tales Around the Pavement* (2008), seven artists produced context-specific works and ephemeral interventions in the inner-city landscapes of downtown Cairo. The interventions all started from the adoption of improvised tactics and appropriation strategies practised every day in public space by the city's residents themselves. Marwan Fayed, an architect and member of the academic staff at the German University of Cairo, observed the habits and practices of Cairo's residents, taking these as the basis for his solutions for street furniture. In *Paddling the City: Authorization for an Urban Complex* he created new kinds of urban seats from such used materials as drink crates and car tyres. In her interactive project *How to Make your Body Double Overnight,* Malak Helmy transformed a deserted kiosk into a wish-fulfilment machine. Completely covered with golden paper and decorated with a velvet curtain, the kiosk attracted the attention of passers-by and appealed to them to publicly announce their wishes. In the course of the project, the artist discovered that not only was the former kiosk shopkeeper accused of erecting the structure illegally, but that the police also had an eye on her. Although she had persuaded the janitor and members of the nearby mosque to support her project, she was summoned to the police station for questioning.[28] Her intervention revealed yet again the state's restrictive control of public space. Together with the works of other Cairo artists and cultural producers, her works also represent a new generation of artists not prepared to be co-opted by the ideological prescriptions of official cultural policy and, for this reason, producing other images of the megacity themselves.

Translation from German by Andrew Boreham

26 Sherif El Azma, born in the mid-1970s in Manchester, is today living as an experimental filmmaker and media artist in Cairo. In a direct reference to the situationists' derivative, aimless and unoriented urban exploration, he takes experimental walks through Cairo. In a discussion, he described his approach: "If you had a psychogeographical society in Cairo, how would it function? Do you have the authority to survey the city? In a way, this is tied to the state security and paranoia of the 1960s, and the impossibility of going around collecting traces and not getting caught. If you have a psychogeographical society in Cairo, they will come and find you, because what are you looking for? Years ago, New Cairo, which are now wealthy suburbs, were no-go zones. They were military zones, paranoiac zones, and you could not enter them. The military is less than it was since 1973. With the notion of psychogeography, I use it as an excuse to look at how institutions are built, how institutions network, and how people become institutions. It is more about systems, really. It's fun to play with the idea of psychogeography, because it's a form of playing with the city more generally." See Kaelen Wilson-Goldie 2003, Sherif El Azma, *Bidoun. Art and Culture from the Middle East 17*. Retrieved on 23 April 2012 from http://www.bidoun.org/magazine/17-flowers/sherif-el-azma-by-by-kaelen-wilson-goldie/
27 See Ben Wittner, Sascha Thoma 2009, *Arabesque. Graphic Design from the Arab World and Persia*, Berlin.
28 See Contemporary Image Collective 2007, *Tales Around the Pavement,* Cairo

Model Citizens

WOUTER OSTERHOLT AND ELKE UITENTUIS

Since 2005, Dutch art duo Wouter Osterholt and Elke Uitentuis have been developing site-specific projects in public space. Their work focuses on the tensions between regulations, on the one hand, and improvisations, on the other, which become evident in conflicts over public space. In *Model Citizens* (2008), a project realised in cooperation with artists at Cairo's Townhouse Gallery, they investigated the urban microcosm of Antikhane, a popular downtown district. Over the past years, life in the district has radically changed in the wake of such urban planning measures as a forced relocation of businesses and other amenities. The artists' work concentrated on creating an "alternative vision for the future of the quarter which includes changes suggested by the residents themselves."

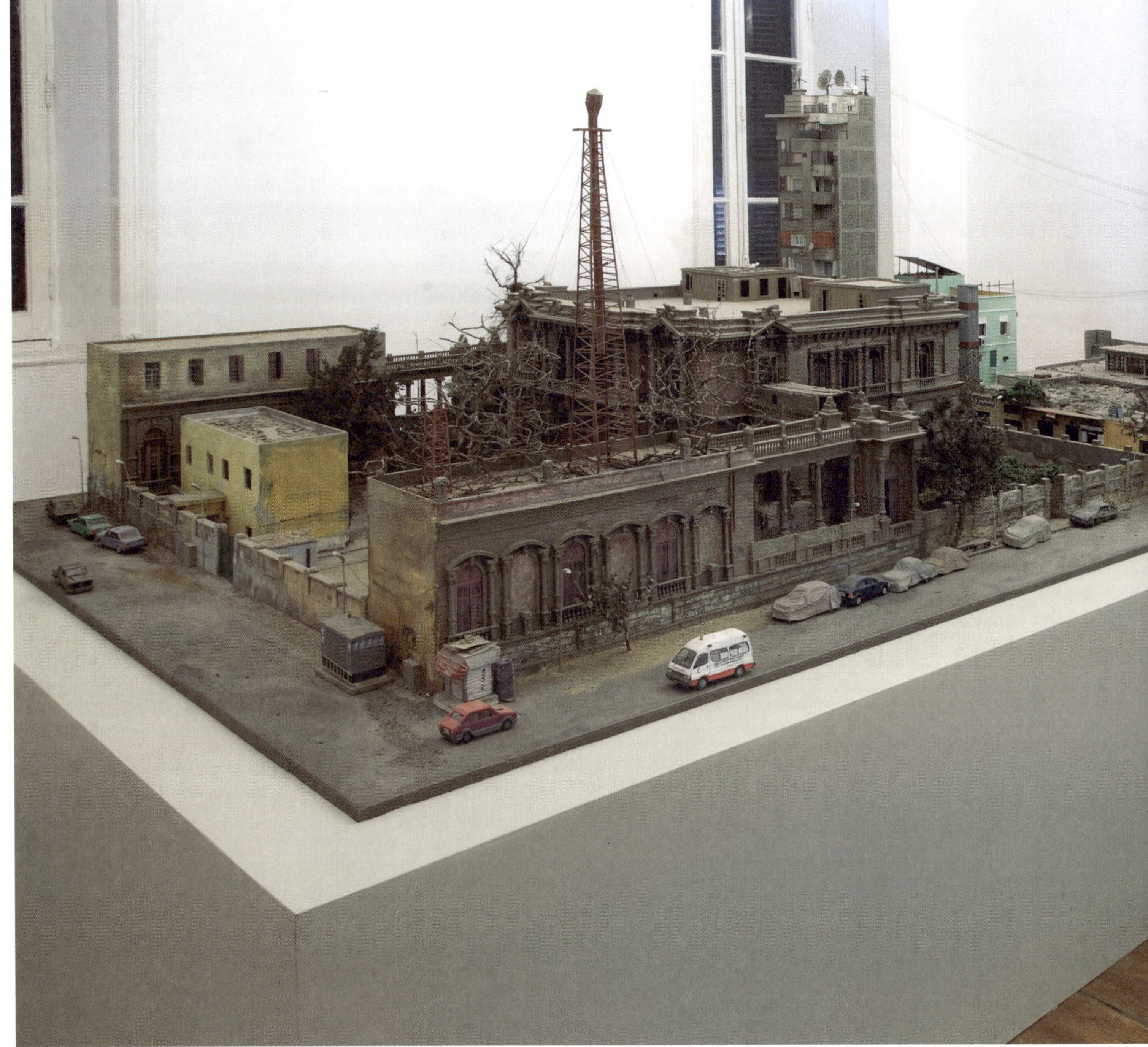

View of the model

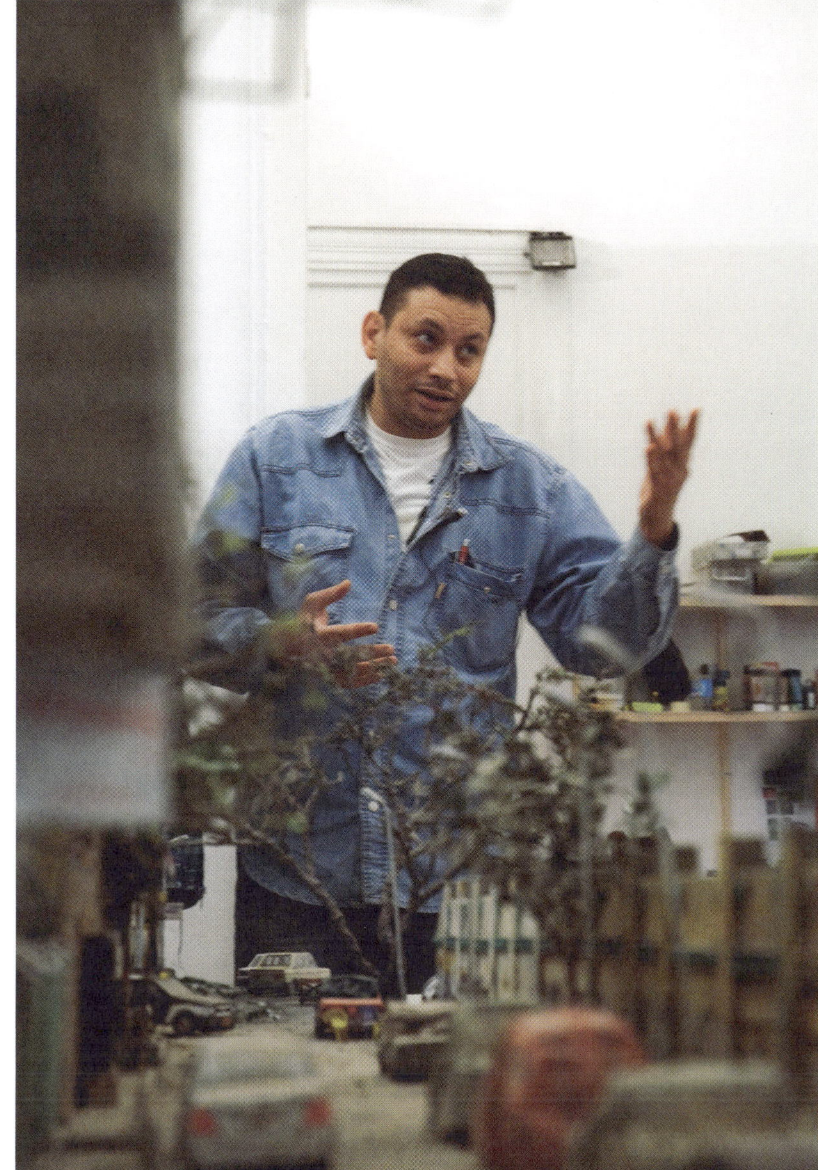

Interview with a workshop participant

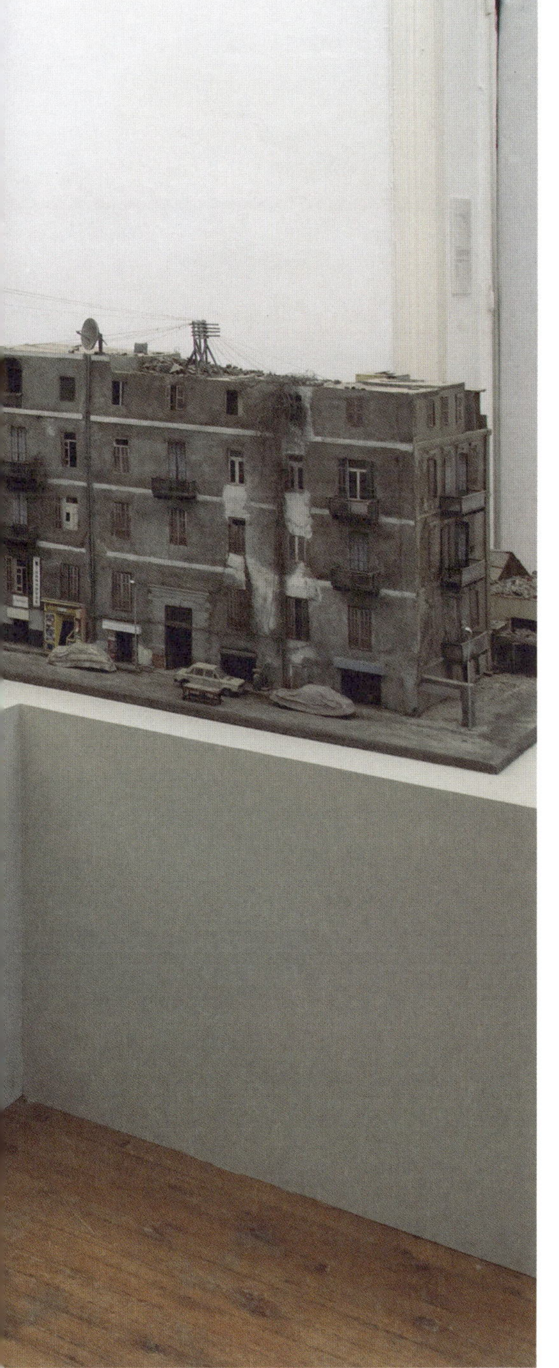

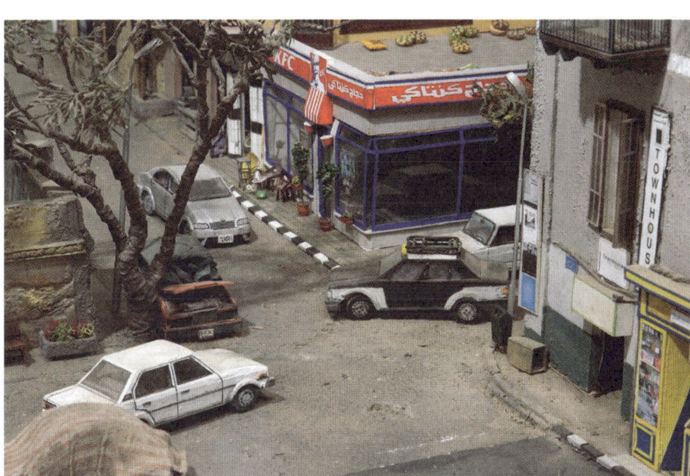

Close-up of the model after the workshop

The *Model Citizens* project explored the urban structure of the Antikhane district in downtown Cairo. An accurate 1:35 model of the district formed a central element in the project, with the miniature landscape serving as a means of encouraging debate. By engaging with the model, members of the community reflected on their everyday environment and considered the changes they would like to see. The artists asked the Antikhane residents about how they saw the quarter's future, and then worked these suggestions into the model.

The Olympic Garden

RANA EL NEMR

Rana El Nemr, co-founder of the Contemporary Image Collective (CIC) in Cairo, mainly works with conceptual photography. She focuses on the city's material nature and the spatial effects generated by changing societal structures. In an experimental approach, she also critiques the significance of the images created. In her long-term project *The Olympic Garden* (2008–2010), Rana El Nemr observed the processes and forms involved in state institutions taking over architecture and public space, and how these were then reappropriated by local residents.

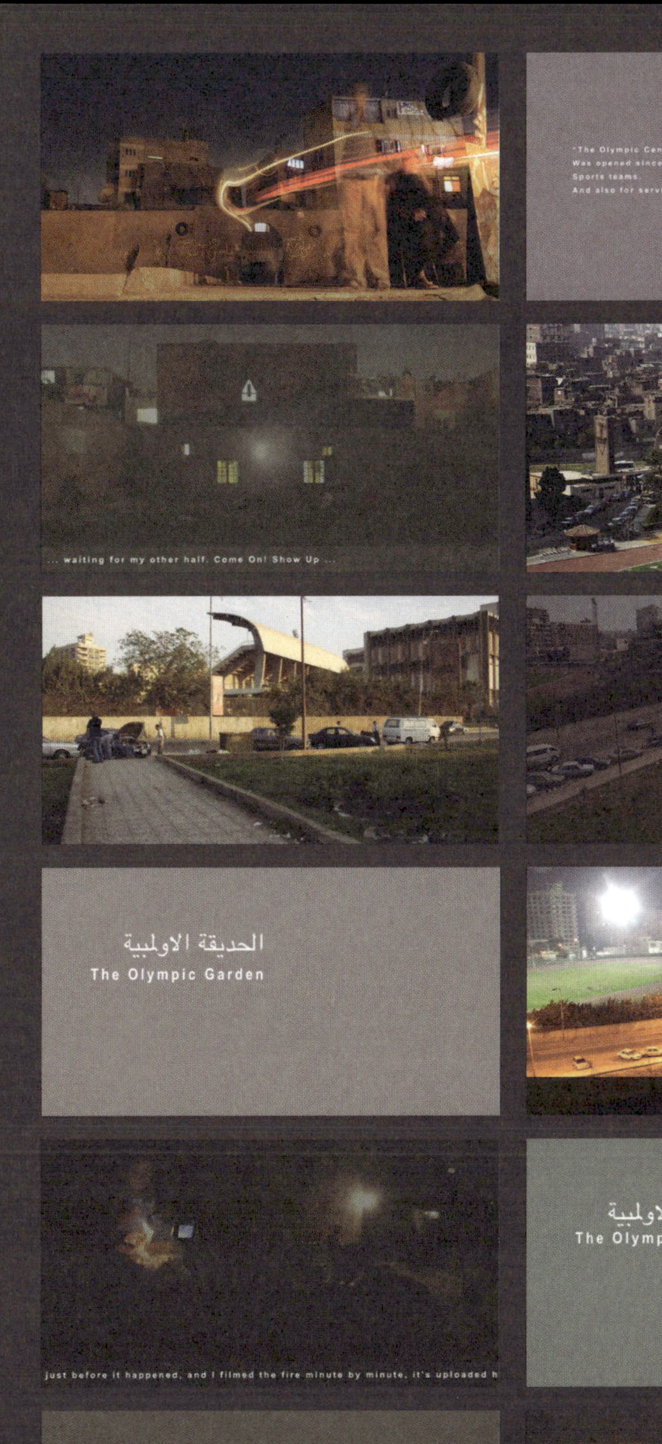

... waiting for my other half. Come On! Show Up ...
just before it happened, and I filmed the fire minute by minute, it's uploaded h
here I am ... waiting for my other half. Come On! Show Up ...
الحديقة الاولمبية
The Olympic Garden

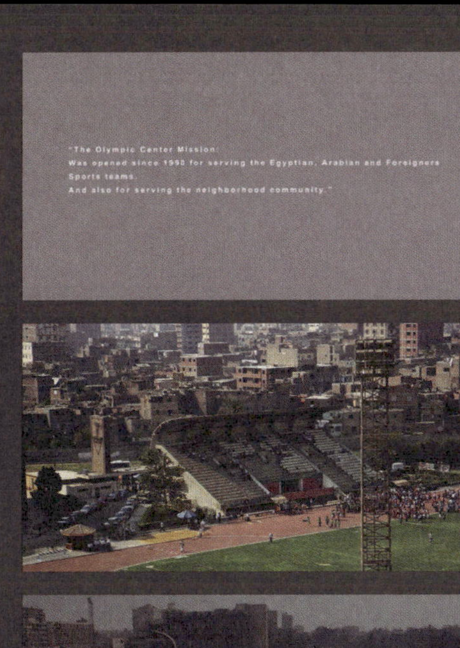

"The Olympic Center Mission:
Was opened since 1990 for serving the Egyptian, Arabian and Foreigners
Sports teams.
And also for serving the neighborhood community."

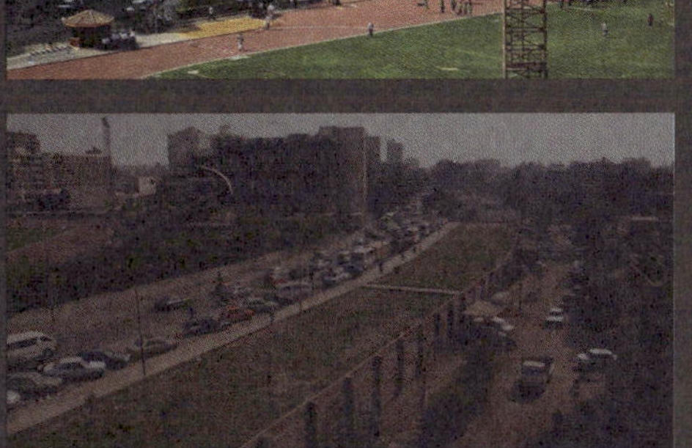

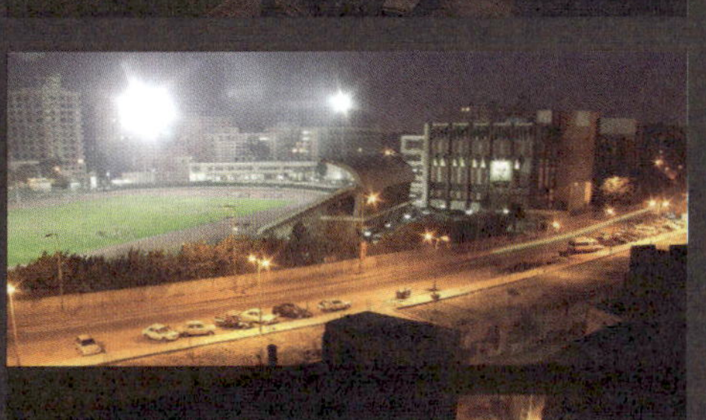

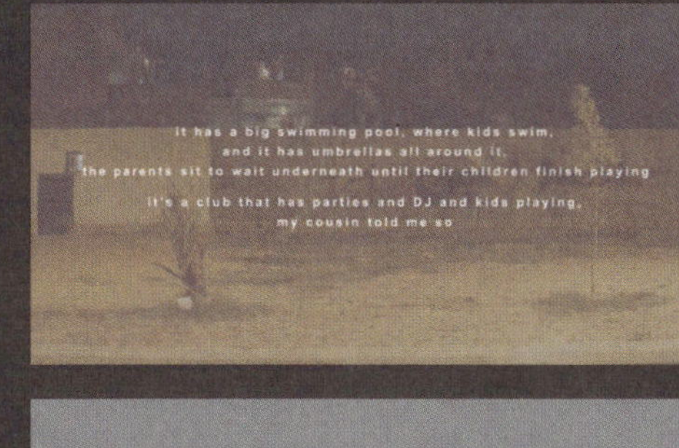

it has a big swimming pool, where kids swim,
and it has umbrellas all around it,
the parents sit to wait underneath until their children finish playing

it's a club that has parties and DJ and kids playing,
my cousin told me so

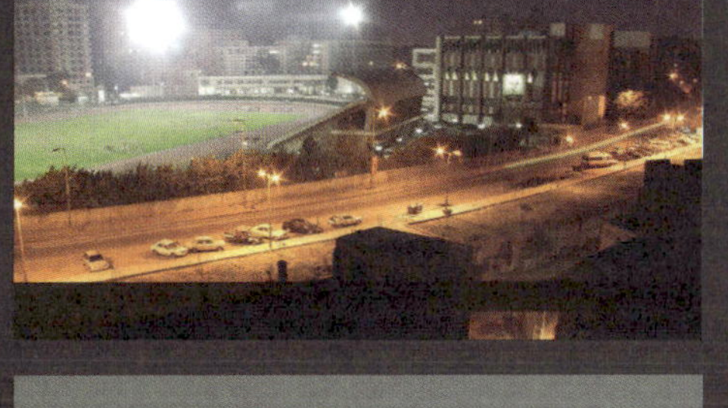

الحديقة الاولمبية
The Olympic Garden

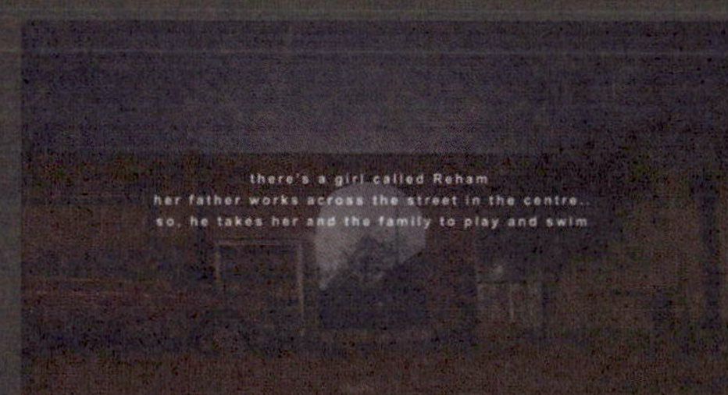

there's a girl called Reham
her father works across the street in the centre.
so, he takes her and the family to play and swim

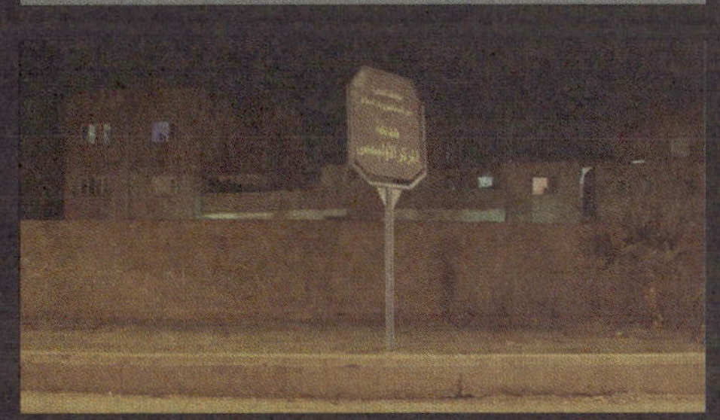

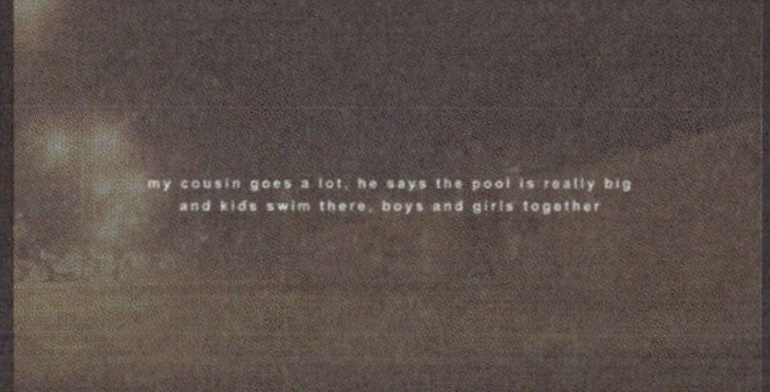

my cousin goes a lot, he says the pool is really big
and kids swim there, boys and girls together.

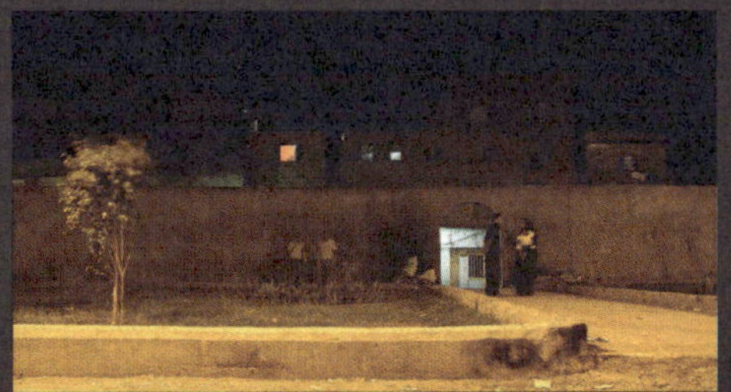

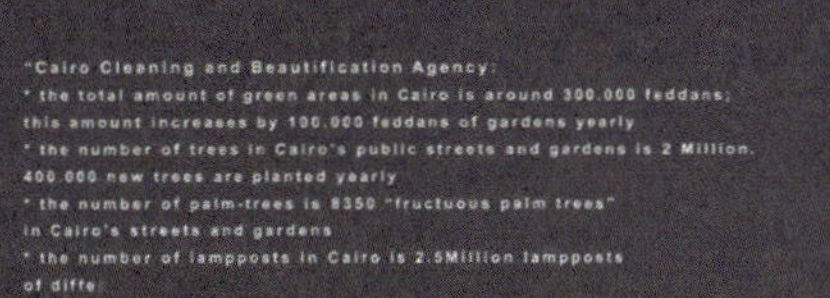

"Cairo Cleaning and Beautification Agency:
* the total amount of green areas in Cairo is around 300.000 feddans;
this amount increases by 100.000 feddans of gardens yearly.
* the number of trees in Cairo's public streets and gardens is 2 Million.
400.000 new trees are planted yearly
* the number of palm-trees is 8550 "fructuous palm trees"
in Cairo's streets and gardens
* the number of lampposts in Cairo is 2.5Million lampposts
of diffe:

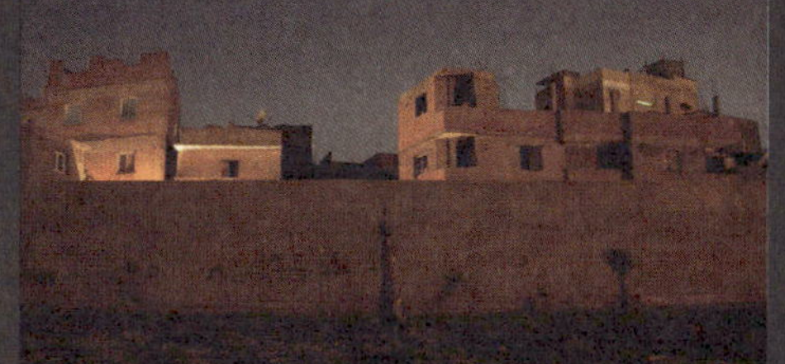

On Refrains, Sets and a Backdrop

HALA ELKOUSSY

Co-founder of the Contemporary Image Collective (CIC) and the PhotoCairo festival, Hala Elkoussy has been an integral part of the independent art scene in Cairo since 2004. The city is a recurring topos in her work. She is particularly interested in the social dynamics underlying Cairo's complex urban structure. In her work, she focuses on the intimate, supposedly banal and frequently overlooked aspects of communal life in the city. In her video installation *We're By The Sea Now* (2006), Cairo becomes the setting for the innumerable personal stories found there every day.

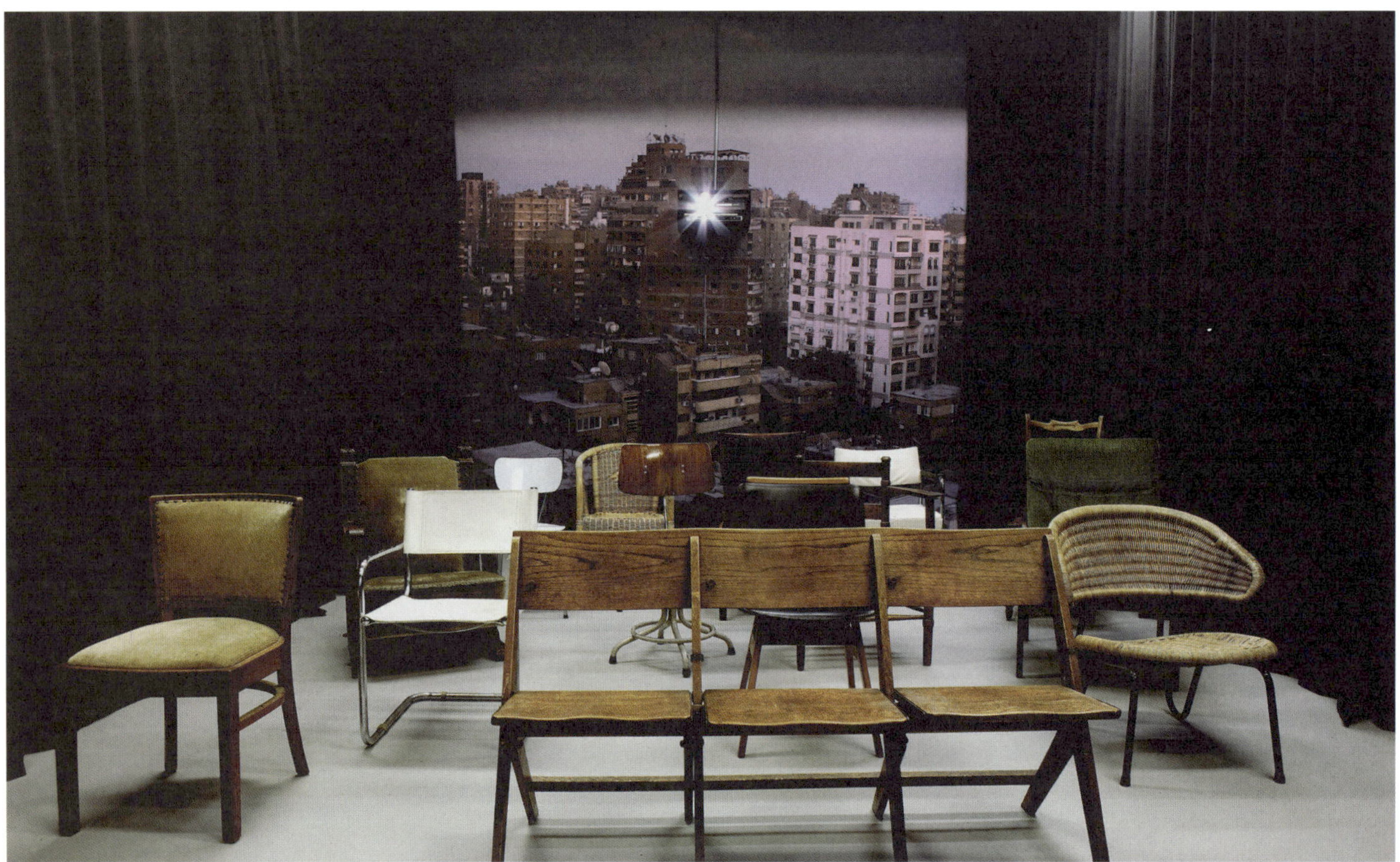

ON REFRAINS, SETS AND A BACKDROP, INSTALLATION VIEW, RIJKSAKADEMIE VAN BEELDENDE KUNSTEN, 2006

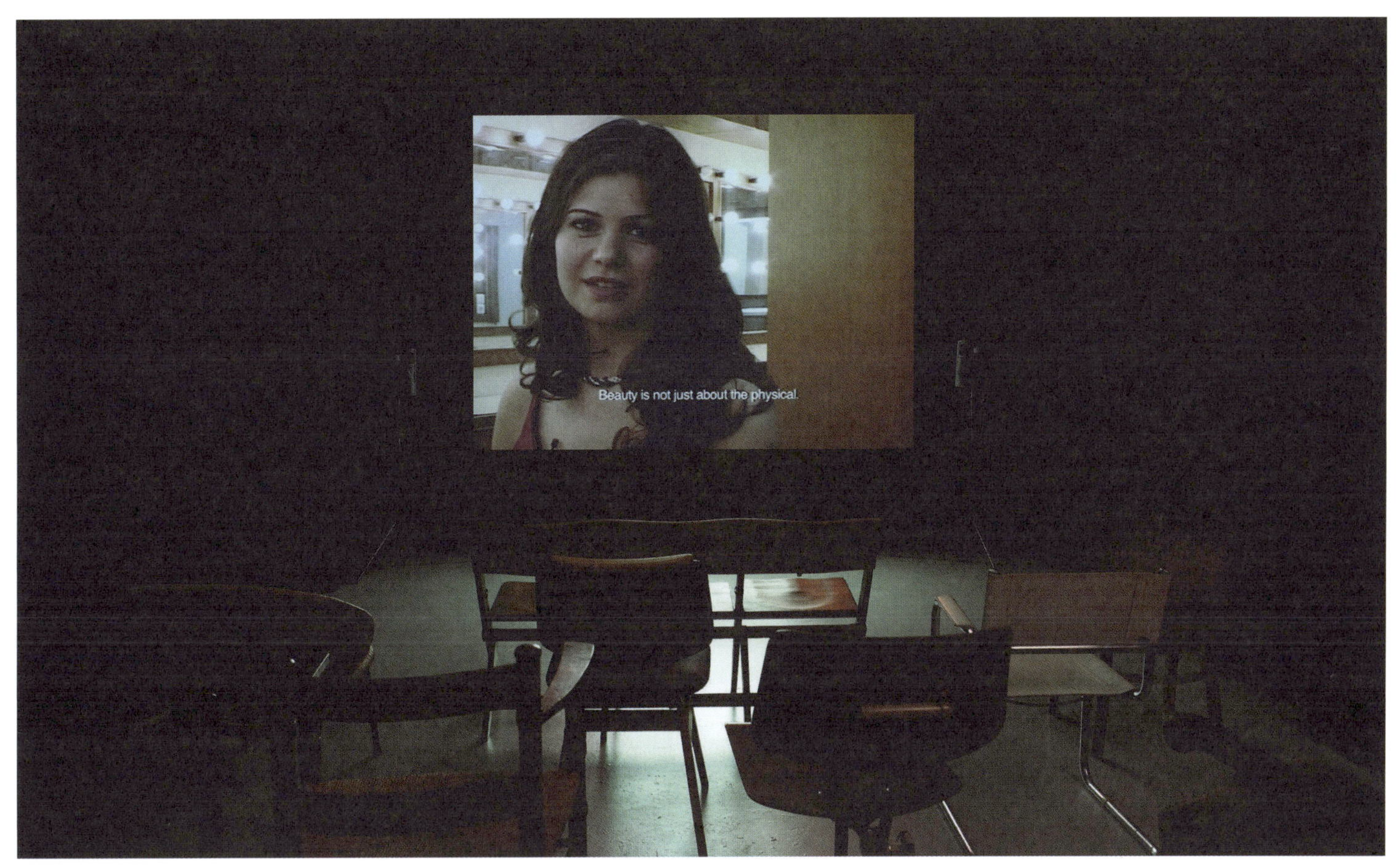

We're By the Sea Now (2006) was filmed in and is about the city of Cairo. Through an array of seemingly disparate anecdotal events, personal accounts, tales and hearsay, Hala Elkoussy focuses on subjective images of the people living in Cairo. Rather than the fragmented structure of the video's 13 vignette-like chapters generating a unilateral stable meaning, it points to gaps and omissions in the production of knowledge.

Hope (Amal)

LARA BALADI

Egyptian-Lebanese artist Lara Baladi was born in Beirut, raised in Cairo and Paris, and educated in London. She has lived and worked in Egypt since 1997. Inside *Tower of Hope* (in Arabic: *Borg El Amal*) a *Donkey Symphony* echoes the cry of the "Red City". As some architects refer to it, this "Red City", Cairo's urban periphery, consists of endless rows of almost identical brick-and-cement buildings, long stretches of often windowless towers, random informal constructions lacking in all amenities. In the midst of the exclusive area of the opera house (which is guarded by the military) and in the context of the biggest art event held by the Ministry of Culture, *Borg El Amal* focusses on the pressing reality of the socio-political situation. Lara Baladi's ephemeral construction and sound installation was awarded the first prize at the 2008 Cairo Biennial.

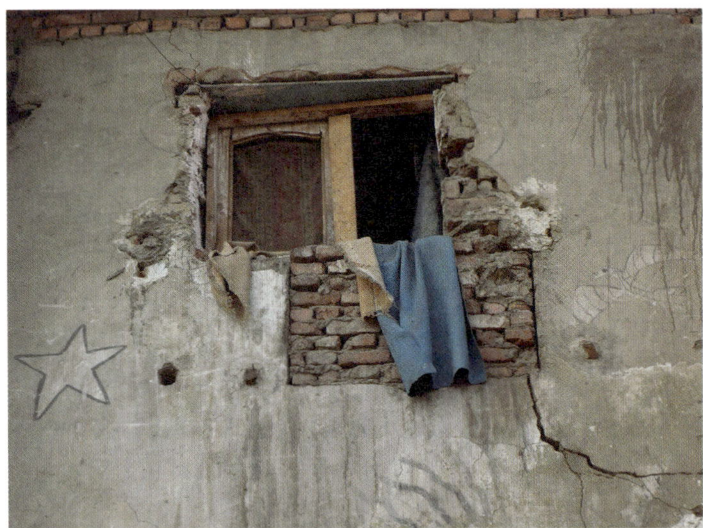
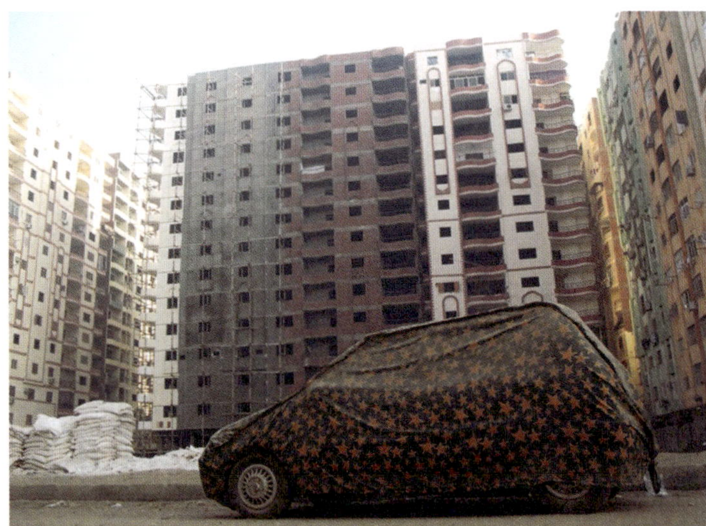
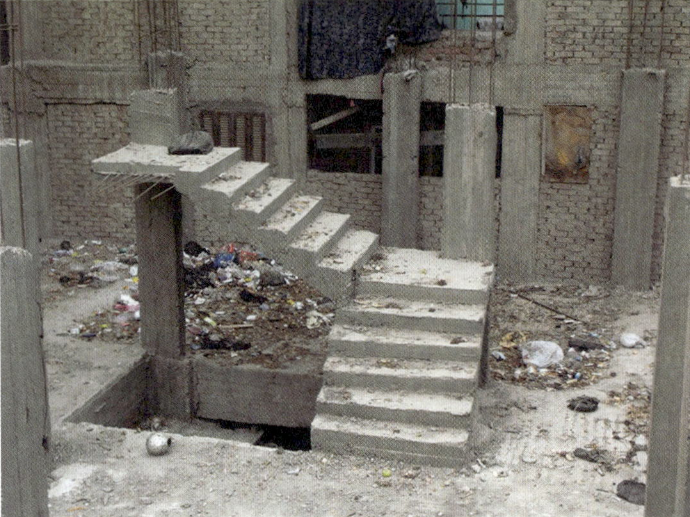
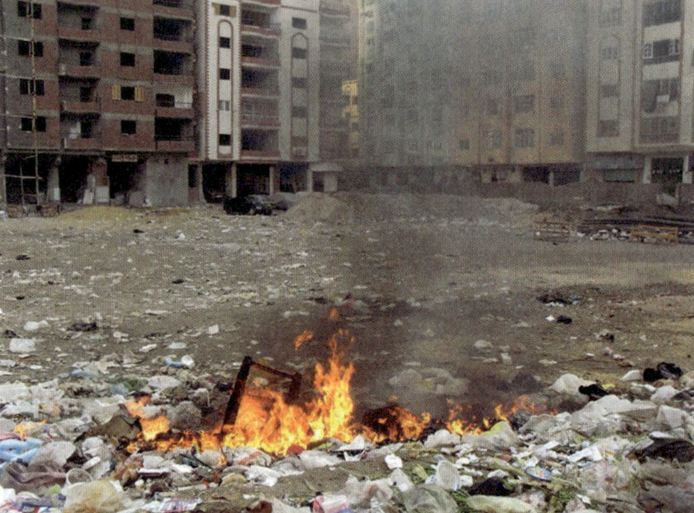

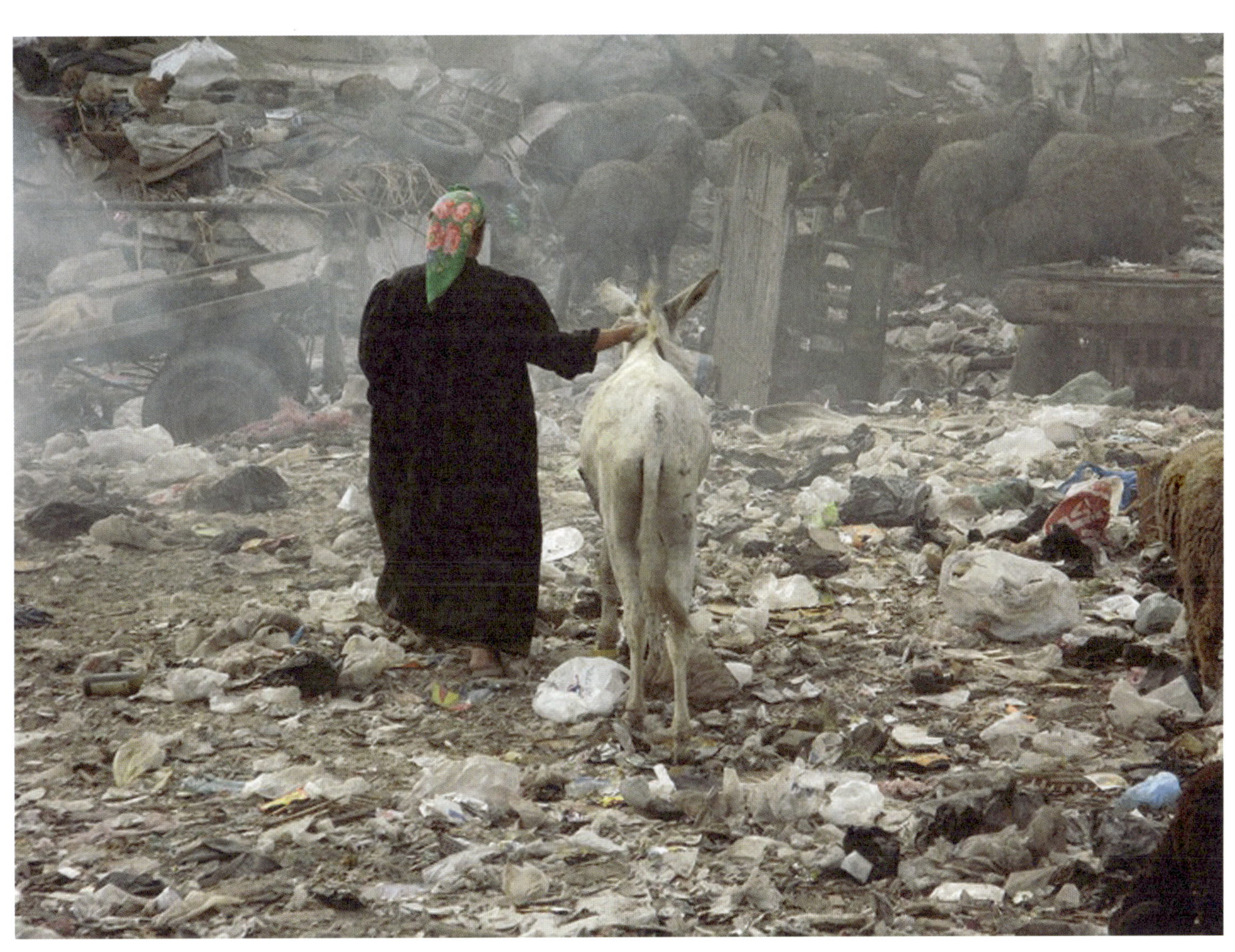

Cultural Palaces

MANDY GEHRT

Mandy Gehrt is an artist living and working in Leipzig. In her *Cultural Palaces* project, she explores the architectural heritage and current state of (former) cultural venues in eastern Germany, Russia, Macedonia and Egypt. Mandy Gehrt's photo works, which defy distinct regional categorisations, were supplemented by short interviews and discussions with artists, cultural producers and functionaries. *Cultural Palaces* was shown at *PhotoCairo4*.

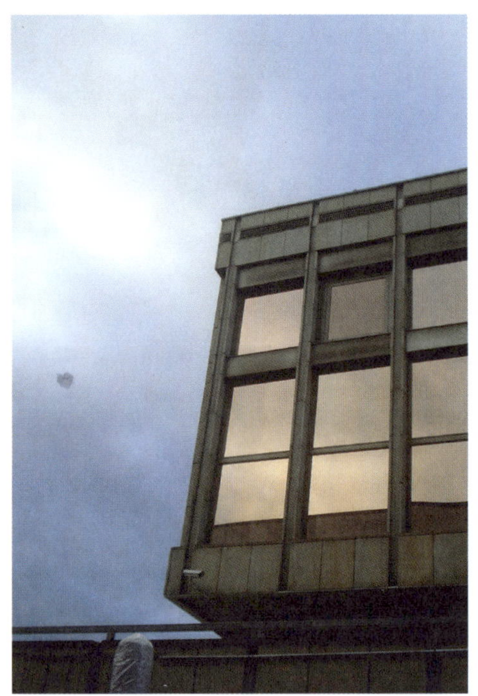
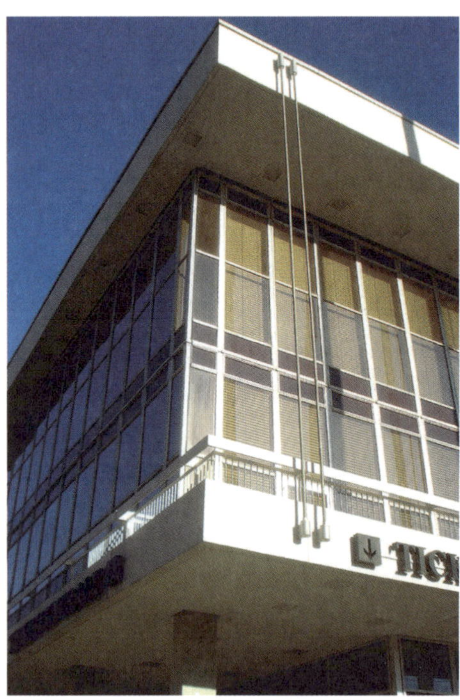

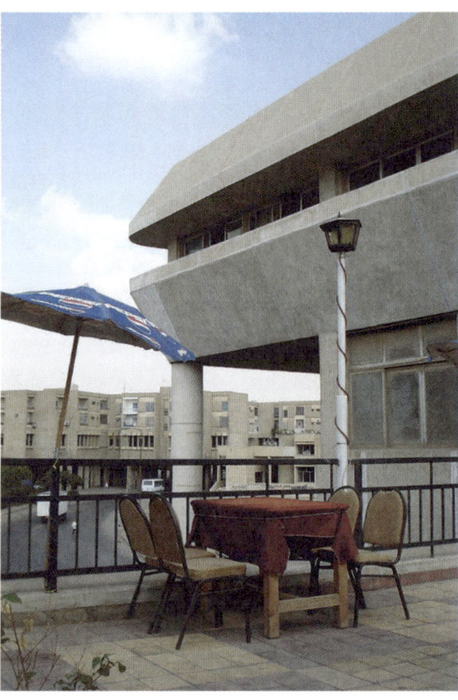
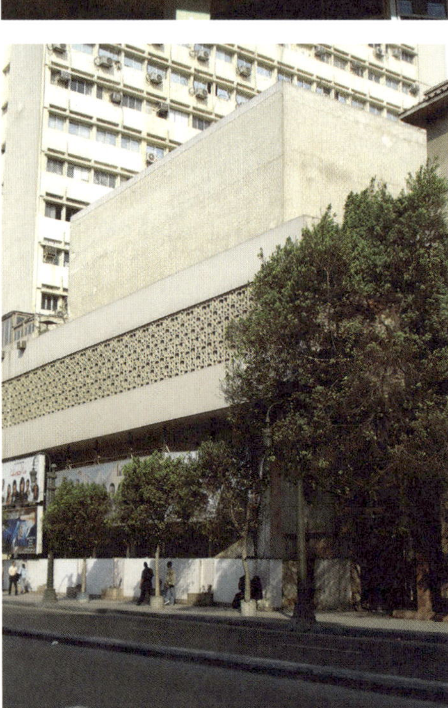
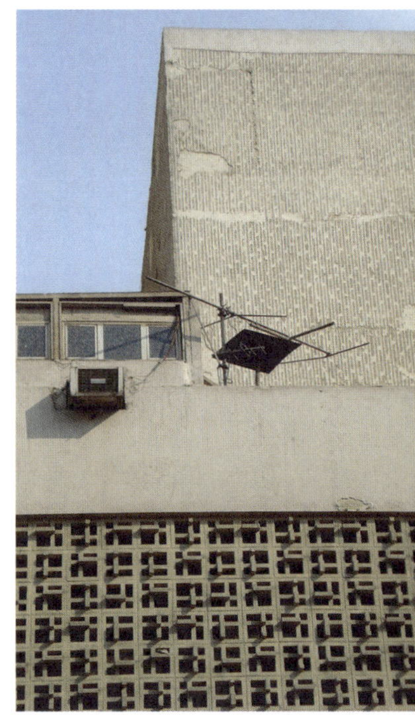

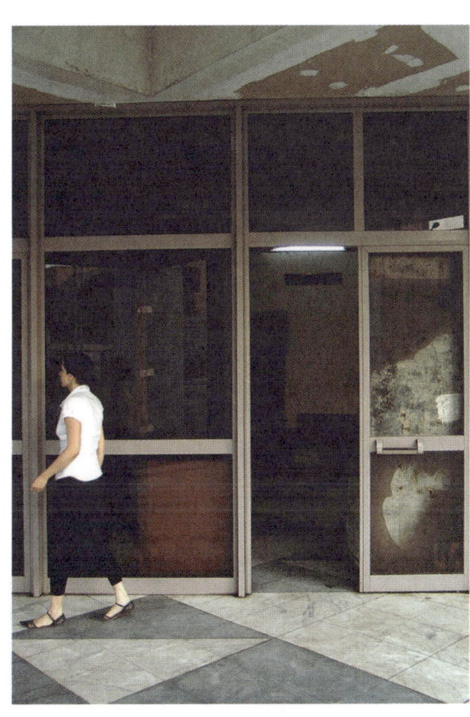
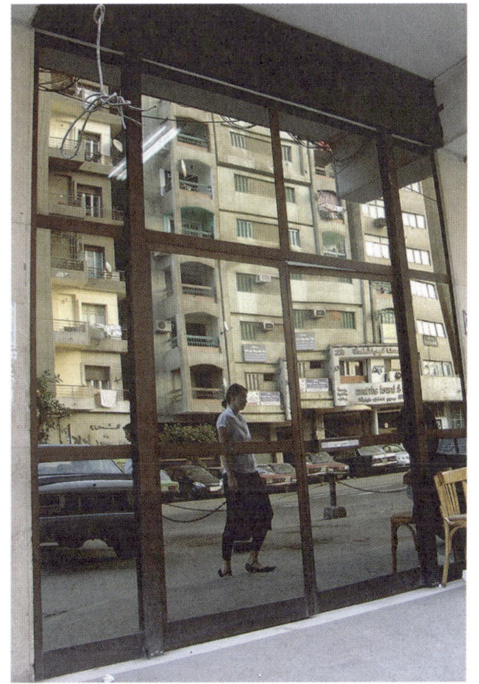
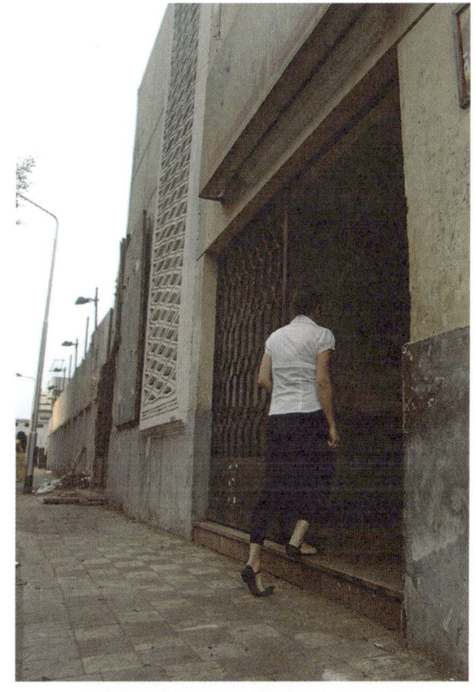
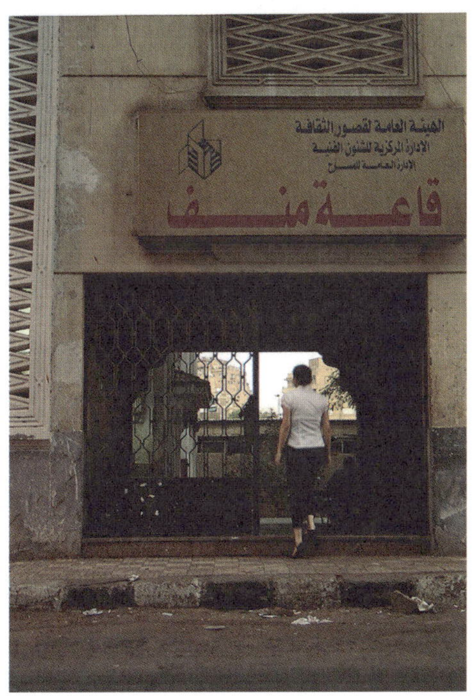

الهيئة العامة لقصور الثقافة
الإدارة المركزية للشؤون الفنية
الإدارة العامة للمسرح
قاعة منف

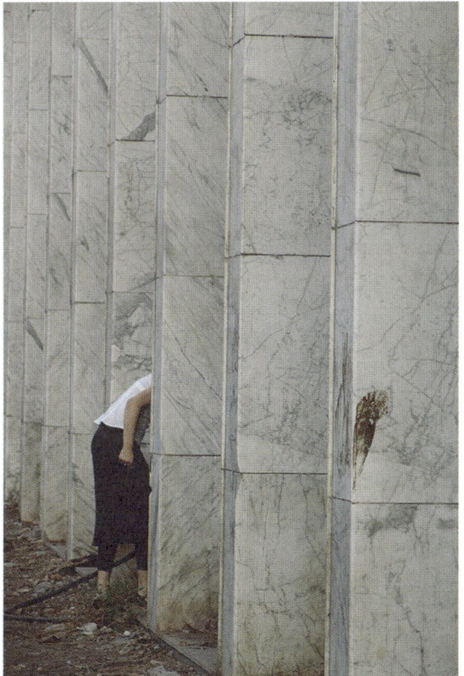
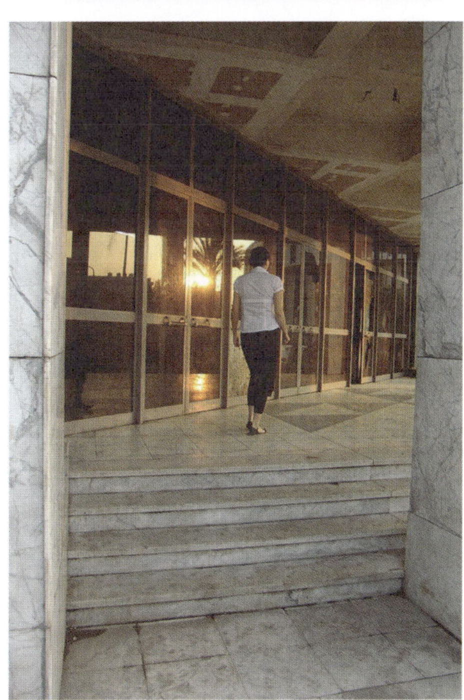

Everyday Heroes

GANZEER

"Mofa" runs the graphic studio Ganzeer: Experimental Arts Unit and the design blog *Ganzeer.* His works range from commercial advertising graphics and product designs to film animation. His magazine *Shakloh,* issued at irregular intervals, has created a platform for designers from Cairo. He also experiments with contemporary Arabic typographies and a mix of Arabic and Latin scripts. In *Everyday Heroes* (2007), he sketched garbage collectors, laundrywomen and messengers – the "service providers" of Cairo's informal world – in the style of classic comic heroes. In collaboration with George Azmy, he has published a comic book about a futuristic Cairo.

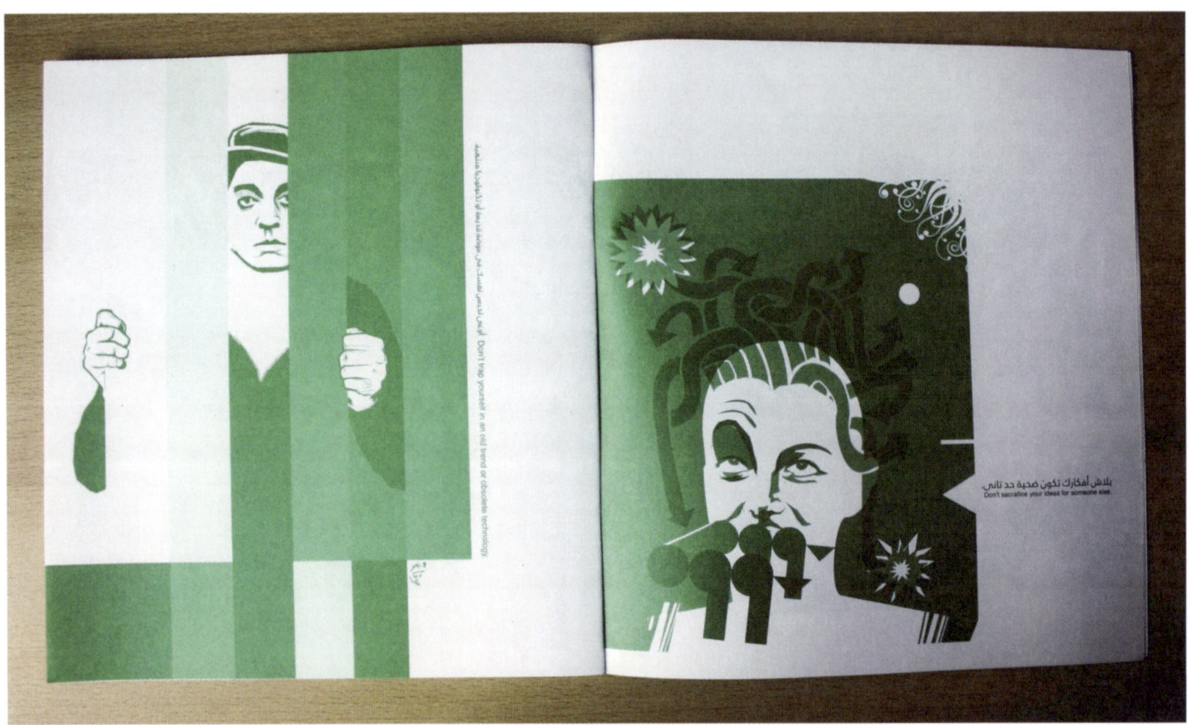

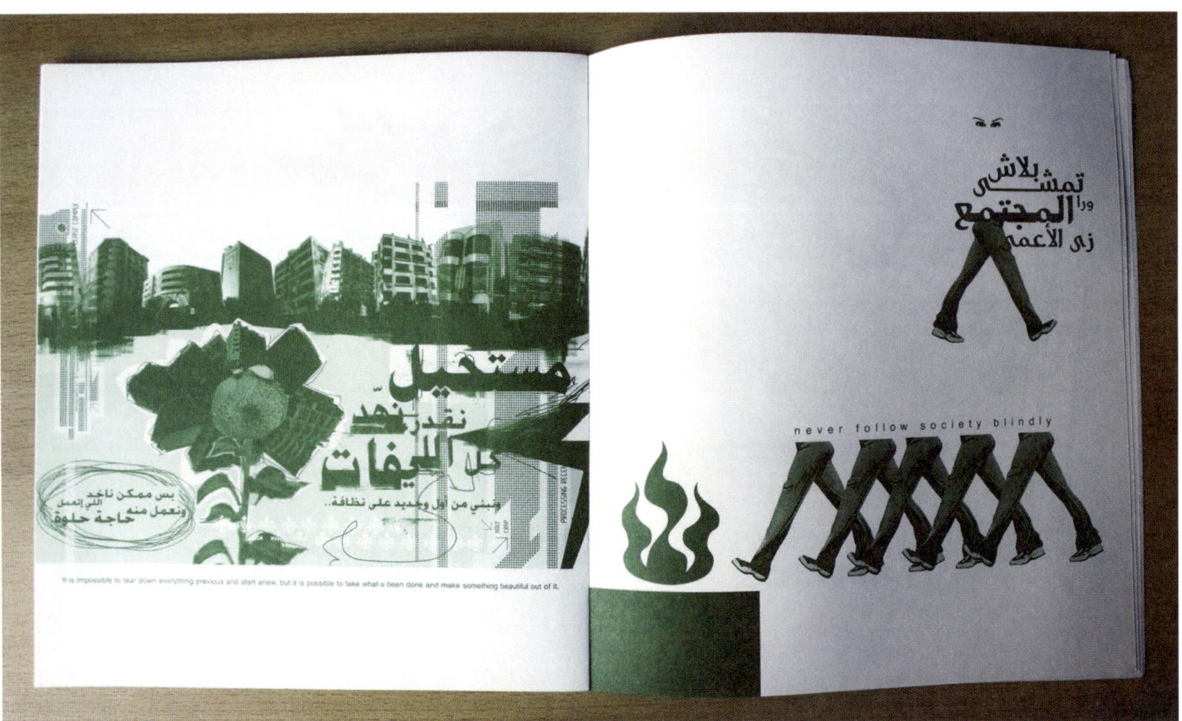

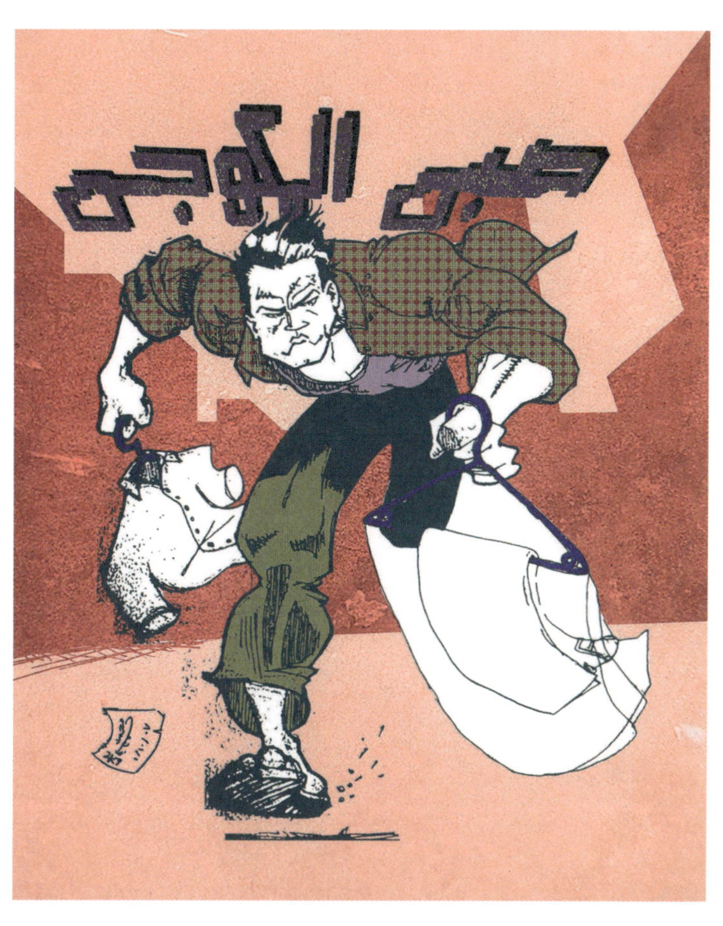

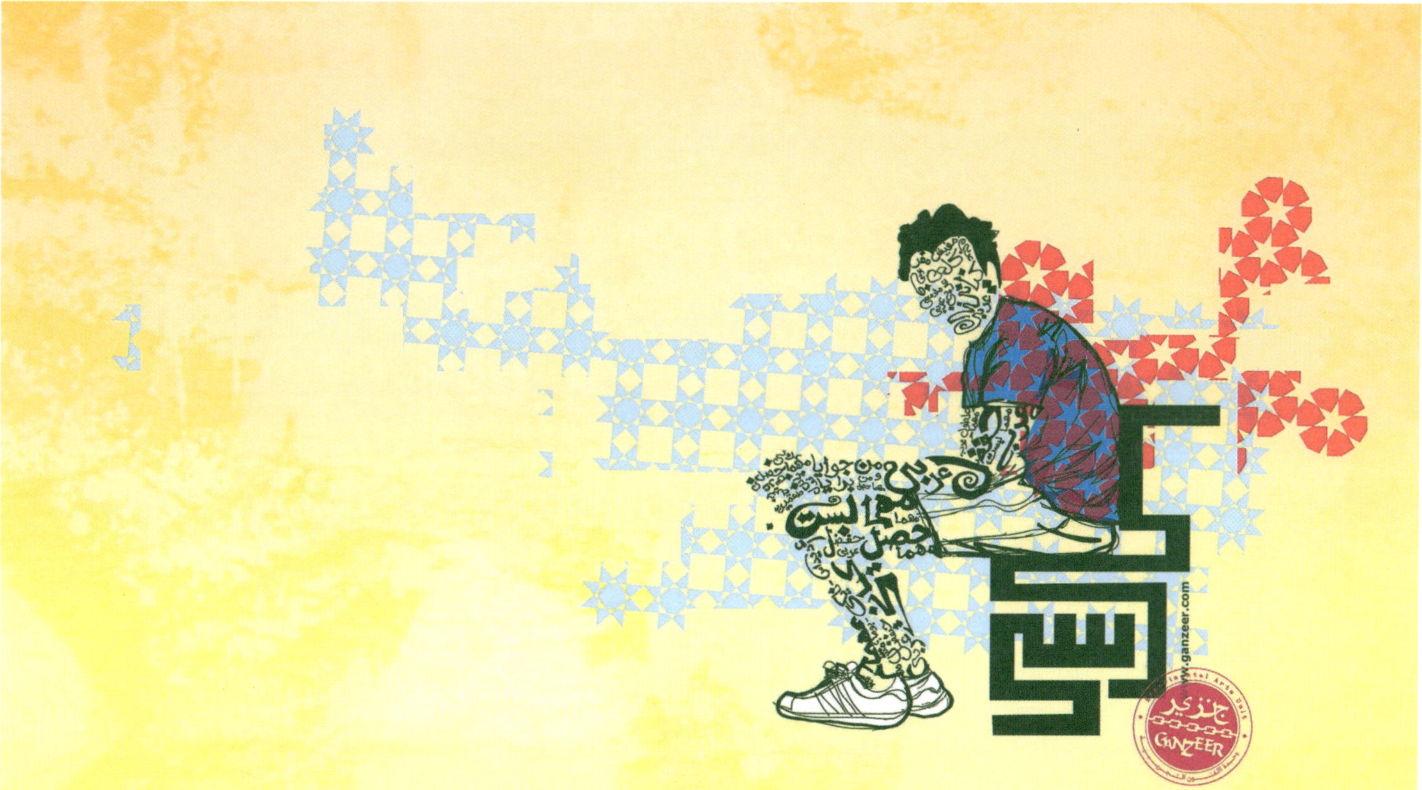

LAGOS

Lagos
All Roads

AKINBODE AKINBIYI

The city constantly changes, time and time again. It grows, becoming denser and more complex. Different authorities try to control it. Illegal and semi-legal structures are torn down, razed to the ground. Attempts are made to combat the omnipresent underlying criminality, to regulate the roads and set up public transport. Hardly are such schemes implemented because those affected avoid and evade them, and find a substitute.

The city is a living organism, but one without a heart to hold it all together. The most vibrant kinds of centres can be found everywhere: markets, junctions, and vast crowds of people which swell ever larger only to simply dissolve and disperse later. Obalende, Ojuelegba, CMS, Race Course, Ijora, Apapa, Yaba Bus Stop, Maryland, Ikeja Bus Stop, Oshodi, Ketu, Mile 12, Amuwo-Odofin, Isolo, Oyingbo, Festac. Places in the city which in the bus, in the *Danfo,* appear to merge into one another, bus stops, without end, without halt.

Many Lagos residents take the bus stops as their sole point of orientation, as the only way they can experience or move around the city. The surface is deceptive, a skin of shimmering temptation. The yellow of the *Danfo* minibuses, the Marina high-rises, the luxury of Phase 1, Lekki Peninsula.

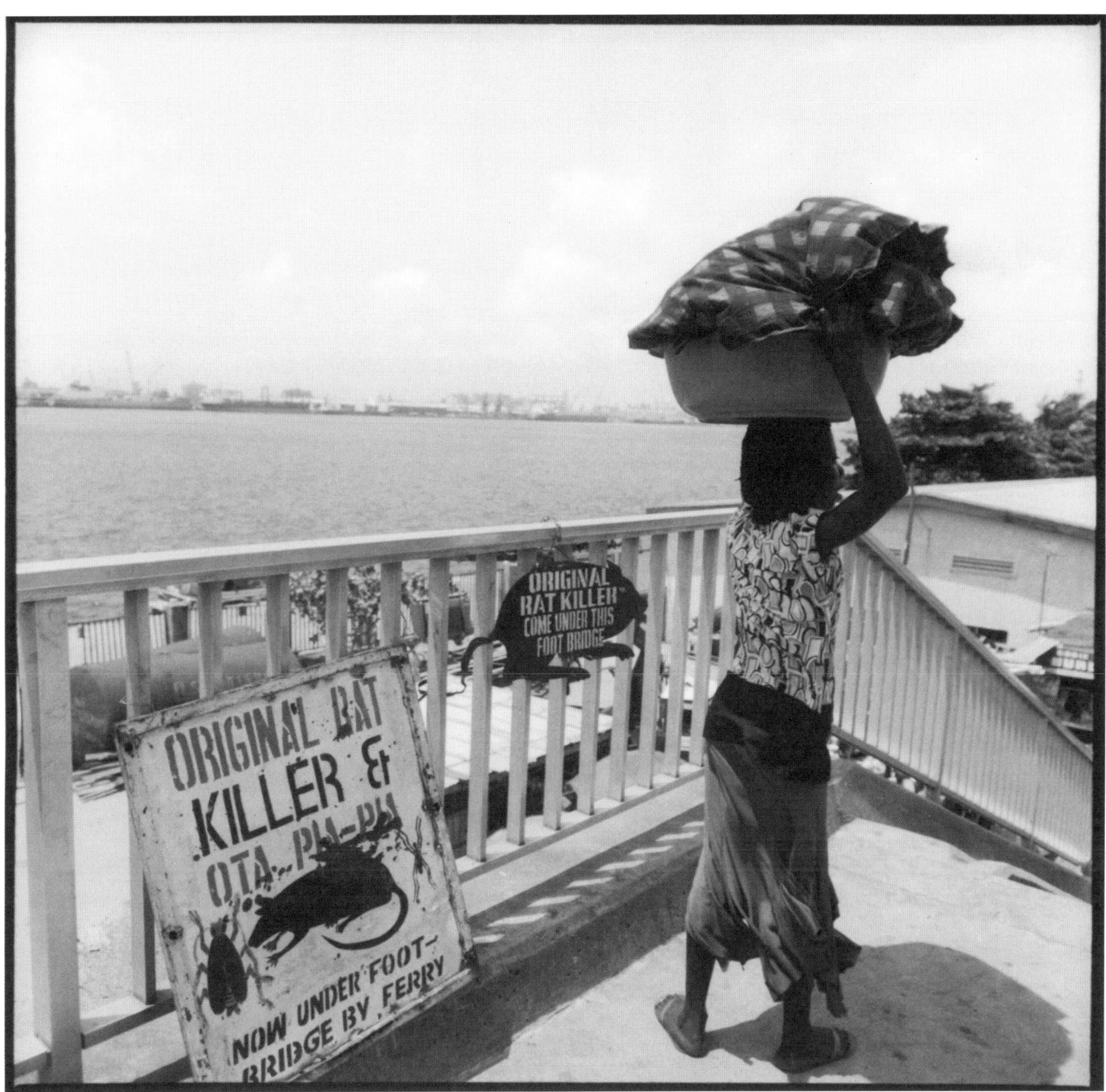

ORIGINAL KILLER, 2010

At some distance away, Apapa harbour is still one of the leading transshipment centres for imported goods in West Africa. The local populations were exploited and robbed through such colonial city harbours, designed more as stores and warehouses than as factories.

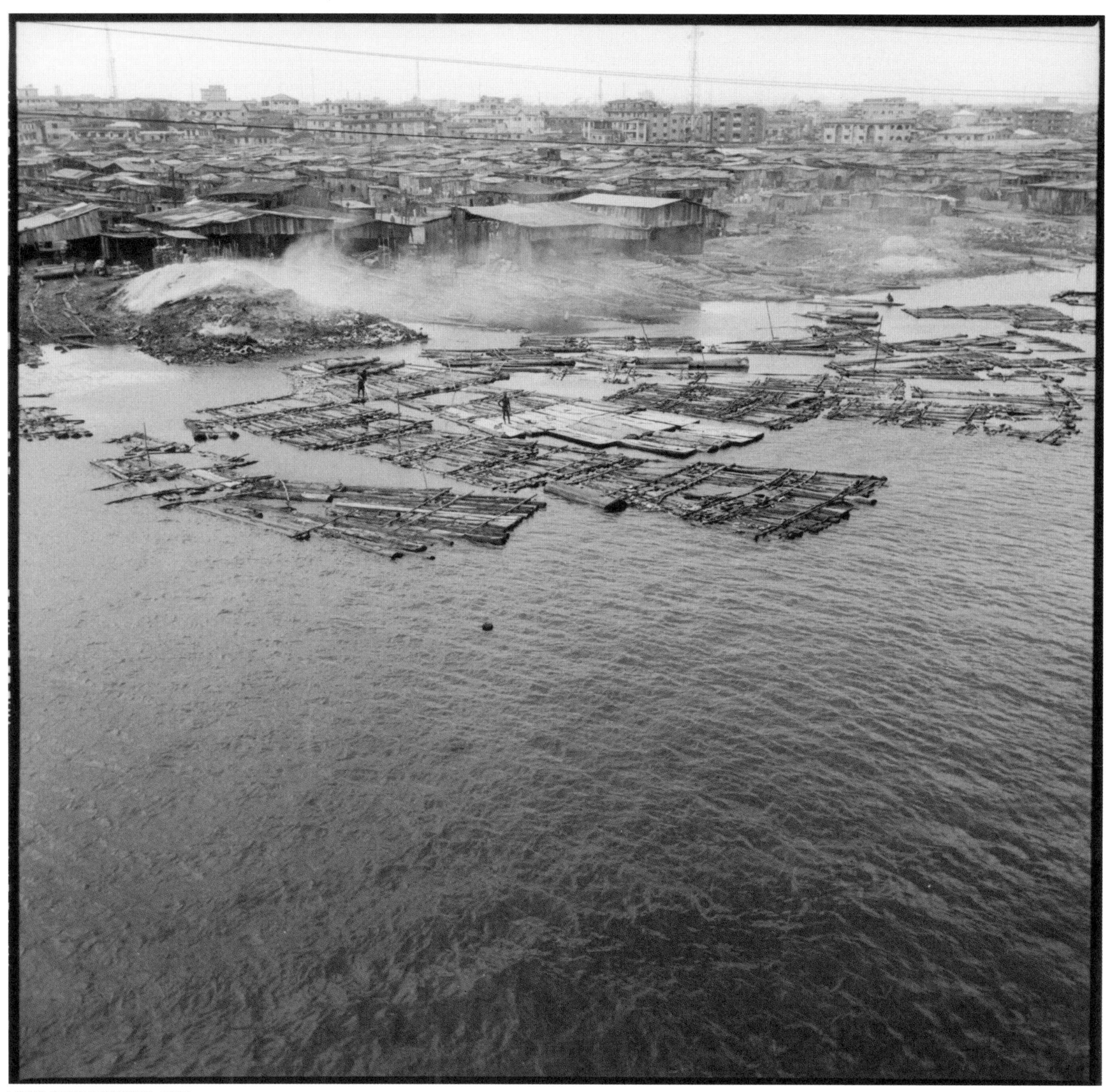

LOGS IN THE WATER, 2010

Driving across the twelve kilometres of Third Mainland Bridge takes twenty minutes when the traffic is flowing; in a jam, it can take several hours. The bridge starts on Ikoyi Island in the south-east, leads over the lagoon to the north to the tollgate and the expressway leading out of the city to Ibadan. Travelling across the bridge, you have an almost cinematic impression of the different parts of the city, as you do of the sawmill, a place where the washed in logs are manually processed. For newcomers, this seems an apocalyptic image, but they overlook the order and the degree of organisation hidden in the smoke.

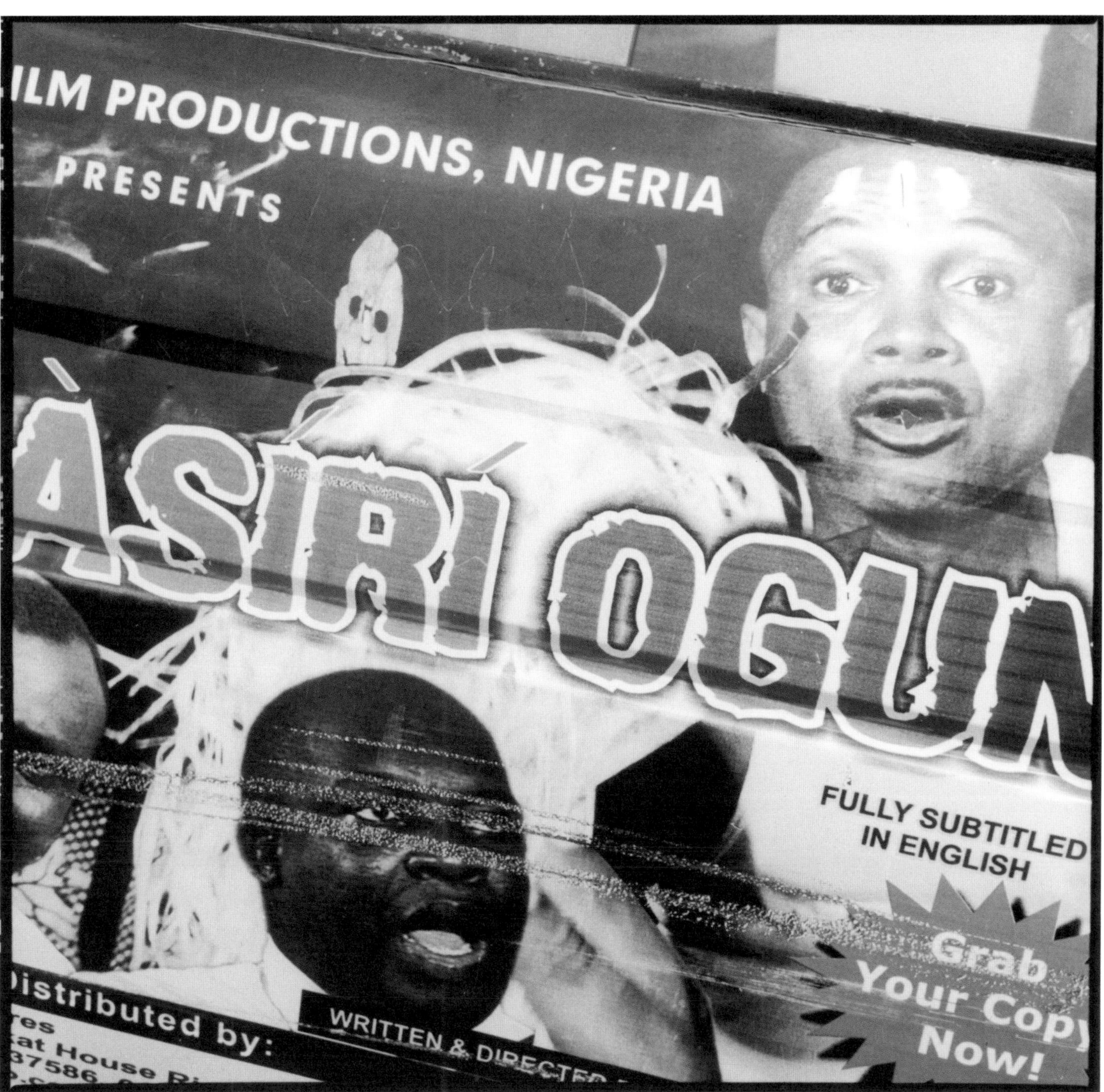

FILM POSTER, 2010

In the early 1990s, the collapse of a once-flourishing film culture led to the establishment of an independent video film industry, now the third largest film industry in the world. Nollywood satisfies the popular desire for entertainment, for a virtual world of illusions.

133

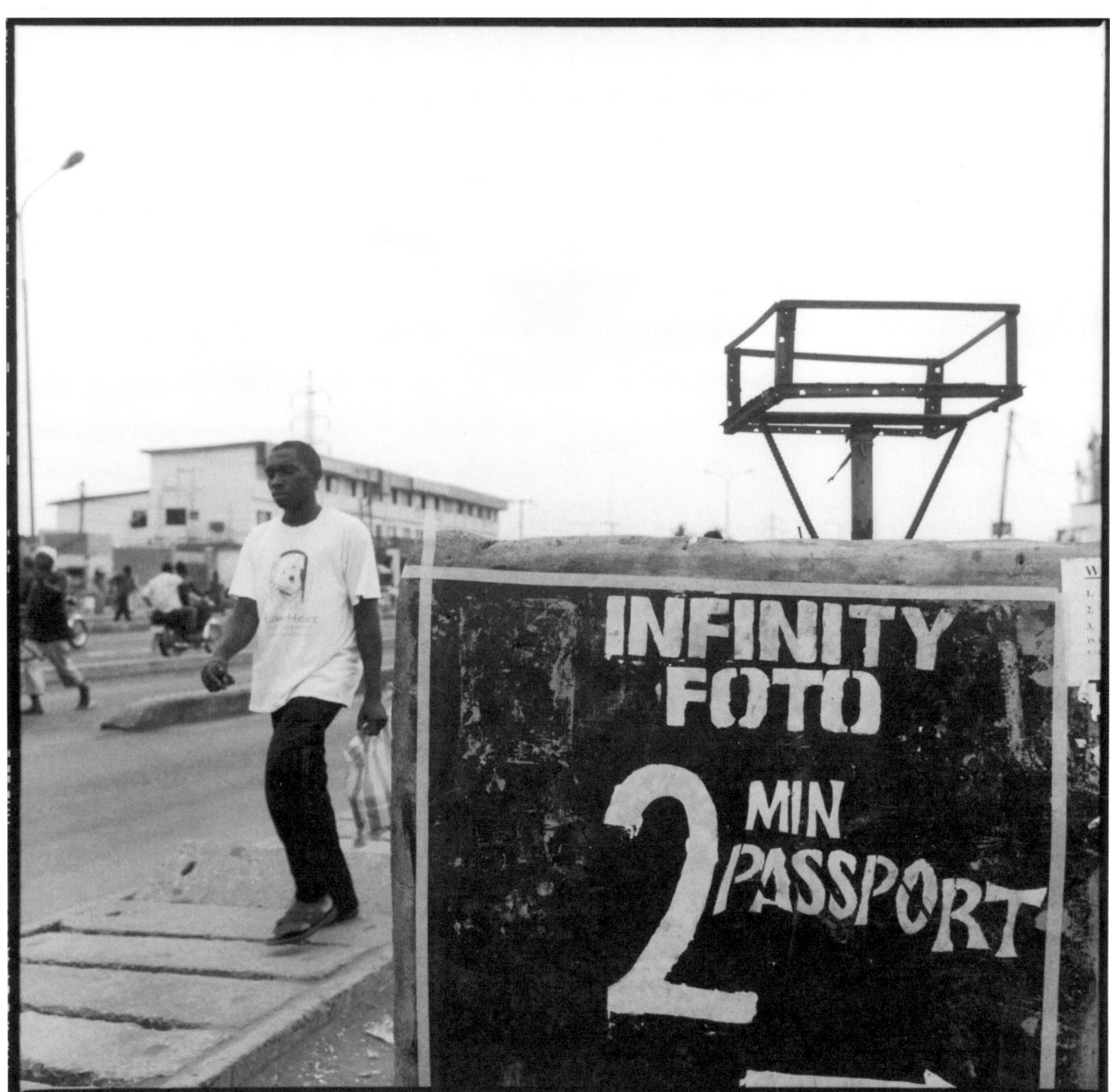

IKORODO ROAD, 2010

Along Ikorodo Road, one of the key transport routes on the mainland

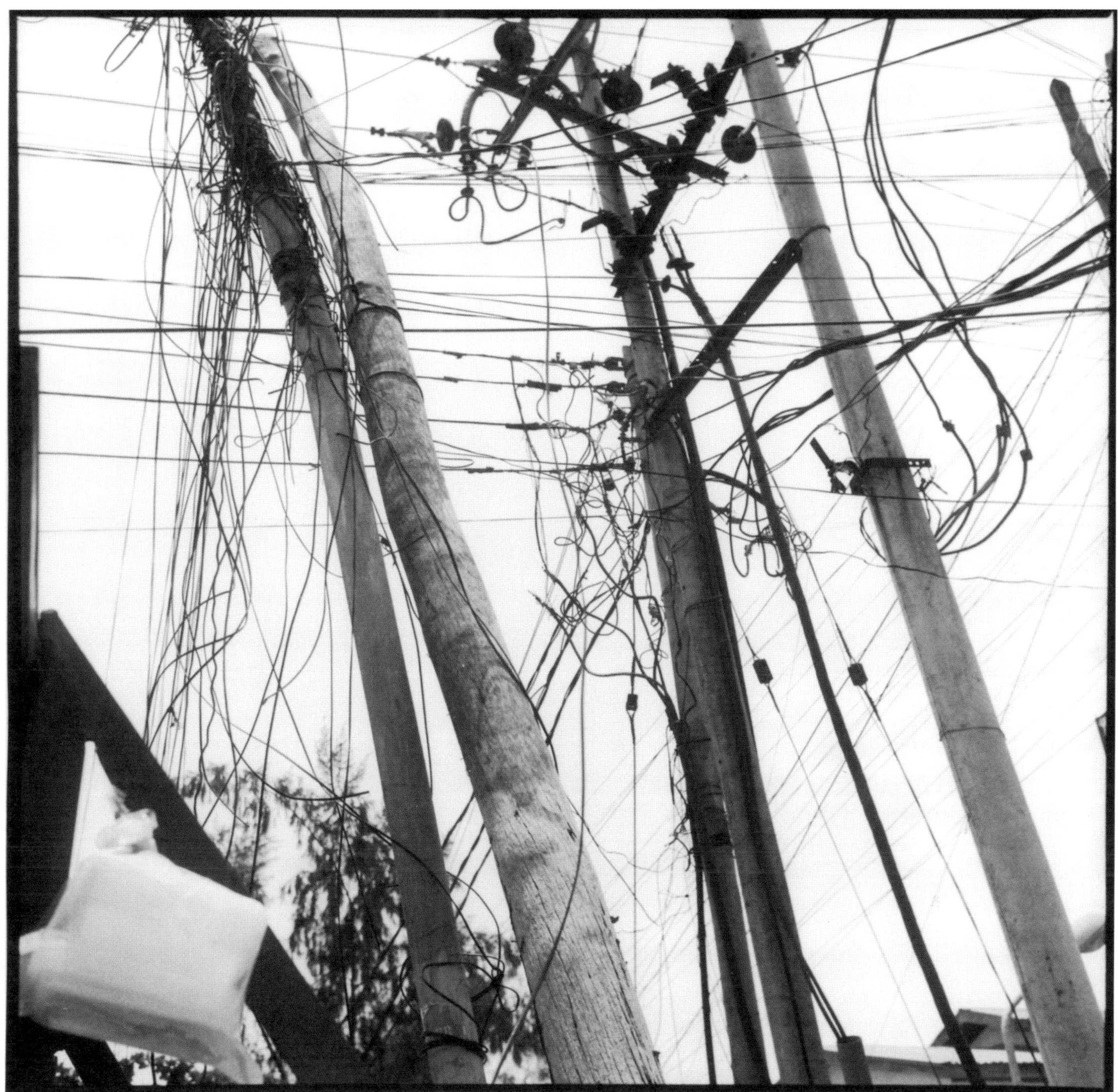

POWER SUPPLY LINES, 2010

The residents' attempts to make something out of what are actually desperate structures and to try to find a solution, lies behind what Western observers often like to call chaos or anarchy. It's rare to have a constant supply of electricity. The jumble of cables testifies to this hidden self-help, the attempt to remain connected.

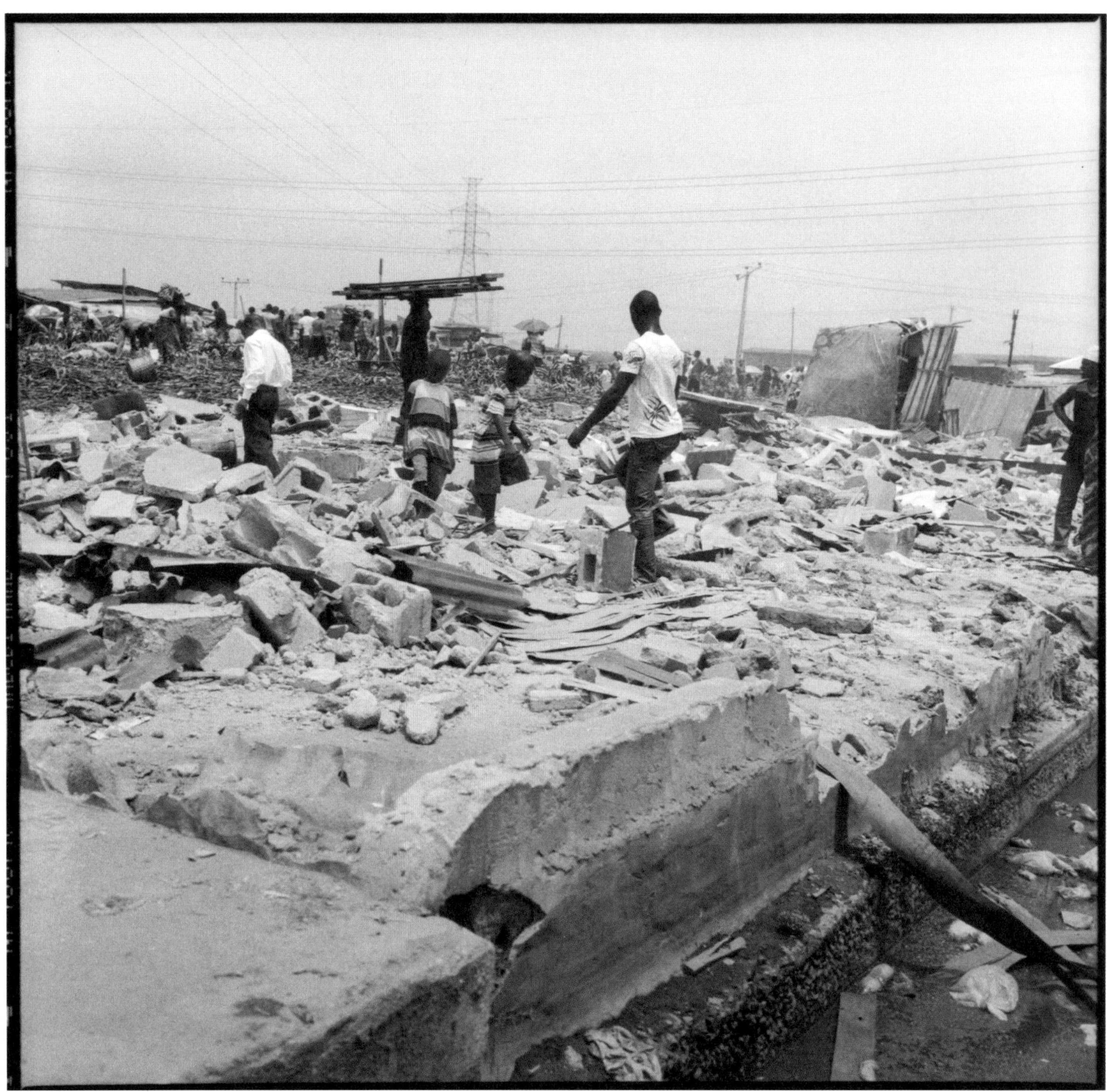

DEMOLISHED NEIGHBOURHOOD, 2010

In Lagos, entire neighbourhoods have often been torn down overnight; for example, the Maroko settlement in July 1990, which housed the cooks, gardeners and other domestic staff working for the rich on Victoria Island. Recently, bulldozers razed this market area near Mile 12 to the ground. Allegedly, petty criminals were sheltering in the area. Every so often, such measures recur, making thousands of families homeless and triggering reactions in the people affected.

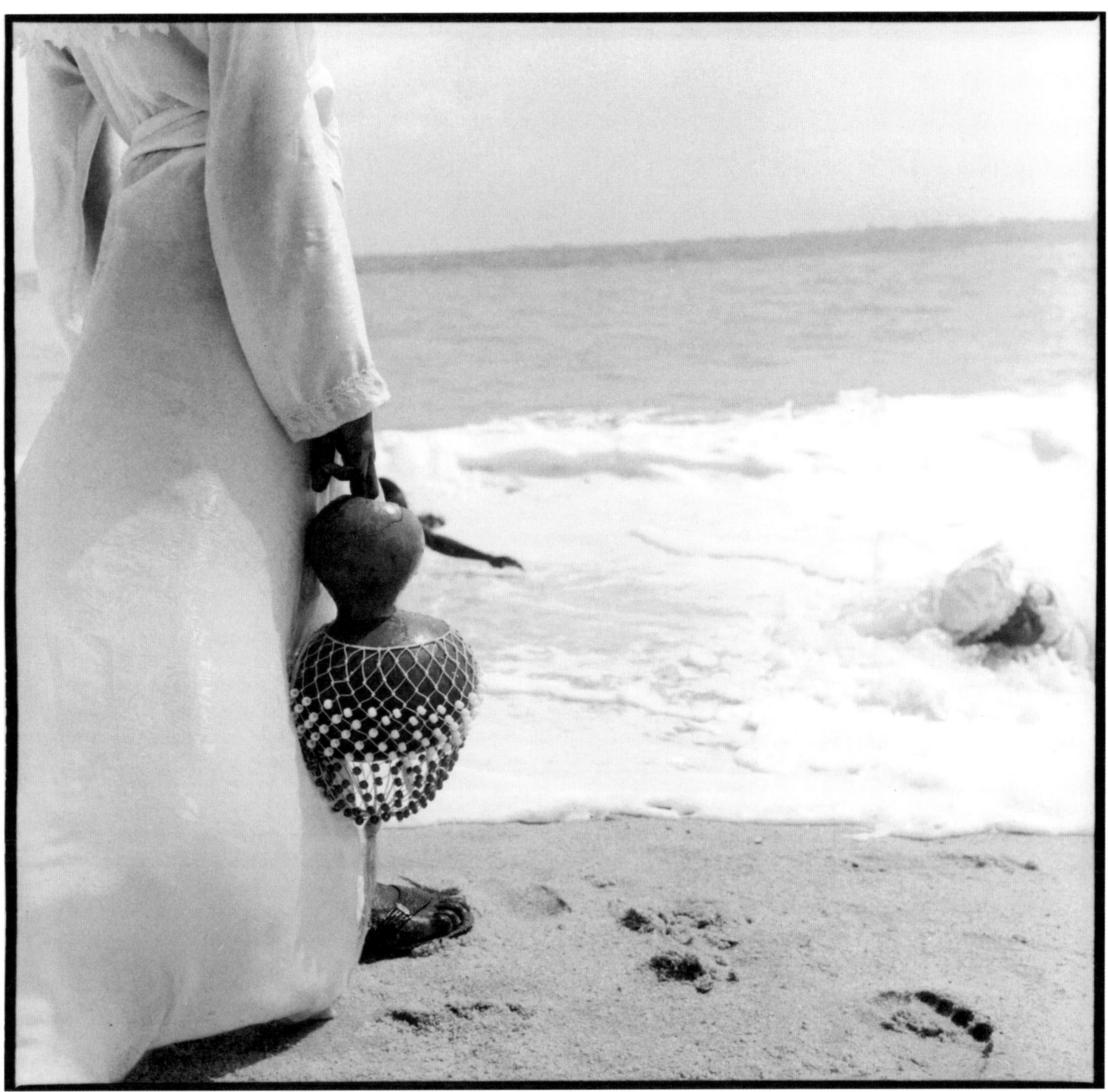

BEACH, 2010

For many followers of the numerous Pentecostal churches, the sea is a place of ritual cleansing, baptism and inner prayer. The Atlantic inundates the coast almost unnoticed, its waves washing the beach away. The British attempted to use massive rocks to protect the coast of Victoria Island, giving it the name of Bar Beach. Today, Lagos has turned away from the sea and is establishing connections to the country's large interior. The beach is only bustling with pleasure-seekers at the weekends and on public holidays – almost the only place of recreation in a metropolis of fifteen million residents.

Translation from German by Andrew Boreham

Lagos – Oshodi
Inspecting
an Urban Icon

PETER PROBST

I

It happened in the early morning hours on Sunday, 4 January 2009. A special operations unit several hundred-strong moved in and cleared Lagos' notorious Oshodi market. Dark clouds of smoke rose as innumerable homemade stalls were pushed together by three bulldozers and set on fire. It took over a hundred trucks to remove the remnants – metal, rubber, plastic and anything else that had survived the flames. In the late afternoon, when the clean-up operation finally came to an end, an incredulous crowd of thousands of people was still standing at the edge of the road. They had witnessed how one of Lagos' best-known urban icons had begun to change.

II

For over thirty years, the view from the outer expressway to the Agege motorway underneath symbolised the dystopia of Lagos: long parallel lines of yellow minibuses surrounded by vast crowds pushing their way past mobile cook shops and market stalls, baskets of meat, fish, vegetables, spices, canisters of palm oil, bundles of firewood, piles of fabrics, plastic bowls and thousands of other goods where it was better neither to know nor ask their origins or use. [→ Fig. A] The ground was a sea of car

tyres and plastic bags, snaking around your feet as you walked, impeding your progress. In amidst the jumble of stalls, traders and goods, hardly visible yet solidly integrated – rail tracks. These were the tracks taking the trains to and from the north. Encased in the clusters of traders, the trains seemed to be virtually absorbed by the market, only to be spat out again at the edges of its vibrant realm. There was no way you could get through the market quickly; it might take hours just to move 500 metres. The scene was an urban coronary, the total collapse of any town planning, a nightmare of policy regulation, and for some simply the "most radical urban condition on the planet".

At least, that was the subtitle chosen for the *Lagos Handbook,* produced under lead researcher and author Rem Koolhaas, a Dutch architect teaching at Harvard University.[1] In the late 1990s, Koolhaas began investigating urban development and organisation in the 21st century. Lagos appeared to be a suitable field of research. With around fifteen million residents and the UN forecasting it would become the world's third largest city by 2020, Lagos promised to offer some significant insights into tomorrow's world: Lagos as a laboratory.

But Koolhaas' Lagos project did not just focus on architecture and urban theory. From the outset, this was also a visual project.[2] One of the works by the team of photographers and filmmakers accompanying Koolhaas showed a foreign world of urban life and survival previously hidden from the Western gaze – admittedly, with Koolhaas' cognisant self-promotion as a fearless researcher in this dark realm. Armed with the cool analysis of systems theory, the audience witnessed a kind of Luhmannian rider in the jungle of Lagos.[3]

Hardly surprising then that Koolhaas' project quickly attracted attention in Europe and the USA, changing the Western perception of Lagos. A city that the West had tended to view as merely the urban signature of a corrupt, mismanaged state was transformed into a projection surface for Western fears about the future. Lagos – and especially Oshodi – became an icon of terror, a hyperversion of Fritz Lang's expressionist nightmare *Metropolis* transformed into reality, spectacularly framed by such phrases as "state of emergency" and "necropolis".[4]

The real findings of Koolhaas' research were less dramatic, but no less idealising. According to Koolhaas, Lagos was neither more nor less than a prime example of urban self-organisation. Viewed from a helicopter, Koolhaas' preferred means of transport, the supposed chaos revealed a hidden order. Not one organised and held together by a state paralysed by corruption, violence and mismanagement. Instead, the actual coherence of the city resulted from the individual citizens, their own creativity, improvisation, and the power of their agency. Despite all the constraints and impossibilities, they were the ones who enabled Lagos to function. And not just in the form of a fixed, stable order:

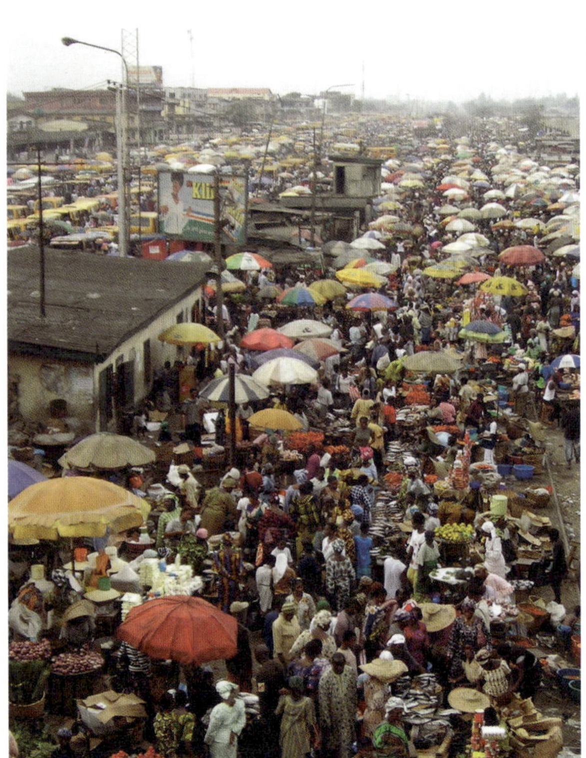

A

Photo: © Peter Probst

1 Pierre Belanger et al (eds) 2000, *Lagos Handbook, or a Brief Description of What May be the Most Radical Urban Condition on the Planet,* Cambridge, Massachusetts

2 Bregtje van der Haak 2003, *Lagos / Koolhaas,* New York, as well as Rem Koolhaas and Bregtje van der Haak 2005, *Lagos Wide and Close,* Submarine Films

3 The list of Koolhaas critics is correspondingly long, see Matthew Gandy 2005, Learning from Lagos, *New Left Review* 33: 36–52.

4 Mike Davis 2004, Planet of Slums. Urban Involution and Informal Proletariat, *New Left Review* 63: 5–34

Lagos' urban signature was far more change and transience, the temporary and transitory generated by circumstances and, at the same time, defying them.

III

Long before Koolhaas' study, Nigerian geographers, architects and urban planners had presented similar analyses and reports.[5] In other words, the base data were already widely known. Founded in 1860, Oshodi belonged to the crescent-shaped development of numerous shanty settlements set up in the course of the 19th century around Lagos, a harbour town born from the slave trade. The first urban boom was triggered by the railway from Lagos to the north, built to support the colonial administration in recruiting thousands of workers from all over the country. With the majority of these workers usually settling in Oshodi, the foundation was laid for the district's cosmopolitan structure. The second major population boom came in the 1950s, when Oshodi's cheap rents made it a popular district for anyone who found a job in the newly constructed factories in Ikeja and Ilupeja. The third period of Lagos' population explosion in the 1970s was ushered in by Nigeria's independence in 1960, the development of the oil industry and the OPEC high-price policy. Nigeria experienced an economic upswing and rapid population growth, with the number of Lagos residents tripling in just ten years.

In an attempt to get on top of the problem of increasing traffic flows, vast amounts were pumped into developing the road infrastructure. The German construction company Julius Berger oversaw the building of new motorways and bridges.

The same company also constructed the clover-leaf junction of Agege and Oworonki, south of the airport, which became home to the Oshodi market. By the 1960s, the market had already developed into one of the key trading centres where the urban population bought food. With burgeoning urban growth and the new road structures, this situation changed as the distribution of labour was added to the distribution of food. As a result, the junction became a massive bus stop where buses and their passengers merged with market stalls and their customers.

The Local Government Council tolerated the spread of market stalls, factoring in the illegality of many stalls as a fixed income from the taxes and receipts of the stall rents. In the 1970s, Nigeria's economic power still significantly exceeded the many other aspiring developing countries, but the boom fuelled by years of high oil prices was followed by an economic and political crash. As oil prices fell, the debts incurred in infrastructure development could no longer be serviced. The military junta, with their power based on violence, corruption and despotism, lacked any kind of legitimacy. The revenues served to secure the state apparatus. As Lagos city ran out of money and state structures collapsed, self-organisation became increasingly widespread.[6]

IV

As indicated above, Koolhaas' analysis fitted in with an existing interpretative pattern. Thus what makes his work on Lagos interesting is not his argument as such, but rather how it impacted the city and what it led to. The external eulogy to Lagos' self-organisation amounted to the city's aesthetic ennoblement. Even if this did not in itself produce new artistic projects by local actors, it did generate a framework allowing such projects to become visible for the West.

The first example here is Depth of Field, or DOF as it is known, a collective of young Nigerian photographers founded in 2001 at the Bamako Photo Biennial. The members include such names as Uche James Iroha and Emeka Okereke whose own work has, in the meantime, also gained international recognition. The DOF Lagos members started to explore the city rather like ethnographers. In contrast to the shots taken by Koolhaas's team, which remained on the surface, their declared aim was to provide a photo-documentary view into the "depth of field". What they found and photographed were and are, first and foremost, everyday scenes and transitory moments, as well as modes of appropriation and creative reinterpretation. These include, for instance, Okadas small motorbikes, used to transport both people and goods, people getting onto one of the yellow Molue buses, once the landmark symbol of Oshodi, or young men collecting scrap metal under motorway bridges to turn it into consumer goods. [→ Fig. **B**]

A second example: Dil Humphrey-Umezulikee, alias Dilomprizulike, self-dubbed "Junkman of Africa" and founder of the "Junkyard Museum of Awkward Things". He was only known to a small circle until the late 1990s, a situation that changed as a result of the interest generated by Koolhaas' work. The material for Dil's works recalls his teacher El Anatsui, probably the best known Nigerian artist in the West at present. Just like Anatsui, Dilom-

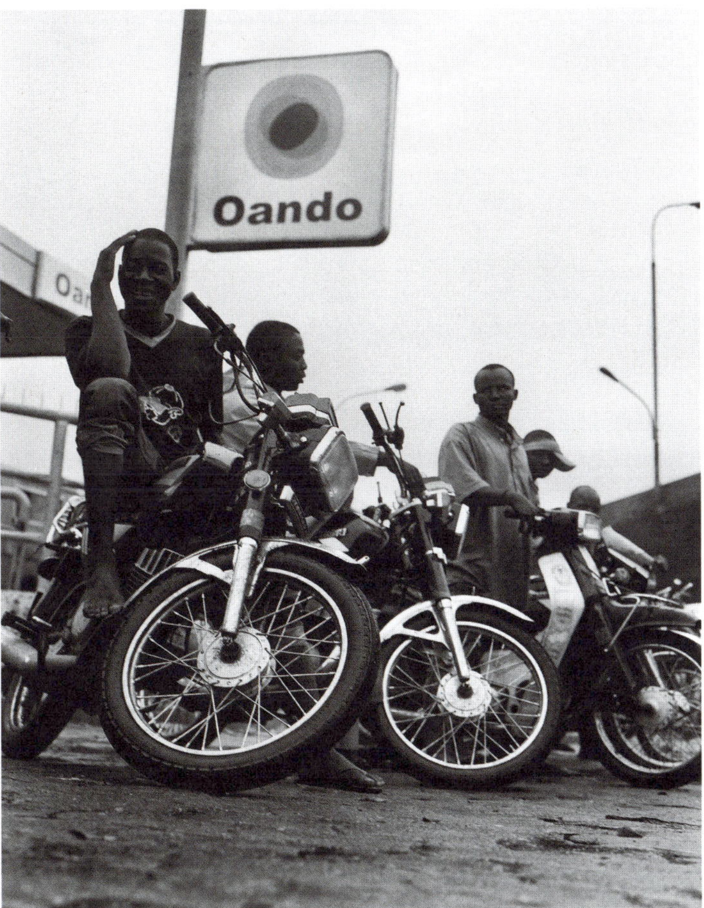

5 One of the central figures was David Aradeon, a photographer and professor of architecture at the University of Lagos. Aradeon was also a member of the Creative Intelligence Agency (CIA), which presented urban planning studies of Lagos. See David Aradeon, 2001, Oshodi: Replanner's Options for a Subcity, *Glendora Review: African Quarterly on the Arts* 2/1: 51–58.

6 Abubahkar Momoh 2000, Youth Culture and Area Boys in Lagos, in: Attahiru Jega (ed.), *Identity Transformations and Identity Politics under Structural Adjustment in Nigeria*, Uppsala, pp.181–203

B UNTITLED, EMEKA OKEREKE

prizulike also recycles objects that have been thrown away. From refuse, old clothes and scrap metal, he constructs such installations and assemblages as *Waiting for the Bus* – a group of people clothed in rags and standing at the edge of the road. But Dil's position is more radical than his teacher. While Anatsui is primarily concerned with formal aesthetics, Dil produces political abject art focused on the processes of discarding, separation and disposal – irrespective of whether person or object. Both can become trash if the society decides to discard them and declares them trash. The shocking thing is not trash itself, but rather the societal processes labelling someone or something trash.

A third example: the *Glendora Review.* The magazine was founded in the mid-1990s by Nigerian publisher Olakunle Tejuoso as a project to counter the intellectual and cultural void under the Abacha military regime. The *Glendora Review* rapidly grew into a key medium for Nigerian art criticism, gaining an international profile in 2001 with an issue dedicated exclusively to Lagos.[7] The majority of articles in the issue explored Lagos' unconventional fascination for the Nigerian general public. According to US-based artist and art historian Dele Jegede, who edited the issue, Lagos is movement and permanent change. Equally feared and admired, the city occupies a very special place in the Nigerian imagination. Celebrating Lagos as a location of ambivalence, correlated with Koolhaas' celebration of uncontrolled forces of development that defy any attempt at planning yet are nonetheless self-organising. This 2001 issue located the *Glendora Review* as a prominent platform for aesthetic reflection on Lagos. In 2005, in a similar vein, the book *Lagos. A City at Work* [→ Fig. C] appeared as a *Glendora* special edition. Koolhaas and photographer Edgar Cleijne in turn planned a volume entitled *Lagos: How it Works* as a response. However, although the book has been announced, it has never been published.

V

The partial dissolution and restructuring of the Oshodi market in early 2009 did not only mark the end of Koolhaas' paradigm, but also the partial dissolution of art forms that took this paradigm as an orientation. Aside from its book *Lagos. A City at Work* published in 2005, the *Glendora Review* has not produced any more issues. Dilomprizulike has moved on from Lagos and is now settled in Germany. In the meantime, the DOF members have also turned to other subjects and themes. [→ Fig. D] Conversely, the last years have seen new artists, curators and philanthropists appearing on the scene with a critical distance to a discourse of state decay, urban creativity and self-organisation.

The traditional centres of this discourse were and have remained such European cultural centres as the Goethe-Institut[8] and the *Maison de France,* though new locations have also become established. One of these is the Artistic License Gallery in the Sandilane Arcade on Victoria Island. In March 2009, only two months after the clean-up operation at the Oshodi market, the gallery showed works by Toyin Omolowo. Omolowo's stringent geometrically structured images based on textile design had as little to do with one of Dilomprizulike's trash installations as the

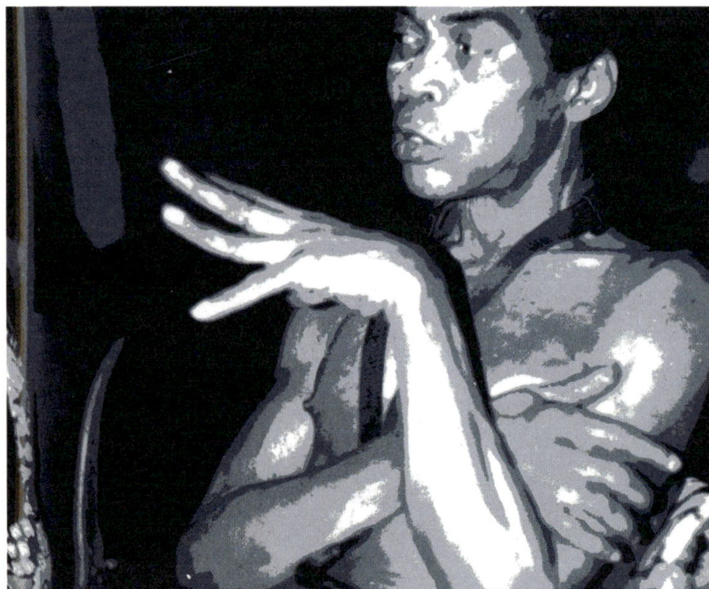

Graphics: © Weyinmi Atigbi; Photo: © Glendora Lagos

C   Double page from *Lagos. A City at Work,* published by Glendora

7   Dele Jegede (ed.) 2001, Lagos: Cognizance, *Glendora Review: African Quarterly on the Arts* 3/2: 5

8   With Goethe-Institut support, for example, the Germany-based artist Emeka Udemba realised two interventions in Lagos in 2005 and 2008, artistically transforming a street (*Lagos Open*) and two churches (*In God We Trust*). Emeka Udemba 2008, *Transforming Public Space. Two Art Interventions in Lagos,* Lagos.

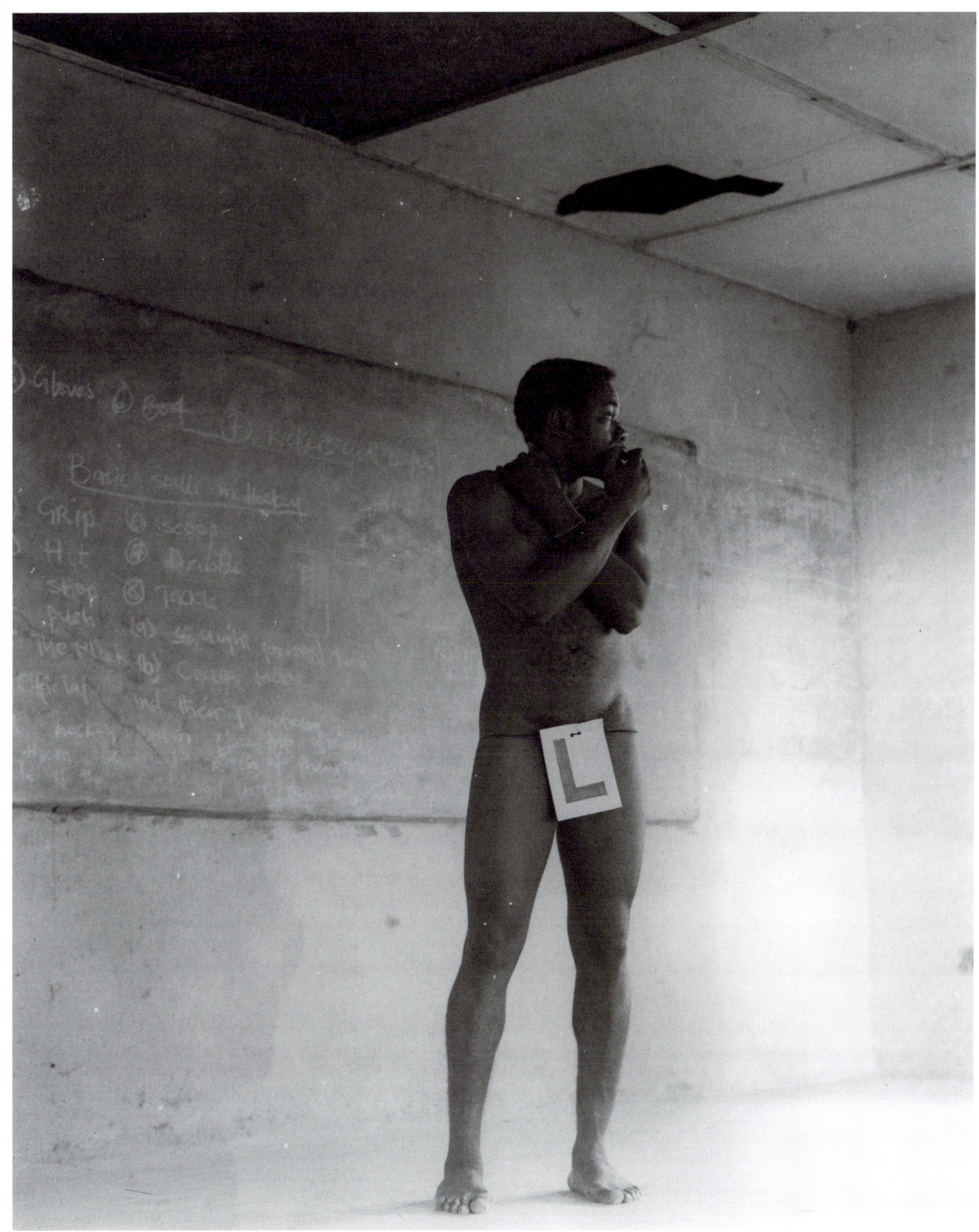

D LEARNER 3, UCHE JAMES IROHA, 2000

rich Victoria Island with the once disreputable Oshodi. In contrast, the most prominent example for the change in the arts scene may well be the Centre for Contemporary Art in McEwen Road, some kilometres south of Oshodi near Lagos University. Founded by Bisi Silva in 2007, the Centre has become one of the leading addresses for contemporary Nigerian art.[9] In its self-defined role as an alternative space for art, it not only functions as a gallery but also as an international meeting point where foreign artists and curators can come together with local actors.[10]

Undoubtedly, many of the new locations, artists and initiatives continue to follow the principle of the temporary and transitory. A location that only opened yesterday may no longer exist today, or have moved and now reside under a different name. But it is precisely this transformation of Lagos that is also a guiding theme – at least as it is exemplified by Babatunde Fashola.

The son of an old and influential Lagos family, Fashola is the governor of Lagos State and, in this capacity, also the mayor of Lagos. He came into office in 2007 – the same year that Bisi Silva opened her Centre for Contemporary Art. With his background as a lawyer, Fashola is linked to the hope for governance and a return of the state. Unlike Nigeria's political elite, Fashola is comparatively young and a new political force. He is, in fact, a political outsider. His vision of Lagos is not fuelled by Fritz Lang's *Metropolis,* but by World Bank funds and his experience in and impressions of Singapore, Dubai and New York. The latter's former mayor Rudolf Guliani belongs to Fashola's stated role models,[11] and just like Guliani, Fashola has also introduced a policy of zero tolerance. He is not only fighting crime, but has started a campaign against urban squalor and street traders. There are now new authorities such as the LAWMA (Lagos Waste Management Authority) and KIA (Kick Against Indiscipline) whose members regularly patrol the city's districts, rigorously taking action against small-time criminals and illegal trash disposal.

The clean-up operation in Oshodi in January 2009 also took place under the auspices of the KIA. In the meantime, the old Oshodi belongs to the past. Under Fashola's new leadership, Lagos today – fifty years after Nigerian independence – is celebrating itself as a project of the future where the federal state motto of "Lagos – Centre of Excellence" is set to become a reality. Lagos State's capital is to be transformed into a modern megacity. Here, the effective publicity displays include such colourful, visually impressive events as the Lagos carnival, [→ Fig. **E**] first held in 2010, rather than critical art space projects such as Emeka Udemba's *Lagos Open.* In the meantime, it has become clear what this means for Oshodi. A process of gentrification has been set in operation. Through the clean-up operation, banishing the notorious "area boys" and installing street lighting, water pipes and sewers, the area has not just become safer and healthier, but also more expensive; rents have risen, and many of the original residents have moved away.

VI

Tunde Kelani has stayed though. After working as a cameraman for Nigerian TV and studying at the London International Film School, he returned to his hometown of Lagos in the late 1970s and set up his first film studio.[12] Kelani's Mainframe Productions are still located in Sehinde Callisto Crescent Road near the Charity bus stop on Apapa Oshodi highway.

Kelani's location in Oshodi and not in the neighbouring Surulere, the centre of the Nigerian film industry, could be read as expressing his distance to Nollywood. The Nollywood films, which were and are quickly churned-out cheap productions, depict the fears and yearnings that are generated by the city and which haunt its residents.[13] [→ Fig. **F**] Kelani's films, though, are not set in Lagos, and do not fit into this genre. Painstakingly produced, they do not follow the Nollywood "hit-and-run" commandment. In a similar way to landscape painting in popular art or works informed by the idea of *Négritude* by academic painters such as Ben Enwonwu, Kelani's cinema morally surveys everyday urban life from the nostalgic, normative-laden perspective of Yoruba culture and tradition. Consequently, Kelani's movies are not located in the urban parvenu of Lagos. Instead, almost without exception, they are set in traditional Yoruba cities such as Ibadan and Abeokuta, a place where Kelani spent his youth and his grandfather still holds the office of *balogun* identifying him as a member of the group that chooses the king's successor and, in case of emergency, also deposes him. The quality of Kelani's films is just as unconventional as his struggle against the infringement of property rights. The goods that once circulated in Oshodi also included pirated copies of Nollywood productions. They both reference each other. Just as Nollywood came of age in the informal sector, it was precisely this

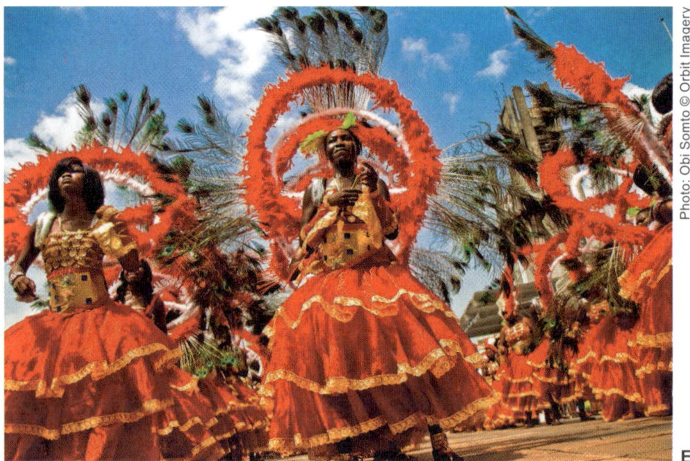

E

9   Bisi Silva 2008, Lagos, *Artforum International* 47/4: 237–239
10 Jazzhole in Awolowo Road in Ikoyi is a second main meeting point.
11 According to Fashola on 12 April 2010 in a lecture at the Harvard Kennedy School of Government

12 For Kelani's biography see Jonathan Haynes 2007, TK in NYC. An Interview with Tunde Kelani, *Postcolonial Text* 3/2: 1–16.
13 Onookome Okome 2002, Writing the Anxious City. Images of Lagos in Nigerian Home Videofilms, in: Okwui Enwezor (ed.), *Under Siege. Four African Cities. Freetown, Johannesburg, Kinshasa, Lagos,* Documenta 11/Platform Four, Ostfildern Ruit, pp. 315–336

sector that also produced practices of appropriation and adaptation. Like other filmmakers too, Kelani suffered from these practices. This changed though with the release of his film *Arugba* in 2009. Here Kelani took a new approach. Like many of his films, *Arugba* is also set in the field of tension between corrupt politics and Yoruba religion as providing a moral authority for sanctions and adjustment. Filmed with Panasonic P2 HD, the film interweaves the contemporary tale of a weak king, primarily set on increasing his wealth, and the story of a young dancer who is trying to win the favour of a young Yoruba priestess.[14]

Unlike Kelani's earlier films, *Arugba* is neither available in the shops, nor exists as a video or DVD. Instead, his film is shown in public spaces. Taking up the tradition of mobile Yoruba street theatre, Kelani and his team travel across the country bringing the film to the audience. After the screening, the team and audience then discuss the film. [→ Fig. **G**]

VII

Fashola's Lagos State government supports Kelani. The state comprises over twenty local governments, and *Arugba* has already been shown in most of them. One can assume that this support is due to more than just the state promotion of the arts. Indebted to the consumer society model, Fashola's government regards Lagos as a company with the city's residents as its customers; yet he also realises that the capitalist machine driving this model produces its own victims. In this context, Kelani's call in his films to retain the existing regional cultural heritage, take it as a point of moral orientation and not – as the members of the Pentecostal churches do – throw it onto the scrapheap of history, functions as a symbolic *vade mecum* on the road to transform Lagos into a modern megacity.

The public welcomes the government's efforts. In January 2010, Nigerian broadsheet *The Nation* led with "From Shame to Shine" as the headline for its review one year on of Fashola's achievements in general and the transformation of Oshodi in particular.[15] What was still an eyesore until very recently is today a reason for pride in the powers of urban renewal. Admittedly, Lagos' notorious "go slow" still exists in many locations across the city, and the introduction of the new red Fashola buses has done nothing to change it. The lustre of the city is, quite literally, crumbling underneath. Lagos is not Dubai, and you would look in vain for such spectacular buildings as Jesse Reiser and Nanako Umemoto's *O-14*. The new buildings here are straightforward off-the-shelf architectural constructions, at times shoddily finished. On 26 April 2010, for instance, a two-storey shopping mall in Oshodi collapsed, burying several people in the rubble. The site had been developed by the Lagos State Government, which then commissioned a private construction company with the

building work. This was already the second accident of its kind; investigations are on-going.

To take up the question asked by Koolhaas and others – can one learn from Lagos? – the only certain answer is simultaneously one of the oldest; as a popular Nigerian saying puts it. "No condition is permanent". In view of the half-life of analyses and images which present Lagos as symbolising the transience of urban planning, it would be advisable to bear that saying in mind.

Translation from German by Andrew Boreham

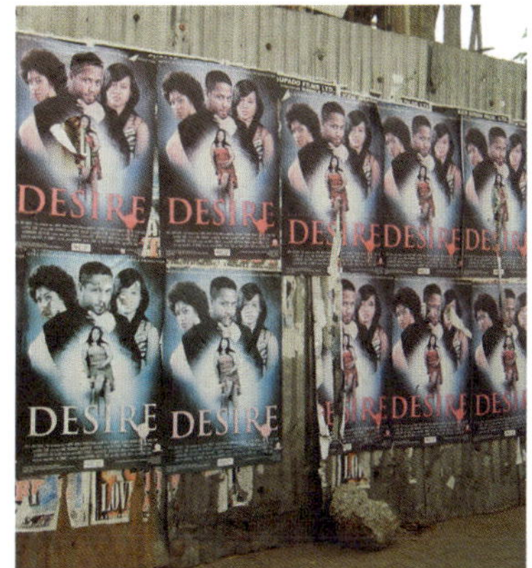

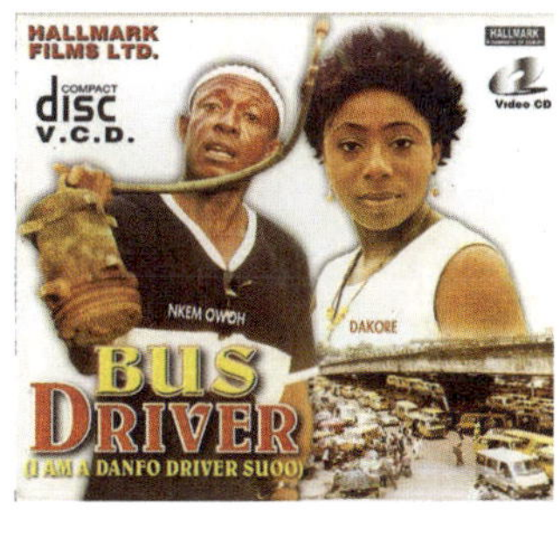

F

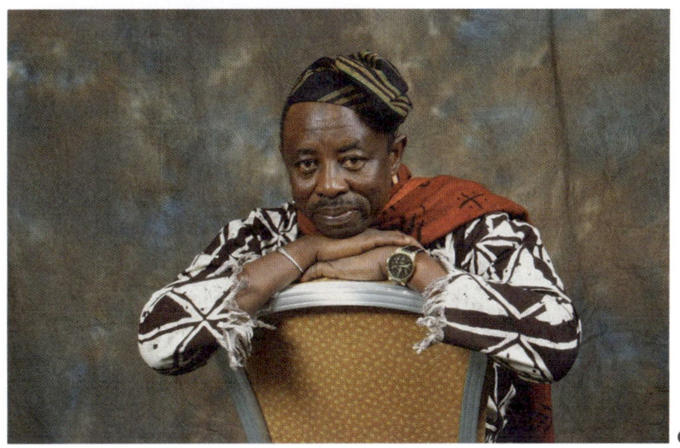

G

14 The film is set in the Yoruba city of Osogbo, with its well-known Osun Festival. On the background here, see Peter Probst 2011, *Osogbo and the Art of Heritage. Monuments, Deities, and Money.* Bloomington.

15 Tosin Adeniran, Oshodi Market. From Shame to Shine, *The Nation,* 1 June 2010

Centre for Contemporary Art, Lagos

A DISCUSSION BETWEEN
BISI SILVA AND KERSTIN PINTHER

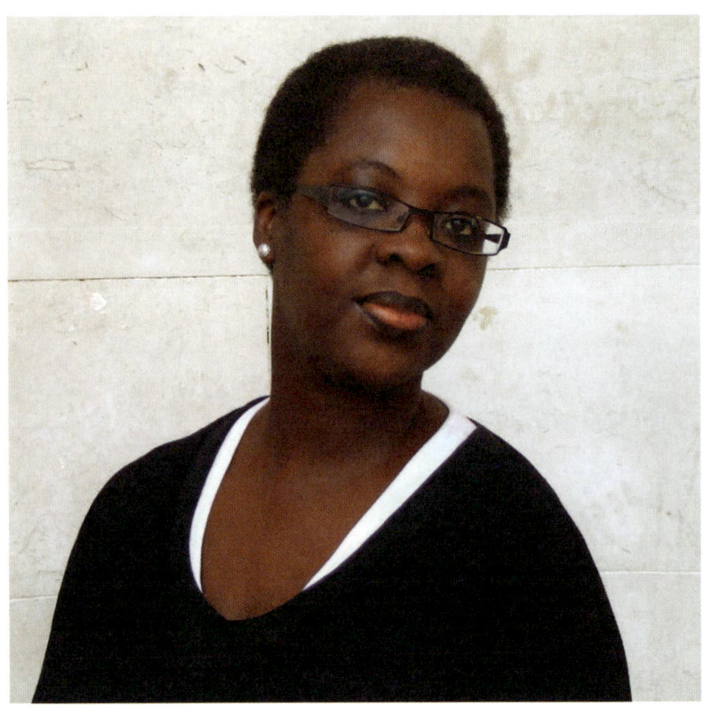

KERSTIN PINTHER: What is your personal background? What did you do before starting CCA, the Centre for Contemporary Art, Lagos?

BISI SILVA: I studied languages with a minor in History of Art at the University of Dijon, France. After that I returned to the UK and did a Masters in Curating of Contemporary Art at the Royal College of Art in London. More or less, I have always worked within the arts, starting off as an art administrator then doing the curatorial course; later I continued work and I did independent curatorial projects in England. About seven years ago, when I moved back to Nigeria, I thought it was important to take time to know the context, which was new for me as I left Lagos as a teenager. I felt that it would be inappropriate to come back and just set something up. I did a few independent projects and then set up the Centre for Contemporary Art, Lagos [CCA, Lagos] in December 2007. We have been open for just over two years and six months.

KERSTIN PINTHER: What made you found CCA, Lagos? What were your ideas and aims?

BISI SILVA: I guess it's something that actually started ten years ago. I've always been interested in starting my own space and in 1998/99 I came to Nigeria on holiday from the UK and I gave a talk at Jazzhole on curatorial practice. I remember somebody saying: "Oh, you Nigerians who live abroad, you don't come back home and interact with us." So I took up the challenge and did a little bit of research and I felt that instead of doing an exhibition, what I thought was lacking was critical discourse, the critical contextualisation of the work that was being created. So instead of focusing on more exhibitions, I thought about organising a series of talks. I approached the *Prince Claus Fund* for funding for a one-year programme that involved bringing art historians, curators, art critics and writers to Nigeria – one person every two months, so about six speakers. It was important that the project was not just Lagos-based but that it could also travel to other parts of the country. The speakers, who included Yacouba Konaté, William Miko, Colin Richards and Eddie Chambers, did not only visit Lagos, they also had the opportunity to travel to the east where we collaborated with the University of Nigeria, Nsukka, and to the north, to Ahmadu Bello University, Zaria. The response was incredibly positive. I remember for the opening lecture, there must have been between 150 and 200 people in attendance (of course including my extended family and friends who came to support me). It is only in retrospect that I can appreciate the profound effect of that first lecture and the entire programme within the local context. The guest was British Art Historian Katy Deepwell, and her talk was on the history of feminist art practice from the 1960s to the present. Of course at that early stage of my interaction with the Nigerian art scene, I was oblivious to the extremely male-dominated Nigerian art world, the suffocating patriarchy of the society and the invisibility of women artists. And to compound the situation, most if not all the images presented a conceptual work which was in most cases unheard of here and practised even less. I am happy to say that despite some angry mutterings from the 'conservatives' I did not feel – at least directly or openly – under attack. In fact the reverse, as people were incredibly interested and open to that lecture and the others that followed. And I am happy to add that it resulted in one of the artists and lecturers at Ahmadu Bello University taking up the history of Nigerian women artists as the subject of his doctoral research which he successfully defended about two years ago.

Therefore, when I finally moved back to Nigeria, the starting point for CCA was always about knowledge production and dissemination. It was about asking: How can we get people to know what's going on within contemporary art not only in Nigeria but also regionally, continent-wide and then globally? And I just felt that there is no point in starting anything without access to knowledge, without that kind of opening up of the minds, without awareness. There is no point in realising an exhibition on beauty if nobody is engaging with the concept of beauty in its wider sense, or if you want to do something on identity or sexuality or the body. There were very few themes and discourses that were being engaged with in-depth, so I thought: "Okay, let me start a library and a research centre, a place where people could come and consult through the books." I wasn't interested in starting a space at that point. I thought I could do exhibitions in different spaces but I felt that the library was important. And if later on, the space came – great! But then I was thinking that people could have been reading about all these things but they won't see it. It would be incomplete, just one part of the view, of the perspective. So I felt that they should have a space where they could experience the conceptual diversity of exhibitions, [and where] they see curatorial practice in practice. They could also look at the way in which artists are dealing with different subjects and issues in very different ways. Also I wanted to provide a platform for artists that may have a less conservative artistic practice. A lot of galleries and spaces may not be open to them, as most galleries here are commercial. So that's how CCA came about.

KERSTIN PINTHER: Could you tell me more about how CCA works? How is it organised and financed? What are the main activities?

BISI SILVA: CCA is first off a specialist visual art library, then we organise exhibitions. We have an art space downstairs and we organise a lot of talks and panel discussions because that's the educational side of what we do – that relates to the books and knowledge production side. We also do workshops in order to provide a platform for professional artistic development. And also by default we encourage young curators. This is a space they can come to and spend time with us to learn about curatorial practice. Then we also do collaborations on different levels with other institutions. We are also interested in taking our projects out of Nigeria. So we've done an exhibition in South Africa and also in Mumbai.

KERSTIN PINTHER: And the CCA is organised as a non-profit organisation?

BISI SILVA: Yes, the CCA is an independent, non-profit-making visual arts organisation. It has a board of trustees, which include Joke Jacobs, one of the top actresses in Nigeria and El Anatsui, one of the internationally recognised artists. Valerie Edozien and Kehinde Oyeleke, for example, are professionals who contribute valuable organisational, managerial and financial skills.

KERSTIN PINTHER: What kind of public does the CCA have? How would you describe it?

BISI SILVA: Artists mainly, art students, but also art enthusiasts, people who are interested in art. The art public in Nigeria is not huge, and less for experimental visual art, so we are not talking about thousands of people. The audience for our programmes is embryonic and we are building more or less from scratch. It is diverse and it is growing as we do try to reach out as widely as possible, we have quite an interesting mailing list. We don't reach the collectors as much, because we don't show collectable work. I can't say art historians, because I don't know any real contemporary art historians. We have a bizarre situation in Nigeria where there are a lot of people with a PhD in Art history but it could be mostly in batik, ceramics, etc. We do interact with Yaba Tech [Yaba College of Art and Technology] as well as the art department at the University of Lagos. From there, postgraduate students come to use the library, not as many as we would like … Once in a while we have the schools around the area here but we don't have the staff to focus just on the schools, so it's sporadic. If we have somebody who is interested in education, we do encourage them to develop that possibility. We did have a staff member who was really interested in working with schools and we started building up a relationship with about four or five schools that would come to our shows but then when he left we didn't have anybody to take over.

KERSTIN PINTHER: How would you describe the contemporary art scene in Lagos?

BISI SILVA: I think that in Africa it's one of the most dynamic, one of the most vibrant. We have a lot of artists and we have probably the largest number of art departments within universities on the continent. Over twenty. Almost each state has an art department, not art schools or academies, mostly art departments. This means that we graduate quite a lot of artists each year. We have a very, very vibrant collectors' base compared to other African countries. So you do have quite a lot of artists who make a good living from selling their work. Lagos is predominantly commercial. The other cities in the country are less commercial because they don't have a market and they are usually attached to a university. However, the Achilles heel to a more widespread visibility, to international penetration, is that art in Nigeria is essentially conservative – the result of academic fine art education in which the curriculum has barely changed. Barely! You know, it hasn't changed over the last fifty years and it definitely hasn't caught up with trends of the late 20th century or early 21st century. I think that the art groups of younger artists are very much interested in being more experimental in their artistic practice and I think that people are now becoming aware that one has to expand the repertoire of artistic medium and also contextual parameters. They are more receptive to the possibilities that are out there. I would say that it's an exciting time because the contemporary art scene is evolving. It is at a very critical and transitional stage and it will be really interesting to see the way in which it develops over the next one or two years.

KERSTIN PINTHER: So besides the public art schools, which other institutions would you consider important in Lagos for the art world?

BISI SILVA: The government has been very, very lax in providing the correct infrastructure that allows arts to grow. I think that this has contributed to the slow growth of the visual arts. You can imagine an oil-rich country that has not yet thought of building a museum of modern art and contemporary art! At the same time it is also one of the countries with one of the richest and oldest cultural heritages, not only in Africa but in the world, so it's problematic and embarrassing. The visual arts – and I'm sure the other arts as well – are not developed at the rate that they could [be]; so there are many difficulties for individuals and organisations to realise and fulfil their potential. This makes it also difficult for Nigeria to take its place properly within the global art community. It is being done, through the efforts of individuals setting up institutions: most of the art activities that you see in Lagos and in Nigeria are the efforts of individuals, whether it's Azu Nwagbogu with his African Artists Foundation or Mrs Chellarams with ArtHouse, which organises the twice-yearly art auction or whether it's CCA, which engages with a more contemporary, conceptual dimension of artistic practice and brings in different artists, curators, and art historians to interact and facilitate cultural dialogue and exchange. Whether it's the commercial galleries that are providing avenues for artists to show their work, sell and make a living. We must not forget foreign institutions like the Goethe-Institut that has been extremely dynamic, especially recently under the former director Arne Schneider as well as the current director Roderik Gross, who is also putting together some interesting programmes and collaborations. The British Council has been in crisis, as far as I'm concerned, for many years. And the sum total of their contribution to the visual arts can be summed up as inconsequential. The Alliance Française, when they were in their bigger building, were very dynamic on all fronts. They still are within the realm of music and dance and they also have a small space for visual arts. When you take the totality of all these individual possibilities, bring it together, it begins to create some kind of a critical mass, which makes for a very vibrant visual art sector.

KERSTIN PINTHER: In this context, how would you consider the impact of people like Okwui Enwezor or Chika Okeke, who are quite influential internationally? What is their impact on the local art scene in Nigeria?

BISI SILVA: Well. I don't know. I have been here for nearly seven years and I don't think I have bumped into them here, which of course doesn't mean they haven't been here. From what I gather, Okwui was here during one of his platforms when he was artistic director of documenta. That visit was around 2000 or 2001. I am not sure as I was still in England. I know that Chika Okeke was here for research purposes a few years ago, maybe three or so years ago. I really don't know if I can say that they had an impact on what's going on in the local art scene. I do know that Enwezor has worked with and commissioned new work from Depth of Field (DOF), the photography collective, in some of the exhibitions he has organised; Seville Biennale and *Snap Judgments* come to mind, however I don't recall if it necessitated a trip here. The wide gap between art professionals here and abroad is quite problematic and we need to find ways to bridge that gap. But then, I think that Nigeria is not an accessible place, just as Lagos. I think that, if people do want to interact, they do have to make the effort to come a few times, get a good grasp of what's going on and then see in which way they can make a contribution that would have a lasting effect. We have texts and books written by people like Enwezor in the library but it is only accessed by a few readers; the majority may recognise the names as being Nigerian but little else beyond that. However that is not to say we don't have Nigerians in the diaspora interacting locally, we do, and in the last three years it is increasingly substantial but mainly artists. We have had Emeka Udemba, Chidi Kuwubiri, Nnenna Okore, Dilomprizulike; we have had visiting artists such as Victor Ekpuk, Wilfred Ukpong, Lawson Oyekan, Anaele Iroh. Academics such as Sylvester Ogbechie and Nkiru Nzegwu have given talks at CCA. There are a lot more – that I may not even know about – coming to Nigeria at least once if not twice a year with an interest in coming more often and engaging with the art scene. And I know of other artists with international visibility who are deeply interested in doing something here.

KERSTIN PINTHER: What do you consider the strength of the contemporary art scene in Nigeria, in Lagos?

BISI SILVA: Its resilience is exemplary. Nigerian artists are ambitious go-getters – almost like modern-day explorers, avid for information, ready to interact and engage across cultures and boundaries. And, as I said, in the absence of government interest, doing whatever it takes to make themselves, their work and their ideas relevant locally, across the continent and globally. I love that spirit. And another aspect that I find interesting is that as an outsider that dynamism, the vibrancy is not visible to the naked eye: you can feel it but you can't see it on the surface. It is only when you sharpen your antennae, go beneath the radar, then you begin to discover incredible things, and the cultural vibe of the city begins to reveal itself. I always find it funny when visiting curators want to come here and they expect to book lots of appointments in advance. They collect names and set up time schedules. You are not going to get any vibe from Lagos that way because you are operating above the radar.

At the moment, outside of the traditional media of painting and sculpture, photography is very important. It is really strong and has the highest potential but it still needs a lot more structure. A large percentage of photographers are self-taught here and self-taught almost in an isolationist kind of way – apart from the mentorship scheme, where young photographers can work for a couple of months with older photographers such as Don Barber, Jide Adeniyi-Jones – and through workshops led by Akinbode Akinbiyi who is based in Germany, as well as the mentorship of Tam Fiofori and Pa Ojeikere. This has created exciting possibilities, and groups such as Depth of Field have been generous in working with even younger artists. We also have the collective Black Box but as a group they have not been able to make the kind of impact that Depth of Field did although individual members of Black Box are doing extremely well, such as Andrew Esiebo, Abraham Ogbohase and Uche Okpa-Iroha who recently won the Seydou-Keita-Prize at the 2009 Bamako Encounters. Video art also has the potential to bring out some exciting possibilities. But I still think that's a few years away as it is an extremely new field within the Nigerian context and we can't yet single out anybody in the medium right now but I know that artists are working hard. I know that there are many artists exploring the medium seriously. That's why in 2009 CCA focus was on video art. We showed the exhibition Identity: An Imagined State and the accompanying publication, which is one of the first documenting only video art in Nigeria. We also have Jelili Atiku whose main medium over the past four [or] five years is performance art, as well as Emeka Ogboh who is creating some really exciting work using sound as the starting point for his artistic practice.

Nigeria is a big country and most artists working in an experimental manner or who think conceptually are really working in isolation. Critical and profound artistic working – outside of traditional painting and sculpture – is a utopian undertaking in many places outside of Lagos, and the two, three other 'art centres' in Nigeria. Of course, we cannot put the Nsukka and Enugu axis in this category which – because of the history of the University of Nigeria, Nsukka, and the impact of El Anatsui – has allowed artists to embrace a more experimental form of practice. Artists such as Lucy Azubuike, Nnenna Okore, Bright Eke, Dilomprizulike, Amuche Ngwu-Nnabueze, Amarachi Okafor, Alozie Onyirioha, just to mention a few, that El Anatsui has either taught or mentored, helping them to make their mark. The rudiments of the content is there but it needs to be harnessed to make an important impact, and if artists realise this and begin to have a strategy that helps and guide them, then I believe, it's going to be extremely exciting.

KERSTIN PINTHER: Are photography and media art taught at the art schools?

BISI SILVA: No, well let me not be categorical in saying that. Let's not say, that they're not. I know they do a certificate at Yaba Tech and that they teach photojournalism at the Nigerian Institute of Journalism. However there are no three-year degree courses in photography or digital media.

KERSTIN PINTHER: What is the present status of painting? Nigeria was or is still very strong in painting. Is there any shift from painting to installation?

BISI SILVA: Painting continues occupying its position at the top of the artistic medium hierarchy in Nigeria. It is the preferred medium of art schools, of artists and of collectors. It reigns supreme. And many Nigerian artists have perfected their technical skills. The problem lies, I feel, in the lack of development of content in which the same themes are regurgitated ad nauseam. The average Nigerian artist spends hours, days and even months in his or her studio, fine-tuning the lines and colours and shades. The contextual aspect is lacking, a lot of themes are not drawn out or developed. So there is still a lot of work that needs to be done. However there are a few artists out there trying to break out like Kainebi Osahenye of course, who had an exhibition at CCA last year. We were interested in using that exhibition as a way of talking about, looking at painting beyond being something decorative that you put in your house, beyond being one- or two-dimensional but something that could actually be in another format, a different medium and that's, I think, when we started an interesting conversation. There are a couple of people who are trying to push the boundaries of painting, and, it'll be interesting to see what comes out in the next years.

KERSTIN PINTHER: How do you see the roles of so-called returnees: artists, filmmakers who return to Lagos for some weeks, some months and who are interested in getting to do something in Lagos?

BISI SILVA: I think a lot of artists have started doing that. You know Akinbode Akinbiyi comes as often as he can. We have Emeka Udemba, who has done some really great projects here. Who else comes? Junkman [Dilomprizulike] who lives abroad – he comes in and does performances here at the Goethe-Institut. So I think that there is a big interest in people coming back and really doing something tangible. It will engender a vibrant sector if you bring both groups together: people who have just a little understanding of the Nigerian situation but also have the wider view, and the locals who have a very deep understanding of their context; that makes a very successful and inclusive scene. So I'm very interested in those possibilities. I'm interested, not only in Nigerians living abroad but also interacting with other Africans. You have to understand that even within Africa we don't know each other very well, so even interacting within the continent I think is extremely important in order to be able to create multiple centres of artistic excellence and activity.

KERSTIN PINTHER: Would you like to add something?

BISI SILVA: CCA, Lagos is open for business. Welcome to our world!

KERSTIN PINTHER: Thank you very much!

The conversation took place in March 2010 at CCA, Lagos.

▦ D.A.REVIEW

April 1977, Vol. 13, no. 100

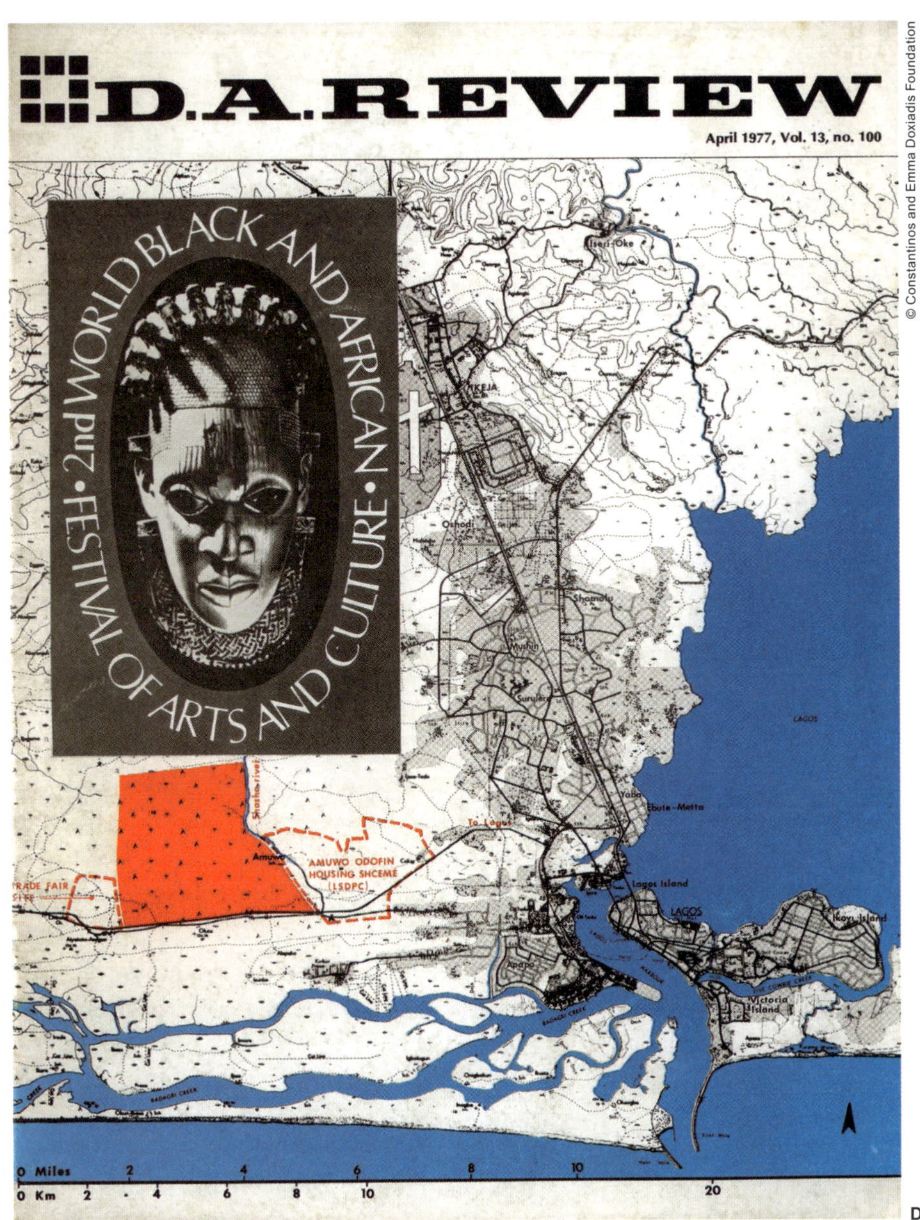

D.A. REVIEW, APRIL 1977

FESTAC '77

From 15 January to 12 February 1977, eleven years after Dakar's *Festival Mondial des Arts Nègres,* Lagos held the second edition of this Pan-African cultural spectacle. FESTAC '77 carried forward the desire to create an independent narrative of African or black culturality and historicity. As part of the expression of Pan-African solidarity, FESTAC '77 also provided an opportunity to host representatives from the global black alliance. During the one-month festival, guests from the black diaspora were offered an unparalleled presentation of 'traditional' culture. The cultural traditions displayed in the form of dance, theatre or archaeological artefacts, often seeming to draw strongly on folklore roots, were the product of a return to Nigeria's pre-colonial culture already underway in the run-up to the event. Meanwhile, at the colloquium held at the same time, theoreticians and intellectuals discussed the black community's intellectual heritage. The display of unity and progress was expressed architecturally in two prestigious building projects: the National Theater and Festac Town. The latter, designed on stringent modernist principles, was constructed specifically to provide accommodation for the international FESTAC guests.

FESTAC '77 was held in the era of Nigeria's meteoric rise to the wealthiest economic power on the African continent. The 1970s oil boom triggered comprehensive state-run development schemes in Nigeria not only aimed at modernising the infrastructure, but also envisaging the revival of a national cultural heritage. As Achille Mbembe wrote in his article *The Dream of a Free Exchange* in the *Tageszeitung* newspaper on 5 June 2010, the aim was less to "foster the creative and expressive potential of its citizens" than "to prescribe certain types of (national) mentalities and behaviours in the name of the official value systems or ideologies". He concluded: "The time is over when Africans idealised differences and local particularities […], [a time] when we believed that only 'authenticity' counted in every form of cultural expression […]. In most cases, the search for something quite our own has led us into a dead end."

The editors

Translation from German by Andrew Boreham

Culture and Modernity Since FESTAC '77

DENIS EKPO

The year 2007 marked the thirtieth anniversary of the Second World Black and African Festival of Arts and Culture, FESTAC '77. The Centre for Black African Arts and Civilization (CBAAC), itself a progenitor of FESTAC and the official institutional custodian of its symbolic capital, had organised a series of commemorative activities including an exhibition at the UNESCO headquarters in Paris. During the exhibition, African cultural materials generated at FESTAC were showcased and there were some commemorative stamps and a few other sundry things. FESTAC '77 was a sixty-nine-nation world event and the ingathering in Lagos, Nigeria, of not only blacks and non-blacks of Africa but also the diasporic remnants of the "black race" scattered all over the world. However, although it was the thirtieth anniversary of celebrations taking place in Nigeria, there was virtually no echo of similar commemorative activities in black and African communities across the other sixty-eight participating nations. Even within Nigeria itself, echoes of FESTAC's anniversary were confined to a few obscure press reports issued by CBAAC. Among the general public in the host country, memories of that grand world event seem to have badly faded or been mangled beyond recognition. For instance, a commemorative survey on the web inviting people in Nigeria and elsewhere to recount their memories of FESTAC attracted only one respondent. And what was his response? He remembered the good old days when Festac Town had good roads and steady power supply compared to today when it has become a slum and a den of robbers.[1] In other words, all that respondent knew of FESTAC was Festac Town, a sprawling housing estate built to accommodate most of FESTAC's participants. The event itself, that which gave birth and name to that town, had faded from memory.

But way back in 1977, all of Africa and the rest of the black world were frolicking to the dithyrambic "Negro rhythms", "tribal drums" and "wild dances" of FESTAC; Lagos had become the mecca of African collective cultural and artistic self-retrieval and self-accreditation. Thirty short years later, it is noteworthy that not only has the memory of that unique event all but faded even in the host country but also, no country in or outside of Africa has hosted a third FESTAC.[2] Given that the interval between the *Festival Mondial des Art Nègres* held in Léopold Sédar Senghor's Senegal in 1966 and the Lagos event was a mere ten years, the conspicuous absence of a follow-up to what was supposed to be a regular revolving celebration of "Africanity", has raised questions not just about the *raison d'être* of the FESTAC jamboree but also about its seemingly troubling hangovers. What was the spirit behind such a gargantuan transnational show-off of "black culture and art"? The more generous reviews of thirty years of FESTAC seem to concentrate on the sheer spectacular exuberances of the mega-event to the exclusion of the undercurrent of ideas, attitudes, anxieties, etc., which at that point in African history called for a FESTAC and justified the enormous expenses required to organise it. Conversely, echoes of the anti-FESTAC hostilities from the then African left can still be heard among reviewers who recall the sheer irrationality of its economic cost to Nigeria and the ruinous and pathetic vainglory of showing off our very weaknesses, including half-naked hysterical dancers and shrieking tribesmen, as if they were our strengths. One reviewer on the web cannot forget what he calls "the bottomless-pit expenses" of FESTAC that nearly ruined the economy of Nigeria.[3] I believe, however, that a less ideologically partisan reassessment of the FESTAC event is both possible and necessary. Perhaps one way to recover one's intellectual balance when remembering FESTAC is to contemplate again the official emblem of the event, the famous Benin mask, and then to imagine what spirit was, or is, concealed behind the exquisite glossy exterior of that celebrative work of "primitive" genius. Though it may be difficult to fully understand the sacred code that produced and indwelt the original Benin mask, it is certainly easy to recapture the sponsoring spirits of FESTAC that reclaimed that mask as its signature emblem. The spirit behind the simulated Benin mask was nothing other than the body of ideas, emotions, worries, memories and hopes that had fired the imagination and armed the hands of those Pan-African cultural ideologues that conceived and engineered the grand event. The term "cultural nationalism" can be said to capture the whole gamut of ideas and anxieties, from the Negro Renaissance movement in America to Negritude and Pan-Africanism[4], through which these black master-thinkers had consistently sought to redeem Africans from the civilisational nonentity where Europe since Hegel had dumped it. FESTAC was all those grand theories of African cultural revivalism removed from books, taken to the marketplace and performed live on the world stage. A confirmatory enactment through performances of Black/African cultural renaissance, it

---

1. *Memories of FESTAC '77*, retrieved on 7 July 2010 from http://www.nairaland.com

2. The French art and culture journal *Africultures* in 2008 devoted an issue to African festivals. See *Africultures* 73 (2008) and my article on FESTAC titled *FESTAC 77 et le projet de la modernité africaine*, p. 26–30, of which the present essay is a modified and enlarged version.

3. Babs Ajayi, *A Strange and Fascinating Nation*, retrieved on 7 July 2010 from http://www.Nigeriaworld.com

4. The Harlem or Negro Renaissance movement (1917–1930) was the first major Black intellectual and cultural movement that sowed the seeds of all subsequent pan-African intellectual as well as cultural-nationalist ideologies such as Négritude, Indigenisme.

was also a strong statement of Africa's assured place in the rendezvous of world civilisations. But beyond these tautological postures of self-confirmation, FESTAC was, perhaps even more significantly, a passionate beckoning to Europe, calling on it to recant its ingrained Hegelian stereotypes about Africa and the black race and to recognise Africa's culture-specific right of way into and within modernity. In other words, beneath the self-intoxicating cultural nationalist drums and dances of FESTAC, the debate with modernity, the coveting of the West's recognition, were the real but concealed leitmotifs. In this essay I want to attempt to recover some occluded meanings and impacts of FESTAC especially with regard to Africa, by reinterrogating that ultra-cultural nationalist event in the light of the ongoing modernity/modernism debate in Africa's postcolonial politics of culture and development.

FESTAC: a Black Riposte to Assaults of a Eurocentric Modernity

Before I tackle how FESTAC connects with the modernity issue, let me say one more word on the ostensible *raison d'être* of that fabulous transnational jamboree. For those who may still be tempted thirty years on to dismiss FESTAC as an unqualifiable "Negro-African" irrationality, a futile show at a time when Africa could hardly feed herself, it might still be necessary to rehearse the conundrum that Africa and the Black world outside Africa did not enter world history by negotiating with Europe or by voyaging to America on the *Mayflower*. Offspring of a defeated, humiliated and offended civilisation, Africans and Blacks of African origin were in modernity, a priori deprived of the privilege of living history as the innocence of becoming. A considerable chunk of modern history is essentially the history of the totalised anthropological disqualification of the black people by white Europe.

The imperial seizure of Africa and the conversion of the sold black man into the manure that grew the foundational economy of the New World are but two of the defining primal wounds that had infected our modernity-consciousness, leading in some cases to severe psychic amputations in cultural self-understanding and historical memory. In the heyday of Pan-African cultural nationalism, leading Black ideologues naturally felt that although newly independent Africa could economically hardly take care of herself, still, the Africans and the New World were summoned by an unenviable fate not to live by bread alone but by first recovering the spiritual/cultural foundations of their civilisational identity claims and then showing them off before a mocking, skeptical modernity that had previously consigned them to an othered non-entity. There was that irresistible existential urge to prove to an Afro-phobic white world that Africans were not civilisational orphans of the New World; that Africa, their ancestral continent, was not a heart of darkness but a treasure house of great ancient civilisations overflowing with great artistic marvels and cultural splendors. FESTAC was the international curating of a global exhibition of the Africans' hitherto misrecognised contributions to the world's cultural heritage.

I believe every African around the globe must have experienced the frisson of a regenerated sense of Africanity; they must have felt a great new collective pride in having successfully rediscovered the millennial heritage of cultural and artistic splendors that once formed the enchanted mytho-poetic backdrop to African civilisation. To the African diaspora in particular, FESTAC must have been the Negro Renaissance dream come true. Being in Lagos and participating in the unique cultural carnival must have been bliss if not heaven. These diasporic blacks must have gone home not only with a heightened sense of re-rootedness in a great civilisation but also a feeling of a more dignified subject-position. To the African in Africa, FESTAC was a celebratory confirmation of what he already intimately knew, namely, the fact that the millennial cultural and artistic genius of Africa had survived the repeated assaults of European cultural vandalism. So gratifying must have been the psycho-existential gains of FESTAC that its Pan-African committee decided to create a custodian institution, CBAAC to perpetuate the memory of the event and disseminate its cultural nationalist spirit and achievements.

The Pathologies of Post-FESTAC Modernity in Africa

The trouble with FESTAC was its morrows. While members of the diaspora went home highly satisfied and satiated with culture and the wonders of Africa, the Africans they left behind had sufficient reasons to gnash their teeth. Once the brief hangover of the hallucinated cultural-nationalist euphoria lived in the prox-

← Collooquium on Negro Art, 1966 Dakar

imity of the FESTAC orgies had dissipated, life in Africa returned to the reality principle, namely, the daily assaults of hunger, violence, underdevelopment. In the host country people necessarily started to wonder what, if anything, had been achieved by such a wild montage of "Africanity" that corresponded to no known reality. Indeed before long, the cultural-nationalist motif of African dignity, pride et cetera was unmasked as a huge collective self-delusion, a massive fraud and arbitrary simulation, because in reality, nothing in post-FESTAC Nigeria/Africa had changed except for the worse. The same seventies and eighties that engendered the cultural nationalist ferment birthing FESTAC were also the periods that saw to the near total dilapidation or in some cases, the total reversal, of the meagre gains of Africa's contact with modernity. Although the happenings that created the anomies of the post-FESTAC years had no direct link to the festival, I want to argue in what follows that the cultural nationalist ethos that got triumphantly dramatised and normalised in FESTAC appeared to have hindered Africa's social, economic and technological modernisation project. In other words, though FESTAC itself was apparently no more than a harmless carnival, the spirit behind its mask, its exacerbated cultural nationalist spirit, when allowed to encroach upon and insinuate itself into the practice of Africa's modernity project, proved pernicious in many respects.

FESTAC had ignited in most of black Africa an intense cultural revivalist fire that pervaded all classes of people. So important was this self-renewal spirit that culture (that is, essentially traditional dance, music and popular theatre) almost replaced the flag as the new symbol of our sovereignty and new-found international pride. So prolific became the use of culture at the hands of the ruling elite that the Nigerian writer Cyprian Ekwensi sarcastically defined culture in those days as what the poor use to entertain the rich.[5] Indeed in most of Africa at that time, no pub-

lic function involving even the obscurest local government official was complete without the ritual culturalist dessert of half-nude dancing maidens or hooting old women clad in raffia, being served red hot. But such self-serving commodification of culture by the elite was nothing compared to what the same elite did with the new-found paradigm of cultural nationalism massively simulated, embellished and legitimised by FESTAC. In the hypertrophy of the FESTAC spirit of cultural nationalism, the political rulers were convinced of the necessity of evolving and pursuing an original African path to modernity in conformity with the cultural/spiritual specificities of the African modernity-consciousness recently rediscovered and celebrated in FESTAC. To underscore the role of FESTAC in promoting the Afro-nationalist path to modernity, one should remember that the nascent African modernity-consciousness was first worked out by the cultural nationalists through the medium of the arts, especially poetry, fiction, painting et cetera. Senghor's Négritude in many respects could be considered Africa's first discourse of its modernity-consciousness because it was an attempt through poetry to recover and integrate native African world views into the modernity heritage.[6] However, the signature tone and the dominant idiosyncrasies of Africa's consciousness of modernity came not from the conciliatory cultural politics of Senghor but from the charismatic accusatory pathos of Chinua Achebe, especially his aesthetico-political characterisation of Europe's advent into Africa as the "falling apart of things".[7] With the success of the *Things Fall Apart* motif in the culture, art and ideology discourses, our modernity-consciousness before FESTAC was already defined almost exclusively in terms of an accusatory, retaliatory strife against European modernity. In FESTAC, within the folds of the cultural nationalist rhetoric and the nativistic flourishes of the performances, the Achebean paranoid modernity-consciousness was inevitably also put on display. After FESTAC, a schizophrenic cultural-nationalist politics founded on, on the one hand, the blaming and coveting of Europe and on the other hand, a going back to the past, led to the emergence or radicalisation of what can be termed the Africanisation ideal as the over-determining spirit and ethos of our commerce with modernity. This ideal, which can be defined as the voluntarist drive to remake the fallen African world in our own Afrocentric image, to tame modernity to our specific cultural needs, became, as a result of the incantatory visuals and rhetoric of FESTAC, powerful pictures etched into the minds of the elite to inspire and dictate the subsequent conception and execution of our modernisation projects. Why were the elite so easily seduced by the cultural-nationalist spirit of FESTAC? The jamboree furnished the feel-good meta-political legitimacy for re-enchanting not just the African past but all that that past stood for in terms of its fundamental difference from, and opposition to, a colonially powered moder-

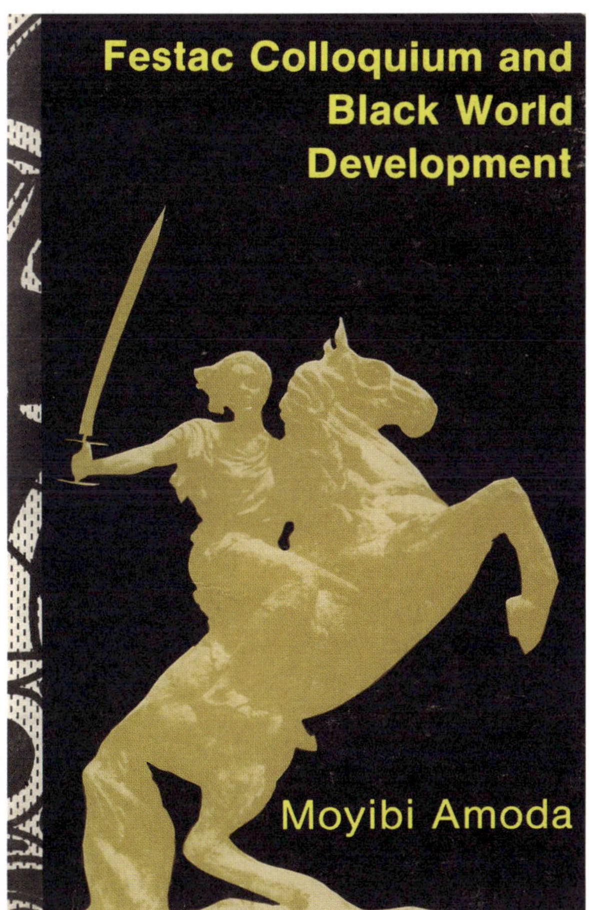

← Festac Colloquium, 1977 Lagos

5   Cyprian Ekwensi was one of Nigeria's pioneer novelists noted mostly for children's stories as well as for city novels such as *Jagua Nana,* amongst others.

6   See Denis Ekpo 2010, Speak Négritude but Think and Act French: The Foundations of Senghor's Political Philosophy, *Third Text* 103 24/2: 227–239.

7   Chinua Achebe's charismatic novel *Things Fall Apart* (1958) was the first major novel that described the civilisational rapture of Africa by Europe in essentially adversary and traumaphiliac terms.

nity. It had helped not only to rouse back to life whole slabs of pre-colonial forms of life but had also embellished and exalted this past to a point where it became performative again and could be woven into the very fabric of our modernisation process. Accordingly, the first major attempt by Africa to define its post-colonial path to modernity, the famous *Lagos Plan of Action* of 1980[8] was infused, from conception to execution, with the cultural-nationalist motifs of FESTAC. In this heroic document of a Négritudian theory of technological modernisation of Africa, what stands out is the preponderance of aesthetico-culturalist visions and paranoid pathos of a "race-proud", nationalist Africa defiantly calling off the imperialist bluff of a Eurocentric modernisation procedure. One may of course sympathise with the Afro-nationalist/anti-imperialist spirit that inspired and drove what was undoubtedly a premature self-reliance ambition in technological modernisation. I note however that it needed a high dose of fiery cultural nationalism for these brave leaders to have convinced themselves that such a Négritudian path to technological modernity was feasible. I have no doubt that the leaders' formative overexposure to the over-heated cultural-nationalism of the

FESTAC days contributed to both the impotent self-reliance hubris and the anti-West paranoia, the combination of which fathered the disastrous voluntarism of the African path to development. This is not to accuse FESTAC of responsibility for the failure of Africa's developmental policies but to highlight the neglected genealogical link between the failed and abandoned African bush path to modernisation and the role played by the cultural nationalist ferment generated in, and sustained by, the psychical hangover of an event like FESTAC. Thus, if at the popular level FESTAC created and generalised the new paradigm of culture as what the poor in Africa use to entertain the rich, it seems that the post-FESTAC cultural nationalism of the rulers became what Africa used to excuse and legitimise its missteps in modernity.

Similarly, in FESTAC a hubristic revenge motif of cultural nationalism was made enticingly present and even provocatively performative in some of the historical re-enactments. An example was the story of the FESTAC emblem itself, the Benin mask stolen by Britain during the Benin massacre of 1897 and kept in the British Museum ever since. The refusal of Britain to return

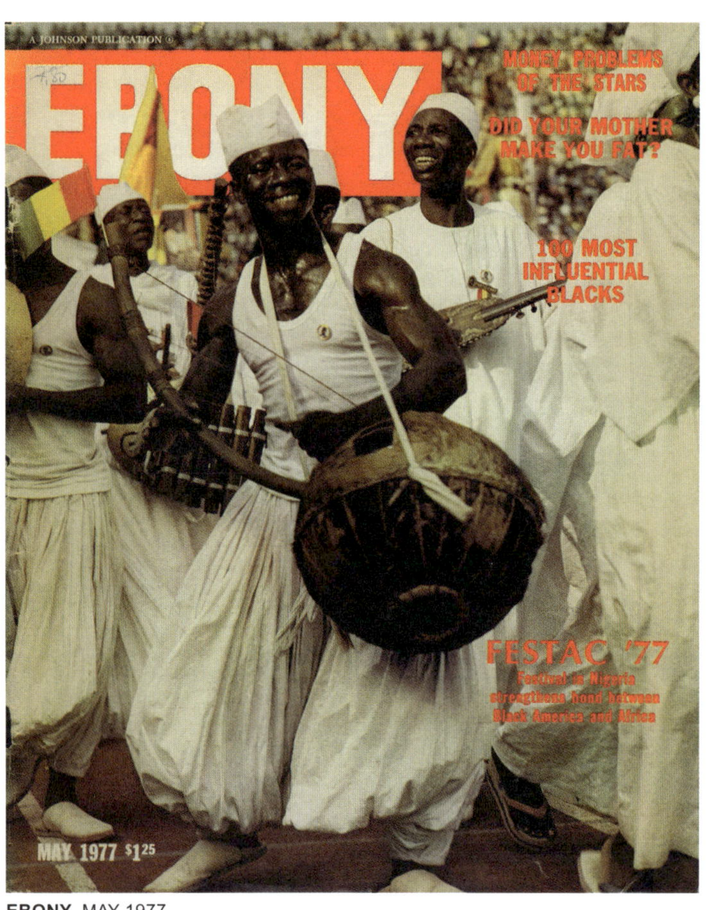

EBONY, MAY 1977

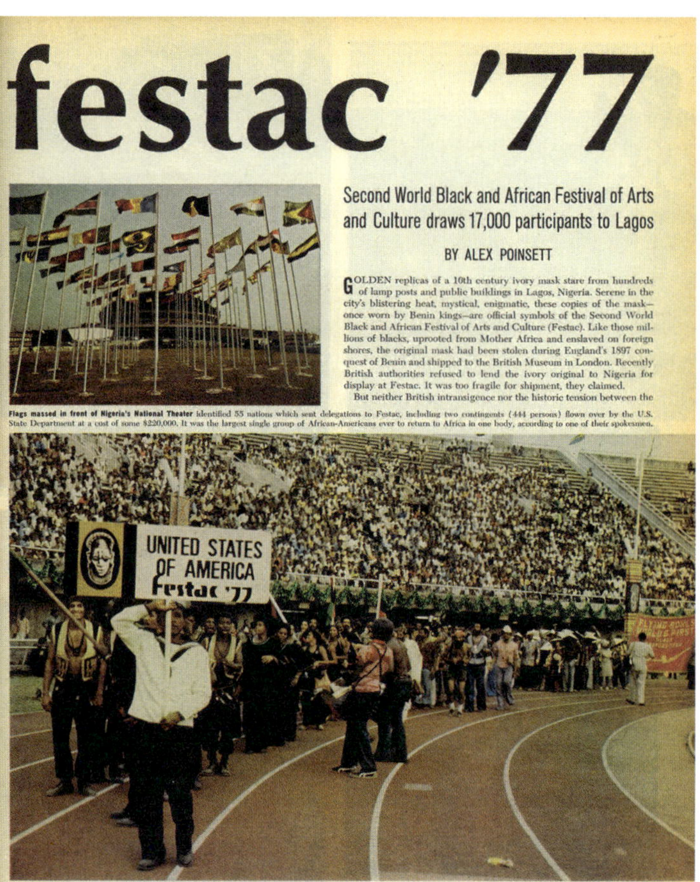

festac '77

Second World Black and African Festival of Arts and Culture draws 17,000 participants to Lagos

BY ALEX POINSETT

GOLDEN replicas of a 16th century ivory mask stare from hundreds of lamp posts and public buildings in Lagos, Nigeria. Serene in the city's blistering heat, mystical, enigmatic, these copies of the mask—once worn by Benin kings—are official symbols of the Second World Black and African Festival of Arts and Culture (Festac). Like those millions of blacks, uprooted from Mother Africa and enslaved on foreign shores, the original mask had been stolen during England's 1897 conquest of Benin and shipped to the British Museum in London. Recently British authorities refused to lend the ivory original to Nigeria for display at Festac. It was too fragile for shipment, they claimed.

But neither British intransigence nor the historic tension between the

Flags massed in front of Nigeria's National Theater identified 55 nations which sent delegations to Festac, including two contingents (444 persons) flown over by the U.S. State Department at a cost of some $220,000. It was the largest single group of African-Americans ever to return to Africa in one body, according to one of their spokesmen.

8   The 1980 *Lagos Plan or The African Path to Development* was the first major blueprint for an independent Afrocentric road map to technological and industrial development.

the original piece thus leading to the use of a mere replica was given maximum hype as the paradigmatic case of Europe's continuing remorseless rape of Africa without compensation. With such arresting and heart-rending reminiscences that flooded the FESTAC talks and shows re-highlighting the historical image of Europe as a villainous plundering pirate, FESTAC did not just cause the bleeding from old scars but also very powerfully re-etched antipathy towards Europe into Africa's postcolonial consciousness.

Nevertheless, worse than some of the leaders' (such as Idi Amin) tragic-comic abuses of Africa's emotional vengefulness towards predatory Europe, were the delayed effects of the FESTAC-inspired wholesale return to, and revival of, some "archaic blood-soaked tribal rites" and other lethal "pagan cult practices". In the vindictive FESTAC spirit of total complacency towards any innate evil in African culture that Europe had tried to eradicate or had merely bad-mouthed, people were actually encouraged, as a gesture of cultural-nationalist defiance, to go back to some of these repulsively pagan ways and fetish practices in order to adequately spite Europe and puncture its arrogance as the salt of the earth. It was indeed fun and highly emotionally gratifying for people to re-convert back to the cult-ridden religiosities of their ancestors. Thus those very rather sordid and most obscurantist aspects of our pagan past, which Christianity as well as secular Western education had done a lot to tame, were suddenly given a new lease of life and a rejuvenated cultural-nationalist legitimacy. FESTAC as the re-enchantment of the whole past was, in a very real sense, the apotheosis of an attempted repaganisation of Africa's culture. Today, however, quite a lot of the old demons resuscitated during FESTAC seem to have remained behind to haunt and pollute not just private quests for sudden wealth but also Africa's postcolonial political culture as a whole. In some African countries, especially Nigeria, ritual murders, human sacrifices and a host of other murderous cult practices performed to obtain political advantage or secure occult invincibility at the hands of political rivals have become the very stuff of political competition especially where democracy is being practised.[9]

I have tried to analyse the concealed linkages between the cultural nationalist demons that were roused back to life during

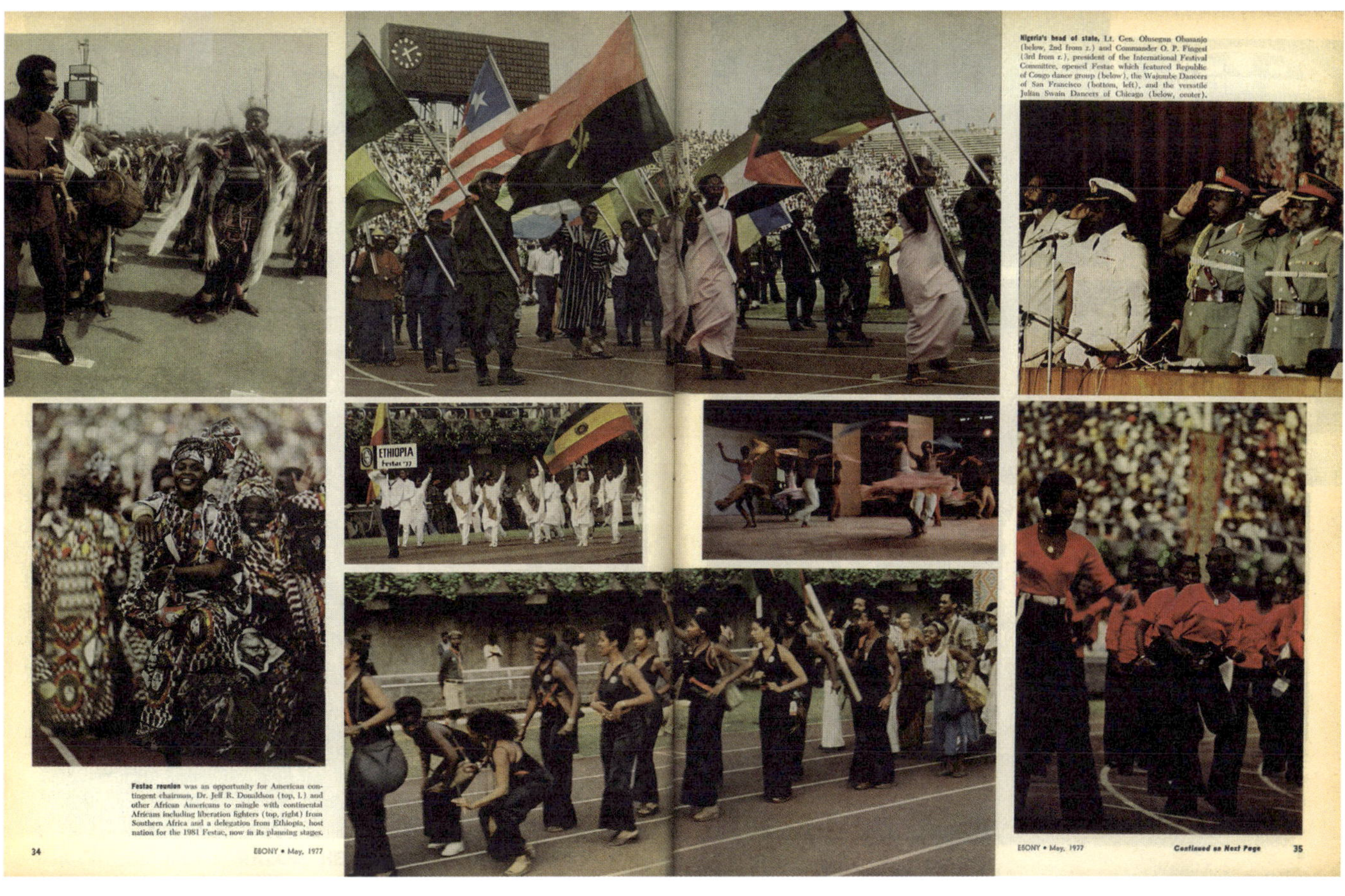

9 In Nigeria during the 2007 elections it was widely reported in the papers how human heads meant for rituals were trafficked from one part of the nation to another. But the most gruesome incident was the discovery of rotting corpses in a shrine in a village in eastern Nigeria called Okija. The peculiarity of this shrine was the discovery that prominent politicians including many state governors were its most fervent clients.

FESTAC, and some of pathologies that resulted from conceptualising and implementing Africa's modernity-project in the horizon of the FESTAC-infested spirit of over-heated cultural nationalism. Of course superficially, FESTAC was about the celebration of a newly reclaimed heritage and not about development or politics. However, one must remember that the heritage reclaimed, invented and celebrated, no matter its intrinsic worth as a legitimate form of life of the old African world, also contained remnants of quaint world views, values and mindsets that when resurrected and made performative again, drastically unlinked us to the spirits that breed the life-forms and language games of modernity/modernisation. While congratulating ourselves during FESTAC on having rediscovered the ancient tribal formulas for Africanising modernity, we were at the same time disconnecting ourselves hubristically from the mindset, the thought patterns, the strategic humilities and other best practices (such as cultivating an unadulterated rational-scientific outlook upon the world) through which other ex-colonies were successfully cracking the modernisation code. In the Afrocentric cultural-nationalist frame of mind maximised by FESTAC, concern for roots, racial dignity and pride appeared to have swarmed and deflected our minds from concern for the real cultural performatives of the modernity spirit, chief among which includes the willingness to let go of a defeated past. When the re-enchanted old tribal spirits rechoreographed by FESTAC became mixed up with the logics of modernisation, the result was the incapacitating baroque muddle – neither modern nor native – the desolated Africa of the late eighties and nineties leading to the quick dismantling of the Afrocentric structures of development and power all over Africa. This is not saying that the FESTAC-infested cultural nationalism of the elite acted alone in precipitating the debacle of development in postcolonial Africa. Indeed, against the thinking of some Western Afro-pessimists[10] who accuse Africa of resorting to Négritude and FESTAC so as to mask its basic incapacity to fructify its contact with modernity, it must be recalled that the colonially transmitted modernity heritage itself had already been rendered almost unusable mostly as a result of the structural perversities of Europe's casual and brutish colonisation which was aggravated no doubt by an even more perverse and precipitate decolonisation. What I am saying is that, to an already dire postcolonial condition replete with colonially inherited incongruities was added a debilitating burden of an excessive historical/cultural consciousness. FESTAC credited this error of getting hung up on the past and on culture at a time when there was sufficient work to be done. Thus the trouble with FESTAC was that in its success lay the very seeds of its hidden harmfulness. The carnivalesque feel-good

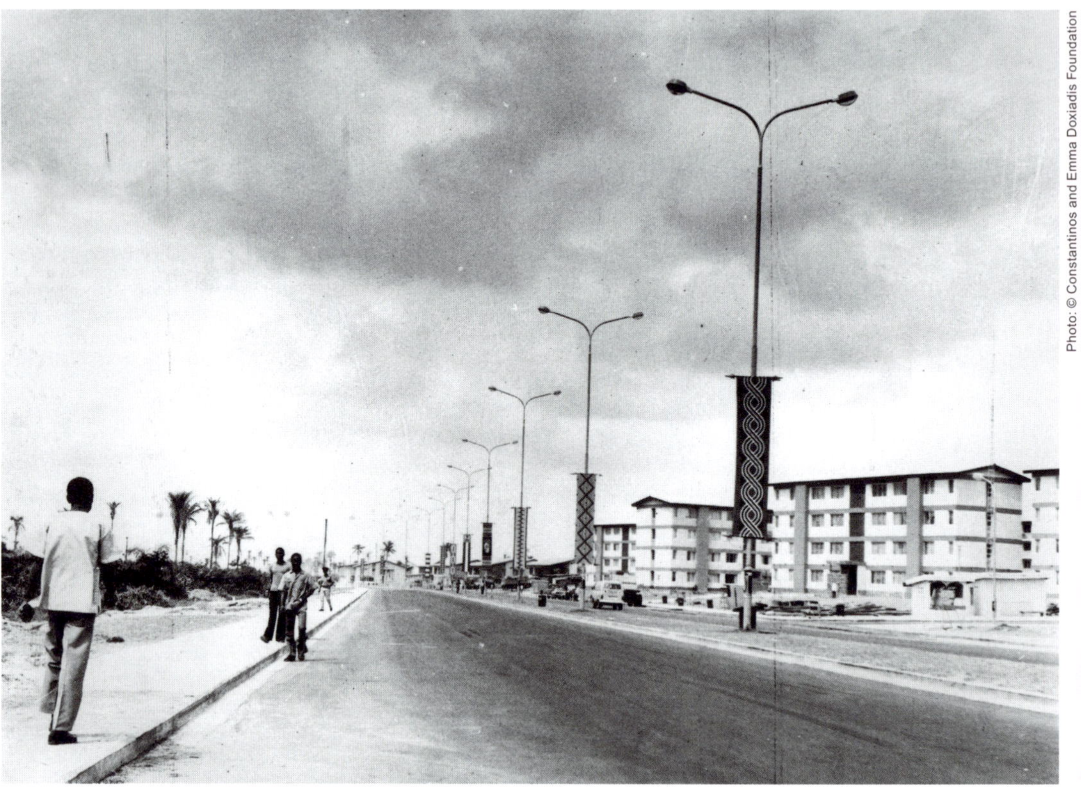

10 A good example is Stephen Smith 2004, *Négrologie: Pourquoi L'Afrique meurt?*, Paris.

atmosphere that pervaded the festival came mostly from our conviction that we had successfully revived and put on display before the whole world not only the cultural foundation of our identity but also the authentic loci of our historical memory. However, a more accurate description of FESTAC would be that it was a grand performance of resuscitation magic for a dead past and/or the montage of an artificial life-support contraption for tribal cultures on their death beds. Because of the self-delusional effects of some of the performances, we easily forget that what in our historical memory and cultural traditions got re-enacted and revived in the course of these magic séances had, by necessity, to be mostly the bad memories, (such as slavery, colonisation), or the bad cultures (such as dead folklores and quaint tribal cults). While it was good that FESTAC graphically cultivated memories of our troubled past and disoriented present, the question is: Would it not have been better if, regarding some episodes and practices of our past and present, Africa and the black world had also cultivated a studied forgetfulness? For a severely wounded and mis-opened continent so keen on recovering its balance and accessing modernity's goodies, it looks like forgetfulness vis-ą-vis a mostly depressive past and unperformative cultural traditions, becomes an existential necessity. The modernity we covet supposes a time consciousness – a form of life and a language game – radically different from the old tribal life forms and world views that we staged at FESTAC to artificially keep it alive. Thus, one hidden negative spirit in FESTAC was an attempt to arrest, through the delusional timelessness of carnival, Africa's inchoate attempts to embed herself more meaningfully in the future-oriented temporalities of a modernity. From the experiences of successful non-Western modernisers, we have learned that no one can come into the order of modernity without a good deal of such mental and cultural change, and that anyone who has successfully adapted to modernity's order of things is necessarily no longer a tribesman. FESTAC, in spite of its modernist cultural/artistic maquillages and choreographies, wanted to legitimise a stagnant or anachronistic identity of the African as tribesman or the "Black man" as the permanent victim.

As a show intended to prove that we were not what the white man thought we were, FESTAC was not a solution to, but the very exacerbation of, the Africans' existential predicament, namely: having to depend on others for an idea of our own worth. The rather masochistic romance with the past, its wounds and its fossilised folklore; the compulsive resort to cultural/artistic evidence as sufficient proof, stemmed directly from the recognition neurosis that had badly afflicted past generations of black cul-

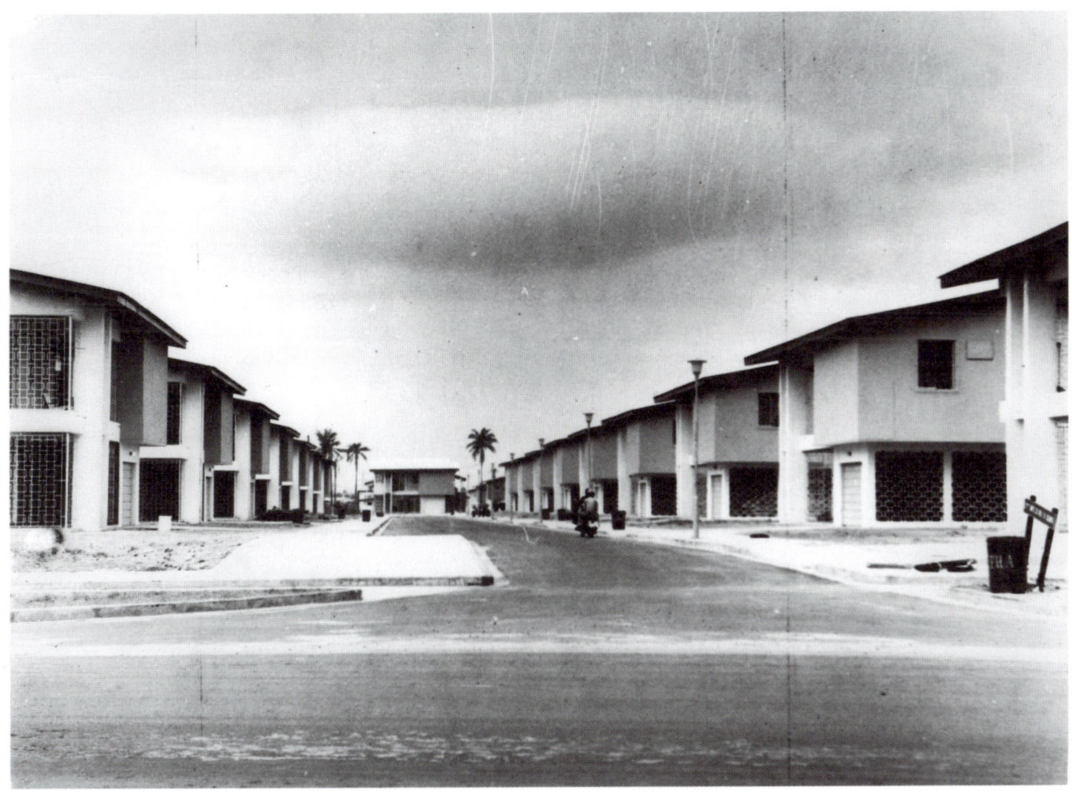

Festac Town

tural nationalists. However, seeking to prove by the richness of our cultural heritage that we were legitimate partners in and even co-creators of modernity seems to have proved the contrary, namely, that the very modernity we both covet and complain about has managed to push us out of its implacable systemic logics. For, to prove a cultural point in capitalist modernity, you must first prove your capacity to succeed economically and technologically, that is, non-culturally. In other words, in the logic of globalised capitalism that drives modernity, a people has to first succeed as an industrial power and then the West would immediately come in search of the hidden ethos in the tribal cultures that serves as a non-modern trigger or a non-Western enabling environment. By putting culture first, FESTAC wanted to be a reversal of the sequence of proofs in postmodernity. Therefore it stood no chance as a performative argument for taking Africans more seriously. A thousand FESTACs can prove nothing regarding our standing in modernity. In the economics of capitalist modernity, organising FESTACs to prove a cultural point, settle an identity crisis or mitigate our psycho-dependency on others, amounts to throwing good money into latrine pits. You prove nothing with half-naked dancers, nor do you undo non-recognition by putting on stage weeping men in chains re-enacting the agonies of slavery or colonisation. Before a modernity that has sold its soul to the devil of capitalism, culture, especially the display of quaint and archaic folk ways, the replay of old agonies, the exhibitionism of victimhood et cetera, is virtually a non-argument.

Festac Town

But now that cultural nationalism has refuted itself as a viable path to modernity, what is the fate of FESTAC? Why has FESTAC not been replicated since 1977? According to the then CBAAC director Professor Duro Oni, the huge cost that Nigeria deployed to host the event has intimidated and scared away other potential hosts. But that could be merely chauvinistic indirect praise of the unmatchable wealth and generosity of Nigeria. I believe that FESTAC cannot be repeated mostly because of the self-invalidation of its sponsoring ideology, namely, cultural-nationalism. The unfolding post-FESTAC forces of postcolonialism and global capitalism had simply refuted narcissistic emotions and crushed on their path atavistic cultures and tribal/racial identity claims. The disastrous debacle of the African path to development was synonymous with the exhaustion of the cultural-nationalist paradigm of self-assertion in modernity. New paradigms such as adherence to global best practices *et cetera* have replaced identity/race politics. In other words, the African/Black cultural politics that created FESTAC no longer exists and probably no longer will. The messianic spokesmen of a Pan-African cultural renaissance – Du Bois, Senghor et cetera – have been replaced by political engineers of an African economic renaissance: Thabo Mbeki has replaced Senghor, FESTAC has given way to NEPAD (New Partnership for Africa's Development).

However, though the forces of history have swallowed up the FESTAC spirit and rendered a repeat performance unlikely, it would be wrong to intone a requiem for everything concerning FESTAC. Even if a third FESTAC is not feasible in the foreseeable future, we should at least be satisfied with its ghostly institutional survival in CBAAC. In this quasi-museumistic repose, FESTAC's wild and economically ruinous cultural-nationalist spirit has successfully been tamed and permanently held captive. What this means is that any African or black American still itching from memories of lost roots can go to CBAAC and indulge in their private FESTAC nostalgia without any more harm to Africa's national economies and overall modernity project.

Above all, though the spirit of FESTAC may be lying in its museumistic repose in CBAAC, the hardest surviving shell of the festival however remains FESTAC Town. Originally conceived as a showpiece of modernity, that is, a modern experimental village fitted with all the devices of a planned urban habitation, it stood in its heyday as an unconscious refutation of the back-to-the-roots philosophy of FESTAC itself. As an island of modern urban planning in the baroque sea of semi-modern and native bric-a-brac that was Lagos then, FESTAC Town with its paved streets, street lights and flower pots on verandas, symbolised, in spite of itself, the victory of modernity over tradition, European-styled urban rationality and order over unplanned native housing *laisser-aller* and chaos.

However, the modernity spirit that had victoriously indwelt FESTAC Town (against the very cultural-nationalist impulse that had driven the conception and execution of the festival) was to be very short lived. For it took a few short years, less than a decade, for same 're-bushing' forces of postcolonism that afflicted the rest of Lagos to swarm FESTAC Town, killing its modernising facade and turning it into the den of robbers that the web respondent talked about. Today FESTAC Town is known mostly as the headquarters of some of the most notorious urban evils plaguing Nigeria, especially armed robbery, pirating of CDs, and the notorious scam business popularly called 419. Infrastructure having decayed and the middle-class residents having fled to either Abuja or the less insane areas of Lagos, the scum of the Lagos urban jungle have invaded FESTAC Town, making it a place where even residents fear to tread and an absolute no-go area for visitors. This uncanny reversal of modernity in FESTAC Town would have continued unabated if not for the near miraculous intervention of the current Lagos state governor whose massive urban renewal programme has also spilled into FESTAC Town. Today FESTAC Town like many other parts of Lagos looks like a huge re-building site with excavations and demolitions blocking the streets with mountains of rubble.

It is hoped that this once highly symbolic modern micro-city in the midst of the unmodern baroque Lagos magma will come out of this remodernisation exercise totally re-kitted and returned to its old glory as the only really unwasted, solid and lasting achievement of the FESTAC jamboree. But while celebrating this imminent rebirth of FESTAC Town, one should also ponder the fertile paradox that both birthed it about thirty years ago and caused its downfall less than a decade later: it was not the cultural-nationalist back-to-the-roots traditionalism of FESTAC that could have created and maintained FESTAC Town but that which had roundly defeated and superseded it, namely, the disrooting, disenchanting and rationalising spirit of modernity.

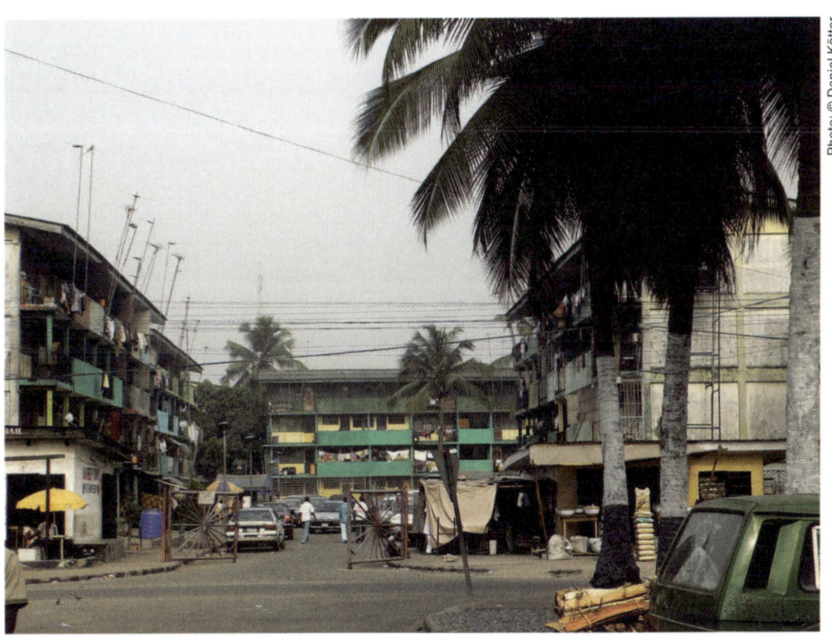

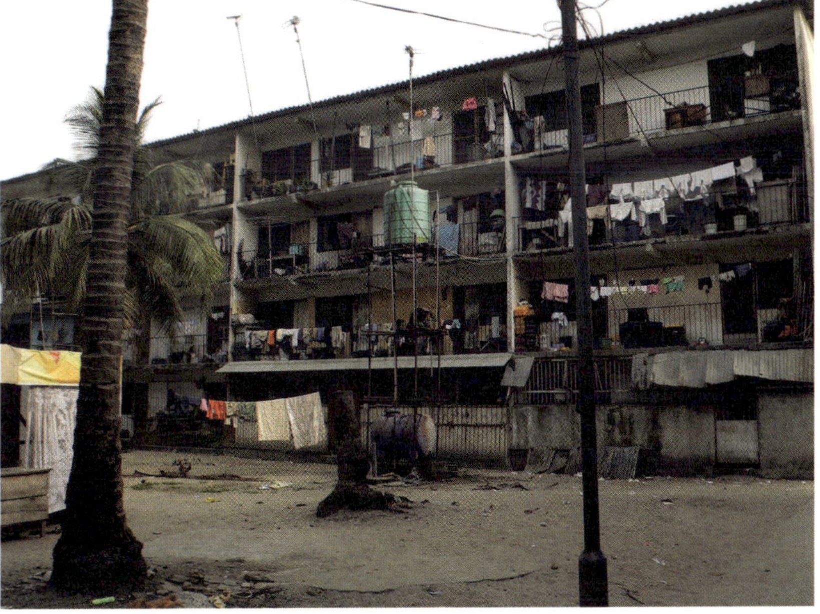

Festac Town today

With Spear in the City
The Adventure of Modernity in the Photo Novels of the 1960s

MATTHIAS KRINGS

In the second half of the 1960s, Lance Spearman alias 'Spear' conquered the cities in anglophone Africa. Spearman started his career in Johannesburg, home to the South African-based *Drum* Publications. Soon though, "Africa's top crime buster" who "has a charming way with the girls" and "a deadly way with thugs", in the words of *Drum* advertising, was also setting the world to rights in Lagos, Accra, Nairobi, Dar es Salaam and Kampala, ridding towns of cat burglars clinging to the facades of buildings and master gangsters with dreams of world domination. The adventures of this elegantly dressed detective appeared as a weekly photo novel distributed in South Africa as *Spear Magazine* and in the rest of Africa under the promising title *African Film.* For the issues printed in Lagos and distributed across West Africa, the publishing run of this transnational 'look-read' was 100,000 issues. "We devoured those things," commented a one-time Nigerian reader in an Internet forum, recalling how he waited at the door of his home every Monday for the vendor so

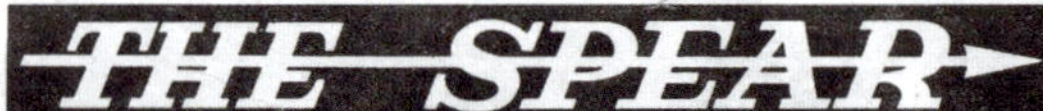

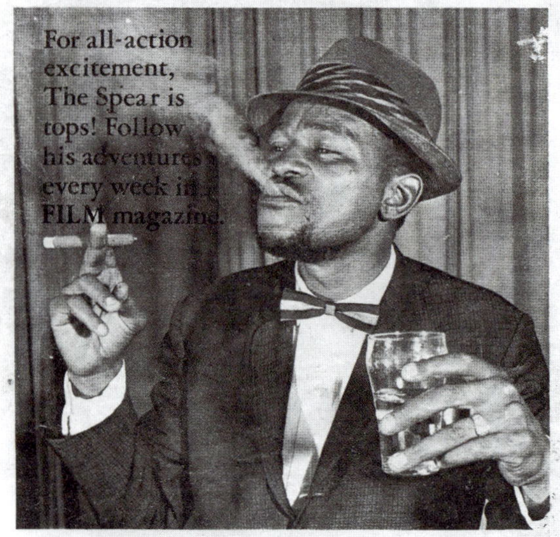

he could finally get his hands on the latest copy. *African Film's* readers were largely young and male, and the magazine offered them the chance to participate in an urban modernity full of nightclubs, elegant interior designs, tough criminals and fast women. The adventure of modern technology was celebrated in car chase scenes, walkie-talkie and phone communication, and fantastic wonder weapons in the hands of mad professors. As Spearman developed into a rolemodel his characteristic features – elegant suit, narrow-brimmed hat, bow-tie, and fondness for cheroots and scotch on the rocks – was much copied in African cities around 1970. [→ Fig. **A**]

In those years, the cities exercised an immense appeal on, above all, young people from the rural areas, resulting in rapidly expanding urban populations. As traditional habits and role clichés changed, cinemas and bars came to be almost paradigmatic locations of urbanity. The new urban culture was characterised by the principle of mixing and interweaving cultural elements from different backgrounds; it also included a prevailing openness towards European and US cultural influences. This new urban lifestyle was expressed in music, dance, posters and bar paintings, travelling theatres and 'market literature', although these forms also explored its downsides. The photo magazine *African Film* could, as it were, easily fit in with these many different genres of popular culture. Not only were Spear's adventures nearly all set in an urban milieu, but they also connected tropes in Western popular culture with genuine African motifs; for example, science fiction technologies from contemporary spy thrillers with the symbolic visual element of the spear.

Production and Distribution:
Johannesburg – Lagos – Nairobi

African Film was produced by South African publisher Jim Bailey. Since the 1950s, he had built *Drum* up into a magazine that was read across all of anglophone Africa and, from its inception, *African Film* was similarly designed for Pan-African distribution. By the time the magazines reached their readers in West and East Africa, they had a long journey behind them. The stories were written in South Africa by around twenty-five authors – many of whom were students at the University of Lesotho – and then turned into scripts in Johannesburg before being sent on to Swaziland for the photo shoots.[1] In the early years, the strips were sent to London where they were mounted and printed before being returned to Africa as a finished product and distributed by the *Drum* subsidiaries in Johannesburg, Lagos and Nairobi. Later, after printing had been organised at the local subsidiaries, the magazines no longer needed to take a detour via Europe. However, until the magazine was discontinued around 1972, the content still came from South Africa.

---

1 Stanley Meisler 1969, Look-reads, *Africa-Report* 14/5–6: 80–83

A Advertising a new role model (*African Film* n.d.)

Given this background, it may seem even more surprising that the photos hardly contain any evidence of their local origin. References to South Africa that may have appeared in the Swaziland street scenes, such as car plates or advertising for South African products, were edited out afterwards. In this way, the magazines could still be sold throughout Africa despite a growing boycott against South Africa, which was largely driven forward by Nigeria.[2] In addition, the publisher's details in the West and East African editions gave no indication of the real origin of the publication, but listed Lagos and Nairobi as the publisher's address and local personnel as editors. In the case of *African Film,* this procedure may have been primarily politically motivated; nonetheless, it was and still is common practice in photo novels, at least for the international market, to edit out concrete location references from the images. To ensure the products are marketable and readable transnationally, the images are photographed as neutrally as possible, leaving only the texts to be translated.[3] This approach, for example, enabled Italian *fotoromanzo* to be launched on the South African market in the early 1960s, triggering a real boom for the genre among the white population.[4] Hence, together with some other photo novels from *Drum* Publications, *African Film,* sold in South Africa as the *Spear Magazine,* can be regarded as the successful adaptation of an originally European format for a black African market. To serve an African audience, the white actors had to be replaced by African models – although, unfortunately, there is almost no information on the actors who played the characters in *African Film.*[5]

Lance Spearman was portrayed by a man named Joe Mkwanazi. Before he was discovered by a photographer working for *Drum* Publications, Mkwanazi had spent his days in Durban as a 'houseboy' and his nights playing the piano in a nightclub. For modelling Spearman, he was paid the equivalent of $215 a month.[6]

African Film cost a shilling, making it affordable for a broad audience. As a result, as early as 1968, the magazine had an Africa-wide circulation of 165,000 copies.[7] Since each issue was also passed from hand to hand, an estimated total readership of half a million would hardly seem to be too high.

Hunter and Hunted

An image of a deserted street at night, with a text block at the top: "Two o'clock in the morning and the city is asleep. Doors are bolted and locked, windows closed or burglar proofed …" A second image underneath shows a man in a suit in the centre of the night scene. His right hand has been replaced by a hook. He casts an eerie shadow. "This city lives in fear […] fear of an unknown terror." Page turn. Four images in medium shot showing the Hook-Hand Killer in action. "A terror that moves in the night and strikes swiftly …" He looks up and thinks: "Ah! That window on the third floor is open." He moves closer to the house – "A terror that strikes the careless … those who do not lock their doors or bar their windows." He looks up at the wall: "Ah! Up the drainpipe. An easy job." On the opposite page, he climbs the house wall "like a cat" until he reaches the open window. Once the page is turned, the readers see a woman asleep. Over the next six pages, the psychopathic, misogynist killer will tie her up and gag her, and finally kill her with his hook hand. All this takes place while Lance Spearman is on holiday in Spain.[8]

Such a thriller-style opening is rather unusual for *African Film,* and belongs to the later development of the series. A typical Lance Spearman story begins with a scene showing the detective at home or relaxing during his free time. If he isn't just lying in the bathtub in his apartment or sipping a drink in his bathrobe, he can either be found sitting at a bar or in his office with his feet on his desk. This peaceful atmosphere is broken by the message that a crime has been committed. A night-time phone call from an old friend or a call from Captain Victor – Spearman's uniformed police contact – or a report in the paper, all tell of past crimes and unusual events that need to be investigated further. [→ Fig. **B**] When looked at more closely, even the first episode of the story about the Hook-Hand Killer follows the same narrative structure, although in this case the 'relax sequence' has simply been moved forwards onto the title page: sitting at a bar, Lance Spearman alias 'Spear' looks out at the reader with a twinkle in his eye, using a gesture to clearly indicate that he regards the background scene of a man schmoozing up to a woman as just part of the good life. The title underneath provides the connection between the cover photo and the story inside: "While Spear relaxes […] The Hook-Hand Killer Strikes!"

In his fight against crime, Lance Spearman is not only aided by Captain Victor, but also helped by Sonia and Lemmy. Sonia is Spear's agile assistant, capable of dispensing impressive karate kicks during hand-to-hand fighting with gangsters; Lemmy, a young boy around twelve years old, rescues Spearman from a range of uncomfortable situations, and not least served as an identification figure for younger readers. A one-time reader from Nigeria remembers exactly how Lemmy was introduced into the cast: "When Spearman took on a young sidekick called Lemmy, many of us almost died of jealousy – we so wanted to be in his shoes."[9]

African Film perfectly fits the category of the suspense novel within Todorov's typology of detective fiction.[10] According to Todorov, this category sits in-between two other categories of crime fiction, the whodunit and the thriller, and combines their prominent properties: the mystery of the absent crime that has to be unravelled through a story of investigation, typical of the

2   Meisler (1969), p. 80–81

3   Ulrike Schimming 2002, *Fotoromane. Analyse eines Massenmediums,* Frankfurt a.M.

4   See also Lily Saint 2010, Not Western: Race, Reading, and the South African Photocomic, *Journal of Southern African Studies* 36/4: 939–958

5   Apparently, Lance Spearman even had two African forerunners in the black twin detectives Bravo and Morgan who featured in *Flash,* a magazine published in South Africa between 1965 and 1967; see Saint (2010), p. 941.

6   Meisler (1969), p. 81

7   Meisler (1969), p. 81

8   *African Film* (n.d.), 172: 1–11

9   Tunde Giwa 2008, *Black like us.* www.chimurengalibrary.co. za/ essay.php?id=26&cid=26_1 retrieved on 29 February 2012

10 Tzvetan Todorov 1977, *The Poetics of Prose,* Oxford, p. 50–51

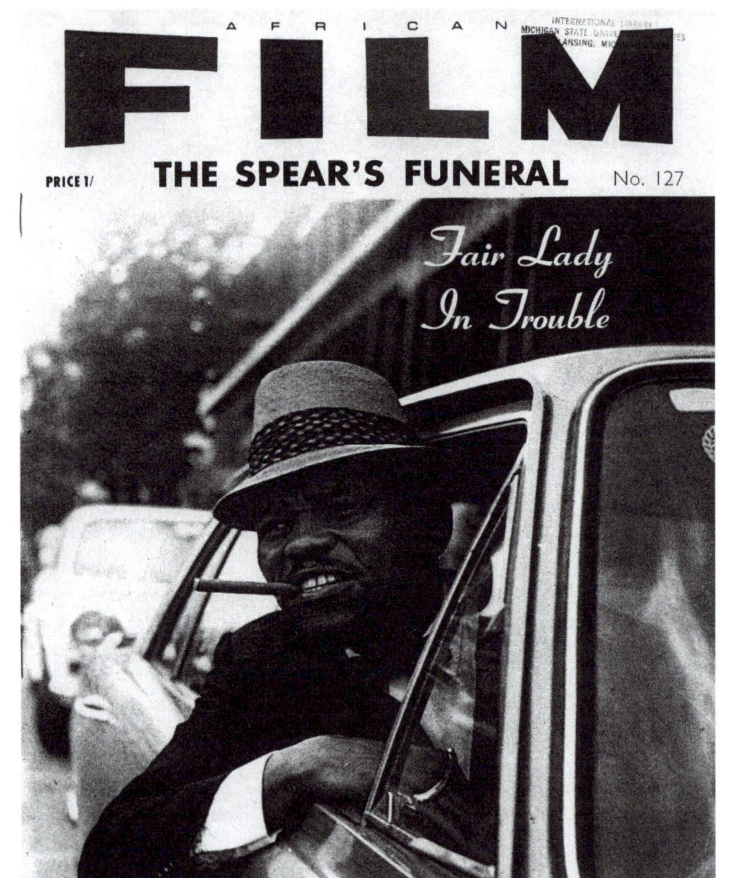

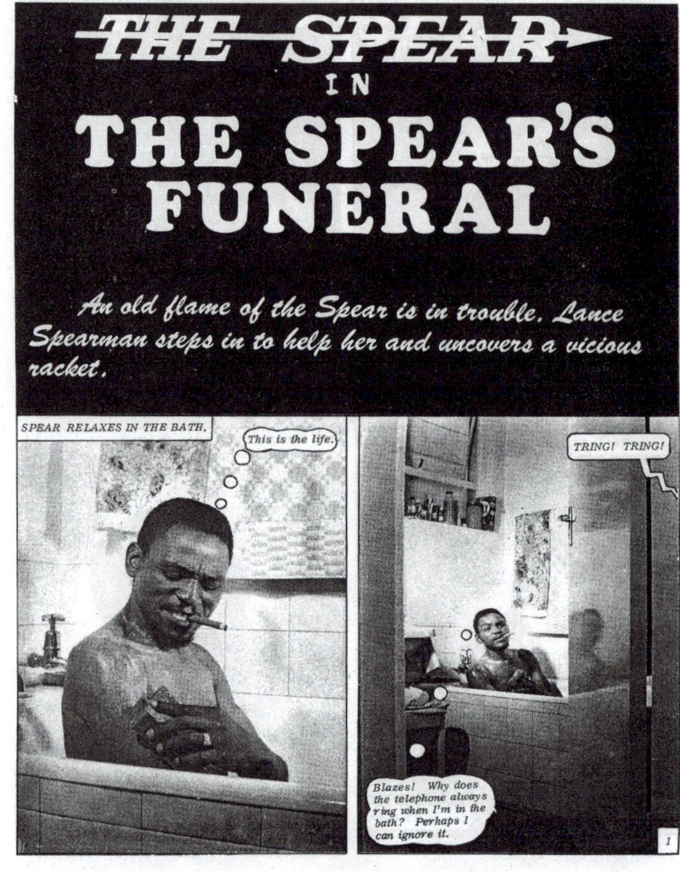

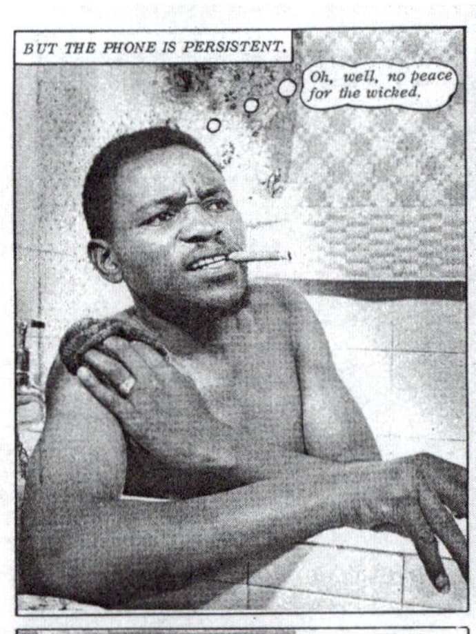

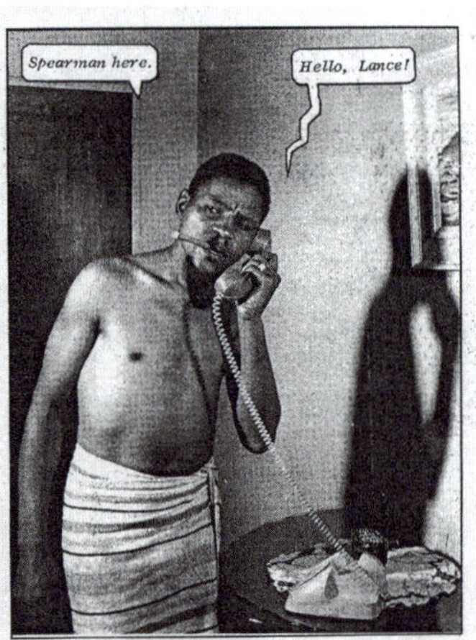

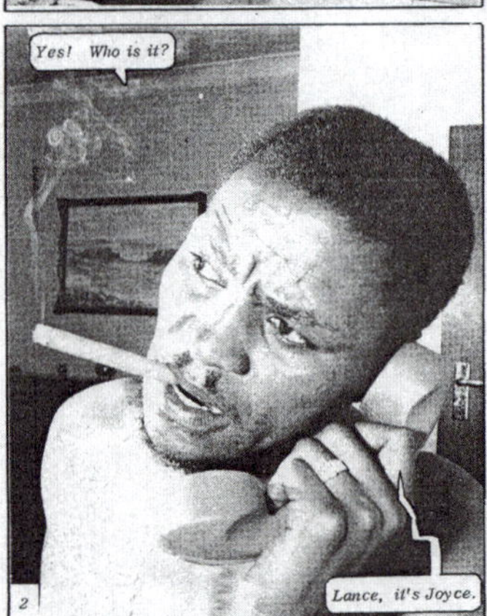

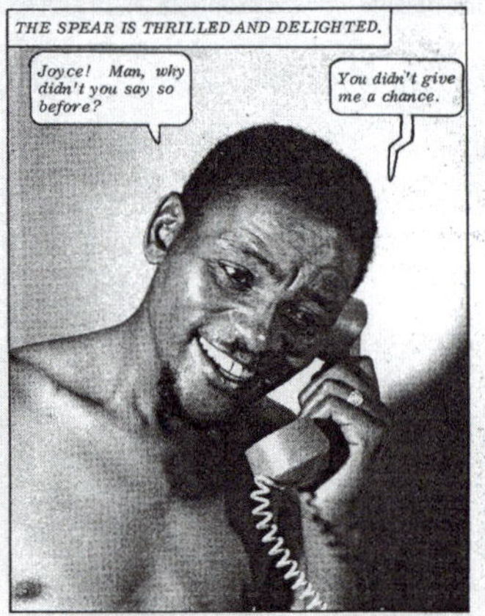

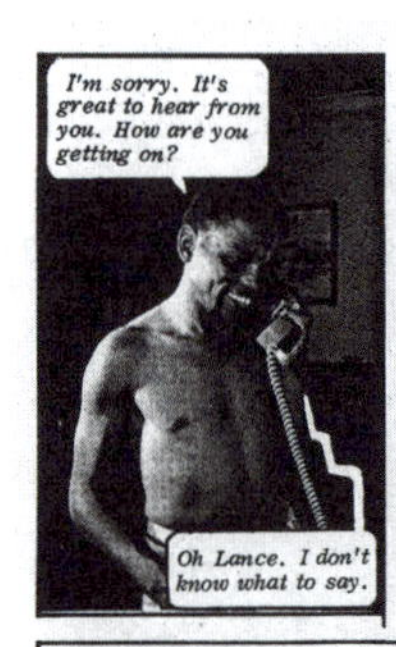

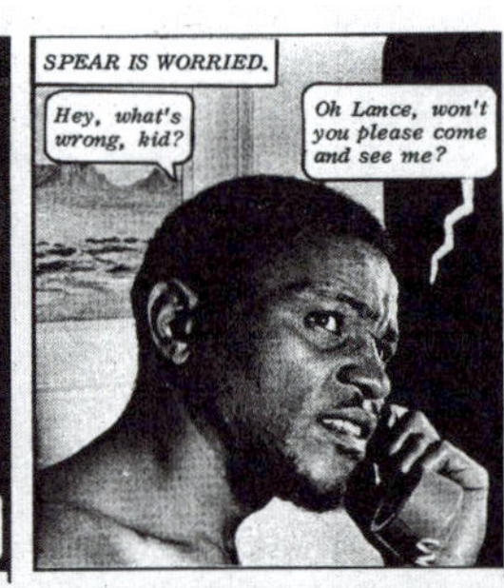

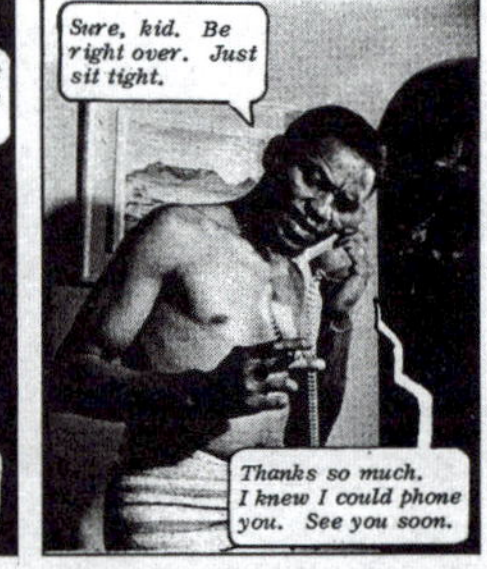

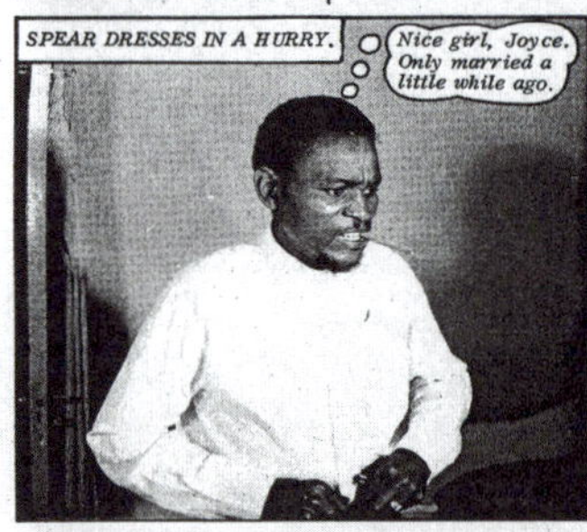

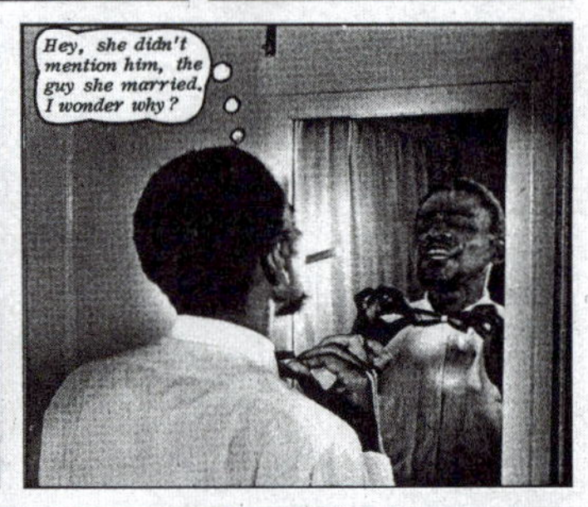

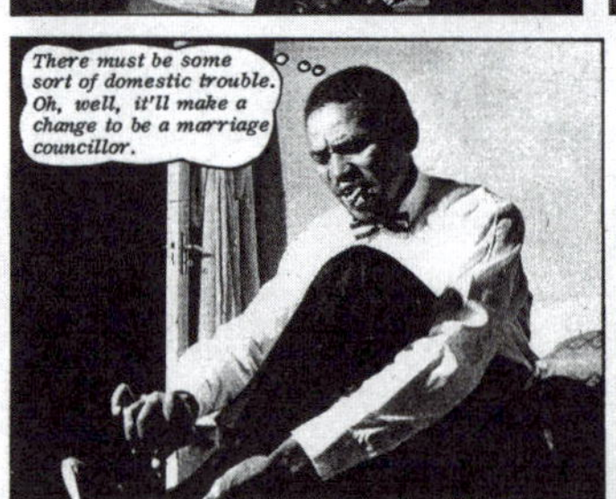

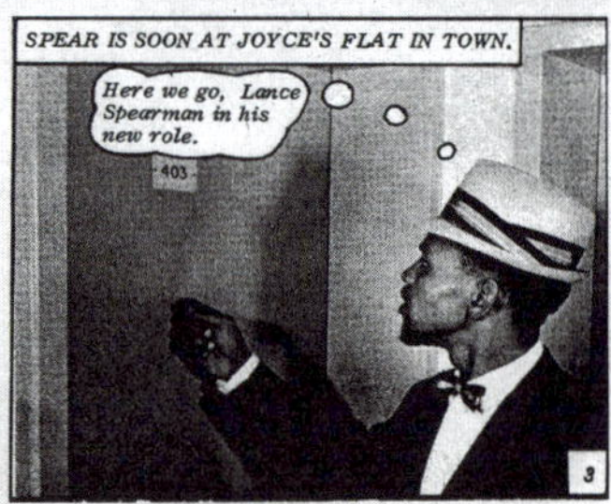

B Beginning of a new adventure (*African Film* n.d., 127)

whodunit, and the emphasis on the present, on crime in the making, typical of the thriller. While the former raises the reader's curiosity, the latter aims at creating suspense. In *African Film,* mystery, the story of a past criminal event that has to be detected, is reduced to a mere point of departure while the main interest derives from the story set in the present, the story that unfolds during Spear's investigations. This coincides perfectly with Todorov's observation that in the suspense novel "[...] the reader is interested not only by what has happened but also by what will happen next; he wonders as much about the future as about the past. The two types of interest are thus united here – there is the curiosity to learn how past events are to be explained; and there is also the suspense: what will happen to the main characters?"[11] As is typical of suspense novels, Spear and the other main characters constantly risk their lives. Although tough and always ultimately the winner, Spear is far from being immune from the fists of those he encounters as the story unfolds. Often he comes out of a fight with severe bruises, aching limbs and a black eye, and has to be bandaged by his assistant Sonia. Suspense is not only created by the plot, but also through a clever employment of the specific properties of the photo-novel medium: the last images at the bottom of many right-hand-side pages serve as cliff hangers, making the reader interested in what happens next when he or she flips the page.

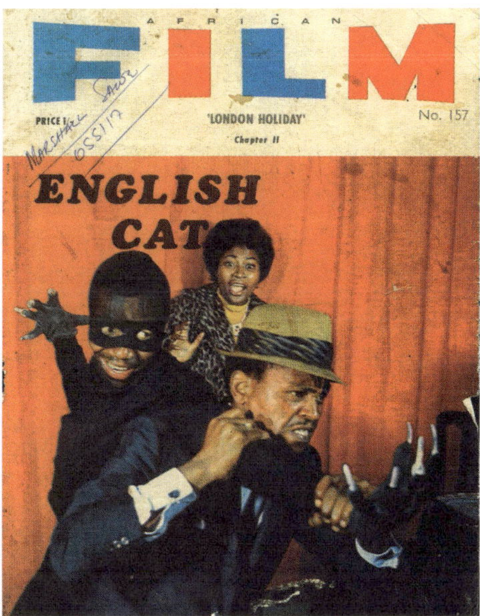

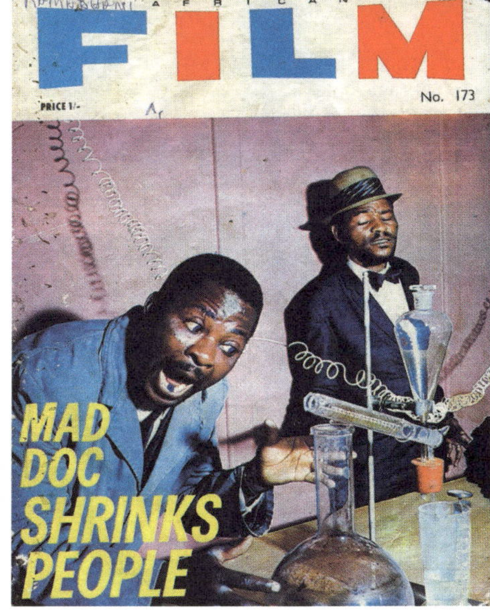

C Title pages with antagonists (*African Film* n.d.)

The spectrum of criminals menacing Spear and his friends ranges from simple diamond thieves to shady insurance agents or power-crazed syndicate bosses determined to take over the town, the country or nothing short of the entire world. There were slightly fewer than 200 issues of *African Film,* and some of Spear's adversaries appear several times. In the early episodes, Lance Spearman frequently has to deal with Rabon Zollo, who loses an eye in a fight with Spear, but he also has recurring problems with the Cats, a gang of cat-burglars in black masks and claw-gloves who are able to climb the highest walls of any building. Over the years, Spear's adversaries and their plans become increasingly fantastic; for example, Dr Devil, who favours a rubber Halloween mask and a red cape and turns out to be a criminal mastermind with plans to rule the world, or the Earth Monster, a submissive giant in a bear costume, misused as an instrument of murder by a syndicate boss. The later episodes also include a solid dose of science fiction in the form of several mad professors; for instance, the Hook-Hand Killer is revealed as the Mad Doc, owner of a special serum able to make people shrink. This category of characters also includes Professor Thor, inventor of a machine that can read people's thoughts, and Professor Rubens, who transplants the organs of animals into people to produce a werewolf. [→ Fig. **C**]

African Film's sources of inspiration can be easily identified. Contemporary observers had already noted Lance Spearman's resemblance to an 'African James Bond' – a similarity not only evident in his taste in clothes, his general style and fondness for ironical remarks, but also in such technical equipment as knife-throwing boots, exploding cigarettes and a walkie-talkie disguised as a wristwatch. Dr Devil has the features of Dr No and, in a similar way, the topos of a menace to the entire world from similar figures also seems to be derived from spy films. Just like those movies, *African Film* is packed with references to contemporary history as well. The Cold War, for instance, appears in the story about the power-crazed tycoon who threatens the world with a nuclear rocket hidden on an island. "Once I have the East and West committed to a nuclear war," he tells Spear, "there will be no difficulty for me to pick up the rest."[12] Dr Devil also reveals a similar plan to his cronies: "Today all the big power countries are trying to land a rocket on the moon." After this clear reference to the year of the first moon landing, he continues: "I will hi-jack these rockets by powerful radio control and send them crashing into the sea." By carefully targeted false information, the governments involved would soon be at each other's throats, and a war would break out. "We will then move in and assassinate the leaders and take over. Each of you will be head of a country."[13]

Aside from the James Bond habitus, Lance Spearman may well have been modelled on Philip Marlowe, Sam Spade or Mike

11 Todorov (1977), p. 51
12 *African Film* (n.d.), 126: 20
13 *African Film* (n.d.), 117: 14–15

Hammer, the hard-boiled private detectives of the classic US detective novels. The group of authors writing *African Film* could well have been familiar with them from Hollywood movies or from thrillers by James Hadley Chase, a British author whose novels were influenced by Raymond Chandler's thrillers. Since Chase was a very popular author throughout Africa, it is hardly surprising that the language of the figures in *African Film* is spiced with the kind of slang that could also have come from Chase. Ultimately, one can also only speculate whether the name of Lemmy, Spear's young sidekick, is a reference to Lemmy Caution, the fictitious FBI agent created by Peter Cheyney and played by Eddie Constantine in French-Italian film productions from 1953.

Images of Urban Modernity

There are three characteristic elements in the prototypical *African Film* city: modern architecture, independent women and criminality. Shots of urban exteriors show people strolling along the pavements of streets lined by shop windows and multistorey buildings. The facilities include public phone booths, public parks and gardens, and even an open-air swimming pool. Modern cars drive down the streets. At times, there are even explicit comments about the architecture. For example, Spear is waiting for the lift in the office building of a fraudulent insurance company, and thinks: "These people seem to be doing all right for themselves. This is quite a building." [→ Fig. **D**] 14 The interior shots, comprising the majority of the images, show bars and nightclubs as well as modern furniture and furnishings: tiled bathrooms, living rooms with a three-piece suite, side tables, bookcases, record players and framed pictures on the walls. Spear's investigations often take him out of the city to remote country houses whose elaborate architecture is in no way inferior to their urban counterpart.

The only references to the old Africa are the detective's first and last name, and a spear decorating his office. Apart from that, *African Film* celebrates an African modernity in which there is no trace of a reference to traditional rural Africa. If the protagonists should join a country outing, as they do in the 'Gold Fever' episode, the landscape is devoid of traditional village buildings. Even the clothes worn by the people in the former gold rush town that Spear and Lemmy visit for a holiday are more reminiscent of cowboys from the American West than residents of rural Africa. Here, a dialogue between Lemmy and Spear in a souvenir shop can be read as a meta-commentary. Lemmy finds a rare piece and calls out: "Gee! Spear, look at that. It's real African art", while Spear laconically replies: "Don't you believe it. It's either made in Birmingham or Hong Kong."15

Independent women are a characteristic element of urban life in *African Film*. They are addressed as "doll", "honey" or "darling" and meet men in bars. As a womaniser, Lance Spearman can easily compete with his British role model. Just as in the James Bond films, seductive women are often working as accomplices for Spear's adversaries, although this does not stop the Spear from having romantic adventures with them. For this reason, the bar scenes frequently lead to scenes in the women's apartments, especially since the *African Film's* female characters are usually self-reliant and comfortably off. On arriving in their apartments, the women first disappear into the bedroom, leaving their visitor in the living room: "You help yourself to a drink while I put on something more comfortable." – "Wow! Thanks, doll." What happens next is usually left to the reader's imagination, which – as in comics – has to fill in the 'gutter', the white space between two panels. In some cases, there may be kisses, but there are rarely even harmless bed scenes. Spear's assistant Sonia is the only woman able to withstand his otherwise irresistible advances. Her rejections of Spear's unequivocal suggestions are standard situations with a high recognition value and are part of the two figures' fixed repertoire found in nearly every issue.

Hilda 'The Head Huntress' represents the dangerous other side of the female norm. In the first scene of the episode about this man-murdering monster, the reader becomes an eyewitness of how her skilful arts of seduction lead "Mister Munn E. Spinna, a rich married man" to his doom.16 The story starts in a "posh nightclub" where the gentleman "is having a night out without his wife knowing about it!" Suddenly he sees "a shapely doll with all the curves in the right places coming towards him". "She gives him a big, friendly smile", which the reader cannot actually see since the woman in the first photo is shown from the back, only emphasising her 'curves' even more. "Wow! That's what I call real sexy!" thinks Mister Munn E. Spinna, and loses his head to Hilda – quite literally, since on the following pages he falls victim to her plans for revenge. Hilda The Head Huntress turns out to be a murderous psychopath determined to get her revenge on a gang that destroyed her entire family. When Lance Spearman finally tracks her down, she has already decorated her living room with the heads of several victims.

The ever-present crime in the prototypical city, however, is not solely caused by Hilda The Head Huntress, the Hook-Hand Killer or other dangerous gangsters, but primarily comes from their henchman or minor gangsters and thugs hanging around in every bar and on every street corner. In this world, only smart, fearless and seasoned fighters such as Spear and his friends can survive. Consequently, a correspondingly large percentage of the images in every issue is devoted to fight scenes. These action scenes are incredibly dynamic, partly because the actors' movements are shot with camera angles usually associated with the cinema. In some cases, speed lines, a stylistic device

14 *African Film* (n.d.), 127: 27
15 *African Film* (n.d.), 146: 5

16 *African Film* (n.d.), 50: 1

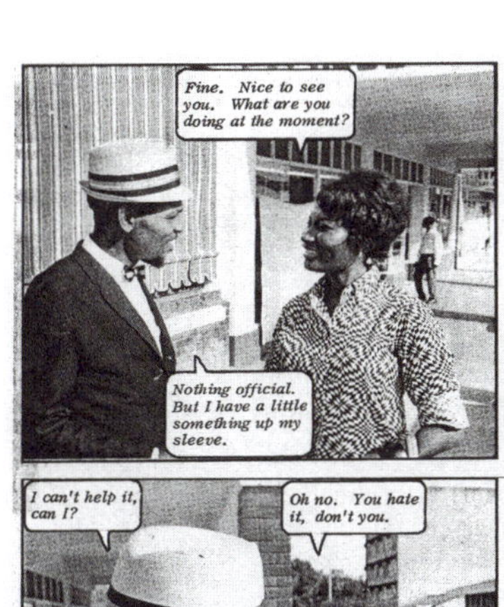

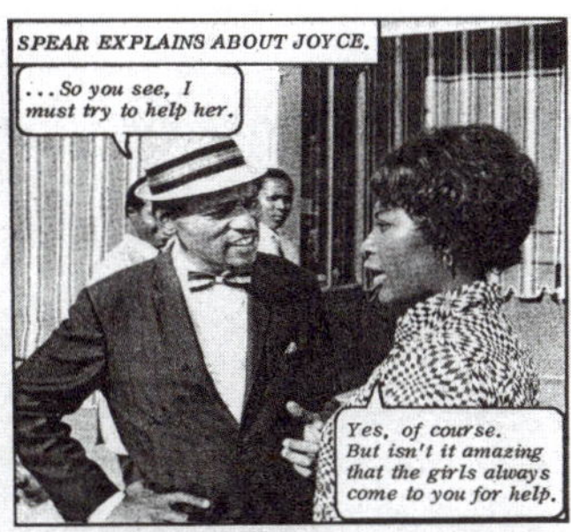

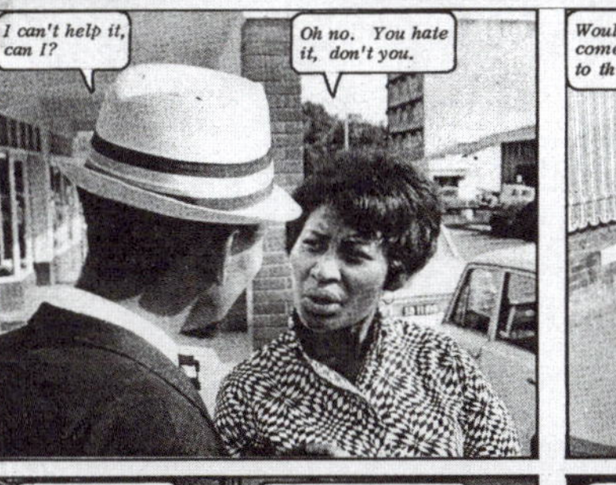

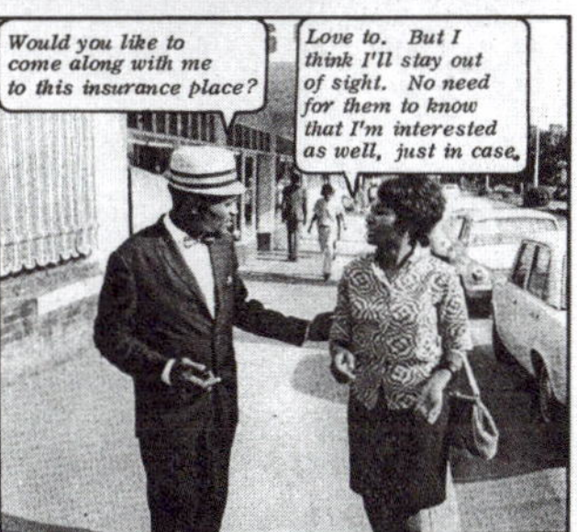

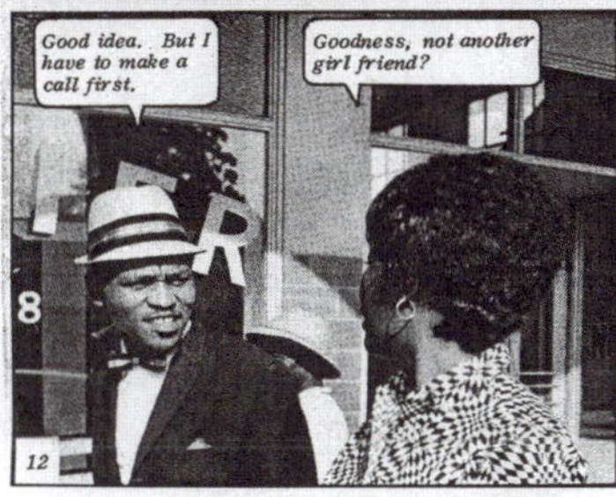

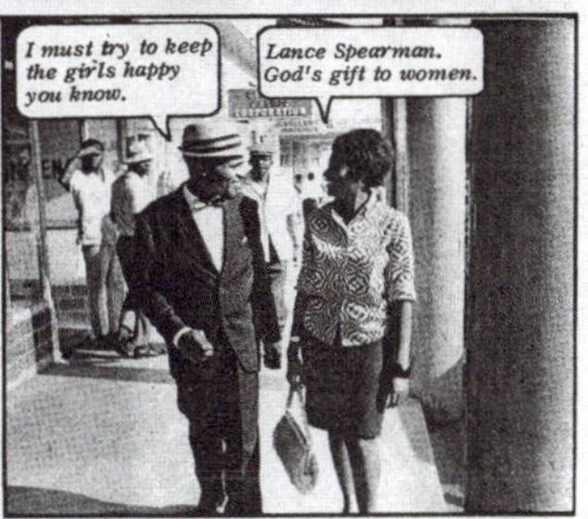

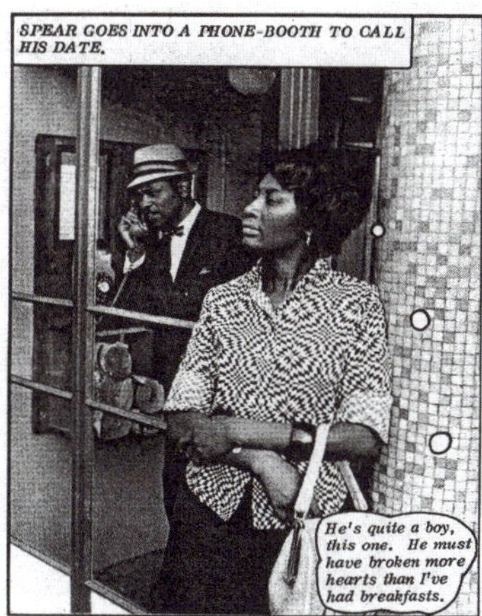

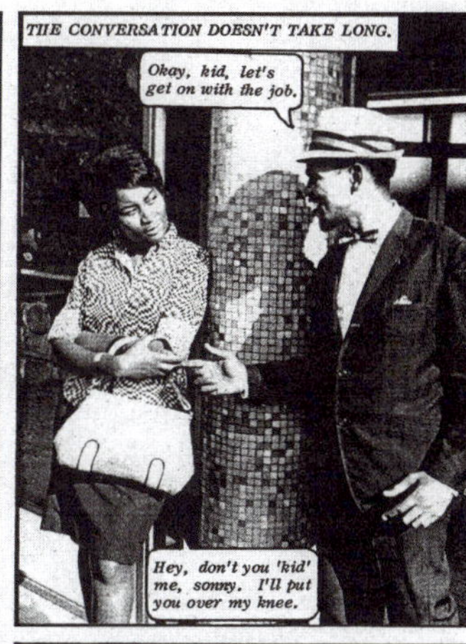

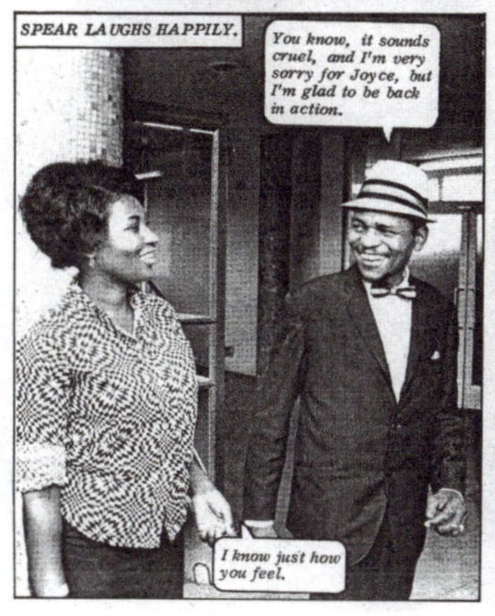

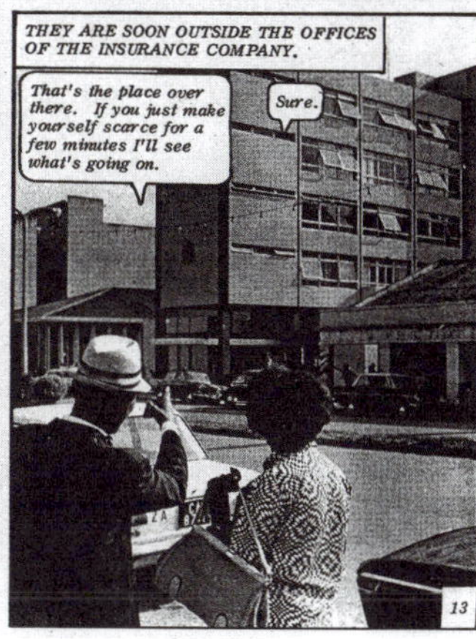

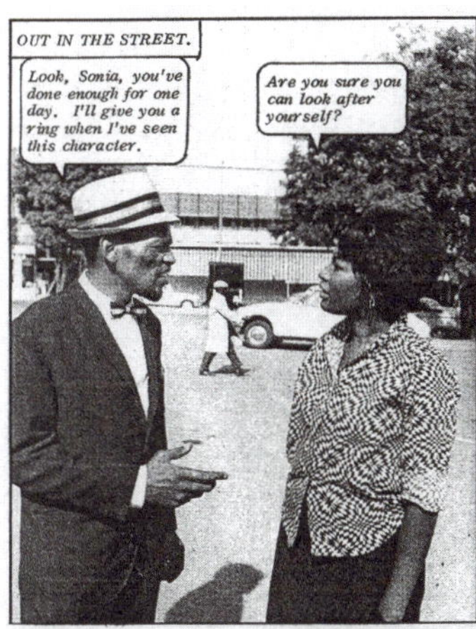

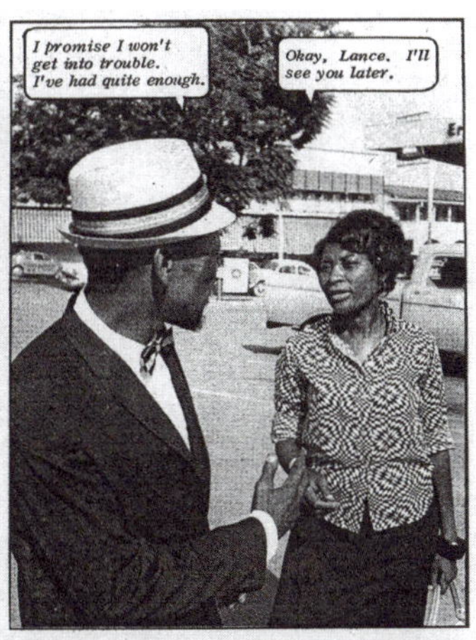

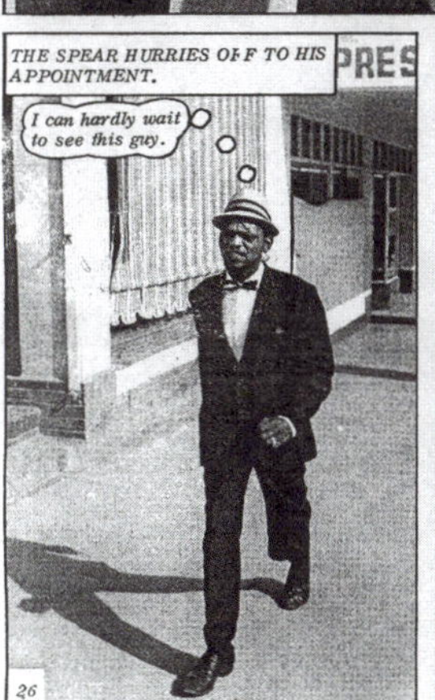

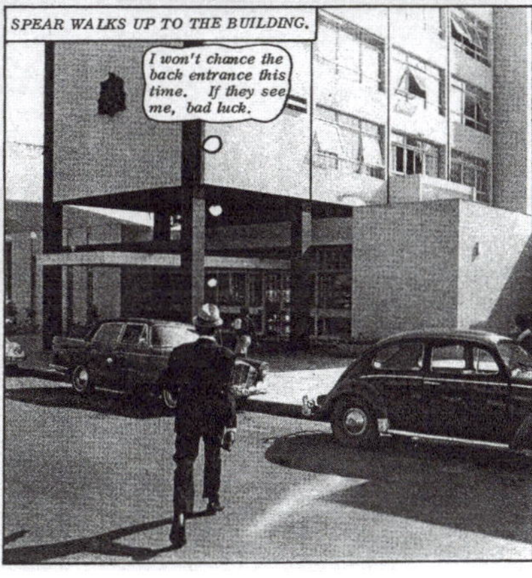

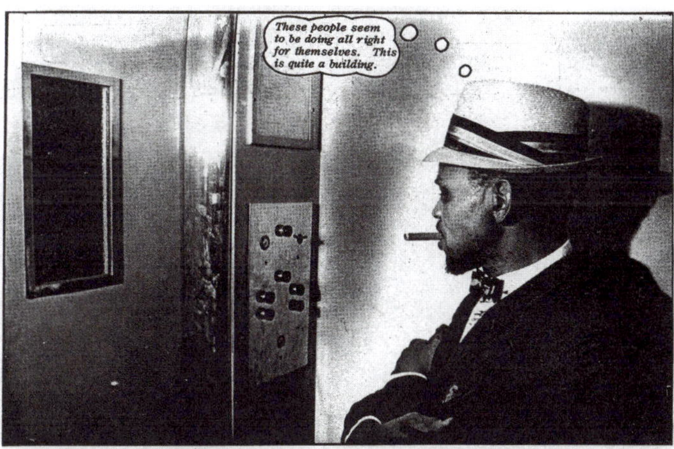

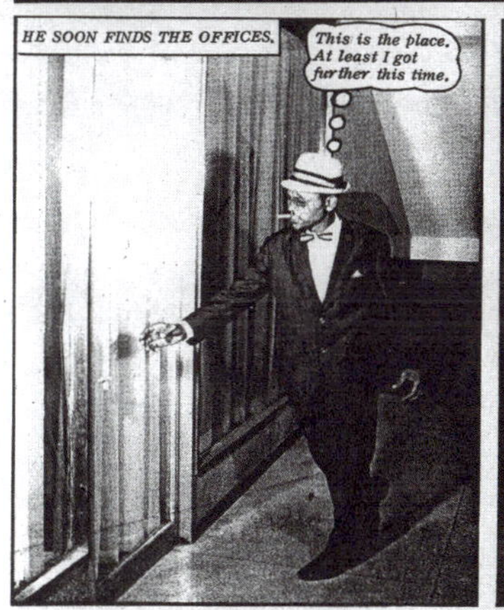

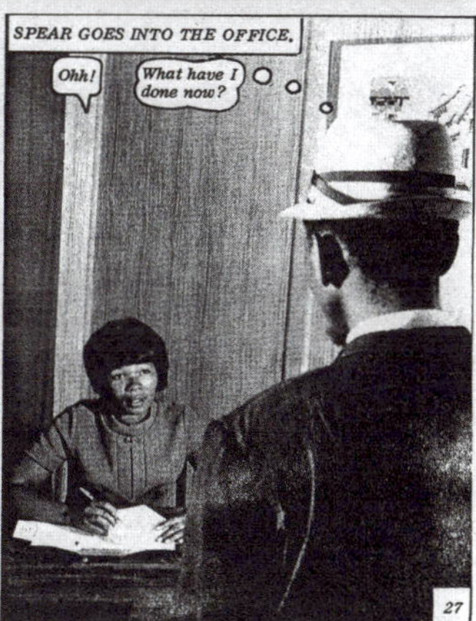

D Spear and Sonia in the City (*African Film* n.d., 127)

borrowed from comics, are also added. The different camera angles and focus of shots, reverse-angle montage and varying picture sizes per panel create a dynamic that approximates the cinematic experience. The liveliness of the images is further enhanced by the actors' vivid facial expressions. Here, *African Film* clearly took a different approach from contemporary European photo novels. In the latter, to make the actors look as perfect as possible, they were shown with closed lips even when they were talking. While images in European photo novels merely functioned to illustrate the text,[17] the images and text in *African Film* were on a more equal footing. In some sequences, such as fight scenes, the images play a leading role. They can even be understood without the texts, which kept the magazine attractive for an audience with limited literacy. For the literate audience familiar with English, the scenes offered additional fun as Spear and his friends spiced up the fights with their essentially ironic comments, giving uppercuts and karate kicks a comic undertone. "Have a knuckle sandwich," Spear announces to one of the thugs before landing a punch on his face. A few pages later, he is shown Bruce-Lee-style in mid-leap as he karate kicks two opponents with the words "You guys look hungry. Have a meal."[18]

Transnational Readership

In 1969, journalist Stanley Meisler, a contemporary observer, wrote: "In almost every English-speaking town of Africa, young men, most with no more than five years of schooling, sit on the sidewalk and avidly read the one-shilling picture magazines that chronicle the adventures every week of Spearman and other heroes …"[19] He described the average reader as young male migrant workers who left their rural homes in search of a better life in the cities. But they have been bitterly disappointed; many doors remain closed to them and they have to make do with casual jobs. "Spear is their imagination given a concrete form. He is the black man – smart, witty, tough – who rules the urban world which they want to enter."[20] Meisler was a foreign correspondent based in Nairobi and his portrait of the readers may well have been informed by his everyday observations there. It could, however, be further refined. In an essay about her childhood in Nairobi, Kenyan journalist Kate Getao describes *African Film* and comics as part of an urban middle-class youth culture. "When I was a youngster, I was lucky to receive exactly five shillings as pocket money. With that amount of money, you could buy two comics, a bar of chocolate, a packet of liquorice allsorts and have change to spare. [...] These comics and film strips were so addictive that a collection of them gave one stature in the community [...]. In those days, you could win friends and influence people by swapping comics. I knew my relatives by what sort of comic collection they possessed, and never resisted visiting anyone who had a large pile of *[African] Film* stored under their bed."[21] Secondary pupils also belonged to the circle of loyal fans, as was confirmed in talks with former readers in Dar es Salaam in 2009. The less affluent had to borrow the magazines, while others – such as Kate Getao – bought them with their own pocket money, and the privileged few even had the magazines bought for them by parents who hoped the 'look-reads' would improve their children's English.[22] But in fact the young readers were most impressed with the stretches of panels filled with fist fights, which they readily transposed into the dusty streets of their hometowns. Fans imitated Spear's style as far as possible, with some even taking up smoking. Interestingly, since the Tanzanian readership of *African Film* assumed it was a Nigerian publication, the prototypical city portrayed in the magazine was identified with Lagos. This may have been reinforced by the magazine's occasional lists of new Spear Fan Club members, which showed that most of them actually did come from Nigeria. Fifty per cent of all new fan club members were Nigerian, with the vast majority of them living in Lagos; the other fifty per cent were split equally between Kenya, Uganda and Tanzania.

In an essay entitled *Black like us,* Tunde Giwa, himself a Nigerian one-time fan of *African Film,* attributed the popularity of Lance Spearman primarily to the stories revolving around a black – and hence African – hero. He notes that comics distributed in Africa in the 1960s either came from the US or Europe and were focused on the deeds of such white heroes as Superman, Tintin or Thor. If the adventures of the white heroes in these stories were set in Africa at all, Africans only appeared at most as part of the local background. "Into this culturally colonised milieu came a new comic [...] called *African Film* featuring Lance Spearman, a raffish and nattily dressed black super cop with an ever-present panama hat. And we all instantly fell deeply in love with him. No one forced Spearman on us.[23] For the first time, we had a comic hero who was actually black like us." Without doubt, the magazine's positive reception also benefited from its contemporary context, appearing at the end of a decade when the majority of African colonies had gained their independence. In an era marked by nationalism and growing self-confidence, a versatile African crime fighter made sense. He could protect the fictive modern nation where his adventures were located from every kind of criminal menace (as the cover of issue 118 announced: "When the country's existence is threatened, its leaders at once call in The Spear"). As Africa's answer to James Bond and the US comic industry superheroes, Lance Spearman, who not only saved the country in his adventures but regularly rescued the entire world, may well have satisfied his postcolonial readership's profound desire for equality.

---

17 Schimming (2002), p. 73

18 *African Film* (n.d.), 107: 10, 23

19 Meisler (1969), p. 81

20 Meisler (1969), p. 81

21 Kate Getao 2008, How I long for those comic book days, *The Nation* (Kenya). www.nation.co.ke/magazines/saturday/-/1216/490922/-/item/0/-/mgydua/-/indey.html retrieved on 4 March 2010

22 Matthias Krings 2010, A Prequel to Nollywood: South African Photo Novels and their Pan-African Consumption in the Late 1960s, *Journal of African Cultural Studies* 22/1: 75–89

23 Giwa (2008)

Between Onitsha Market Literature and Nollywood Videos

At that time, the sketch of an urban African modernity as developed in the photo novels was almost unrivalled – at least in terms of visual mass media. African film production was still in its infancy, and the cinemas were showing Hollywood movies, Italo-Westerns or Indian schmaltz. In the majority of countries with the exception of Nigeria, TV was only introduced later; even where it did already exist, reception was still uneven. As the title implies, the issues of *African Film* were something like a portable movie substitute. The staged photos had very little to do with the actual reality of African cities, but far from being seen as a shortcoming, this was the reason for their particular attraction. The achievement of *African Film* was its adaptation of Western genres, thus enabling the audience to connect with global contemporary popular culture. Anyone more interested in local stories – at least in southwest Nigeria – could buy or borrow the local language photo novels published by the West African Book Publishers in Lagos. These were primarily adapted plays from the Yoruba tradition of travelling theatre, and although they also addressed modernity, they had strong references to local traditions.

African Film can be most viably located between the two genuinely Nigerian genres of Onitsha Market Literature and Nollywood video films which, in contrast to the Yoruba photo plays, similarly appeared in English and were marked by a general openness toward outside influences. Just as in *African Film,* these two genres also took the perils of modern city life as their theme, warning against the deceitful arts of seduction of independent women or the occult machinations of wealthy gangsters. *African Film* may not contain explicit advice on how to deal with money and women or how to cope with life in the city in general, as was characteristic in the 1960s Onitsha Market Literature, but it can nevertheless be read as a didactic medium: anyone who locks their doors and windows at night lives longer, and whoever adopts Spear's stylishness and ironic directness needs nothing more for success with women. Both Nollywood video films and *African Film* turn their audience into an eyewitness of events, with both genres enabling their customers to experience criminal machinations at first hand. Moreover, as a precursor of the popular African cinema as represented by today's Nollywood films, *African Film* already anticipated a near Pan-African reception. Against this background, it is hardly surprising that you can come across exchanges like this one in a Nigerian Internet forum: "Do I remember Spear you ask? Man, Lance Spearman should be made into a movie for real!" The answer gives reason for hope: "I actually DID start writing a Lance Spearman screenplay a few years ago, but then I changed the character into an original creation because I wasn't sure what the situation was with the rights to the Spear character. I actually should look into that [...] because I think that movie should be made, if not by me then by someone else. (But preferably by me)."

Translation from German by Andrew Boreham

State-Theatre [1] – Lagos

DANIEL KÖTTER AND CONSTANZE FISCHBECK

Some of the works by Daniel Kötter and Constanze Fischbeck connect their interest in researching theatre's medial and social conditions with video installation and film. As part of their intensive research into Lagos' urban structures, Kötter and Fischbeck went several times to view the National Theatre, which was built specifically for the FESTAC. The contrast between the gigantic, dusty and empty auditorium and the city's complex performative street life led them to create their *State-Theatre: Lagos/Teheran/Berlin* (2009–2010) project that explores how spatial conditions provide a basis for theatre. This work is Daniel Kötter and Constanze Fischbeck's second cooperation.

The National Theatre in Lagos is Nigeria's only publicly funded location for the performing arts. In the midst of the diversity of artistic methods and discourses, the building's monumental character expresses its aspiration to promote and showcase a national culture. The theatre's jutting presence in urban space also shapes the conception and horizon of expectations for the material possibilities of performative practice in Lagos.

After the air conditioning broke down in 1992 and the roof started to leak, the main auditorium, the heart of the building, was not used for fifteen years. Since then, the smaller rooms set around it, designed as cinemas, exhibition and conference halls have been infrequently used as venues for theatre and dance performances, wedding receptions and parties. The theatre's present empty state offers a surface for projections and speculations, a conceptual space for alternative uses, future theatre forms and performative practices.

The National Theatre

"Capable of seating 5,000 people, the Main Hall consists of a collapsible stage and an auditorium. When in proscenium the hall has a capacity for 3,500 seats. The cinema screen in the Hall is fixed to the ceiling and can be lowered by remote control. The stage has three rows of curtains, a backdrop and a double cyclorama for creating silhouette effects. It is easily amenable to any directional concepts. It is ideal for major musical concerts, drama and film shows. Such is the versatility of this huge hall that it also handles indoor sporting activities like table tennis, wrestling, boxing, etc."

(Source: *The National Theatre of Nigeria*, 1970s advertising brochure)

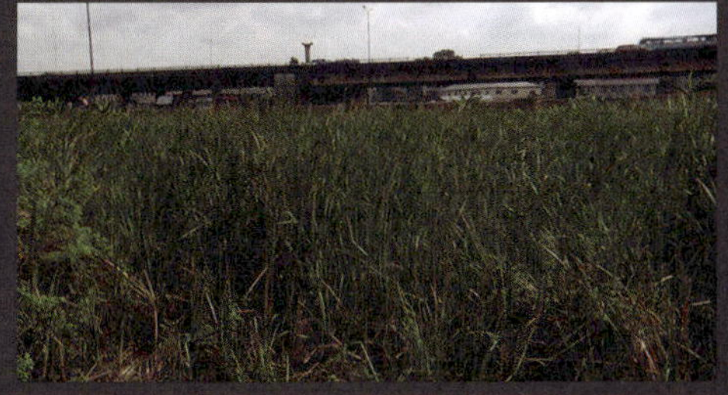
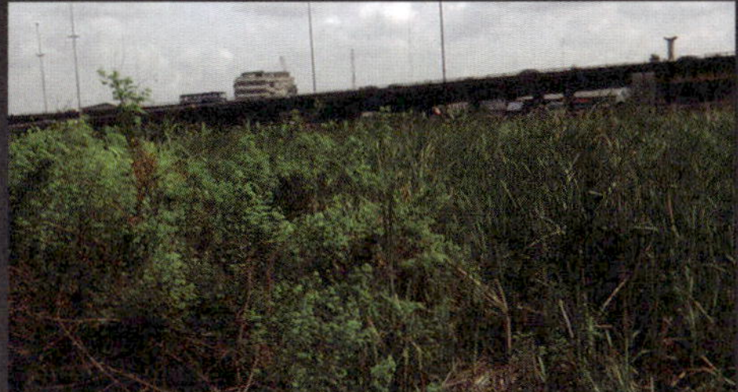
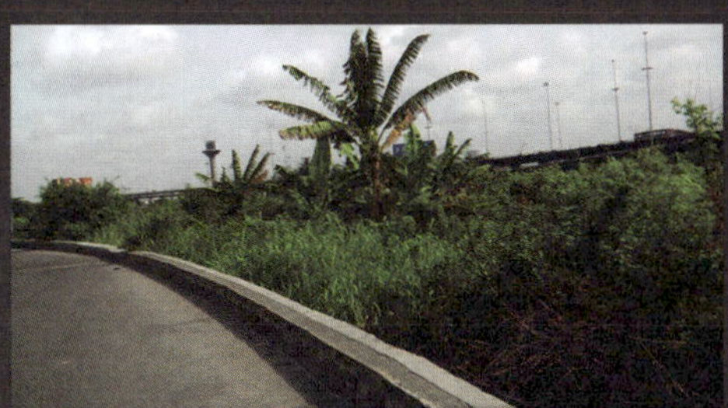
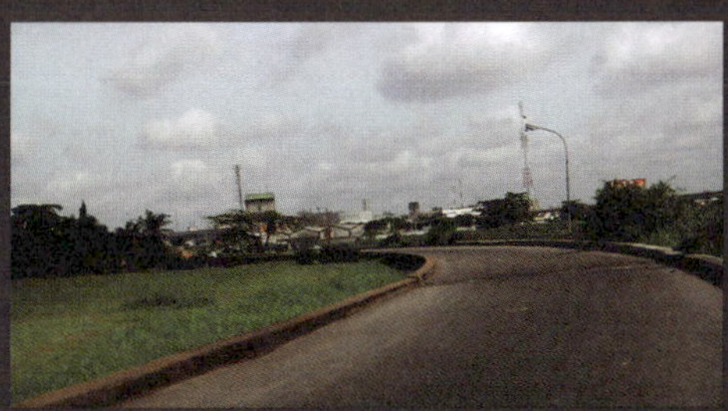
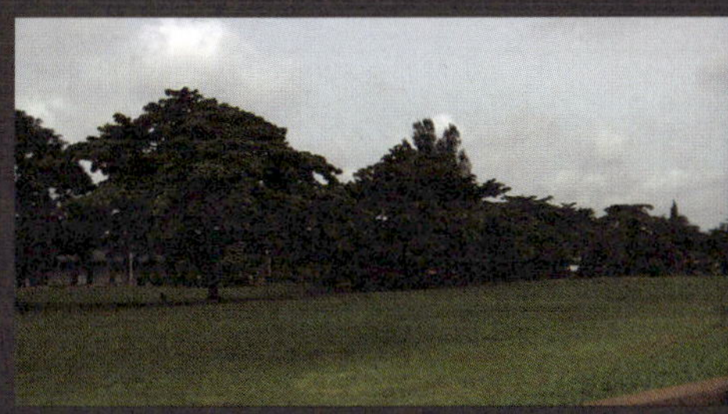
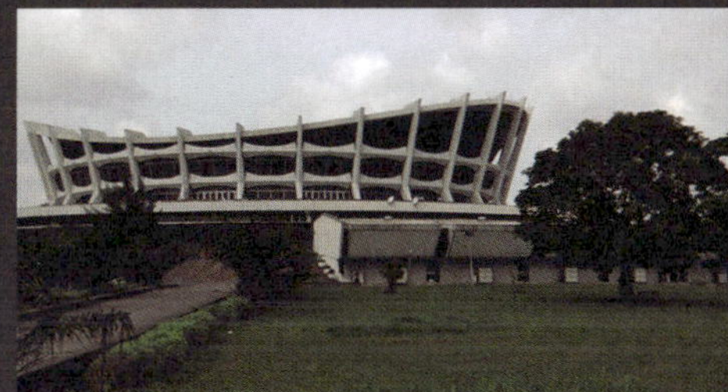
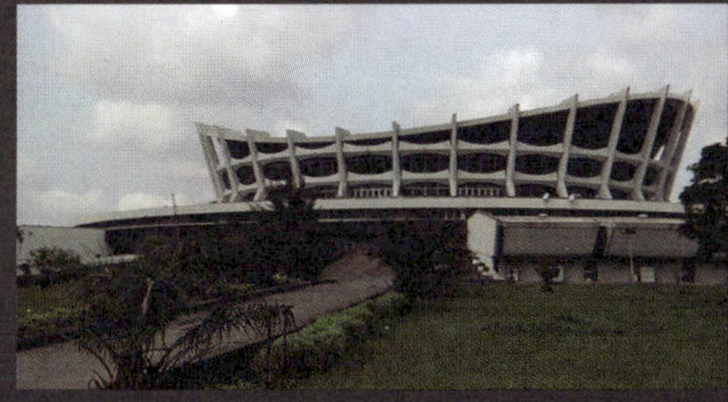

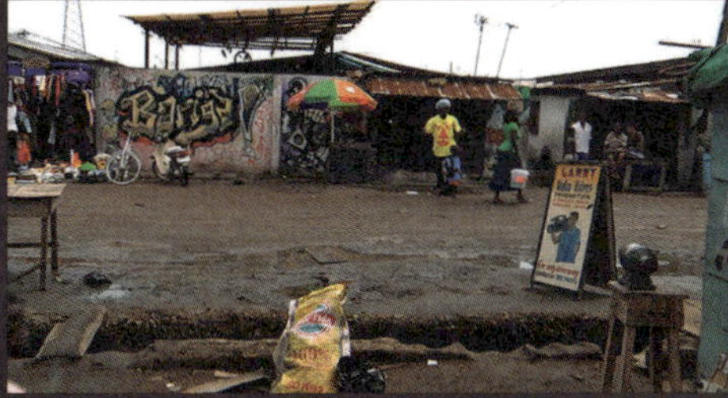

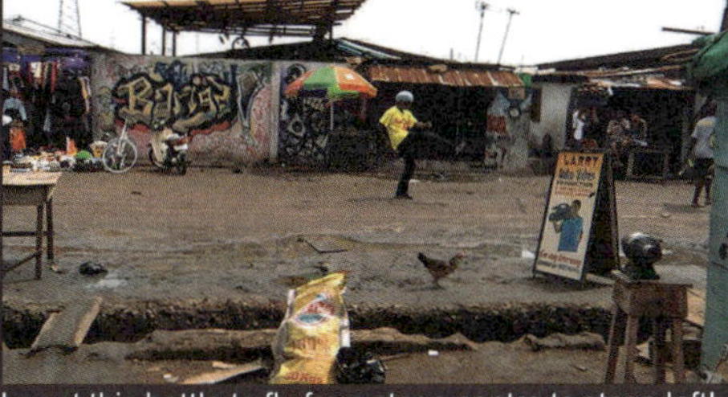

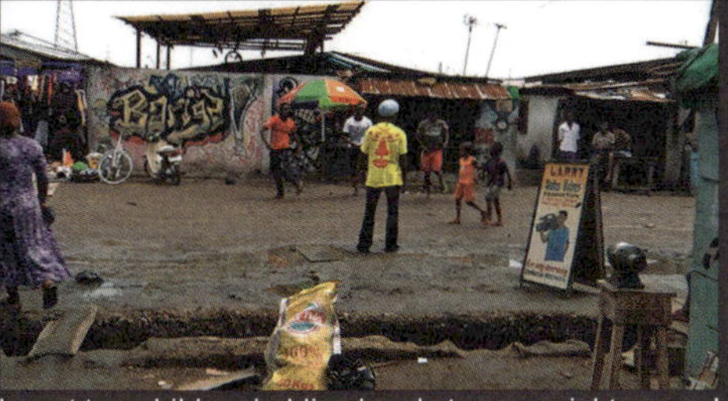

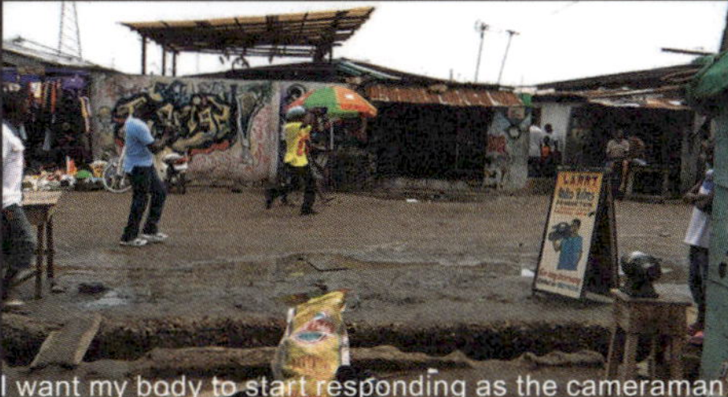

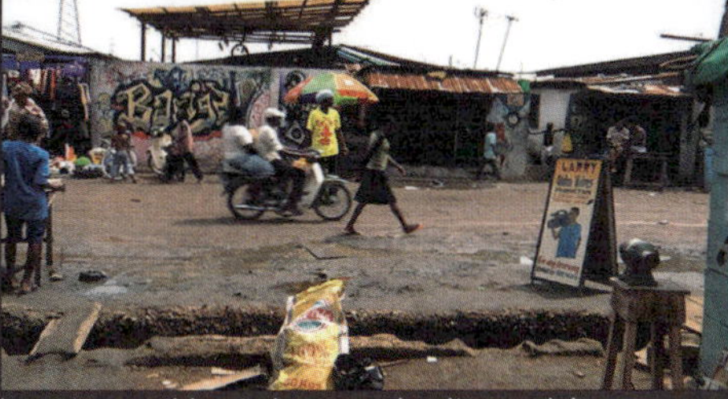

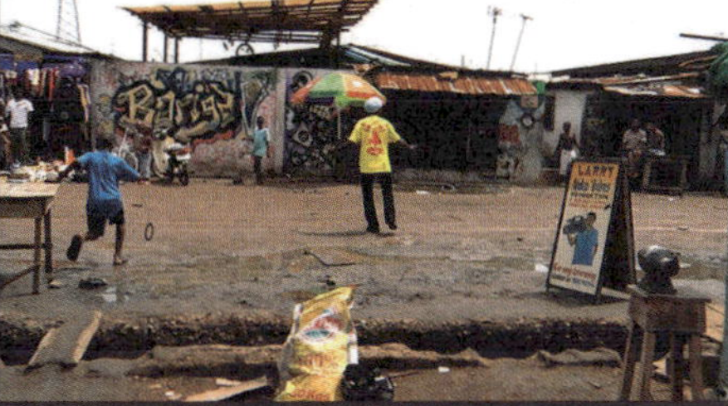

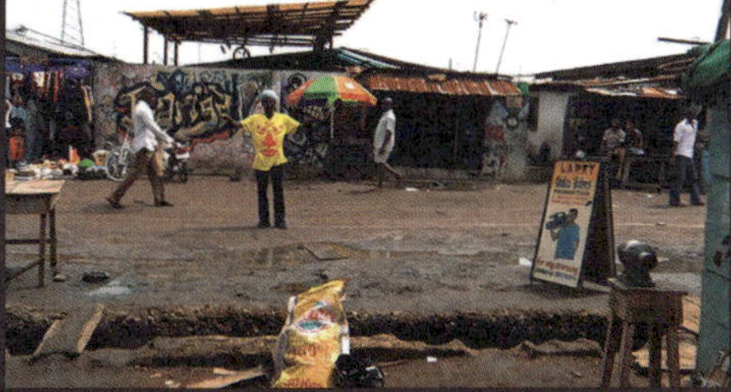

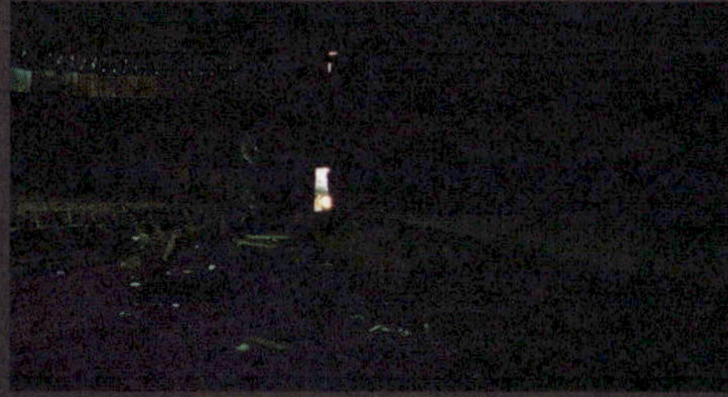
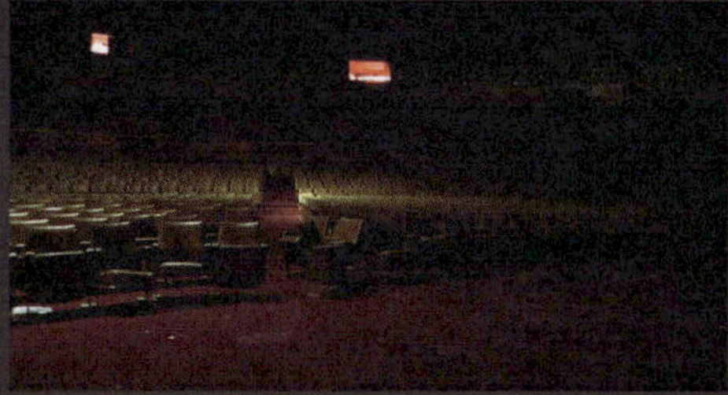
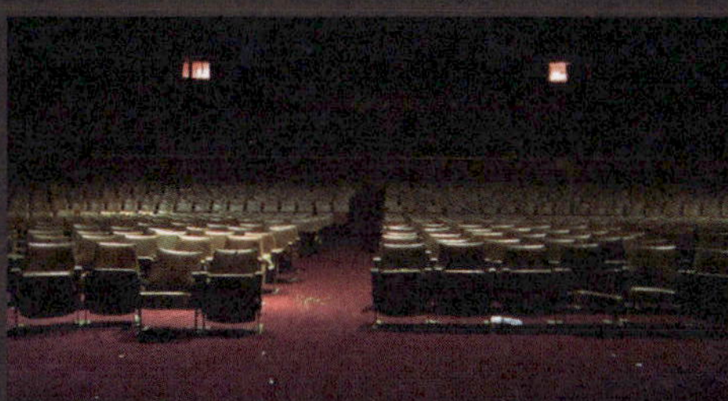
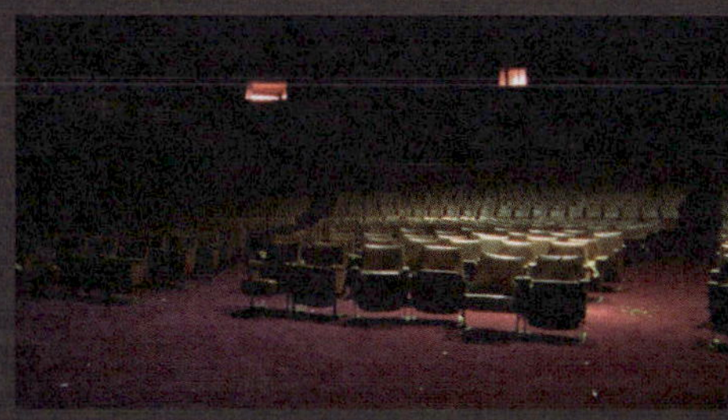
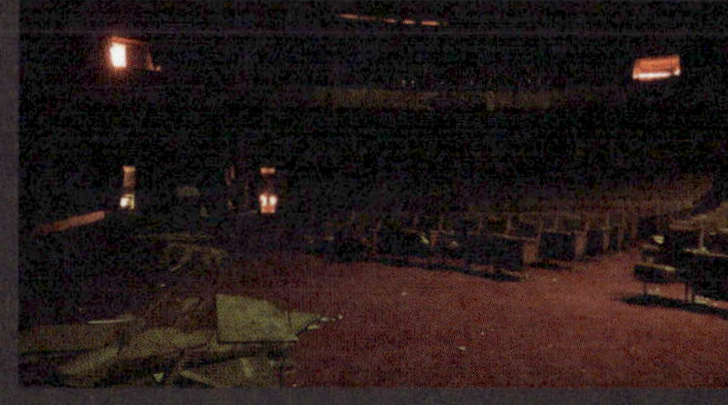

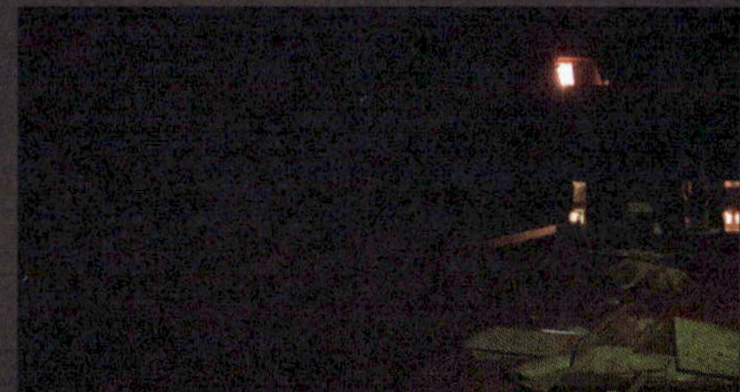

STATE-THEATRE [1] – LAGOS, VIDEOSTILLS, 2010

Casualties

KAINEBI OSAHENYE

Kainebi Osahenye has been working as an artist for nearly twenty years. During this time, he has become primarily associated with the medium of painting. Recently, Osahenye has increasingly begun to integrate conceptual approaches in his works. His installations, usually large scale, are created from found objects – empty plastic bottles, beer cans and squashed tubes of colour. The visual impressions of the city, gathered on his walks through Lagos, lend his works a specifically urban aesthetic. In *Casualties* (2008), he has arranged thousands of old beer cans to create an over life-size cascading curtain.

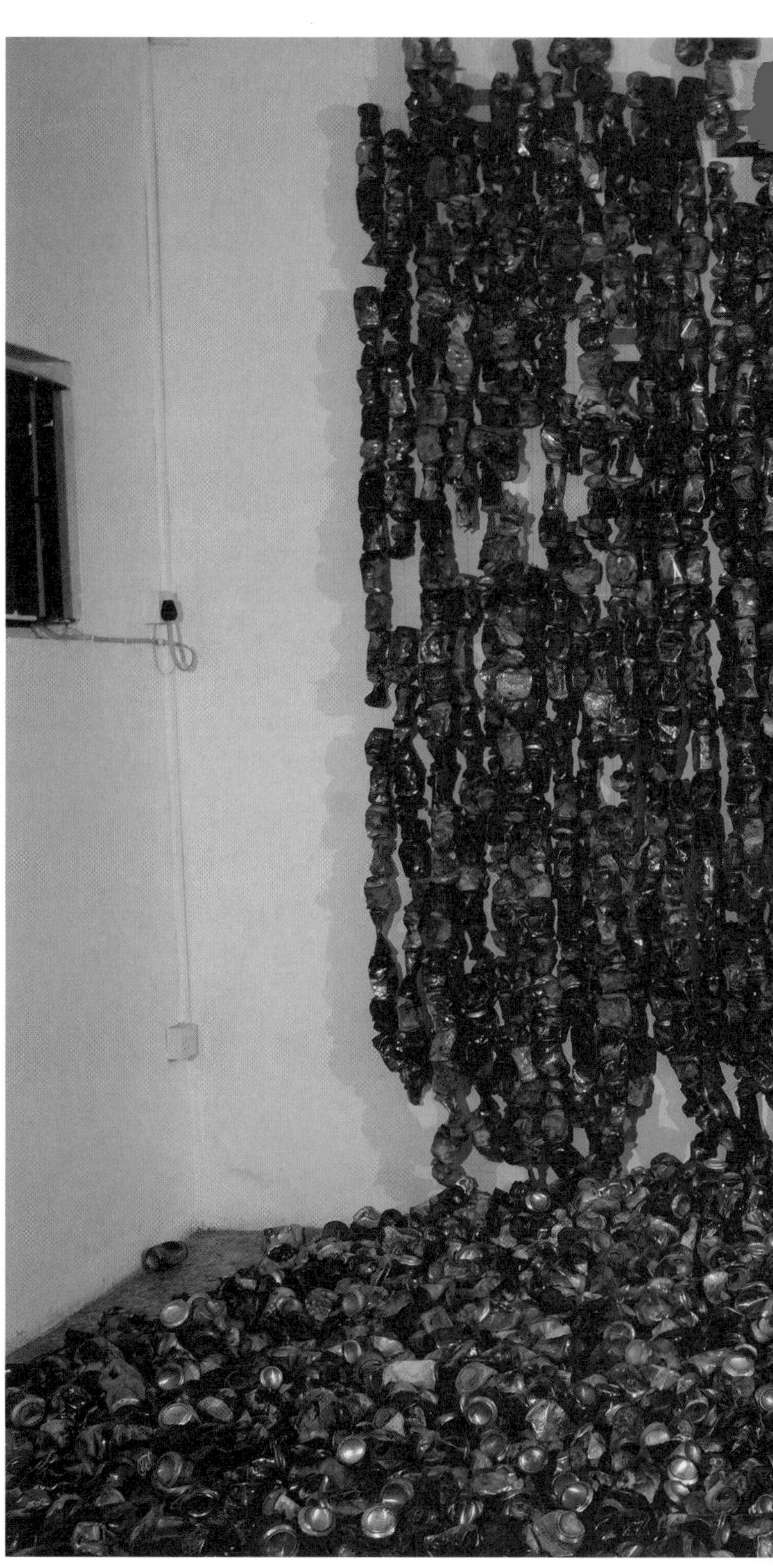

CASUALTIES, CANS, FISHING LINE, FLAGS, VARIABLE HEIGHT, 2008

Lagos Soundscape

EMEKA OGBOH

Since 2007, graphic designer Emeka Ogboh has been an active member of the small but steadily growing media art scene in Lagos. His current projects, which focus on using auditory media to explore Lagos' acoustic cityscape, have culminated in the ongoing multimedia project *Lagos Soundscape.* (www.lagossoundscape.com)

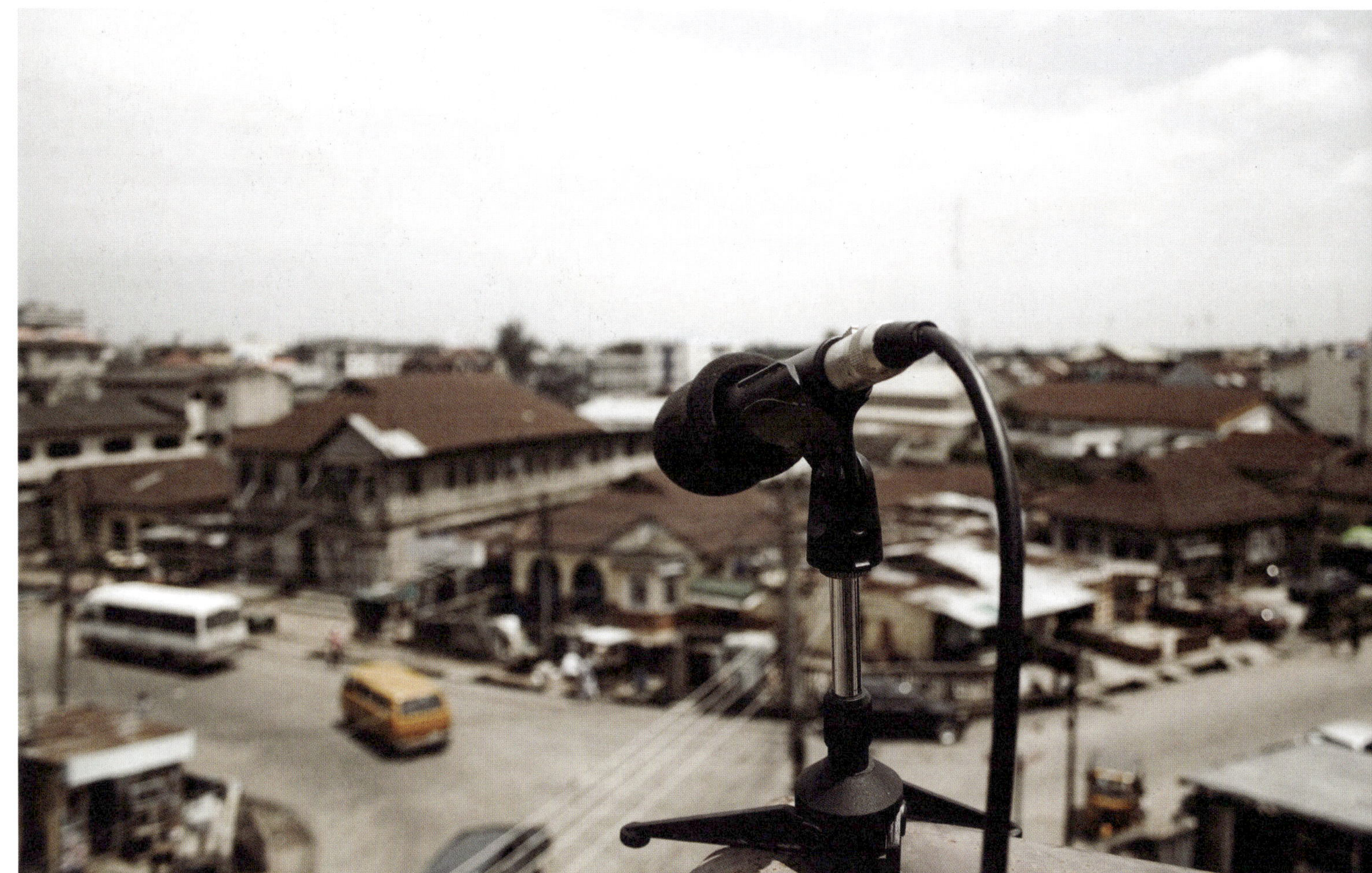

LAGOS SOUNDSCAPE, 2008

It is hard to imagine Lagos without its characteristic Danfo mini-buses. These cadmium yellow VW minibuses with horizontal black stripes provide a means of connecting points on the map of a city seeming forever on the move.
The Danfo minibuses first appeared on the streets of the city in the 1970s. Since then, they have become Lagos' archetypical transport medium, carrying masses of people every day from one location to another. A Danfo may look like any other commercial minibus, but it stands out through its own particular cacophony of sounds: melodious horns hooting in an acoustic landscape created by the drivers shouting the stops; ear-blasting radios blaring out the latest Yoruba songs; the strident sounds of local and imported hip-hop or afrobeats; vendors not only touting wares, but also rumours; mini-entrepreneurship on the move; jibes about "ethnic characteristics", mobile calls at full volume; dialogues, monologues, and other forms of self-assertion. The mix continues with fiery speeches by fervent preachers and neighbourly banter, creating a sound landscape with an overlay of opinions occasionally spiced by choice urban phrases – and for a moment, it all seems to be echoing around the small square of space dubbed a Danfo.
In these minibuses, where everyone can call themselves a specialist on any topic, you only need pay the standard fare to get an "expert" analysis of politics, finance, sport and religion.
This is where the life of the city happens, nearly twenty-four hours a day.

LAGOS BY BUS, 2010

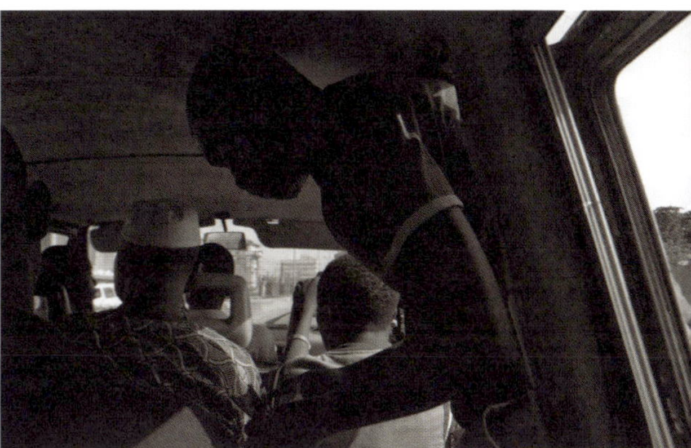

All photos: © Olusola Otori

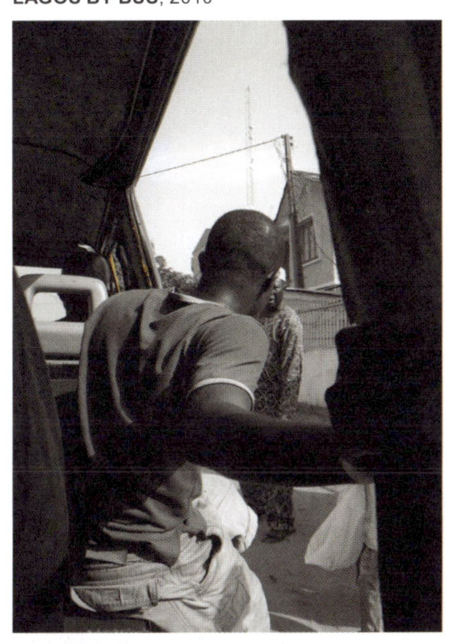

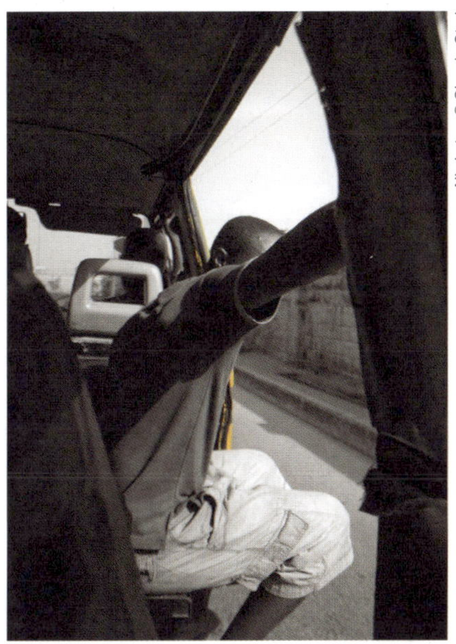

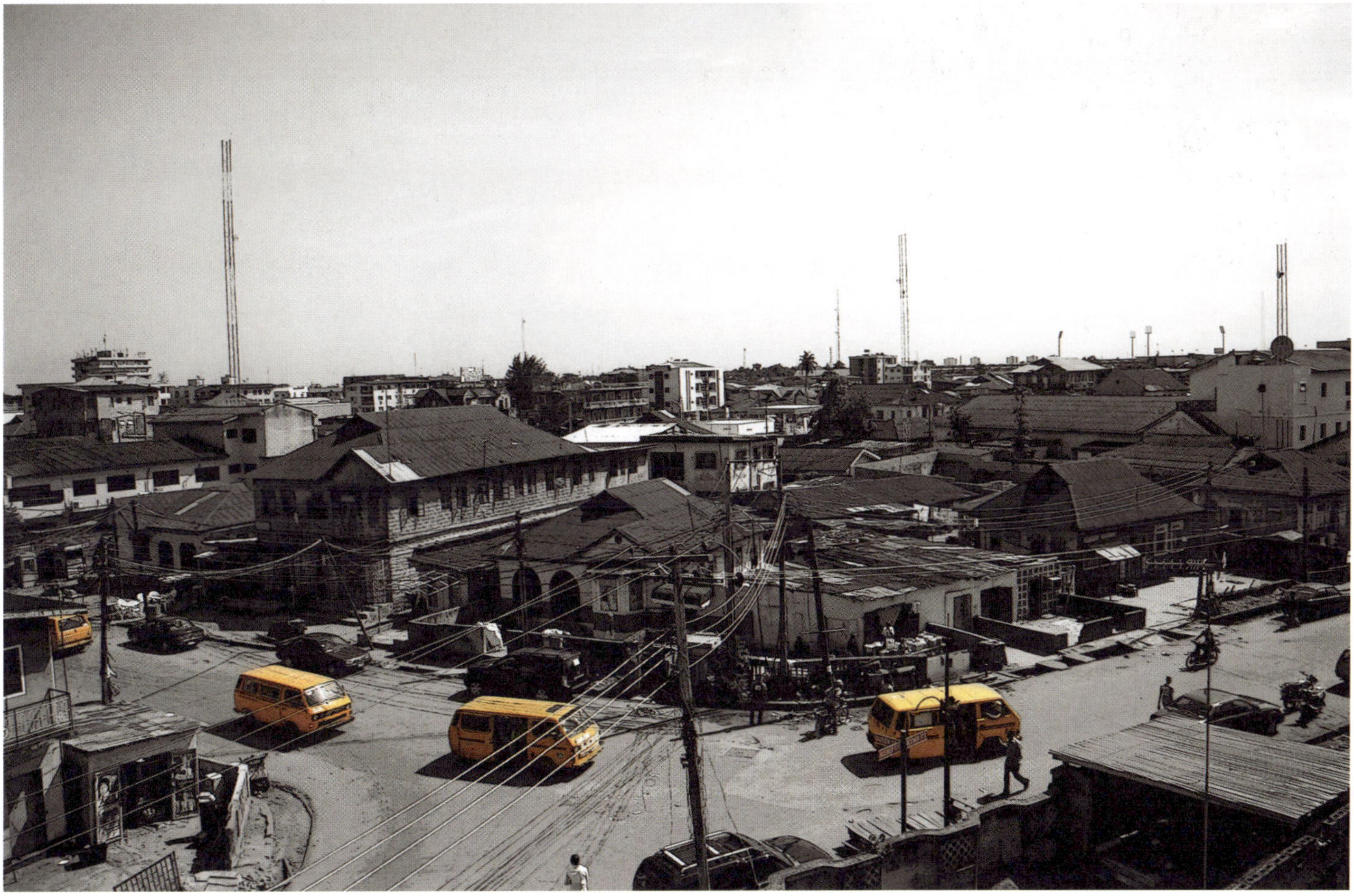

Under Bridge Life

UCHE OKPA-IROHA

Lagos photographer Uche Okpa-Iroha is a founding member of the Black Box photography collective. His work primarily explores the everyday lives of the city's residents and their interaction in public space. In 2008, his photo series *Under Bridge Life* was awarded the Seydou Keita Grand Prix at the 8th African Biennial of Photography in Bamako (*Rencontres de la photographie africaine*), Mali.

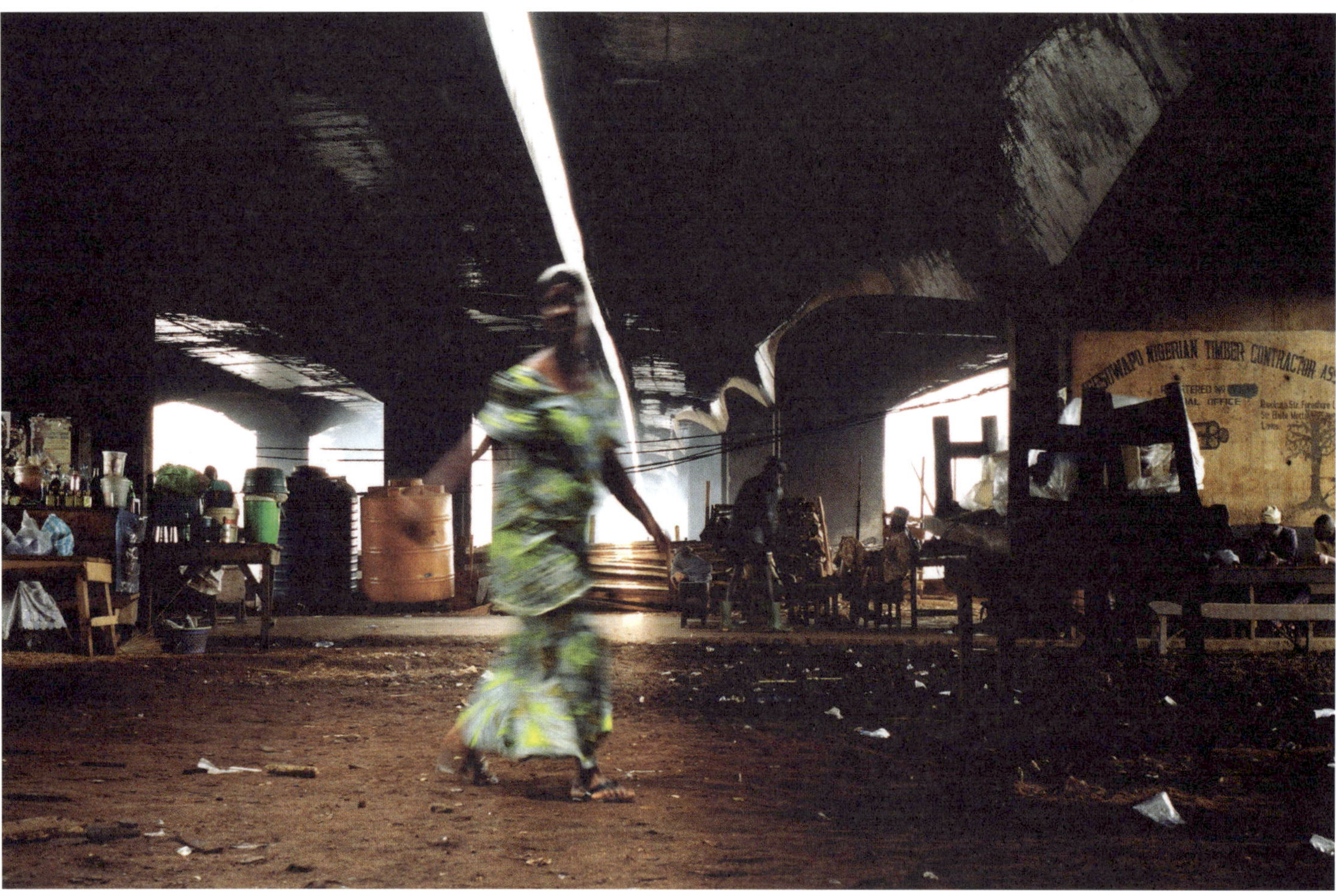

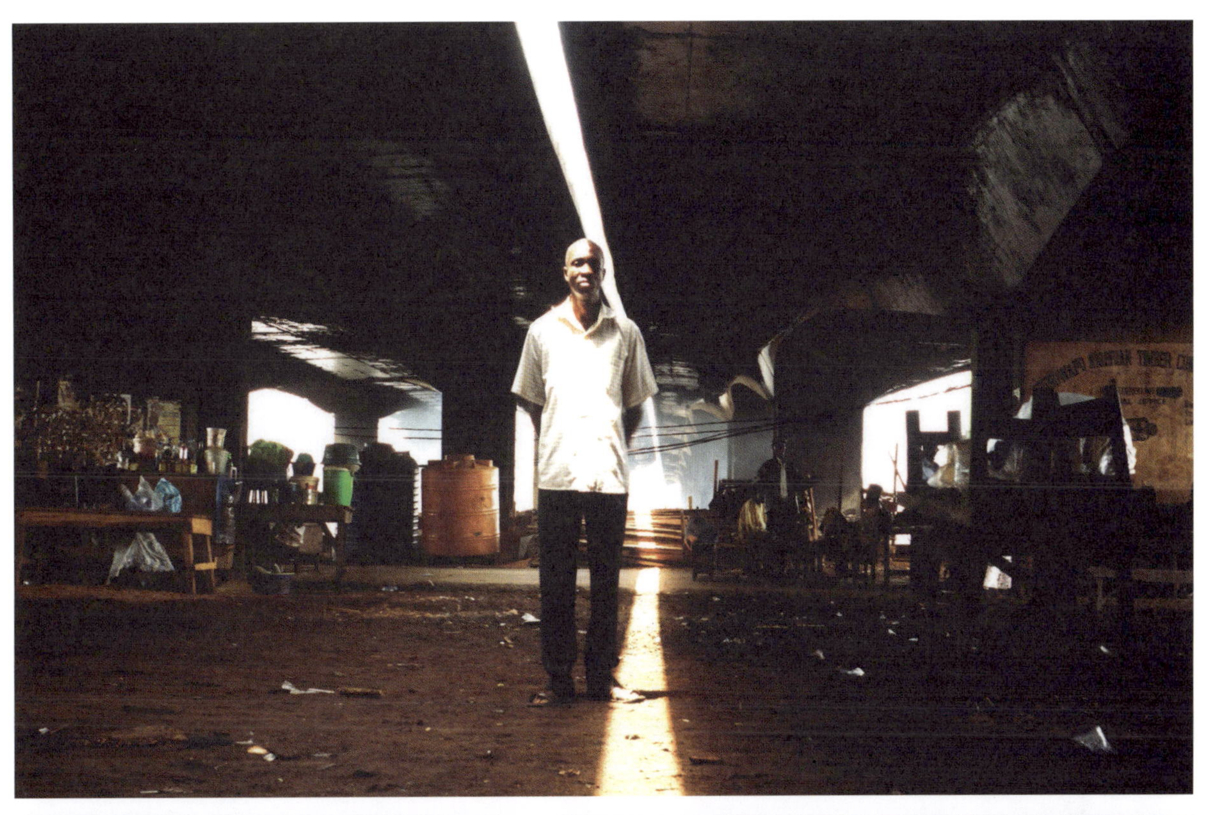

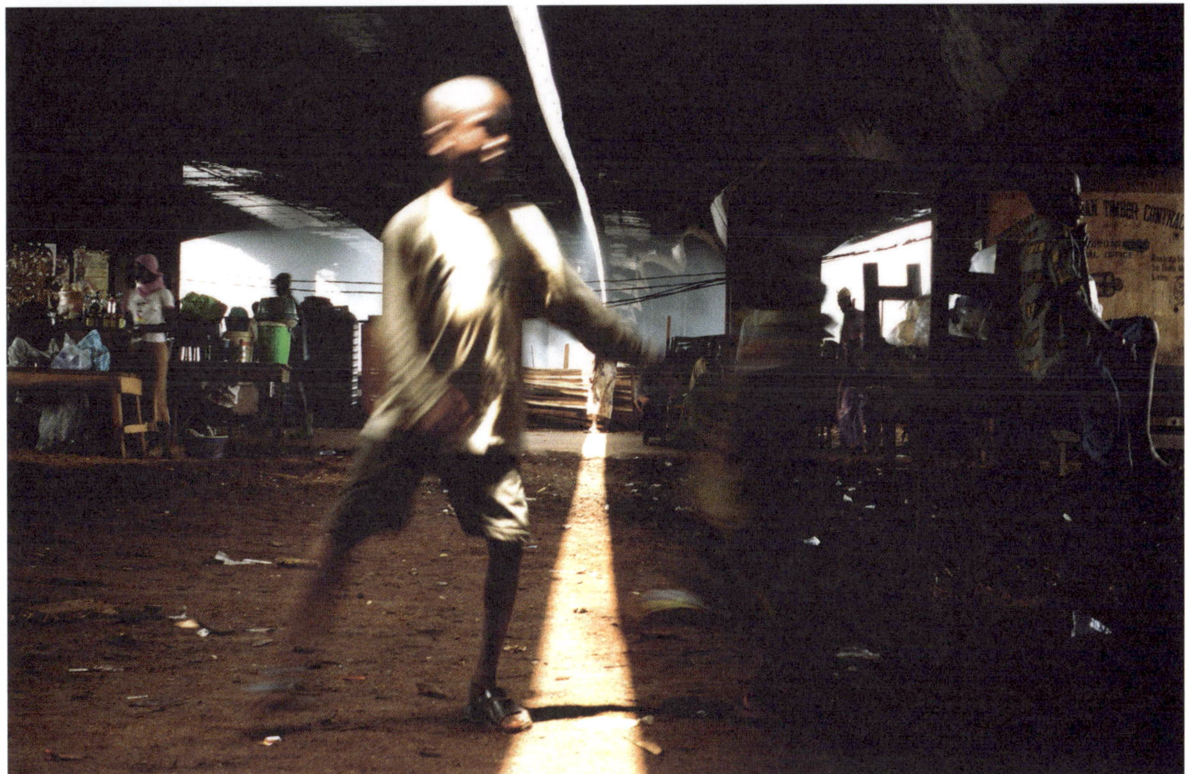

Big Hope

OLAKUNLE TEJUOSO AND WEYINMI ATIGBI

Olakunle Tejuoso and Weyinmi Atigbi are cultural producers from Lagos. Olakunle Tejuoso operates the Glendora / Jazzhole bookshop and music store; Weyinmi Atigbi is a graphic designer and photographer. In 2005, working together and in cooperation with other artists, scholars and photographers based in Lagos, they designed and published the book *Lagos. A City at Work. Big Hope,* the work they created for *Afropolis,* continues and extends their research at that time. While they previously concentrated mainly on Lagos' visual culture, the focus is now on the hope of changes fuelled both by politicians and the widespread desire for a better urban policy for all.

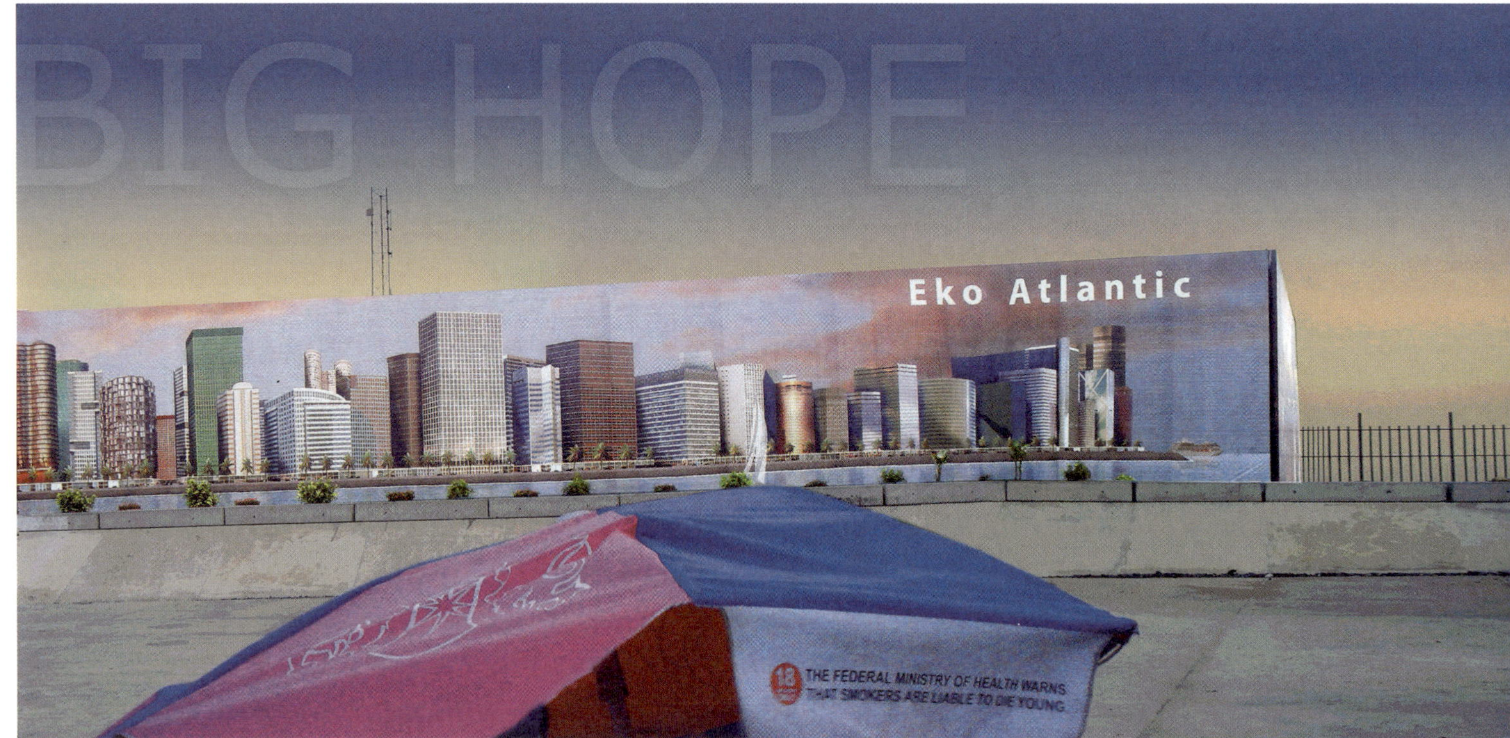

On the Horizon: A BIG HOPE …

The approach in *Lagos. A City at Work* is decisively influenced by the assumption of a life-cycle theory. This theory can help understand the incredible dynamism of this mega-metropolis … HOPE, TENSION, CHOKE, CONFLICT, RELEASE, REFLECTION, then again cautious hope. Since then intense research has been carried out into these tensions, setbacks and conflicts. But now we can see how the dynamic of 'urban self-assertion' becomes newly established every day on a different level though without necessarily being 'positive' or 'negative', but rather in the sense of a system's natural expression which constantly renews itself like the skin, incessantly creates itself anew, and finds a new identity. The dream of Lagos' future identity is extolled as the BIG HOPE. Whenever we record the highly diverse visions that feed on this hope (whether the object

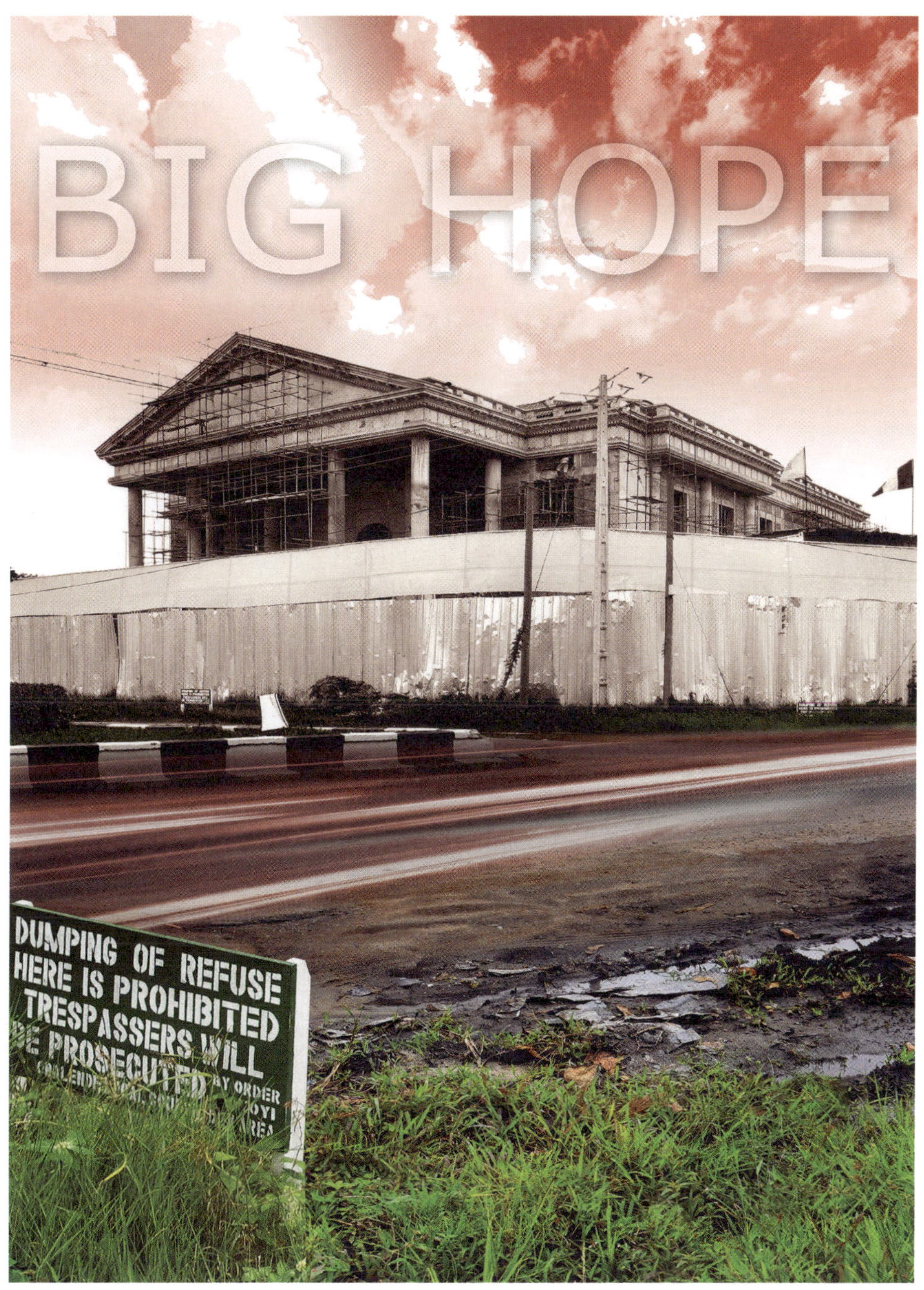

of that desire is a new Florida in the heart of Lagos or a sky-scraper skyline à la Dubai), we find these projects have just as many fervent supporters as opponents. And then there are the undecided. And another question is: Which elements of the BIG DREAM have already become a reality, and which have faded?

But ultimately, the BIG HOPE will anyway have to come to terms with the new identify emerging from the successes and failures of this major urban planning project. This much is clear: this identity must be linked at all costs to a profound sense of responsibility. In this process, it does not matter much whether this sense is mainly derived from practical necessity and – understandable – interests or altruistic motives. After all, in the end what now looks like a reconciliation of interests will only fuel the continuation of the great drama.

Weyinmi Atigbi

Lagos Open

EMEKA UDEMBA

Emeka Udemba is a graphic artist and curator living and working in Germany and Nigeria. *Lagos Open* (Goethe-Institut Lagos, 2005), the art project he curated, explores how art production and artistic interaction can support the development of new strategies and different perspectives on existing structures, as well as alternatives to or fantasies about them.

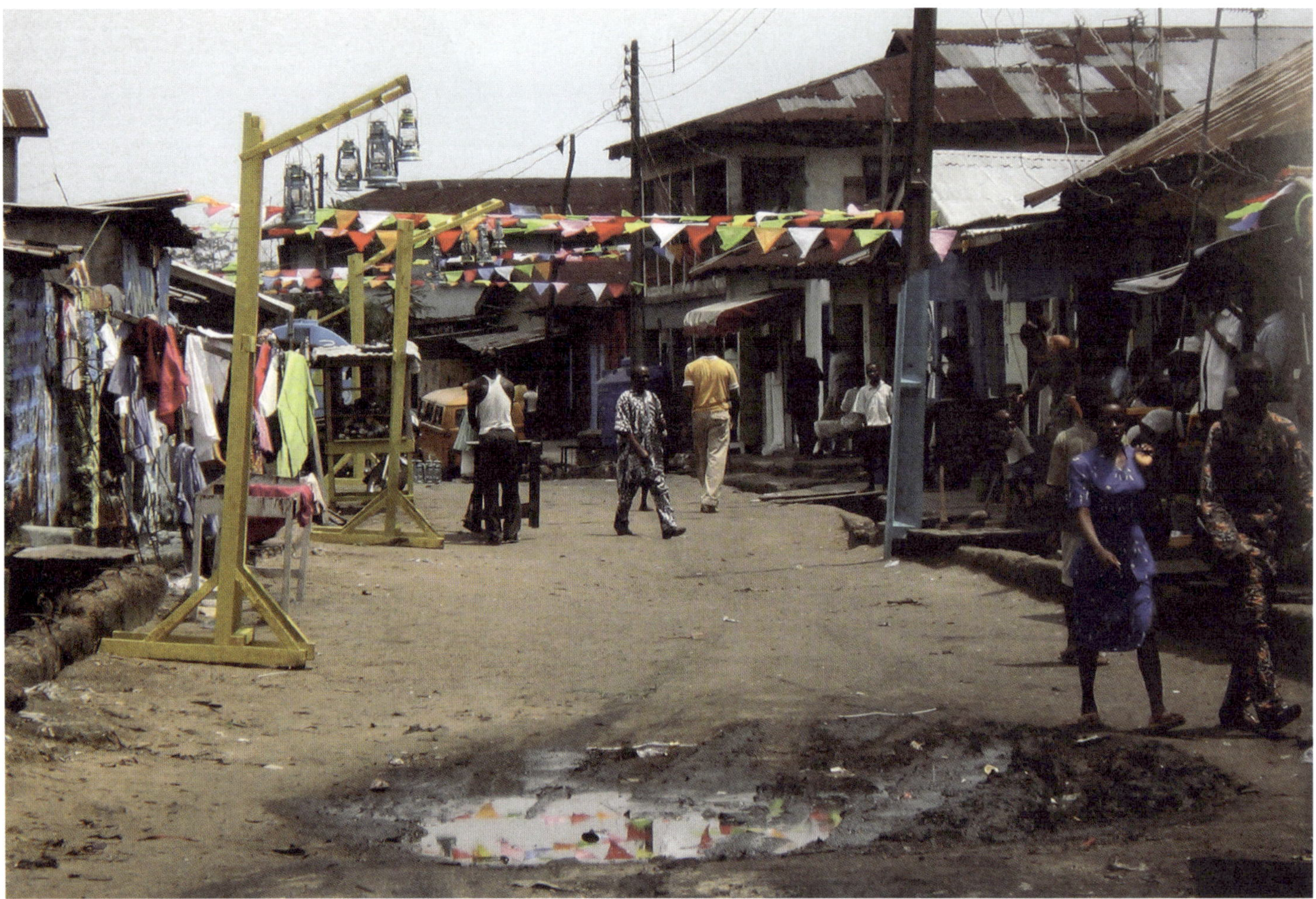

[…] One crucial aspect of the unusual *Lagos Open* project was the focus on linking art practice and expression in public space to questions about more comprehensive social development. The project was realised in Goriola Street in Ajegunle, a marginalised residential quarter in Lagos.

[…] What happens when public space becomes the material an art work should shape and form? To what extent do such spaces make a statement about the condition, conflicts and desires of a community?

In Goriola Street, eleven artists living and working in Lagos took part in a multi-disciplinary discourse with no fixed guidelines on materials or methods. […] Goriola Street was transformed into a fantasy landscape: graffiti and murals decorated simple kiosks selling food and miscellaneous items; a fake sign indicated the presence of a fictional transport system under Goriola Street; kerosene lamps attached to a wooden construction became street lamps and there were live performances and poetry recitals. All of this formed a structure around the complex web of life as it is lived in Lagos – a life that could also exist in any other African city where art often offers people solace and support.

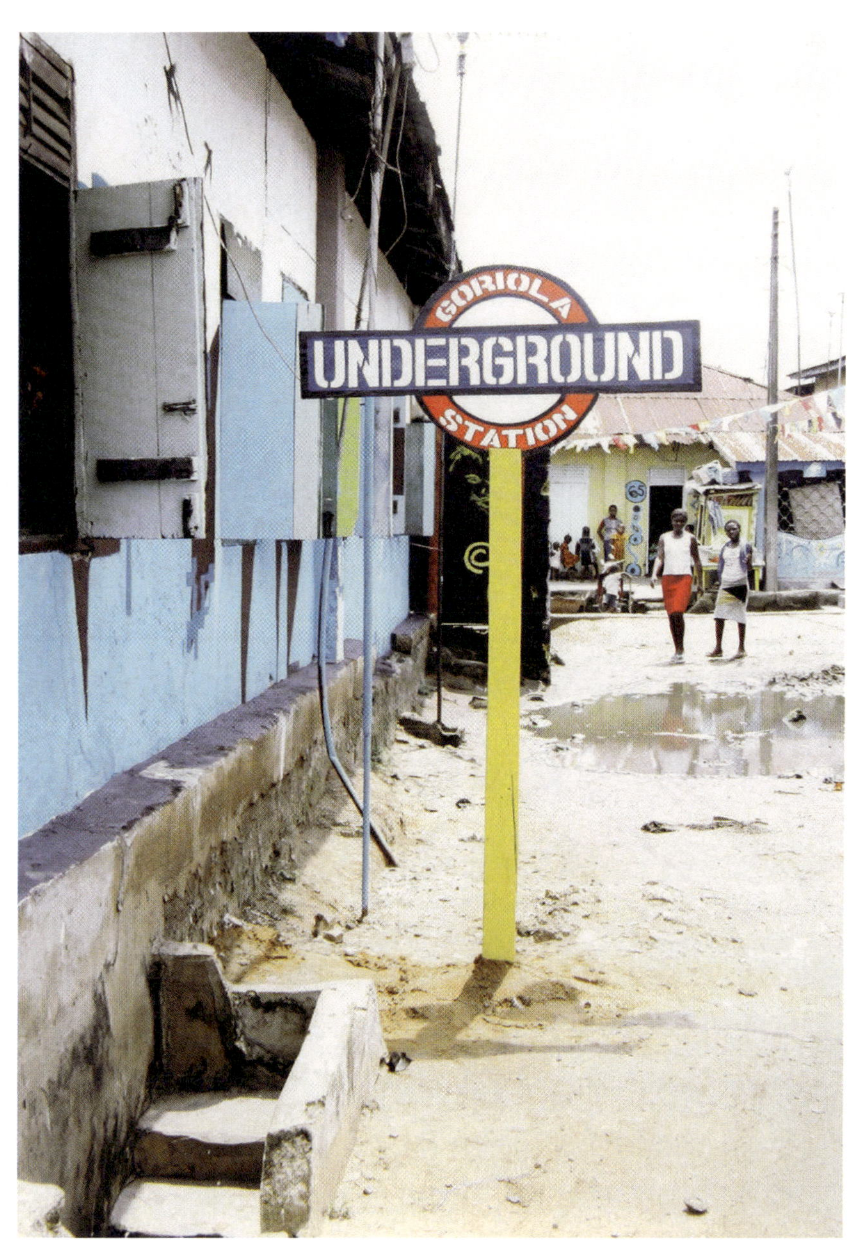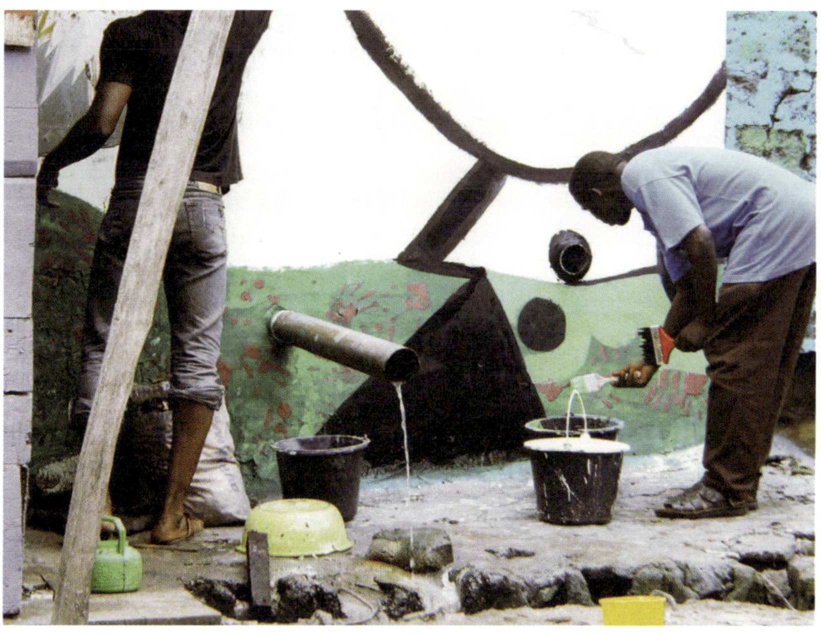

GORIOLA
UNDERGROUND
STATION

NAIROBI

Public Action and Privatisation of Land in Nairobi, Kenya
The Example of Mathare 4A Slum Upgrading Project

DEYSSI RODRIGUEZ-TORRES

The goal of *Mathare 4A Slum Upgrading Project* was to construct houses, renovate shacks and install public services in Mathare 4A, a subdivision of a large slum in the Mathare Valley in Nairobi. Approved by the Kenyan government, financed by the German government and administered by the Catholic Church, this public project began in 1992. Conflict erupted in 1997 when the beneficiaries learned that the land destined for the project, owned by the state and occupied by people since the 1940s, had been given over to the Catholic Church. This transfer was rejected, especially by the owners of the structures who did not want to lose revenues earned from the rental of shacks. Encouraged by local politicians in search of supporters, these property owners in need of revenues together with their renters, who were demanding that ownership of the land be awarded to them, started a protest movement whose main complaint was the transfer of property to the Catholic Church. Afterwards, the competing interests of landlords, politicians and their clientele undermined the execution of the project to the point of blocking it entirely.

In order to understand the sources of the rejection and failure of this policy we will examine firstly the evolution of Nairobi which was built upon racist criteria and became a city dominated by social segregation. Nairobi has over three and a half million inhabitants[1], of which roughly seventy-five per cent live in five per cent of the total urban area. An analysis of modes of access to land use will permit us to understand the origin and the evolution of the conflict instigated by the implementation of *Mathare 4A Slum Upgrading Project*. Finally, we will explore how public and private sectors contributed to the creation of a public problem. The quasi-failure of this project appears thus as the result of the role of public powers that, in contemporary Kenya, do not elaborate policies to the benefit of poor citizens, but rather manage an elitist public agenda based on a system of political and administrative favouritism. Appropriation of land parcels, speculation and selective policies would constitute the structural axis of a logic of self-interest that has guided Kenyan public actions since independence.

1. Modes of Access to Urban Lands

In 1899 the English constructed a railway transport station (on the site of Enkare, Nairobi) that eventually came to fill the role of a town. Like other capital cities founded for and by the Whites, Nairobi was the administrative centre, seat of power and place of domicile for a settler colony. Promoted to the rank of East African Township in 1903, Nairobi acquired city status in 1950. Colonial urban policies were based on racial segregation; according to this logic, Nairobi was divided into three residential areas. The north and west (Westlands) were assigned to White settlement. The south, a part of the east and the commercial centre

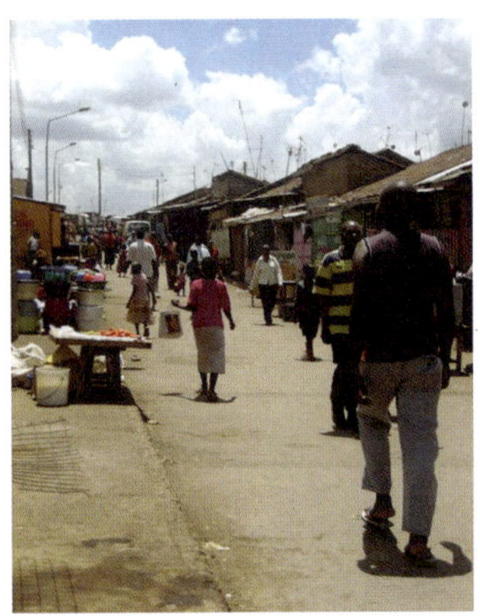

Main road in Mathare A4

---

1   In 2001 Nairobi had 2,143,254 inhabitants. Source: Republic of Kenya, 2001: *The 1999 Population and Housing Census. Counting our People for Development,* Kenya

were assigned to Indians and Pakistanis. African workers possessing a special pass, the *Kipande,* resided in the east (Eastlands) in dormitories and small houses known as Low-Cost Municipal Housing. Rural migrants and Africans expelled from other areas of Nairobi settled in Eastlands. These immigrants or displaced persons, workers or squatters surviving from earnings made on legal or illegal activities, settled in what were called Native Locations and founded slums where they did not have access to land ownership. Thus, towards 1919, Africans (especially the Kikuyu) from the rural areas or who were expelled from other neighbourhoods came to live illegally[2] on lands that today correspond to the large Mathare Valley slum.

From Racial to Social Segregation

In the 1920s, the colonial government began to construct neighbourhoods and bedroom communities for employees. The Site and Services Schemes and Low-Cost Municipal Housing appeared at this time. In these programmes, developed in Eastlands, the government would prepare and build on lots, of which it would retain ownership and the units were rented to individual tenants. It was as such a Site and Services Schemes that Pumwani became the first official African neighbourhood. Low-Cost Municipal Housing projects have given rise to Majenga, Kaloleni, Shauri Moyo, etc.

Eastlands therefore recalls the history of urban settlement marked noticeably by racial segregation and the beginning of the construction of an urban identity. This fundamentally African urban space witnessed two types of mobilisation: that of poor citizens in search of land, housing and employment, and that of public institutions that would plan projects often subcontracted to other non-governmental organisations. After independence (1963), the urban policies initiated by President Kenyatta led to a reconfiguration of the city: Africans were henceforth free to move and the *Kipande* ceased to exist. The passage from racial to social segregation[3] took shape following the departure of the Europeans when the new Kenyan elites moved into the northwest of Nairobi, the middle class into the southwest, while the poor continued to crowd into the Eastlands slums.

Public Action and the Enriching of Developers

This urban redevelopment occurred in a 'natural' way through the political and economic power structure and influences of both sides. A new class of land speculators, supported by the state, played a determining role in this process of restructuring urban areas, where public action was envisaged according to the logic of financial accumulation based on land appropriation. As it stands, in post-independence Kenya, Africans have the right to acquire land. The Registered Land Act of 1987 made the notion of property titles official, replacing Land Certificates which did not guarantee ownership of the property to the landholders.[4] In Nairobi, the prerogatives of the City Council[5] are defined by the *Local Government Act Cap. 265 of the Laws of Kenya,* enacted in 1977, which authorised them to plan the construction of housing, to divide parcels and to expropriate land if necessary for urban development. As during the colonial era, the City Council is authorised to demolish buildings and illegal dwellings as well as evict their inhabitants.

The first housing policies were elaborated in Nairobi following a report[6] undertaken by the United Nations in which the creation of semi-public agencies were envisaged, such as the National Housing Corporation (NHC) which replaced the Colonial Central Housing Board; the Housing, Finance Company of Kenya (HFCK) and the National Cooperative Housing Union (NACHU). Thus, the City Council abandoned the colonial programmes of Low-Cost Municipal Housing and reinforced the Site and Services Schemes in which it remained the land owner, leasing or selling parcels. In these programmes, the administration partially finances the construction of infrastructures, the finishing work on installations falling to the beneficiaries who, depending on the case, should pay a monthly rent to the City Council or the interest fee on the mortgage.

These new Site and Services Schemes were intended for the poorest neighbourhoods, including those in Eastlands. However, some of the housing constructed through these programmes was not occupied by their designated recipients who, instead, found themselves unable to cover the costs of self-construction and/or to afford the fees. In these informal and often illegal neighbourhoods, where a majority of residents had neither employment nor stable revenues, low-cost housing construction policy was doomed to fail. The developers did not anticipate the financial difficulties of the beneficiaries, many of whom had to return to the slums. Politicians, officers of the municipality or ministry concerned by the programmes along with their supporters, expected the departure or even expulsion of the bidders in order to take possession of the housing units. The transfer of a unit that was first assigned to the poorest city dwellers and then into the hands of other people with regular earnings or political support, contributed to the structuring of urban space in accordance with a logic of social class division as well as to the creation of a small middle class. Familial or associative networks, along with favouritism and political patronage, have played a determining role in this process of consolidation of social and residential segregation.

This type of diversion of public projects has established the basis of a 'new urban order' including housing policies as well. Thus, in the 1980s, sixty per cent of the housing inscribed within the

2   David Etherton 1971, *Mathare Valley. A Case Study of Uncontrolled Settlement in Nairobi,* Nairobi

3   Deyssi Rodriguez-Torres 1995, *Nairobi: le bidonville face à la ville,* Cahiers du Cide, Brussels, p. 24

4   Simeon Hongo Ominde 1984, *Population and Development in Kenya,* Nairobi

5   Government of Kenya, *Sessional Paper No. 5 of 1966/67 on Housing Policy for Kenya,* Nairobi

6   Lawrence Bloomberg, Charles Abrams 1964, *United Nations Mission to Kenya on Housing: Prepared for the Government of Kenya,* New York

programmes in Nairobi was diverted and only twenty per cent was occupied by their designated recipients.[7] Patronage and organised networks, diversion of projects and corruption became established modes of political and economic survival for numerous decision-makers and other municipal officers. Most of the projects conceived by the City Council in the 1970s and 1980s in Eastlands have become large public housing blocks whose profits go to the officers who signed the contracts, their close connections and to political clientele. The Site and Service Schemes intended for the poor have been failures that have revealed the inability of public authorities to establish and execute public agendas. The situation has not changed with time: in the 1990s, the Tenant Purchase Scheme, financed by the government and financial backers, reproduced the same political insider trading.

2. Privatisation of Land and Private Sector Transfer of Urban Development Policy

Since the end of the 1980s, the City Council has found itself blocked, on one hand, by constraints imposed by structural adjustment programmes which, incidentally, have amplified land speculation and aggravated the divide between rich and poor, and, on the other hand, through a lack of political will, corruption and illegal privatisation of land. At the same time, state land that was often built on by squatters or individuals, poor areas and slums have continued to expand. Politicians and members of government use Temporary Occupation Licences to allocate housing and state land to individuals. "Public land has been allocated by Officers and other personalities who have no legal authority to allocate it. Thus, there are situations where land has been allocated by Chiefs, District Officers, District Commissioners, Provincial Commissioners and even Members of Parliament. With the entry of these Officers in the public land allocation process, impunity is thus complicating the problem even further […]."[8]

The granting of Temporary Occupation Licences provides financial incentives to citizens who become "structure owners"; they do not pay rent for the land because the allocation is the result of an agreement made with a politician within the framework of patron-client relations. These structure owners, active in poor neighbourhoods, build shacks where each room houses an entire family. They fix the rents they collect by persuasive or violent measures and lead the life of slum landlords. Adapted to rental speculation, protected by politics, they are known as "structure owners without property title to the land". This system of state land allocation has become polished with time and will allow an economic profit to be earned while helping politicians and functionaries ensure the loyalty of proprietors who, in turn, offer them allegiance and votes during elections. Temporary land attribution therefore contributes to extending a system of political patronage, and Nairobi thus becomes a city where land use varies according to political interests.[9] Currently, there are three types of properties in Nairobi: private property in the strict sense of the term; housing built on public lands; and public lands occupied by squatters or renters who give their rent to a structure owner. Public action is thus not based on the principles of a social state, rather on the elite interests of politicians. This explains why, during the 1990s, sixty per cent of public land had already been privatised with the City Council controlling only five per cent of urban land.

Within this context, the government, under popular pressure, is looking for ways to resolve the problem of squatters, renters and the homeless, whose growth in numbers parallels urban growth. To realise urban projects, the government has often solicited the aid of lenders and the private sector, all while delegating infrastructure projects to the private sector, non-governmental organisations and the churches. In fact, the churches have a long tradition of involvement in urban social projects and are perceived as reputable guarantors by lenders because funds are not diverted. The Church, which possesses a social base founded on ties created through its education, health and other programmes in sectors where the state does not penetrate, would have the capacity to attract funds from international aid organisations and fill the void left by the state.

Politics Delegates its Projects: The Realisation of *Mathare 4A Slum Upgrading Project*

It is within this historical and political context that the public sector delegates social policies. With *Mathare 4A Slum Upgrading Project,* the Catholic Church would replace the state at Mathare A4, a village constructed by squatters (in the 1940s) on state land in Mathare Valley, a slum sheltering more than 500,000 residents.

At Mathare 4A, as in Mathare Valley, there has never been any investment by public authorities. Here, families of five and more reside in one-room huts (fifty square feet) with no separate cooking area or sanitary facilities. Only two sanitary blocks exist in the slum for the entire population. There is no potable drinking water; baths, laundry and dishes are done with the same water bought by residents in plastic litre jugs. The shacks and alleys have no public lighting. The streets, like the floors of the shacks, are dirt. The municipality does not collect garbage; garbage containers are nonexistent and household waste, dirty water and domestic garbage are thrown into the street. According to a study done by the GITEC (1995), serving as a basis for the realisation of *Mathare 4A Slum Upgrading Project,* in the beginning of the 1990s Mathare 4A had 21,600 residents lodged in roughly 8,000 structures. The average monthly salary by

7   Gervase Chris Macoloo 2000, The State and Low-income Urban Housing Production and Consumption in Kenya, in: Robert A. Obudho, Jackton B. Ojwang (eds), *Issues in Resource Management and Development in Kenya,* Nairobi, p. 247–257, Paul M. Syagga 2000, Trends in Urban Housing Strategy for Kenya into the Next Century, in: Robert A. Obudho, Jackton B. Ojwang (eds), *Issues in Resource Management and Development in Kenya,* Nairobi, p. 258–270

8   Republic of Kenya 2004, *Report of the Commission of Inquiry into the Illegal/Irregular Allocation of Public Land,* Nairobi, p. 14

9   Isaac Karanja Mwangi 2002, Challenges for Urban Land-use Planning and managing Development in the City of Nairobi and Bordering Urban Areas, in: Washington H. A. Olima, Volker Kreibich (eds), *Urban Land Management in Africa,* Spring Research Series 40, Dortmund, p. 198–211

household was about 3,370 Ksh.[10] More than seventy per cent of the shacks belonged to landlords who did not live in the slum. Ten per cent of the residents were structure owners and ninety per cent were renters, each household paying a monthly rent of between 100 and 300 Ksh.

The St Benedictine Church, located in the slum, is well established here having constructed a church (eighty per cent of the residents are self-declared, practising Catholics), organised social projects such as the school, the day-care, a health-care centre, sport activities for adolescents, reintegration programmes for street children, and proposed training programmes (in computer science, office management, and social work) or scholarships for indigent young people, etc. This church was run by Father Klaus Braunreute (Father Klaus) who, involved in the social projects and familiar with the poverty of slum residents, identifies the uncertainty of the housing situation as their main problem. Through the Church, he proposed to develop a programme intended to provide slum residents with both houses and public services. In 1989 Father Klaus began discussions with the Archdiocese of Nairobi, municipal engineers, legal representatives, the German Embassy and Zacharia Maina, the Circumscription / Regional Deputy. Mr Maina, supporter of KANU,[11] gave support to the project and the structure owners, both those residing and not residing at Mathare 4A.

In 1990, as the political campaign for the first multi-party general elections of December 1992 got underway, the project became a reality. While the Church sought financing for the programme, the candidates for the post of Regional Deputy made efforts to defend residents, prevent evictions and protect structure owners. Although these candidates were Kikuyu, they promised to support all the residents of Mathare A4 of which half were Luos. The new Deputy, M. Muraya, would participate during discussions by positioning himself on the side of the residents.

The Church obtained financing from the German government which, through the *Kreditanstalt für Wiederaufbau* (KfW), accorded funds estimated at 610 million Ksh.[12] The Kenyan government authorised the execution of the project on state land and the creation of a joint venture between the Kenyan and German governments, which entrusted the funds, execution and management of the project to the Archdiocese of Nairobi, which in turn named Father Klaus as manager of Amani Housing Trust, the agency created to execute the project.

The *Mathare A4 Slum Upgrading Project* was put on the agenda in 1992 and the tenants and structure or land owners were informed of the programme. They were notified and invited to designate their spokesperson against the Amani Housing Trust and also against the Catholic Church, both of which represented the Kenyan government, the KfW and the Archdiocese of Nairobi at Mathare 4A. The programme, which was to start in 1993 and be completed by 2001, had three goals. Firstly, the construction of 8,000 one-room houses, with residents retaining their status as tenants with rents, by house, fixed in a range of 350 to 450 Ksh. Secondly, the land and structure owners would be expropriated and indemnified, retaining no claim to property rights. Thirdly, Amani Housing Trust would construct public services (sidewalks, gutters, roads, toilets, wash houses, etc.). The project was begun in 1993, when Amani Housing Trust, with Father Klaus as programme director, installed their offices at Mathare 4A. To begin construction, it was necessary to demolish existing huts; however, residents and owners often resisted such demolitions. To deal with this situation, the company sent in police and gangs of young people recruited on site: the police gave orders and chased the residents away while the gangs destroyed whatever they found in their paths and drove out those who refused to leave.

Civil Dissent

Dissent appeared at the very beginning of the project. While structure owners rejected the project because it had deprived them of their means of subsistence, tenants denounced police violence and the attribution of new houses to people who did not reside in the slum. Most forcefully, the dissenters supported the right to maintain the status quo: the rights of proprietors to collect rents and the rights of tenants to live under a roof – even while paying rent. Proclaiming their rights, structure owners and tenants drew closer and their demands became political. They were joined by successive deputies at Mathare A4 who, no longer able to allocate land in the slum to build their clientele base, increased their backing of the proprietors who wanted to retain their huts.

The first phase of the programme (which was supposed to last until 1997) unfolded in the midst of such altercations, which were mostly peaceful and confined to the area of the slum. The Church had initiated the reimbursement of former owners, presented construction plans to tenants and begun to demolish and build. When the first houses were allocated, the tenants were supposed to pay the rent, 420 Ksh per house, to Church revenue collectors. This is when dissent intensified with inhabitants denouncing the quality of the housing and refusing to pay rent.

1994–1997

Opposition to the project became a gathering point for everyone with interests in Mathare A4. Structure owners, both residents and non-residents of the slum – the rich in this case – expressed their disapproval because they did not have access to the programme's houses. They had been expropriated and had received reimbursements, but demanded the augmentation of

---

10 100 Ksh = 1 Euro or $1.31
11 Kenya African National Union (KANU), main political party
    in power until December 2002
12 *The Standard,* 21 February 1994

compensation and access to the new houses. In reality, the common theme of opposition from the structure owners was that *Mathare 4A Slum Upgrading Project* had destroyed their livelihoods: shack rentals.

The tenants – the poor – refused the one-room houses that offered virtually nothing different from their former dwellings because it meant they still would have had to crowd into a single, dirt-floored room. They complained about rents which rose to 800 Ksh per house, double what they had paid previously. Since the tenants knew that houses were in the process of being expropriated, those who still lived in the old housing no longer paid rent to the structure owners. The latter, who were the big losers in the project, initiated the protests. Once they clarified their goal – to be allocated land through purchase or through governmental concession – tenants joined the action. Structure owners, with the support of the deputy and the Area Councillors, became spokespeople for the dissenters. Thus a triad of owners, tenants and politicians was created that undertook legal action demanding the allocation of land parcels and funding to inhabitants and proprietors. Rents to structure owners or to the Church ceased to be paid. The boycott of the project had begun.

The committee representing the dissenters requested the Archdiocese to accord it the parcels of land, and funds to renovate dwellings itself, but the Church rejected the petitions and dialogue broke down. In 1995, the committee lodged a suit against the Archdiocese before the Makadara Court; it demanded the return of structures and programme funds to residents, and offered to the government to buy the land, which the committee intended to pay with the money that people had collected in a special fund. According to their proposal, along with funds given by the German government, the neighbours would pay for the land and redevelop the slum in light of their own needs. After six months of debate, the court denied the committee's petition, con-

firming the Archdiocese in its role as programme manager.

The decision of the Makadara Court spurred on dissent. A new appeal, exhorting all the neighbours to unite against the project, would prove to be extremely efficient. It was no longer a matter of defending the interests of the Luos (the majority of tenants) or the Kikuyus (the majority of the structure owners), but of everyone together.

The resistance movement begun by ruined small proprietors transformed into a conflict following the adhesion of an interethnic majority of residents and local personalities. The resistance united around a new strategy: onsite attacks on the Amani Housing Trust and its director. Organised in each neighbourhood and involving owners, tenants, women's associations, sects, the unemployed, street children, etc., new demonstrations began. This new phase of the protest did not ameliorate the crisis. Faced with the passivity of the public sector, which took no action, the Church sought a solution. In 1996, with the endorsement of the Kenyan government, the Archdiocese created a study group that would examine the protesters' petitions. However, at that moment, the citizens learned that the government had awarded land at Mathare 4A to the Catholic Church in trust for ninety-nine years. The study group's conclusions were negatively impacted. From then on, all one spoke about at Mathare 4A was "the appropriation of land by the Church".

1997–1999

With this allocation of land, the project became bogged down and what would have become an open conflict between local social groups (the rich against the poor) transformed itself into a force of unification among inhabitants. The protesters called for a boycott of the programme, accusing the government of treason and demanding the departure of the Church and its employees from the slum. The contents of the demands evolved, eventually no longer concerning the size of the houses or the rents demanded. The slogan was to demand that the land parcels be restored to the residents of Mathare 4A, to Kenyans. The tone of the discourse was nationalistic; the government, the Church and Father Klaus became the targets for denunciation. The leaders accused the Church of having changed its Christian, moral and ethical principles by doing business deals with the state against the people, and they reiterated that the role of the Church is to defend its children, not to rob them of their possessions. Father Klaus, together with the project staff, became Public Enemy Number One.

In the meantime and even though slowed, work on the project continued and new houses were assigned; collectors demanded rent and tenants still refused to pay. To correct this, managers did not hesitate to use force; for example, evicting the residents

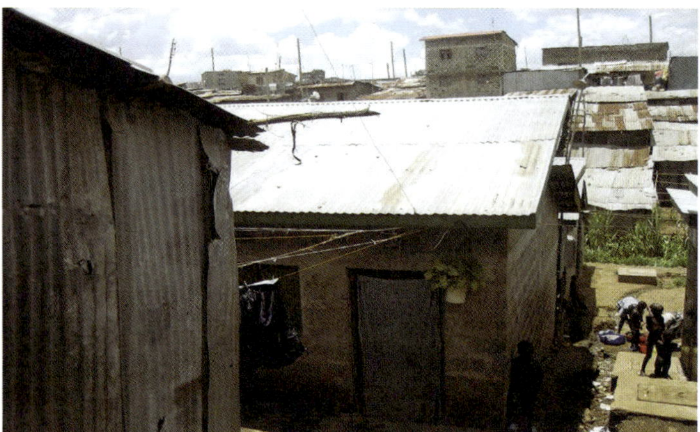

Paths through houses of the upgrading-programme in Mathare A4

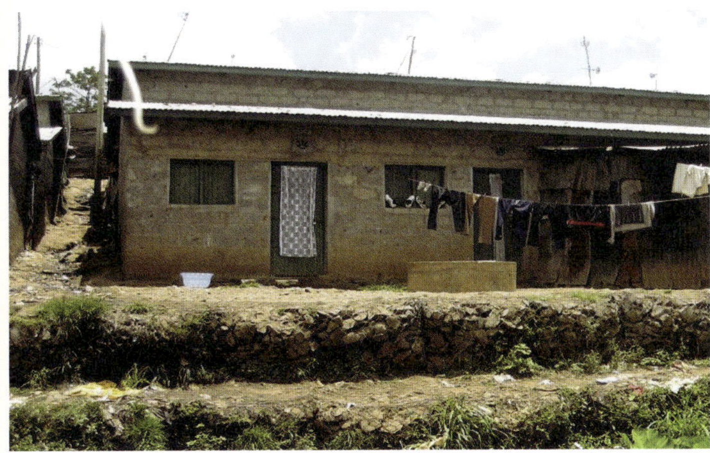

One of the last houses built within the scope of the programme

and demolishing the houses with the help of bats, clubs and bulldozers.

The crisis grew and violent clashes erupted in the slum in November 1998, requiring police deployment and resulting in many being injured. In December of that year, a brigade of some fifty men, mobilised by Amani Housing Trust, headed for Mathare 4A. Wielding bats and clubs, the police and young thugs hired for the occasion evicted the inhabitants, throwing their belongings outside and demolishing more than forty shacks. The first objective of *Mathare 4A Slum Upgrading Project* – to procure housing for all the inhabitants of the slum – was thus totally distorted.

In January of 1999, Amani Housing Trust had already spent some 122 million Ksh. The demolitions allowed the work to continue, but amplified opposition as well as complaints[13] against violence and the misallocation of houses.

1999–2001

After assisting on the sidelines during almost six years of conflict, the public authorities finally decided to intervene in January 1999. They ordered the temporary suspension of the project and created a task force that would identify the problems encountered during the conception of the programme. This group concluded that, with time, the protesters' demands had not changed; they continued to demand ownership of the land and to criticise the quality of the new construction: for them, the project came down to replacing a one-room shack with a one-room house whose rent would cost more than 420 Ksh.

In the course of discussions, new estimates for the work-in-progress were presented by the Archdiocese of Nairobi. In the beginning of the 1990s, ninety-two per cent of Mathare 4A residents were tenants who paid rents to structure owners who had been reimbursed by the Church. Incidentally, even if the law

does not require that reparations be made for illegal usufruct, it does not prevent the awarding of compensation. The Church thus awarded compensation in amounts ranging from 5,000 to 550,000 Ksh. In 1999, the project had paid out more than thirty million Ksh in indemnities for more than 5,000 houses, and 3.7 million Ksh had also been reserved to reimburse 745 shack owners.

The task force discussions came to a close in February 1999 and its decisions were communicated: Amani Housing Trust would restart its work, the lands and houses would no longer be sold due to the poverty of the inhabitants, and it would be impossible to convert the project into a Tenant Purchase Scheme. The rents were fixed according to economic indices, etc. The result of negotiations would thus be marked by renewed dissent in which other actors in the associative and religious community joined. The programme boycott would be followed by civil disobedience. With varying degrees of violence, opposition to the programme and demonstrations continued throughout 1999 and 2000. In late 2000, the protests took another turn when confrontations between neighbours and police resulted in two dead and numerous injured.

3. The Construction of a Public Problem

Opposition to the project changed form, taking on a much more political character and motivating other citizens and some pressure groups to join (for example, the Kenya Human Rights Commission Kituo Cha Sheria) and invest themselves in the defence of Mathare 4A residents. Starting in 1999, these organisations tried to restore a dialogue between the parties in conflict, intervened to ensure indemnification of owners, and offered legal assistance to people appearing in court or sent to prison, and tenants who demanded access to land ownership. The local churches accompanied people during demonstrations, counselled them on negotiation strategies, and gathered money to help pay the costs of lawyers and fees when they were arrested.

The implementation of this policy created a non-violent community movement. The inhabitants of other marginal sectors, notified of the danger they faced of having their living quarters taken over by the private sector, prepared for the defence of their homes. Slum residents monitored the project's evolution very closely, confirming that they lived under the same conditions as their neighbours in Mathare 4A and were likewise in danger of losing their shacks and the lands they occupied. The residents thus decided to join together and found new associations whose goal was to protect against this type of project. For example, at Mathare 4B, the neighbourhood abutting Mathare 4A, where the Church had planned to execute a similar project, residents founded a cooperative in 1995 that they fund today with their

13 "In the matter of the […] Civil case N°488 of 1988, the plaintiffs were a group of over 1,000 residents living in Mathare 4A […]. When residents began objecting the corruption that had infected the project and the displacement of many valid residents, the implementing agency hired by the Church started to systematically and forcibly demolish dissenting residents' structures […] Violent confrontations become the order of the day and the situation culminated in several weeks of bloody violence when the Archdiocese refused to cease using intimidation, force and violence in order to collect rents and taking over existing structures of people opposed to the project […] The court dismissed the application holding that because the plaintiffs were 'squatters' who did not have title deeds they could make no legal or equitable claim for the land […]", Christine Bodewes, Ndaisi Kwinga 2003, The Kenyan Perspective on Housing Rights, in: Scott Leckie (ed.), *National Perspectives on Housing Rights,* The Hague, p. 221–240, here p. 237

meagre savings. Its objective is to show that they have a formal organisation through which they intend to negotiate the purchase of land still in state ownership with the public authorities. In Mathare B, the project never saw the light of day. Organisations similar to the one at Mathare 4B were created in other slums like Gitari Marigu, Huruma Estate, Korogocho and Mukuru.

The impact of *Mathare 4A Slum Upgrading Project* can thus be gleaned from studying the entire development of the programme and from the crisis provoked by the decisions of the task force where, instead of leading to the realisation of public policy, it actually generated a public problem. For the administrators, the quasi-failure of the project led to civil and criminal unrest that necessitated the use of force. For tenants and structure owners, it was not only a matter of lost revenues and living areas, but also the loss of control over what happened in their living areas. For tenants, the problem was also financial; they lived below the poverty line in a country where fifty-eight per cent of the population survives on less than a dollar a day.[14] Thus, the crisis at Mathare 4A was not provoked uniquely by the effects of the *Mathare 4A Slum Upgrading Project,* but rather this project helped to reveal structural problems the residents had been experiencing. The crisis demonstrated also that the effects of the project did not correspond to those expected. The event therefore became the manifestation of endemic problems that fed a sentiment of exclusion[15], producing unintended results that triggered the creation of a public problem. The attribution of land to the Church revealed a problem to which the public authorities were knowingly blind. To acknowledge the problem and resolve it would require the public authorities to establish a programme of distribution-legalisation of urban lands occupied by poor social sectors. At present, the political establishment is not ready to initiate this kind of reform because, at Mathare 4A, as in Kenya at large, land is a valuable pillar of a system of favouritism and a source of enrichment for the few.

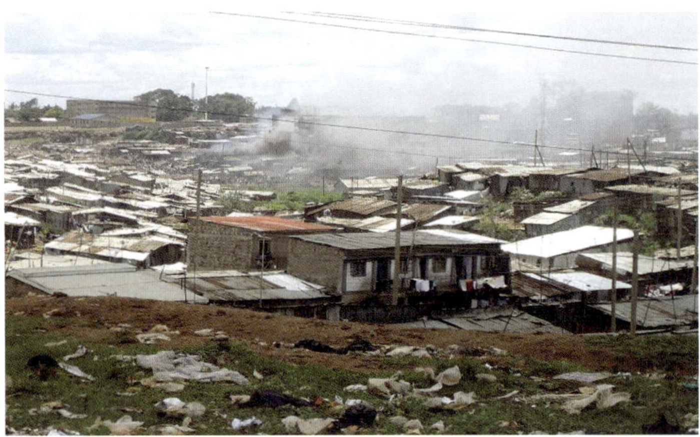

View over Mathare A4

Conclusion

Public policy in Nairobi favours the enrichment of politicians and the maintenance of a network of political clientele. Accusations of corruption, so frequent on the local political scene, are concerned in particular with access to land. It is thus quite logical that the Mathare 4A project would head toward failure, that its objectives would be diverted, and that it would end in paralysis.

In the evolution of public action, the private sector prevails over the public. This is confirmed when one sees that neither the City Council nor the organisations charged with urban development have any active role in construction, thus leaving the path open to new joint ventures managed by the private sector. This shows that public authorities do not manage urban governance, illustrates the lack of political will power to develop housing policies that would benefit poor inhabitants and, finally, proves that public agendas are not based on investments but rather on elitist interests.

Concerning the protest movement against *Mathare 4A Slum Upgrading Project,* it did not succeed in either eliciting the political establishment or in constituting a political force. It resulted in an action that tended to guarantee the economic and political survival of a select number of residents and politicians. These subjects vigorously maintain their authority over public lands in order to barter land parcels and temporary leases against votes and individual profit.

Within this framework, land symbolises the war booty that politicians need for elections. This in turn generates a permanent struggle for the occupation of the land, resulting in squatters, tenants and common folk opposing land and structure owners who collect rents and are politically linked. Thus, specifically in Nairobi, a social class of real estate speculators establishes itself by developing the area with the function of rent and state support. Since the state and appropriation are ways to use land to enrich oneself, 'order' exists behind the apparent 'disorder': chasing away or displacing poor slum dwellers functions as a means of accumulation for politicians and the upper class that live, in fact, from land rent.

Finally, *Mathare 4A Slum Upgrading Project* could not be called a public policy that sought compromise between differing interests; neither mediation nor negotiation took place between the parties. This public policy is more of a regulatory scheme on the social level and corresponds to an elitist model[16] whose objective was none other than conserving the status quo.

Translation from French by Lucy R. McNair

14 PNUD 2007, *Human Development Index 2007–2008,* New York

15 Deborah A. Stone 1989, Causal Stories and the Formation of Policy Agendas, *Political Science Quarterly* 104/2: 281–300

16 Nicholas Henry 2004, *Public Administration and Public Affairs,* New Delhi

Nairobi Matatu[1]
as Social-Cultural Matrix

MBUGUA WA MUNGAI

Introduction:
Field Notes of a *Matatu* Researcher

Bena lives in Kahawa Wendani, a low-income residential estate 15 kilometres from Nairobi facing a military garrison, which in turn neighbours a university, Kenyatta – popularly known as KU, which is where most of his clients come from. Bena – the name is a stylisation of Bernard – works as a conductor on a *matatu,* and I met him during one of my fieldwork excursions on Nairobi roads. He is in his late twenties and has been working on this particular *matatu,* named Akademiks, for two years, and on Route 45 (Nairobi-KU) for seven. His is one of the hundreds of thousands of vans and minibuses that sometimes literally 'fly' on and off Kenyan roads on account of their great speeds. By the end of the day, his employer expects the *matatu* to have made a minimum of ten trips from Nairobi's city centre to the university, but then this is not always the case given the vagaries of Nairobi roads – prone to accidents both minor and major, extremely nerve-wracking traffic jams (especially when roads are cordoned off to allow the president unhindered passage to some destination or other, or when it suddenly rains), police crackdowns on 'un-roadworthy' vehicles (only passenger service vehicles inevitably bear the brunt of such efforts) occasioning a strike by *matatu* workers claiming "police harassment" and sometimes there might be violent confrontation between these *matatu* men and the various route-control criminal gangs and other cartels that seek to control the passenger transport business in the city, its suburbs and even some parts of

rural Kenya. For seven years Bena has taken this erratic character of his work space – the road – in his stride and he still goes about his business with great charm and cheer. On this particular day he is rather stylishly dressed in an Enyce Shirt, blue Levi's jeans and expensive Timberland boots. I notice that Bena is popular with his female passengers, mainly young students from the university. Noticing my bemusement, he cockily lifts his right eyebrow and in Kiswahili states matter-of-factly: *"Matunda ya maisha!"* ("picking life's ripe fruits!"). His *matatu* is by now full, and the driver is impatiently revving eager to zoom off as Bena bids me a hasty goodbye with the promise of catching up later. I next saw him two years later in the city centre and he had since graduated from being a *matatu* conductor to working on a *Citi Hoppa*[2] bus operating on Route 125 to Rongai. He was clad in a maroon uniform, having shed his former *'shine'*[3] to comply fully with the requirements of the *'Michuki* Rules'[4]. Bena had come far indeed.

Driving, or being driven, on Nairobi roads presents one with endless opportunities to scrutinise and contemplate road interactions between motorists. These are perhaps the most interesting and anxiety-inducing relations because they involve *matatu* – public transport vehicles that are the hub of passenger transport in Kenya even though, ironically, they are privately owned.[5] These vehicles are assigned specific route numbers by the city Transport Licensing Board but it is common to find a vehicle pirating on undesignated routes. However, flouting the law in such blatant terms is quite risky for *matatu* crews as this becomes a 'justifiable' basis for police officers to demand bribes from them. Also, illegal route-control gangs such as *Mungiki, Taliban* and *Kamjesh* who usually impose a 'protection fee' for vehicles licensed to operate on specific routes usually take this as a turf infringement and it can lead to either violent repulsion of offending *matatu* crews or they could be asked to pay a hefty one-off fee. What this shows is that there is considerable tension amongst players in the informal *matatu* sector that necessitates an analysis of *matatu* work beyond economic terms. Proceeding from the above assertion, it might be said that interactions on Kenyan roads, as in other parts of the world[6], operate according to patterns of logic that might not be immediately evident but which might become clearer upon closer scrutiny of motorists' mannerisms. Road behaviour tells us as much about economic relations as it does about social and political aspects of life, not just in Nairobi but also in Kenya. For instance, the fact some people drive short distances to work while others have to catch a *matatu* to get there is not simply a question of class but

---

1   *Matatu* are privately owned vans and minibuses that carry between fourteen and twenty-five fare-paying passengers depending on the licensed carrying capacity. *Matatu* is a plural non-count noun meaning three and is derived from the Gikuyu phrase *"mang'otore matatū"* (thirty cents) which was the fare from Nairobi to outlying areas when the earliest forms of pirate taxis are reckoned to have begun operating in 1953. (Gibson Aduwo 1990, *The role, efficiency and quality of service of the Matatu mode of public transport in Nairobi: A geographical analysis,* unpublished M.A. Thesis, Nairobi).

2   The name of one of the bus companies that sprung up in the void created by the collapse of Kenya Bus Service

3   This word has the same meaning as 'gear', meaning fashionable wear. The terms are in *Sheng,* a predominantly urban sociolect that works mainly by affixing elements from other languages to Kiswahili word stems. Among other processes it also involves the appropriation of whole words, invention of

new ones, metathesis, and giving new meanings to old words (for a full discussion see among others Peter Githinji 2008, Sexism and (Mis)Representation of Women in Sheng, *Journal of African Cultural Studies* 20/1 (June): 15–32, Peter Githinji 2006, Bazes and their Shibboleths: Lexical Variation and Sheng Speakers' Identity in Nairobi, *Nordic Journal of African Studies* 15/4: 443–476, Nathan Oyori Ogechi 2007, Building Bridges through Trichotomous Youth Identities in Kenya: Evidence from Code-choice, in: Kimani Njogu (ed.), *Cultural Production and Social Change in Kenya: Building Bridges,* Nairobi, p.129–150, Chega Githiora 2002, Sheng: Peer Language, Swahili dialect or Emerging Creole?, *Journal of African Culture Studies* 15/3: 159–181, David Samper 2002, *Talking Sheng: The Role of a Hybrid Language in the Construction of Identity and Youth Culture in Nairobi, Kenya,* unpublished Ph.D. dissertation, University of Pennsylvania). *Sheng* is arguably the vernacular of *matatu* workers especially in Nairobi.

also one of choice. Some people opt to leave their vehicles at home and ride a *matatu* to Nairobi not just because it is economical to do so but also because they prefer to have someone else – the *matatu* driver – battling it out with other drivers for control and domination of road space. This 'battle' is, in itself, a way of being in the city that has critical implications upon individuals' survival in Nairobi. As Bena's case demonstrates, *matatu* might enable us to think about not just crews who work on these vehicles but also about mobility – physical and social – and Nairobi urban life. The opening anecdote illustrates important connections between *matatu* life and gender and class but it also makes evident some important aspects of the nature of urban culture and modern life in Kenya. The young men who work on these vehicles are the thread that holds all these aspects together and, as such, a discussion of *matatu* as a factor of social-economic mobility might begin by paying attention to the gender dynamics of the occupation.

"Men only!": *Matatu* as Gendered Space

One of the most striking characteristics of *matatu* work is the fact that it is a heavily gendered occupation. After the introduction in 2003 of rules aimed at regulating *matatu* work, a number of women ventured into the business but as the rules were increasingly ignored, the number of female workers began dwindling and today only very few may be found.[7] The majority of *matatu* crews are young men in their twenties.[8] Traditionally this type of work is seen as the domain of the 'uneducated' given that a majority of the labour force hold at best a secondary school level of education while a significant majority are primary school drop-outs.[9] It is true that some of these men are rough-cut but this has only served to buttress the perception that their occupation is a domain for 'unpolished' young men. This negativity has made it impossible for women to take up *matatu* work because society expects them to be 'proper' women who are therefore expected to undertake only 'decent' jobs. Of course, the basis of such thinking is to be found in traditional beliefs about women that are commonly found in communities across Kenya. Such communities define(d) women's roles within a dichotomisation that understands men in relation to the space outside the homestead and women as being solely meant to occupy the domestic field. Understood this way, it is apparent that the opposition to female entry into the *matatu* sector has had little to do with doubts about female capability to perform these jobs and more to do with the perception that they are encroaching upon distinctly male space. The disapproval with which society looks upon women who might engage in *matatu* work is part of the moral censure that aims at directing them towards other careers.

However there are differentiations in the roles played by men in the *matatu* sector. The actual owners of these vehicles are generally older men who often have other sources of income, the surplus of which they then invest in *matatu*. To purchase a fourteen-seater Toyota van and pay all the official and unofficial fees (the latter going to route-control cartels) requires approximately 20,000 USD. Even though a bank loan can be obtained for these purposes, it is usually a costly option and most investors thus prefer to use their own savings to finance their initial investment. It is noticeable that younger men are joining the business because they have access to credit lines but this is largely an exception. As a general rule only financially well-heeled men (and some women) have this kind of capital and as a result command a lot of respect. They are usually referred to in Kiswahili as *wazee* (elders) by the younger men whom they employ to run their vehicles. *Matatu* drivers tend to be older (late twenties to forties) while the conductors tend to be in their early to mid-twenties; running to catch up with the vehicle as the driver unexpectedly speeds off, or having to jump on and off it to assist passengers often with their heavy loads, requires agility levels that most of the older men cannot manage. This is one reason, too, why *matatu* owners will generally avoid hiring female workers, who are perceived not to have the requisite physical stamina.

On the whole, the *matatu* man's job might not be attractive but he plays a role that is central enough in Nairobi's economic life for him to command some level of attention. Bena and his colleagues, fully aware of their important role in facilitating mobility for a large section of society, are often quick to take advantage of their placement to cultivate significant social capital. It is for this reason that Bena takes pride in the fact that he has a lot of female admirers, a situation which inevitably leads to all manner of social negotiations. For instance, schoolgirls are an especially prized category of commuters for *matatu* men and they receive favours ranging from free rides – known as *sare* in *Sheng* – to lunches, pocket money and evening outings. Romantic liaisons often crop up around these negotiations and even though it is true the men tend to have the economic upper hand, the girls too are not powerless in the transactions as has been asserted elsewhere.[10] There is an intriguing irony about Kenyans' social attitudes towards *matatu* men; whereas parents will never warn their daughters against riding to school in

4   Known as the '*Michuki* Rules' (Legal Notice No. 164 of October 2003), laid strict rules specify among other requirements that *matatu* men should have work uniform. Vehicles' bodies are to be painted the one colour stated in the log book and they should be fitted with speed governors.

5   Kenya has not had a government-owned public transport system since the early 1990s when the Nyayo Bus Service Corporation collapsed due to mismanagement, see Jennifer Widner 1992, *The Rise of a Party-State in Kenya: From "Harambee" to "Nyayo"*, Berkeley. The Kenya Bus Service Company, which began its Nairobi operations in 1935, faced with stiff competition from *matatu* and citing heavy maintenance costs for its fleet eventually folded in 2006. In either case it is significant that the presence of both bus companies was largely felt only in urban centres. Rural Kenya has always been *matatu* country.

6   See Daniel Miller 2001, *Driven Societies. Car Cultures*, Oxford, Charles Edward Case 1992, Bumper Stickers and Car Signs Ideology and Identity, *Journal of Popular Culture* 26/3: 179–190, Adalberto Aguirre Jr 1990, Social Communication and Self Identification: Participatory Behavior on the Freeway, *Journal of Popular Culture*, 24/2: 91–101.

7   Legal Notice No. 164 was aimed at bringing some sense of order in what was otherwise regarded as the lawless *matatu* sector. Amongst other things, one was required to obtain a certificate of good conduct from the police. What this meant was that potentially anyone with a clean record could be licensed to work on *matatu* and, given the acute unemployment levels in the country, it was natural that women would move to take advantage of this regulation. In time, *matatu* men went back to their old rough ways and the women who had joined this sector gradually left.

8   Meleckidzedeck Khayesi 1999, *Matatu Workers in Nairobi, Thika and Ruiru, Kenya: An Analysis of their Socio-Economic Characteristics, Career Patterns and Conditions of Work*, Nairobi

9   Meleckidzedeck Khayesi 2002, The Struggle for Socio-economic Niche and Control in the *Matatu* Industry in Kenya, *DPMN Bulletin* IX/2 (May): 1–6

10   Fatuma Chege, Zippora Rimbui and Waveney Olembo 1994, *Traveling to and from School in Nairobi: Girls and the Painful 'Matatu' Ride*, Nairobi

matatu, they will be quick to point out the dangers of marrying a *matatu* worker. This largely points to anxieties about class. This will be examined next.

"Stay in your place!": *Matatu* and the Travelling Class

Generally Kenyans have been socialised to think about modernity's finer material goods – nice cars and houses, expensive schools for their children, holidays and hospitals abroad – as the ultimate markers of social success. School is one of the key institutions through which this ideology is inculcated: the acquisition of degrees leads to highly-paying white-collar jobs and hence success. Ben Blasto Obulawayo's song *Someni vijana*, played to Kenyan school children during lessons conducted via radio broadcast, has been instrumental in shaping this kind of thinking. Be that as it may, there is usually undue pressure for individuals to acquire material markers of success and to do so quickly. The car occupies a significant place amongst these objects. Those who ride in *matatu* are perceived to be doing poorly financially while those who drive their own cars are envied their good fortune. However it is not always true that *matatu* passengers are poor people; some leave their vehicles behind for the simple reason that it is pointless to hassle through traffic only to go and park the car for the whole day. By the same token, some who insist on taking their cars to the city daily do so in order to strike the impression of success – they might quite literally own nothing else apart from the vehicle which was bought through a loan. But even then, such impressions are considered to be important because they open doors to other networks – social, economic and sometimes political depending on what type of car is being driven. Young male drivers are particularly keen on using their vehicles as a charm strategy with women. In this sense, car ownership is taken to index class and the possibility for social-economic mobility.

But there is also a twist to the practices of car ownership and mobility in Nairobi. Schooling has enabled women to forge ahead in terms of careers and with these financial fortunes. This has meant that whereas large numbers of boys drop out of school, a significant number of girls go on to complete higher levels of schooling. They land well-paying jobs and acquire some financial muscle, something that inevitably has implications on ideas of gender discussed above as well as on these women's class positioning.[11] Consequently the fact that they now drive around in flashy cars – or even own a car at all, regardless of its state – is one of the conspicuous reminders, especially to men, of how far women have travelled from the traditional gender roles that tied them to the homestead. For those *matatu* men who dropped out of primary school these socially mobile women are a cause for anxiety as they are perceived to represent the material success that the men failed to achieve. This is one of the explanations that might be offered for the hostility – where evinced in verbal or physical aggression – that *matatu* men direct especially at female car owners on Nairobi roads. Inevitably out of this bitterness amongst *matatu* men and their allies in other urban social networks, a discourse arises of perceived marginalisation and persecution. Whether through language or the popular music of Nairobi youth culture there emerges a distinctly class-marked world-view in which the *matatu* man (as a self-perceived victim) is ranged against the rest of society (chiefly police, government, politicians, the elite class and everyone else who can be 'othered'). At this point it becomes necessary to examine *matatu* as a mediation of other city subcultures.

Generation *Malebo*[12]: The Matrix of Contemporary Nairobi Subcultures

Given that *matatu* work is predominated by the youth, the sector is very tightly linked to Nairobi youth culture. This culture is defined by fashion labels, music, a brash attitude towards life and a general loudness that calls attention to these youth. It is not incidental, then, that youth music is loud, a loudness that is demonstrated at two levels. The first relates to the music's literal aspects: popular with young *matatu* passengers it is usually played at very high volume. Even if anyone wanted to ignore *matatu* men and their passengers, the extremely loud sound systems installed in these vehicles are guaranteed to attract attention – but it is risky, too, because the police use this as a basis for either arresting crew members or for negotiating bribes. Regardless of its perils this self-gesturing is considered an attractive option by the youth who consider the rest of society to have deliberately shut their ears to the youth who want to be heard. The second significant level at which this music operates is that of content. Again, it is significant that generally this music tends to be of the 'rebellious' variety, particularly because its beginnings were rooted in American rap and hip hop culture. Reminiscent of the 'moral panic' that was occasioned by the advent of rap in the US, the emergence of Kenyan urban music modelled on American rap has sparked great anxiety amongst members of the conservative mainstream society; epithets such as 'decadent', 'immoral', 'dirty' have been hurled with abandon at this music since the rapper Hardstone, who is credited with pioneering the genre in Kenya in 1998, performed a remix version of Marvin Gaye's 1982 track *Sexual Healing*.

What the birth of rap in its Kenyan iterations did was to offer young people a creative space within which they could be heard. This new possibility has been aided by access to recording

---

11 Bancy Wangui 2008, *Alarm over high Boys' School Dropout in Central, The Standard online edition*. Retrieved on 11 September 2008 from www.standardmedia.co.ke/insidePage. php? [accessed on 11.09.2008]

12 *Malebo* is the Sheng plural word for 'label' and refers to designer names on clothes.

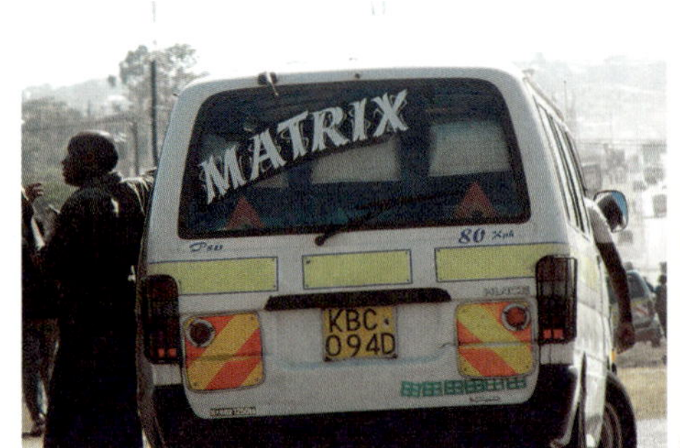

A

technology outside established studios, which are expensive. In this way, youth, who otherwise might not ever have recorded their music, found an infrastructure through which their creativity could flower. *Matatu* have been at the core of this system in a critical way. Some underground Nairobi rappers – they record music in home studios and hawk it on *matatu* and at discotheques – have had stints as *matatu* crew, a fact that places them strategically to understand the everyday realities of urban life, especially in relation to young people. Marginality, a popular theme within the urban youth community, inevitably is a predominant element of urban pop music. *Matatu* might thus be seen as being both a space for inspiring creativity as well as a platform for its dispersal. Much of the underground music distributed through *matatu* networks never gets to be played in the mainstream studios, and this mechanism is an important way through which the youth can circumnavigate around matters of taste censorship by the mainstream culture. Given that thousands of youth ride on *matatu* daily in Nairobi, it might be seen that the messages in this music have wide reception. Other than rap, reggae in its various forms is popular among both *matatu* crews and some passengers.

Even though urban music is heavy with ideas of romance, the theme of revolution is equally dominant. In this regard a correspondence might be seen between the latter point – rebellion against the formal scheme of things – and the dominance of anti-mainstream fashion tastes among the youth who form the bulk of *matatu* clientele at the same time as they constitute a majority of the labour force on these vehicles. Sagging pants, exposed bellies, over-size shirts and unkempt hair are some of the more overt ways through which youth subcultural revolt against taste is expressed. One can then see the tension that such forms of dress might provoke amongst members of the dominant culture who are more comfortable with conservative dress codes – business suits for men and non-revealing (modest) attire for women.

This 'offence' directed against society might also be seen in vehicle decorations done by *matatu* crews – almost always egged on by young passengers and sometimes in order to attract and retain them. Any writings and drawings on *matatu* – which mainstream society considers "graffiti" but which the youth regard as "artistic expression" – are never to be taken for granted. In themselves, whether individual words like 'Matrix' [→ Fig. **A**], phrases clipped from other forms of creative expression (*Can't Touch This* – clipped from rapper MC Hammer's song of the same title – or a bible quotation) or drawings of animals, [→ Fig. **B**] *matatu* decoration is a shorthand by which *matatu* men evoke ideas and practices in politics, religion, culture and current affairs, local and international, even though some of the elements depict near-impossible situations as Obama promoting hip "gear". [→ Fig. **C**]

In conclusion, as the vehicle name *Matrix* cited above suggests, it is necessary to examine the totality of the environment in which *matatu* operate in order to comprehend the contexts of its subculture. At the same time this environment acts as a mould, a constitutive framework that can be considered to shape some of the behaviour of *matatu* crews and their passengers. As might be seen from the illustrations immediately above, *matatu* enable a discourse informed by elements drawn from both local and global sources. How people position themselves to appreciate or participate in representations of such discourse is largely determined by where they are positioned in terms of class and gender. *Matatu* men, realising that some Kenyans do not take them seriously, often resort to mocking reflexive monikers such as *Joker*, [→ Fig. **D**] but only a person who is totally oblivious to the intense struggles that take place around *matatu* mobility would take this aspect of Kenyan life as a joke. After all, dealing the joker card in a game can have disastrous results for an opponent. On the whole, to read *matatu* and the subculture that grows around these vehicles is to begin to unpick some of the threads that help to tell some of the important stories about Kenyan life.

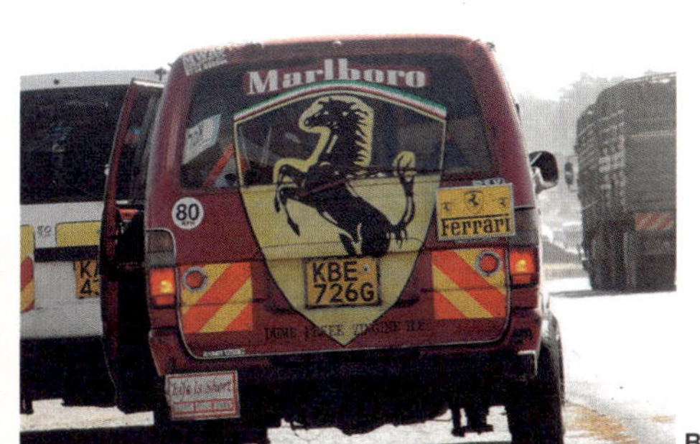

B

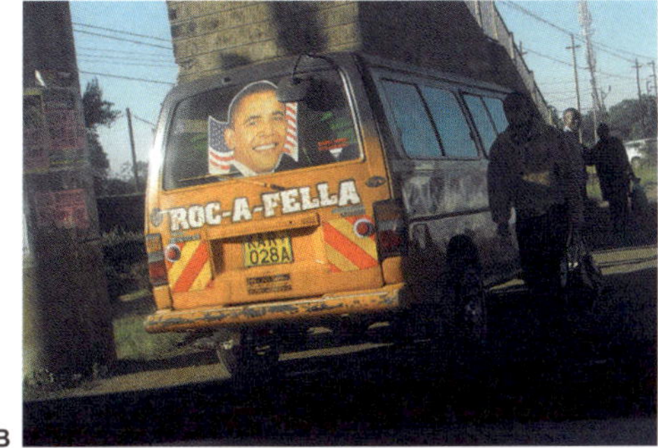

C

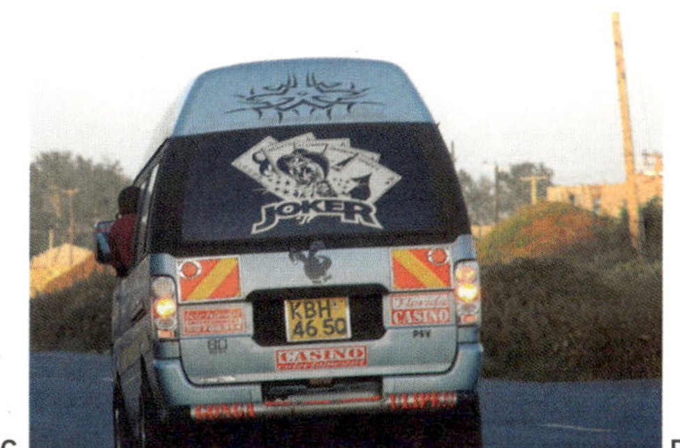

D

Sketches
of Postcolonial
Kenyan Literature
Cultural Anthropology
or Creative Fiction?

TOM ODHIAMBO

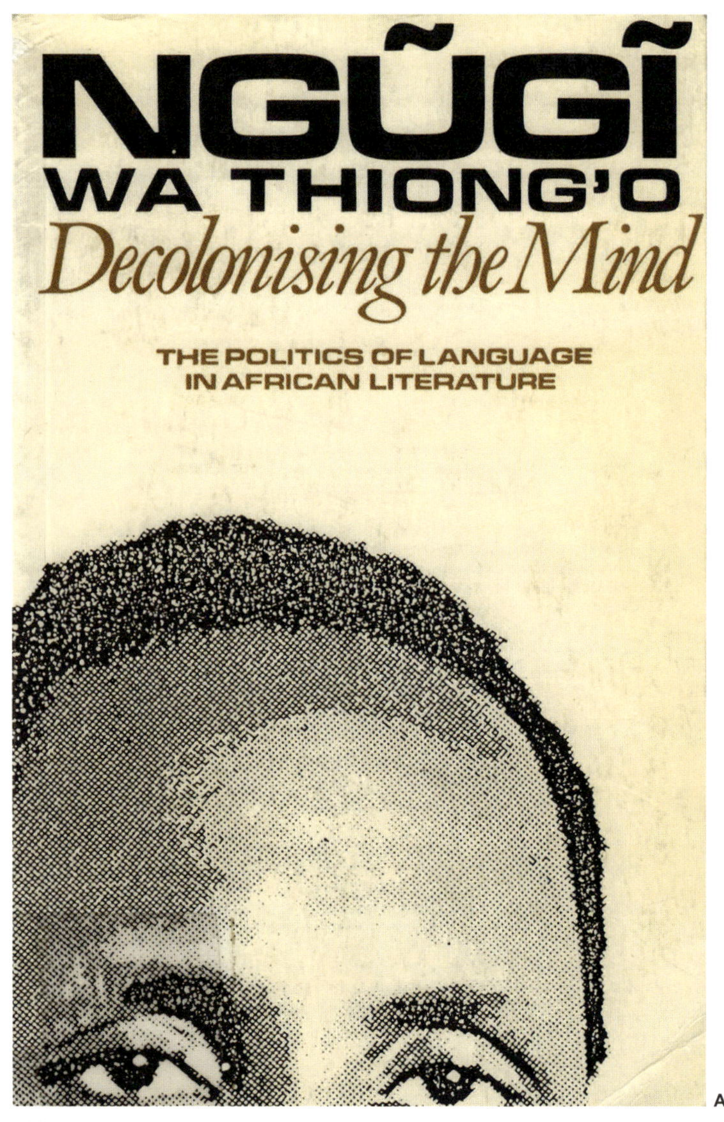

The influence of Kenya's most celebrated writer Ngũgĩ wa Thiong'o on literary and cultural production, consumption and scholarship in Kenya is likely to continue to be more profound in the future than it is today. The reason for such speculation is because over time, and in spite of the government's misguided efforts to marginalise local languages supposedly because they encourage negative ethnicity, advances in communication and the spread of the FM radio has led to a significant rebirth of interest in and use of local languages. Radio stations now broadcast in *Dholuo, Gikuyu, Kamba, Luhya, Kalenjin, Gusii,* or *kiMeru* – languages that are, amongst others, of the more than fifty speech communities in Kenya. This phenomenon reminds one of Ngũgĩ wa Thiongo's most enduring argument for the "decolonisation of African cultures and languages". Ngũgĩ's thesis is that to attain proper decolonisation, Africans would have to recuperate their languages and cultures from the influences of colonialism. This process would enable Africans, and other former colonised peoples, to regain their individual and collective identities. Of course Ngũgĩ's thesis derived very much from the line of thinking that had been instrumental in the emancipation struggles of Afro-American intellectuals and writers, epitomised by W.E.B. Du Bois and the seminal Afrocentric theories of Frantz Fanon. The ethos of these founding fathers of the philosophy of African liberation informs much of the earlier writing in Africa in the immediate postcolonial era. In Kenya, Ngũgĩ himself led from the front in the struggle to free Africans from colonial culture. His writing and that of many of his contemporaries in Kenya functioned as statements of cultural affirmation and political intention; the intention being to not only assert the Africans' new statehood but also to celebrate the success of the anti-colonial struggle.

Ngũgĩ's *The River Between, Weep Not Child, A Grain of Wheat, Petals of Blood,* and *Devil on the Cross,* all share a significant characteristic.[1] In each of these books Ngũgĩ seeks to highlight a peoples' relationship to land. Land as a key factor of production in an agricultural economy, which is what most settler colonies were all about, is therefore an integral element of the identity of the community Ngũgĩ writes about. Therefore, the *Gikuyu* people, who were most affected by the white settler economy, have to wage the war of liberation fuelled by the need to reclaim their land. As a result the *Mau Mau* war of liberation was largely fought in areas occupied by the *Gikuyu* speakers and the war forms a significant trope in Ngũgĩ's fiction. The choice to write about the *Gikuyu* naturally conditioned Ngũgĩ, like many of the early generation of African writers such as Chinua Achebe, Tim Aluko or Ferdinand Oyono, to engage in the production of the anthropology of his people. Thus *The River Between* and *Weep Not Child* are peppered with details of the traditions and customs of the author's people, information that can be found in Jomo Kenyatta's

1   *The River Between,* 1965, *Weep Not Child,* 1964, *A Grain of Wheat,* 1967, *Petals of Blood,* Berlin 1977, *Devil on the Cross,* 1982 (all published in London) [editor's note]

Facing Mount Kenya, which is about the ways of life of the Agikuyu. This emphasis on the cultures of his people, or on the African cultures and languages, was later at the core of Ngũgĩ's critical essays especially in *Decolonizing the Mind: the Politics of Language in African Literature* (1986) [→ Fig. **A**] 2 and *Moving the Centre: The Struggle for Cultural Freedoms* (1993). 3

Some of the fiction by Grace Ogot and Henry ole Kulet is also structured on the customs and traditions of the Luo and Maasai peoples from whom the two writers come, respectively. Ogot's *The Promised Land* and *Land without Thunder* and Kulet's *Moran No More* or *Daughter of Maa* are texts that are steeped in the *Luo* and *Maasai* worldview respectively. They offer the reader entry into the authors' communities, detailing rituals and philosophies of life. To read these books is to immerse oneself into the *Luo* and *Maasai* cultures not just by the narratives themselves but also by the strength of the idiomatic language used. Read within the historical context of postcolonial Kenya in which the state stressed the need to suppress ethnic identities, in the name of nation-making, and to celebrate the newly forged identity of Kenya through the adoption of English and Kiswahili, the narratives in these texts challenge the suggested state hegemony. At the same time these stories best illustrate the contradictions and complexities that shadowed the process of 'inventing new traditions' in Kenya in the postcolonial period; on the one hand the state felt that emphasis on African languages would contribute to ethno-nationalistic tendencies, yet on the other hand Kenyans were exhorted to celebrate their cultures, which were mainly signified through their languages. In addition, the education policy encouraged the use of African languages, especially in the countryside, for instruction in the lower classes, thus many elementary language books and literature readers were written in African languages. Although the works of the likes of Ogot and ole Kulet were written with the intention to challenge a Western worldview and offer an African one, or even to signify the creativity of Africans, this writing tended to produce and reproduce binaries such as African versus European; Black versus White; Traditional versus Modern; Old versus New, etc., all of which cast the early literary texts as anthropology or fiction.

The Literature of Individualism, Hedonism and Dystopia

The 1970s was a period of socio-economic, cultural and political convulsions in East Africa and Kenya. The second decade of independence from British rule was characterised by poor returns from the sale of agricultural products, in Kenya's case mainly coffee and tea, a rise in the price of petrol, political realignments in the country with some of the pre-independence political ideals being discarded and replaced by ethnic preferences in government, new ideological positions, adoption of capitalistic economic policies and outright theft of public resources. The independence party Kenya African National Union (KANU) had fractured and the government in power was seemingly unable to deliver on its pre-independence promises to create jobs, resettle the landless and guarantee equal access to opportunities to all Kenyans.

The natural consequence of this state of affairs was the rise of a sense of despair, alienation and marginalisation of different social groups and classes including the youth, low cadre workers in sectors such as the civil service, the industrial sector and agriculture. The contemporary literature of the time, from writers such as Charles Mangua and David Maillu, graphically captures the overwhelming socio-economic inequalities in many forms. Mangua's novel *Son of Woman* and its sequel *Son of Woman in Mombasa* are compelling dramas of the hedonism adopted by those who had high hopes that a state governed by fellow Africans would be more equitable. However, the cynical anti-hero of *Son of Woman* is arguably a prototype of the major characters in works of many of the writers whose fiction Roger Kurtz 4 characterises as Kenyan "urban literature". The heroes, heroines and anti-heroes of books such as Maillu's *After 4.30, Unfit for Human Consumption* or *My Dear Bottle,* or Meja Mwangi's *Going Down River Road,* [→ Fig. **B**] *Kill Me Quick* or *Cockroach Dance* all, in one way or another, occupy a world in which morality is defined by the individual and where individual happiness or gain are more important than communal welfare.

Going Down
River Road

Meja Mwangi

B

2 Ngũgĩ wa Thiong'o 1986, *Decolonizing the Mind: The Politics of Language in African Literature,* London
3 Ngũgĩ wa Thiong'o 1993, *Moving the Centre: the Struggle for Cultural Freedoms,* London
4 Roger J. Kurtz 1998, *Urban Obsessions, Urban Fears: the Postcolonial Kenyan Novel,* Oxford

The language of these novels raises attention to itself and the subject matter, especially in its overt reference to consumption, hedonistic behaviour and social anomie. For instance Maillu's *After 4.30, Unfit for Human Consumption* and *My Dear Bottle* are all concerned with the social conduct and consumptive desires of the emergent working-class Kenyans in the 1960s and 1970s. The title *After 4.30* signals whatever workers do after hours; *Unfit for Human Consumption* dramatises the sexual escapades of the urbanised and socially mobile classes, whilst *My Dear Bottle* is an ode to the value of alcohol in the lives of the newly urbanised.

Thus the language and ethos of this literature largely challenge the 'cultural nationalism' of the earlier writing that had sought to project an "imagined community" that was united in purpose and in which individuals were willing to sacrifice their personal identities and aspirations for the welfare of all. The decline in the economic welfare of Kenyans, as captured in Colin Leys' book *Underdevelopment in Kenya: The Political Economy of Neo-Colonialism* (1975)[5], engendered widespread moral degeneration as manifested in novels such as *My Life in Crime* and *My Life with a Criminal* by John Kiriamiti, *The Life and Times of a Bank Robber* by John Kiggia Kimani; for instance, all of these novels unashamedly celebrate the use of violent robbery to earn a living. Other novels such as *Going Down River Road* and *Kill Me Quick* may vary the theme of social anomie but all generally tend to argue that when the underdog is pushed into a corner and is faced with extreme deprivation she or he will instinctively resort to socially unsanctioned means to survive. In other words, the viciousness and depravity of urban life for many Kenyans naturally turns them into social predators of the socio-economically well off who, in turn, prey on the poor and are partly to blame for the widening socio-economic gap between the two groups. This cyclic drama of prey-turned-predator, predator-turned-prey is most dramatised in the urban literature that we have referred to above.

The *Sheng-* and *Kwani*?-Generation and Yearning for a Different Identity

Kwani? [→ Fig. C] is a word that evokes mixed emotions in several Kenyans with an interest in literature and culture. This is because of the daring character of those who founded the magazine, and on their seeming intention to question the established literary culture in Kenya as expressed in their proclamations to revolutionise the production and consumption of literature and culture in Kenya. This generation of writers is mostly made up of individuals born in the late 1970s and early 1980s. The choice of language – *Sheng* (a mixture of Kiswahili and English, the two official languages in Kenya, and other Kenyan languages) – signals their difference from the earlier generation of post-independence writers. Apart from conveying the fact that users of *Sheng* are made up mainly of urban dwellers, this generation imagined itself as less tied to the ethno-linguistic backgrounds of their parents. *Sheng,* although relying on English and Kiswahili for its root structure, also incorporated words from other Kenyan languages such as *Gikuyu, Luhya, Luo* or *Maasai.* Thus its users may have been disavowing their ethnic affiliations whilst at the same time being tied to those languages and cultures by the acts of borrowing idioms from them.

Generally *Sheng* appeared in writing mainly meant for young readers, even when some of the writing was by adults. The late Wahome Mutahi who wrote a humour column, *Whispers,* in both *The Standard* and *The Nation,* the leading Kenyan daily and weekend newspapers, generally used *Sheng* to denote the "changing times" in which the idea of a cosmopolitanism driven by urbanisation was being celebrated. He had the desire to include the youth in his writing and the wish to exclude the censorship of the then repressive state. Mutahi's humour column, his subsequent plays (mostly written in *Gikuyu*) and novels, especially *Three Days on the Cross* and *Merchants of Death,* in a way speak of the upheavals of a Kenya in a tight grip of an intolerable government from the 1980s into the 1990s. His writing, especially its language, is probably one of the most satirical in Kenyan literature, but it also set the precedent to question convention, to contest the authority of the state, to challenge acquiescence, which the *Kwani?*-generation later fully exploited. Preceding Mutahi, and often regenerating conterminously with his writing and theatre, was the *matatu* genre (see Mbugua wa Mungai's essay in this volume), which popularised pithy everyday wisdom, commenting on the hardships of life as well as how to survive for another day. The innocuous politics of the *matatu* provided mobile albeit temporary space in which the tout, the driver and the passengers could meditate on their fate beyond the reach of the state. The *matatu* literary genre remains thriving, ever innovative, borrowing from and commenting on local and global issues and retaining the youth as its core audiences.

Kwani? meaning "so what?" was a most daring statement to be made by a group of young writers who were completely unknown at the time when the eponymous literary magazine was launched in 2003. The founding editor, Binyavanga Wainaina, had just won the *Caine Prize for African Writing* with his short story *Discovering Home*[6]. He relocated from Cape Town, South Africa, to Nairobi and started *Kwani?*. The magazine's stated aim was to shake the Kenyan literary and cultural scene by publishing the writing of new and young writers, with whom it deemed the established writers were unwilling to work. *Kwani?* innovated in many ways. It accepted both creative fiction and what it

5 Colin Leys 1975, *Underdevelopment in Kenya: the Political Economy of Neo-Colonialism,* London

6 Binyavanga Wainaina 2001, Discovering Home, *Neue Rundschau* 2/2009: 72–93

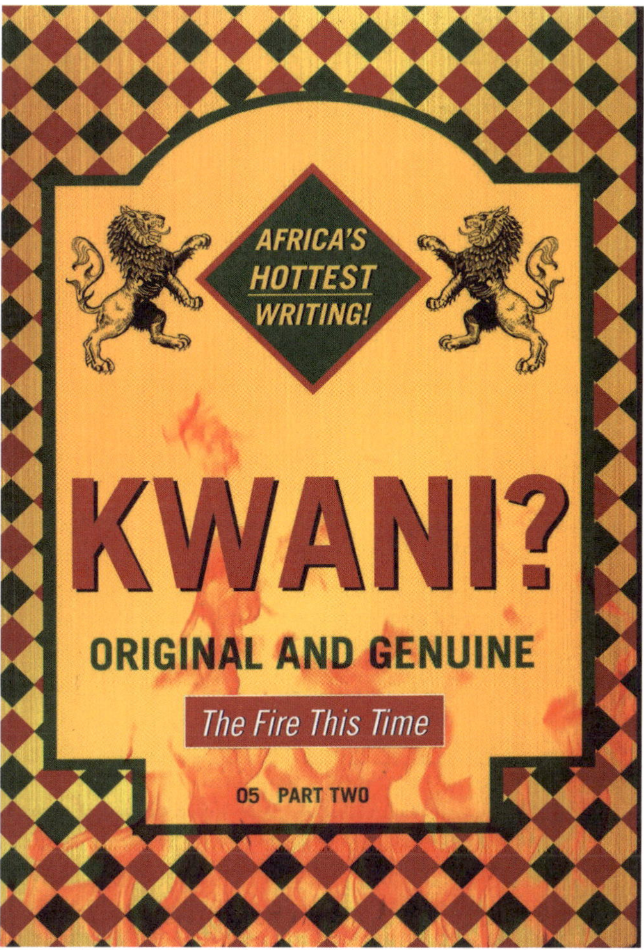

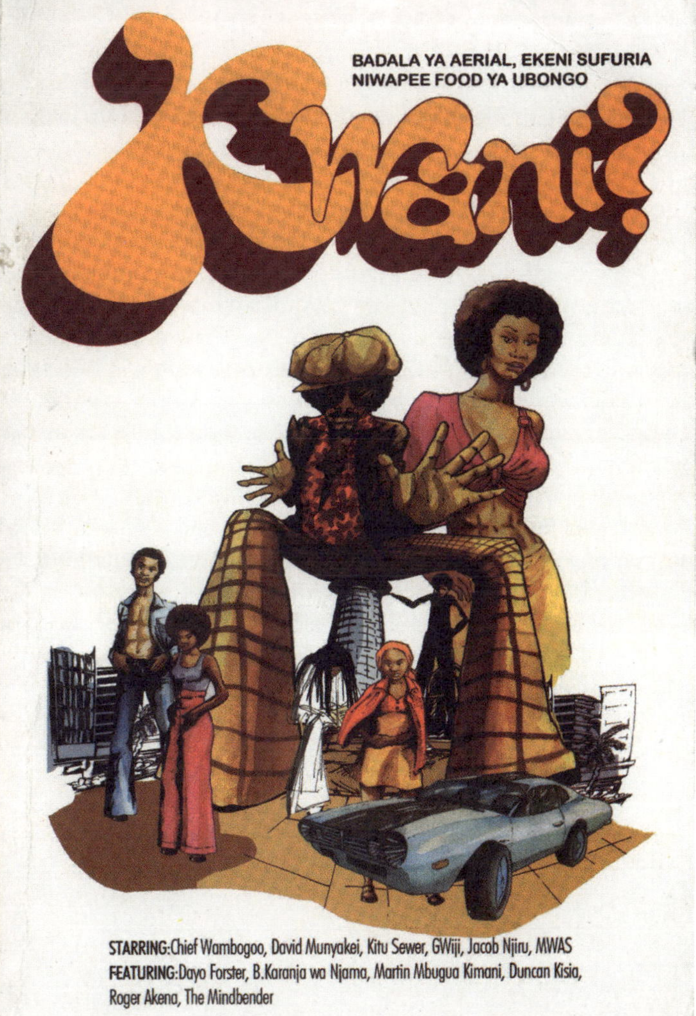

popularised in Kenya as creative non-fiction – journalistic writing, reportage and essays on topics ranging from politics, religion, ethnic relations, to Pan-African issues.

The use of texts in a mix of media including photographs, cartoons, poetry, email exchanges on topical subjects, academic essays alongside the creative fiction for which it was primarily launched, depicted an image of an unconventional literary magazine. As a result *Kwani?* was able to claim a significant institutional profile. On the one hand it sought to project itself as Kenyan, yet on the other hand some of its contributors were drawn from other parts of the world, which gave it a transnational image. A consequence of this dual identity is that *Kwani?* could not speak in a Kenyan tone only. The tone of its language was partially influenced by its contributors – whose writings tended to cast the magazine as Pan-African, international or worldly, urban, or educated – and its audiences from beyond Kenya.

Even the writing of some of the emerging and celebrated figures published by *Kwani?* such as Binyavanga, Parselelo, Yvonne Owuor, Muthoni Garland or Billy Kahora, has tended to speak about Kenya to both a Kenyan and a foreign audience. There is a sense in which one feels that this kind of writing may be influenced not only globally – especially by literary practices around prizes, networking of young writers through workshops and conferences and circulation of texts – but also by a desire to chart a new literary course in Kenya, a definitive statement of new imaginaries around how to make sense of a postcolonial state that is still caught in struggles to define itself. This is one sense from which one can attempt to understand Binyavanga's story *Discovering Home.* Written as diary sketches of his travel from Cape Town to Nairobi to Uganda to attend the 60th wedding anniversary of his maternal grandfather, Binyavanga's journey of self-discovery is also a voyage through the social, economic, political and cultural landscapes and heritages of East Africa. On the one hand it is an invitation to the reader, especially the post-1960 generation of Kenyans, to reflect on what makes the collective identity of the Kenyan nation-state, in a country where one's ethnic origins often significantly determine one's destiny in life in matters such as where to go to school, getting employment, who to marry and where to live. On the other hand, *Discovering Home* is a fascinating tale of the possibilities that travel and mobility offer individuals to remake themselves – Binyavanga becomes someone else, a writer, after living in Cape Town but also by making his diary available to us. He is a child of a father and a mother who travelled beyond her native home. Binyavanga's relatives – collected in his father's home – come from different corners of the world, where travel had originally deposited them.

Thoughts on the Future of Kenyan Literature

The performance of Kenyan literature in international literary competitions such as the *Caine Prize for African Writing* and the *Commonwealth Prize for African Writing* evokes mixed reactions from literary enthusiasts, critics, writers and publishers. Binyavanga Wainaina's *Caine Prize* win in 2002 followed by Yvonne Owuor's win in 2003 and the subsequent short-listing of Parselelo Kantai (2004 and 2009), Mukoma wa Ngũgĩ (2009) and Lily Mabura (2010) give the impression that Kenyan writers are not doing badly. But the absence of Kenyan novels from the *Commonwealth Prize* entries for several years has often been used by critics as justification for an argument that Kenyan literature is in decline. Granted, compared to South Africa or Nigeria, Kenyan literature's global profile is indeed low. There are more novels, for instance, published in each of those two countries than are published in Kenya annually. Yet it is not very productive to compare the three countries on equal terms. South Africa has a more sophisticated and established publishing industry and literary culture than both Nigeria and Kenya. Nigeria has a bigger population and therefore more potential readers than Kenya and South Africa. South Africa and Nigeria publish a lot more in African languages than Kenya does. But even in Kenya there are significant novels and anthologies of short stories published in Kiswahili, which are generally read by fewer people than those who read books in English. Although Kiswahili is more spoken in everyday social transactions than English, it is less privileged than the latter. The Kenyan publishing industry also prefers to invest in textbooks for schools rather than investing in creative writing. These downsides to creative writing in Kenya often tend to be highlighted and the positives that could be built on to improve the quality of Kenyan literary works and engender a widespread literary culture are understated.

It is safe to speculate that Kenyan literature will significantly benefit from technological advancements such as those that have made it possible to publish-on-demand, Internet-based literary magazines and e-books, as well as resources that enhance the quality of manuscript editing and its preparation. The increase in vanity publishing and the rise of indigenous publishers such as *Kwani Trust, Storymoja, Focus Books* and *WordAlive,* whose profiles have been enhanced by their affiliation to an international network of like-minded local publishers in other African countries, portend well for Kenyan writers. A recent short story competition for young Kenyan writers by *Kwani?,* for which I was a judge, revealed that a significant number of Kenyan writers are not just willing to write but also experiment with style. *Kwani?* has encouraged such writers to submit their work for consideration in a literary and publishing culture that would have frowned on such experiments as being misplaced.

A Last Word

Technological innovations have extraordinarily rearranged the structures that produced, disseminate and aid in the consumption of cultural products. Books and other related material, including cultural artefacts, have significantly benefitted from revolutions in technology. Website publishing and do-it-yourself software for preparation of manuscripts may not be universally in use in Africa, or even in most parts of the world, but such developments will chip away at the privilege of the traditional publisher and once more 'resurrect' the author. For the African author, especially in a country such as Kenya, the chance to publish at low cost, reach a bigger audience and even be able to receive royalties has been enhanced by technology. Technology has also allowed for experimentation, especially with form. Many unpublished African authors start off with the short story and eventually turn it into a full-length novel – as is the case with Binyavanga Wainaina, who is working on a novel in which its first parts were the *Discovering Home* story. The freedom facilitated by the Internet also mean that an author can write without restrictions of language that traditional publishers may have imposed on him or her. Thus social networking sites associated with particular ethno-linguistic communities such as www.Jaluo.com or www.Kisii.com have short stories and poetry in *Dholuo* or *Gusii.* Such sites are able to project their own, often essentialised, politics of identity based on ethnic affiliation, even in a globalising world where one would imagine that such identities are limiting or are likely to be impacted and fractured in discrete sub-identities by the same technological and related global forces that drive Internet connectivity and networking. Thus one hopes that the traditional publishing industry in Kenya – both multinationals and locals – will exploit technology to expand the range of literature published in the country and therefore give more voice to writers and texts to readers across the racial, ethnic, religious, gender, age, and socio-economic divides. One hopes that in future it will be possible to produce a proper cartography of Kenyan literature. But as of now there is still less agreement on what stands for the canon of Kenyan literature, its popular versions and others; in other words critics and readers of Kenyan literature are not agreed on its foundational identity. For instance David Maillu, Mwangi Ruheni and Charles Mangua still do not feature on the reading lists of literature courses in departments of literature in Kenyan universities because they are deemed to be 'popular' rather than serious. This exclusion from the university curriculum is a reflection of long-lasting politics of intellectual differentiation between the university educated elite, especially those from departments of literature and writers who are not products of those departments. Yet these writers are some of the most prolific and insightful chroniclers of Kenya's postcolonial history. They are probably even more sensitive to the plight of the poor than policy planners, economists or sociologists. The city though, just like elsewhere in Africa, will remain an integral site of imagination for Kenyan writers given the expansion of urbanisation in Kenya. One reason for this preoccupation with the city is because it is the one place that offers hope for many unemployed young men and women, although it generally delivers desperation and anomie as illustrated in Meja Mwangi's *Kill Me Quick,* where incarceration and death are easier to find than employment. But it is also in the cities that political, economic and cultural futures of Africa are and will continue to be forged; and this is where Kenyan literature will mainly derive its inspiration and subject matter.

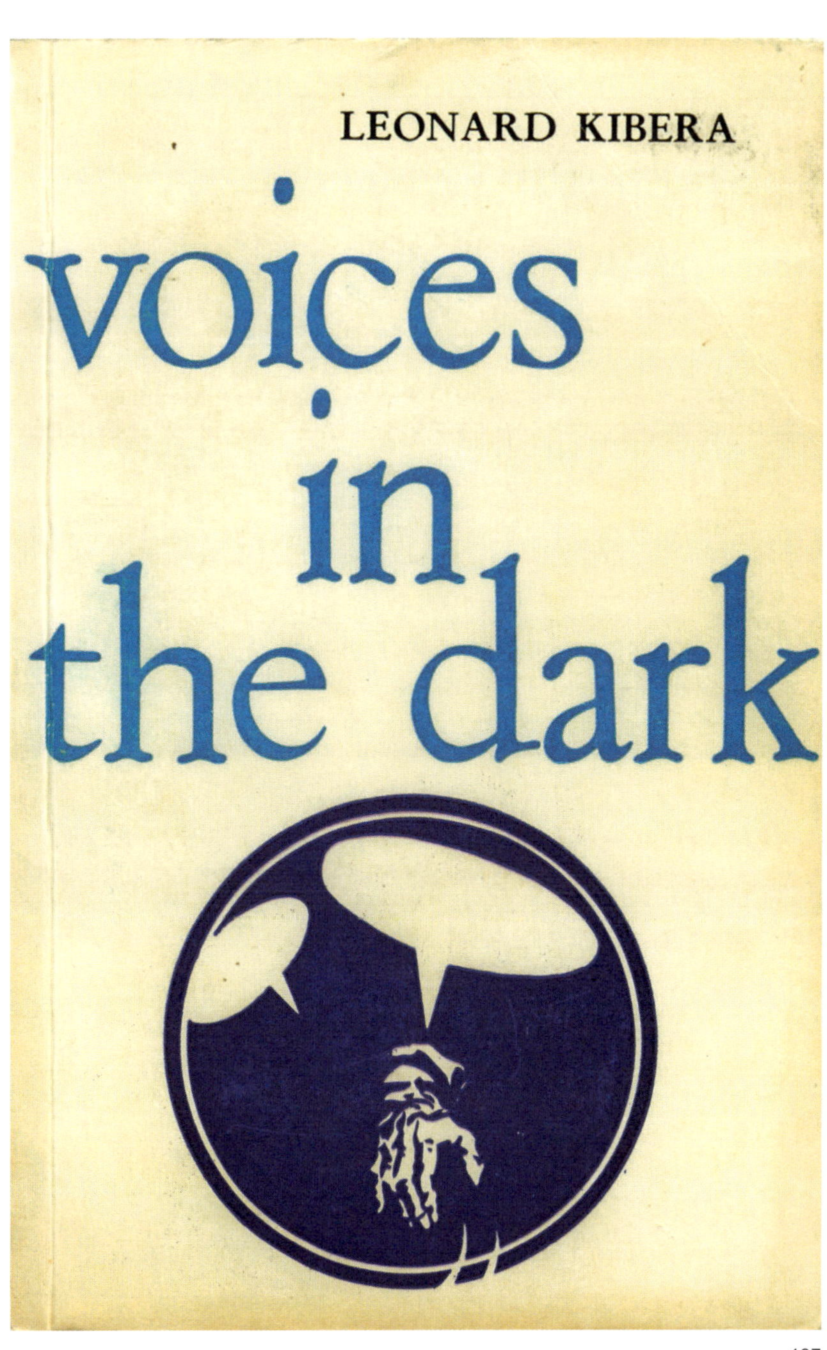

Somali Refugees in Eastleigh, Nairobi

MANUEL HERZ

Refugees generally belong to the weakest, most vulnerable and least influential groups in a society. They are treated as an undifferentiated 'faceless' mass, organised and administered in refugee camps with neither the power to autonomously influence their living conditions nor even, in many cases, their own lives. The specific locations of the camps are an important factor in creating the powerlessness of the refugees. In most cases, refugee camps are set up in a country's remote areas, far from social, cultural or economic life. Such a setting, where refugees have extremely limited possibilities, generates a dependency on aid and humanitarian organisations. In contrast, cities and urban regions can offer refugees the chance to trade, exchange and achieve independence. However, since politicians and local populations regard refugees as 'unfair' competition, many countries ban them from settling in urban regions. Such an approach creates a consciously controlled powerlessness which only reinforces the image of refugees as passive recipients of charity. Numerically, urban refugees remain an exception. Even in Africa, the continent that currently has the largest number of refugees and internally displaced persons, only approximately ten per cent of the refugees live within cities. The few examples of urban refugees, though, do refute the widespread prejudice of the refugee as a parasitical profiteer. The pressure on refugees to make a living, their regional or international networks, their enforced openness and willingness to leverage niches result in intensely vibrant structures that not only benefit the refugees themselves but local populations as well.

Eastleigh

It has rained in the night. The air is still humid, saturated with the odour of rotting food and human sweat. The smell is overlaid by the spreading stench of densely viscous diesel fumes pumping out of the exhausts of thousands of minibuses and trucks as they fight their way through the narrow streets. After the rain, the streets are ankle-deep in mud. Densely packed crowds constantly force their way through the narrow spaces left by the stream of vehicles. Everywhere, people are selling their wares. Street vendors hawk plastic buckets and coat hangers, or T-shirts and jeans. The occasional free spaces are taken by women selling plastic jewellery or household goods. The pavements, few and far between, are jammed with pick-up trucks unloading goods or repacking them onto hazardous-looking constructions on the vehicles' loading platforms and roofs. The streets are flanked by lines of shopping plazas, one after the other.

This is First Avenue in Eastleigh, a district of the Kenyan capital two kilometres east of the city centre. The refugees living here, primarily from Somalia, have turned this into one of Nairobi's most vibrant and remarkable locations, and made it the hub of a trading network spanning the globe. In addition, this area, dubbed 'Little Mogadishu', is the displaced ersatz capital of a disintegrated country.

Eastleigh has approximately 100,000 residents, making it one of the largest Somali cities and the second largest contiguous Somali community outside Somalia itself. Thanks to the relatively well-established infrastructure in Eastleigh in particular and Nairobi in general, the district has assumed the functions of a capital city in place of the barely operational Mogadishu. Eastleigh is not only where a major percentage of Somali trade is coordinated, but also headquarters one of the few working Somali banks, is a centre of Somali financial transactions, and the location where Somali ministers and politicians from diverse parties meet and discuss the future (and fate) of this tragic country. Mainly home to non-registered refugees, often with no

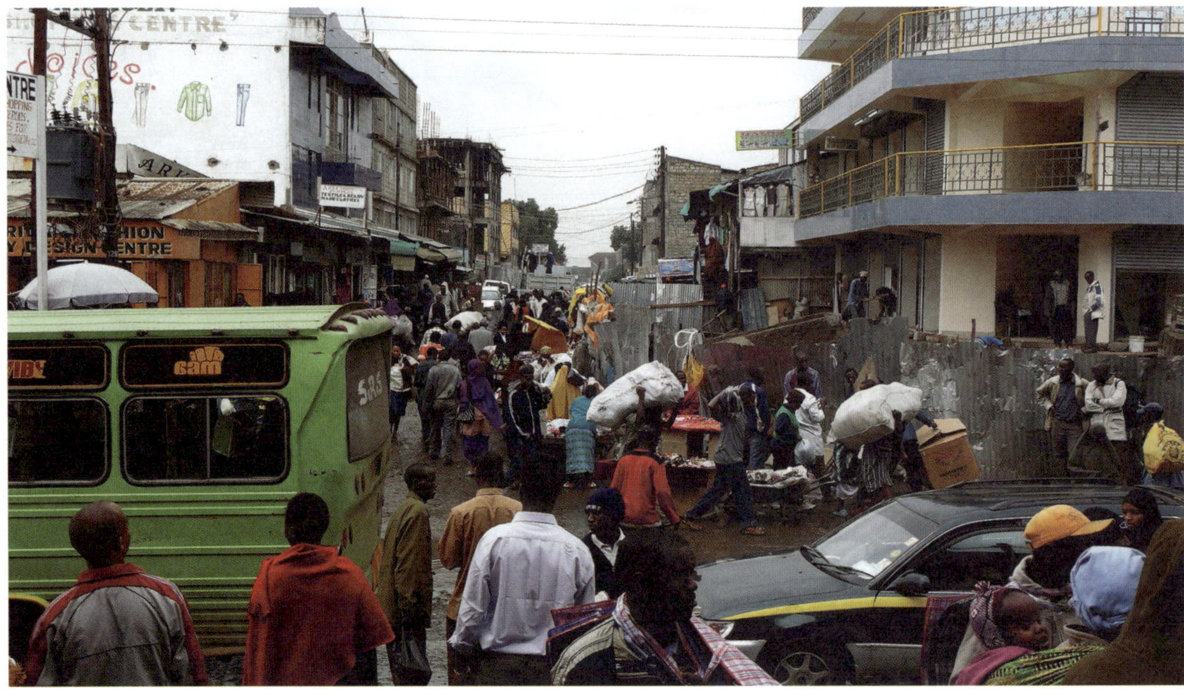

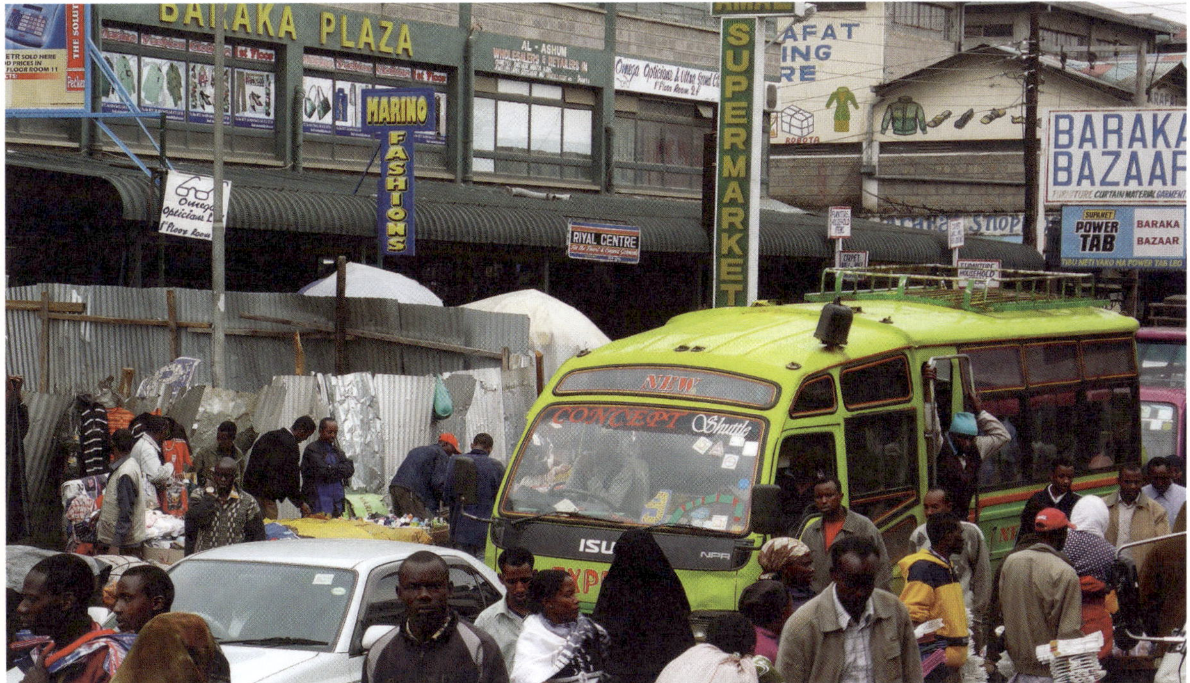

documents or only forged ones and living here informally or illegally, this district in the heart of Nairobi is largely ignored by the Kenyan capital's official authorities, its residents invisible to the public gaze.

Historical Development

In the first decades after Nairobi was founded, it was an Asian city. Nairobi goes back to 1896, established as a station on the East African Railway, halfway between Mombasa on the Indian Ocean and Kisumu on Lake Victoria. The first Indian traders began settling a few years later, a time when hardly any of the local Kenyan population lived in Nairobi. Kenyans were only allowed to stay in the city if they were male and could prove full employment with one of the white settlers or one of the city's businesses. If they were married, they had to leave their families behind in the villages outside the city, or in other parts of the country. For centuries, Indian and Arab merchants dominated trade along the East African coast. They also played a major part in constructing the railway line, settling in a number of places, including Eastleigh. The (prosperous) white settlers established neighbourhoods where the climate was better on the higher ground to the west of Nairobi in a region with forests and winding valleys, similarly winding roads and an abundance of little brooks and streams. In contrast, Eastleigh was located in the dusty eastern area, laid out during the 1920s in a checkerboard pattern with six broad northsouth avenues intersected by fifteen streets aligned eastwest. There, the Indian traders built their courtyard houses, developed efficient trading structures and soon dominated commercial life throughout Nairobi.

In the 1940s, a new law allowed Kenyans to move to Nairobi with their families. In those days, the Asian trading community also enjoyed sufficient prosperity to facilitate a move to the neighbourhoods of Westlands and Parklands further west, offering a more pleasant climate. The east of Nairobi, and Eastleigh in particular, again became an 'immigrant's' quarter, this time inhabited by local Kenyans. When Kenya achieved political independence in 1963 and the policy of ethnically segregated neighbourhoods came to an end, Nairobi's population rose dramatically. As Kenyans moved in from rural areas, the first Somali traders also settled in Eastleigh. The old courtyard-style residences built by the Indian merchants were familiar to the Somalis, who had lived in similar houses in Mogadishu and their home regions around the Horn of Africa.

In 1992, former Somali President Siad Barre was deposed and exiled. As Somalia became embroiled in a crippling civil war, the country steadily fell apart. In just a few years, with famine raging and Somalia gradually sliding into a permanent state of anarchy, hundreds of thousands of people fled across the borders to Kenya. There, they were placed in refugee camps near Dadaab in eastern Kenya where they eked out a dismal existence in extreme poverty. The Kenyan government had initially operated a liberal refugee policy granting refugees freedom of movement across the entire country. But with the growing flood of refugees, it limited movement and required all registered refugees to remain inside the camps. They were also forbidden from taking on any paid work. In the far east of the country and with a poorly developed infrastructure making access difficult, the refugee camps resembled virtual prisons.

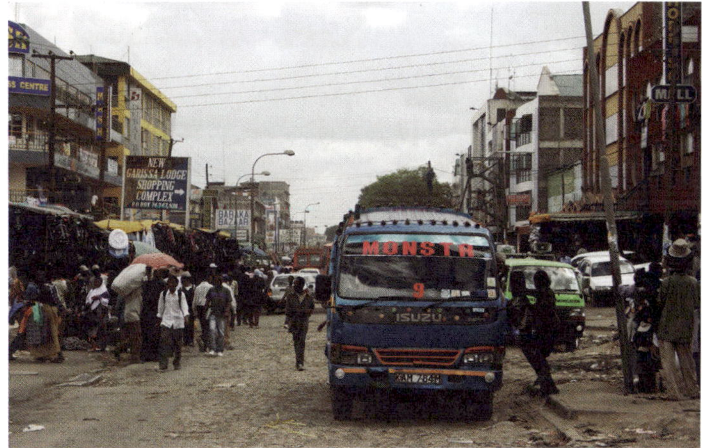

A large percentage of the Somali refugees were relatively prosperous traders from Mogadishu, Somalia's capital city. With their urban background, they were unfamiliar with the rural lifestyle of the camps. Before they left Somalia, they sold their goods and real estate, arriving in Kenya with gold and cash. Used to city life and with no opportunities to earn a living from business in the refugee camps around Dadaab, they soon started moving unofficially to Nairobi. Since they had contacts to the Somalis already living in Nairobi, they also settled in Eastleigh. In this way, Eastleigh became an 'immigrant district' for a third time – this time as a home for illegal Somali refugees.

Initially, the Somali refugees arriving in Nairobi planned to sort out their administrative affairs and emigrate as quickly as possible to London, Dubai or the United States. Guesthouses and other accommodation were built, and there they spent their time waiting for their exit visas. One of these guesthouses was Garissa Lodge on First Avenue. Since exit visas commonly took months to be granted, the Somali merchants started trading to bridge the time. With no desire or opportunity to rent trading space, and no commercial infrastructure to leverage, they simply began trading out of their hotel rooms. Gradually, Garissa Lodge was transformed from a guesthouse into a trading centre. A Somali business woman, now notorious, spotted this trend. In no time she had bought up Garissa Lodge and completely converted it into a shopping mall. Her original idea for the Somali trading centres in Eastleigh was quickly copied, and variations appeared all down the main road through the district. These commercial activities were a magnet, drawing many more Somali refugees to the district. Today, around 100,000 people are thought to live in the streets of 'Little Mogadishu'.

Shopping Malls

The Amal Shopping Centre is currently considered to be the most sophisticated style of shopping mall in Eastleigh, offering the ultimate shopping experience in this urban 'refugee settlement'. Located next to the Bangkok Shopping Mall (the former Garissa Lodge), the Amal Shopping Centre has five floors packed with goods from across the world. The prices are affordable, and the presentation of the goods across the mall follows a specific curatorial concept. The ground floor is dedicated to cheap mass-produced textiles. Many of the individual shop units, each around six square metres, are crammed with textiles from floor to ceiling. The goods are either sold from a small niche within the shop or in the corridor in front. These shops do not have any functional separation between storage and sales. The ground floor comprises 160 densely packed businesses selling their wares. The more upmarket clothing is sold on the first floor, including jeans from China for 500 Kenyan shillings (around five euros) or T-shirts for a fraction of the price. On the second floor, individual shops are combined into larger units focused on shoes, sports shoes and suits. This is also where you find the electronics stores with hi-fi systems, TVs and the ubiquitous mobile phones. The third floor is dedicated to service outlets with travel agents offering flights across the world, a Western Union branch and offices arranging the hawala Islamic money exchange, various other moneychangers, an Afghani fast-food restaurant, a mosque, and a clinic operated by the Aga Khan Trust. The top floor is occupied by the management's offices, which are separated from the rest of the shopping mall.

The Amal Shopping Centre's individual floors are connected by a succession of intersecting double staircases, ramps, bridges, spiral staircases, lifts and arcade-like corridors and galleries. There is a series of air spaces and atriums to channel daylight down through the building to the ground floor. This design creates a complex three-dimensional structure of shopping, access and recreational areas. The building's architecture combines informal and improvised aspects with the formal and conventional. Elements of the standard repertoire of shopping malls such as galleries and atriums are condensed and merged with other spaces and functions, such as mosques, ramps or sales areas.

There are three parallel and intertwined access systems which have different functions: the stairs, used by the majority, of the mall's customers and visitors; the ramps, where goods are rolled or lugged to the particular floors and the individual shops, and which also provide general access; and two lifts, primarily constructed to enhance the mall's image since they were the first lifts in Eastleigh and a visible sign of modernity and comfort. In fact, though, the lifts are rarely used in everyday life. All three of these circulation systems are intertwined and include direction changes, sometimes running upwards and sometimes down-

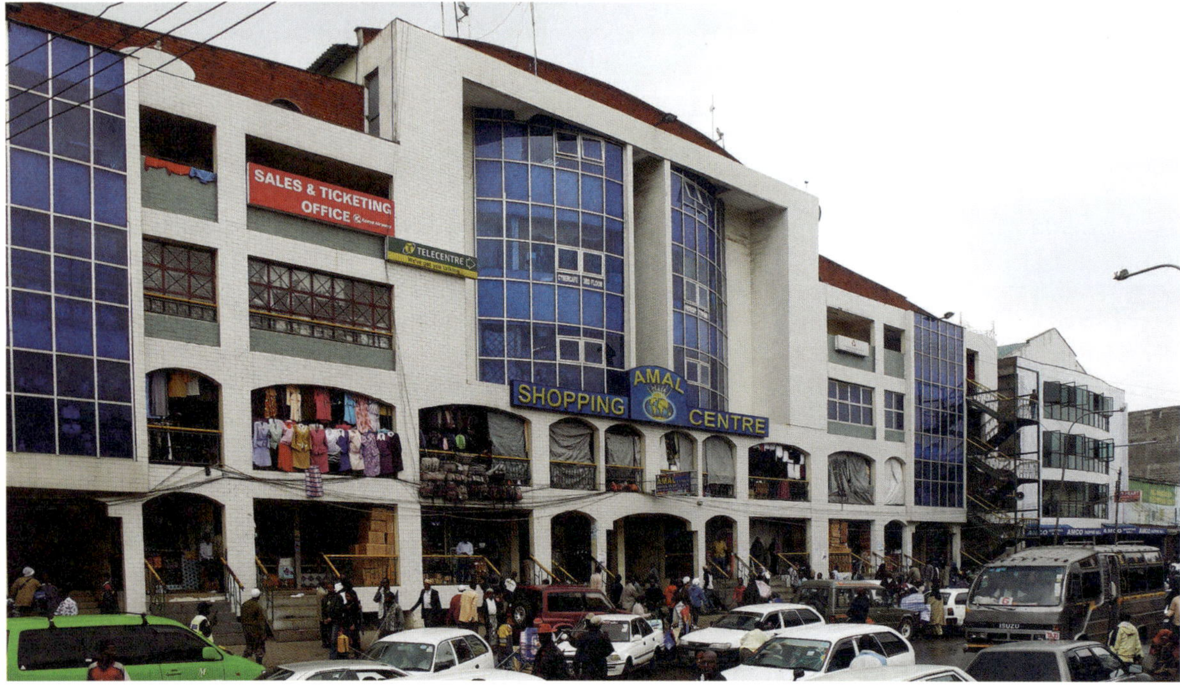

wards. Together with the adjoining open areas, atriums and galleries, they create a very complex space apparently allowing movement freely in all directions and in all three dimensions. Here, selling, shopping, warehousing, delivering, storing, sorting, trading bargaining, trying on goods and concluding sales all take place simultaneously – a shopping centre on speed.

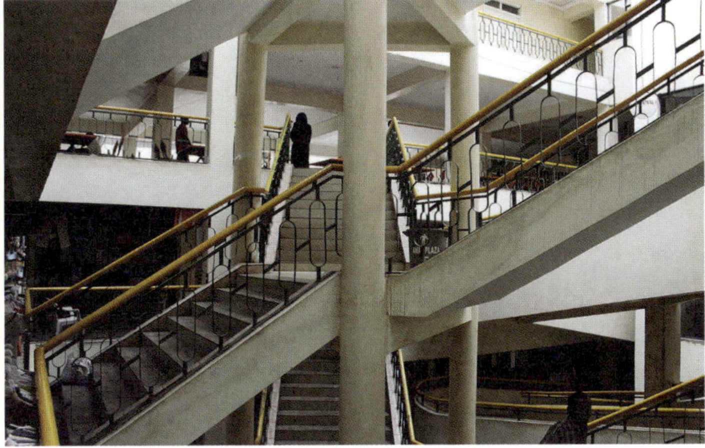

The Amal Shopping Centre was built in 2003. Since then several new shopping malls have opened, and others are in planning or undergoing construction. Shopping malls have recognised architecture's role as a means of identification and a unique selling point for customers. They seek to outdo each other in size, and compete with the flashiest facades, window designs, and stair and ramp systems to bring in the customers. The shopping malls are financed and built by Somali investors living in Nairobi who are usually also refugees of the civil war. During the funding phase, they sell off the rights of use for the future shops for between 10,000 and 21,000 US dollars to interested traders or small investors. The traders all come from the Somali community in Eastleigh, and are often chosen by the investors on tribal lines. Since the sums raised by the investors during the funding phase often exceed the construction costs, simply building the shopping mall already generates a profit. After purchasing a right of use, a trader only has to pay a minimal rent on the shop space for ten or fifteen years. In some cases, these share certificates are sold on to other traders. This funding system facilitates the construction of large and complex building projects and guarantees manageable investment costs for all those involved. The mutual dependency inherent in the funding system and the close-knit Somali community networks provide a high security against any loan default. Although the system is purely profit-oriented and based on the rules of the free market economy, with its low capital input in relative terms it is ideally designed for the conditions of the Somali refugees.

A Global Trading Network

The continuing civil war in Somali since 1992 has created a Somali diaspora around the whole world. There are groups of Somali refugees across Africa, on the Arabian Peninsula, in North America, Europe, Australia and East Asia, making this one of the most scattered ethnic groups in the world. The Somali diaspora has created a global trading system with centres that include Eastleigh. Transactions are prepared and executed by phone through middlemen and Somali contacts in Dubai, Hong Kong, Minneapolis or London.

In Eastleigh, hardly any of the goods for sale are produced in Africa. They usually reach Eastleigh via Dubai. If they are sent by ship, they are offloaded in Mombasa, Kenya's only harbour, and then trucked to Nairobi. If the goods from all across the world are airfreighted in, the planes land in Eldoret, 300 kilometres northwest of Nairobi, to avoid paying customs duty. Every day, trucks laden with merchandise roll into Eastleigh to supply the individual shops. The district has no central distribution points; as in the individual shops, there is no separation between retailer, wholesaler, sales and storage. Overseas containers transported on 18-wheeler trucks squeeze through Eastleigh's narrow streets. When they stop at a shopping mall, the goods, offloaded by hand, are taken through the mall's main entrance and packed into the small shop units. The streets are blocked for hours, leaving the traffic gridlocked.

It is not only the goods that come from all around the world. Initially, Eastleigh was a local market hardly known outside the city, but it soon had an impact on trade in the entire region. The Somali traders in Eastleigh keep prices down by leveraging global price differences in wholesale goods, cutting transport costs and frequently avoiding customs duties. Attracted by the low prices of the Somali trader network, cost-conscious customers come here from across Nairobi to find a bargain. And it is not only the Nairobi residents who are aware of the possible savings in Eastleigh. In the meantime, this Somali district in Nairobi attracts middlemen and individual customers from across Kenya, Uganda, Tanzania and Ruanda who buy goods in bulk and then sell them on in their domestic markets. As a result, Eastleigh, this densely packed, dirty and vibrant district of Somali refugees, has become one of the key trading centres for the entire East African region. Since this development runs across all the business areas of textiles, clothing, household and electronic goods traditionally held by the Indian merchants, it has significantly weakened their dominance in Nairobi's commercial life.

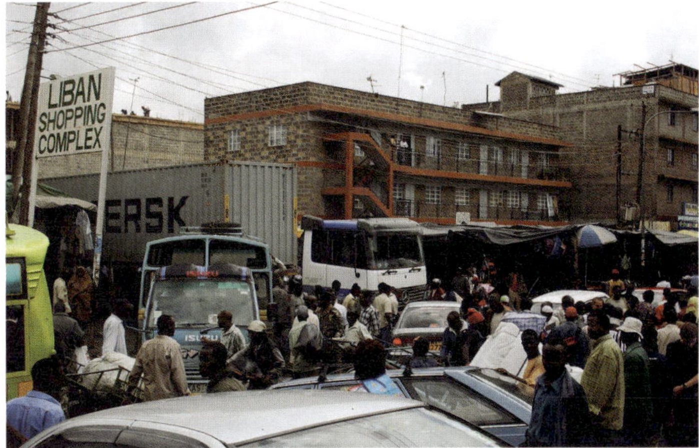

In December 2000, Garissa Lodge, a highly symbolic shopping mall, burned down. Although the evidence showed that the fire was caused by arson, the perpetrator was never caught. This led, in turn, to a belief that the attack was masterminded in the Indian business community as a warning to the Somalis. Despite or perhaps because of the commercial success of the Somali refugees, their situation in Eastleigh remains uneasy and uncertain. The assumed arson attack on Garissa Lodge by the Indian business community is the most prominent sign of pressure from Somali competitors. Other traders in Nairobi submit complaints to the City Council in an attempt to influence it and undermine the position of the Somali traders. The Somalis' evident business success combined in many cases with an illegal residence status as refugees in Nairobi makes them easy victims of bribery and extortion. The Nairobi police, notorious for their corruption, regularly check residency permits in the area and demand a 'fine' of between thirty and two hundred euros if a person's papers are not fully in order. Somalis are apprehended, kept in police custody or prison cells, and only released when their family pay a 'fee' of a similar amount. If the documents of Somali business people are in order, they are then charged 'taxes' instead. Some years ago, the local police changed their approach and instead of demanding various forms of protection money, started openly stealing goods, regularly taking wares from the individual shops. The dealers have sought to combat extortion and the exploitation of their insecure status by founding the Eastleigh Business Community as an organisation to represent their interests.

But the local police force is only one of the dangers facing the refugees. Given the large number of Somalis and Ogaden (ethnic Somali Ethiopians) living in Eastleigh, and the conflicts and political persecution they are subject to in their home countries, the district is rife with foreign secret services and agents. Informers from hostile groups or with opposing political beliefs infiltrate the community and seek to kidnap or physically threaten Somalis or Ogaden. As a result, the regional African crises and wars are projected onto this Nairobi district, thus finding a counterpart in everyday life.

But global conflicts also resonate on the streets of Eastleigh. After the September 11 attacks on the World Trade Center in 2001, the US secret service infiltrated and investigated affairs in Eastleigh, claiming the district was home to al-Quaeda sympathisers and it needed to uncover money flows to the organisation. A number of hawala were forced to close their businesses and US agents detained and interrogated various local residents. Under this direct yet diffuse pressure from foreign powers, the district experienced a prevailing and constant mood of mistrust. Foreign visitors were not welcome and people with cameras (for example, the author of this article) were immediately met with distrust and suspicion, with people hardly willing to answer questions even about ordinary, everyday matters. Although the Somali district of Eastleigh is intense and vibrant, with business activities always revolving around communication and trust, the Somali are today suspicious of people from outside and limit communication to the absolute minimum.

Refugees as Spatial Actors

Somali refugees in Kenya are very conscious of the spatial level of their actions. They can draw on a broad network of support bases inside and outside their host country, optimally leveraging their different potentials. In particular, there are structural dependencies between Eastleigh and the refugee camps around Dadaab which, with a population of around 180,000 people, are nearly twice as large as the Somali community in Nairobi. Refugee families in the camps usually send their sons to specific destinations ranging from Garissa, in the vicinity of the camp, to Nairobi or, if possible, Dubai. Once there, they are supposed to sound out possibilities, gather information on business opportunities, personal security and the quality of life, and financially support family members remaining in the camp. Every month, transfers of money – known as remittances – ranging from fifty to several hundred dollars are sent from Nairobi to the family members in the camps. Despite temporary Somali residents in Eastleigh often opting to stay permanently, many view the district just as a place to earn money as migrant workers and support their families. In the long term, they plan to return home.

Since the Somali refugees in Eastleigh are registered as refugee camp residents, they regularly have to go back to the camps. At intervals, the United Nations High Commissioner for Refugees (UNHCR) carries out a headcount of refugees there. The refugees need to be present during the headcounts which are always announced some days in advance, since these are taken as the basis for food distribution and other forms of support. A headcount is big business for the travel and coach companies in Eastleigh offering daily connections to the refugee camps and destinations in many other regions of East Africa. On the evening before the headcount, the packed streets in Eastleigh are even more jammed with people than usual, with hundreds if not thousands of refugees making the journey across the country to be registered in the Ifo, Dagahaley and Hagadera camps as UNHCR refugees, to then travel back to Nairobi the next day. Although Eastleigh is one of the most impressive districts in Nairobi, in a certain sense it is an outpost of the refugee camps in the east of the country.

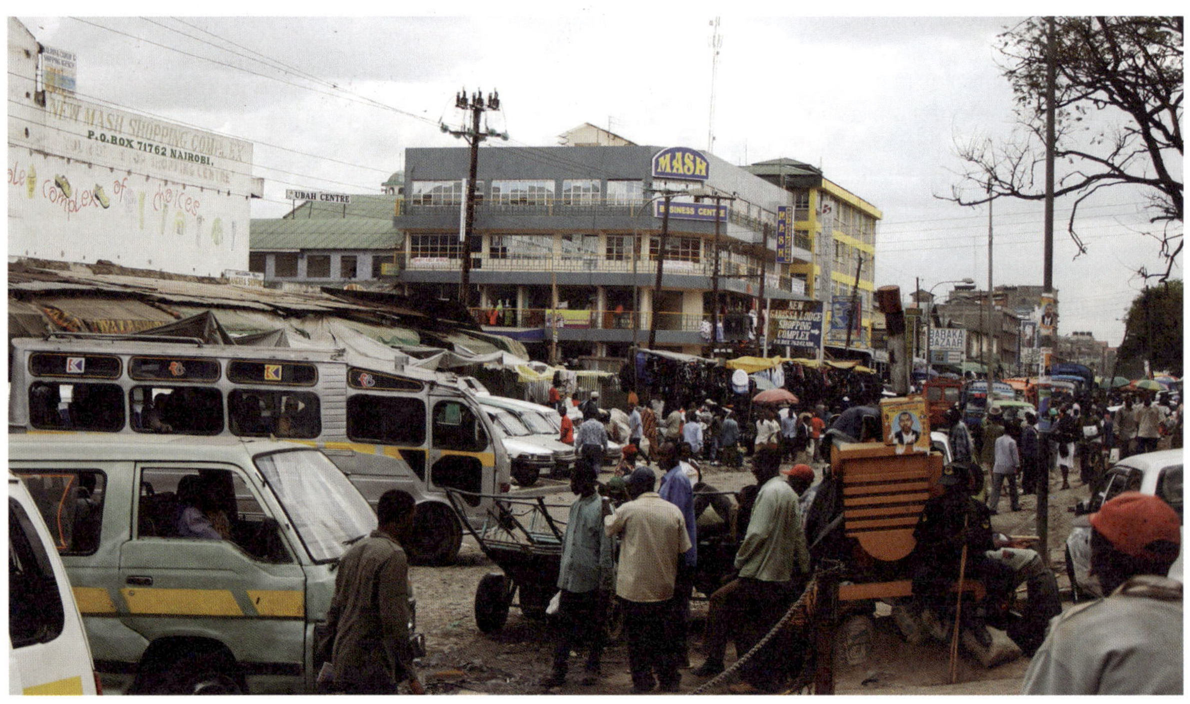

Despite the close-knit, intense, vibrant and urban community in Eastleigh, which is almost unique in Nairobi, the living conditions are highly problematic. The air is heavily polluted from the exhaust fumes of the old diesel engines in the cars, minibuses and trucks, children have nowhere to play, there are no green areas or leisure facilities, and the houses are dilapidated and the sanitation poor. Nonetheless, the rents have risen rapidly over the last years. Although the residents are almost exclusively Somalis, many of the apartment blocks are not Somali owned. Today, Somalis feel it was a mistake to have primarily invested in commerce, and not put enough into property. With the high density of residents and the importance Somali refugees attach to living together, Kenyan property owners can hike rents as they like, and the rental price bears no relation to the quality of the accommodation provided.

Given the district's high residential density, rising rents, poor quality of life and lack of possible areas for expansion, it seems pertinent to ask how Eastleigh will develop over the next years. With no provisions for coping with the district's population growth and a lack of space for expanding the commercial centre further, the district and its residents clearly need to develop new strategies. First Avenue simply does not have the space for additional shopping centres. The head of the local community-services department at UNCHR is responsible for Somali refugees in Nairobi and therefore concerned with the precise question of where Nairobi's next Eastleigh will be located. The Somali refugees and investors are already reacting to this trend, and have taken three different approaches to starting new 'branches' of their district.

Inside Nairobi itself, they are beginning to exploit new streets outside Eastleigh – and, in the process, move ever deeper into territory traditionally belonging to the Indian business community. They take over individual shops in the streets near the Central Business District and quickly expand; soon they control a large section of the street, and it somehow becomes a dislocated part of Eastleigh, with all its density, intensity and distinctive noises, smells and visual impressions. In contrast, the individual investors and shopping mall owners constrained by the limits to growth inside Eastleigh itself have larger-scale plans for expansion. The pioneer here, once again, is the Amal Shopping Centre. With the mall limited to approximately 4,000 square metres of plot area, and with no possibility of developing on site, the Amal Shopping Centre opened a branch in Johannesburg four years ago. At present, the management is in the process of 'settling' cities in its own homeland. A Mogadishu branch has already been opened, and planning for two other shopping malls is on-going in the Somali cities of Bosaso and Galkaio. In an odd reversal of the location process, Somali refugees are now settling their own country from Nairobi and establishing one of the few functioning structures there; a domestic "diasporisation".

The Eastleigh Business Community is also currently considering which smaller cities near Nairobi could be potential new settlement areas for Somali refugees and traders, how to establish such settlements and how to develop trading structures. The cities highest on their agenda are Thika, twenty-five kilometres to the northeast, and Athi River, twenty-five kilometres to the southwest. In these two towns, Somali refugees would have a pioneering role in a metropolitanisation process that the Nairobi City Council has long planned, but failed to realise. Kenya's capital city has long since expanded outside its relatively tight administrative borders. To create a coherent scenario for growth and urbanisation, the City Council developed a Master Plan incorporating the surrounding municipalities. So far, though, the cooperation between the individual towns and municipal authorities has been less than satisfactory. There is a certain irony in the fact that it is the Somali refugees, unwanted by the state in urban regions, who are now driving forward the metropolitanisation process more vigorously and proactively than the Nairobi City Council itself seems capable of.

The Somali refugees in Eastleigh have developed a remarkable city district whose urban qualities, as well as its problems and deficits, are hard to find anywhere else in Nairobi. As a bustling, vibrant, efficient and very professionally managed global trading network that supplies all of East Africa with goods, but also as one of Nairobi's most urban districts, and moreover one established by residents without a legal right of residence, Eastleigh may well be unique in its present form. The spatial practices and urban operations here seem conscious and goal-directed. The refugees have settled strategically in diverse areas within the city, leveraging the potential of Nairobi's connection to the neighbouring countries in East Africa. They regard Eastleigh as an outpost of the refugee camps, developing 'branches' in the region, and arranging an 'outsourcing' of services and the district itself. They have recognised the advantages of an expanded metropolitan region far sooner than Nairobi City Council, and long before the inflexible local authority can develop its own concrete expansion plan. Born from a mix of distress, necessity, economic interests and an international trading network, the Somali refugees have become real-life urban planners.

Translation from German by Andrew Boreham

Warosho

MASAI MBILI (TWO MASAI)

Is an artists' collective founded in 2001, using shared studio rooms in Kibera, Nairobi. *Warosho* is a series of painted signs informed by the tradition of the local population unofficially nicknaming certain locations in the city. The names are signs of how these locations have been appropriated and transformed into general points of orientation for the urban population. *Warosho,* Sheng for: back street, investigates the significance of these popular names.

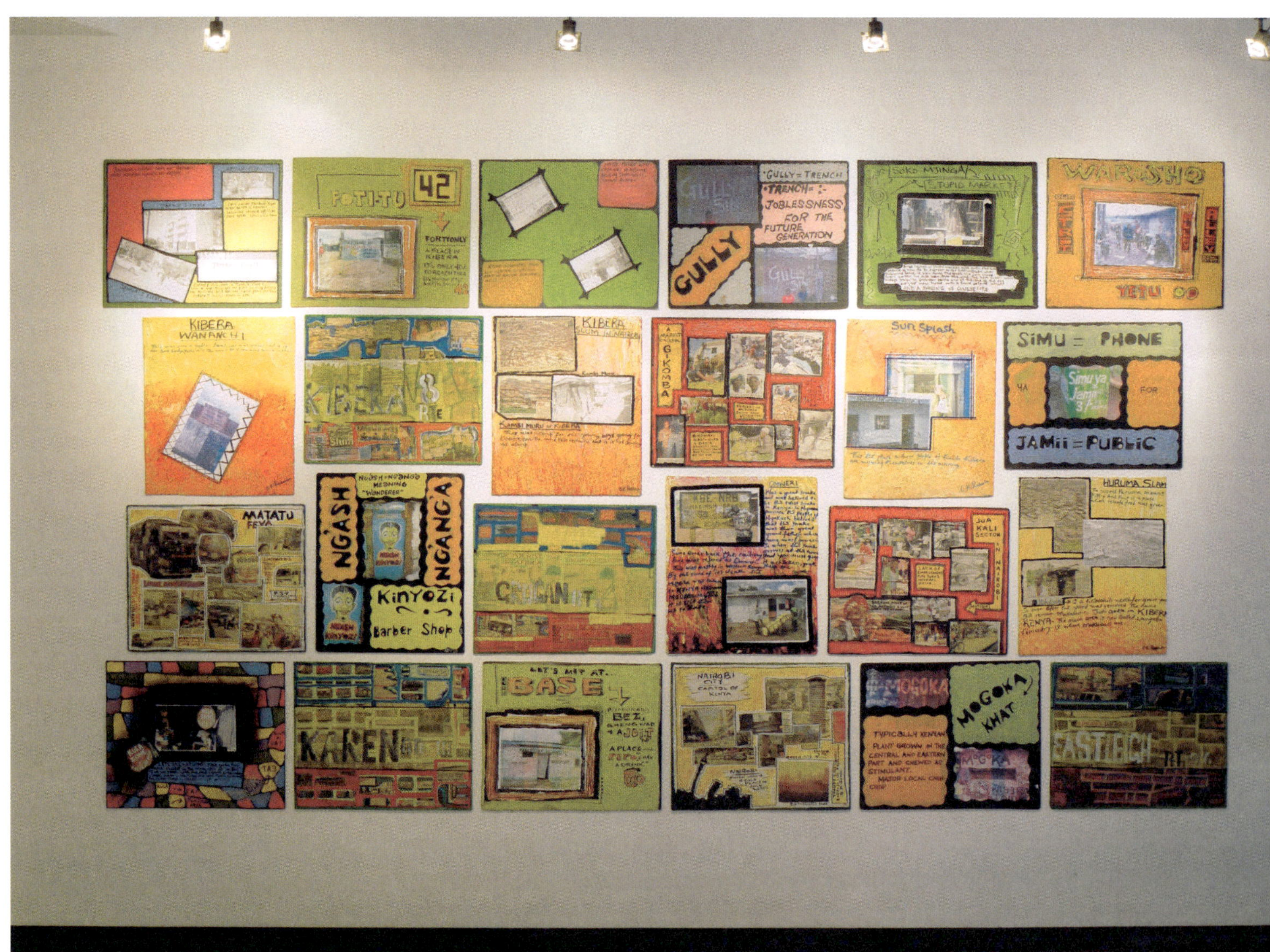

WAROSHO, PAINTING AND COLLAGE ON PLYWOOD, EACH APPROXIMATELY 50 × 60 CM, 2010

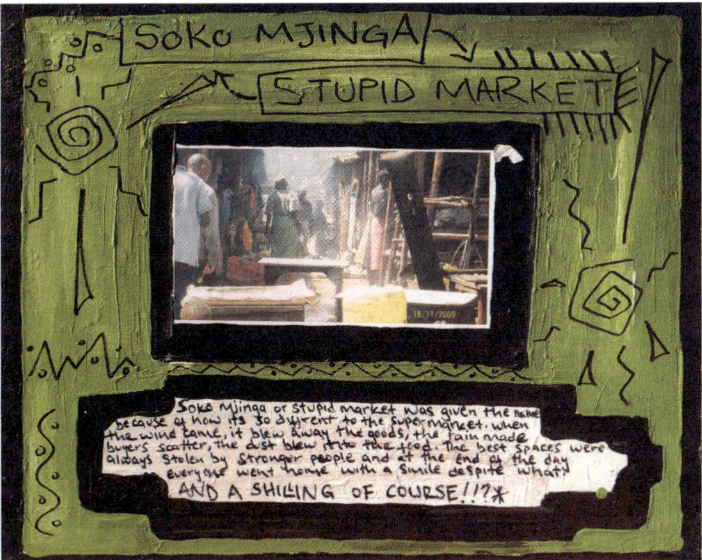

← The *Soko Mjinga* or Stupid Market is very different from a normal supermarket – and that difference is reflected in the name. When it was windy, the goods for sale were blown away, dust got into the food and the rain drove the customers away. The best stalls were always taken by the strongest, yet nonetheless in the evenings everyone went home with a smile on their lips and, of course, a shilling in their pockets!!

Matatu Feva, initially, every journey cost thirty KSh. Licensed to give passengers a thrilling ride; main features: videos, mobile disco, maximum speeds, and graffiti. ↓

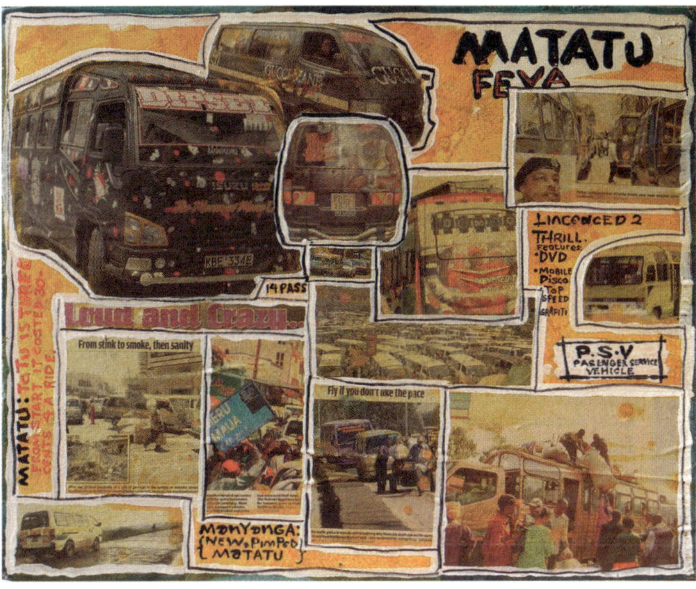

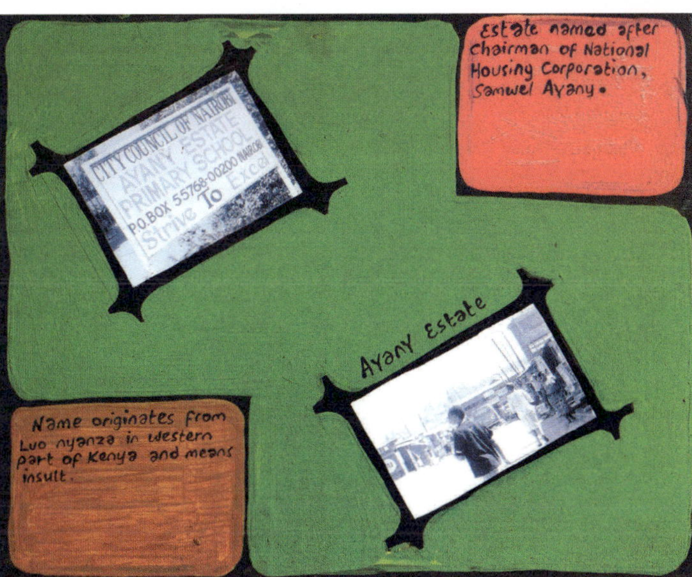

← *Ayany Estate,* a settlement named after Samuel Ayany, National Housing Corporation Chairman. The name, which is a swear word, originally comes from Luo Nyanza in western Kenya.

Jamhuri – the Swahili word for "republic". The Republic of Kenya was proclaimed on 12 December 1964. Jamhuri Park, the second official park after the Uhuru Gardens (Freedom Gardens), was named five years after the Republic of Kenya was founded. Five years later, the Jamhuri I estate was built next to the park as one of the first African residential quarters. Work on the Jamhuri II development started in 1991. ↓

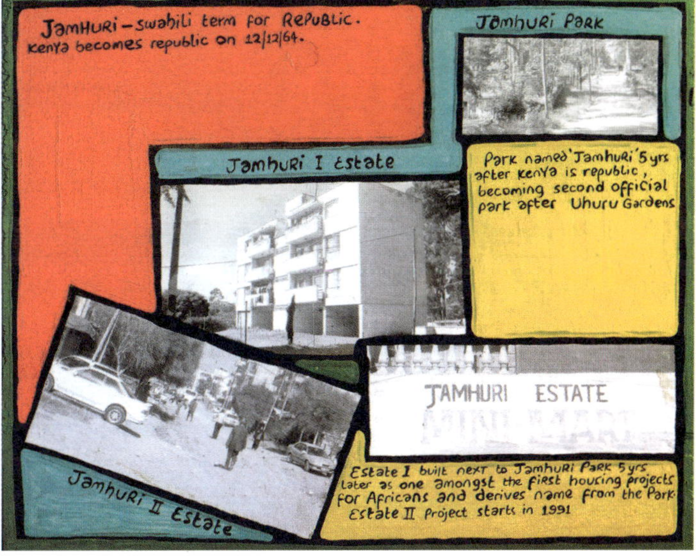

Kibera – 8, Kibera is derived from the Arabic word *kibra*. The first inhabitants of the Kibera slum were Arabic-speaking Nubians, Second World War veterans settled there by the British colonial government. The area was part of the *Ngong* forest, and *kibra* means 'forest' in Arabic. Later, Kenyans also settled around the village, and changed the name to Kibera. ↓

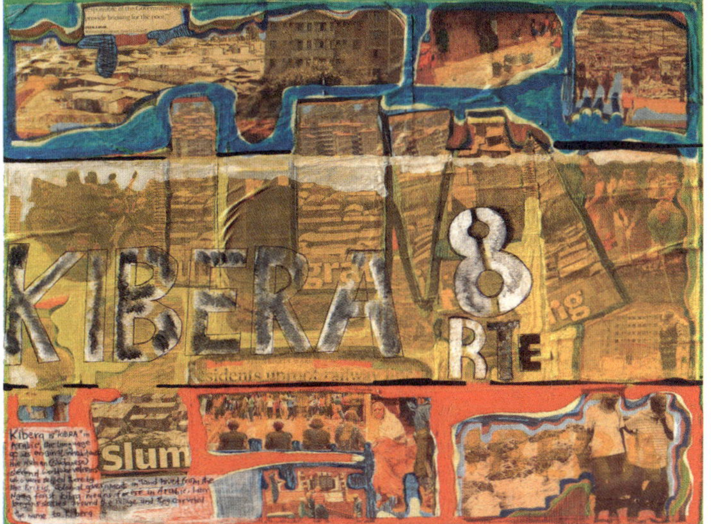

Upgradasion

SLUM-TV

Slum-TV is a grass-roots initiative founded in 2006 in Mathare, Nairobi, primarily dedicated to producing documentary video clips. The *Upgradasion* video installation shows fragments of a soap which, through its scenario of a slum development project, offers an insight into the complex slum economies and power relations. *Upgradasion* was produced by Sam Hopkins with Charles Njoroge Matathia (screenplay), Hawa Essuman (director) and Chris King (editor).

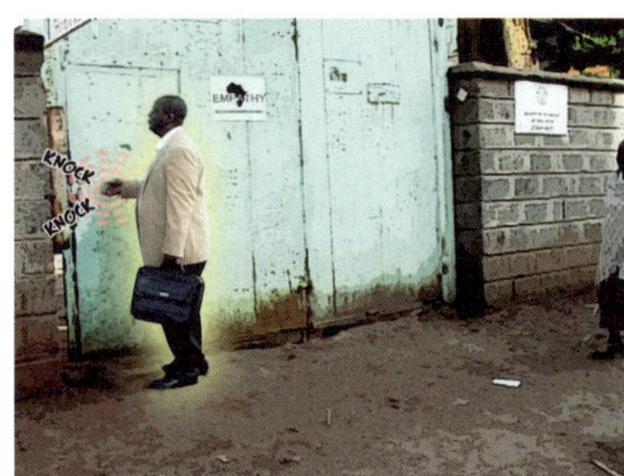

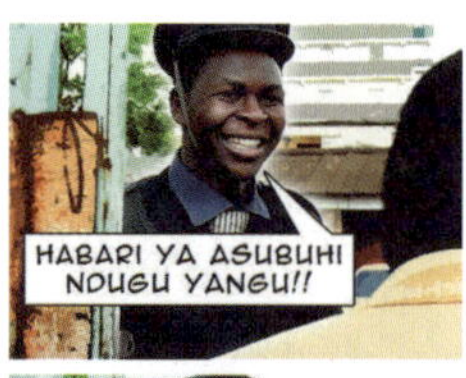

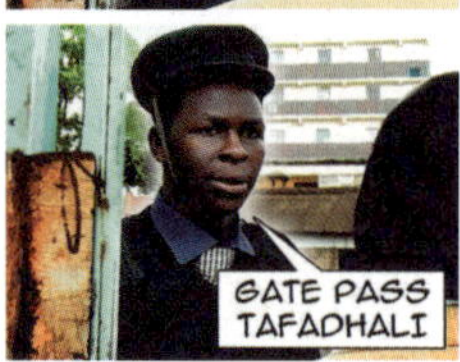

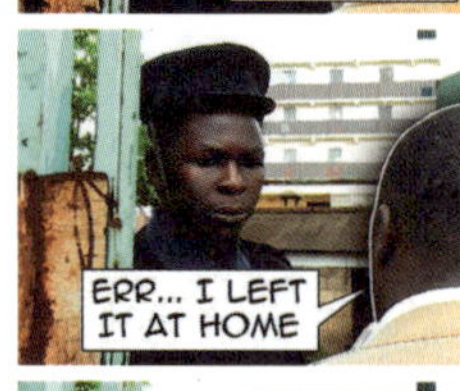

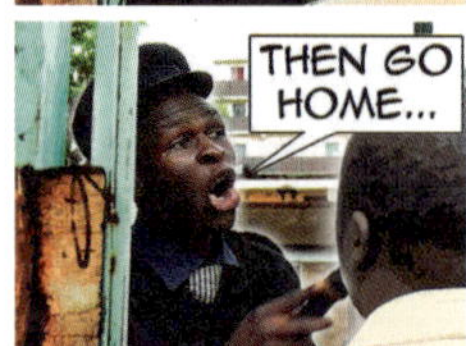

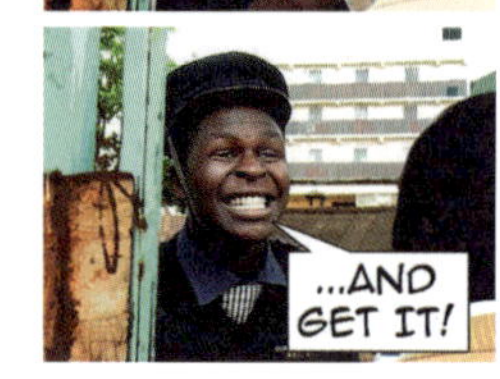

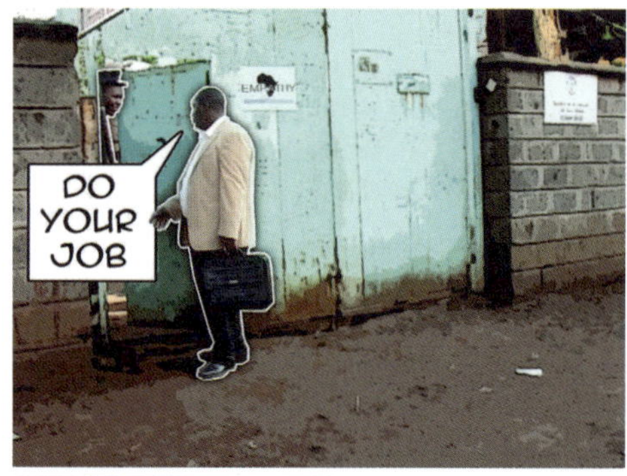

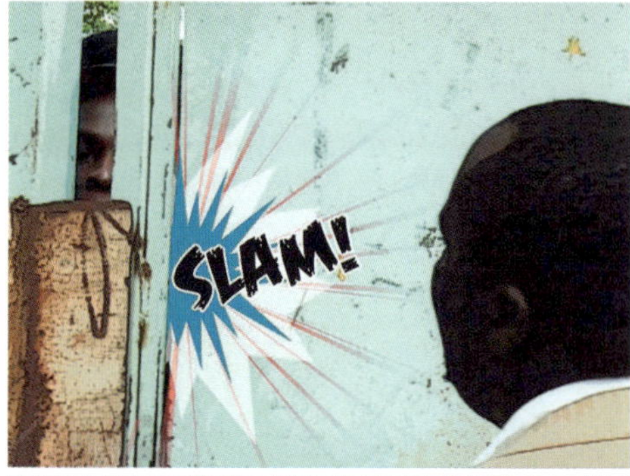

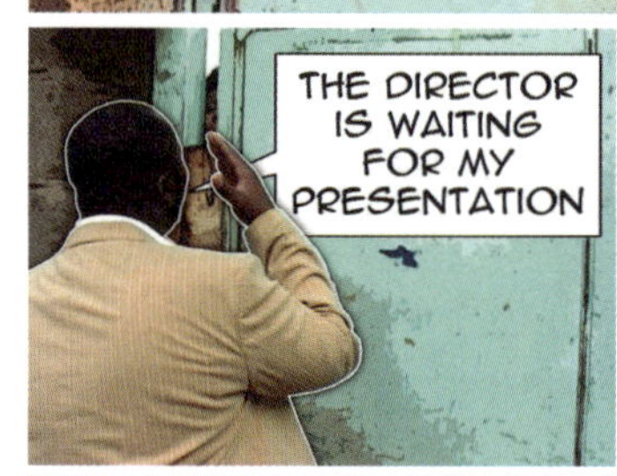

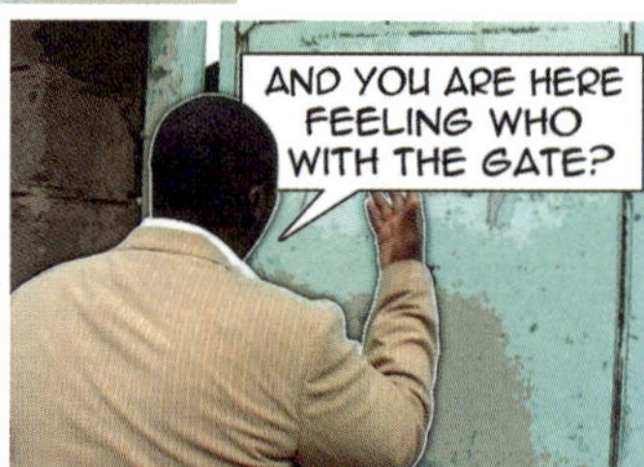

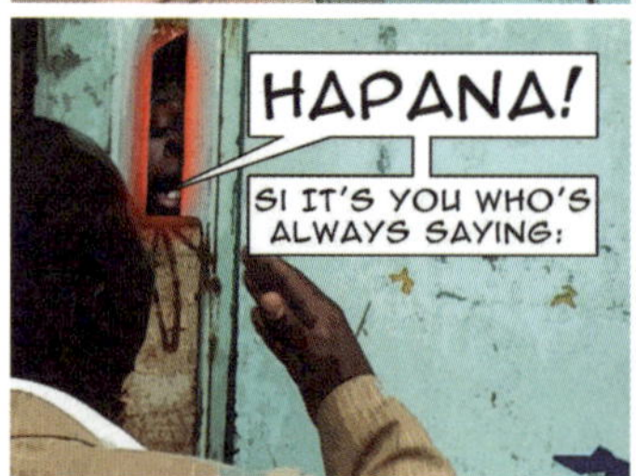

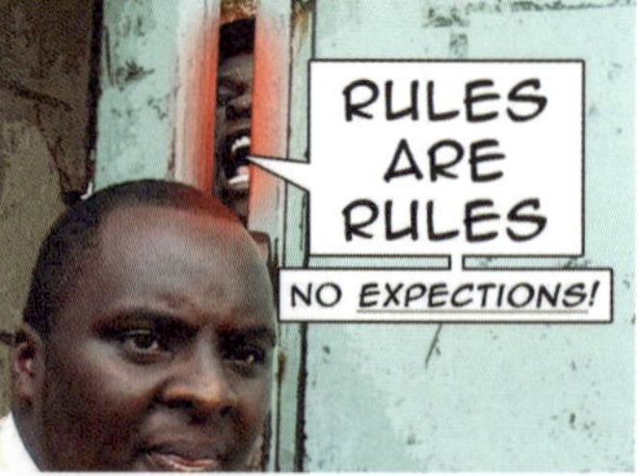

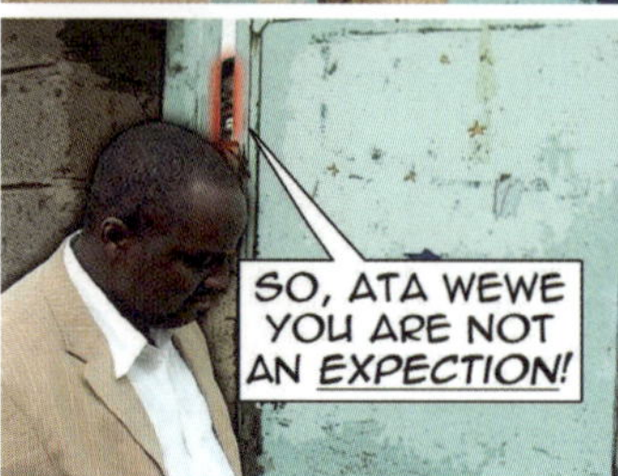

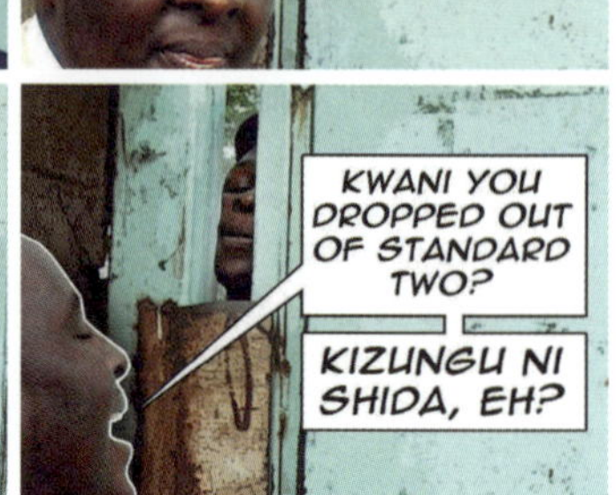

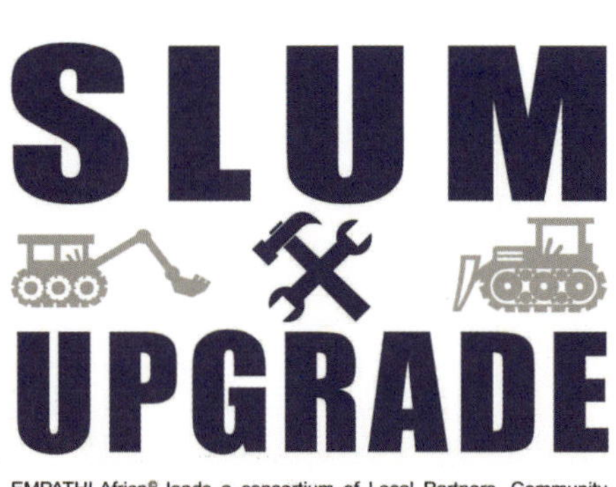

EMPATHI-Africa© leads a consortium of Local Partners, Community Organisations and Collaborators in the quest for a better future for all dwellers of Matherani slum: *The Largest Slum in Africa.*

Phase 1 will be implemented as of 1st December 2010 with the aim of:

Adequate Housing Provision
Livelihood Enhancement
Economic Resiliency
Capacity Building
Disease Mitigation

Esteemed Chief Karanja of Matherani, along with EMPATHI officials, will be hosting an UPGRADE RALLY at Matherani Chief's Camp, 3pm on Friday 21st May. COME SHOW YOUR SUPPORT!!!

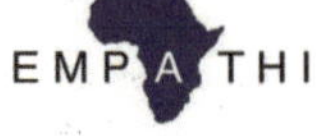

EMPATHI
EMPowering Africa THrough Innovation

UPGRADASION, CHRIS KING, POSTER, 2010

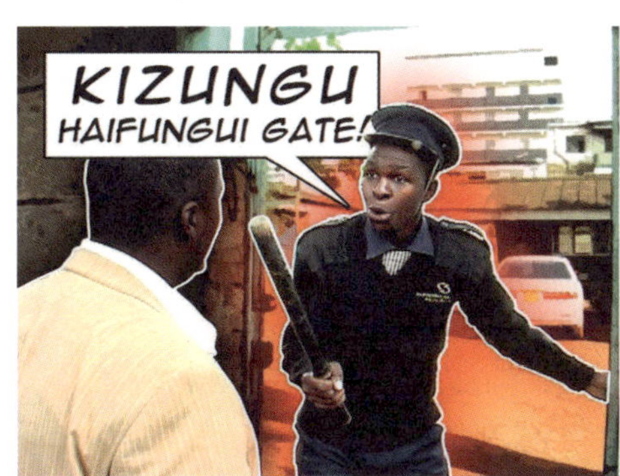

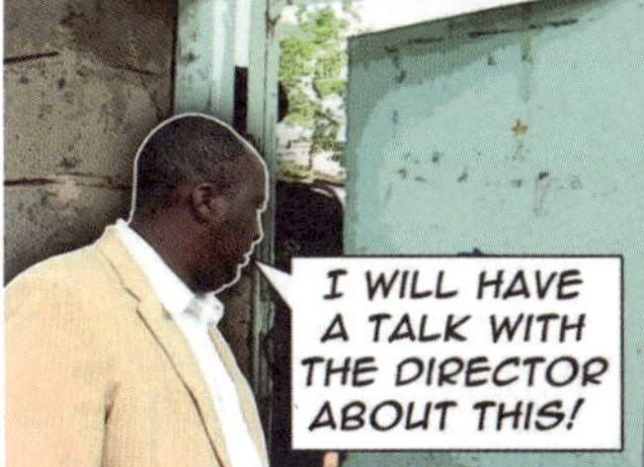

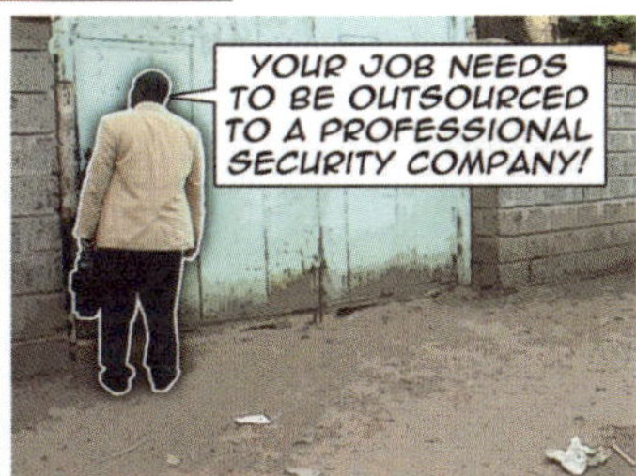

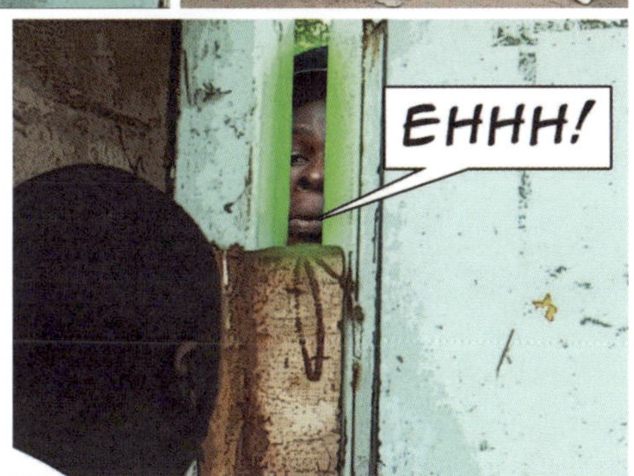

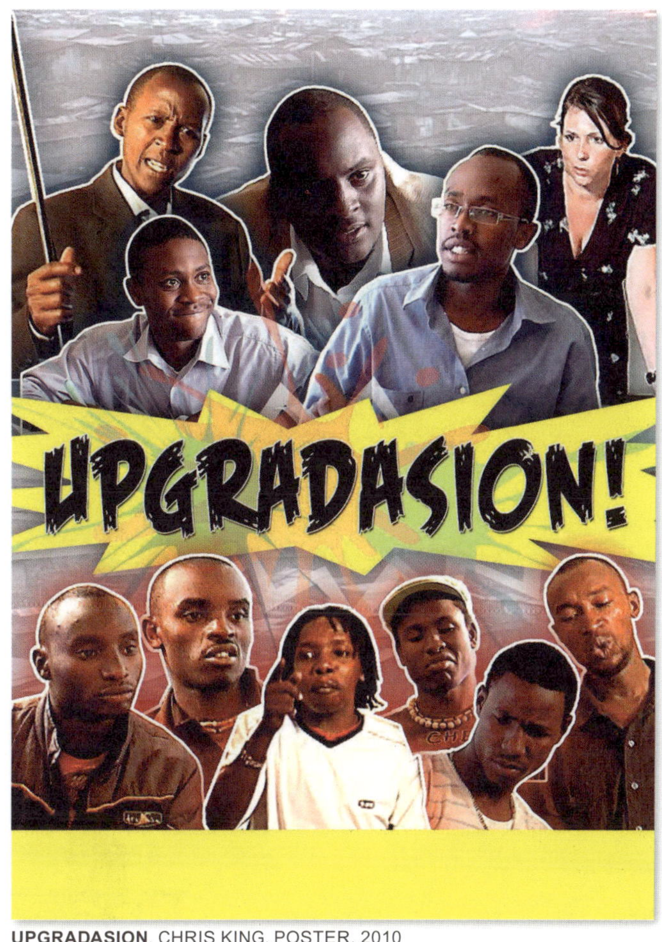

UPGRADASION, CHRIS KING, POSTER, 2010

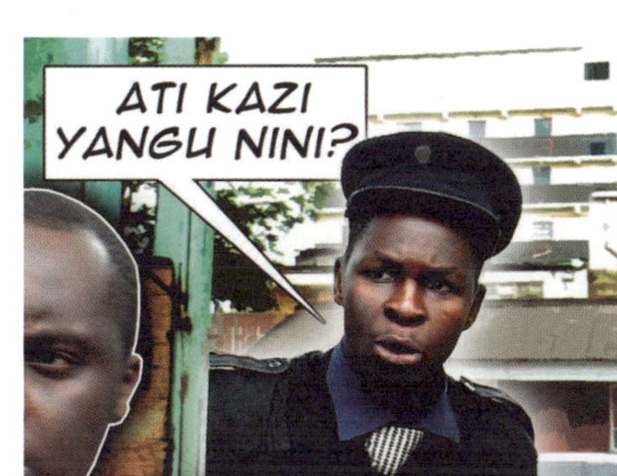

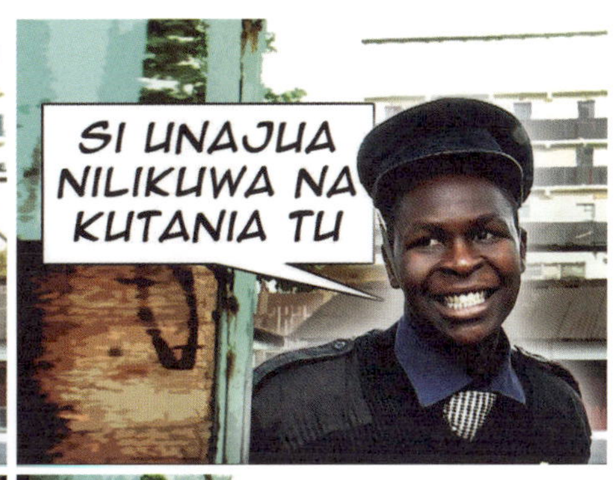

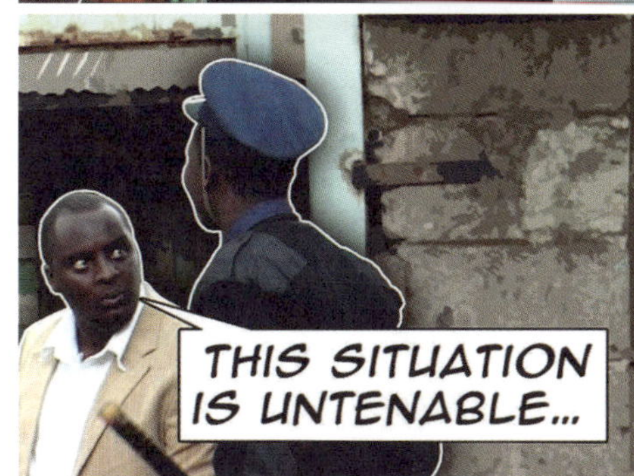

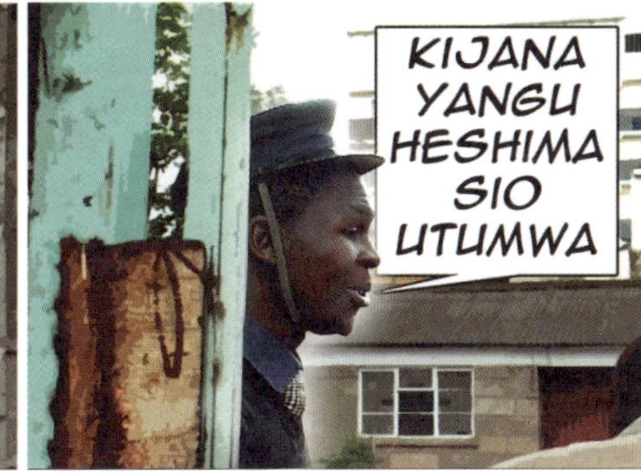

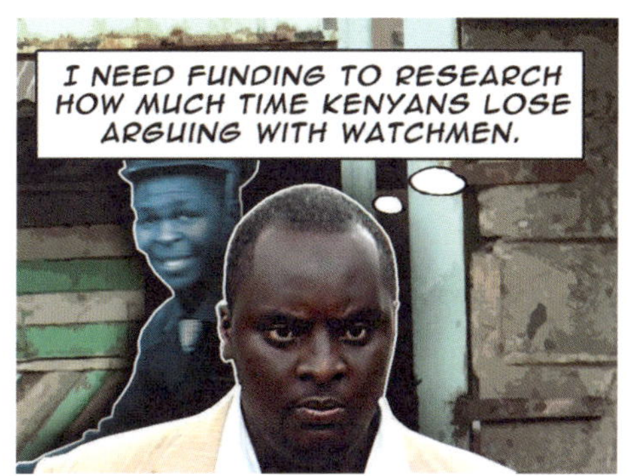

UPGRADASION, VIDEO INSTALLATION, 2010

Roomah

SAM HOPKINS

In his work, Nairobi-based artist Sam Hopkins addresses issues around public space. *Roomah* explores the culture of Nairobi's legendary *matatus,* the pimped minibus taxis, which from outside are most notable for elaborate designs and very loud music. However, *matatus* are above all sites where social and gender relations are negotiated and urban mythologies produced. In the *Roomah* sound installation, Sam Hopkins takes a closer look at the rumours circulating in and about *matatus.*

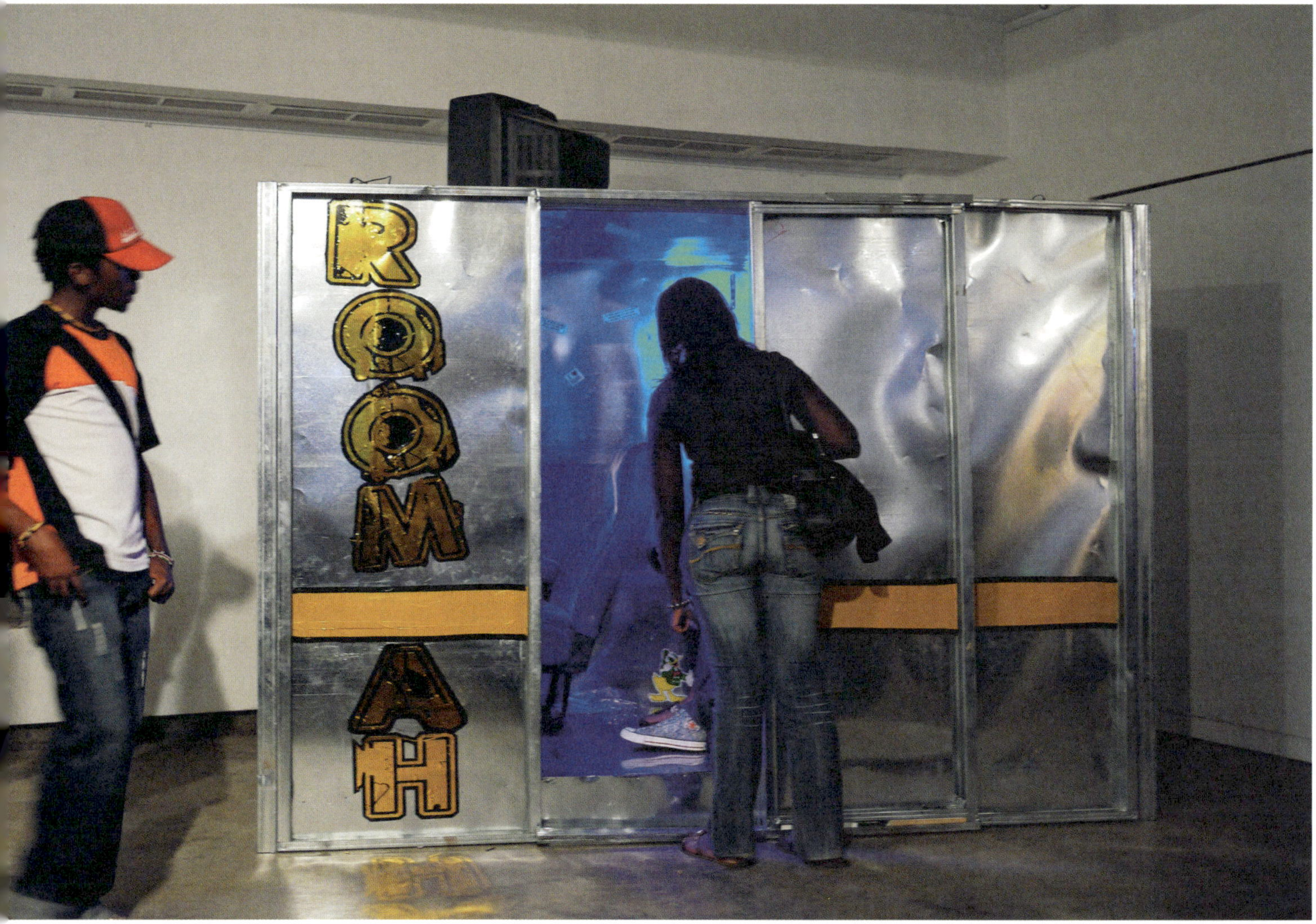

ROOMAH, INSTALLATION, 2010

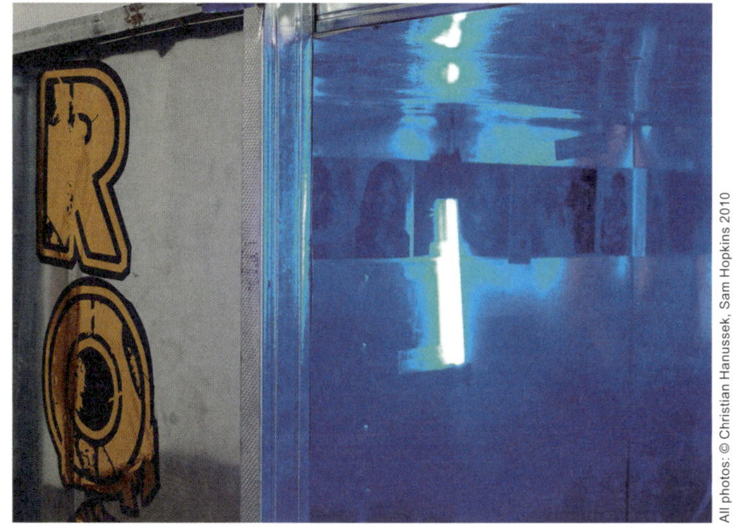

[01:00:00;00–01:00:11;15]
CN: Five years ago if you lived in 44 everyone respects you because you live where the best matatus in Kenya live.

[01:00:11;15–01:00:21;10]
SO: For example you find that Route 28 has the most boring cars, while 58 has best cars.

[01:00:21;10–01:00:26;25]
VN: 44 started it, but people from Buruburu have much money, so they better it.

[01:00:26;25–01:00:40;13]
SO: Ok, we have Baby, no. 9, and we have Baby Fat. So route 14 we have Baby Fat and the latest car which is now running the town is Chihuahua.

[01:00:40;13–01:00:48;03]
GO: There's this one it's called … it was called … Outlaw … I think it's from 58 also.

[01:01:45;01–01:01:57;28]
CN: And also there's another one, from Eastleigh. The first matatu to have a satellite dish. … it's called 'if you can't stand the heat, stay away from the kitchen'.

[01:01:57;28–01:02:06;01]
KI: And when u get inside it's like, it's amazing, because you can find as many as like 10 TV screens.

[01:02:06;01–01:02:12;00]
MM: So this vehicle has a big big screen. It's almost 100 inches.

[01:02:12;00–01:02:25;05]
KI: And some are like very big. You have like one big one, or three big ones.

[01:02:25;05–01:02:31;28]
MM: The whole window at the back, like emergency door, emergency window, is blocked. Big big movie.

[01:02:31;28–01:02:38;10]
KI: Sometimes the screens face outside. So when the traffic is there and you are walking you can just watch the videos.

[01:02:38;10–01:02:49;10]
MM: So for me what is most interesting is that when it's going away, you can't see the vehicle, it's totally black. You just see the movie and the little lights.

[01:03:40;13–01:03:51;07]
MM: I know in Buruburu, I have cousins there, girls, who just run around to town, and back to Buruburu, to town … Cos they think it's cool to be in a matatu with the best music.

[01:03:51;07–01:04:04;01]
GO: But you can just find a woman going to town, sitting with the driver, to and fro … to and fro … And she's just there … just changing, at that time it was the tapes.

[01:04:04;01–01:04:10;09]
CN: You know like, many of the girls they dropped school because of those matatus.

[01:04:10;09–01:04:15;17]
GO: Even girls loved the touts more than us.

[01:04:15;17–01:04:28;16]
CN: I know one of the girls, they have a lot of money … but she ended up to marry a makanga because the makanga has a nice matatu.

[01:04:28;16–01:04:32;23]
MM: … they wore the flashest clothes, they had the nicest girls …

[01:04:32;23–01:04:43;19]
CN: They are celebrities! Makanga of 44, Buruburu, Eastleigh, the makanga there are celebrities.

[01:04:43;19–01:04:53;14]
JM: …coz you know, I was young, so I used to enjoy sitting next to a girl, and it's a crammed matatu, so she half sits on me, and that felt really good … I hope I'm not …

[01:04:53;14–01:05:04;28]
CN: You know makangas have big mouths. So when a lady hear … I love that man with the big mouth, I'll be secure.

[01:05:04;28 - 01:05:18;19]
JM: But you know, that was cool, and we'd have conversations … and even older people would admit and say, 'Hey, I was sitting next to this girl and it was really cool' and you know, anyway … I think they enjoyed it too …

[01:06:31;22–01:06:37;01]
KI: … drivers I think … they are very professional. Coz it's like Safari Rally.

[01:06:37;01–01:06:44;03]
DM: I don't know where those drivers come from. But those people are just good! Those people are good yanni.

[01:06:44;03–01:06:47;22]
They are matatu drivers … not just drivers.

[01:06:47;22–01:06:59;05]
DM: It's like play station. If you sit in front of a matatu it's like play station … coz these guys do some wicked things and you think damm that's nice!

[01:06:59;05–01:07:11;27]
JM: A matatu is not just about driving, it's more than driving, coz you know, it's about manouevring, finding short cuts, the squads …

[01:07:11;27–01:07:26;16]
CN: So, if you see anyone driving no. 17, being a lady or a gentleman, believe that guy or lady is hardcore!

[01:07:26;16–01:07:31;12]
DM: It's not about the pretty matatu and everything, it's just the hardheadedness.

[01:07:31;12–01:07:38;10]
CN: Kayole, there's police … police that don't follow rules.

[01:07:38;10–01:07:53;09]
DM: They call them operations … operations is when the police just feel like we are short of dough, or something and they decide now to let's go and operate.

[01:07:53;09–01:08:05;00]
CN: And police there they are the same as the thugs. They wear the same, they talk the same. You'll know that he's a police when he arrests you.

[01:08:05;00–01:08:28;15]
DM: Matatus get away with it coz there are different rules for different matatus. If it's not owned by policeman, it's owned by maybe mungiki or it's owned by politicians … and if you try to trace it back to the person you claim owns it there's not, trace back to them.

[01:08:28;15–01:08:49;13]
Now that bus, the one with the satellite dish. It used to carry cops. Like one day the carjacker hijack it, they (police) remove their firegun. Ba bam … everyone slipped down … they gunned them down.

[01:11:52;18–01:12:07;05]
It's so cool, you see these sort of glittering specs, floating inside the matatu, and as people walk out you see the specs sort of light on their clothes … whatever you feel about it, that's innovation. Bottom line.

[01:12:07;05–01:12:18;27]
SO: Like, number 9, it's always full until you find people, students, hanging outside. Why? The music's there, the car is pimped and whenever you alight from that vehicle, you feel proud.

[01:12:18;27–01:12:27;25]
DM: It's something for me that I say if I become rich I would pimp a matatu and just have it … coz I love it.

[01:12:27;25–01:12:36;17]
JM: It's innovation, respected. That person is going ahead. That's innovation, and if you can't catch up you better say, 'hey, you got it'.

[01:12:36;17–01:12:43;14]
DM: Yanni, it's corrupt … but it's sweet.

TRANSCRIPTIONS: **ROOMAH**, 2010

Nairobizm

X-LIMITS DESIGN

X-Limits Design is one of the leading *matatu* workshops in Nairobi. This is where *matatus* are revamped to incorporate the latest design trends and technological developments.

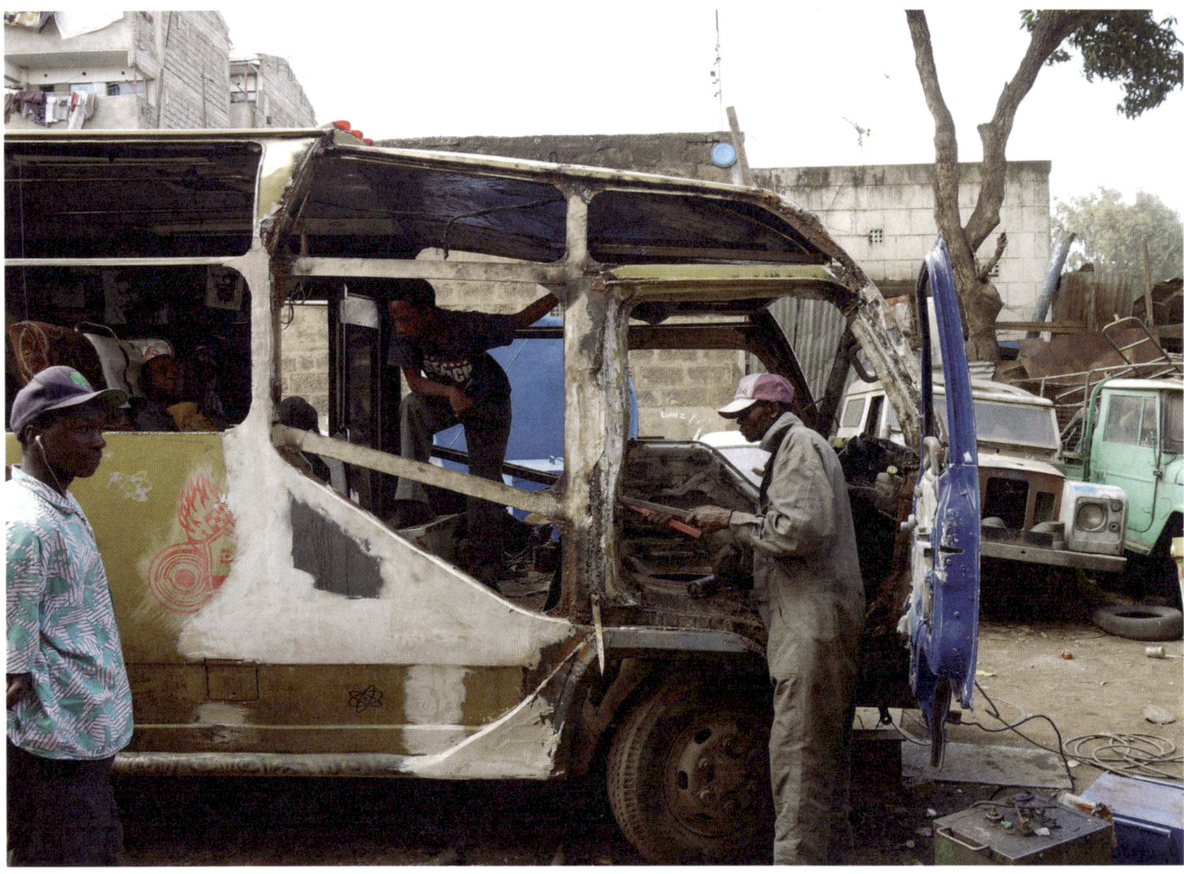

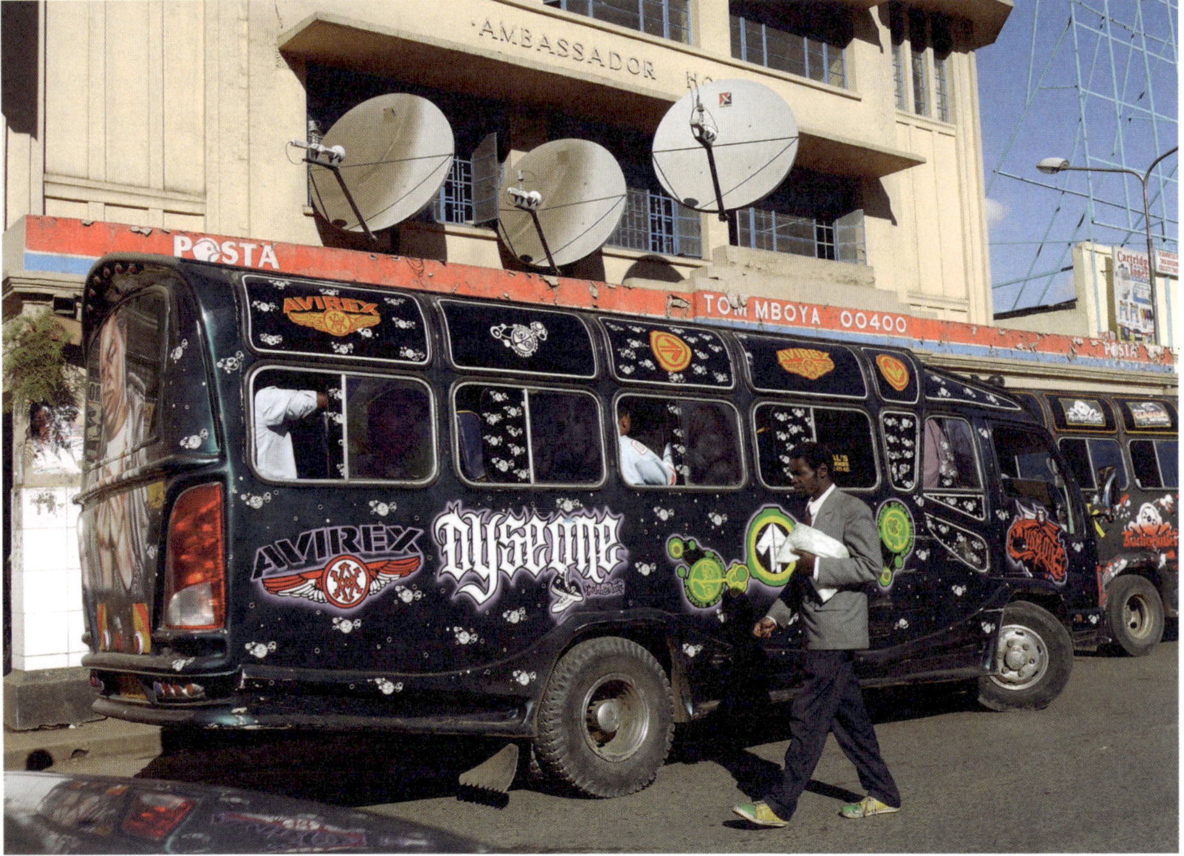

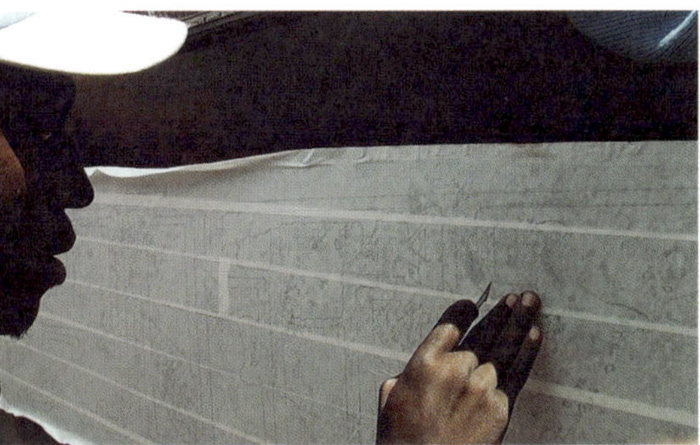

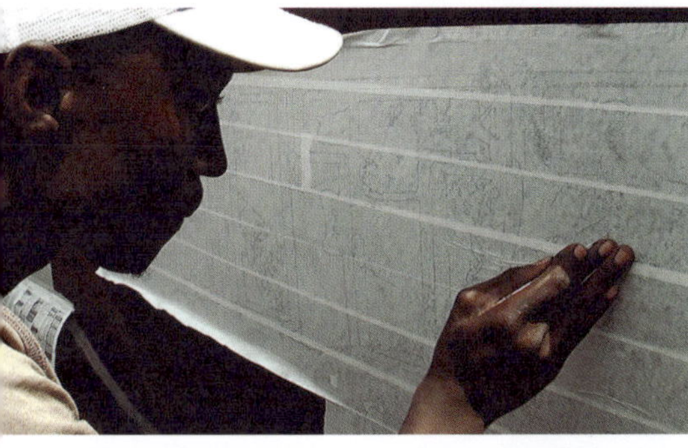

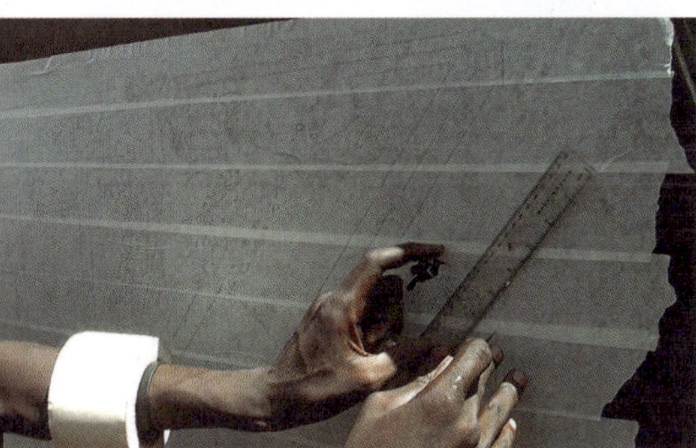

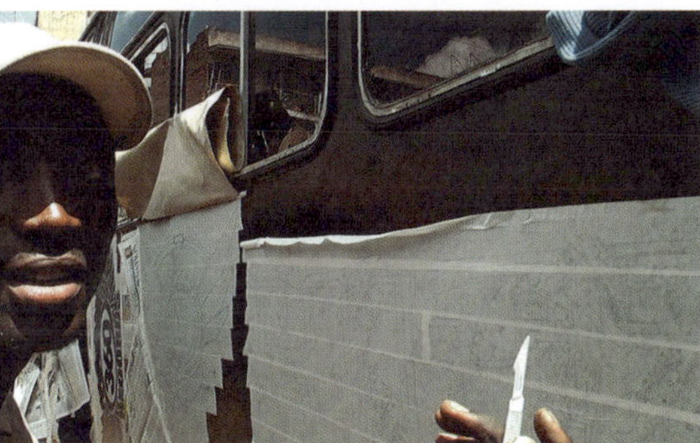

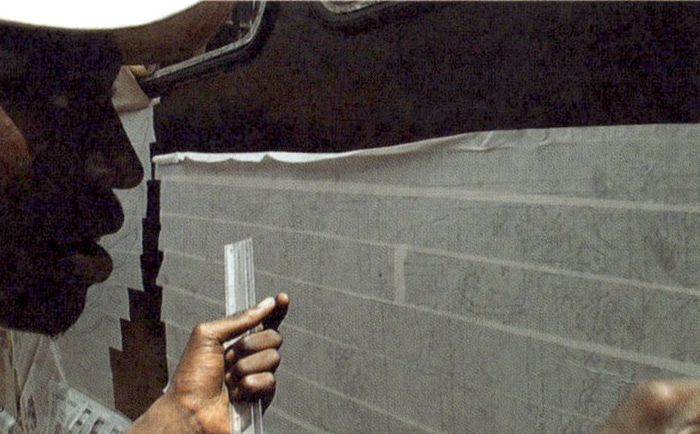

ZEDDY: Right now I'm doing the cutting; I use this blade, a scalpel, which is normally used in the operation theatre. I use it to get a fine, delicate cut, so the paint can run into it. First I cut and then take off the stencil so that we can paint.

CHRISTIAN: But before you start, you must get a picture from somewhere; as I understand you look on the Web for interesting images and then work them over.

ZEDDY: We enlarge them and then we do the drawing on the boards.

CHRISTIAN: What makes your style special?

ZEDDY: I can say we take our time to do this, you see, I'm going slowly, but the final work will be a great job, everybody likes it. We take our time, also by doing the research on the Net.

CHRISTIAN: How did you begin doing this? Did you do graphics before? Or was it through the *matatu* that you started?

ZEDDY: I started doing the *matatu,* because I grew up loving *matatus* – and I knew how to draw. That's how I got into that business.

CHRISTIAN: And you are just doing the graphic design? Do you have other specialists for the body-design and interiors?

ZEDDY: I also do the interior design, like putting pictures in the interior and making it look good. I also can do some other things but I'm specialised in the *matatu* graphics. It is an artwork and you have to be a special artist to do this kind of art.

CHRISTIAN: Does the cutting take most of the time or is it the spraying later?

ZEDDY: You can say that the cutting, the tracing of it and the enlargement take a lot of time. For the spraying I just use a compress and a gun. I mask where I'm supposed to mask so I apply different colours, so it's also kind of a long process.

CHRISTIAN: And for one *matatu* are there quite a number of people working on it?

ZEDDY: Yes, usually there are four of us and it takes – let's say – a week to complete the work.

CHRISTIAN: And that includes everything: the bodywork, interiors and the graphics?

ZEDDY: Yes, we are working like ten hours a day.

CHRISTIAN: And the *matatus,* they are kind of recycled? Do they get reworked from time to time?

ZEDDY: Yes, you can say they go for renovations.

CHRISTIAN: So how long would a *matatu* run, after you finished your work?

ZEDDY: Like one year.

CHRISTIAN: One year and then it gets reworked?

ZEDDY: Jah Jah.

The Way You Walk

LAURA HORELLI

In her video works, Berlin-based artist Laura Horelli primarily explores the interface between public and private spheres. *The Way You Walk* takes the artist back to places in Nairobi, where she spent several years as a child. She immerses herself in the world of the expatriates, the international specialists who work for the UN – as her own parents did – and for NGOs, and investigates the contradictions arising from their idealistic goals and the reality of their life and work.

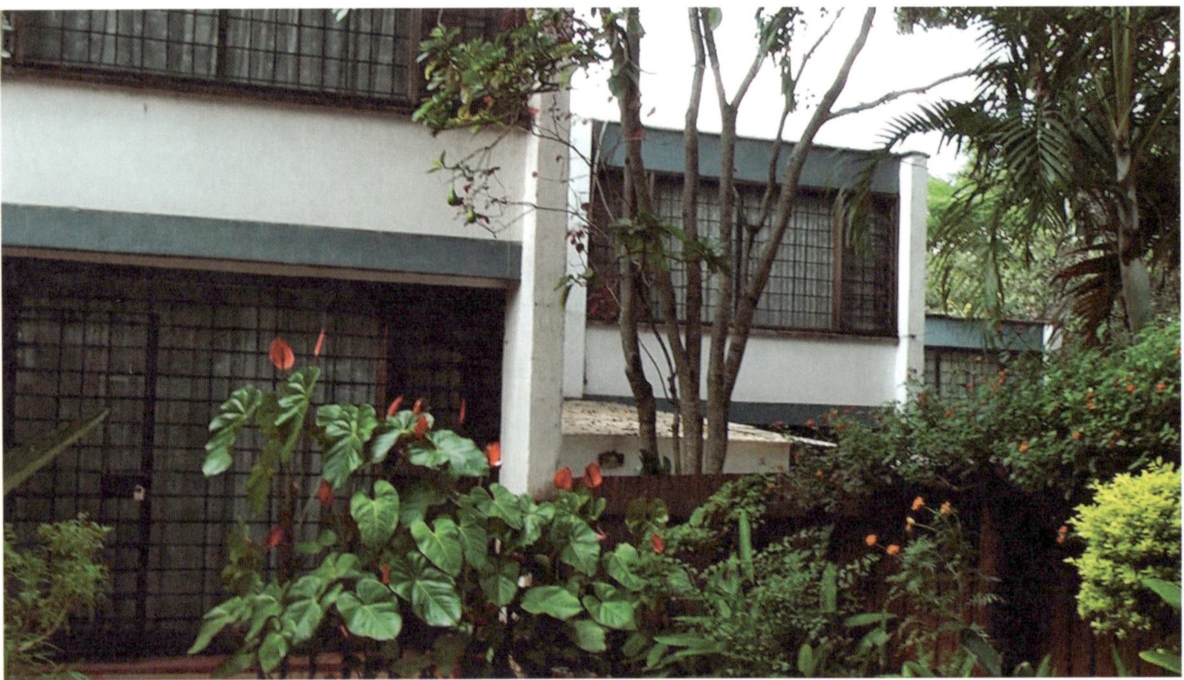

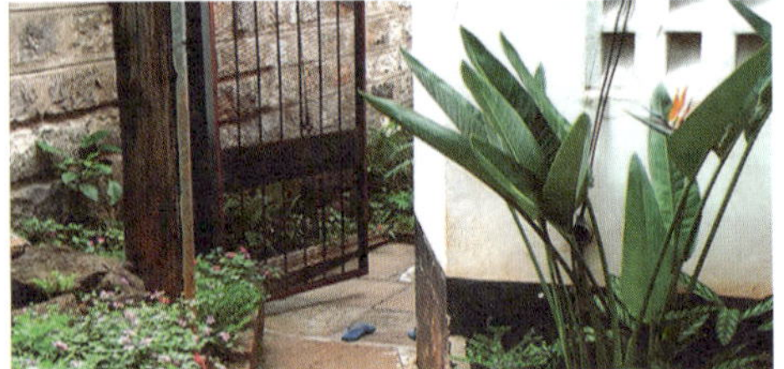

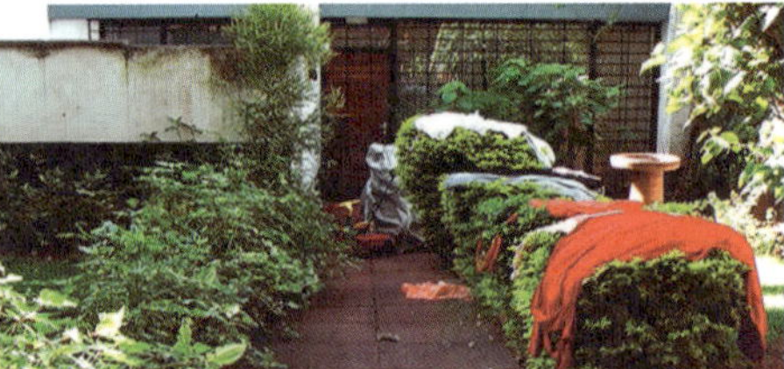

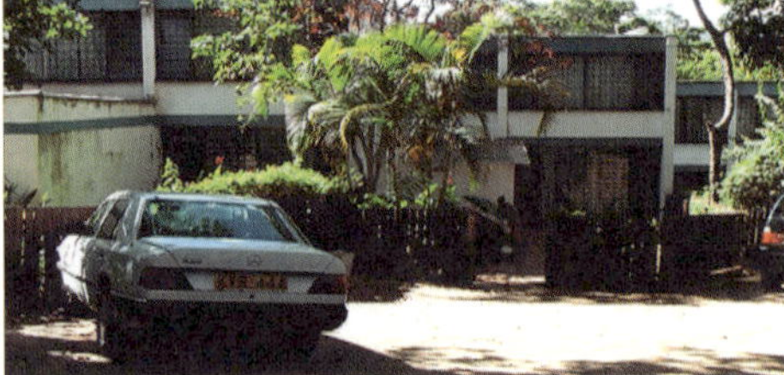

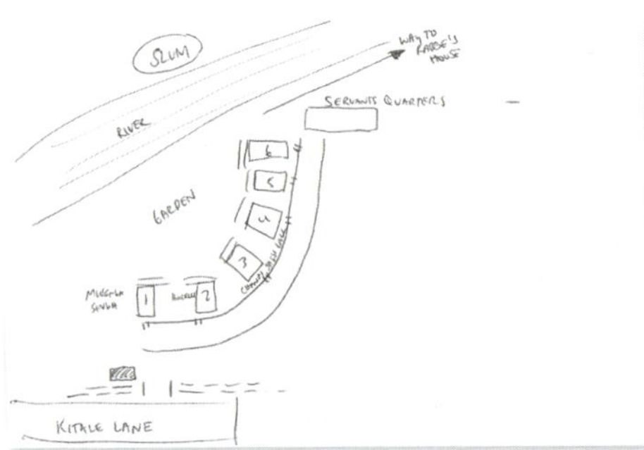

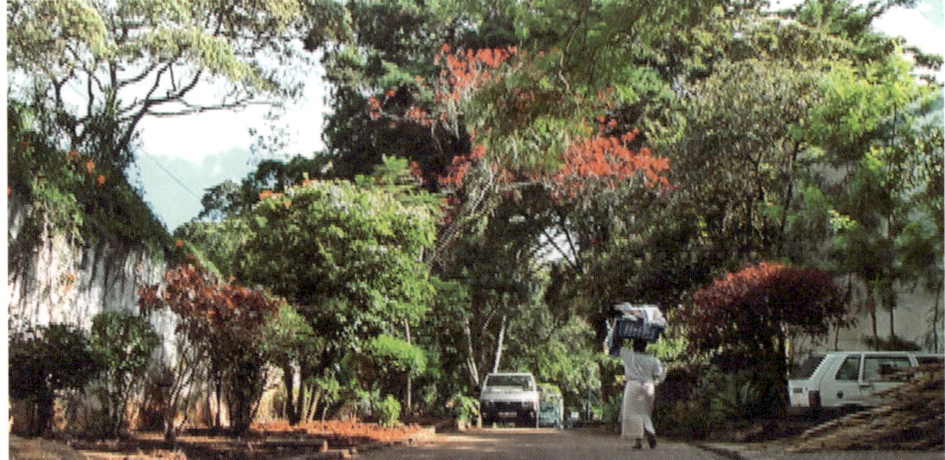

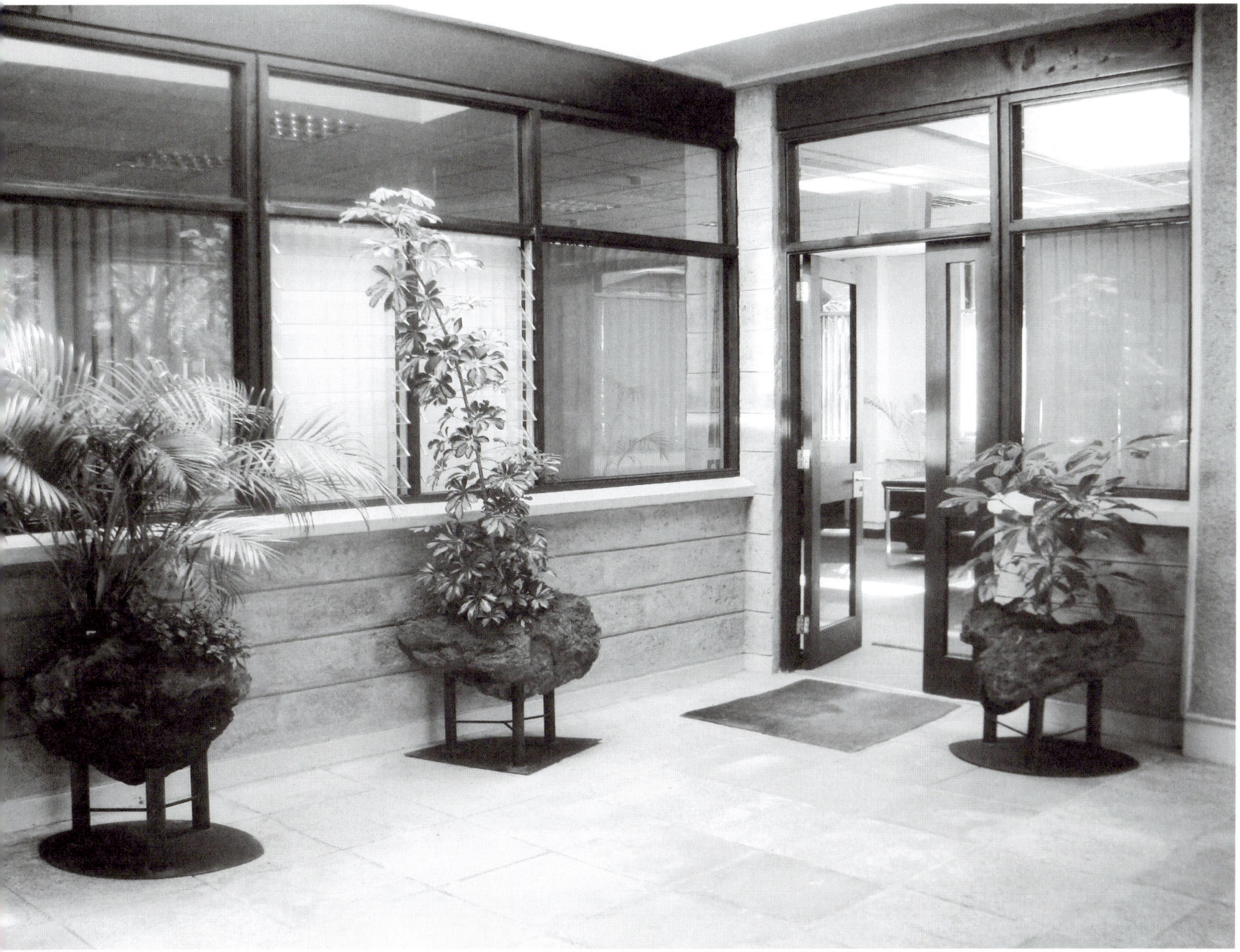

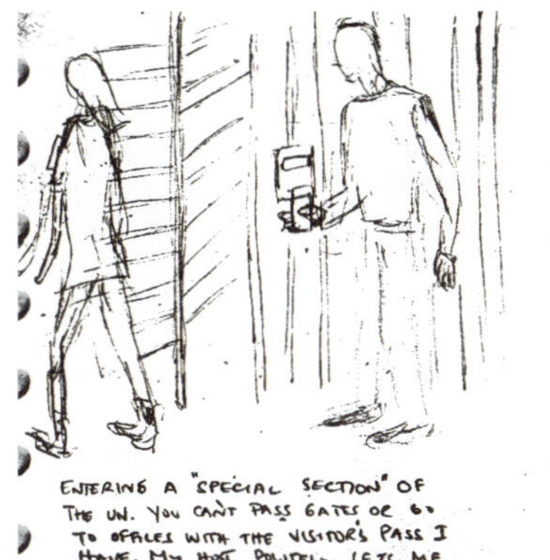

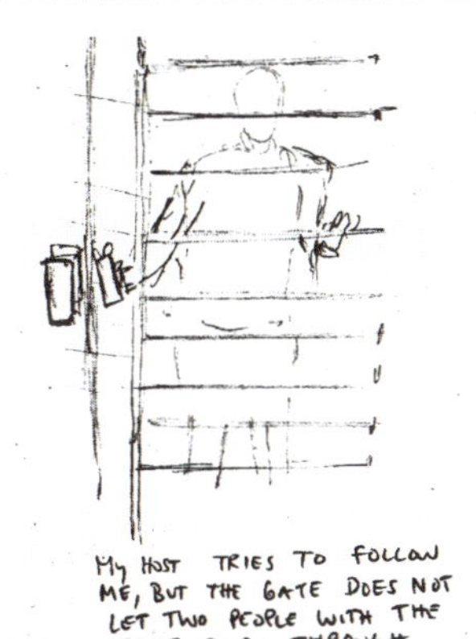

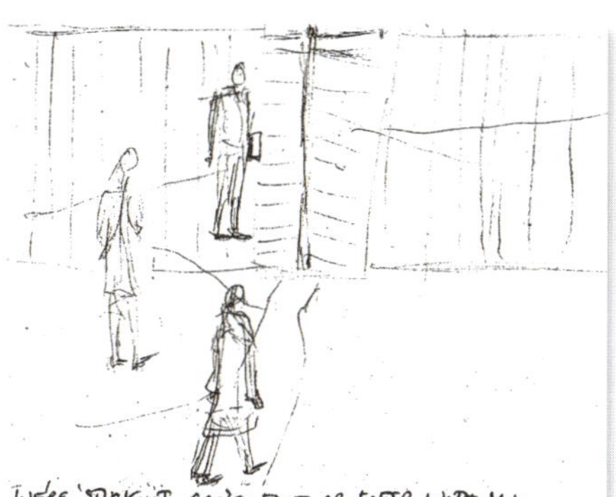

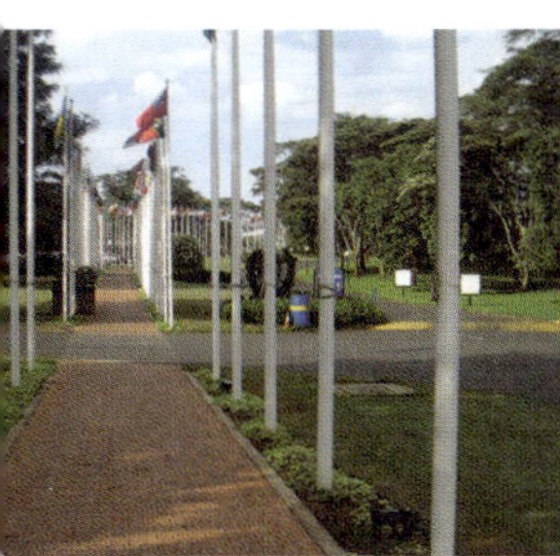

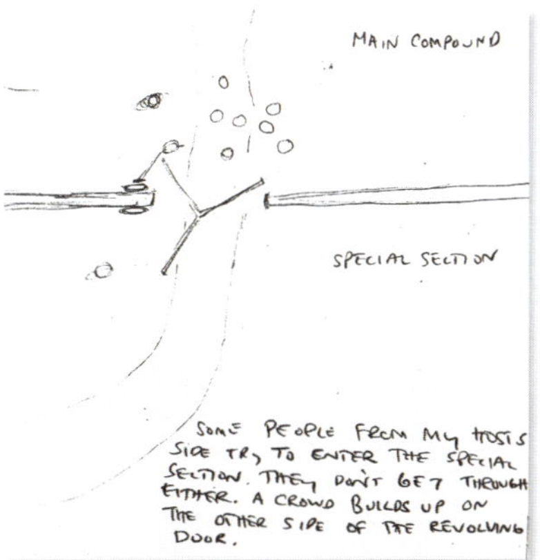

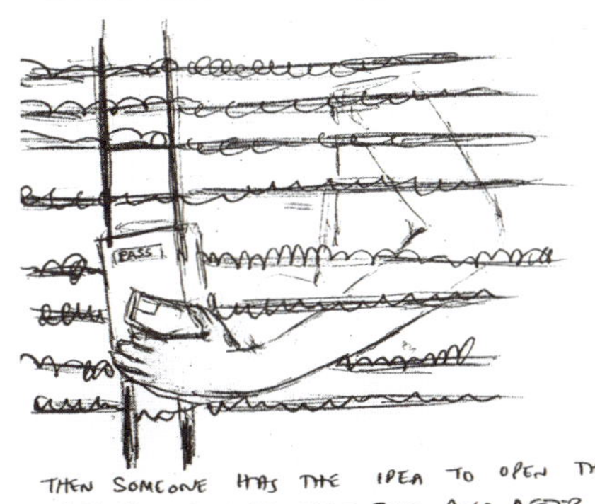

THE WAY YOU WALK,
PHOTOS AND DRAWINGS, 2010

Migration Shaping Nairobi
Case Studies of Specificity

ETH STUDIO BASEL

The ETH Studio Basel comprises Jacques Herzog, Pierre de Meuron, Manuel Herz, Shadi Rahbaran, Ligia Nobre and students from the Swiss Federal Institute of Technology Zurich (ETH) and Harvard GSD. The ETH Studio Basel is an Institute of Urban Research in the Department of Architecture investigating transformation processes in contemporary cities. One of its central theses maintains that the specific character of cities is further developed under the influence of globalisation.

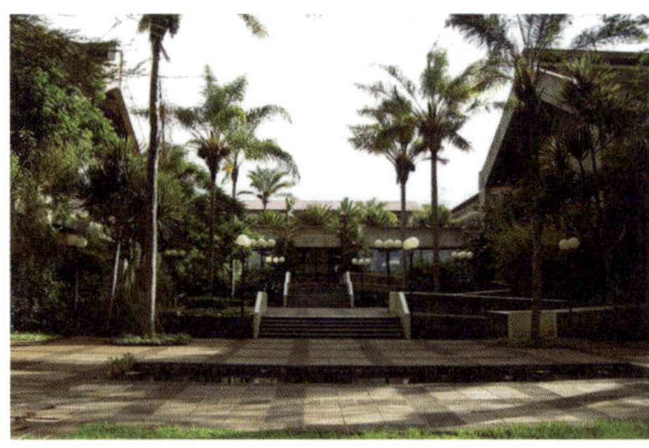

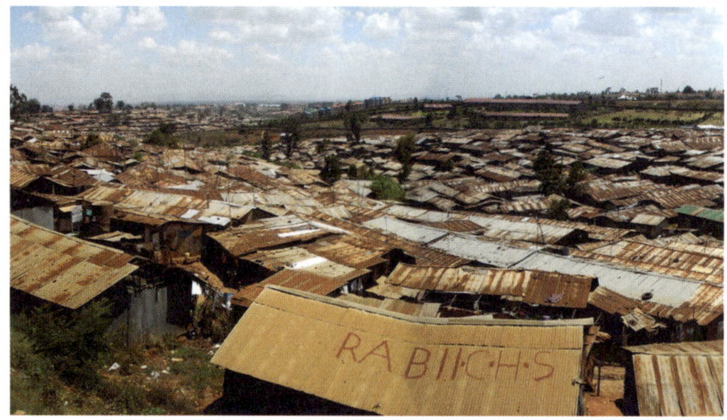

↑ Nairobi, as home to the headquarters of such UN organisations as UN-Habitat and UNEP in addition to numerous international NGOs, plays a leading role in the global economic and knowledge transfer network.

The rural population migrating to the city heads for slum areas such as Kibera. ↗

Nairobi was founded as a railway supply depot in the early 20th century. Under the influence of diverse waves of immigration, the city developed into the seat of the colonial government. After independence, Nairobi became one of the most cosmopolitan cities worldwide. The ETH Studio Basel research provides a basis for studying how different waves of migration impact the built city structure. →

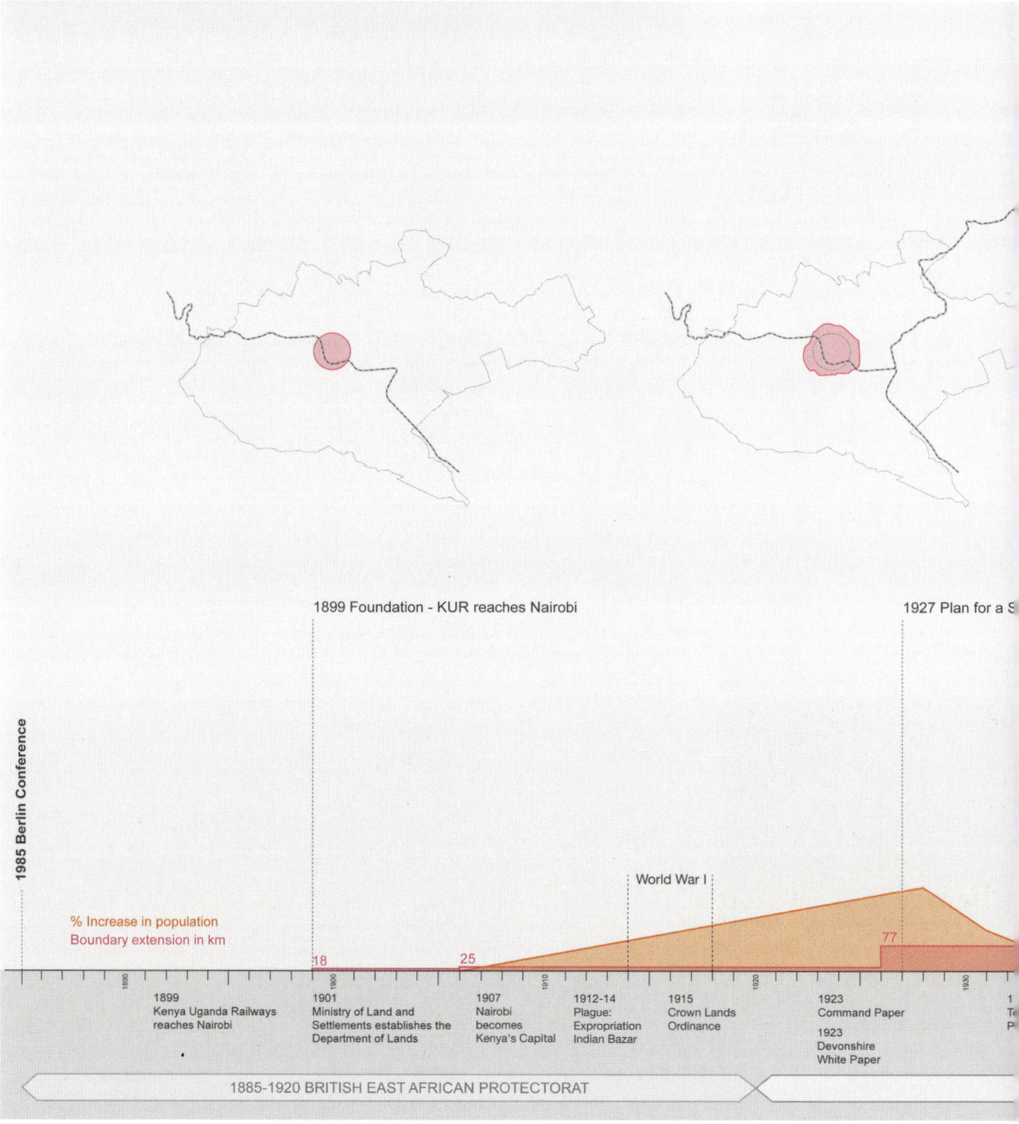

Thanks to an influx of Somali refugees, the city district of Eastleigh has developed into one of East Africa's leading trading centres. →

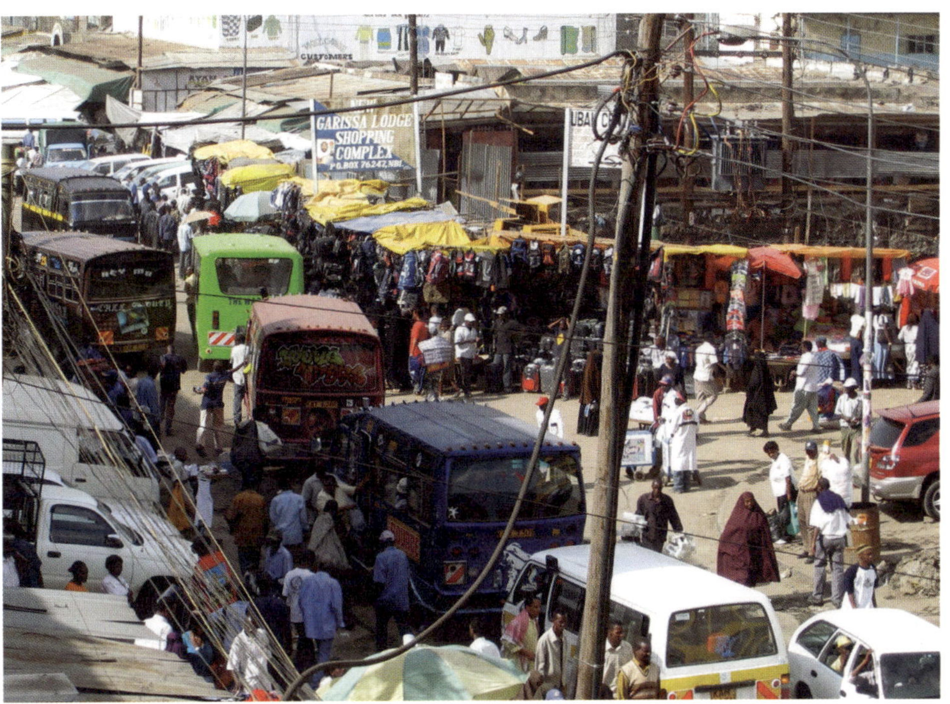

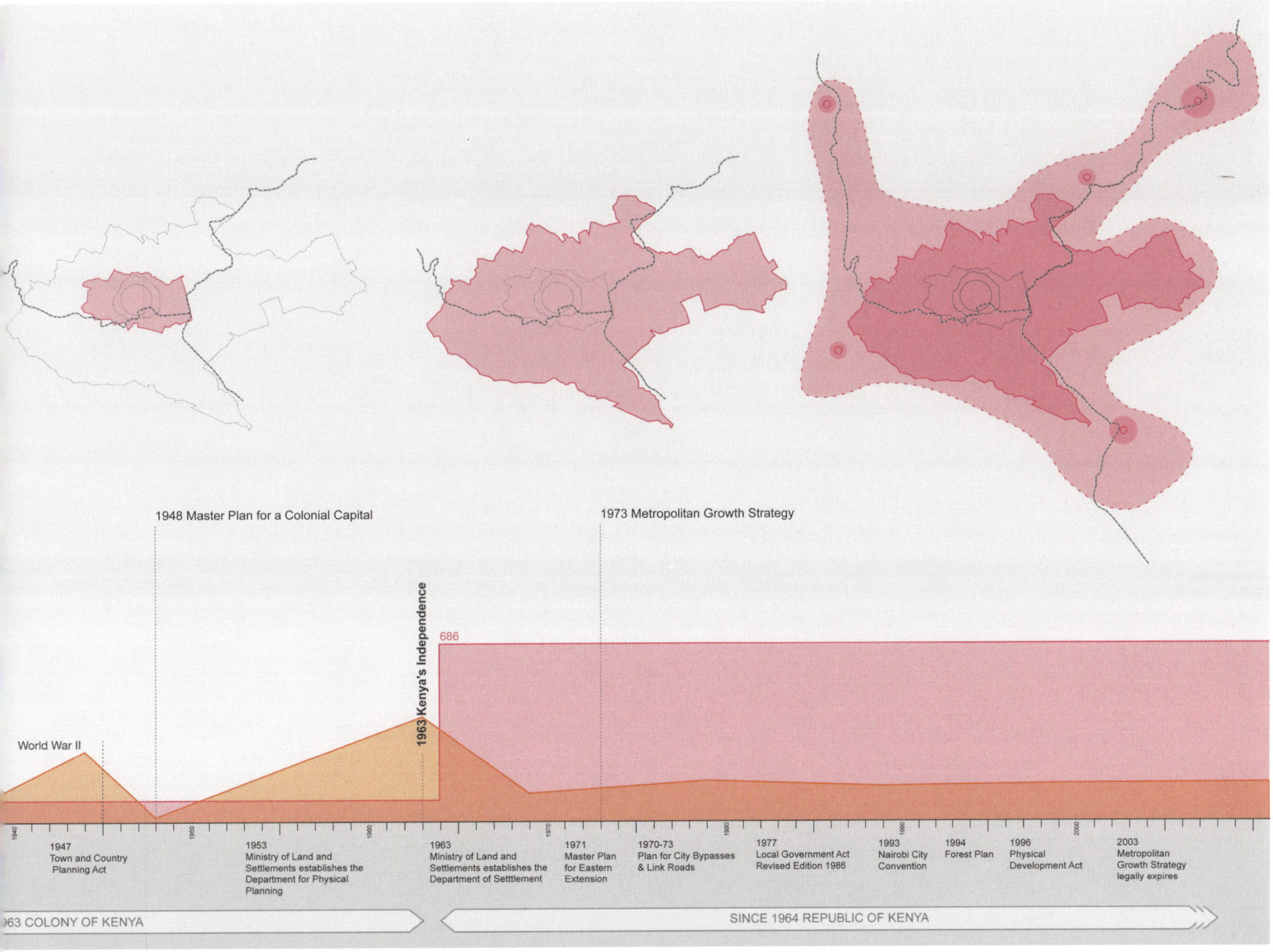

KINSHASA

Tropical Cowboys
Western Movies and the Making of Kinshasa's Bills

CHARLES DIDIER GONDOLA

Kinshasa, the capital of the Democratic Republic of the Congo, has had a long, uninterrupted tradition of interstitial youth peer groups, from the time the city expanded as a colonial economic hub in the 1910s to the present.[1] In the early 1920s, a Belgian Scheutist missionary railed against *"les gamins kleptomanes"* (child thieves) and *"les malandrins"* (scoundrels) who huddled in bands to roam the streets of the booming city and whose meanness brought mayhem to the urban colonial order.[2] With each passing year and decade, youth gangs would wane and wax, come and go, and with each new generation of gangs the same semiotics of violence wreaked havoc in what became one of the largest and most hybrid African metropolises. Today, the latest and most feared youth gang movement is known as *kuluna* (Kikongo for 'military platoon') and is responsible for a large number of petty crimes committed daily in Kinshasa. *Kuluna* has become a byword for insecurity, crime and havoc that even trumps references to armed soldiers or police force.

Starting in the late 1940s, a new youth movement spread in most of Kinshasa's townships (*quartiers*). It became the epitome of youth culture, masculinity and violence. The *Bills* or *Yankees,* as they dubbed themselves, accumulated over a period of two decades a cultural lexicon that supplied Kinshasa's youth cultures with all the paraphernalia that came to define them, from their cosmopolitan vernacular to their sartorial antics. What is known today as *Lingala ya ba Yankee* owes much to Hindoubill, a cryptic argot by design[3] that the *Bills* created in the 1950s to conceal many of their illicit activities. The *Bills* – a take on the eponymous hero, Buffalo Bill, whose films were widely distributed in the makeshift movie parlours that sprouted in every corner of Kinshasa's townships – drew their lifestyle from the Hollywood rendition of the bygone American Far West as well as from local cultural patterns that extolled the virtue of toughness, courage and resourcefulness. Drawing from a cultural studies' notion that youths' delinquency and social transgressions should be viewed as cultural practices through which they display agency[4], this author argues that Kinshasa's postwar culture of masculinity was mediated through the interplay of two phenomena: the *Bills'* tropicalisation of the 'Wild West' (as seen through Hollywood's lenses) on one hand, and their ritualisation of colonial and postcolonial violence, on the other.

The *Bills* were amongst a number of youth groups in colonial Africa that unyoked the lore of Western films from the screens to the streets. In Dar es Salaam, for example, "young scamps, living on their wits and without any form of parental or other control"[5] acquired "the idioms of tough speech, the slouch, the walk of the 'dangerous man' of the films; the ever-popular Western films teach [them] in detail the items of clothes that go with the part"[6]. Even rural Eastern Nigeria claimed its own 'cowboys' who decked themselves out in cowboy gear including "a gun worn in a belt, either a toy gun firing explosive caps, or a wooden model of a gun carved in the village"[7]. In exchange for "small presents of drink, food, and money" they would entertain the village on Saturday evenings with their elaborate repertoire of folk songs.

Yet, the *Bill* was one of a kind, creating a masculine ethos that continues to suffuse Kinshasa's culture. The movement also cut across socio-economic, ethnic and linguistic lines. Finally, the importance of the *Bills* cannot be overstated for not only did their culture of violence mobilise and channel "the social forces from the margin," by contributing to "the establishment of one of the most powerful forms of expression in Kinshasa's flamboyant popular culture"[8], but it also acted as a wedge that opened Kinshasa's townships to the possibility of insurrection,[9] thus accelerating the decolonisation process.[10]

Hollywood Meets the Colonial Tropics

Immediately following the war, emerging gangs of "tropical cowboys" staged ritualised violence in Kinshasa's *quartiers* in an attempt to erect and police the borders that defined youth, gender and masculinity. Inherent juvenile fascination with violence may have served as a backdrop to the emergence of Kinshasa's gangs, but it was a postwar colonial urban context, which could no longer shield *l'empire du silence*[11] and hold global cultural flows at bay, that provided the impetus. As Belgian missionaries took centre stage in dealing with neutralising and channelling this youthful exuberance through films, they also unwittingly sowed the seed of indiscipline and subversion. Of all the films promoted by the missionaries, including Tarzan movies, Chaplin's tramp character and war propagandas, it was the Hollywood renditions

1   For a partial genealogy of youth groups in Kinshasa, see Tshikala Kayembe Biaya 1997, Les paradoxes de la masculinité africaine moderne. Une histoire de violences, d'immigration et de crises, *Canada Folklore* 19: 89–112

2   Raphaël de la Kethulle 1922, Le vagabondage à Kinshasa, *Congo, Revue générale de la colonie:* 727–730

3   Roland Kiessling and Maarten Mous 2004, Urban Youth Languages in Africa, *Anthropological Linguistics* 46/3 (Fall): 303–341, Sesep, N'sial Bal-Nsien 1990, *Langage, normes et répertoire en milieu urbain africain: L'indoubil,* Québec

4   Mary Bucholtz 2002, Youth and Cultural Practice, *Annual Review of Anthropology* 31: 525–552, here p. 531

5   Andrew Burton 2001, Urchins, Loafers and the Cult of the Cowboy: Urbanization and Delinquency in Dar es Salaam, 1919–61, *Journal of African History* 42: 199–216, here p. 201

6   Burton (2001), p. 214

7   Paul E.H. Hair 2001, The Cowboys: A Nigerian Acculturative Institution (ca. 1950), *History in Africa* 28: 83–93, here p. 84

8   Filip De Boeck and Marie-Françoise Plissart 2005, *Kinshasa: Tales of the Invisible City,* Tervuren, p. 38

9   Charles Didier Gondola 1999, La contestation politique des jeunes à Kinshasa à travers l'exemple du mouvement 'Kindoubill' (1950–1959), *Brood & Rozen, Tijdschrift voor de Geschiedenis van Sociale Bewegingen* 2 (January): 171–183

10 Charles Didier Gondola 2009, Tropical Cowboys: Westerns, Violence, and Masculinity among the Young Bills of Kinshasa, *Afrique & Histoire* 7 (May): 75–98, here p. 77

11 Belgian writer and anti-colonial activist Oscar-Paul Gilbert coined this expression in his 1947 scathing depiction of Belgian colonial society in which Africans chafed under a system reminiscent of South Africa's apartheid; *L'empire du silence: Congo 1946,* Brussels.

of the Far West lore in such films as *The Lone Ranger*[12] that had, by far, the most lasting and dramatic impact on the young people of Kinshasa. The idea behind the promotion of these genres was, of course, predicated on colonial racism. Congolese supposedly lacked subtlety and sharpness that were required of most viewers to enjoy unadulterated and uncensored cinematographic experiences. Time and again, Europeans, be they colonial officials, missionaries or private entrepreneurs, derided the natives' inability to enjoy, let alone comprehend, films other than *Tarzan* and the like.[13] As one Belgian missionary bluntly opined, "cinematographic conventions confuse him; psychological nuances escape him; and the rapid flow of sequences overwhelm him"[14]. Thus, cowboy films seemed tailored to the native's primitive mind and became the staples of most theatres. Missionaries went to great length to censor these movies and expunge, for instance, scenes in which white male characters behaved badly or scenes in which hapless white females fell prey to lewd and unknowable Indians or other non-whites.[15] Yet, in spite of their best effort to purge these films of scenes of violence and incivility, they remained potentially powerful and were likely to stir into action an already volatile group of disenfranchised youth. These European film promoters were so blinded by colonial racism that they brushed aside any thoughts that such images could impact these young audiences differently than they had anticipated. When it became evident that youth violence in several Congolese cities directly followed patterns exhibited in Western films and gave way to tightly structured gangs, colonial reports attempted to address the crisis. In 1953, for example, a colonial report lamented the "real danger" caused by Western films on such immature and emotionally feeble minds.

A New Vernacular of Urban Violence

The *Bills* drew much of their lifestyle from what they considered authentic cowboy culture although, as we will examine further, their lifestyle was also shaped by local rituals and individual idiosyncrasies. In 1957, a Belgian colonial district commissioner delineated in what came to be known as the *Rapport Bissot*[16] much of what the *Bills* stood for: gang activities, including marauding, drug trafficking and consumption, and sexual debauchery.

Cowboys du Farwest

One of the main gangs investigated by Bissot, *Cowboys du Farwest,* grouped teenage boys who had fallen through the cracks of the colonial regimen, along with adolescent girls, most of whom had been smuggled by pirogue from Brazzaville. This gang had formed in 1950 on Kinshasa's eastside, first as a bunch of rebellious youngsters. Many amongst these tropical cowboys had

been reduced to eke out a living well within the confines of illicit activities. Long hours spent watching cowboy movies and reading comic books fostered among them a camaraderie and collective fascination with the aesthetics of violence.[17]

As the band grew in size so did its predacious activities, which included smoking marijuana, inter-gang feuding and stealing. Gang members met regularly at the hangout of their leader, an older teenager named Bulu who styled himself "Windy".[18] There, these disillusioned youths found temporary solace and recreated a sense of belonging which the city had failed to afford them. Following a practice that became widespread in most gangs in the late 1950s, *Cowboys du Farwest* subjected its new recruits to hazing and initiation rites involving oath taking and smoking marijuana. It was only after successfully passing such rites that the new gang member could choose a sobriquet from the vast lexicon of authentic and imagined heroes. Nicknames such as John Wayne, Gary, Opalon (Hopalong), Buffalo, Pecos, Mijos Bill and Sinatra, to name a few, gained popularity among the *Bills*.

By 1956, *Cowboys du Farwest* was eradicated due to colonial repression. Some of its members were deported back to their villages while others had been forcibly whisked away into juvenile detention wards. Yet the *Bill* movement continued unabated. Many other gangs ebbed and flowed to such an extent that in the late 1950s most townships had developed a "gang problem" that neither colonial repression nor parental control could curb. By then, the movement had touched large juvenile segments that found social acceptance as gang members.[19]

Beyond Ethnicity

If ethnic affiliations did not account for the way gangs formed and acquired their own singular identity, it was instead an acute sense of place, loyalty and belonging to a *quartier* that shaped the *Bill* movement in 1950s Kinshasa.[20] As they vied for "territories" within the African townships, some gangs managed to control an entire *quartier,* as the following case of Camp Luka exemplifies. In the late 1950s, Camp Luka exhibited few urban features, clearly indicating a phenomenon of *villagisation* that became the quintessence of the postcolonial urban experience.[21] Located on Kinshasa's southwestern periphery, it consisted entirely of scantily built brick-and-tin shacks. It had no running water, sewage system, or electricity and least of all no zoning regulations or public amenities. Most of its residents were latecomers to the city and, therefore, had little choice but to occupy the wooded, undeveloped areas around the capital illegally. Camp Luka was also peculiar in another respect. The majority of its residents were ethnic Bayaka from the Kwango province, a group that had been relegated to the lower rungs of the colonial ladder. Bayaka took on the menial jobs that earlier migrants shunned. They could

12 Invariably, informants cite *The Lone Ranger* or rather its French version, *Le dernier des fédérés,* as the quintessential Western film that influenced them the most. The Lone Ranger first appeared as a radio series in 1933 and was later (1949–1957) adapted to a television series that starred Clayton Moore as the masked Texas Ranger who rides along with his faithful, laconic Indian sidekick, Tonto, to enforce law and order and set up cliffhanger shootout denouements.

13 Francis Ramirez and Christian Rolot 1985, *Histoire du cinéma colonial au Zaïre, au Rwanda et au Burundi,* Tervuren, p. 277

14 L. Van Bever 1952, *Le cinéma pour Africains,* Brussels, p 6

15 Gondola (2009), p. 83

16 L. Bissot 1958 (1957), *Étude qualitative sur la délinquance juvénile à Léopoldville,* Léopoldville

17 Some theatres were operated by bar owners and adjacent to these alcohol outlets. Once the show was over, the crowd, including some older *Bills*, would move into the bars and indulge in drinking extravaganzas; Vieux Fantomas, interview with the author, Kinshasa, 10 July 2005.

18 Jacques Babillon 1957, *Léopoldville. Étude générale du problème de la jeunesse autochtone,* Louvain, p. 119

19 Sesep puts at 60,000 the number of young people between twenty and twenty-five who considered themselves gang members; Sesep (1990), p. 21.

20 More than anything, soccer tournaments provided many opportunities for different township teams to match up their skills and display their loyalty to their neighborhood.

21 De Boeck and Plissart (2005), p. 34

be found carrying water, collecting and selling firewood and, more commonly, working as domestics for the emerging African petit bourgeoisie. Few of them had even a veneer of colonial education and could not therefore jockey for the subaltern positions left vacant for Africans to fill within the colonial administration. Camp Luka's ethnic homogeneity and its heightened ethnic identity did not hinder the emergence of *Bills*. Not only did a gang form there, but it also operated without any reference to ethnicity although, as can be safely assumed, many of its members were young Bayaka. They shared a common *Bill* culture with other township gangs, a culture that put them at odds with the ethnic solidarity that older Bayaka cultivated in Camp Luka. They clashed with other gangs not so much because of ethnicity but as a result of their marginalised urban experience. Thus, what set Camp Luka's gang apart was its loyalty to a locality rather than its allegiance to a particular ethnicity.

Performing the Male Body

Although *Bills* greatly contributed to the creation of a township culture and life that ran counter to the prevailing ethno-nationalism, and often served as "big brothers" to younger residents, both boys and girls, some of them also actively engaged in fiendish sexual behaviour. Desire to enhance one's status as a gang leader or to inflate one's reputation as a tough guy ("*dur des durs*") led *Bills* to practices that might be considered as ancillaries to sexual violence.

Kintulu

One such practice was called *kintulu* (bodybuilding) and those *Bills* who faithfully partook in it were known as *Apollons*. In the late 1950s, young *Apollons* flexing their muscles in their hangouts drew huge crowds of onlookers, some sitting on top of walls, others perched in trees to have a better view of these formidable scenes. Many in the crowd were girls who, just as the younger boys, were attracted by the capers, the bulging torsos and the raucous atmosphere that these sessions of *kintulu* exhibited. Pictures of *Apollons* provide a glimpse into this underworld, revealing the tight connection between *kintulu* and masculinity, especially as it intersected with notions of courtship, seduction, and sex appeal. In one of them, taken by Congolese photographer Jean Depara at the *quartier* Citas (or Casamar) in 1963, a young *Apollon* is depicted in a typical bodybuilding pose with

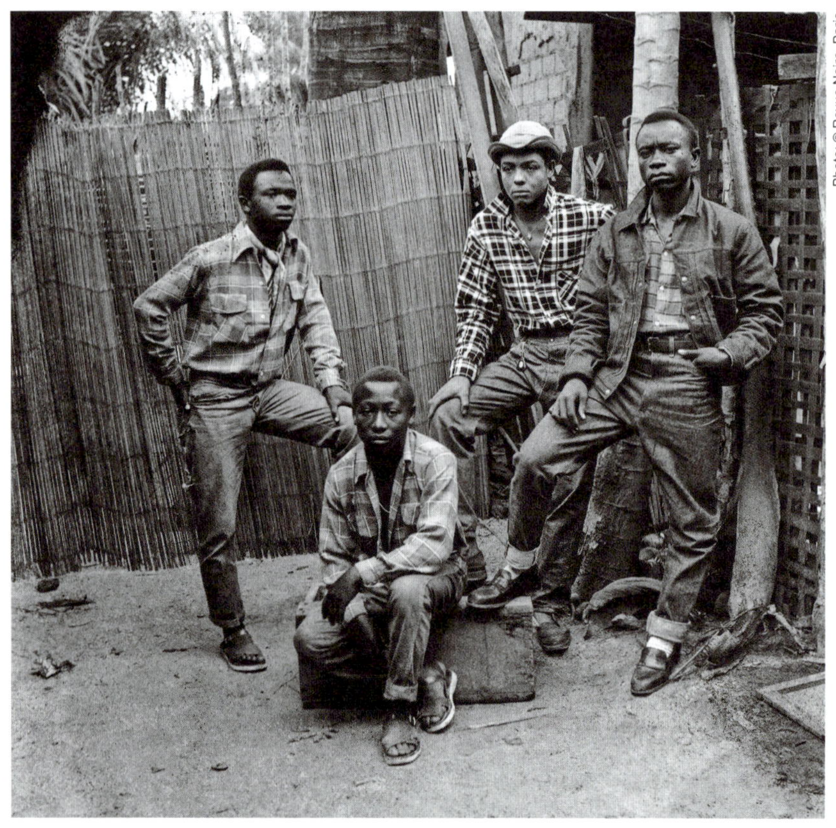

BILLS, JEAN DEPARA, CA. 1960

two young women flanked on each side. The gender dichotomy is all too apparent. The two women are fully clad in 'conventional' urban attire that conceal the shape of their bodies and enhance their femininity. They shyly gaze at the *Apollon* with unfeigned admiration and meek demeanour as though he had cast a spell on them. By contrast, the *Apollon* looks larger than life with his naked upper body flexed to the extreme. It is indeed this juxtaposition of the male naked body exuding confidence and his two female companions cast in 'traditional' feminine postures that enhance the young *Apollon's* masculinity. Yet, what the picture intends to do goes beyond a mere glorification of maleness. Depara's composition recycles many familiar themes. There is no doubt that Depara, himself a former *Bill*-turned-photographer, intended, perhaps unconsciously, to portray the *Apollon* in his best role, as a protector of female chastity and a rampart against intruding predators. It is precisely for this reason that his two female companions are not lusting after his body but rather looking straight in his eyes in gratitude. However, this seemingly innocuous composition reveals also another theme when one looks at the *Apollon's* interaction with his two female companions. He is holding the hand of one of them while staring intensely at the other one, suggesting troubling sexual innuendos.

Kamô

In addition to *kintulu, Yankees* partook in a magical ritual known as *kamô*. Although physical strength and stamina undoubtedly played a role in one's ability to get the upper hand in *billings* (Hindoubill for 'fights') between rival gangs, it was *kamô* that was thought to determine the outcome. For a little less than five francs, *Bills* would go to older *Bills* (*Grands Bills*) such as Degazin, Debarron, Eboma, Moruma (known as "*le roi du kamô*") and Verre Cassé (Broken Glass) in search for 'traditional' medicine to increase their physical abilities. Many would cross the river to neighbouring Brazzaville not only to indulge in a drinking spree[22] but also to have potent medicine applied to their wrists, ankles, thorax, or temples. Fantomas, who turned twenty-two in 1950, occasionally went to see a certain Makoubounzou in Brazzaville to have powerful *kamôs* for just one CFA franc[23] while Jean Christian Matabul, who was nicknamed "Poison" because of his unmerciful tantrums, only trusted a certain Aimant (Magnet) for strong *kamôs* and serious training.[24]

The *kamô* ritual involved two distinct procedures. First, minor incisions (*nzoloko*) would be made on the aforementioned parts of the body. For example, two or three (rarely more) parallel incisions

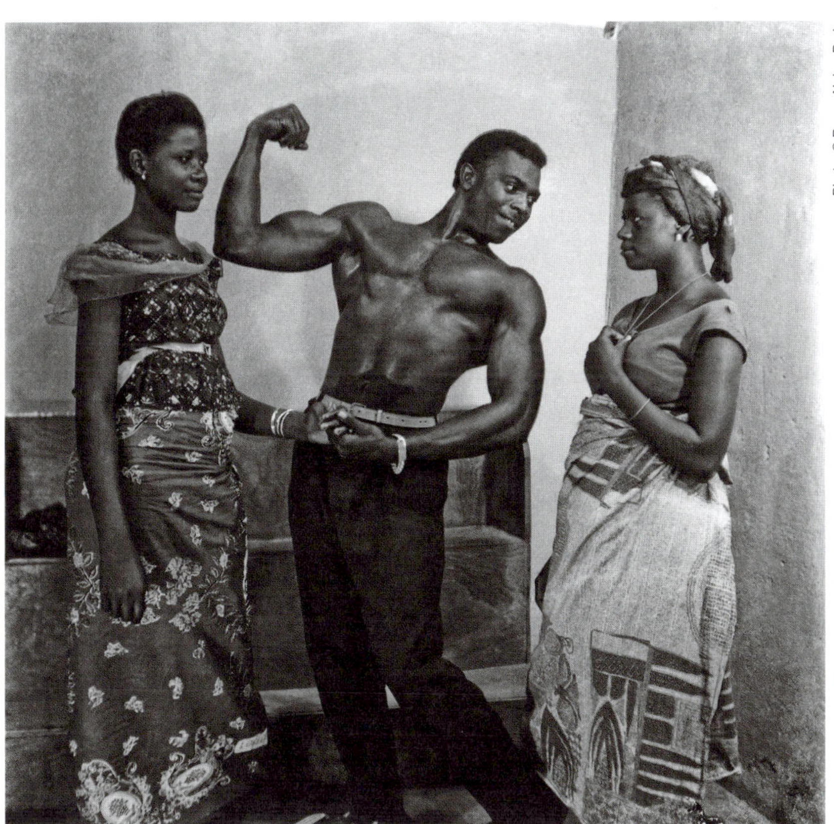

APOLLON, JEAN DEPARA, 1963

22 On 23 July 1932, the general government passed a decree authorising Congolese natives to consume alcohol sold in bars operated by "coloured people" (*personnes de couleur*). However, unless they were *immatriculés* (registered) or holders of the carte du *mérite civique* they were not allowed to drink wine until the 18 April 1955 decree. Congolese across the river, in neighbouring French Congo, had no such restrictions; Charles Didier Gondola 1997, *Villes miroirs: migrations et identités urbaines à Brazzaville et Kinshasa 1930–1970*, Paris, p. 256

23 Vieux Fantomas, interview with the author, Kinshasa (Kasa-Vubu), 10 July 2005

24 Jean-Christian Matabul (aka Poison), interview with the author, Kinshasa (Lemba), 23 July 2005

measuring each half an inch could be done on one's wrist resulting in small bloodletting. Then, depending on who cut the *kamô* or the type of strength one was seeking, a particular mixture of burnt powder (*nkisi*) would be applied to the open wound. Degazin invariably used a speck of leopard fur, lion's nails, gorilla pelt, the bone of a river fish known in Lingala as *mina,* and some tree bark. When a customer requested, for instance, the ability to strike devastating head butts, Degazin would also throw in razor blades, nails and needles and cook the whole thing in a small cast-iron skillet until most ingredients had been reduced to ashes. Others mixed in the bone of a snake's head. After the hot mixture had cooled down, ashes would be applied to the *nzoloko*. Degazin, who has been at the head of Congo's organisation of tradi-practitioners for the past two decades, learned the trade as a child and perfected it as he watched Eboma (whom he affectionately called "*Vieux Ebo*") cut *kamôs* in *quartier* Mofewana (or Farwest). By the time Degazin got into his own profitable business, his following grew at such a rate that he quickly eclipsed his old master.

Degazin and some of the people who flocked to him to receive *kamôs,* including Nimy Mayidika (former *Bill* and President Mobutu's chief of staff), lionise *kamô* as the quintessential masculine brand. All young people, even the "brainy" such as Jean-Jacques Kande[25], Bomina Nsoni[26], Paul Kabaidi[27], and Nimy Mayidika himself resorted to *kamô*. "We all cut *kamô*", recalls Bomina-Nsoni, and "we all believed in its power."[28] The power of *kamô* was both mystical and physical as it shielded and sanctuarised the masculine body. Immediately after administering *kamô*, Degazin would break bottles on the head of his clients, who by then had already fallen into a trance. He would then have them swallow broken glass. Some would bring packs of brand new Gillette razor blades, which they would crush with their teeth, chew and swallow, sometimes in front of bewildered crowds.

Ingesting nails, needles, bullets, razor blades, broken glass and other sharp objects has its counterpart in local "witchcraft" rituals. For the *Bills,* internal absorption of sharp objects was also intended as an act of defiance and magical fortitude that mirrored external cutting (*nzoloko*). Furthermore, it embodied a vision of manliness which, as Mansfield reminds us, evokes the Greek word ανδρεία, a term the Greeks used also for "courage, the virtue concerned with controlling fear"[29]. *Kamô* was less about physical invincibility than it was about taming one's inner vulnerability by daring to do the unthinkable.

Zoumbel

Indeed, *kamô* provided many *Yankees* or *Bills* the same exhilarating sensations that marijuana did and, perhaps, a justification for some of their most wayward antics. Both cutting *kamô* and smoking marijuana became the two compulsory rites of passage in Kinshasa's *quartiers* in the 1950s. Yet, smoking marijuana (*zoumbel* in Hindoubill), because it remained a concealed activity beyond the law, provided even a stronger bond among *Yankees*. To be admitted in any formal or informal gang of *Bills,* one had to partake in this social rite. When I asked former ambassador Bomina Nsoni why older *Yankees* in his *quartier* coaxed him to smoke his first joint, he told me that they resented his intellectual airs and wanted him to be like them. "The focal point [of the movement]," he added, "was marijuana. The true *Bill* was into marijuana" ("*Le vrai Bill était dans le chanvre*"). Even Father Jeff de Laet, the white Belgian missionary who befriended the *Bills* and endeavoured to steer them away from interstitial nihilism and back into the Catholic fold, had to go through the *zoumbel* ritual in order to be accepted by the *Bills*. Père Buffalo, as the *Bills* had nicknamed him, set up a JOC (*Jeunesse Ouvrière Chrétienne*) Centre on Movenda Avenue in Ngiri-Ngiri. There, he gradually wooed *Grands Bills* Billy and Néron who were active in Dynamique and Mofewana *quartiers,* respectively. He quickly learned Hindoubill, compiled a rudimentary thesaurus and, at one point, even mused about translating the Bible into Hindoubill. The sight of this young Scheutist missionary, clad in a white robe, breaking bread, dancing, and frolicking with Black youngsters in one of the roughest African townships did not sit too well with the European establishment as it breached the Belgian strict colon bar. Yet, it was not until he had tasted weed surreptitiously stuffed in his pipe by one of his protégés that Père Buffalo was inducted into the *Bill* brotherhood.[30]

Zoumbel[31] was not just an illegal, yet a readily available substance[32] that served to bond bands of *Bills*. Just as with *kamô* it also allowed them to dull the pain that dereliction at the bottom rung of the urban ladder inflicted upon them. But *Bills* were not just at the receiving end of this social violence that wreaked havoc in Kinshasa's *quartiers*. They were, as Honwana and De Boeck have posited, "makers and breakers of society"[33], in an ambivalent posture where they acted as agents of change by shaping the ideological, social and material world around them, but where they also bore the brunt of changes that affected their society. Especially in the 1950s context of apocalyptic *fin d'empire,* at a time when a new grammar of international violence ushered the Cold War in Congo, *Yankees* felt little control over the direction their country was heading and, therefore, reasserted their power over their *quartiers*.

Kintulu, kamô and *zoumbel* provide evidence to what has been articulated time and again as attempts by juveniles to frame their bodies as "subversive sites"[34]. What is more, these bodies display an aesthetic of selfhood realisation as much as they counter and subvert dominant paradigms about manhood, culture in general and the contentious notion of body politics. There is no doubt

25 Kande started a career as a journalist in 1950 and it was in that capacity that he befriended Mobutu who was then himself an aspiring journalist before joining the army and going into politics. Kande made a name for himself by writing a controversial article on the *Bills* after a thorough investigation into their underworld. He went on to become Mobutu's trusted collaborator and his first Minister of Information in 1965, a post he was to keep until the early 1970s.

26 Bomina Nsoni served as Congo's ambassador to Gabon and the OAU (Organisation of African Unity). He ended his diplomatic career after a short-lived appointment as Congo's ambassador to the UN in 1997.

27 Kabaidi served as Governor of Kinshasa for most of the 1970s. An important figure in Kinshasa's political scene he singlehandedly brought many *Bills* to Mobutu regime's fold through the CVR (*Corps des Volontaires de la République*) he helped establish in 1967.

28 Bomina Nsoni, interview with the author, Kinshasa, 2 August 2009. In any given day, Degazin claims that at least forty to fifty "clients" would visit his practice in Saint-Jean (now Lingwala); Jean Sumbuka Bigonda (aka Degazin), interview with the author, Kinshasa, 29 February 2009.

29 Harvey C. Mansfield 2006, *Manliness*, New Haven, p. 18

30 Gondola (2009), p. 94

31 Raymaekers has identified at least 75 such terms, including *zoumbel, nua, boul, likeke, lititi* (Paul Raymaekers 1963, *L'organisation des zones de squatting,* Louvain, p. 299). This creative process could come about as follows: "Sometimes, we just sat together and discussed how people started to understand what *nua* meant. Let's make it *diato* from now on. Then we all adopted *diato*. We constantly changed those terms." Petit Moloch, interview with the author, Kinshasa (Ngiri Ngiri), 16 July 2007.

that to examine the manifold use of the *Bill's* body is to disentangle one thread at a time the inextricable symbiosis of aesthetics and politics. It is to peel away layers of quiescence in order to uncover concealed patterns of subversion and indiscipline.

Conclusion

In the early 1960s, as Congo became the most emblematic battleground of the Cold War and reeled from the devastation caused by widespread rebellions, the *Bill* movement continued unabated. Their hold on the *quartiers,* in which they vied for control and power, mirrored developments taking place on the war fronts where soldiers and militiamen increasingly targeted civilians, especially women. Similarly, some gang members resorted to rape and sexual violence in their attempts to cope with a "crisis of masculinity" that unfolded in the city and to impose their own brand of hypermasculinity in their *quartiers.* Although likely rape victims were girls (*nzele* in Hindoubill) who belonged to other "territories" or *quartiers, Bills* did not hesitate to turn against their own township girls once they started *kolúka* ("to wander") and to flout gender rules by refusing to comport themselves in public according to a colonial ideology that hardly tolerated the visibility and assertiveness of women in the public space.

By the time Mobutu took over in 1965 and brought centripetal ethnic forces under control with an iron fist, the *Bill* movement also came to an end. Many older *Bills* were co-opted within Mobutu's incipient regime. They made up the backbone of Mobutu's CVR (*Corps des Volontaires de la République*), the precursor to Zaire's youth party (JMPR). According to Paul Kabaidi, a former *Bill* himself who was appointed governor of Kinshasa in the 1980s, Mobutu recruited a large cohort of former *Bills* in several key positions in the armed forces and government; Mobutu's longtime chief of staff, Nimy Mayidika, was a *Bill* and so was General Mahele Lyoko Bokungu, Mobutu's army chief of staff. Other *Bills* decided to hang up their spurs as a result of Père Buffalo's 'redemptive ministry. Père Buffalo had long exalted Jesus as the *Grands Bill* par excellence, using stories in the New Testament, such as when Jesus drives the moneychangers out of the temple (Matthew 21:12), to show Jesus' *Bill* pedigree and thus attract *Bills* to the Gospel. In Ngiri Ngiri (Mofewana *quartier*), he created a centre where *Bills* could learn a trade, socialise and eventually transition into mainstream society. Still, other *Yankees* just outgrew the *Bills'* juvenile lifestyle and decided it was time to seek more gratifying opportunities in the 'adult' world. The movement then had not only lost its emphasis on violence but also its gang culture. Yet, the *Bill* philosophy continues to define youth cultures in Kinshasa and remains a behavioural repertoire for its plethora of youth living in a state that has failed them,[35] a postcolonial Chronos (*Χρόνος*) devouring its own children.

32 *Cannabis indica* was smuggled into Kinshasa in fishermen's canoes from Brazzaville and the Upper-Congo region. The market for marijuana seemed to have increased around 1959 prompting some local farmers to grow it in cassava (or manioc) plots; Raymaekers (1963), p. 300.

33 Alcinda Honwana and Filip De Boeck (eds) 2005, *Makers and Breakers: Children and Youth in Postcolonial Africa.* Trenton

34 Honwana and De Boeck (2005), p. 11

35 Theodore Trefon 2004, *Reinventing Order in the Congo. How People Respond to State Failure in Kinshasa,* London

Congo Music

GARY STEWART

tween champion George Foreman and challenger Muhammad Ali. [→ Fig. **A**] The music on the stage and the mayhem in the ring would show the world that Zaire was aimed for greatness. That this was the summit, that from this point Zaire would fall more rapidly, and perhaps more disastrously than it had risen, would not be known for a few more years. In 1974 it was time to recognise what appeared to be the country's tremendous progress, the most enduring elements of which, it turned out, came from the realm of the arts. And what better way to celebrate than to showcase the nation's stellar musicians alongside their famous counterparts from abroad. After all, Zaire's musicians already dominated the popular music scene in Africa. Two of its biggest stars, Tabu Ley and Abeti, had even played the renowned Olympia concert hall in Paris. The rest of the world should know about this Zairean treasure. [→ Fig. **B, C**]

The music that Ley and Abeti and their immensely popular peers had raised to a level of virtuosity rivalling their international colleagues came to be called Congolese Rumba or simply Congo Music: strains of the Cuban *Son* repatriated on radios and records and re-Africanised with a pinch of jazz and a dash of cabaret. This new music, which was sung in Lingala and played primarily

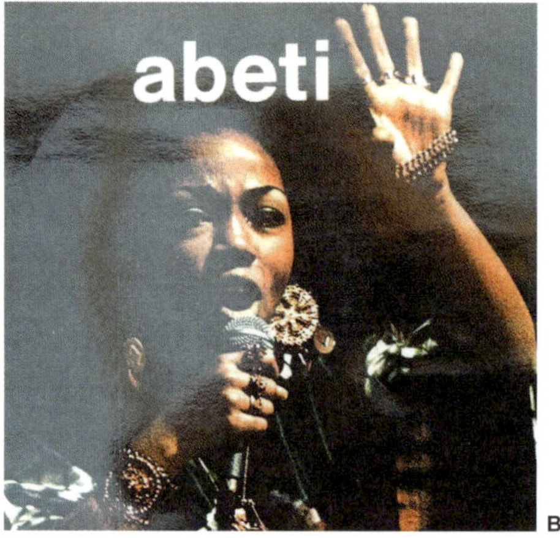

B

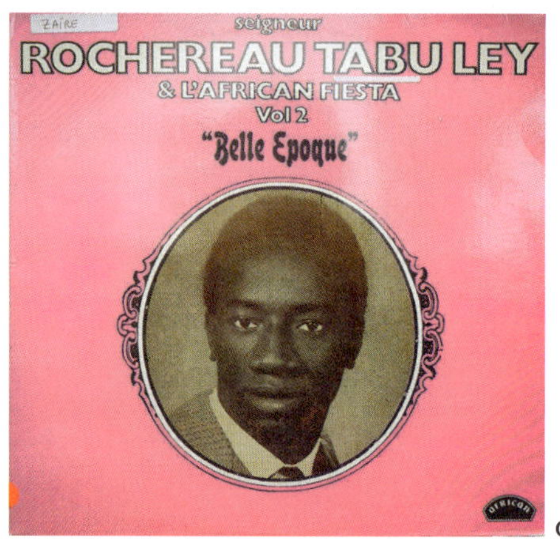

C

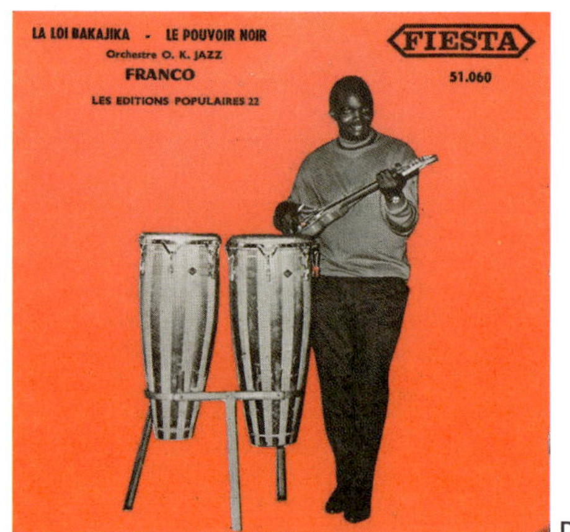

D

In 1974, a party invitation issued from central Africa: the time was late September. The place: Zaire – the old Belgian Congo renamed by its autocratic president, Mobutu Sese Seko. Many of the preeminent entertainers of the latter half of the 20th century – James Brown, Celia Cruz, Miriam Makeba, and more, along with home-grown stars like Franco, Abeti, and Tabu Ley Rochereau – would come to the capital, Kinshasa, to perform in a three-day extravaganza prior to a heavyweight title fight be-

A

on guitars, transcended barriers of ethnicity and culture and helped to bind disparate peoples together. The Congolese Rumba was a product of Kinshasa's urban milieu, but the city itself, in no small measure, was a product of the music too.

The musical accomplishments that reached full flower in Mobutu's Congo-Zaire could be traced to a process of urbanisation unintentionally set off during the notorious 19th century rule of Belgium's King Leopold II. Forced labour in the countryside – the collection of wild rubber and ivory to support the king's lavish spending at home – irreparably disrupted rural life. The transfer of the king's personal African plantation to the control of the Belgian government in 1908 abated the worst of the Congo's outrages, but life could never return to the way it had been before the coming of the white man. Two world wars demanded more from rural Africans, who were required to cultivate the land and mine its precious minerals to help supply the armies of Europe. Some were recruited to join the fighting; others to work in the factories that sprang up near river banks and rail heads in new cities.

The Belgian government recruited its own citizens to bring their skills and entrepreneurial spirit to the colony. Other Europeans – whether seeking refuge from the Great Depression or simply thirsting for adventure – came to the Congo for a fresh start. Most of these newcomers gravitated to the burgeoning cities where they started businesses, worked in factories, or staffed the colonial bureaucracy.

For both Africans and Europeans the biggest attraction was Léopoldville, today's Kinshasa, a town on the banks of a wide place in the Congo River some 240 miles upstream from the Atlantic. Quite rapidly the town became a city, more so after it was made the colony's capital in 1930. Colonial authorities tried mightily to limit its growth, but the numbers of people abandoning rural life and its hardships swamped their efforts.

Nearly all the musicians who would go on to win the hearts of the entire continent emigrated to Léopoldville or were born to parents who had already made the journey from the countryside.

Franco, the guitarist who led the legendary band O.K. Jazz for more than thirty years, came from Sona Bata, south of Léopoldville, as a boy in the 1940s. [→ Fig. D] Dr Nico, a leader in seminal groups African Jazz and African Fiesta, moved with his parents from Kasai Province to the east. Tabu Ley's family had come to town from Bagata along the Kwilu River to the north. As a young girl, Abeti fled to Léopoldville with her mother in the wake of violence in Stanleyville (Kisangani) during the unrest that attended Congolese independence. [→ Fig. E] Singer Sam Mangwana's parents had escaped an authoritarian Portuguese regime in Angola to start over under the somewhat less repressive Belgians. Several musicians, like clarinettist Jean Serge Essous and singer Edo Ganga who would work in O.K. Jazz, crossed the river from Brazzaville in the French Congo. Similar stories could have been told by a million others.

Europeans contributed to Léopoldville's fertile mix, although in the evenings they kept themselves separate. "After nine o'clock you are not allowed to be in the white part of town," musician Ray Braynck recalled. "They blew a bugle horn for you to get out of there."[1] According to Braynck, the curfew failed to deter him; he and a friend would sometimes remain, hiding until after midnight, so they could steal coconuts. During the day the white area opened to all, for there much of the colony's business transpired. The white-owned shops needed African customers in order to prosper. Along with necessities like food and clothing, some merchants stocked cheap guitars, foreign records and the machines to play them, and radios that could secure a link to the outside world.

Among Léopoldville's entrepreneurs, one of the earliest to recognise that a certain synergy might develop between music and commerce, was a Belgian ex-army sergeant named Jean Hourdebise. He established a radio station called Congolia in 1939 and supplemented its coverage by erecting a series of loudspeakers in African quarters of the city to reach the many who could not afford radios. To attract African listeners he began to

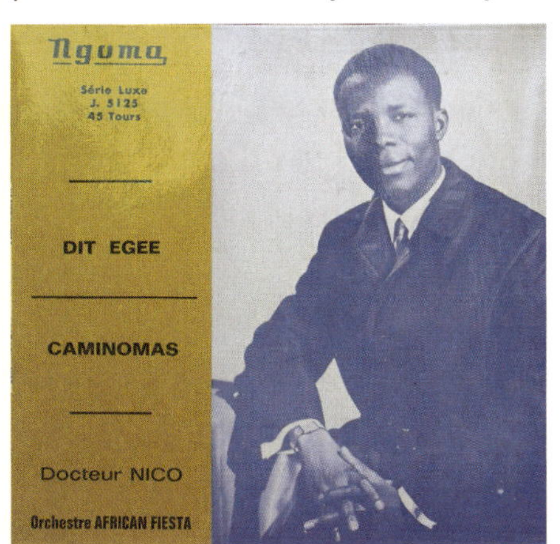

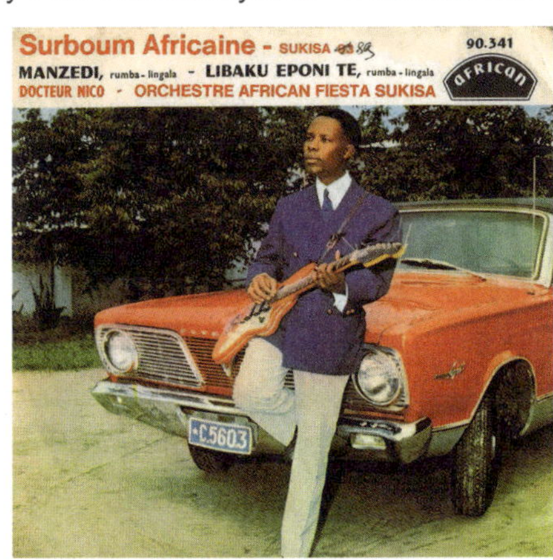

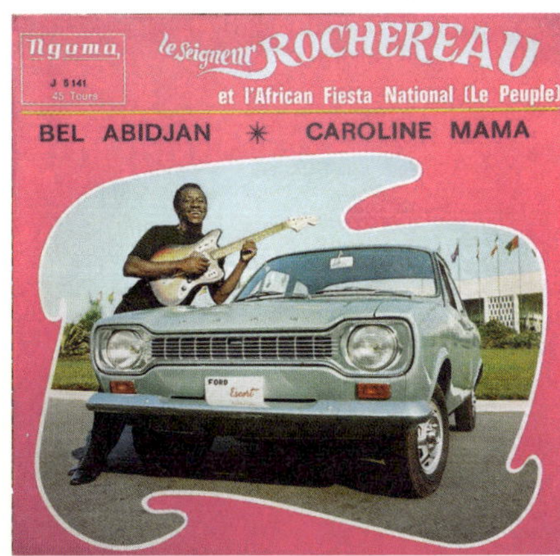

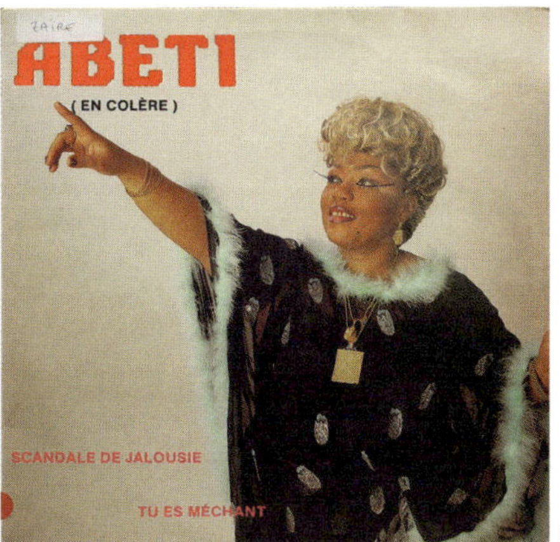

E

1 Raymond "Ray Braynck" Kalonji, interview with the author, Washington, D.C., 1 September 1994

Les meilleurs enregistrements AFRICAINS
DISQUES Ngoma
CONGO YA SIKA
BOSENGE BAR
Chez AMUZU
OLEREE BAR
TAHITI
MINC BAR
Kongo Bar
AU RECORD
DEPOT BAR
KIMPWANZA BAR
ZEKA BAR
BAR TALA TALA
ELYSÉES BAR
INDEPENDANCE BAR

21
SÉRIE DES NOUVEAUTÉS
Ngoma
MAKAMBO YA MWASI OYO
AMI PAUVRE VIDA
par
ONÈMA PASCAL
avec l'orchestre
JECOKAT
CHRISELINA MOKE
YOKERO KERO PANTA
par
G. ROSSIGNOL & I. RAPHAËL
avec l'orchestre
JECOKAT
SUPER 45 TOURS

1040
SÉRIE DES GRANDS SUCCÈS
Ngoma
SANGO YA BANA NGOMA
Polka pika
BOYOKAKA MALOBA YA MAMA
Polka pika
VICTORIA APIKI DRAPEAU
Polka pika
KOMBO WA BISO BITEKE SUZANNE
Rumba
TRIO BOW
et le
GROUPE RYTHMIQUE NGOMA
SUPER 45 TOURS

Ngoma
WENDO
MWANGA Paul
B.P. 74 Léopoldville
Rep. du Congo
Ngoma
JDN 8
FACE 2
MA SULU MANKATU LUTIMA
MWANGA Paul
et l'Orchestre JAZZ VENUS
BEGUEN Band
MUNDANDA Antoine
Emm. O'OLIVEIRA
LAISO
Succès africains

48
Série des Nouveautés
Ngoma
NALOTI LOUISE MOKE
CHARLOTTE BONI KO?
por
PHIL-PHILO
et l'Orchestre JAZZ BABALOU
LOLA BAILA RYTHMO
TIKA NALELA CHARLOTTE
por
PHIL-PHILO
et l'Orchestre JAZZ BABALOU
SUPER 45 TOURS

1011
Série des Grands Succès
Ngoma
MARIE LOUISE
PAUL KAMBA ATIKI BISO
MARIE LOUISE
WASERO ERUGA
par
WENDO
SUPER 45 TOURS

SUPER 45 TOURS
80
Ngoma
K. P. FLAMMY, M. OLIVEIRA, FREITAS. & LAU.
et l'Orchestre JAZZ BEGUEN
SONGI SONGI EZALIMABE
TATA SENDUE NA KATANGA
ANGOLA NSIETO
TUSAMBILA NZAMBI

Ngoma
Ngoma
23
MARIE-LOUISE
Lingala
chanté par
WENDO
(2 guitares)
SONDREM
NGOMA vous présente toujours un répertoire incomparable sur NGOMA le vrai disque Africain !
NGOMA le disque des meilleures vedettes de toute l'Afrique !
NGOMA moto wa liboso ayokisi bino lolaka ya bino na diski ya fono !
NGOMA Champion des Disques

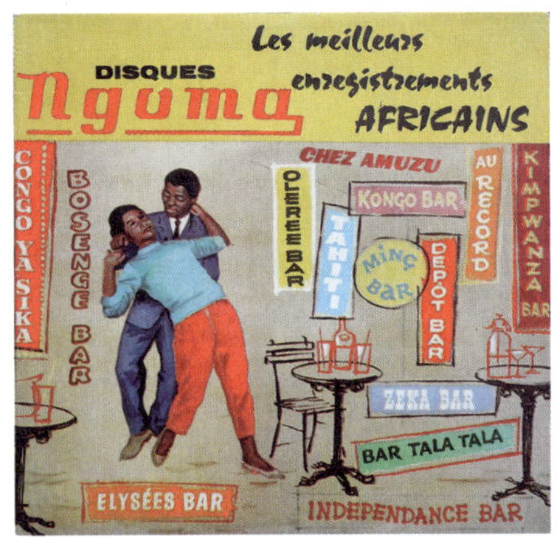

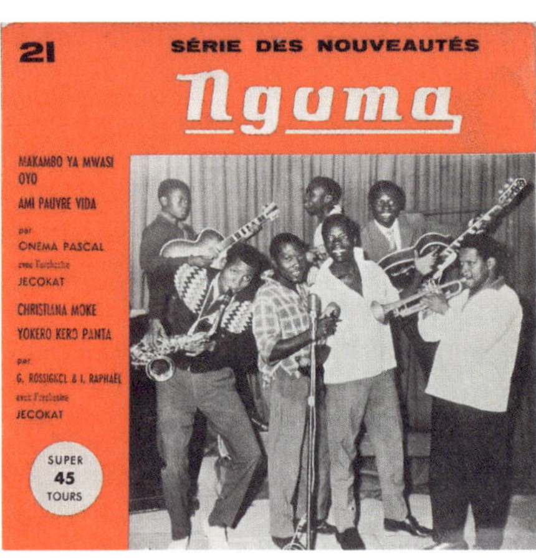

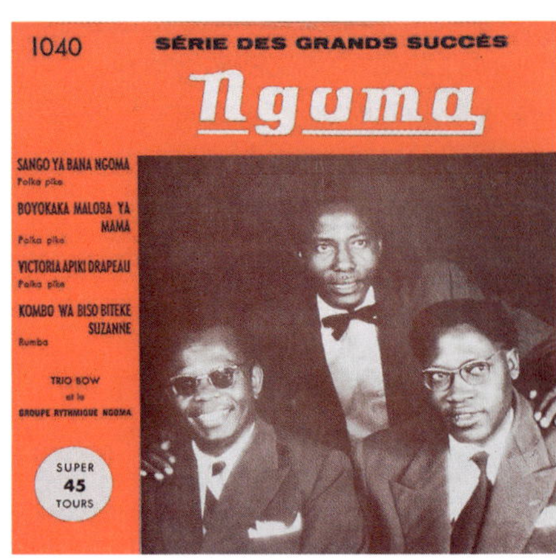

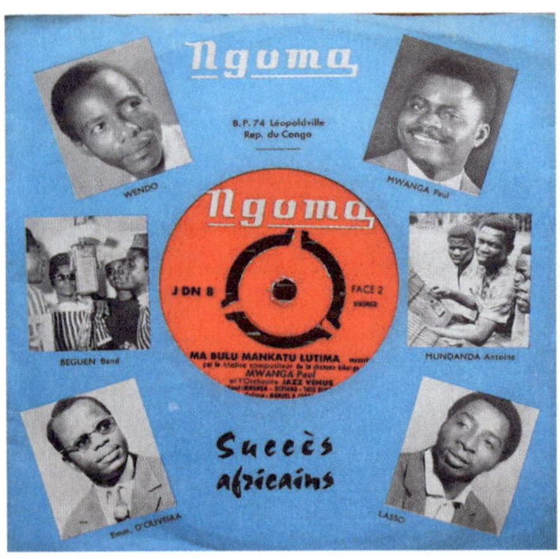

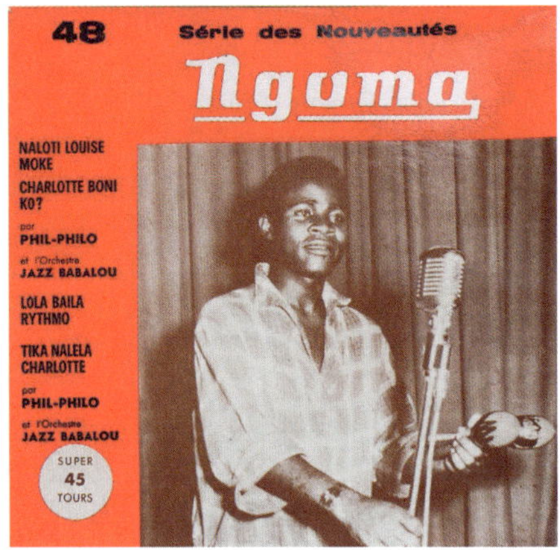

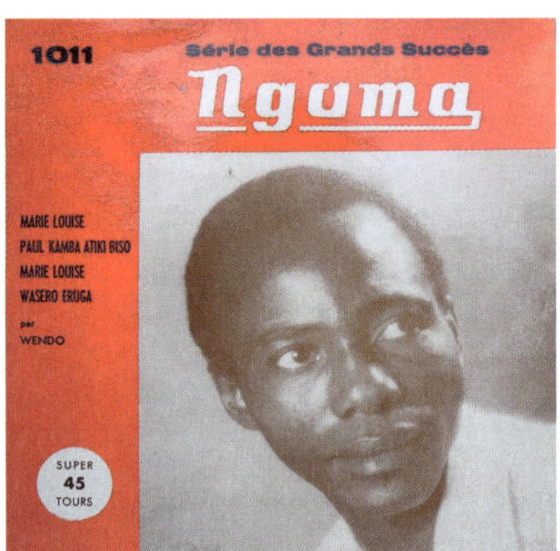

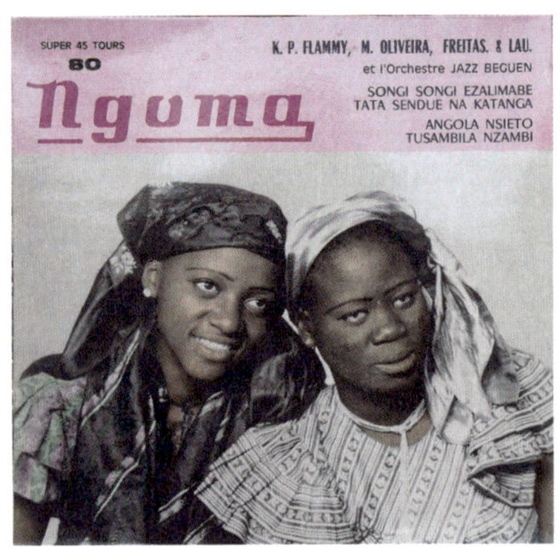

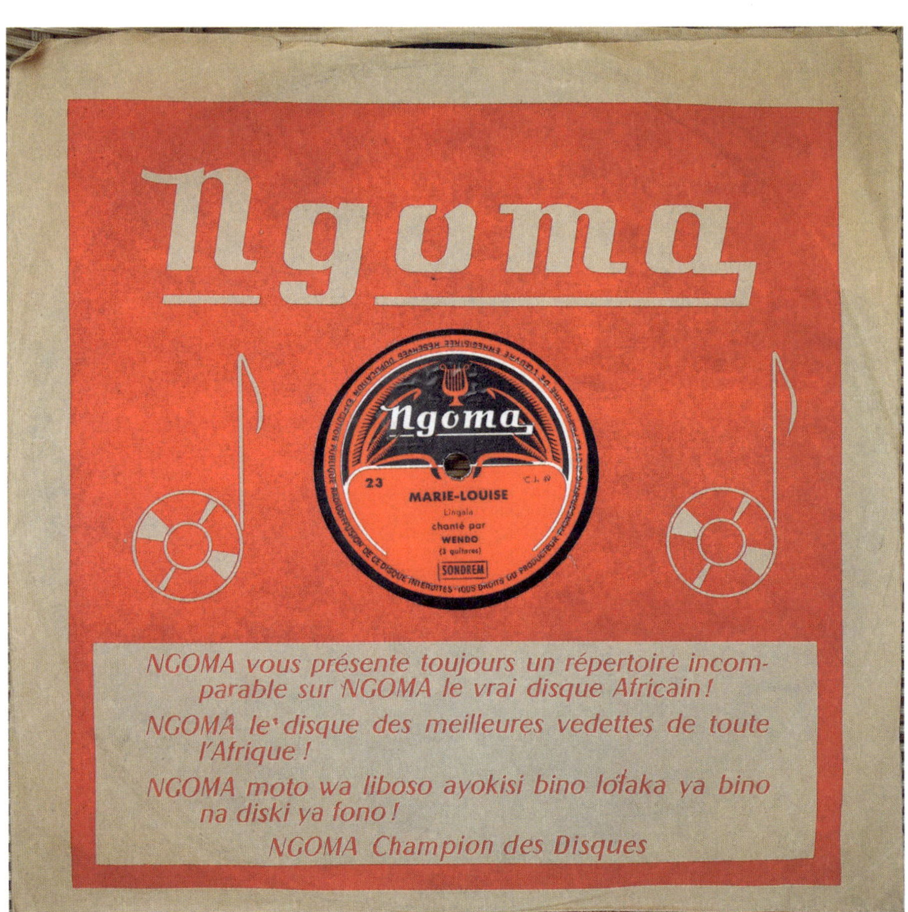

F

record African musicians and then play their works on the air. The number of listeners increased following this innovation, and that attracted merchants who were willing to pay to have their firms mentioned on Congolia's programmes. One of the first to sing on the radio was a boatman named Antoine Wendo Kolosoyi, who would parlay the opportunity into a successful career that continued for more than sixty years.

Another to link music and commerce was Nicolas Jeronimidis, a general merchant who opened Léopoldville's first recording studio in 1947. Called Ngoma, the studio recorded Congolese music's earliest pop stars, including Wendo, another singer-guitarist named Henri Bowane, and dozens more. [→ Fig. F] "We had a large machine to make recordings on acetate disks," Nikiforos Cavvadias, a brother-in-law of Jeronimidis, remembered. "We sent the acetate disks to Europe, to Belgium, to make the matrix and press the records."[2] By recording the music and selling the records, Ngoma won a far broader audience for its musicians than they had been able to reach on their own. The records, in turn, inspired more musicians to approach the studio for work and brought more customers to the Jeronimidis shop. Soon Jeronimidis stocked EMI gramophones from England and the needles they required from Germany; Bush radios and Vidor batteries to power them; and a steadily increasing catalogue of Ngoma records produced by an expanding roster of musicians. His network of dealers selling Ngoma records eventually covered the entire country and extended to West and East Africa.

Ngoma's success led other merchants to join the competition. The Benetar brothers, like Jeronimidis, were of Greek origin. They opened Opika in 1949, a studio that launched the first bona fide (but fleeting) musical sensation Jhimmy "the Hawaiian" (who had never been out of Africa). Opika also nurtured a more substantial talent in singer Joseph Kabasele, the man many consider to be the father of modern Congolese music. [→ Fig. G] The competition intensified in 1950 when two Greek cousins named Papadimitriou opened a third studio they called Loningisa.

A Belgian jazz musician, Fud Candrix, introduced the saxophone when he sat in on several recording sessions at Opika in 1952. A year later, Bill Alexandre, another Belgian jazz player, electrified the music – and its fans – when he plugged in his sleek new Gibson guitar.

The Congolese music business and Léopoldville's population were expanding so rapidly that toward the end of the 1950s the Belgian company, Fonior, built the colony's first record-pressing factory. In addition to the manufacture of records, Fonior invited groups to Brussels to record in studios far superior to the rudimentary establishments in Léopoldville. Speaking of Fonior's owner, one Willy Pelgrims, Cameroonian Manu Dibango, [→ Fig. H] who performed in Kinshasa, recalled that "when Pelgrims invited people to Brussels he bought all the equipment, new equip-

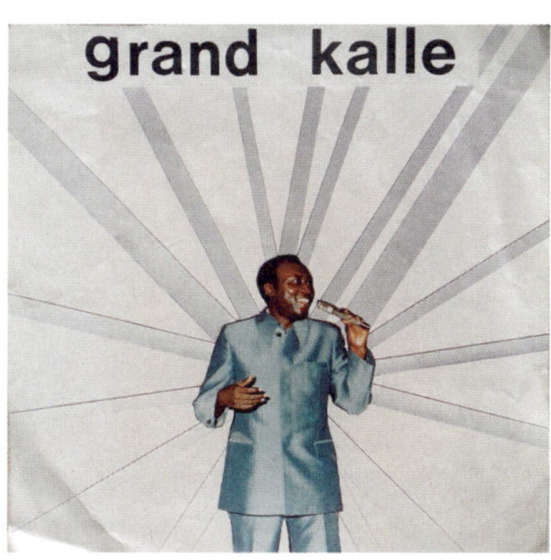

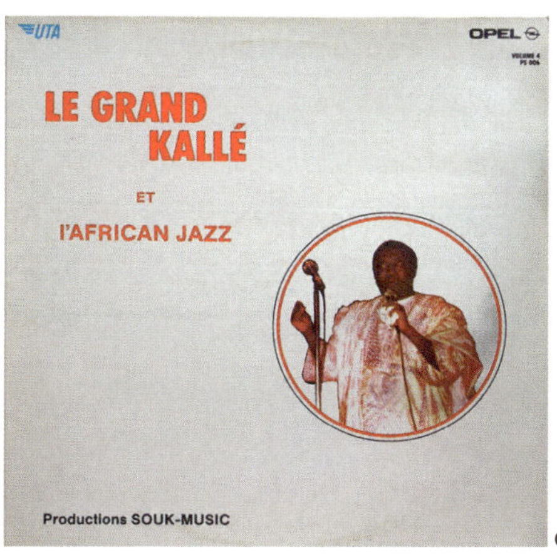

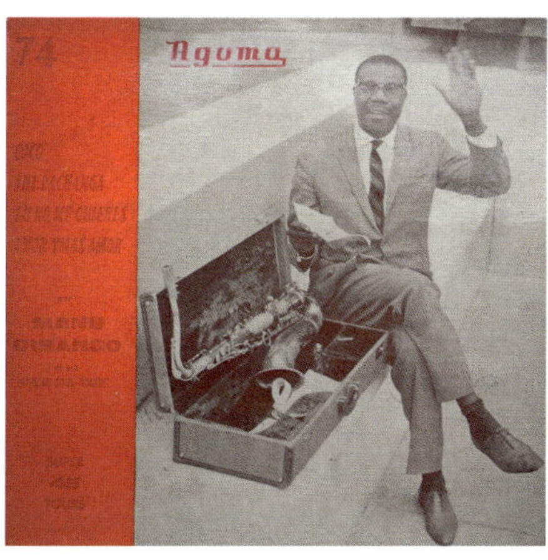

2 Nikiforos Cavvadias, interview with the author, Brussels, 3 January 1997

ment. The musicians brought the stuff back to Congo, and the other musicians they saw that, 'Wow! Fantastic!' So there was inter-reaction and competition – in a good way."[3]

In addition to its shops, both white and black, that furnished the capital's essentials, the city gave birth to a number of bars that relieved the pressure, if only temporarily, of the new urban life. These establishments opened in the African *cité,* across the park and past the zoo from the white *ville* that curled along the river bank. Some had a kind of makeshift feel, nothing much more than someone's backyard dotted with tables and trimmed with lanterns, perhaps a sound system, and fridge to chill the beer. Better places could be found indoors, real saloons with a bar and dance floor. Records provided the music in most, but many booked live bands too. "We were doing such great stuff that in the evening we would fool our boss' watchman to get out of the studio with the instruments, and we would go to the *cité* to perform in a bar," Edo Ganga recalled. "People really liked our music, what we were doing. Because we were selling records."[4] The growing number of bars and recording studios attracted more musicians, and more and more people wanted to hear them. Factory jobs weren't the only ones to be had.

Under colonial rule the mixing of Congo's nearly 200 ethnic groups accelerated in the cities as members of nearly all of them streamed in. In this regard, anthropologist Colin Turnbull once wrote – in a passage that was perhaps overly pessimistic – that in the city an African "quickly discovers that here he is no longer a member of a family, even of a tribe; that his neighbour is not bound by the same beliefs that bind him, and so can not be relied on to behave as a reasonable man. The only sensible and safe thing to do is to mistrust one's neighbour, to think for oneself alone, to have no consideration for others."[5]

Still, the breaking of old bonds presented opportunities for new ones to be forged. One such bridging of old ways to new could be found in the adoption of Lingala, a pidgin that had evolved among traders and boatmen to facilitate communication among various groups along the rivers. Largely because it bore little ethnic or cultural baggage, Lingala soon spread to become a lingua franca – along with the French of colonial administrators – especially in Léopoldville. Nearly all of Léopoldville's musicians adopted Lingala for their compositions. As records sold outward, away from the capital, they helped to spread the language to rural areas, thus abetting a growing sense of a broader Congolese nationhood. But it would take more than shared language and music to make a country.

When the Congolese won independence in 1960, people celebrated to the exuberant sounds of *Indépendance Cha Cha* by Joseph Kabasele and African Jazz (as did Africans across the continent when their own times came). But celebrations were short-lived as subversion of Congo's new democracy by outside powers and the resort to ethnic-based alliances among Congolese politicians plunged the country into chaos. Post-independence Léopoldville sprawled uncontrollably as people poured into the city to escape political violence in the countryside. What emerged from the upheaval was a Congo united by a ruthless dictator.

Colonel Joseph Mobutu exerted his will through the army and secret police, but he manipulated his country through cultural means as well, not the least of which was music. Mobutu began replacing European designations with African ones in 1966 with the announcement that Léopoldville would henceforth be Kinshasa. He launched his *Mouvement Populaire de la Révolution* the following year, and, his hand unseen, he raided O.K. Jazz to form the nucleus of a new group called *Orchestre Révolution*. The band didn't last, so Mobutu gradually began to cultivate ties with Franco, who was leader of the band he had raided. Franco supported Mobutu's 1970 'election' as president in song, as did other groups, in what would become an often-repeated ritual aimed at remaining on the good side of the regime. [→ Fig. **I, J**]

Politics aside, Congolese music was mostly fun. "The songs we sang were very nice songs artistically, because we were very close artistically," said Sam Mangwana. "At that time we had a group spirit. You must be close to make nice music."[6] Manu Dibango remembered that "nightlife was very powerful in Congo at that time." Music and beer were abundant he said. "It was a good life."[7]

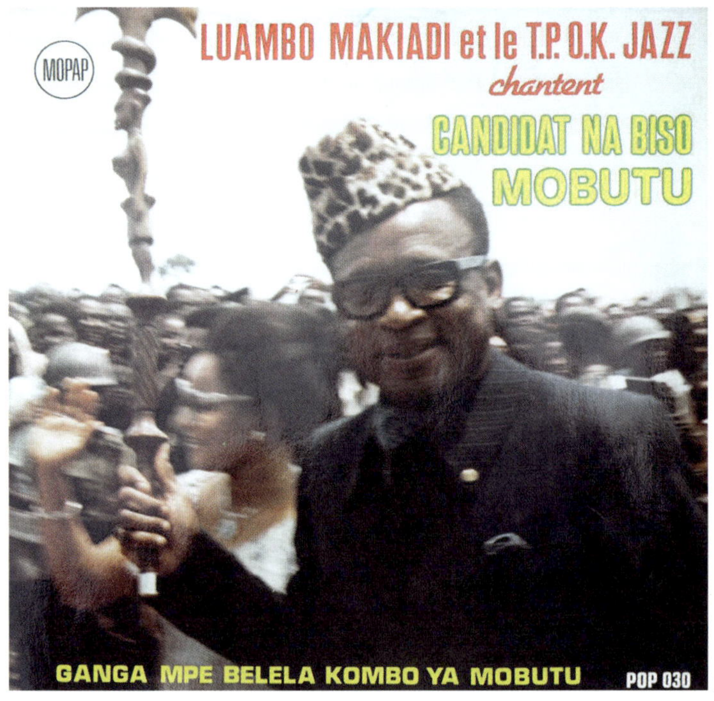

3   Manu Dibango, interview with the author, Paris, 24 August 1991
4   Edo Ganga, interview with the author, Brazzaville, 7 June 1993
5   Colin M. Turnbull 1962, *The Lonely African,* New York, p. 125
6   Sam Mangwana, interview with the author, Silver Spring, Maryland, 15 October 1990
7   Dibango (1991)

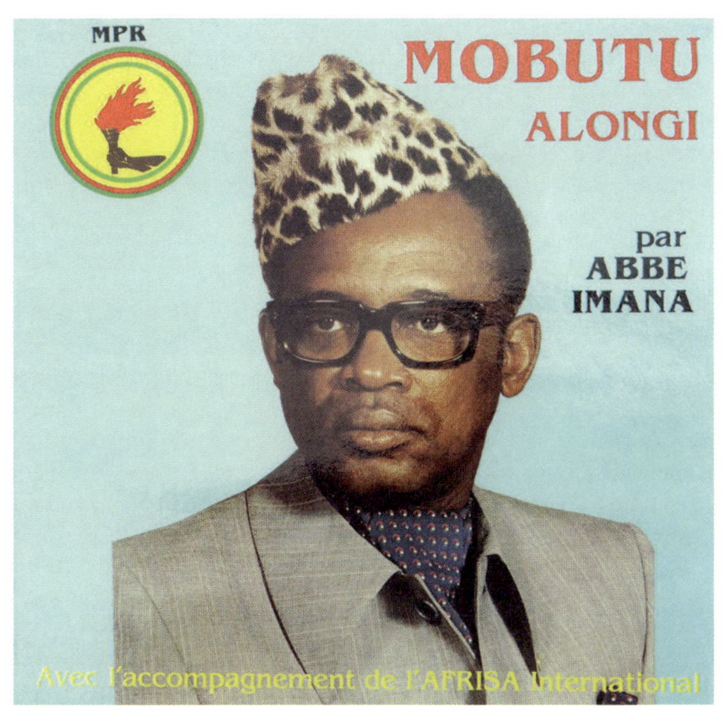

MPR
MOBUTU
ALONGI
par
ABBE
IMANA
Avec l'accompagnement de l'AFRISA International

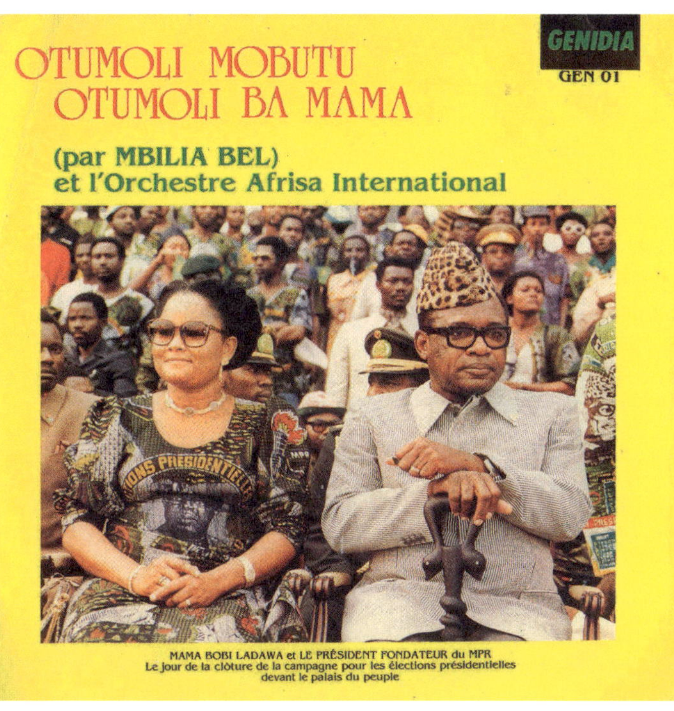

GENIDIA
GEN 01
OTUMOLI MOBUTU
OTUMOLI BA MAMA
(par MBILIA BEL)
et l'Orchestre Afrisa International
MAMA BOBI LADAWA et LE PRÉSIDENT FONDATEUR du MPR
Le jour de la clôture de la campagne pour les élections présidentielles
devant le palais du peuple

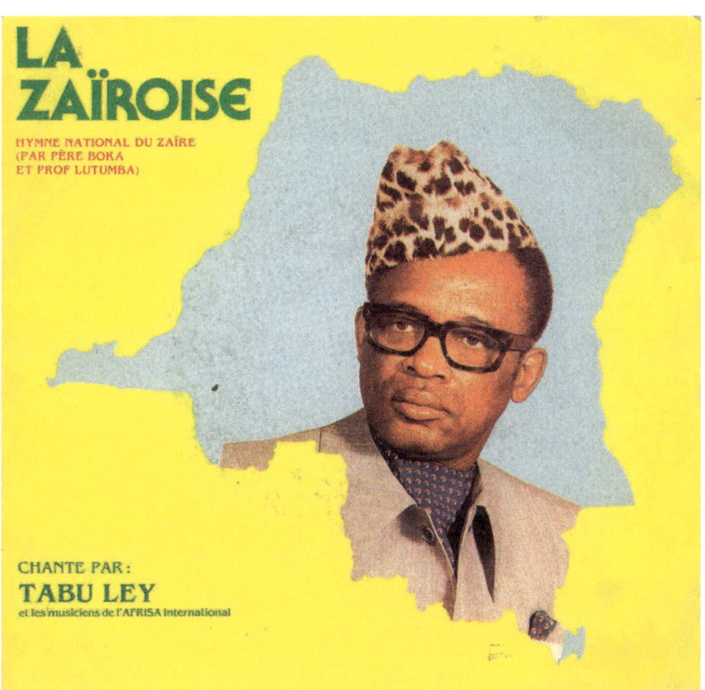

LA ZAÏROISE
HYMNE NATIONAL DU ZAÏRE
(PAR PÈRE BOKA
ET PROF LUTUMBA)
CHANTE PAR :
TABU LEY
et les musiciens de l'AFRISA International

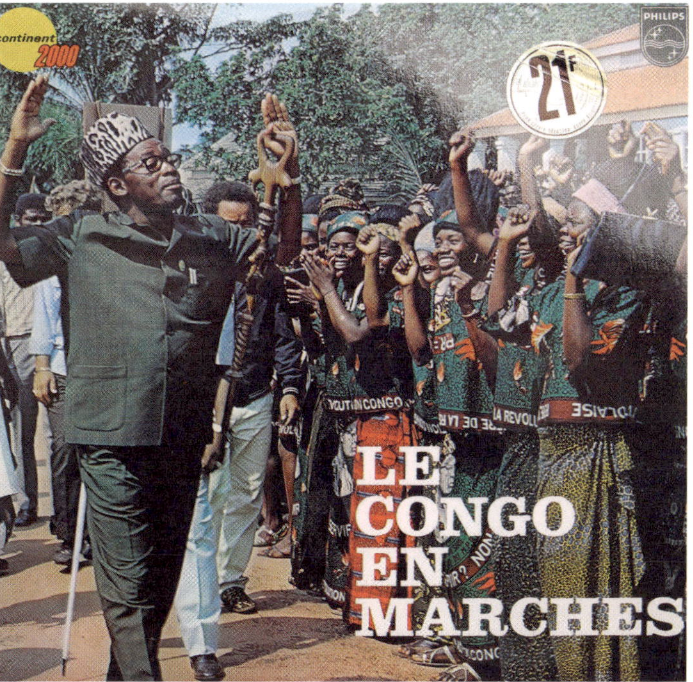

continent 2000
PHILIPS
21 F
LE
CONGO
EN
MARCHES

Kinshasa's relentless population growth gave rise to a new concentration of entertainment establishments in an area called Matonge, close to the centre of the city's well-stretched boundaries. There a beer salesman named Raymond Franck opened the *Vis-à-Vis* nightclub, the district's showplace. Franco built his *Un-Deux-Trois* club in Matonge, and Tabu Ley followed with a club he called the Type K. Dozens upon dozens of other bars dotted the area along with record kiosks and food stands and other businesses that catered to the flourishing night life. And dozens upon dozens of bands sprang up to help sate the people's thirst for music.

Despite the fun that could be had, Kinshasa failed to fulfil its promise of jobs, at least in quantities sufficient to keep up with the exploding population. As a result, a degree of alienation had set in among the city's unemployed youth, even before independence. Many of them called themselves *Bills* after the heroes of American cowboy movies. They talked in a kind of slang called Hindoubill, named in part for the Hindu of Indian movies that were also popular at the time. Post-independence counterparts to the *Bills* were the somewhat more prosperous *Yé-yés*, named for the "yeah, yeah" cries of rock and roll. The *Yé-yés* had their own style and slang, which together with Hindoubill infused and invigorated the music and helped give birth to a new youthful generation of musical groups.

The first such band to gain widespread notoriety, Zaiko Langa Langa, made its debut in 1970. Zaiko's frequent personnel changes spawned a number of offspring, the remnants of which carry on to this day. The youth movement also inspired a craze for high-fashion clothing called *la sape*. Musicians and their fans who indulged in this very expensive competition came to be known as *sapeurs*. Zaiko alumnus and leading *sapeur,* Papa Wemba, said what most who participated must have been thinking: "I had to set myself apart from the others. I had to have a look."[8]

Life in the city imposed its frustrations as the *Bills* and *Yé-yés* could attest, but anyone who experienced the Kinshasa of the early seventies couldn't help feeling the city's overall sense of optimism and perhaps could understand why it would require a heroic effort for anyone to pull up stakes and return to the countryside.

President Mobutu's own optimism seemed to correspond with his consolidation of control and the concentration of cash in his bank accounts. His vision for himself and his country was expansive. Late in 1971 he announced that the name of the country would be changed to Zaire. Early the next year he decreed that all who carried a European-sounding name must shed it in favour of one authentically African (he became Mobutu Sese Seko). This was necessary, Mobutu would later explain, to give the Zairian "back his human dignity which colonisation had com-

pletely destroyed by imposing assimilation and alienation. The dazzling development of Zairian arts since that time may be considered a renaissance, and proves the wisdom of our program."[9] The principal Zairian art Mobutu surely had in mind was his country's sensational music. Its artists changed their names and rushed to promote the new *authenticité*. [→ Fig. **K**] Franco recorded with old-timer Camille Feruzi, an accordionist popular in the 1940s. Others dropped their electric guitars in favour of the heretofore passé acoustic models, at least until the novelty wore off. Nearly everyone – save for the Catholic Church which tried mightily to defend 'Christian' names – seemed to think that the exercise was one of Mobutu's better ideas.

Perhaps buoyed by the success of *authenticité,* Mobutu began to overreach. There had already been signs that the foundations of Zairian progress were less solid than they appeared. Mobutu's next move ensured that they would crumble. Toward the end of 1973 he announced that he would deliver Zaire from foreign control by turning all commercial establishments over to "sons of the country." Although he promised just compensation for the foreign business owners, the transaction was largely one of confiscation. Franco was awarded control of the Fonior record-pressing factory, but most who took over the foreign firms were ill-equipped to manage them.

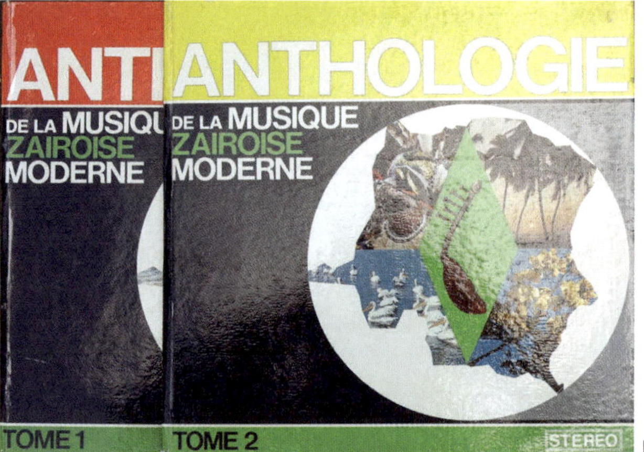

K

By the time the boxing match party invitations went out in 1974, it was clear that 'Zairianisation', as it was called, had turned into a disaster. Many businesses simply closed, their inventories sold and the proceeds pocketed by the new owners. Foreign exchange to finance imports of raw materials dried up. Franco's record-pressing factory ran at reduced capacity, often resorting to the collection of old records to be melted down for pressing into new ones. Musicians could still make money in the clubs, but their record earnings evaporated.

Mobutu scrambled to undo the damage, but it was too late to recover. The experience of Loningisa proprietor Basile Papadimitriou was, perhaps, typical. "In 1976, a new order gave us the

8   Papa Wemba, interview with the author, Paris, 30 August
    1991

9   Jean-Louis Remilleux 1989, *Mobutu: Dignity for Africa,* Paris,
    p. 107

10 Basile Papadimitriou, letter to the author, 10 November 1993

right to return to Kinshasa to pick up our business again, the president not being happy with the result of the 'Zairianisation' of business," he recalled. "I returned and proceeded to inventory the goods turned over, the result of which was not good."[10] Papadimitriou and most other foreign businessmen decided not to stay in Zaire.

Oblivious to the unfolding disaster, festival planners forged ahead. The spectacle of Zaire '74 with its astonishing array of musicians and the Ali-Foreman fight a month later (Ali won) introduced Kinshasa to the world. But it was a city whose glory days were dwindling. Television viewers couldn't see that the musicians were playing to a largely empty stadium. Most Zairians couldn't afford the price of a ticket. Over the next few years the city's best musicians would move on to the more promising capitals of Paris and Brussels where Congolese music enjoyed a brief renaissance. [→ Fig. L] Back home the party would wind down for a few more years, but Matonge would soon be just another remnant of an urban carcass. Kinshasa's golden era was coming to an end.

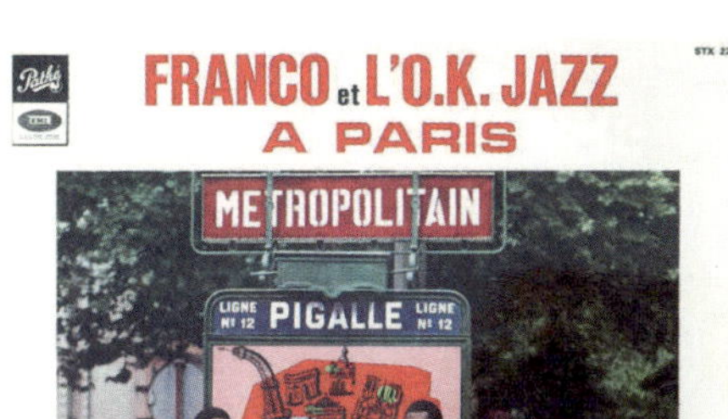

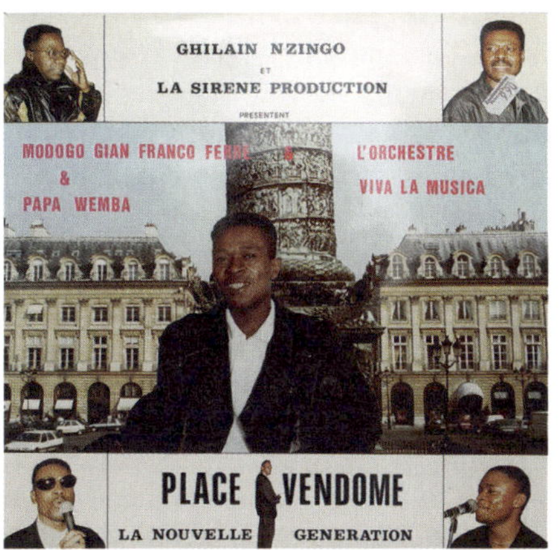

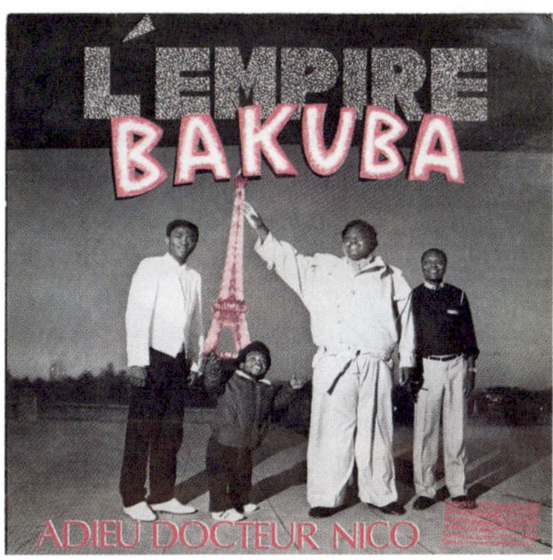

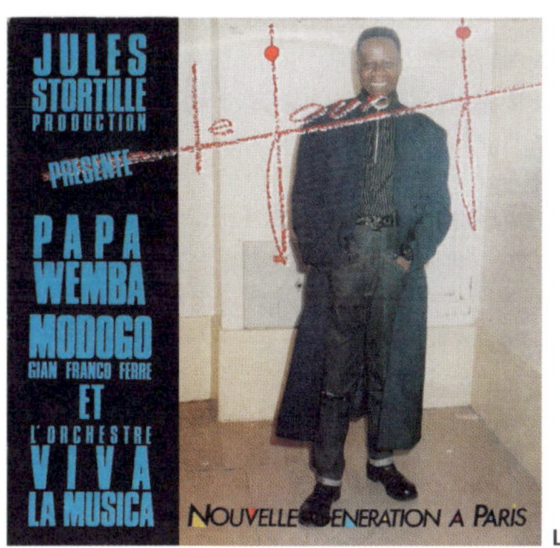

Rumble in Kinshasa

DOMINIQUE MALAQUAIS

Weigh-In

In 1974, Kinshasa hosted a historic sporting event: the now iconic Muhammad Ali-George Foreman boxing match.[1] While other much-followed bouts between internationally recognised boxers had taken place in Africa previously and others have been held on the continent since, this singular event is unrivalled. Thousands of pages have been written and three films have been produced about the fight; an extraordinary number of photographs documenting it, original, re-tooled and bootlegged, are in circulation, in print and on the Internet; numerous works of art, from paintings to video installations and performances memorialise its highlights. Why then write further about the 'Fight of the Century'? The reason is at once straightforward and profoundly fraught. The overwhelming majority of words and images disseminated over the past thirty-five years about the Ali-Foreman "Rumble in the Jungle" (an expression coined by Ali) privilege one point of view: they position the event as a matter of import for and interest within American culture and history specifically. Mainstream, mostly white, chroniclers, as well as writers, photographers and artists whose primary but broader focus is African-American battles for civil liberties and recognition, have firmly situated the match as a US-centred phenomenon that is relevant to a large extent insofar only as it speaks to North American concerns and sensibilities. While the Rumble – or, more precisely, Ali's role in it – does indeed deserve a great deal of attention in this regard, such attention, to date, has resulted in a highly problematic elision: Kinshasa, the place where the match took place, is largely absent from the stories told about the event. Indeed, of the city and the newly independent nation to which it belonged, of the man at Zaire's helm and behind the event – President Mobutu Sese Seko – and, most importantly, of the local constituencies involved, we do not hear much except what relates directly to the experiences of US participants and onlookers.

What place does the Rumble occupy in Congolese histories, imaginaries and constructions of identity? What was – and what is now – the nature of its political economy? What stakes were involved and for what manner of stakeholders? By what forces were these stakes shaped, how and why? A key event associated with the match – *Zaire '74,* a festival that brought together musicians from three continents, from James Brown to Miriam Makeba and the biggest Congolese Rumba stars of the day – was funded by the iron-fisted Tolbert brothers then ruling Liberia. The match made news and waves from Cape Town to Cairo and across Asia as well, with Pakistani and Indian children taken out of school to watch Ali, the American Muslim, fight for the heavyweight championship of the world.[2] Little of this is mentioned in accounts of the Rumble to date. This shows, in no uncertain terms, that the Ali-Foreman fight was far more than the principally American event it is commonly presented as; it also underscores the fact that this was far more than a mere sporting event. The Rumble's reception, instrumentalisation and – a point largely ignored by chroniclers – both its long-term and its present-day resonance outside the US make it a global event, in the most complex, political sense of the term – an event that speaks, as few others do, to the extraordinary complexities of the postcolonial condition.

These matters and a wide range of questions they raise are at the heart of an ongoing project: a trans-media and trans-disciplinary undertaking focused on the match and titled Barnburner, which brings together some twenty contributors – scholars, writers of fiction and faction, and artists in multiple fields, from photography and video to experimental cartography, performance and hip hop.[3] What follows is an overview of some of the core questions addressed by the Barnburner project.

Round One: Match of the Century

The plan was not, initially, to hold the match in Africa. The United States (New York City) and Great Britain (London) were both vying to host the event. Kinshasa, however, beat them both to the punch – and some punch it was… The sponsors of the match had arranged for 357 giant screens to be arrayed around the world, each of which would serve as a platform for a closed-circuit projection of the fight; over two million people would be watching the match live on these screens – each of them a paying viewer. The amount of money involved was staggering for the 1970s. Ali and Foreman were both slated to receive five million dollars. The purse was to be paid out by Zaire.

All of this, and much more, was announced on 1 April 1974 at a packed conference convened by President Mobutu's press secretary, Bula Mandungu. Much was made, in this setting, of the president's very personal involvement in bringing the match to Zaire and ensuring that it would be an unmitigated success. The announcement was largely for foreign consumption. In Zaire, and in Kinshasa in particular, it was old news: for months, the state-controlled press had been filled with communiqués about preparations for the upcoming fight, relayed, notably, by *Elima*

---

1 Earlier versions of this text, in both French and English, appear in the journals *Africultures* (no. 73, 2008) and *Chimurenga* (no. 14, 2009). For their support, suggestions and inspiration in the writing of these and related pages (see note 3), many thanks to Bob White, Cédric Vincent, Mowoso Collective, Bart Legum, Adam Haupt, Vera Grant, Zimitri Erasmus, Sophie Duvernoy, Kadiatou Diallo and Cameron Leader-Picone.

2 Amin Gulgee, personal communication, 13 March 2010

3 The Barnburner project is generously supported by the W.E.B. Du Bois Institute for African and African-American Studies, Harvard University. Its first incarnation is a publication (2011) co-edited by Dominique Malaquais and Kadiatou Diallo for SPARCK – Space for Pan-African Research, Creation and Knowledge. SPARCK is an experimental multi-sited, transdisciplinary programme of artist residencies, public in-the-city interventions, performances and exhibitions, workshops, colloquia and publications at work throughout Africa and her diasporas. It is a programme of the Africa Centre, a South-Africa-based contemporary arts and culture NGO.

and *Salongo,* the two principal daily newspapers affiliated with the country's only legal political party – the president's party, MPR (*Mouvement Populaire de la Révolution*).

In the United States as well, there was quite a buzz, though of a different kind. At its heart was, of course, Ali, whose positions on racism, civil rights and the Vietnam War, to say nothing of his identity as a Muslim convert and a vocal member of Elijah Muhammad's Nation of Islam, had netted him an extraordinary number of enemies in white America as well as sectors of the emergent black middle class. At the heart of the maelstrom too, capitalising on the country's fascination-cum-hatred of Ali, was a dubious character: Don King. Today, King's is a household name. At the time, he was little known in boxing circles. His area of expertise was, rather, the numbers racket, with a sideline in less than limpid work in the entertainment field. He had beaten to death a man who owed him money and, for this, spent time behind bars. It was reputed that King entertained close ties with the Italian Mafia, and had earned a well-deserved reputation as both a thoroughly crooked and charismatic businessman.

Just as the personalities involved were complex, so too were the political, economic and social contexts in which the match was being set afoot. The US has just begun extracting itself from the filth of segregation and the country remained intensely racist. For King, in this context, raising funds for the match had proven a high-wire act: quite simply, and as he was wont to remind with great gusto any and all who would listen, it was amazing that he had managed to. In Zaire, things were, to say the very least, complicated as well. In 1960, the Belgian colonial regime had finally been ousted. The country was left in shreds. A year later, Patrice Lumumba, the man who had led the country to Independence, was murdered by Belgian soldiers with the active help of the CIA, following a *coup d'état* by Mobutu, who was then at the helm of the army. Aided and abetted by the world's richest nation and by the ex-coloniser, the country headed full-tilt into anarchy. In 1965, following a second coup supported by Washington, Mobutu took over once and for all. He would remain in power, ruling with an iron fist, until 1997.

Like Don King, Mobutu was given to high-wire acts. He had an uncanny ability to mix and match the most extraordinary positions. Behind him, through much of his reign, lurked Washington and Paris, both of which saw in him a rampart against Communism (or what passed for such) and as a means of imposing order – their order – in the immensely lucrative business of raping the region of its mineral wealth. Mobutu worked hand in hand with the 'West', yet simultaneously drew inspiration from Maoist China and lent his support to 'anti-Western' insurrection movements in Angola, Chad and Sudan. While the US and France were busy celebrating their 'dear friend's' capitalist spirit, in 1966 he nationalised dozens of companies, among which were some of the country's most lucrative enterprises, such as diamond and copper mines in the Katanga region. In doing so, Mobutu deployed a more or less "socialist" (or "socialising") rhetoric, but in fact the move had one purpose only: to put money – huge amounts of it – in the bank accounts of the small, local nomenclature that had come to surround him and to line the pockets of his associates in the 'West'. Western Europe and the US made out like bandits and Mobutu shortly emerged as one of the wealthiest men on the planet.

Throughout, the Zairian leader showed a remarkable ability to juggle with the ideas, slogans and needs of multiple, often opposed, parties, from whom he managed to obtain just about everything he wanted. To do so, he developed two strategies, both of which need to be taken into consideration when addressing the Ali-Foreman match. To the first of these strategies he gave the name *"Recours à l'authenticité"* ("recourse to authenticity") or, in other contexts, simply *"Mobutisme"*.[4]

"Mobutisme", he explained, was a return to the country's roots. The people were to seek strength and direction in their ancestral past. In order to build a nation that was authentically theirs, they were instructed to look not to concepts imported from Europe, but to ideas and traditions of their forefathers.[5] With this in mind, Mobutu changed the country's name – Congo became Zaire – and renamed many cities as well (Léopoldville, for example, became Kinshasa) and, on 5 January 1972, Mobutu ordered all citizens to abandon their European (Christian) names for names that he insisted should be "authentically African". To refuse – to continue to go by the name Paul, or Anne or Jean – was to run a real danger: a stiff fine and prison sentence, or worse. Mobutu himself – whose *nom de baptême* was Joseph Désiré – changed appellations: he became Mobutu Sese Seko Kuku Ngbendu wa za Banga. "Sese Seko", in Lingala, signifies "which knows no end / that which will never cease being"; "Banga" means "fear". The message was clear.

In the beginning of his reign, in the second half of the 1960s and the very early 1970s, Mobutu was quite popular in the country. In part, this was due to Zaire's economic success.[6] Between 1967 and 1970, economic growth was in the ten per cent range and, thereafter, until 1973/74 it stood at about five per cent. These numbers were largely a result of the high price of copper on the world market: the Vietnam War was in full swing and there was strong demand for the red metal by weapons manufacturers. Also significant was a massive currency devaluation, which, in thorough contradiction with his party's rhetoric, Mobutu imposed in order to make Zairian exports affordable for his 'Western' partners. The economic windfall did not last, though. On 30 November 1973, Mobutu introduced the second of the two strategies that marked the first decade of his reign: "Zairianisation". The latter called for an expropriation of small and mid-

4   There are, in fact, distinctions between the *"Authenticité"* campaign and "Mobutisme." I eschew a discussion of these here, as they do not seem to me fundamental to the issue at hand. For a specialist of Congolese history, however, it will be clear that what follows contains significant (and perhaps not entirely excusable) ellipses.

5   "Roots", "ancestral past" and "traditions" are, needless to say, Mobutu's terms, not my own.

6   For an overview of the Zairian economy and its political ramifications under Mobutu, see Charles Didier Gondola, *The History of Congo*, Westport, USA and Georges Nazongola-Ntalaja 2002, *The Congo from Leopold to Kabila: A People's History,* London.

sized businesses belonging to foreigners – European, Asian and West African businesspeople, whose shops and small factories were turned over to members of the Mobutu clan. The result was disastrous. Most of the new owners had no financial experience, and a year later all of the expropriated businesses were nationalised. This move, the government referred to as *"la radicalisation"*; there was, however, nothing radical about it: the new owners stayed in charge, but under government supervision. Graft on a massive scale ensued and the economy went into a tailspin from which it never recovered. This tailspin was accelerated by a series of gargantuan construction and *mise-en-valeur* projects, each more useless than the next, among which was the creation of huge presidential parks and architectural sites. A case in point was the presidential domain of Mount Ngaliema, a sprawling marble palace overlooking Kinshasa designed by Fernand Tala-Ngai (1938–2006).[7] The Ali-Foreman match belongs to this series of projects. It is in this context, quite specifically, that it must be considered.

The economy was falling apart and the Zairian people were beginning to feel the effects of this cruelly. Mobutu, meanwhile, was getting more and more caught up in the 'authenticity' strategy that he had developed. The president, he had taken to stating, is akin to a 'traditional leader'. From whole cloth, he created the concept of a 'national chief', whose power knew no limits and whose role was to act as a 'father' (or, in still another iteration, a 'guide') for his people – a simultaneously severe and benevolent patriarch. Mobutu was less and less open to criticism – of any kind. As the economic situation worsened, he relied increasingly on the police, the army and a panoply of secret service outfits to silence a population becoming more and more hostile to his rule. 1974, the year of the fight, marked the beginning of the end: at this point, the downhill slide had become irreversible.

Round Two: In the Arena

The stadium where the Ali-Foreman match was to take place was the very incarnation of the debacle now underway. Its name was *Stade du 20 Mai*. This, however, had not always been the case. Initially, the arena was called *Stade du Roi Beaudoin*, after King Beaudoin I of Belgium. It was built even as Belgium was losing its hold on Congo – as a last hurrah by the embattled coloniser. This was in 1952, a few years before the coming of Independence. Beaudoin – a young man – had just acceded to the throne following the abdication of his father, Leopold III. Following the Second World War, in the face of the great powers, Belgium had nothing – nothing but its vast empire, which the young monarch could not fathom losing. Since the 1940s, Congo had been the site of a deeply engaged independence movement despite the fact that, across Africa, the colonial era was clearly coming to an end. However, Beaudoin would have none of it. He launched a colony-wide construction campaign, commissioning thoroughly useless structures in cities across Congo. Among these was a spanking new stadium for Léopoldville – Léopoldville, which, as we have seen, would soon become Kinshasa. Naturally, he named the new stadium after himself.

In 1955, Beaudoin travelled to Congo. A sumptuous celebration was organised to herald his arrival. Meant to be a crowning moment for Belgian colonisation, it took place in the stadium, before a crowd of 70,000 people. The event was immortalised in countless photographs seen around the globe. They were the last of an era: never again would the world press dare sing the praises of Belgian colonialism. Congo was about to explode, and the stadium was about to play an important role.

The first concrete signs that the end was coming occurred a little less than two years later on 16 June 1957, at an ordinary football match being played in the stadium. An unfortunate call by a referee caused a fight to break out between African and European members of the public. Things got out of hand and a few white folks' cars were set on fire. Anywhere else, this would hardly have been an issue, but in Congo it was something new: never had resentment for the colonial invader been expressed quite as publicly. The Belgian establishment was shocked and responded violently. In retrospect, the clash can be seen as fundamental: it marks quite clearly the beginning of the end. A second related event, also at the stadium, proved to be the nail in the coffin. It took place in 1959 – on 4 January. A football match again – a championship meet between the team of record in Léopoldville, Vita Club, and a little-known military crew called Mikado. Against all expectations, Mikado won, three goals to one, and walked away with the championship title. The atmosphere was tense as tens of thousands of fans streamed out of the stadium. Outside, the anger of the Vita supporters met another wave of anger: the Belgian authorities had just banned a meeting of ABAKO (*Alliances des Bakongo*), the most visible nationalist party in the capital. In the violently unequal social context of late 1950s Léopoldville, frustration from inside and outside the stadium became one. It was the straw that broke the camel's back.

All hell broke loose. Three days of riots ensued, in the course of which colonial monuments, schools and religious establishments were sacked. The Belgian government sent in the army. Predictably, the result was a bloodbath: forty-two dead and 250 wounded, all of them Congolese. ABAKO was dissolved. But it was too late. Nine days later, Beaudoin was forced to announce that Belgium was leaving Congo. Officially, the colonial era came to an end six months later, on 30 June 1960.

Clearly, this stadium where Ali and Foreman were to meet in 1974 was no ordinary place. Mobutu was eminently aware of this, and had been for some time. Two years after the coup that put an end

---

7   Tala-Ngai was responsible for a number of other "white elephant" construction projects of the period, among which the Ministry of Foreign Affairs and Supreme Court buildings, as well as the vast enclave where the now eponymous FIKIN (*Foire Internationale de Kinshasa*) takes place, with its yearly battle-of-the-bands, in which such acts as Papa Wemba and J.B. Mpiana go up against each other in night-long, near-apocalyptic encounters of sound, movement, gender violence and displays of fashion as a weapon.

8   Norman Mailer 1975, *The Fight*, New York, cited from version 1997, p.112

to the career – and the life – of Patrice Lumumba, Mobutu (the Guide) gave a new name to the arena: *Stade du 20 Mai*. The name refers to 20 May 1967, the day on which Mobutu published the *N'Sele Manifesto* – his party's charter, on the basis of which he went on to govern Zaire for the following two decades.

Freshly renamed, the stadium emerged as a key site for the first part of the Mobutu era: a gigantic theatre which Mobutu used to stage events around himself – rallies, military parades and the like, in front of captive crowds of tens of thousands of men, women and children. Well aware of its symbolic heft and of the political uses to which architecture can be put, in the run-up to the Ali-Foreman match, Mobutu instrumentalised the stadium to ensure that everyone understood the extent of his power – to underscore why it was that he had chosen to include the word Banga ("fear") in his newly minted Zairianised name.

The year 1973, as previously noted, marked the final period of the Zairian economic boom; by 1974, the downward spiral had begun. By all accounts, you could feel it on the street. Thefts and armed robbery were becoming common. A few Europeans had ended up on the wrong side of a knuckle or knife. The match was coming up and Mobutu wanted nothing that might mar the great moment he was planning. To this end, he came up with a plan that would make the stadium the centre of terrifying rumours. Norman Mailer, one of the great writers on boxing and the author of a book on the Ali-Foreman fight, offers the following on the subject:

"Late last spring, the crime wave grew so intense that thieves were posing as policemen. The wives of Americans were getting raped. A nightmare for Mobutu if foreigners should arrive for the fight and get mugged en masse. So his police round up in a hurry three hundred of the worst criminals they can find and lock them up in some of the holding rooms under the stadium. Then fifty of the three hundred were killed. For all we know, some of them could have been shot in the dressing rooms of the fighters. The key to the execution was that it took place at random [...] They just eliminated the nearest fifty. The random destruction was more desirable. Fear among the criminal population would then go deeper. Good connections with the police are worthless in such an unstructured situation. For much the same reason the other two hundred and fifty criminals were let go. So they could tell their friends of the massacre. The crime rate for this brief period is down. Mobutism."[8]

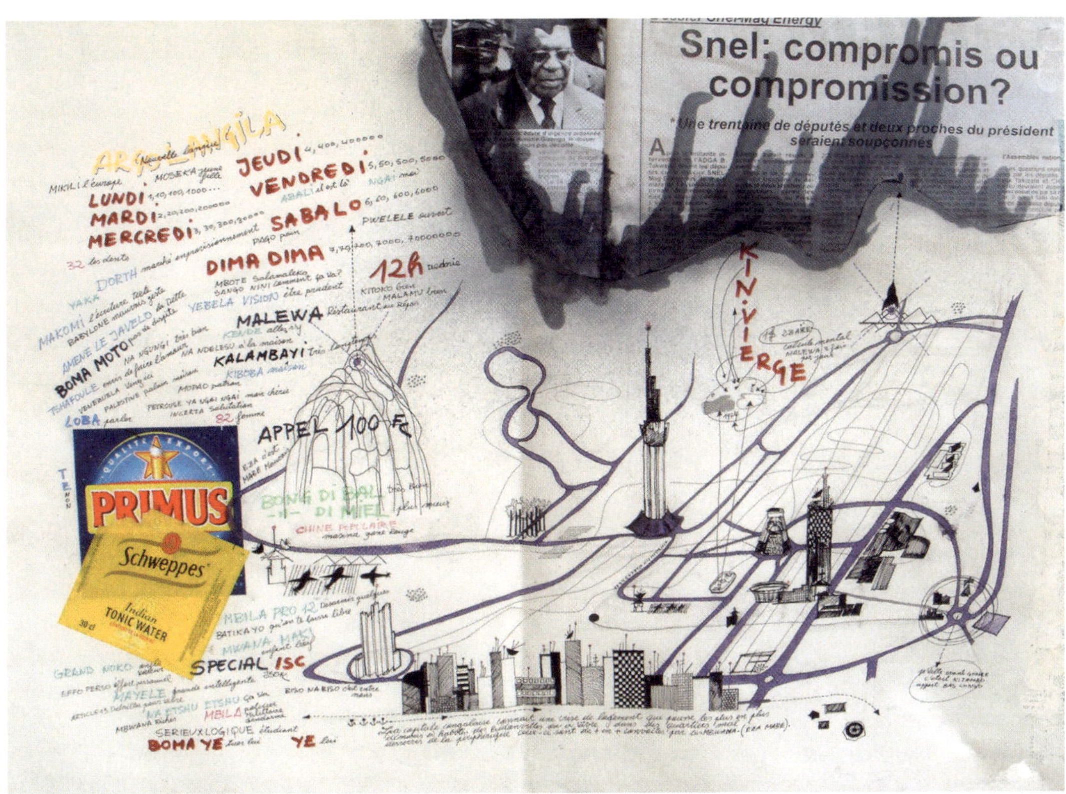

MÉGA MINGIEDI, **UNTITLED**, DRAWING AND COLLAGE ON PAPER, 2008

↑ An experimental map of Kinshasa, tracing the way the artist and the author took to the stadium where the Ali-Foreman "Rumble in the Jungle" took place in 1974.

The extraordinary thing, in all of this, is that no one has ever been able to establish beyond a doubt that these executions took place – or even that there was, in fact, a warren of cells under the stadium. Mobutu was a master in the art of manipulating rumour. It is quite possible (though again there is no proof one way or the other) that he created an architectural rumour and that this rumour functioned (most effectively) on two levels: on the imaginary of foreigners coming to Kinshasa for the fight and on the imaginary of the local population, who, already, was having to face on a daily basis the terror inflicted by Mobutu's police, army and secret services.

Indeed, it seems, talk of blood at the stadium went even further than Mailer may have been aware and, with this, Mobutu's manipulation of rumour. The Guide, Mbala Nkanga[9] notes, was notoriously interested in witchcraft. With this in mind, many Kinois saw a double symbolism in the bloodbath said to be taking place at the stadium. There were the surface explanations – Mobutu's determination to bring crime to heel, official worry that fear would keep foreign viewers away; and then there was the "true" (or in any event the more fundamental) reason: the executions were in fact sacrifices performed at Mobutu's behest to ensure that the event would be a success. According to *radio trottoir* – the story on the street – the blood of throats slit was sprinkled at strategic points around the ring. When, a few weeks later (as we shall see), the bout had to be postponed, rumours abounded of fresh blood spilt and sprinkled; Mobutu, it was said, was increasingly concerned that the fight would not happen at all. The image is, to say the very least, striking …

Outside, for the whole world to see, was a spanking new stadium (Mobutu, as the press reported daily, had had the entire structure refurbished by engineers brought in from across the world). Inside, hidden from view, as in a monster's inner sanctum, was a place where bodies were being butchered. And hidden still further, visible only to those blessed with "second sight" – *ndoki*, "seers" – blood drunk by the earth all about the ring where the boxers were to meet. If the goal was to cause a scare, the ploy (rumour or not) was wildly successful: twenty-five years after the fact, in a documentary on the fight, Mailer and others were still talking about the bloodletting.[10]

Round Three: Kin La Belle

The stadium was not the only structure that Mobutu refurbished in preparation for the fight. He also had the city's two fanciest hotels – the Memling and the Intercontinental – upgraded, as well as the public transport system for getting around the nicer

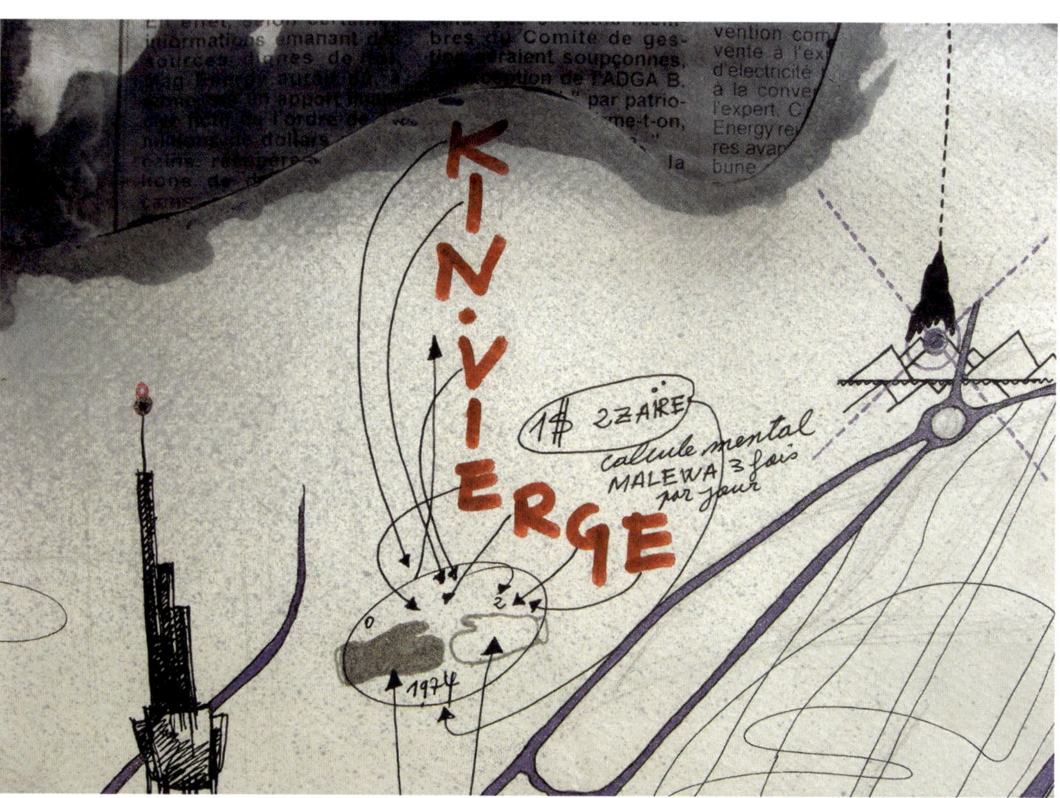

MÉGA MINGIEDI, **UNTITLED**, DRAWING AND COLLAGE ON PAPER, 2008 (DETAIL)

9   Personal communication, Chicago, 15 November 2008; Mbala Nkanga is a theatre director and scholar. He has taught directing, scenography and dramaturgical analysis at the *Institut National des Arts* in Kinshasa (DRC) and is currently professor for theatre studies at the University of Michigan. [editor's note]

10 Leon Gast (director) 1996, *When We Were Kings*

parts of town. On 7 August, *Elima* reported:

> "As of this moment, Kinshasa is ready and able to feed over 12,000 people three times a day. The Zairian capital can lodge over 9,000 foreigners. [...] The commission handling preparations for the match has acquired 105 buses, each with 80 seats, 100 twelve-seat minibuses and 100 Kombis for the press. At last count, there are also 2,500 taxis …"

In the stadium itself, Mobutu had had five hundred telephone lines installed, built darkrooms so photos could be developed onsite and erected towering light pylons, to ensure that news footage and documentaries could be filmed unhindered. All of this was explained in painstaking detail in the columns of *Elima* – this and the fact that the Guide had decided, on the occasion of the match, to bring colour TV to Zaire. This was no little feat when one considers that elsewhere in Central Africa (in Cameroon, for instance) the TV period only made its way onto the scene in the early 1980s.[11]

Why all of this spending? Why did Mobutu decide that he had to host the 'Fight of the Century' in Kinshasa? The answer is in part economic: The Guide was bent on attracting foreign investors.

Above all, however, the decision was political. For Mobutu, this was first and foremost an image-building project – Zaire's image, of course, but also (and most saliently) his own image. It was an exercise in monument construction: in erecting a monument to his power and persona.

Here, we find again the remarkable ability that Mobutu had juggling with ideas that at first glance seem wholly unrelated, or altogether contradictory. On the one hand, and very clear from the official press, Mobutu was intent on presenting his country as the incarnation of – the very window onto – a 'modern' Africa. References to *modernité* appear over and over again in newspapers of the day, along with the statement, often repeated, that Zaire would be able to welcome its American visitors "as if they were in their own country". At the very same time, in what would appear to be a thorough contradiction, the official press, the radio and posters placarded across the city were full of references to "authenticity". In *Elima* in February 1974, one could read the following:

> "We plan to make our country into a paradise on earth, a 'natural nature', as the President puts it, where humankind can come face to face with all things wild – the very wilderness that the human race has learned to destroy in the name of industrial civilization."

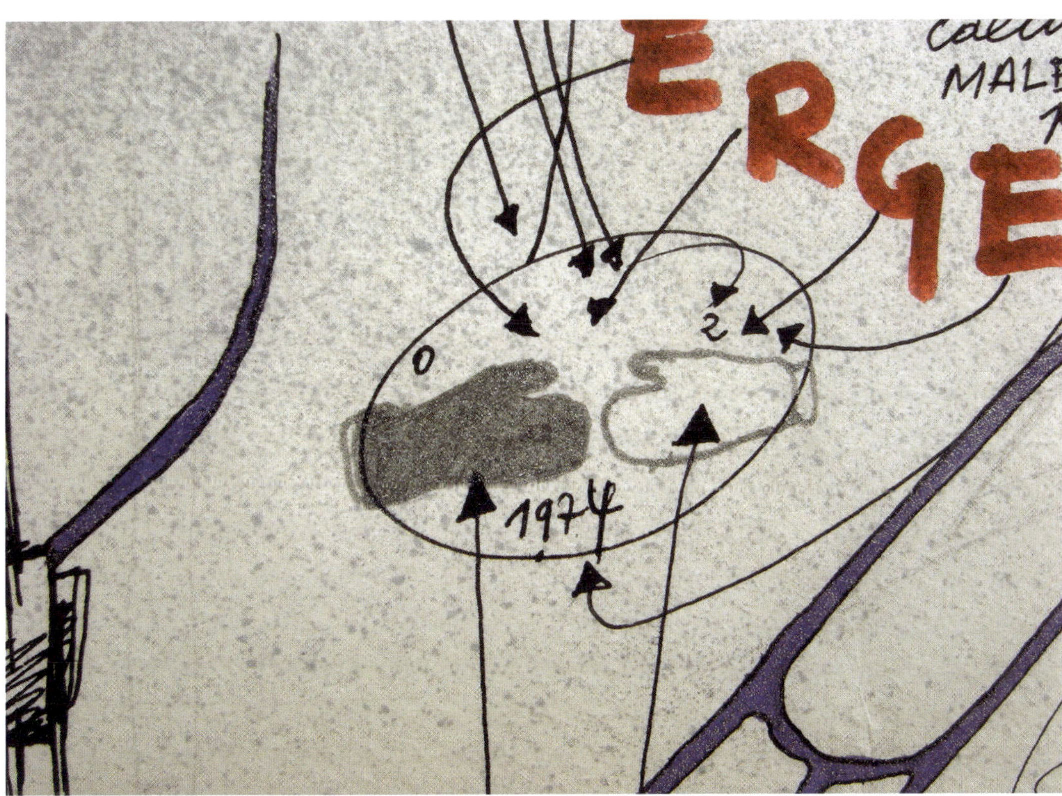

MÉGA MINGIEDI, **UNTITLED**, DRAWING AND COLLAGE ON PAPER, 2008 (DETAIL)

11 Mbala, Personal Communication, Chicago, 15 November 2008: What the papers did not report was the fate of another TV-related move by the Guide. At major intersections, Mbala recounts, Mobutu had had public monitors installed – four in each of the city's twenty-four wards. The idea was that people would gather there to watch the match. In short order, however, these public viewing stations became loci for the production and exchange of rumour, much of it directed against the president. On the monitors, one could watch the news. And on the news – state-run, of course – were brief clips about Zaire imported from Europe. If people had hoped that some sense of the regime's increasing violence was making its way through to the *métropole,* they were soon disabused. The news of Kinshasa from abroad was all of grand and much-appreciated preparations for the fight. As weeks passed, people began to gather around the public TV sets not to watch, but to make, the news: to exchange views about actual and, in their estimation, more relevant goings on in the city. Mobutu's viewing points had become nodes for the dissemination of criticism about his rule. Eventually, the monitors started disappearing. Understandably, the government did little about the thefts – if, indeed, this was a matter of thievery. The TV sets were not replaced. By late 1974, not a single monitor was left. A year later, even the metal structures to which the monitors had been bolted were gone.

Self-evidently, a contradiction is at hand, here – claims of "modernity" versus "authenticity", celebrations of the city as a space equipped with all the comforts of Western urban enclaves versus indictments of "industrial civilisation". Precisely the same kinds of contradictions attended Mobutu's expropriation and nationalisation of foreign businesses in 1973 and his simultaneous dependence for survival on the active help of capitalist governments and their armed minions – capitalist entities that he privately wined and dined and, for local consumption, publicly excoriated, accusing them (quite rightly, one might add, but in what were no more than rhetorical flourishes) of robbing his country and continent blind.

Round Four: The Greatest

In the context of the Ali-Foreman fight, the Guide managed with brio to reconcile such contradictions. This he set about doing in a very original way. He aligned himself on the discourse of one man: Muhammad Ali.

Ali, of course, was more – much more – than just a boxer. He was a man of honour and considerable courage. In 1968, he saw his heavyweight champion of the world title revoked after he refused to fight in the Vietnam War. "No Vietcong," he famously stated, "ever called me a nigger." At Malcolm X's side, he took a very public stand against racism in the US and, for this, was violently attacked by much of America. Still more trouble and violence came his way as a result of his conversion to the Muslim faith and his embrace of the Nation of Islam. Mobutu, whose popularity (like the Zairian economy) was in a tailspin, decided to pattern himself on Ali. He used the official press to suggest parallels between his vision of the world and Ali's – Ali, who, because of the positions he had espoused in the US, had become a hero in the eyes of many Zairians and across Africa more generally. On 12 February 1974, *Elima* printed the following:

> "We [meaning, of course, "I, Mobutu"] are determined to reverse, by all means possible […] the domination and the exploitation of the Black man, on the very soil of his ancestors, by foreigners."

A day later, the same newspaper reminded its readers that Ali held similar ideas:

> "For the oppressed of the world, Ali is not just a boxer: he is the defender of all Black people. Always in the service of his Black brothers, this great boxer is the idol of the oppressed. In him, Black Americans see a saviour; thanks to him, they know, at times, moments of joy. For this reason, Ali is friend to all peoples dedicated to justice, to all who would see racial segregation disappear for all time from the face of the earth."

And, again, a few days later:

> "Muhammad Ali is known as the great defender of the Black race. He is among those who do not hesitate to condemn racial segregation and who hope to see it disappear forever in the very near future. To make it so, he does not hesitate to help his brothers […] hostile (as he is) to people. As we too are great defenders of the Black race and powerful enemies of racism, it is only natural that we should be a centre of attention, a magnet for Muhammad Ali […] The Guide has once again (as he always does) acted in an eloquently powerful way…"

On 9 August, *Elima* said of Ali: "He is the greatest because his personality, his admirable will and his conviction can make miracles come to pass." The words were virtually identical to those used to describe the Guide in the written press and on the country's official radio station, *La Voix du Zaïre.* They were followed, on 15 September in *Elima,* by still another parallel drawn between Ali and Mobutu:

> "This super-championship […] is a triumph without precedent for Zaire. Thanks to this grandiose event, hundreds of millions of people across the planet will discover a young state determined to progress. A state that, like Muhammad Ali, will continue to surprise […] all nations."

Foreman, in contradistinction, was used by the Mobutu machine as a scarecrow – a straw man set up to assist in building up the president's stature. The official press deployed an image of Ali's opponent that took its lead from key sectors of the African-American press. In 1968, the year Ali was divested of his title because of his refusal to fight in Vietnam, Foreman won a medal – a gold medal, at the Mexico City Olympics. Many remember the '68 Olympics for the grand gesture that shocked the world: Tommie Smith and John Carlos, on the winners' podium, raising gloved fists in the name of Black Power, drawing the world's attention to the extreme racism still throttling the US at the time. At these same Olympics, Foreman had a rather different gesture: he waved a little American flag in celebration of his victory. Neither the Panthers nor the Black Power Movement forgave him.

Echoes of the foregoing appeared in the official *Zaïrois* press in 1974. Readers were reminded that between Mobutu, "defender of all Black peoples" and Foreman, apologist for America, there was a chasm. The point was underscored by an interview that *Elima* reprinted, in which Foreman celebrated the American dream, noting that he grew up in abject poverty, was a vandal wanted by the police, and that, thanks to the US government Job Corps, he discovered his passion – boxing – and, in the process, the path to righteousness. "So let no one criticise the United States to my face," he was quoted as saying. The situation is certainly fascinating.

With every passing day, in the official press, one can follow the process: a more and more effective instrumentalisation of Foreman by the Mobutu regime to political ends. Early on, most bets were on Foreman. He was younger than Ali, he was the reigning champion and had just managed to knock out Ken Norton – a giant of a man – in a fight that lasted less than a minute. Foreman was expected to win, but as the day of the fight approached, there was more and more talk about Ali triumphing as a result of his "moral courage". As fight night drew closer, talk of parallels increased between this courage and that attributed to another "fighter" – Mobutu Sese Seko. The sentence that had appeared in *Elima* is worth repeating, used as it was, in virtually the same form, to describe both men: "He is the greatest because his personality, his admirable will and his conviction can make miracles come to pass." No little irony here: Mobutu was celebrated by his own press for what allegedly differentiated him from Foreman and likened him to Ali, when, in fact – great friend to the CIA and hosted in great pomp at the White House in 1973 – it was indisputably with Foreman, and not with Ali, that he had the most in common.

Mobutu's "authenticity" politics had a lot to do with all of this. Unlike Foreman, who, as the countdown to fight-night began was depicted in the *Zaïrois* press over and over again as the man's man (Ali himself got involved, accusing Foreman of being a Belgian), his opponent was described as being "at home in Africa". "Here in my city of Kinshasa," Ali told the press, "all of my Zairian brothers – there will be thousands of them at the fight – will help me win back my title." *Elima* went so far as to announce that he was planning to settle in Zaire, to make it his home.

To reinforce this image – and its link to the image that Mobutu was busy building of himself – the press turned to an interesting use of photography. Every Sunday, *Elima* – quite a large-format publication – dedicated an entire page to the photograph of a famous person: a sports figure, a musician or (naturally) a picture of the Guide himself. On 9 September – a Monday, exceptionally – not one but two full-page photos appeared: they were of Ali and Foreman. Foreman is photographed from the back. He looks over his right shoulder, straight into the camera. The background is dark. It is a fairly typical pose for the newspaper: people are commonly shown either against a neutral, dark background or in such a way as to underscore an interest in things deemed modern – an "American" look, if possible, such as is seen in many portraits by the Kinois photographer Depara.[12]

Foreman, thus, appears in his official press photo against a neutral background, with his back to the camera. For Ali, the situation is radically different. "The People's Champion" – so Ali was known, as opposed to Foreman: "The World Champion" – appears straight on, head and torso facing the camera directly, surrounded by works of African art that have been chosen, quite explicitly, to reference ideas of "authenticity": a Tsaye mask from lower Zaire, a Kuba mask from the Kasai region and a Luba sculpture. The image is eloquent: the only other person whom one sees in the official press accompanied by African objects presented as "authentic" is Mobutu, who almost always appears with a carved cane intended to underscore his invented identity as a "traditional" chief and patriarch. Surrounded by masks and sculptures, Ali is theatricalised, *mise en scène* in a staging of the links Mobutu means to create between himself and Ali, via references to wholly invented notions of "authenticity".

This image of Ali surrounded by works of African art has a very particular origin. It belongs to a highly specific context, a fascinating chapter of Mobutu's reign that draws rather less attention than it merits. The Zairian president was the first African leader to officially raise the question of repatriation – the first to demand that ritual objects pillaged during the colonial era be returned to Africa. He did so in a speech delivered before the General Assembly of the United Nations in 1974 – a speech that was the subject of much commentary in the press and on the radio in Kinshasa.[13] Throughout 1974, the year of the fight, articles appeared in the *Zaïrois* press on a national museum planned by Mobutu, in which he intended to exhibit the works he wanted repatriated – a museum that was to be the embodiment of the "authenticity" he claimed for his regime. During this same period, he launched an acquisition campaign in which objects (ritual and otherwise) were bought in villages throughout the country, to be placed in the museum before European and American collectors could spirit them away.

The Ali portrayed in the official press was presented, thus, not merely as an ally of Mobutu, but also (and more importantly) as the very incarnation of Mobutu's politics of "authenticity" – an Ali who, according to *Elima,* referred to Zaire as "the land of his ancestors", whereas (*dixit* Ali) Foreman would "always feel like a foreigner here". On both the Zairian and the American side, much was made of this trope – this constructed "return to the homeland". Suddenly, weeks before the fight, everyone was singing the song of "authenticity". Mobutu presented Ali's alleged "return" as a gift that he, the president, was giving to his people. Posters plastered all over the city said so in so many words. Don King picked up on the idea and used it to clothe an economic move in ethical garb. King was not a Black Power figure. He was (and would remain throughout his career) a businessman, a cheerleader for the "American dream"; the defence of African-American rights was not at the top of his list. But he had a fight to sell, and he wanted to sell it to one public in particular: the

---

12 This interest in an "American look" is linked to a particular context: young men of the day who referred to themselves as *Bills*, Kinois who modelled their dress and gestures on cowboys seen in American Westerns and were deeply involved in the booming music culture of the time – jazz and rumba orchestras that were at the heart of Kinshasa's cultural life, a point I return to shortly.

13 Once again, however, Mbala notes, the official *Zaïrois* news media failed to report that the image of Mobutu abroad was not entirely rosy. Mobutu's speech at the UN was filmed. The uncut version, which of course was not broadcast "back home". Mbala points out, shows people in the audience shouting at the Guide in protest at the killings going on in Kinshasa.

emergent Black bourgeoisie in early 1970s North America. To do this, he launched a publicity campaign that played on precisely the same kinds of tropes as Mobutu's "authenticity" campaign – the same, feigned interest in origins and in protecting Africans from white greed. Hence the campaign's slogan, seen in posters designed for the occasion: "From Slaveship to Championship." Thanks to King, the poster suggested that African America was returning to its roots, reclaiming the place its people occupied before they were enslaved by Europe and North America. King was appropriating the rhetoric of movements such as the Nation of Islam, to which Ali belonged, in order to give a completely fictitious content – a Mobutuesque "authenticity" – to an enterprise whose sole reason of being was pecuniary and several of whose backers (beginning with the World Boxing Federation) were both white and (at best) thoroughly uninterested in the fate of African America.[14]

The "From Slaveship to Championship" poster centred on the fight, but it also referenced another aspect of the event organised by King: a brilliant move that turned the endeavour into much more than a boxing match. Around the fight, King had built up a remarkable music festival.

Over twelve bands were coming from the States to Kinshasa, among which were some of the biggest acts around. All were to appear at the stadium in the days preceding the match. James Brown, the King of Soul, would be there, as well as B.B. King and the Pointer Sisters. Miriam Makeba and Hugh Masekela – two heroes of the battle against apartheid both of whom at the time were living in exile were also to appear. All agree: this was an event like nothing anyone had ever managed to pull off before. Whatever one thinks of Don King, honour is due: in an America that was still, at this time, profoundly racist, whose body politic and social fabric were falling apart under the pressure of the Vietnam War – a war in which hundreds of thousands of young Black men were being deployed as so much cannon fodder – King had managed a miracle. That, in the process and in mounting the fight in the first place, as Bennetta Jules-Rosette underscores, he (like Mobutu and the white backers associated with both men) was actively putting to use, for his own benefit, racist preconceptions of the Black body, makes all of this quite complicated.[15]

Nothing, in the fight-cum-music festival that would come to be known as the Rumble in the Jungle was simple. On the Zairian side, the music festival was appropriated by Mobutu in the name, as ever, of "authenticity". Hence *Elima,* had this to say on the subject:

> "The public will discover still another marvel. A grand musical festival which the President of the Republic, General Mobutu, wishes to give as a gift to all of those fighting at his side in Zaire and across the African continent. The greatest names in Zairian music will

join hands with the greatest American voices: it will be like nothing the world has ever known."

King invited US acts to take part. This also played the "authenticity" card, reinventing "tradition" as they went. In the American musicians' entourage, (women and men, black and white) were seen sporting cloths emblazoned with Mobutu's effigy, convinced that, in so doing, they were becoming one with their host country. *Elima* was delighted:

> "This year, we see authenticity triumph as Black stars gather in Zaire for a music festival unlike any seen before – the 'festival of the century'."

> "It will be a great festival of Negro arts," the official newspaper intoned, in a hyperbolic reference to the *Festival des Arts Nègres* organised by Léopold Sédar Senghor ten years earlier in Dakar.

> "This gathering of Black American artists is not a simple festival. It is a festival that will allow our brothers [*"nos frères de race"*] to relive the realities of Africa after three hundred years of exile."

Mobutu, as the foregoing suggests, was singing the same song as Don King: "From Slaveship to Championship." Both men were constructing self-portraits that spoke of themselves as rendering a crucial service to a vast portion of humankind.

Present at the festival also, though they were given a far less prominent place than their brethren from the US, were key Zairian musicians. Among them were bands such as O.K. Jazz, the Stukas Boys, Zaiko Langa Langa, Tabu Ley Rochereau and Afrisa Orchestra, all of which, some against their will, in the 1970s and 1980s, were actively instrumentalised by Mobutu, who used them, when needed, as griots for his reign.[16] The situation was bizarre. Many of the American musicians, as previously mentioned, were seen in Kinshasa's swanky hotel lobbies wearing what they (mistakenly) took to be typical "African" garb (dresses, dashikis and assorted *abacosts* adorned with Mobutu's face). Meanwhile, on stage as on their album covers, many of the Zairian musicians patterned their look on what they perceived as a typical "American" look – this even as they were being presented by Mobutu's publicity apparatus as incarnations of "authenticity". Other events were planned around the fight and the music festival, all of which were advertised in the same "authenticity" register:

> "Alongside the [music] festival [*Elima* reports] there will be a strong participation from cultural groups, who will be arrayed around the city. They will show that

14 The poster served not only as an advertisement for the match, but also as a campaign for King himself, whose likeness is given as much prominence in its design as that of either fighter. The World Boxing Federation got a nice piece of advertising out of the widely distributed poster as well; indeed, it came out looking quite good, when, in fact, one would have been hard put to identify a more racist major business venture in the US at the time.

15 Bennetta Jules-Rosette, Personnal Communication, US-Europe telephone exchange, 12 November 2008

16 Bob White 2008, *Rumba Rules: The Politics of Dance Music in Mobutu's Zaire,* Durham, USA

this population of ours, which sings and dances, is very welcoming and is happy to collaborate with anyone […] as long as its authenticity is respected."

Still another event planned was an art exhibition at the *Parc de la Révolution,* where painters, potters and sculptors would show their work. The artists selected were all friends of the regime. The star was Liyolo, a sculptor whose œuvre centred on the Mobutist "revolution" and the peace and prosperity that the Guide claimed were his primary goals.

This type of work – a largely derivative and uninspired mix of Euro-American modernist sources – was explicitly what Mobutu wanted to show, mostly for foreign consumption. Little, if anything, else was given room to appear:

"Freedom of expression and authenticity will be fundamental themes in the exhibition [the press states]. To avoid any deviations from these lofty goals, however, it has been decided that, throughout the show, all other exhibition venues and all crafts markets where artwork is sold will be closed. This will ensure that all eyes are on the exhibit at *Parc de la Révolution*."

All of these events – and others still, including a conference on African-American literature and a show at the Intercontinental Hotel of works by another artist-griot of the Mobutu regime, Nkusu Felelo – were intended to take place at the same time, so as to create a massive synergy: a "mega festival" in celebration of Mobutist Zaire. But things did not go to plan. The schedule was thrown out of whack a few days before the fight. While training, Foreman had an accident and suffered a bad cut to his eyebrow. The fight had to be put off by six weeks.

Round Five: Knock-Out

It would take place, in the end, on 30 October. This complicated matters seriously, but at the same time made things more interesting – or in any event opened them up to the unexpected. Initially, Mobutu panicked. He was certain that his mega festival was going to collapse and, to avert this, grounded all flights: no one could leave the country. This prompted some hysteria among American guests, but eventually things calmed down. The foreign press left and returned six weeks later. Many foreign musicians left as well, but some stayed. People in Kinshasa at the time report extraordinary jam sessions and impromptu collaborations between *Zaïrois* and US musicians, most of which we have traces of today only in oral accounts.[17] Ali and Foreman were not amused, but remained and continued to train.

When finally the day, 30 October, came, the atmosphere in the city was electric. I will not, here, describe the match – most readers likely have a sense of how it unfolded – except to underscore a tactic deployed by Ali: a change of strategy mid-match that had a decisive effect. As the bout progressed, Ali realised that he could not beat Foreman through use of strength. The younger man was physically much stronger. And so Ali threw himself against the ropes and let Foreman exhaust himself, pummelling his older opponent nonstop. When Ali could, he returned punches, but at his own rhythm, and using the give of the ropes to absorb the violence of Foreman's hits. Ali was deploying his now-famous "rope-a-dope" trick.

This lasted for several rounds. Ali took a drubbing, but as Foreman hit and hit, his body tired and his movements became heavier and slower. Ali, meanwhile, stayed on the ropes, but began hitting back more often and faster – faster and faster and faster. Finally, the moment came when Ali sensed that Foreman was nearing the end of his tether. At this point he came off the ropes and turned the situation around, forcing Foreman into the position he himself had occupied for most of the fight. Foreman, exhausted, had not seen this coming.

Mailer picks up the story: "What a dislocation [for Foreman]: the axes of his existence were reversed! He was the man on the ropes! Then a big projectile exactly the size of a fist in a glove drove into the middle of Foreman's mind, the best punch of that startled night, the blow Ali saved for a career. Foreman's arms flew out to the side like a man with a parachute jumping out of a plane, and in this doubled-over position he tried to wander out to the centre of the ring. All the while his eyes were on Ali […] Vertigo took George Foreman, […] eyes on Muhammad Ali all the way, he started to tumble and topple and fall […] He went over like a six-foot sixty-year-old butler who has just heard tragic news […] Down came the Champion in sections and Ali revolved with him in a close circle, hand primed to hit him one more time, and never the need, a wholly intimate escort to the floor."[18]

A whole body of symbolism is at play here. Foreman, the man they said was the white man's man, the man everyone thought would win the fight, crumbled to the ground, felled by the man whom the press has dubbed "the Black man's hope". One would be hard put not to see – and most do see – in this moment a metaphor of Africa: Africa who, backed up against the ropes of history, battles the Leviathan – the 'West' – who would have the continent crumble, but instead finds itself face to face with Africa's fierce refusal to give in.

The next day, Mobutu welcomed Ali in his private residence. He would see Foreman too, but only the day after. It was with Ali first that he exhibited himself; he, Mobutu the winner, alongside Ali the winner; Mobutu the self-proclaimed hero who had brought to his people and to the world a festival that none would forget. He, Mobutu, who, in this year, 1974, proclaimed himself the sole leader of a single party leading one people, undivided, into the future and into history. Into a reign that he claimed would last one hundred years.

---

17 Anonymous source, Personal Communication, Kinshasa, 25 July 2008   18 Mailer (1975), p. 207 ff

Death Matters
Intimacy, Violence, and the Production of Social Knowledge by Urban Youth in the Democratic Republic of the Congo

FILIP DE BOECK

Introduction:
Children of Disorder in the Cemetery State

April 2008 – Kinshasa, the cemetery of Kintambo.[1] As I find myself walking on top of human remains, often hastily buried, the sickly smell of rotting corpses is undeniable. The cemetery of Kintambo, once the main cemetery of Léopoldville, and in use since the 1930s at least, is literally overflowing with corpses. In the late 1980s already, the urban authorities closed this cemetery down, but today, after two more official closures, the inhabitants of the neighbouring *quartiers,* the populated slum areas of Camp Luka, Quartier Congo and the slightly more upscale Jamaïk, still continue to bury their dead there. Every day, more corpses arrive in this cemetery that has long been abandoned by the city's authorities.[2] No longer taken care of, the cemetery has become, in the words of the Kinois, "a forest where snakes lay their eggs". The original ground-plan of the cemetery has totally disappeared. It has made place for lush vegetation that has totally overgrown this Thanatopolis, burying the dead for a second time. Here indeed, one dies twice: tombs and coffins are looted, or washed away by the rainy season's torrential storms, causing the dead bodies to disappear as rapidly as they were buried. Often, also, graves are recycled and different corpses are buried on top of each other for lack of space. Other tombs are destroyed to make place for illegal housing constructions, for in this urban jungle the living and the dead are engaged in a some-times fierce competition over land. The living and the dead live in close proximity; their lives seem intimately related. Kids play football between eroded graves; tombstones along the road serve as shop windows for second-hand clothes, bottles of palm wine, or plastic vessels made in China, which vendors with loud voices try to sell to passers-by; women harvest the corn and ground-nuts that grow from the bellies of the dead; mortuary houses in-side the cemetery are used as shelters by street children (whom Kinois refer to as *société morte,* dead society), while grave-diggers turn tombstones along the main road into their personal office space. In fact, through an informal commoditisation of death, the cemetery has become a market, a place to satisfy one's "thirst for money" (*lokoso*). Youngsters offer their services to the family members of the deceased or to the gravediggers. The latter are organised in a "stable" (*écurie*).[3]

More important, however, than the cemetery's decaying material infrastructure, or the seeming informalisation of death's econ-omy that is performed on the graveyard's surface, is the fact that the management of death and the labour of loss is no longer controlled and performed by elders, but is increasingly in the hands of children and youngsters. Whereas before children and youngsters were physically barred and protected by their parents and elders from contact with the dead, they now seem to have developed the most intimate connection with death.

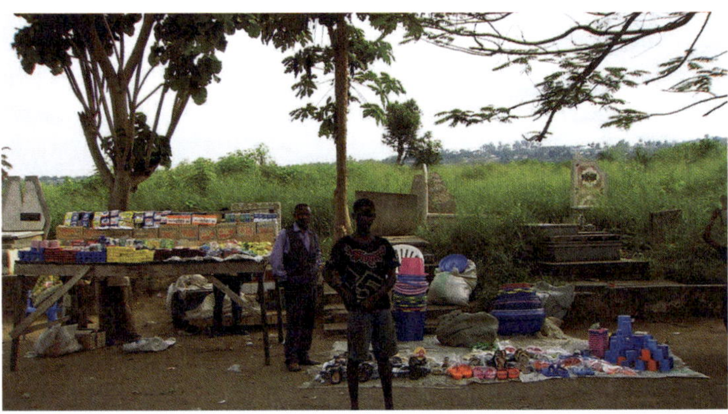

The presence of death has indeed profoundly reconfigured the access and use of public space in the urban setting. Some de-cades ago, in Kinshasa, placing the body of a deceased person

1   My ethnography builds on several years of field research in the city of Kinshasa. Research in Congo was made possible by a number of grants from the Flemish Fund for Scientific Research (FWO-Vlaanderen) as well as by a grant from the Flemish Community to develop an exhibition project entitled *Kinshasa, the imaginary city* (see Filip De Boeck and Marie-Françoise Plissart 2004, *Kinshasa. Tales of the Invisible City,* Tervuren). More recently, for several months between 2005 and 2008, I carried out research in a number of cemeteries in Kinshasa. Most of this field research was conducted in the cemetery of Kintambo, located between two of Kinshasa's more popular, populous and poor neighbourhoods (see Filip De Boeck 2008, "Dead Society" in a "Cemetery City": The Transformation of Burial Rites in Kinshasa, in: Lieven De Decauter und Michiel Dehaene (ed.), *Heterotopia and the City: Public Space in a Postcivil Society,* London, p. 297–308). I also directed a documentary film about Kintambo cemetery entitled *Cemetery State* (2009). Other cemeteries in Kinshasa and its periphery include Kimbanseke and Gombe (named after the commune where they are located), Kinsuka and Kimwenza (both in the commune of Mont Ngafula), Mbenseke and Mitendi (on the road to Matadi and the Lower Congo), Kisenzo (on the border between the communes of Mont Ngafula and Kisenzo), Kingampio, CIFORCO (ex-CIFORZAL) (in Masina, near the international airport), Mikonga (on the road towards Maluku), Kinkole (in the commune of Nsele), and Gombe Lutete. Some of these cemeteries were opened by the (post)colonial authorities, others were originally tradi-tional burial grounds of the Teke-Humbu, the local landow-ners and original inhabitants of Kinshasa (such as the ce-meteries of Kingampio, Kimwenza, Mikonga and Sans Fil in Masina). Some cemeteries such as Kanza, Sans Fil and Makala have ceased to exist in the meantime, while others are menaced by the uncontrolled and rapid urban sprawl

in the middle of the street would have been unthinkable. In the 1960s and 1970s mourning rituals took place inside the compounds, while children and youngsters were barred from any contact with death itself. If a funeral procession passed through the street, mothers would call their children indoors: children were not supposed to come into contact with death, since they represent the beginning of life and should not be contaminated by its end. Today, however, for lack of space within the compounds, the body of the deceased is often placed upon a bier in the middle of the street, under a funeral chapel, and people gather around the body to mourn the deceased and hold nocturnal wakes accessible to all. Streets are blocked and palm leaves are placed at their entrance. As such, the dead, also because they have become so numerous, have quite literally taken possession of the urban public space and have redefined its meaning and its use in the process.

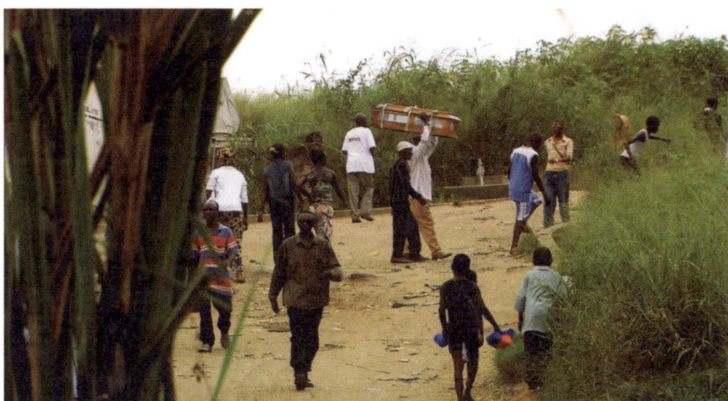

Today, children and youngsters have taken over the control of the mourning and burial rituals. They are also the ones to accompany the deceased on their last journey from the compound to the cemetery. This phenomenon might be observed throughout the city, but it is especially the case in Camp Luka, an overpopulated slum area that borders on the cemetery of Kintambo and which grew out of an illegal squatting area in the 1970s. Among its inhabitants Camp Luka is known as "The State" (*leta*). Camp Luka's youngsters, who call themselves the "children of the State" (*bana état*) or "the children of disorder" (*bana désordre*) impose disorder, their law, the unruly "law" of this strange and ragged state onto the cemetery and indeed the rest of the city. They do so in effervescent ways, ludic and violent at once, during the mourning rituals (*matanga*) and funerals, and through the materiality and aesthetics of the body – both their own and that of the dead.

My contribution is situated at the nexus between (corporeal) intimacy, violence, and the production of social knowledge by urban youth in Congo. More specifically, I focus on the ways in which, in this urban setting, the vitality of the youthful body and

the "life of the corpse", to use the phrase by the Mexican artist Teresa Margolles.[4] Youth and death are two categories that normally exclude each other, but that have become intimately connected in Kinshasa. It is this connection that provokes us to think about the seemingly counterintuitive ways in which young people confronted with powerful societal problems articulate their "law", their sociality, out of the very source of their desperation. By eliding life and death, by placing us in the presence of death, Kinois youngsters forcefully remove the distance we would normally place between ourselves and the dead, and give a new identity to themselves as well as to the city.

If, as Lévi-Strauss famously remarked in the concluding pages of *Tristes Tropiques,* cities are machines *"destinées à produire de l'inertie à un rythme et dans une proportion infiniment plus élevée que la quantité d'organisation qu'ils impliquent"*[5], the cemetery of Kintambo seems indeed to be the right place to redefine anthropology as *entropology, "une discipline vouée à étudier dans ses manifestations les plus hautes ce processus de désintégration".*[6] But is this what is really going on in Kinshasa's burial grounds? It is easy to read a space such as the cemetery of Kintambo, with its infrastructural degradation and the breakdown of cultural norms and longstanding notions of social order that accompany this material decay, as a general metaphor for the zombified state of a city and a country that, in the words of Kinois, "died" or "rotted a long time ago" (*mboka ekufi, mboka ebebi*), or are conceived of as terminally ill and

and 21.47 per cent in 2004. That means that 23.65 per cent of all of Kinshasa's deceased for these years was buried in a cemetery that no longer exists officially. (I have only received figures for the first nine months of 2005, and none for later years.)

3   In the cemetery of Kintambo the main "stable" is called Shamukwale, the name of a village near the Angolan border. At this location people enter into Angola in order to engage in clandestine artisanal diamond mining. Grave digging is here compared, not without irony, to diamond digging. The Écurie Shamukwale, an informal overarching association, consists of a number of separate smaller groups, such as the Écurie Bana cimetière, Écurie État-Major or Camp Kawele, Écurie Camp PM (Military Police), Écurie Camp Police et cetera. The person recognised by most as the head of the informal Shamukwale association is the older brother of one of the cemetery administrative officials, who resort under the city governor's authority. These officials are supposed to register the dead and collect certain taxes. The members of the informal gravedigger groups are all young boys and men from the surrounding neighbourhoods. Other youngsters who offer informal services in and around the cemetery are often also organised in similar *écurie* structures. These various groups at the cemetery of Kintambo offer specific services (digging graves, fabricating crosses, maintaining the tombs, and so forth). Some of these youngsters also offer their services for clandestine burials. Very often, people who cannot afford to finance a burial are forced to bury their dead in a secret and non-official way. This happens more frequently when the deceased is a young child. Along the dust road that cuts through the cemetery and forms the access to the neighbourhood of Camp Luka, a small group of male adolescents, members of the Écurie Tshico, wait to be contacted by parents who want to bury their child without registering with the authorities and by bypassing the regular formalities. In such a case the burial is carried out at nightfall. Other groups of youngsters spend their days waiting along the cemetery to be hired as singers and drummers during the funeral. Others still await nightfall to dig up and steal the coffins of those who were buried during the day. These coffins are subsequently resold (see De Boeck and Plissart (2004), p. 136). Finally, some youngsters await the night to pillage the graves in the hope of laying their hands on clothes and jewellery.

(Kinsuka, Kisenso). Some cemeteries are also threatened by erosions (Kisenso) or were officially closed by the authorities (as in the case of Kasavubu, where the cemetery subsequently became a huge vegetable garden). Finally, numerous burial sites in and around the city of Kinshasa are not known to the city's authorities.

2   A lot of burials are still taking place at the cemetery of Kintambo. At the Division Urbaine of Kinshasa, the city's administrative unit responsible for all of Kinshasa's cemeteries, no official statistics are kept about the amount of burials performed every year throughout the city. However, since 2002, the new head of the Service d'Inhumation keeps track himself of the number of burials, and arrives at a yearly average of 21,968 deaths (until 2005). The cemetery of Tsuengu (Masina SIFORCO) seems to absorb more bodies than any other cemetery, but Kintambo still ranks second, with 25.17 per cent of the city's burials in 2002, 24.31 per cent in 2003

4   See Udo Kittelmann and Klaus Görner (eds) 2004, *Teresa Margolles: Muerte sin Fin,* Ostfildern-Ruit.
5   Claude Lévi-Strauss 1974, *Tristes Tropiques,* New York, p. 413
6   Lévi-Strauss (1974), p. 414

cadavéré.[7] But are notions of entropy, chaos, disorder or dissipation of energy adequate tools to understand the dynamics of a place such as the cemetery of Kintambo? Do they have sufficient explanatory power to fully capture the meanings embedded in the new mourning and funeral practices that have developed around it? It is indeed tempting, perhaps even too obvious, to understand Kinshasa's postcolonial cemetery as a mere zone of social abandonment, to use Biehl's term[8], a zone of abandonment with specific Agamben-esque connotations, in which the law is in force but no longer has substantive meaning.[9] The cemetery of Kintambo and its surrounding slums indeed offer an almost camp-like infrastructure (as Camp Luka's name already indicates in itself), which exemplifies the state of exception that has become the rule in postcolonial Congo. This abandonment illustrates to what extent Kinois are turned into *homines sacri,* collectively reduced to the specific forms of *vie nue,* the raw bare life as described by Agamben, that is a politicised form of natural life, a life exposed and subjugated to death, placed outside both the divine and the profane law.

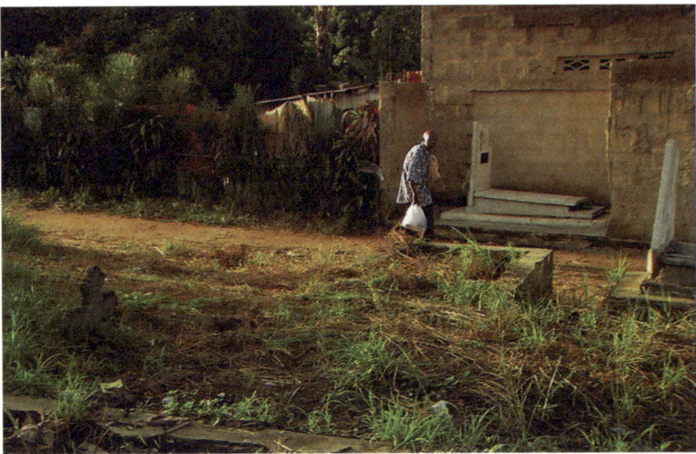

In this contribution, I want to analyse how youngsters, through their cohabitation with death and the generation of new forms of mourning and coping with dispersal and loss, reframe the conditions of such bare life into something else. Through an ethnographic description of their – sometimes violent – involvement in matters pertaining to death, I will analyse specific local attempts made by Kinshasa's youth to turn the aporia of this naked life-form into more euphoric solutions, or at least explore the possibility of (re-)introducing *sacrifice* to give meaning to their own death. In the process, I argue, urban youngsters reconceptualise the camp, the very territory of death itself, in terms of a more heterotopic space. This effort enables Kinois youth to contest and rethink the time of the state and the postcolonial political order, and in so doing express their longing for new political futures.[10] It also offers them the possibility to redefine Congo's ongoing economic and socio-political crisis in terms of a primarily moral critique of the specific necropolitics that underpins the postcolonial state of exception.[11]

Youth, Religion and Death in the Apocalyptic Interlude

For decades now, Congo has been in the grip of a profound crisis that makes itself felt in every field and on every level of Congolese society: politically, economically, socially and culturally.[12] In fact, the crisis is so multiform and omnipresent that there hardly seems to be a way out of the harsh living conditions it has created. "We live like animals" (Lingala: *tokomi kovivre lokola banyama*) is an often heard remark in Kinshasa's streets. One of the only available answers to face the hardships imposed by this widespread crisis is provided by religion. Over the past two decades, as elsewhere in Congo and indeed Africa, Kinshasa has witnessed the rapid spread of Christian fundamentalist churches. Replacing to an important extent the "traditional" Catholic and Protestant religious practices that were introduced during colonial times, Pentecostalism, churches of awakening, charismatic renewal churches and other millenarian movements have deeply penetrated the lives of city dwellers. It is this Christian fundamentalism that has imposed its logic and its temporality onto the city.

However, the very field of death, and the practices that are generated around it, seem to escape, at least to some extent, the hegemony and control of the churches, whether of Pentecostalist, Catholic or Protestant signature. The funeral processions that accompany the deceased to his or her last resting place in the cemetery have often turned into moments of contestation of existing, religious as well as political, figures and structures of authority.[13] When the coffin with the corpse is carried through the streets, especially if the deceased was a young person, children and youth flock around it to sing songs with an outspoken political character: *Toyei, toyei matanga, toboyi baconseillers, soki olingi koteya, teya bandimi na yo. Soki olingi koteya teya bana na yo. Soki olingi koteya teya na ndako na yo* ("We go, we go to the mourning ritual. We refuse the councillors – the elders' authority. If you want to preach, preach for your believers. If you want to preach, preach for your own children. If you want to preach, preach in your own house"). Other songs have a clearly political content: *Bana na diplome bakei koteka mayi, bana na diplome bakeyi koteka boudin. Pays riche lokumu ezali wapi?* ("Children with a diploma sell water, children with a diploma sell sausages. A rich country, but where is dignity?"). Sometimes they even give voice to a nostalgia for the former Mobutist regime: *Mobutu Mobutu tango okenda loso na loso* ("Mobutu ever since you left, we only eat rice [we are hungry]").

7   Filip De Boeck 1998, Beyond the Grave: History, Memory and Death in Postcolonial Congo/Zaire, in: Richard Werbner (ed.), *Memory and the Postcolony. African Anthropology and the Critique of Power,* London, p. 21–57, Filip De Boeck 2005, The Apocalyptic Interlude: Revealing Death in Kinshasa, *African Studies Review* 48/2: 11–32

8   João Biehl 2005, *Vita. Life in a Zone of Social Abandonment,* Berkeley

9   Giorgio Agamben 2005, *State of Exception,* Chicago

10 See Bogumil Jewsiewicki and Bob White 2005, Introduction. *African Studies Review* 48/2: 1–9. [Special issue on mourning and the Imagination of Political Time in Contemporary Central Africa]

11 Achille Mbembe 2003, Necropolitics, *Public Culture* 15/1: 11–40

12 Theodore Trefon (ed) 2004, *Reinventing Order in the Congo. How People Respond to State Failure in Kinshasa,* London

13 Ivan Vangu Ngimbi 1997, *Jeunesse, funérailles et contestation socio-politique en Afrique,* Paris

Funerals, however, have become much more than moments of contestation for a rebellious urban youth. Their social and political criticism reaches far beyond the level of official state politics, and touches on deeply moral issues, related to much more intimate domains. Their actions pose fundamental questions with regard to the possibility of inter-subjective relations; possible reconfigurations of what kinship might mean and of the dividing lines between insider and stranger; or the very definition of the notion of ancestrality, and the feasibility of continued intergenerational transmission of social knowledge. All of this comes to the surface during the *matanga,* the mourning rituals that accompany the death and burial of a parent, a beloved one, a friend or a neighbour.

Youth, Death and Witchcraft Accusations in the Urban Public Realm

Matanga have always been extremely important communal moments of encounter, creating wide-ranging social networks that are regenerated from one *matanga* to the next. As Durham and Klaits remark with regard to funerals in Botswana, "people find themselves connected in their very physical wellbeing through emotional states and sentimental connections recognised and

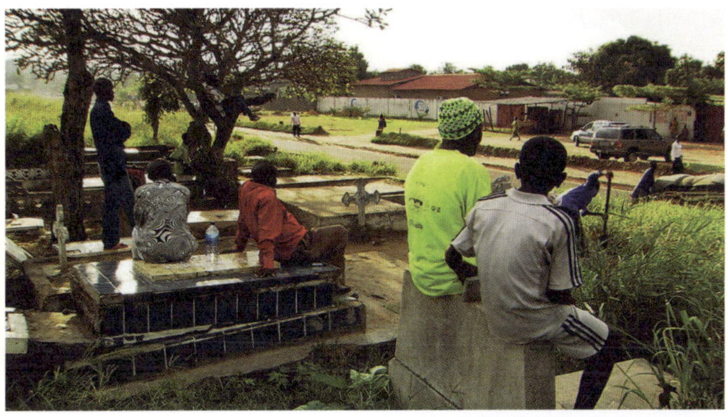

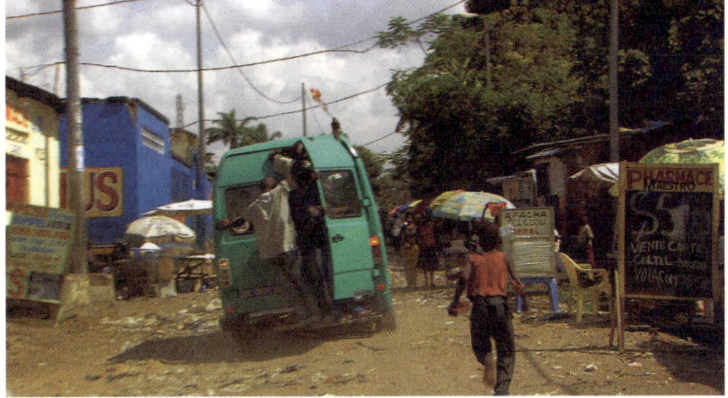

forged in public space".[14] What produces the connectedness between all those present is the sense of shared, collective *Trauerarbeit,* shaping up around an intimate, often corporeal and tactile, and always highly emotional relationship with the very body of the deceased. Family members, friends and neighbours gather around the dead body, weep, sing, address the deceased, touch and embrace the body, dance around it and take care of it during a whole night of mourning, until its burial the next day. That does not exclude this collective labour of loss from being a ludic happening as well. *Matanga* invariably also offer occasions for laughter, amusement, flirting and excitement; they hold out the promise of new encounters, or the joy of meeting up with old friends and acquaintances. At the same time, *matanga* are very weighty occasions in which existing hierarchies and power relations within and between families, lineages and clans are reaffirmed or contested. Usually, the maternal uncles of the deceased are the ones in charge of the funeral. They decide upon the time and place of burial, raise the necessary money, hire chairs, an orchestra and/or choir, contact the authorities, take care of the formalities for burial, meet the cemetery authorities, supervise the unfolding of the mourning period until the burial, assemble the deceased's family (the mother's and father's side, and the in-laws), conduct the palavers surrounding heritage and funeral contributions, and, most importantly, establish the cause of death, certainly in cases where witchcraft is suspected to be at the origin of a person's death.

In Kinshasa today, *matanga* often continue to be important motors for the production and renewal of the cohesion of social networks, especially if the deceased is an adult person or elder. The *matanga* is the nocturnal time-space in which the whole social landscape that unfolds between people during the day is constructed. It sets the scene for the replenishing of the social weave which unfolds during the day.

Matanga lose their broader integrative force, however, when a young person dies. In that case, suspicions about witchcraft are quick to surge to the surface. Youngsters in particular are quick to blame the deceased's parents, uncles and elders for this death (*balei ye, babomi ye:* "they ate him", "they killed him"). Usually, such accusations tend to drastically alter the course of the funeral itself. The *matanga* almost invariably "turns into disorder" (*matanga ekomi désordre, pito-pale*) and becomes an intergenerational battlefield. When that happens, the deceased's friends, his or her classmates, or just any youngster living in the same neighbourhood, are likely to take over the control of the *matanga* and of the funeral rituals. These groups of youngsters, the "people of disorder" (*bato ya désordre*), sometimes in collaboration with local youth gangs, referred to as the "strong people" (*bato ya makassi*) or *yanke* (from "yankee")[15], often start to throw stones at all who are present on the site of mourning. They up-

14 Deborah Durham and Frederick Klaits 2002, Funerals and the Public Space of Sentiment in Botswana, *Journal of Southern African Studies* 28/4: 777–796, here p. 778

15 Kristien Geenen 2009, "Sleep Occupies no Space". The Use of Public Space by Street Gangs in Kinshasa, *Africa* 79/3: 347–368, Katrien Pype 2007, Fighting Boys, Strong Men, and Gorillas. Notes on the Imagination of Masculinities in Postcolonial Kinshasa (DR Congo), *Africa* 77/2: 250–271

root the trees in the compound, or attack the deceased's parental home, often destroying or burning it down in the process,
while beating up or chasing away the parents, uncles, aunts and
preachers who are gathered there to mourn the deceased. The
general atmosphere quickly turns into a chaotic and often violent mood, further enhanced by the youngsters' singing and
dancing (in ways inspired by South-African toyi-toying), and the
lavish use of marijuana and locally brewed alcohol (*lungwuila,
chichampa* or *lotoko*).

Invading the scene of mourning they will single out certain elders while singing: *Tango mosusu ndoki ye yo ye yo* ("Maybe
the witch is this one or that one"). The youngsters will then con-
fiscate the abandoned dead body, block the street and erect a
"frontier" (*barrière*). In this way they "colonise" public space to
establish their "state", their "rule", which is marked by the order
of disorder.[16] They force passers-by to make a monetary contribution. In case they refuse they risk, at the very least, to be
dirtied with a mixture of burned rubber and palm oil. The money
thus extracted is often spent on the burial itself.

Clearly, at that point, the deceased's family members no longer
control the funeral, and do not risk showing up at the funeral itself. Frequently, it is only after completion of the burial that the
responsibility for the dead person is handed over again to his or
her family, and not without long negotiations over whom the
muziku, the money raised by the *matanga's* participants, should
go to. Sometimes the family of the deceased tries to mobilise
the police to regain control over the corpse during the funeral
procedures, but often the policemen refuse to get involved. And
when they do, their intervention often leads to a further deterio-
ration of the situation. Not infrequently, youngsters are hit by
police bullets on such occasions.

Under these circumstances, the funeral itself inevitably turns
into a highly chaotic event. Minibuses and cars are routinely
confiscated in the street by youths. Sitting on the car's rooftop or
hanging out of the windows while singing and shouting, they
use these hijacked cars to drive to the cemetery at high speed.
Often the coffin with the corpse is paraded through the streets,
carried by the deceased's friends and surrounded by dancing
boys and girls singing lewd songs, full of sexual license, while
revealing certain body parts and making obscene gestures:
Lelo libola etuli, lelo libola ekei kopola ("Today the vagina no
longer works, today, the vagina will rot away"). Other songs include: *Awa ezali hotel. Oyei, osali, ya premier coup ezalaka
direct* ("Here [the cemetery] it is a hotel. You come, you make
love, and from the very first shot it is goal!"] or *Mayi! Mayi! Mayi
mibali, mayi mayi mikongo, mayi mayi! Soki nakangi yo nakocha
yo etsubeli, etsubeli, etsubeli! Nakosiba yo!* ("Water, men's water,
water from the backbone [sperm], water, water! When I catch
you, I will put my penis inside you, the penis, the penis, I will fuck
you!").

Often, also, during these unruly funeral processions, the young
carriers of the body perform a divinatory ritual on the corpse,
asking the dead person to direct them to those responsible for
his death (namely his family elders).

The same frenzied atmosphere characterises the burial itself.
Here youngsters often start to dance on the graves, while undressing and exposing their genital parts (*mutakala, nzoto libanda*).

Youth and the Resacralisation of Death

At first glance, death seems to have become a banal reality in
the urban context, when compared to the elaborate funeral rituals and mortuary prescriptions that existed in the rural hinter-
land surrounding Kinshasa until recently.[17] Youngsters will no
longer use the more respectful Lingala word *kufa,* to die, but will
speak instead of *dayé* (from the English "to die"), to show their
indifference or even disdain for death. This seeming banalisation, and according to many older Kinois, even desecration of
death, expresses itself in various ways: not only in the language
youngsters use to denote death, but also in the general attitude
towards the dead who no longer inspire fear, awe and respect,
or in the mere fact that the dividing line between the living and
the dead has become so difficult to trace. As Kinois say: "We
(the living and the dead) are all the same" (*biso nionso bato
moko*). For most youngsters, and in spite of the influence of
Pentecostalism, death signifies the end. There is nothing beyond
death, one just disappears. This attitude sharply contrasts with
former autochthonous beliefs in ancestrality. Today, however, it
seems as if the production of ancestors, at least in the mind of
these youngsters, has ground to a standstill. No longer the prerogative of elders, the management of death is used by the
young to contest the authority of ancestors, and by extension,
adults: "If you do not watch out," they threaten their elders, "we
will make you eat the shovel" (*okoliya mpau*), meaning: we will

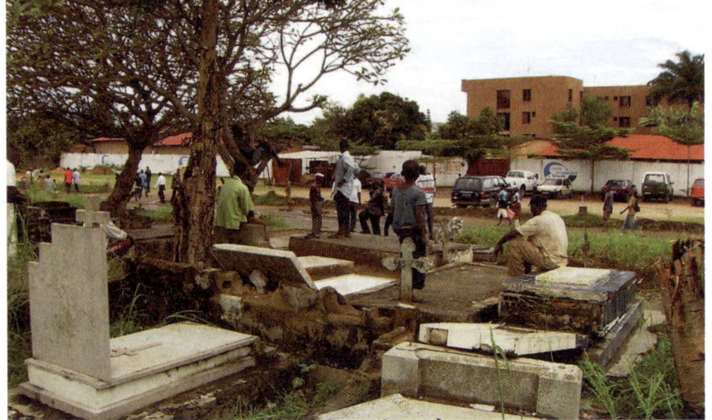

16 This phenomenon, which some Kinois interpret as a privati-
    sation of the *matanga* as public event, is known as *kuluna,*
    a word derived from the Lingala verb *kolona*: to plant, to sow,
    to cultivate. The verb is, of course, itself a derivative of the
    French *coloniser.* In this way, youth's unruly law constitutes
    a particular example of the coincidence of disorder with the
    fixation on the legal that characterises postcolonial reali-
    ties; see John Comaroff and Jean Comaroff 2006, *Law and
    Disorder in the Postcolony,* Chicago.

17 René Devisch and Wauthier de Mahieu 1979, *Mort, Deuil et
    compensations mortuaires chez les Komo et les Yaka du
    nord au Zaïre,* Tervuren

bury you. "How can we still respect the elders?" youngsters told me. "They are the ones who should uphold tradition, who tell us about the important place of the ancestors, but when you see how they cope with the dead who will become the ancestors, when you observe how their corpses are put in the street, how they are buried hastily, how can you continue to believe this? Our elders have turned the process of dying into a *fait-divers*, and they have started to treat the dead with disrespect. So why should we still respect the elders?" Funerals, in this way, have not only become a means for political contestation, but in a much broader sense death has become an occasion for youngsters to criticise the role of parents and elders who have *démissioné*, who have given up, who no longer seem to be able to fulfil their promises, and whose moral authority has vanished. In the light of this failure of gerontocracy, "corpses have become the responsibility of the youngsters of the neighbourhood" (*bibembe ekoma ya bana quartier*). The dead have become their "toy" (*eloko ya jeu*), and the coffin, so this urban youth claims, has become like a football that one tosses up and plays with. Youngsters, in short, have become "the directors" (*bazali kodiriger*) and have taken over the control of the dead, while elders "have become little children" (*bakomi bana mike*).

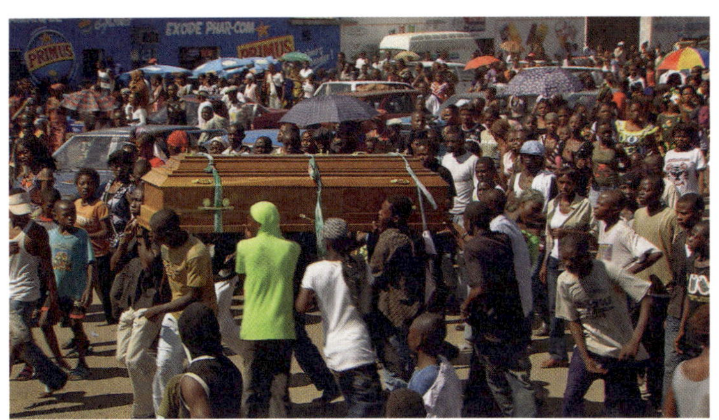

These are radical societal shifts, which accompany a disturbing demographic reality: not only is death and its management no longer the prerogative of elders, they are also no longer the only ones to die. Life expectancy in Congo is among the globe's lowest, and the young die in great numbers. The intimate connection between youth and death provokes us to think differently about the seemingly counterintuitive ways in which young people in Kinshasa confronted with powerful problems articulate a semblance of sociality out of the very source of their desperation. In fact, what appears to be a desacralisation and banalisation of death by youngsters hides a totally different register. In the face of economic ruin, homelessness, apocalyptic predictions, and baseless hopes, young Kinois have designed a new architecture of urban survival for which death, and the very materiality and aesthetics of the dead body, by seeping so visibly and violently into the fabric of life, now serves as an inspirational force, a structural support, a framing device for negotiating social relationships and constructing identities. In a world where mourning has reconfigured meaning, where cemeteries have become dwellings for the living, and where coffins are likened to the footballs that boys toss around, the only way to live is to manage death. For young Kinois who deal with dead bodies on a routine basis, dying is no longer a departure from life, it has become that which gives life its significance, density, and directionality. Life in fact cannot be lived, nor spoken, nor even imagined, outside of the space of death.

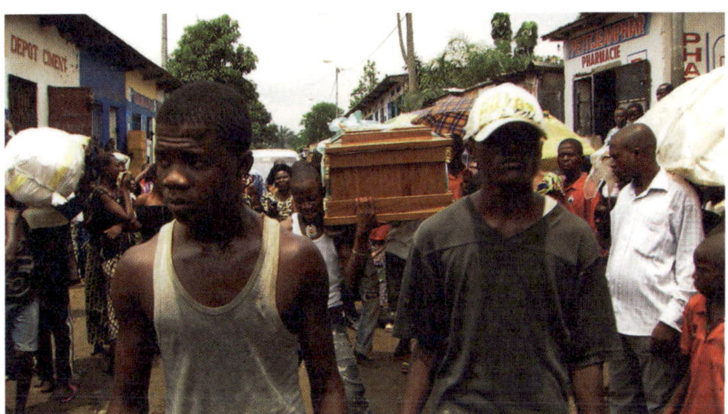

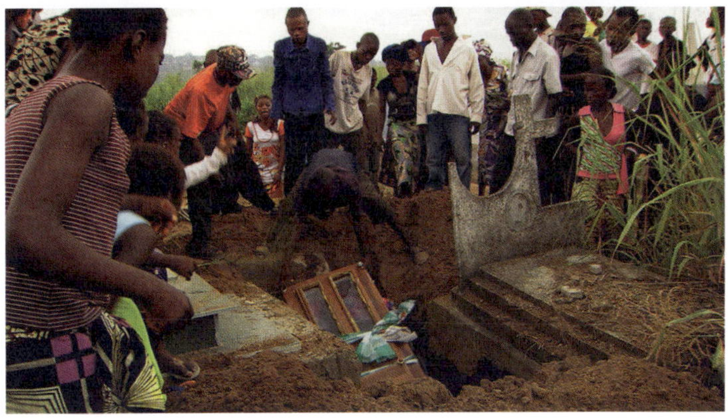

Conclusion: Youth, the Morality of Disorder and the Ethics of Being Human

The repositioning of death enables youngsters in Kinshasa to break away from older models and to redraw the social and moral landscapes of urban public life. Firstly, funerals offer the possibility to reject current official political and religious order (all the more surprising given the thorough grasp of the millennial churches on all other aspects of public life in Congo today). Secondly, funerals form key moments to contest the role of the elders, who are perceived to have abandoned their responsibilities and have failed to live up to the expectations of the young they are supposed to guide and protect. Mourning rituals and funerals thus bear witness of the profound crisis of intergenerational transmission and of existing structures of family and kinship. Funerals, in their guise of ritualised moments of rebellion against the established order, allow youngsters to design an alternative political and also moral landscape. By replacing the rule of the state, the church, the ancestor and the elder with their own rule, which is characterised by "disorder", young Kinois reshape the city's outlook and draw an alternative cartography of the urban public sphere. They abandon older prescriptions, taboos, norms and forms surrounding death and mourning and are thus perceived by the generations of their parents and grandparents as sacrificers of the sacred, as desecrators of the dead, and therefore as highly immoral actors in an urban universe that is otherwise characterised by the high moral discourses of Pentecostalism.

Paradoxically, though, the same young urban actors reintroduce other aspects of much older, pre-urban ritual dynamics, in an "enactment of moral sentiment".[18] The lewd songs and insults which were mentioned above, the exposure of body parts, the whole play with the body's surface and its politics of undress[19] are very "heterotopian", in that they constitute a Turnerian antistructural moment of ritual reversal quite common in a number of Central-African rituals.[20] In this sense, also, one should understand the way in which youngsters ritually ridicule death and disease, by performing dances in front of the corpse of their dead friend, by imitating physically impaired people, thereby keeping death, disease and misfortune itself at bay. Other ways in which tradition is recycled, for example, is through the performance of dances such as *musangu,* a dance traditionally only performed by Lunda and Yaka elders on important political occasions. In the urban context this dance is performed by the young friends of the deceased as a form to salute and praise him.

In various ways, then, Kinois youngsters shape a future for more traditional ritual forms of which they often do not even have firsthand knowledge, but which they nonetheless reinvent single-handedly in the urban context. Against the order of the state and the church, with their promotion of what essentially remains a very colonialist modernity, urban youth introduces its own moralities, while rejecting the moral codes of church and state and the modernity it promotes. In using the body of the dead as an alternative political platform to speak out, they introduce their own bodies as tools for self-making and for exercising their critique against older forms of authority. In this they seem to exemplify what Bogumil Jewsiewicki and Bob White write in their introduction to a special issue of *African Studies Review* on "mourning" in Central Africa: "As death seems increasingly present in the lives of people in many parts of Africa, emerging forms of social mourning echo the need for new political futures, and mourning shows itself as an important terrain for the social production of meaning."[21]

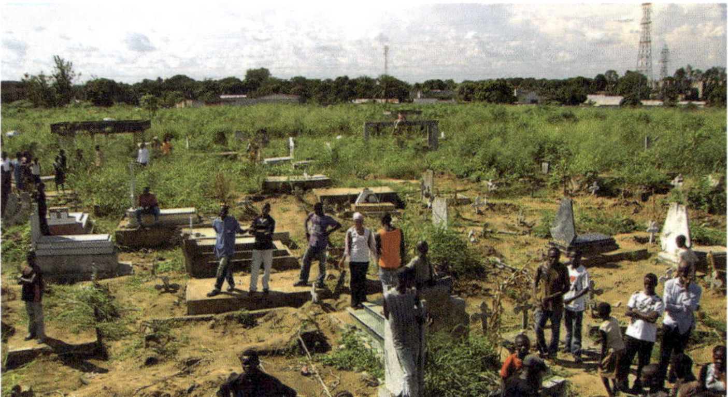

Kinois youth's criticism, though, transcends the mere political level. Theirs is essentially a moral criticism of the world they live in. The outside, the urban public sphere is criticised, reshaped by positing it against its opposite: the intimate corporeal space of inner self and inter-subjective relations. Through a discourse and songs that refer to love-making, sexuality and play, and by means of a powerful and transgressive act of symbolic copulation between two bodies, i.e. the strong and youthful body and the corpse, with all of its – rotting, disintegrating, dissolving, smelly – immediacy, youngsters shout this basic question to Kinois society as a whole: what does it mean to be human in the light of the constant threat of sudden disappearance and annihilation, in a context of systematic abandon and generalised, material as well as spiritual, insecurity?

Against the omnipresence of death, and the constant threat of being annihilated and forgotten, the corporeal dimension of juvenile vocabularies of self-realisation powerfully posits the city in the immediate time-frame of the moment, the now, to celebrate its vitality and life and to offer an alternative to this degradation. This urban life saturated with deadness which numbs everything and everyone, stands paradoxically against what is

---

18 Julie Livingstone 2008, Disgust, Bodily Aesthetics and the Ethics of Being Human, *Africa (Journal of the International African Institute)* 78/2: 288–307, here p. 293

19 See Adeline Masquelier (ed.) 2005, *Dirt, Undress and difference. Critical Perspectives on the Body's Surface,* Bloomington.

20 See Victor Turner 1969, *The Ritual Process. Structure and Anti-Structure,* New York.

21 Jewsiewicki and White (2005), p. 1

shown as the generative dimension of death, that is the power
that death has not simply to mortify life but in fact to *enliven* it.
At the same time, the strange cartel between youth and death
forces the city to stare into the face of its own death, and thereby into the darkest corners of its own modalities of existence.
Juvenile bodies, whether dead or alive, here appear as lucid,
ludic but also subversive sites and frontiers of re-territorialisa-
tion, not only of official cultural and political programmes, but
also of the much deeper and darker sides of what constitutes
humanity in this urban setting. They struggle to redefine the *vie
nue,* with all of the horror and disgust that come with it, and re-
animate this bare life with new forms of profane and divine law.
That is also the new meaning of the graveyard. It provides urban
youth with a heterotopic space to express the crisis, and to find
forms to both *embody* and overcome the disintegration of their
state, their city, their society and its moral values.

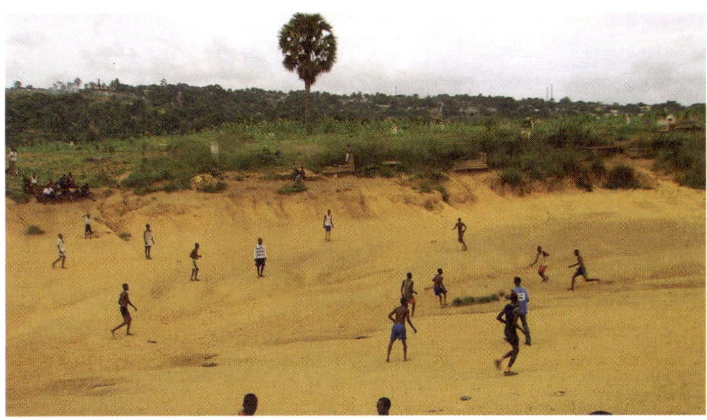

All photos: STILLS FROM **CEMETERY STATE**, DOKUMENTARY FILM 72 MIN, 2010

Tozokende Wapi?

SADI (Solidarité des Artistes pour le Développement Intégral)

SADI is an artists' collective founded in 2005 in Kinshasa with Alain Polo Nzuzi, Yves Sambu, Fransix Tenda, Trésor Mukonkole and Didier Besongo. *Tozokende Wapi? (Where are we going?)* was an intervention in 2009 in Kindele, a southern district of Kinshasa, where murals were painted on the ruins of houses left uninhabitable by soil erosion. For *Afropolis,* SADI created an installation of objects that the Kindele residents abandoned when they had to leave their collapsing houses.

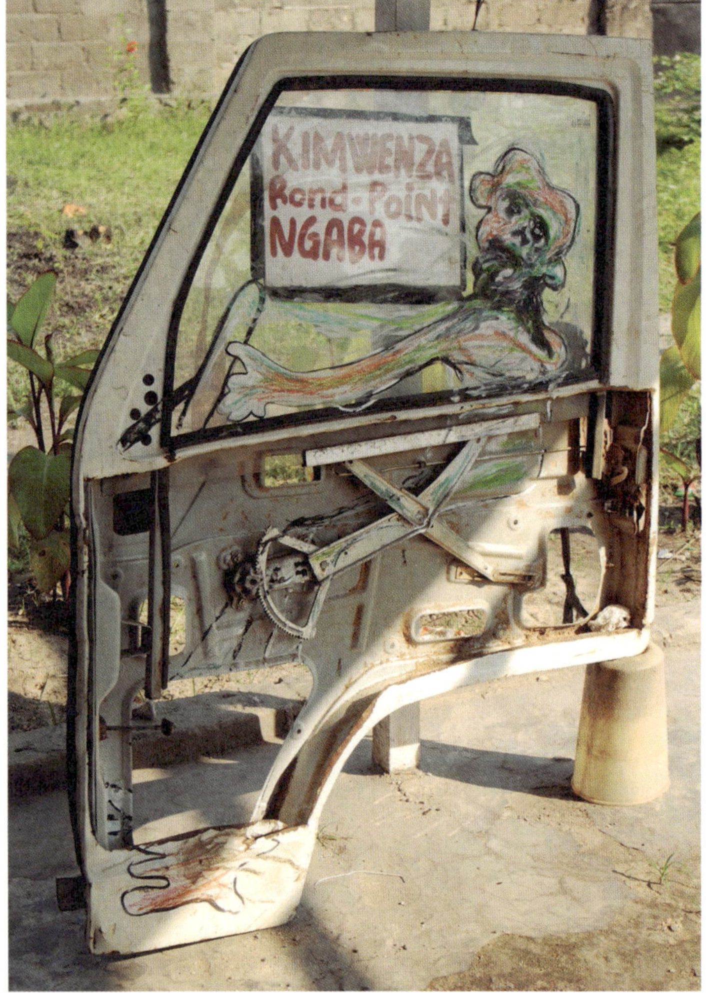

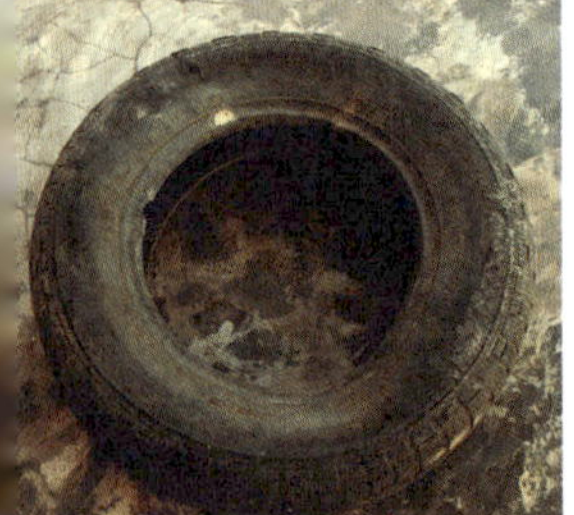

↑ The door of a minibus, a car tyre, a bus timetable. We discover something about the section of the route (Kimwenza/Rond-point Ngaba/Arrêt Makaya) that the bus travelled every day before it also became a casualty of the rains.

The boots belonged to police officers stationed in the district to protect the residents. ↓

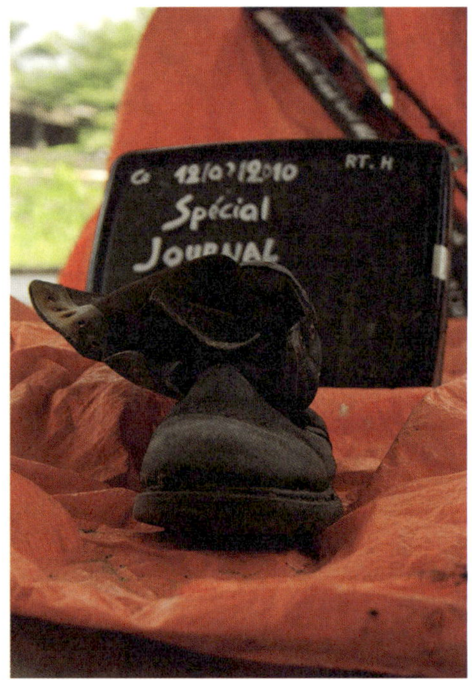

A wrecked computer monitor and a TV tube evoke the many occasions when they did not work, passed on no information, showed no films and were unable to connect to the rest of the world since the electricity pylons had also been swept away by the mudslides. The monitor references the story of Kindele's Internet café, which we have renamed *Cyber Port au Prince* (Haiti) to put the ruined houses in Kinshasa into a global context. →

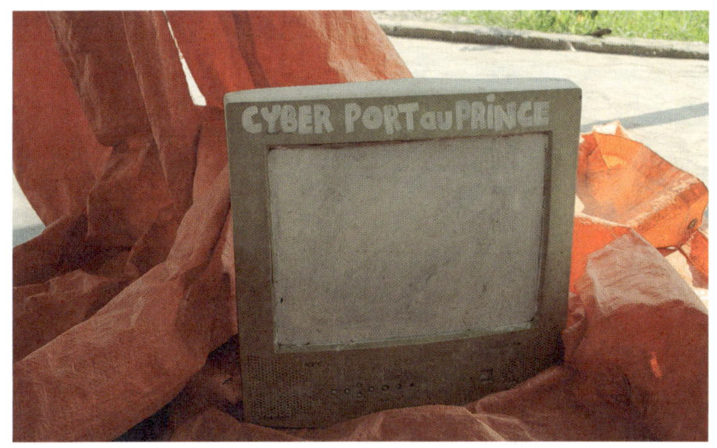

The bed belonged to the Silu family, who had rented accommodation on the road to Kimwenza. The bed was taken outside in the course of a quarrel. The house owner had died of a weak heart and the tenant's children were accused of playing a part in the owner's death. The tensions and frictions led to the tenants being hounded out of the house with all their furniture. They went but left the bed behind. The owner's family decided to throw the bed out in memory of their dead father. ↓

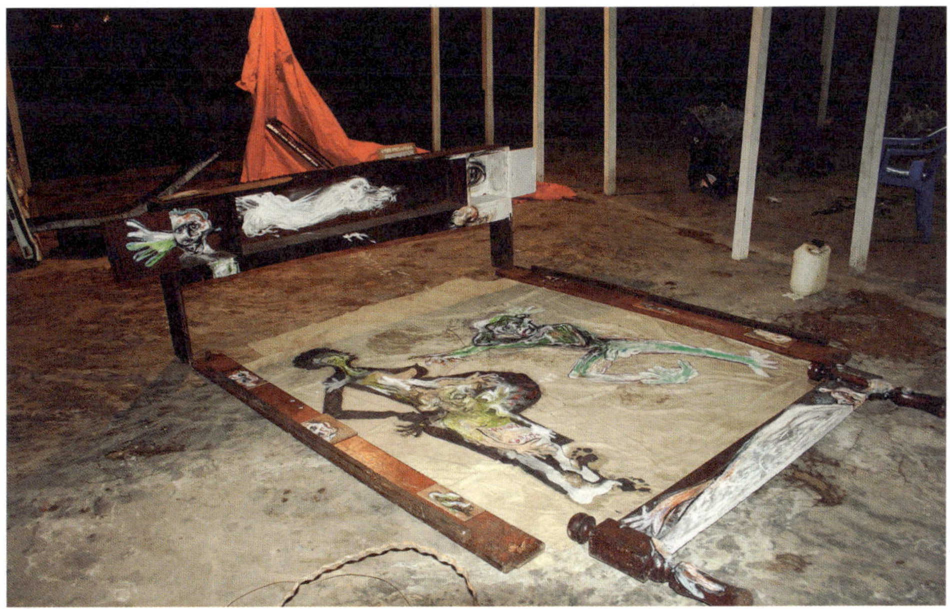

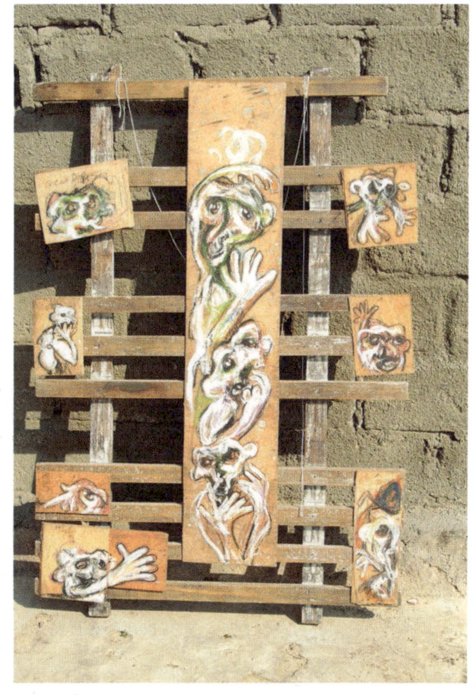

A slatted bed frame on which we've painted all the people who had something to do with the bed; it tells of an entire family life involving ten people separated when their house collapsed. →

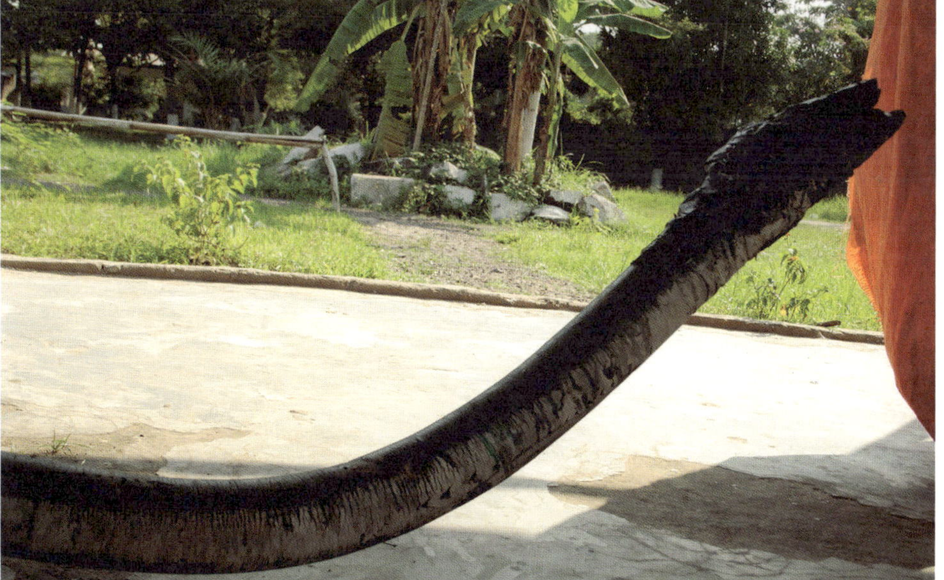

A black tube (the black snake) recounts the story of a superstitious belief in an imaginary snake. The snake is ascribed a mythical and destructive power and – as is said in Kindele – becomes active when it rains. Then it leaves its lair and gnaws at the earth until it breaks away; the snake has also given the ravine its own serpentine shape. →

La cité touristique

PUME BYLEX

Pume Bylex is the pseudonym of Francis Pume, who has created his own universe in Kinshasa with drawings, costumes and models. *La cité touristique* (*The tourist city*) is a model of an ideal utopian city that meets all the needs of its visitors. In the video, Bylex explains the functions of the individual buildings such as the *dome royal,* the central domed building in the *cité touristique,* which houses a global museum where visitors can engage with questions about life and morality.

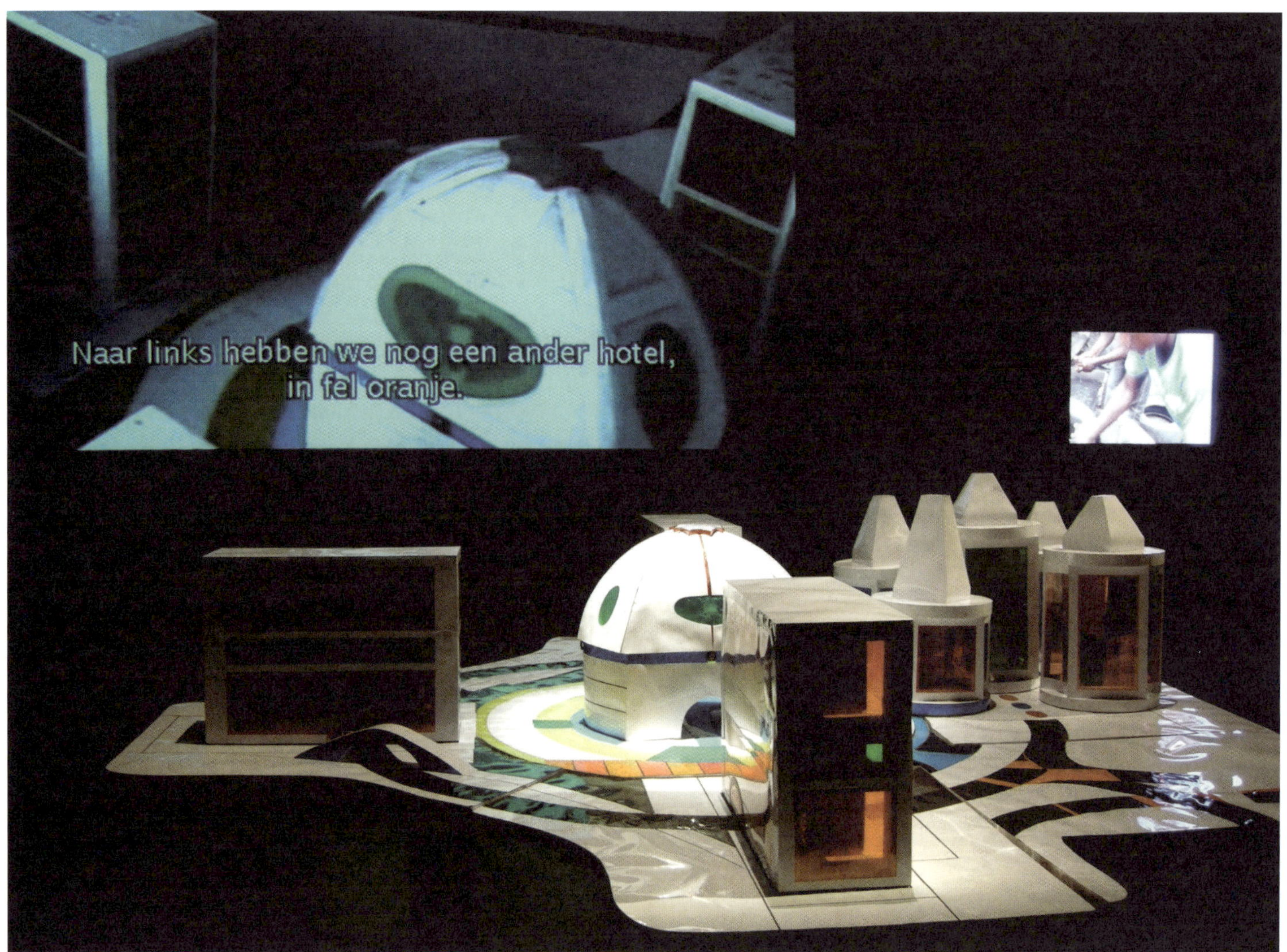

LA CITÉ TOURISTIQUE, VIEW OF THE MODEL OF THE CITY AND VIDEO INSTALLATION, 2008

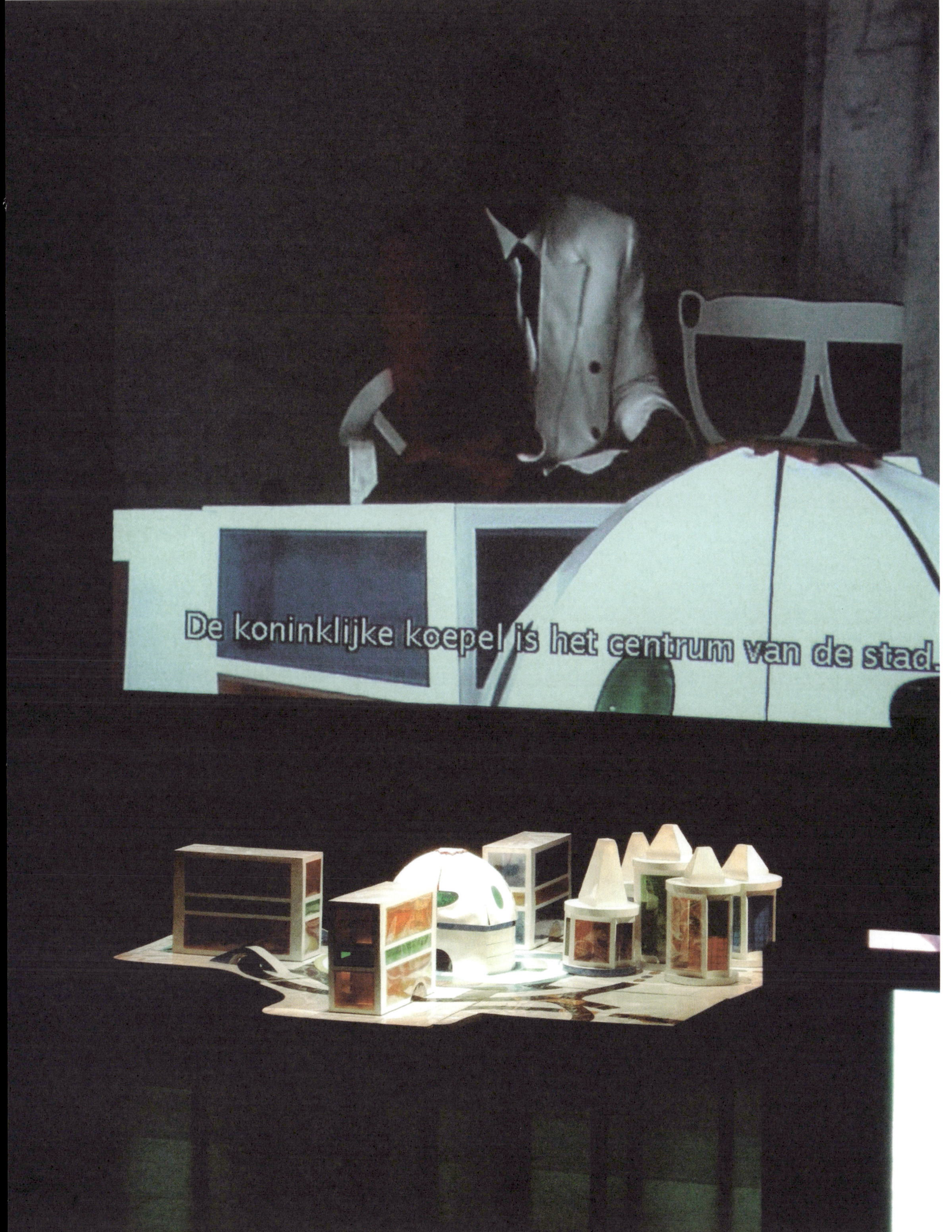

De koninklijke koepel is het centrum van de stad.

Kin Delestage

MÉGA MINGIEDI

Usually working in large-format drawings/collages, Méga Mingiedi creates imaginary vistas of Kinshasa, the city where he lives. Between the abstractly depicted rows of tower blocks in the *ville* and the agglomeration of little houses in the *cité,* Méga not only enters historical events and their settings onto his map, but also the city's potential future.

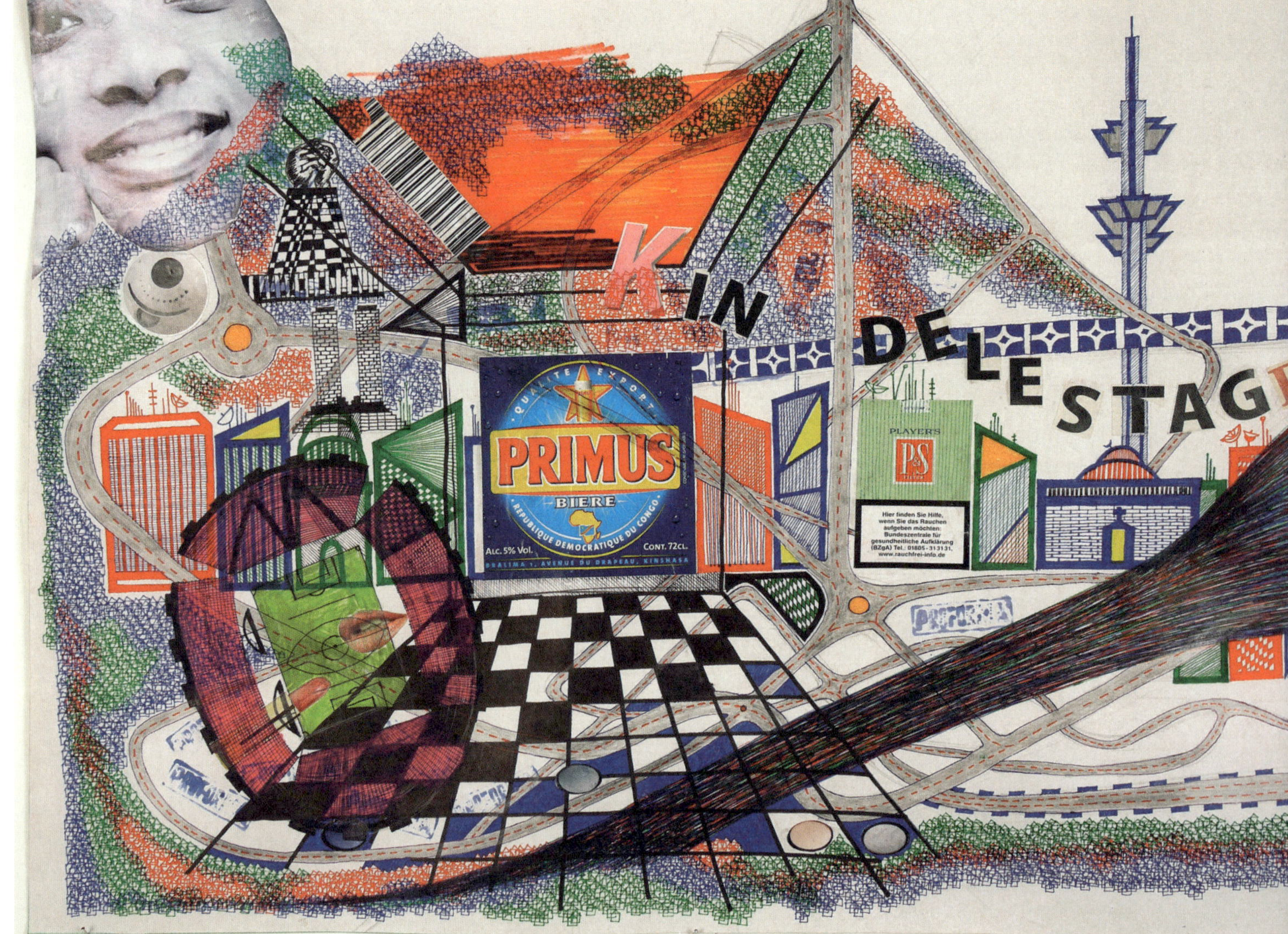

KIN DELESTAGE, DRAWING AND COLLAGE ON PAPER, 44 × 125 CM, 2010

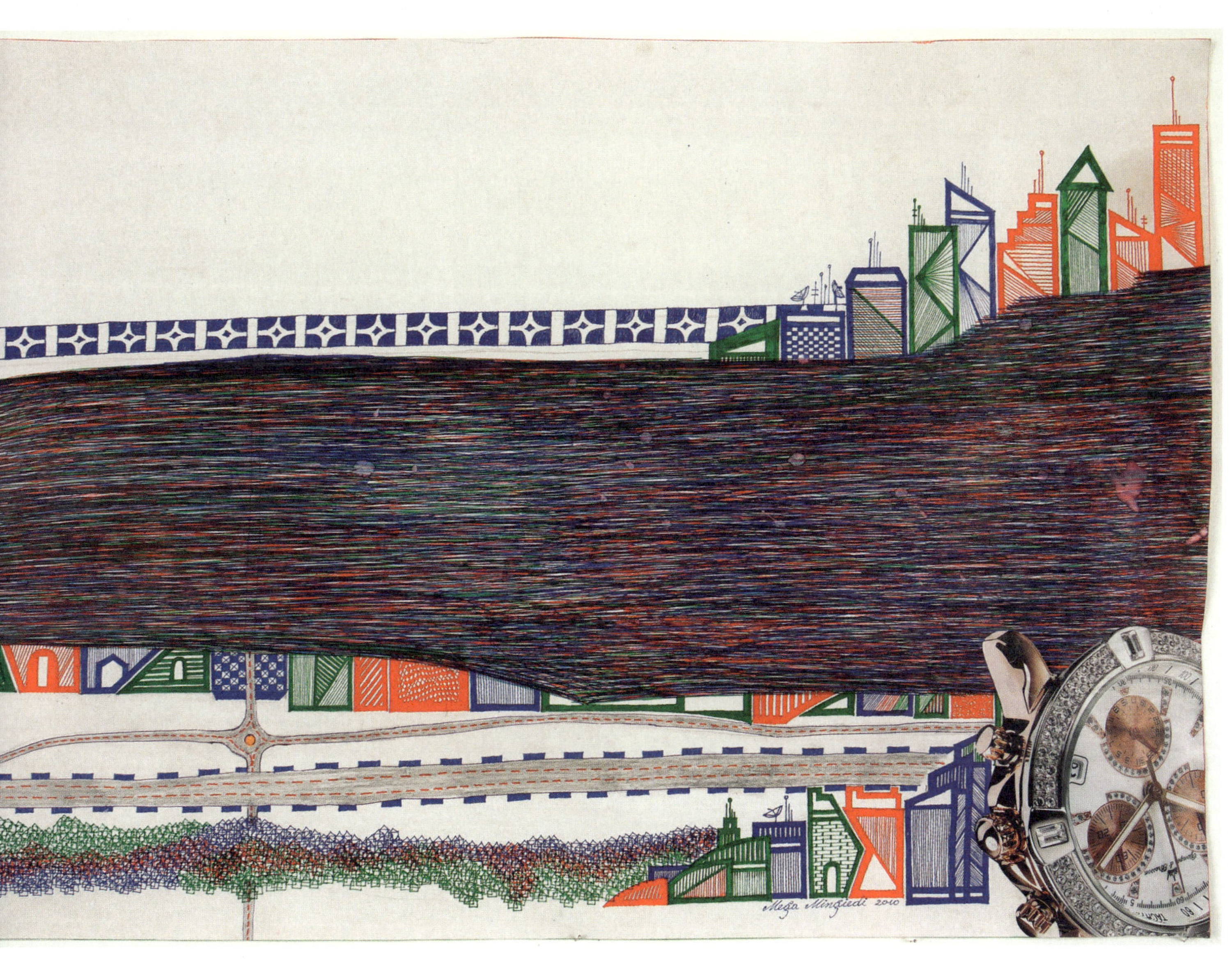

Mega Mingiedi 2010

Les divas de la honte

CÉDRICK NZOLO

As a designer, Cédrick Nzolo created a range of projects for street furniture and worked as a photographer in Kinshasa, primarily at night. In a city where electricity is scarce, the diverse light sources take on a special meaning. The flames from homemade paraffin lamps shroud stalls in a flickering, yellow light while individual light bulbs or neon lamps give off a blinding, garish light in the general darkness around them.

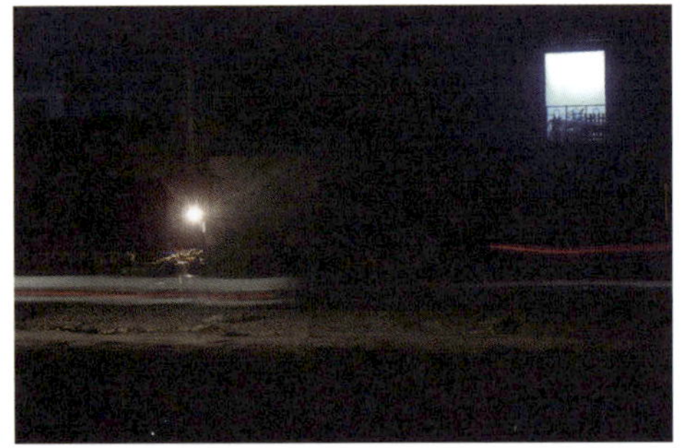 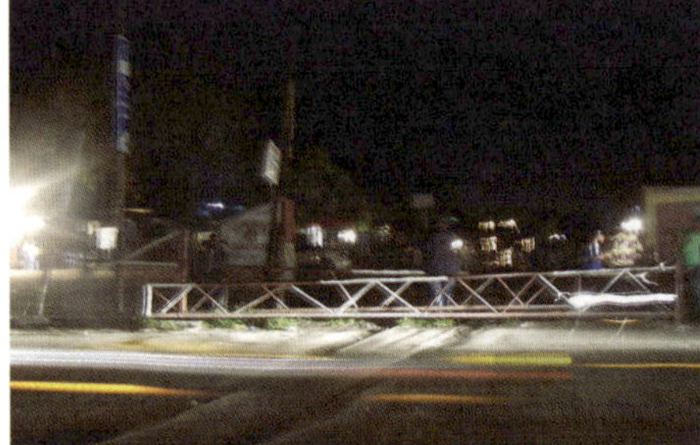 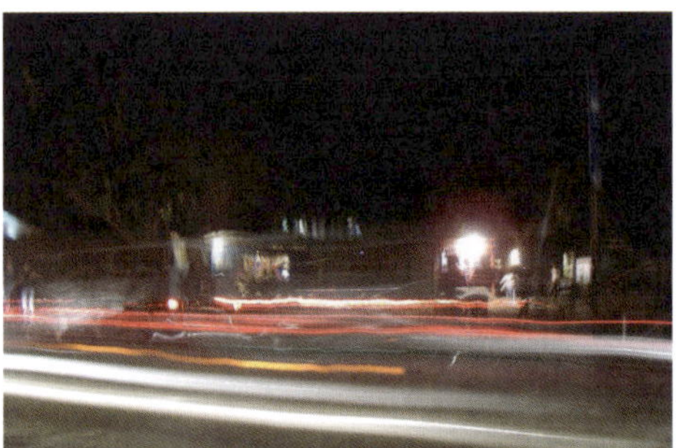

BA NZELA, TRIPTYCH, EACH 45 × 30 CM, 2008

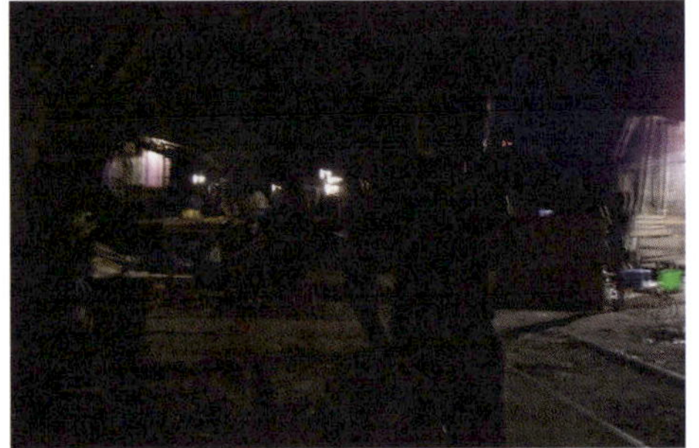 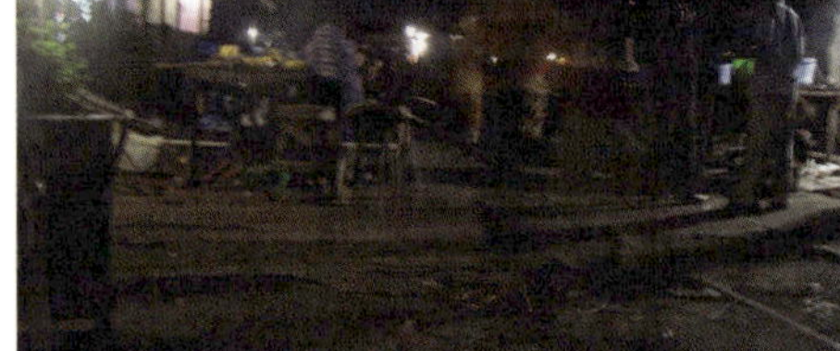 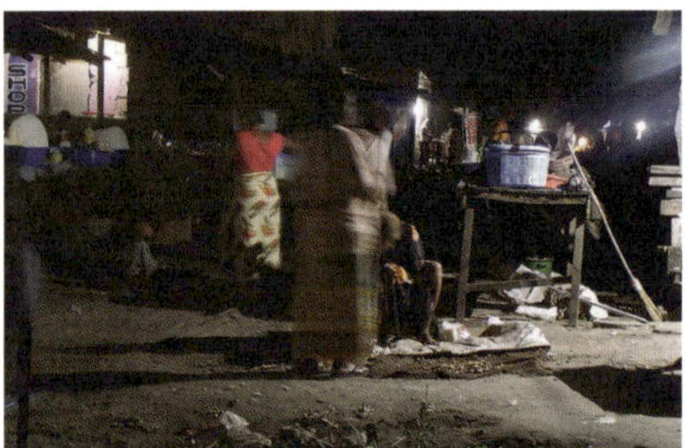

STORA MINOU, TRIPTYCH, EACH 45 × 30 CM, 2008

 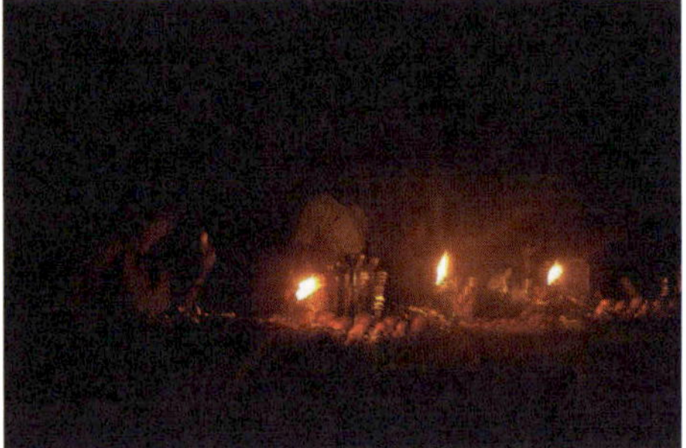 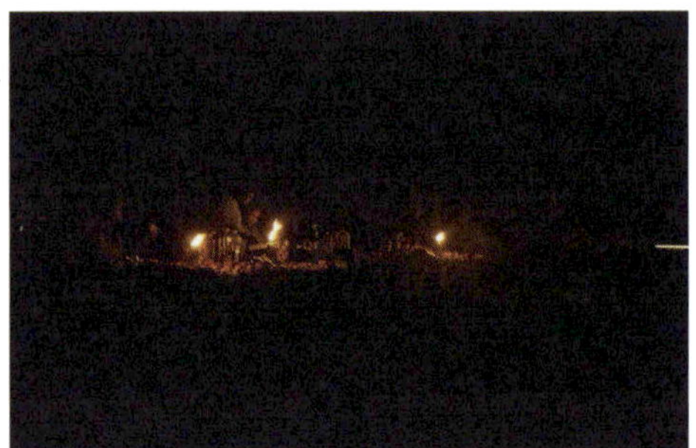

ECURIE PELOU, TRIPTYCH, EACH 45 × 30 CM, 2008

Divas of Shame

This is the story of individual lamps symbolically illuminating many streets in the capital city of Kinshasa. The lamps all have names telling of shameful stories. But given a choice between necessity and shame, necessity wins out since without lamps many places would be almost deserted; businesses need lamps to serve customers in the evening hours. Private people manage to conjure up a public-private light out of nothing – a white-hot lamp on a street corner, paraffin lamps on tables, the lights of car headlights tracing out the route we are following …

Discover the story of the lamps from their synonyms; they are called, for example:
Bipelapela: "Keeps on going out"
Faute ya mobali: "It's the irresponsible husband's fault"
Mbongopasi: "Money is hard to come by"
Mwinda ya koteka: "Lamp for lighting poor people's businesses"
Mwinda ya wenze: "Lamp for lighting neighbourhood market stalls"
Penepene: "Close up"

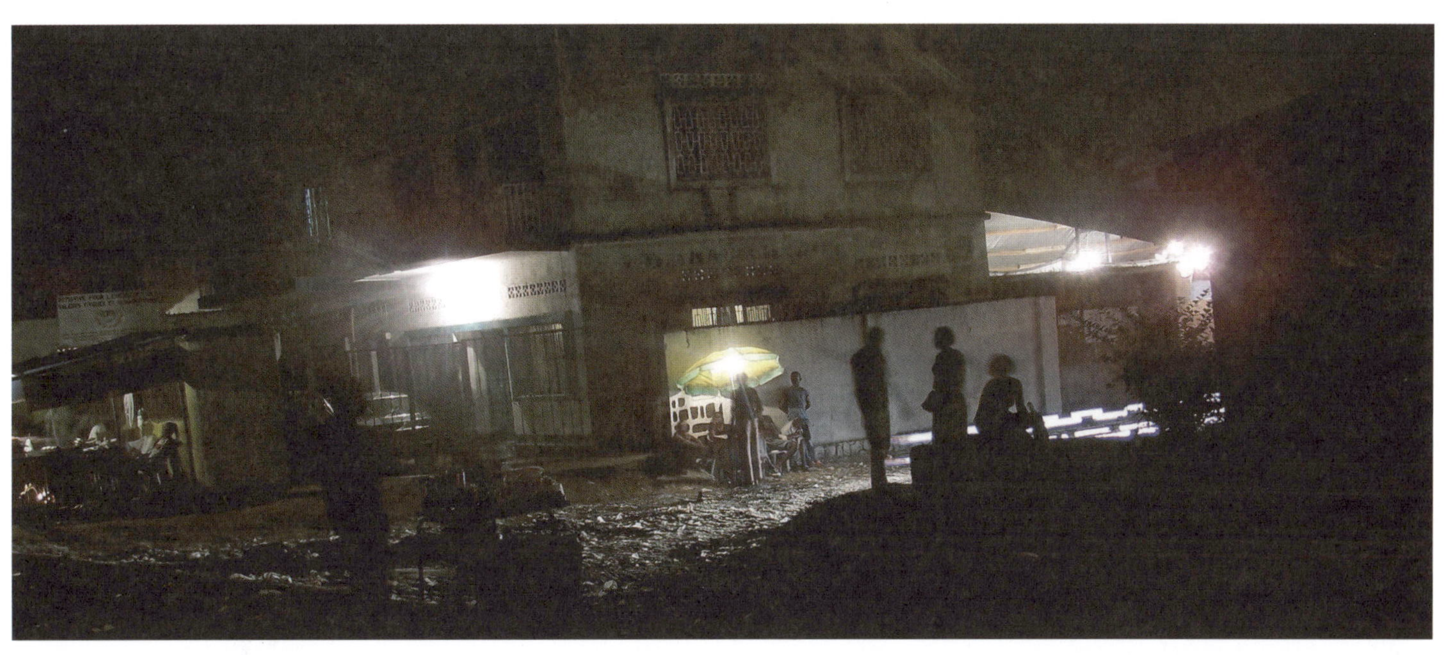

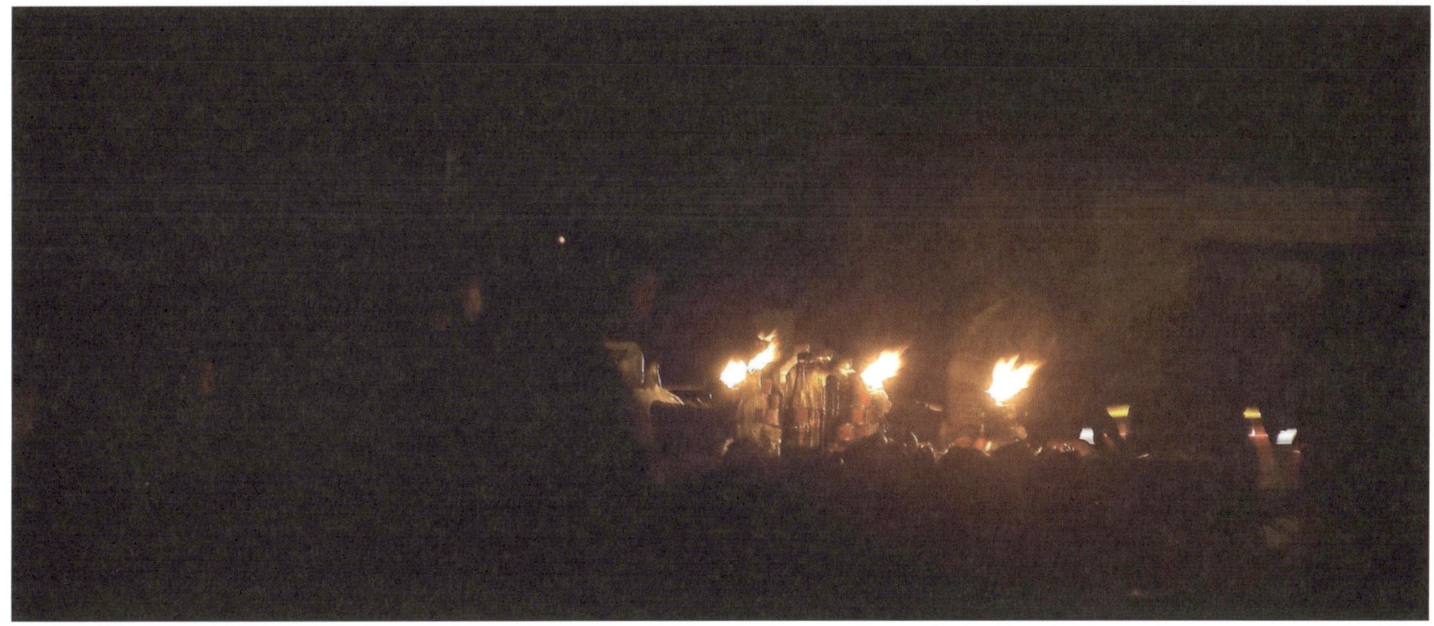

LES DIVAS DE LA HONTE, 2008

Ground/Overground/Underground

MOWOSO

Mowoso is a multidisciplinary collective founded in 2006, and is centred in and around Kinshasa. The collective comprises artists and scholars whose works explore the collision of physical and virtual worlds. *Ground/Overground/Underground* is an Afro-futuristic installation of videos and audio recordings, robots and spaceships, taking visitors to the imaginary worlds of *mikili.* The project artists are Eléonore Hellio (media), Dikoko Boketshu (musician and video artist) and Bienvenue Nanga (post-industrial machines).

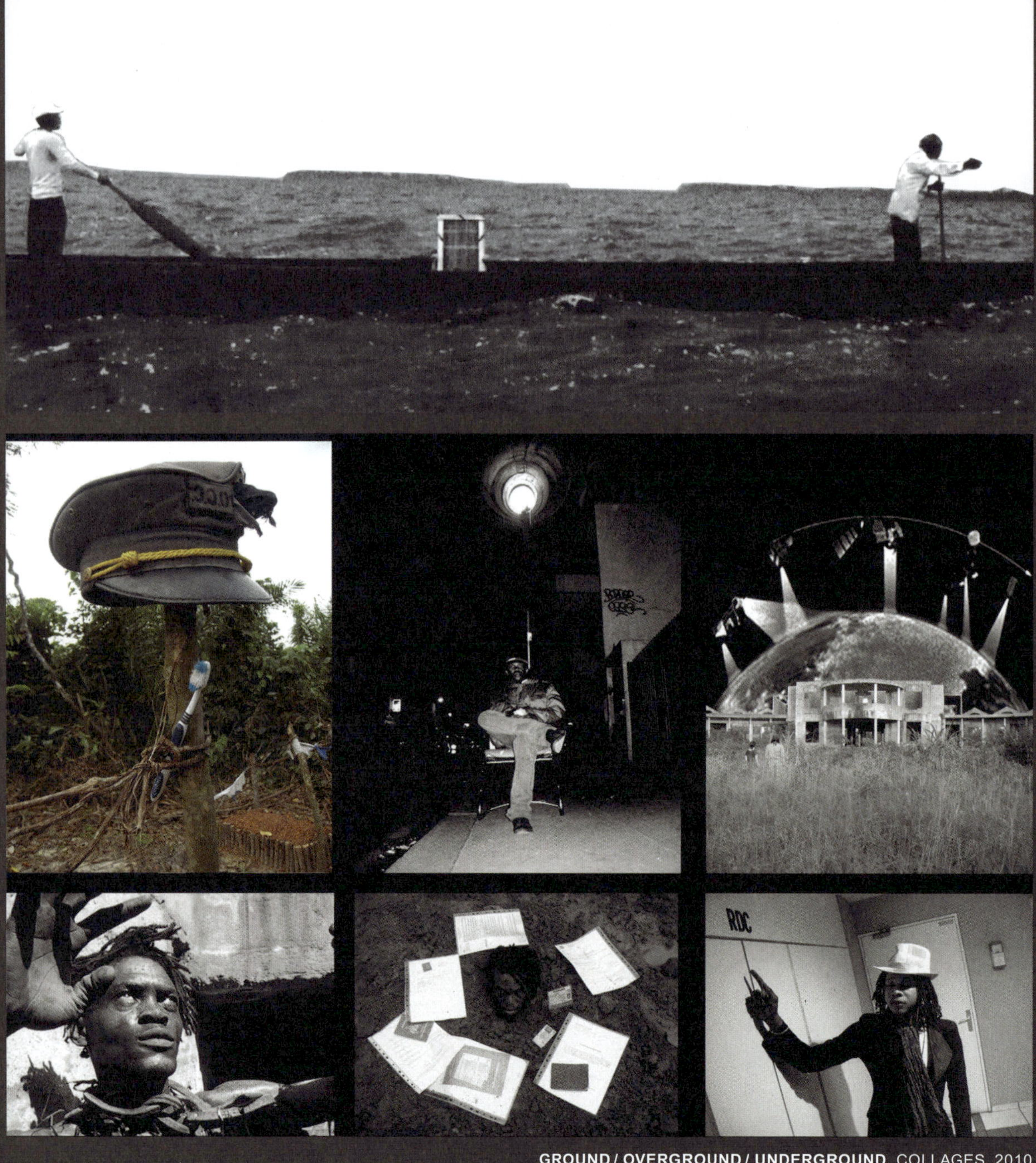

GROUND / OVERGROUND / UNDERGROUND, COLLAGES, 2010

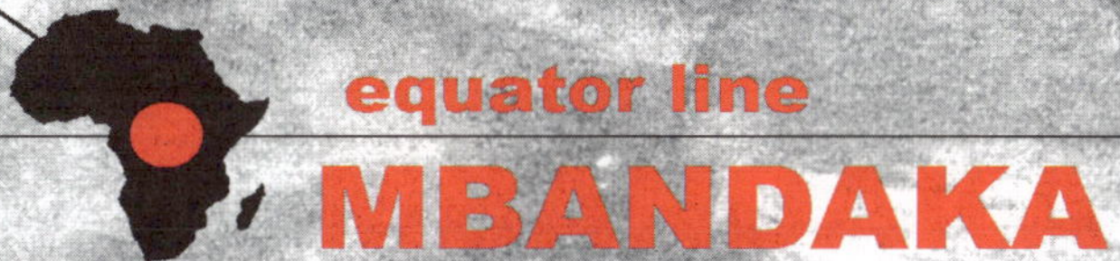
cosmic and virtual realms

equator geostationary orbit machines

OVERGROUND

dreamscape
imaginary of elsewhere

MIKILI WORLDS

capital city of RDC
KINSHASA

capital city of MIKILI
PARIS

intimate politics
postcolonial dilemmas

GROUND

equator line
MBANDAKA

dreamtime psychic processing

UNDERGROUND

multidimensional travel pipelines

invisible knowledge

Mapping Kinshasa

DEPARTMENT OF ARCHITECTURE AND URBAN PLANNING UGENT

In *Mapping Kinshasa,* Luce Beeckmans, Johan Lagae, Guy Châtel and students from the Ghent University (abbreviated to UGent) investigate the history of the spatial elements that have structured Kinshasa's urban space: *Avenue des Héros Nationaux/Boulevard du 30 juin, Zone neutre, Avenue Kasa-Vubu, Cités Planifiés, Rond point Victoire,* and *Chemin de fer.*

1. NEUTRAL ZONE

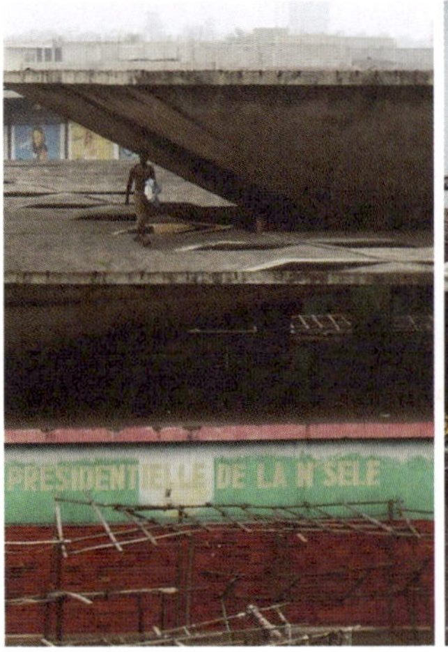

2. RAILWAY

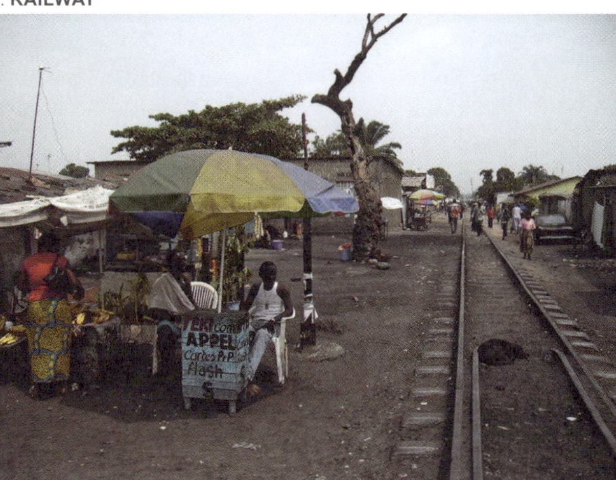

3. BRIDGE *KASA-VUBU*

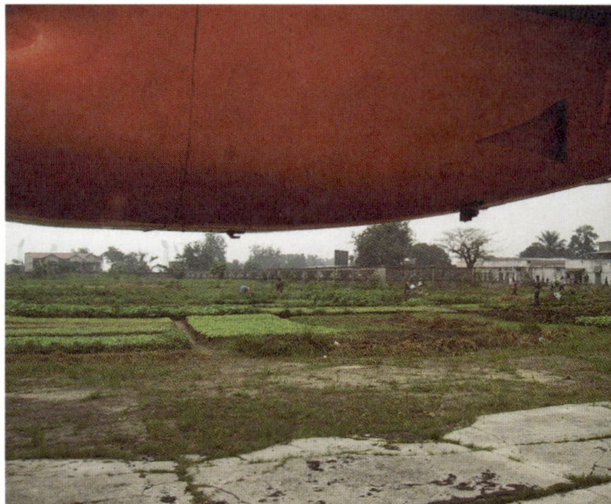

1. NEUTRAL ZONE

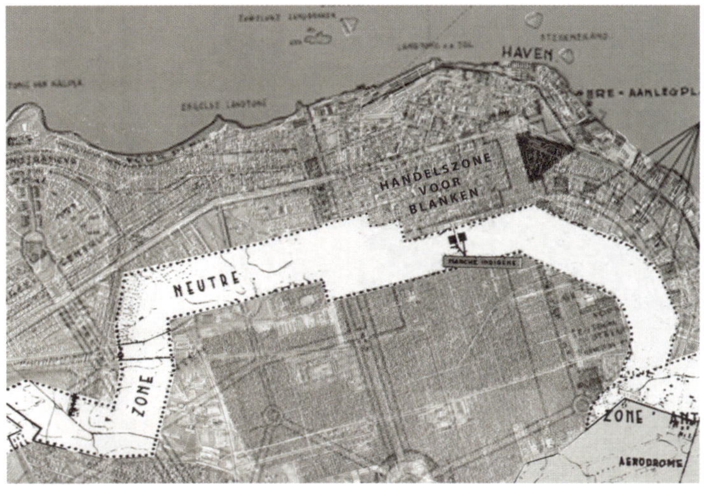

"Ideally the neutral zone has to comprise a broad 800-metre segregation strip. Experience in Congo has shown that a strip of 400 metres, as prescribed by the sanitary regulations, is not sufficient; even this, however, will significantly reduce the danger of infection."
Pierre Ryckmans, Governor-General of Belgian Congo, 1945

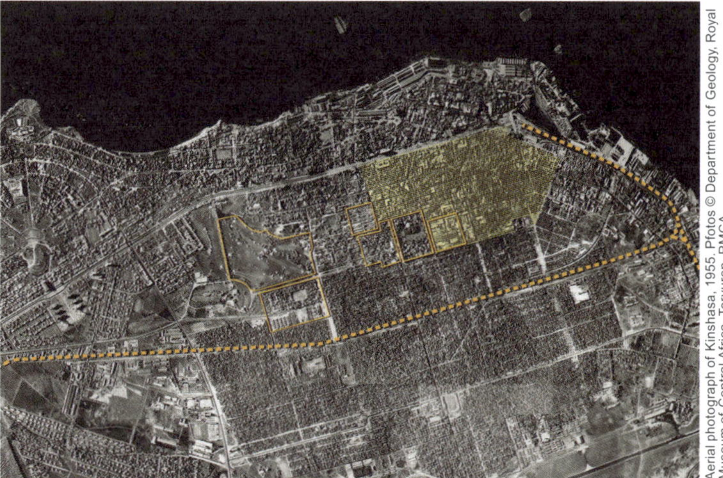

"In practice, Léopoldville has not observed and does not observe the regulations on neutral zones."
Maurice Heymans, 1949

Aerial photograph of Kinshasa, 1955. Photos © Department of Geology, Royal Museum of Central Africa, Tervuren, RMCA

Our involvement with the architecture and planning of the former Léopoldville and today's Kinshasa, the capital of the Democratic Republic of the Congo, derives from a growing interest in Africa's cities which goes beyond any single discipline. In focusing on the materiality of urban space, we are attempting to map the design and structure of Congolese cities to gain an insight into how these urban centres became established and developed. With the help of a range of diverse sources (including historical maps, photographs, architectural planning documents and ar-chives), together with field research and interviews, we are seeking to understand the urban structure of these cities today, and highlight the forces that played a part in their formation over time. We focus on deviations between the draft plans and sketches for the future and the actual construction of the city, as well as between planning discourse, policy and implementation, since realising projects inevitably faces the 'chaotic reality' of decision-making processes. In our view, Kinshasa's present ur-ban landscape is a patchwork and a palimpsest. It is a patchwork

4. PLANNED CITY

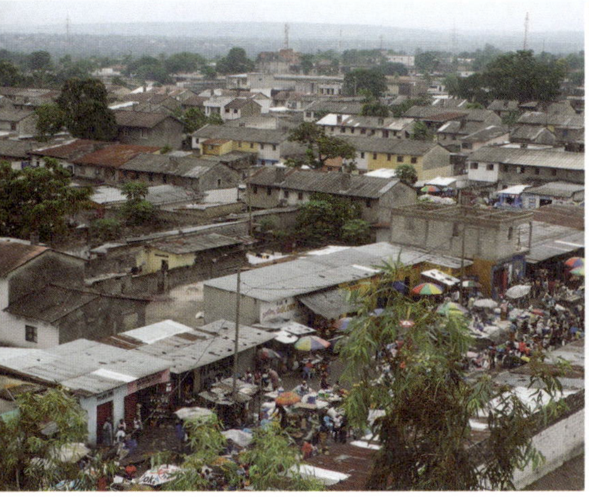

5. ROTARY TRAFFIC *VICTOIRE*

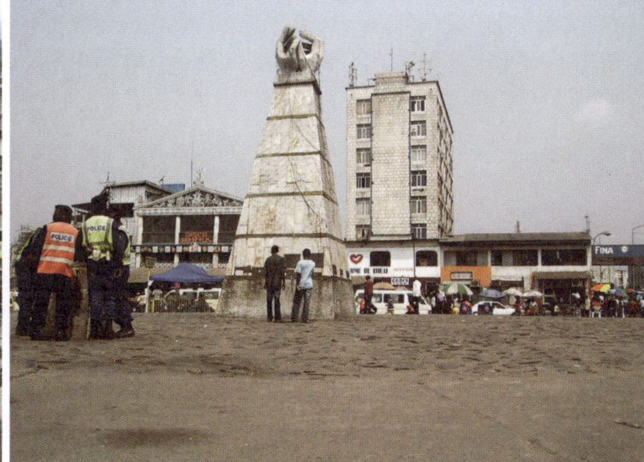

6. MONUMENTAL AXES

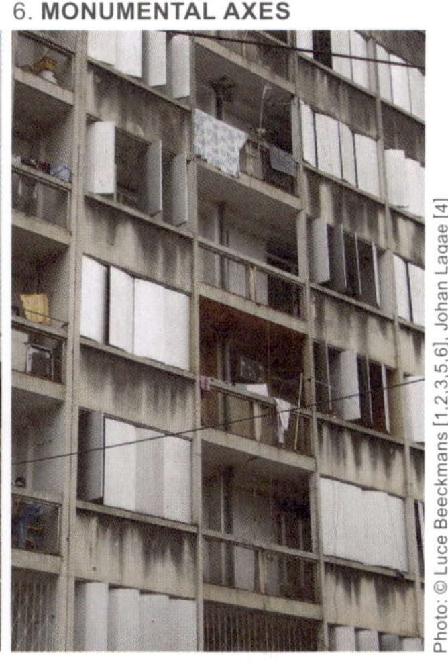

3. BRIDGE *KASA-VUBU*

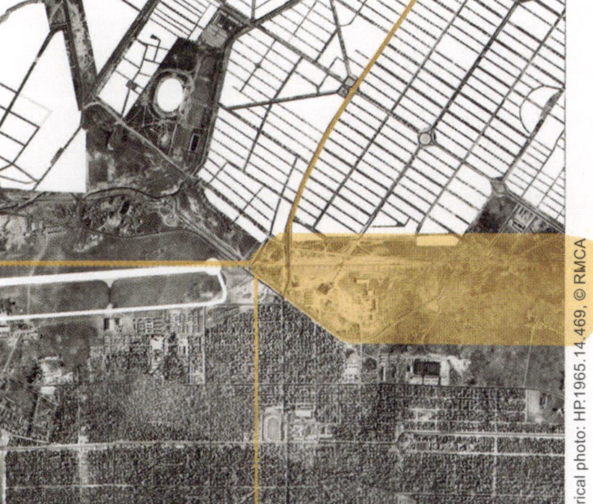

"It was important that the city's regional plan gave the city a heart; it chose the location for what is today called the city centre."
Mission Française d'Urbanisme, 1970

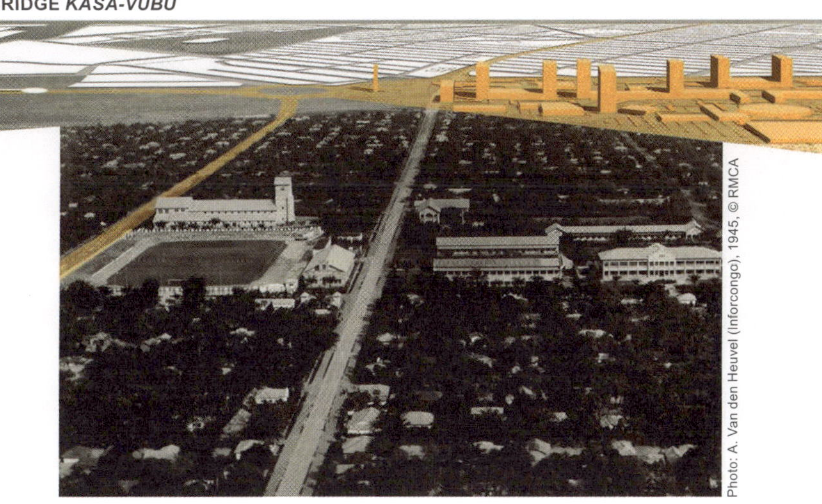

"A monumental city centre was planned. But this divided the popular section of the city, the *cités* and their extensions, where the Kinshasa residents pursue their everyday lives."
René de Maximy, 1984

because the city developed and grew without the colonial planning authorities being able to implement a masterplan (as far as one existed at all) in its entirety. Instead, the planning and construction of colonial Kinshasa was largely informed by pragmatism, short-term political goals, ad-hoc solutions and uncontrolled growth, and to all appearances, even after independence, everything continues in the same way. The reading of Kinshasa as a palimpsest is based on deconstructing the existing urban territory into its constitutive layers, and investigating those elements that have structured urban growth over the course of time, and determined its development and use. Here, we are presenting two fragments of analytical maps produced as part of the *Mapping Kinshasa* seminar at the Department of Architecture and Urban Planning at the University of Gent (spring 2010); they focus on six spatial segments that have shaped Kinshasa's urban landscape since the colonial era.

JOHANNES BURG

The Spatial Politics of the Past and the Present
A Brief History of Alexandra[1]

NOOR NIEFTAGODIEN

When Alexandra was established in 1912, Johannesburg had been in existence for only twenty-five years. During that time the city had grown exponentially from a mining camp into a global centre of a mining capital. Johannesburg was the epicentre of the country's capitalist development: by the mid 20th century it was the hub of the industrial economy and by the end of the century was arguably the financial capital of the African continent. Until recently, the 'City of Gold' (or 'Egoli' in isiZulu) epitomised white wealth, power and privilege. In contrast, the history of most residents of Alexandra was characterised by a perennial struggle for the right to be in the city. The township[2] survived on the margins of this booming city, as a neglected space in which some blacks were permitted to own property. Over time the place became a mecca of black urban life, marked by overcrowding, poverty, a vibrant social life and rebelliousness. Between the early 1930s and late 1970s the Johannesburg Municipality and central government, supported by the middle-class white population in the suburbs surrounding Alexandra, attempted first to excise this 'black spot' from the white city and then, in recognition of its utility as a source of labour, to transform it into a dormitory town for migrants. The authorities continuously attempted to shape and control the township to suit the needs of the powerful and privileged. However, the Alexandrans responded by insisting, in their daily lives and through collective struggles, on defining their own destinies in the city.

The declaration of Alexandra as a freehold township[3] for Africans and coloureds[4] [→ Fig. **A**] in 1912 was deliberate manoeuvre by the landowner, Herbert Papenfus, to avoid the restrictions of the infamous Land Act (promulgated in 1913), which confined African land ownership to a few designated rural areas and effectively prohibited Africans from owning land in the urban areas. Cities and towns were perceived as spaces of white privilege and power. However, a number of localities on the periphery of the Pretoria-Witwatersrand-Vereeniging region (PWV, now the province of Gauteng) that were deemed unsuitable for white occupation were granted freehold status for urban Africans before the passage of the Act. Property ownership was an important symbol of status and of permanence in the urban areas for the hundreds of families who could afford to purchase property in places like Alexandra. A salient characteristic of the early life of Alexandra was the refusal of the Department of Native Affairs (central state), the Transvaal Provincial Administration (provincial state), or the City of Johannesburg to assume responsibility for the area. Residents sarcastically referred to the township as, "Nobody's Baby". Official abdication of responsibility had two principal consequences for Alexandra: on the one hand, state neglect resulted in a lack of investment in basic infrastructure, such as electricity, which added the more well-known moniker to the place, namely, "Dark City"; on the other hand, the lack of state intervention allowed the township relative autonomy from official surveillance and control. One important dimension of the latter was that Alexandrans could elect representatives onto the Health Committee, which was responsible for the management of the area until the late 1950s. These features made Alexandra distinctive from other localities and, as a result, a much sought-after place for Africans wishing to find a foothold in Johannesburg.

The first twenty years of Alexandra's history reflected the steady increase in African urbanisation in general. Between 1916 and 1924 the number of families living in the area increased from 900 to 2,640 and five years later the figure had increased to approximately 7,200 families.[5] From the early 1930s (especially after the passage of the Slums Act in 1934[6]) the City of Johannesburg expelled thousands of black squatters from inner-city slums and attempted to relocate them to new municipal locations. But many of these people eschewed the tightly controlled locations and opted to live in freehold areas, especially Alexandra that, as a consequence, experienced an influx of about 5,000 ex-slum dwellers between 1931 and 1935. By 1936 the official population of the area stood at 16,747, which increased to between 40,000 and 45,000 in the early 1940s.[7] The majority of residents now consisted of tenants and subtenants. [→ Fig. **B**]

Over the next decade and a half Alexandra's population exploded due to a massive influx of new arrivals from the rural areas, triggered in part by a surge in industrial development linked to the Second World War. Rapid industrial development meant

---

1 This paper is based on: Philip Bonner and Noor Nieftagodien 2008, *Alexandra. A History*, Johannesburg.

2 In South Africa, 'township' refers to the urban residential spaces that, under the apartheid regime, were reserved for African people. Many years before, the townships were called '(native) locations' or *lokasies* (in Afrikaans). Even today, townships and locations are common terms, though usually with a different connotation; see the article by Sarah Nuttall in this volume [editor's note].

3 In a freehold township, it was possible for a private person to buy a plot of land, something not permitted in other townships [editor's note].

4 'Coloureds' refers/referred to a heterogeneous 'racial' group, often with both black/African and white/European ancestry, but also including descendants of the early inhabitants of this regions, the Khoisan, as well as of Malay slaves. Although the racist laws of the apartheid regime were also later based on this kind of categorisation, even today 'coloured' is used as an independent term. [editor's note]

5 Report of the Johannesburg and Germiston Boundary Commission, 1936–1937, quoted in Philip Bonner and Noor Nieftagodien (2008), p. 23.

6 The Slums Act sought to eradicate all inner-city slums.

7 Slums Act 1934, p. 60

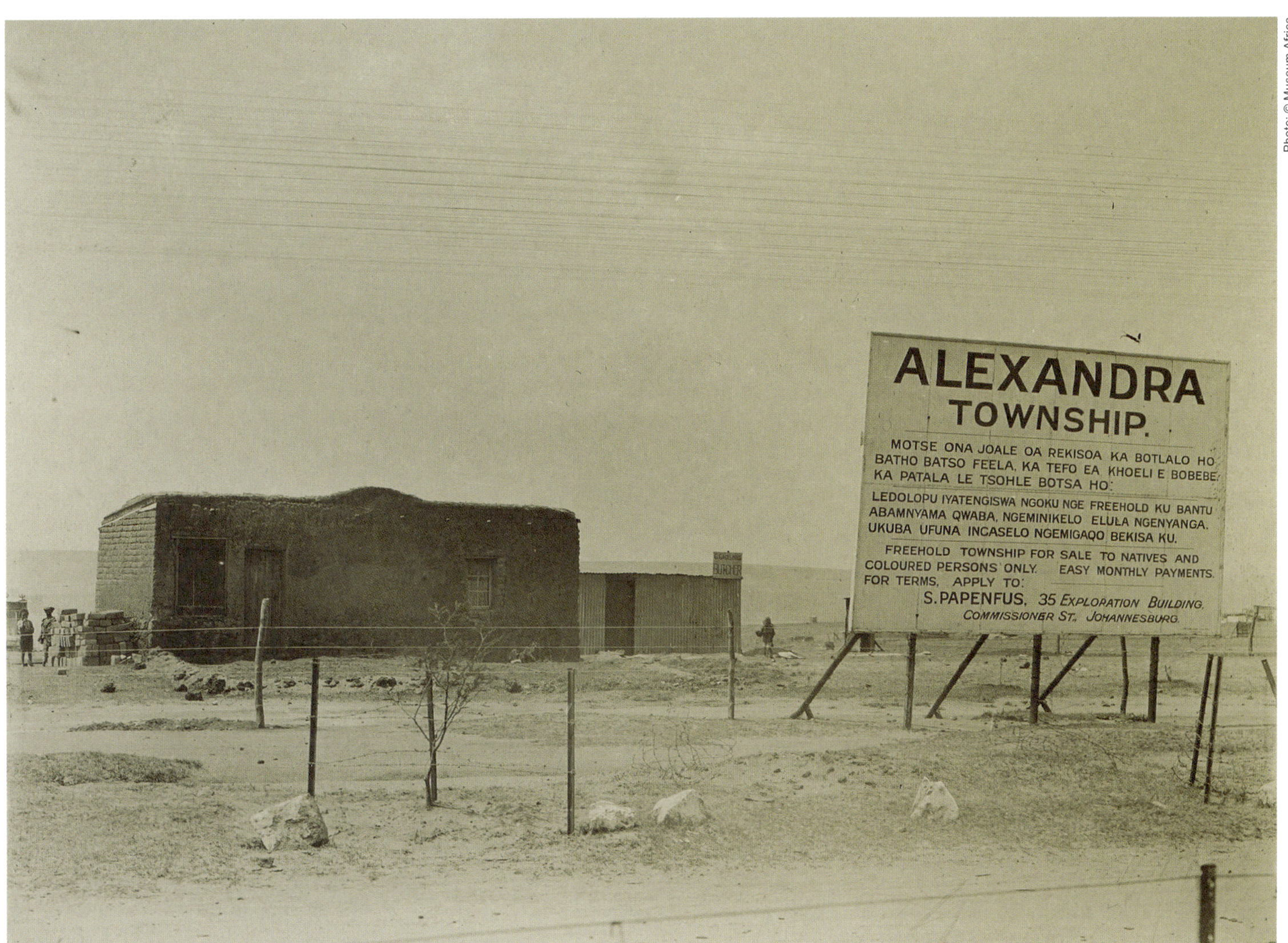

Photo: © Museum Africa

A From the time it was founded, Alexandra was one of the few urban townships where black people could own freehold property. (1914)

that in 1943, for the first time, manufacturing outstripped mining in its contribution to GDP. The demand for black labour surged: the number of African men employed in industry increased by more than 100 per cent from 272,641 to 590,929 between 1936 and 1951. As a consequence African urbanisation registered major growth nationally; in the decade between 1936 and 1946, the African urban population increased by fifty per cent from 1,141,642 to 1,794,212. Notwithstanding a plethora of measures instituted by the government to stem the tide of urbanisation, the African urban population soared even higher in the late forties and fifties, reaching a total of 3.5 million in 1960.[8] Thousands of work-seekers flocked to the Witwatersrand[9], and Johannesburg in particular, the key centres of the industrial revolution in the country. Many of these people chose Alexandra as their urban home, causing the township's population to increase sharply to about 100,000 by the end of the 1940s. By contrast, the population of the more well-known township of Sophiatown, in the west of Johannesburg, stood at a mere 39,186 in 1950.[10] The acceleration in the growth of Alexandra's population coincided with the expansion of white suburbia in the north of Johannesburg, so that by the early 1950s the one and a half square miles of this township was virtually surrounded by middle-class residential areas. From a segregationist perspective the incongruity of having a freehold black location etched into the white urban landscape became increasingly untenable. Calls from the suburban population for the removal of Alexandra that had started in the 1930s grew louder. Echoing earlier discourses of the "sanitation syndrome"[11], suburbanites and city officials

8 Robert Fine and Denis Davis 1991, *Beyond Apartheid*, Johannesburg, p. 14, 156

9 Johannesburg was constructed along the Witwatersrand range of rocky hills. The Witwatersrand range contains major South African gold reserves, and has also given its name to the 'Rand', South Africa's currency [editor's note].

10 David Goodhew 2004, *Respectability and Resistance: A History of Sophiatown*, Westport, p. 66

11 For this notion see Maynard W. Swanson 1977, The Sanitation Syndrome: Bubonic Plague and Urban Native Policy in the Cape Colony, 1900–1909, *Journal of African History*, XVIII/3: 387–410; Maynard Swanson argued that concerns about public health (especially infectious disease) played an important part in the development of racial segregation ideology in South Africa in the early part of the 20th century. He uses the term "sanitation syndrome" in reference to the public health discourse among British (colonial) authorities and urban planners triggered by such factors as growing urban population density [editor's note].

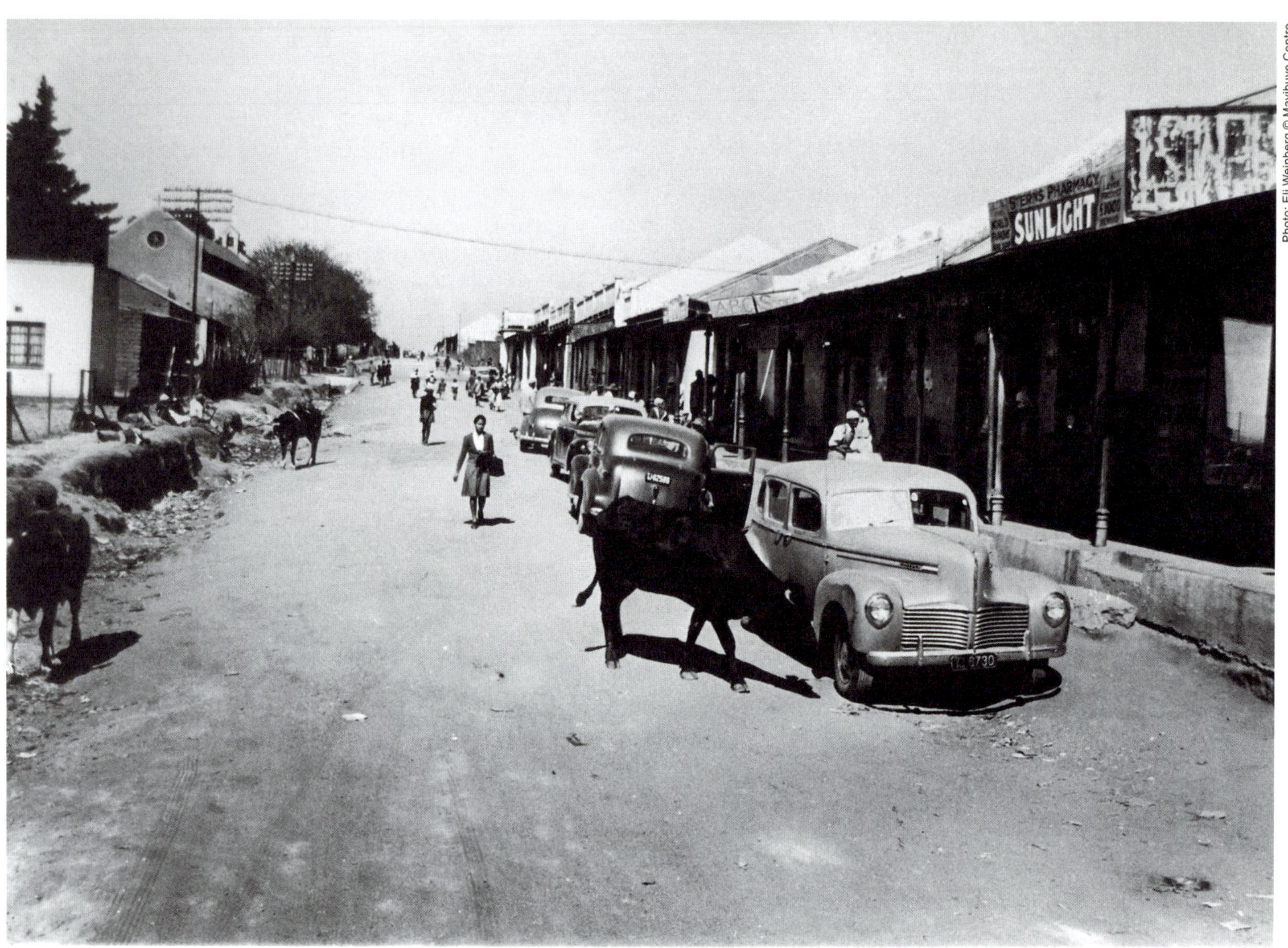

Photo: Eli Weinberg © Mayibuye Centre

B First Avenue, Alexandra's business centre, in the 1940s

complained about the health hazard Alexandra posed to the surrounding white population. However, the combination of various factors, including resistance from Alexandrans and the unwillingness of any part of the state to carry the cost of removing the entire township, prevented the realisation of the demands for removal of the township. Moreover, Alexandra had become an important source of labour for industries and households in the northern suburbs and Johannesburg generally. A big proportion of African women washed laundry or was engaged in domestic service in the Norwood and Rosebank areas, and more than a quarter of the township's population was employed in Johannesburg proper.[12]

Alexandra's rapid transformation created conditions for the radicalisation of local politics, especially around issues affecting the urban existence of Africans. In the mid-1930s a number of new organisations were formed in the township, partly in response to the removal plans. The Alexandra Township Standholders' Protection and Vigilance Association was formed in 1935, the Alexandra Workers' Union in 1937 and a year or so later a branch of the Communist Youth League of South Africa. A proposal in 1940 to create an all-white Health Committee triggered an angry and unified response from residents, culminating in a public rally attended by 8,000 residents.[13]

No other struggle defined the politics of Alexandrans, and arguably of urban Africans in general, than the bus boycotts. Between 1940 and 1945 the private bus companies attempted almost annually to increase the fares of trips between the township and Johannesburg. Each time the commuters responded by mount-

12 National Archives of South Africa, JUS 234 3/40/60, Stephanus Papenfus, Chairman Alexandra Township Company to Director of Native Labour, 22 June 1916

13 National Archives of South Africa TAB 1138 TA 13/8933, Alexandra United Front Committee to Administrator Transvaal, 28 August 1940

ing a boycott, forcing the authorities to back down. In 1944, for example, the Public Utility Transport Company (PUTCO) raised fares from four to five pence a trip (that is, an additional two pennies a day). Considering the low wages earned by most African workers this apparently marginal increase posed a serious threat to their livelihoods. The ensuing boycott involved thousands of people walking twelve kilometres to and from work daily for weeks, making it one of the most significant demonstrations of the power of the emerging black urban working class. Lillian Tshabalala, one of the emerging female radicals of the time, was one of the main leaders in this struggle. Eddy Roux, a leading political figure in Left politics at the time, described the boycott as the most significant moment of African resistance in the Second World War.[14] Nelson Mandela experienced his first taste of an urban mass movement during the bus boycott. "This campaign had a great effect on me," he recalled. "In a small way, I had departed from the role as an observer and become a participant. I found that to march with one's people was exhilarating and inspiring."[15]

By the mid-1940s black locations were hugely overcrowded, as the state failed to meet the growing demand for housing by newly urbanised Africans. This triggered a series of intense struggles over housing, the most significant of which were the squatter movements. Perhaps the most significant of these was James Mpanza's movement in Soweto in which thousands of people occupied vacant land to demand houses, which was correctly perceived as a basic right and an assertion of their permanence in the urban areas. A similar movement occurred in Alexandra, led by the local Communist Party chairman, Schreiner Baduza.[16] Alexandra also established itself as home to several left-wing movements as a variety of Socialist groupings vied with the Communist Party and Africanists for political influence. This political heterogeneity was matched by the township's colourful social life.

Alexandra, like Sophiatown, was a hub of black urban life. Its mixed character – comprising educated elite, property owners, tenants, a constant influx of new immigrants and a growing number of women and families – created cultural and social vibrancy. Beer brewing and selling were ubiquitous as African women struggled to find means to survive and in the process created spaces of social interaction – the shebeen. The growing number of children placed a premium on education, which was provided by several independent missionary schools. By the late 1940s there were 8,000 pupils in twenty-one schools, although a similar number could not be accommodated in schools in the area.[17] Local sport flourished in the 1940s and 1950s, with football and boxing attracting the most support. 'Moroka Lions', 'Young Fighters' and 'Rangers' were the main football teams, while boxers such as Richard 'Black Hawk' Hlubi became

provincial champions. During the same period Alexandra earned notoriety as a centre of gangsterism. Early gangs included the 'Tuta Ranch', 'Zorro's Fighting Legion' and the 'Berlins'. In the 1950s Alexandra was terrorised by infamous 'Spoilers' and then 'Msomis'. Alexandra was one of the foremost places in which an urban black working-class identity was being forged, which found expression in new social and cultural forms and, importantly, also in militant class politics.

Alexandra played a major role in the mass struggles of the 1950s such as the May 1950 General Strike, the Defiance Campaign of 1952[18], the Freedom Charter movement of 1955[19] and the anti-pass campaign, among others. Prominent political figures like Gaur Radebe, Moses Kotane, Josiah Madzunya and Dan Mokonyane lived and operated in the area. The bus boycott of 1957 marked the high point of local mass mobilisation, and arguably of popular political struggle in Johannesburg as a whole. Lasting three months, the boycott reiterated the mass mobilisation of the 1940s and involved thousands of commuters daily walking to and from Johannesburg. [→ Fig. C] In the end the community was again victorious. Ironically, this political victory also hastened the central government's decision to bring Alexandra under its control, an intervention that occurred in the context of an important ideological shift by the ruling National Party to pursue a doctrinaire of apartheid.

The period from the late 1950s to the early 1970s is termed the era of 'high apartheid', defined by the state's zealous efforts to halt and reverse African urbanisation and the promotion of the homelands system. These policies threatened the distinctive character of Alexandra that had developed over nearly half a century. In 1958 the state disbanded the Health Committee and replaced it with the state body, the Peri-Urban Areas Board. Alexandrans suddenly found themselves subjected to unprecedented pass and permit controls that undermined the relative autonomy enjoyed by the township. At the same time the state implemented a removals scheme, in line with its overall strategy to remove so-called 'black spots' from the white urban landscape. Within four years 45,000 Alexandrans (mostly tenants) were relocated to Soweto and Tembisa.[20]

Following this large-scale removal, the remaining residents, especially property owners, hoped their position would be secure because they had the protection of tenure in the urban areas. Indeed the state had intimated that the township would not be 'disestablished' (the official euphemism for the complete destruction of locations) because it was an important reservoir of labour for Johannesburg's northern suburbs. However, in 1963 the state decided to convert Alexandra into a hostel city, that is, a dormitory township for male and female migrants. To achieve this it planned to remove the remaining residents from the area, to terminate property ownership, demolish family houses and on

14 Eddy Roux 1945, Alexandra Bus Boycott, in: *The South African Treasurer,* 21 September, p. 39

15 Nelson Mandela 1997, *Long Walk To Freedom,* Frankfurt, p. 123

16 Alf Stadler 1979, Birds in the Cornfield: Squatter Movements in Johannesburg, 1944–1947, *Journal of Southern African Studies,* 6/1: 93–123

17 John Nauright 1992. *'Black Island in a White Sea': Black and White in the Making of Alexandra Township, South Africa, 1912–1948,* Ph.D. Thesis, Queens University, Kingston/Ontario, p. 39, 64

18 The Defiance of Unjust Laws Campaign was a civil disobedience campaign against the apartheid regime's racist laws [editor's note].

19 The Freedom Charter was officially adopted on 26/27 June 1955 in Kliptown/Soweto. It called for equal rights for black and white South Africans, and for many years remained the core agenda of the African National Congress. [editor's note]

20 Mike Sarakinsky 1984, *From 'freehold' to 'model' township,* Honours Dissertation, University of the Witwatersrand, Johannesburg, p. 25–27

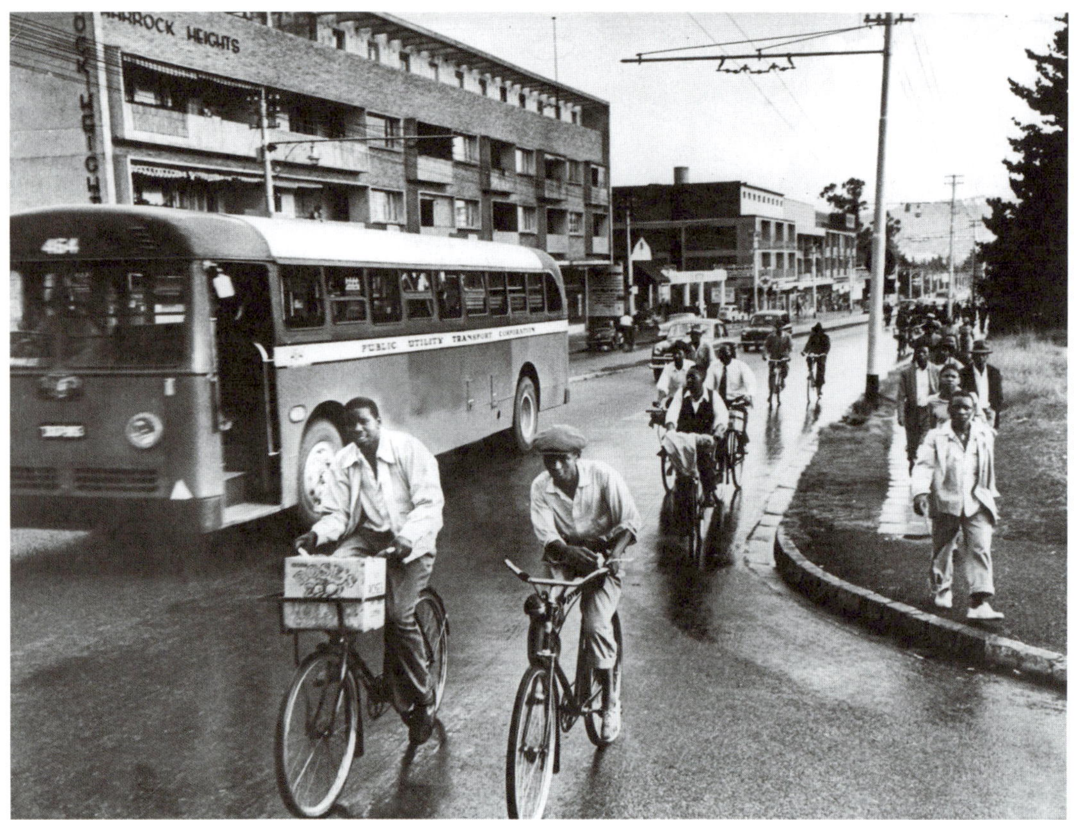

C For a month, thousands of people from Alexandra walked and cycled to Johannesburg and back. Their 'bus boycott' was aimed at forcing down the exorbitant ticket prices (1957).

their ruins erect single-sex hostels. Alexandrans, who cherished their urban status, suddenly found their urban existence rendered extremely precarious. Like their counterparts in the newly established townships, these residents had to comply with various laws in order to be legally present in urban areas and were constantly under threat of deportation to the homelands. It took nearly a decade for the hostels to be completed, during which time Alexandrans experienced mounting poverty and deep anxiety about their future.[21] Yet a strong spirit of self-help allowed residents to endure these hardships. Deborah Mabitsela ('the Mother of Alexandra'), Marjorie Manganyi ('Mother Teresa of Alexandra'), both community welfare activists, and many other women, were pivotal in tending to the needs of the community. When the hostels were eventually opened in the early 1970s the state immediately renewed its plans to remove all non-migrants from the township. In December 1974 hundreds of property owners were given less than one month's notice to vacate their properties. But this high-handed action triggered immediate resistance. Initially comprising individual acts of defiance, which delayed the planned removals, the movement gathered momentum and within a couple of years enjoyed widespread support in and outside the township. By this time the political landscape of

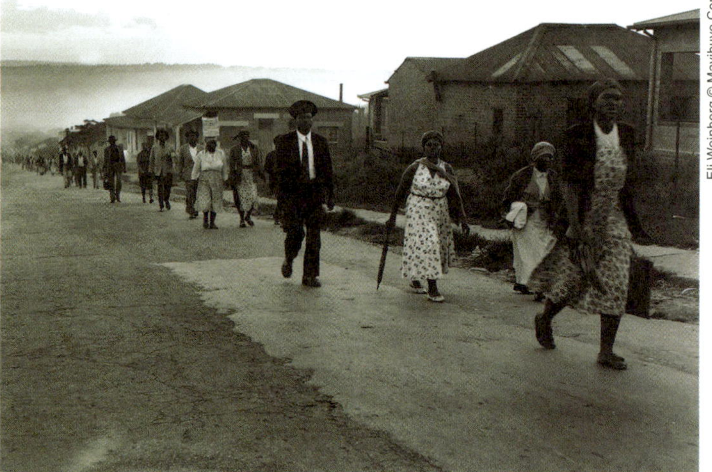

the country had been fundamentally transformed by the June 1976 student revolt, in which Alexandra students played a major part. The new mood of defiance was injected into the Anti-Removal Campaign (led by the Alexandra Liaison Committee), which eventually forced the government in 1979 to abandon its plan to

21 See Mark Mathabane 1986, *Kaffir Boy. The True Story of a Black Youth's Coming of Age in Apartheid South Africa,* New York. This book vividly captures the traumas of this era in the township.

'disestablish' Alexandra. This was a major victory and represented an admission by the state of the failure of its plan to convert the township into a migrant dormitory area. Alexandra – a township of permanently urbanised Africans – was now firmly entrenched in the heart of Johannesburg.

The late 1970s also marked a critical turning point in the country's history: over the next decade the major urban areas experienced complete transformation, a process in which Johannesburg and Alexandra would play a critical part. Prior to the 1976 uprising apartheid appeared hugely successful: the 1960s were characterised by robust economic growth, which resulted in massive accumulation of wealth by the white minority, black political resistance had been largely driven underground and into exile, and key aspects of the state's policies, such as influx control, seemed effective. White privilege and power were intact and flourishing. But the apparent stability of the system was shattered in 1976 and from the late 1970s came under renewed pressure from the mounting tide of migration of African people to the cities as well as the proliferation of anti-apartheid struggles.

When the government announced the reprieve of Alexandra it also undertook to implement a 'master plan' to redevelop the area and especially to construct new houses. Residents were hopeful that a new era had dawned for the township that would witness the restoration of property rights and a general upliftment of living conditions. But the state reneged on its promise, precisely at the point when thousands of new immigrants began to stream into the area to make a life for themselves in the 'City of Gold'. Initially the state responded with characteristic violence against the new arrivals, demolishing their make-shift abodes in the early hours of the morning and sending them back to the rural areas. But this was a futile exercise and in 1986 the state officially abandoned influx control. In 1983 Alexandra's population was estimated between 50,000 and 70,000, but by the end of the 1980s, the figure had increased to between 200,000 and 300,000, registering an astounding increase of about 400 per cent in less than a decade. Without the provision of formal housing the vast majority of these people were forced to live in shacks in the yards of old houses, on the pavements, river banks and in free-standing squatter camps. Alexandra had effectively been transformed into a squatter township and was probably the most congested residential area in the country. In 1986 the population density in the township was about 340 people per hectare, compared to the generally acceptable level of 90 people per hectare.[22]

Alexandra was once again beyond the control of the government. Its rebellious state was further confirmed when in the mid-1980s the national township uprising against apartheid reached a climax in the area with the Six Day War of 1986. Led by the Alexandra Action Committee and based on elected yard and street committees that encompassed the entire township, residents defiantly challenged the authority of the government and replaced the state-sponsored local authority with "organs of people's power". In response the state unleashed a reign of terror on Alexandra, which caused some setbacks, but failed to break the resolve of the community and its representatives. By the end of the 1980s the local civic movement led a campaign to transform the governance of Johannesburg by demanding a single tax base and major investment into the upgrading of townships. In the early 1990s the local leaders of Alexandra played a key role in the negotiations to create new and democratic local authorities that aimed to place the wellbeing of township residents at the centre of any new dispensation.[23]

This project suffered a temporary but critical setback when the townships of the Reef, including Alexandra, were engulfed by internecine violence between Inkatha-supporting hostel dwellers and township residents.[24] In Alexandra, the strength of the civic organisation allowed for effective political mobilisation and self-defence against this state-sponsored violence. By the time of the first democratic elections in 1994 Alexandra was relatively peaceful and the tens of thousands of people who cast their ballots were understandably optimistic that their lives would be transformed in the new South Africa.

However, several years after these historic elections Alexandra was still a centre of abject poverty. Overcrowding and congestion remained ubiquitous, with the number of shacks[25] estimated at about 34,000 at the beginning of the 21st century. In the late 1990s South Africa entered a period of vigorous economic growth, especially of its financial sector. Across from Alexandra, the suburb of Sandton (the country's financial heartland and perhaps the most opulent piece of real estate on the African continent) experienced exponential growth as witnessed in the construction of several new skyscrapers, including gaudy Tuscan-style buildings. [→ Fig. D] On the other side of the motorway, the economic boom made little impact on the poor of Alexandra. Unemployment remained very high at about thirty per cent, while the seventy per cent who were employed were categorised as unskilled, earning less than 1,000 rand per month.[26]

In response to this deepening local crisis the government in 2001 launched the ambitious 1.3 billion-rand Alexandra Renewal Project (ARP), which aimed to transform the township through multiple developmental interventions, including Local Economic Development, and to generate economic activity aimed at lifting income levels and reducing unemployment. The principal objective, however, was to "accommodate 350,000 through upgrading of existing dwellings, de-densification, the creation of new housing on greenfield sites, upgrading of free-standing informal settlements and redevelopment of hostels."[27] Provincial politicians promised to construct between 50,000 and 66,000 new

22 Paramasvaran Narainsamy Pillay 1983, Alexandra: An Analysis of Socio-Economic Conditions in an Urban Ghetto, *Carnegie Conference Paper* 19: 1

23 Mzwanele Mayekiso 1996, *Township Politics. Civic Struggles for a new South Africa,* New York

24 Since many hostel residents were Zulu speakers, they supported the mainly Zulu-based Inkatha Freedom Party (IFP). The conflicts between IFP and ANC supporters played into the hands of the apartheid regime [editor's note].

25 In the South African context, 'shacks' are, for example, corrugated-iron huts and similar makeshift shelters, usually homemade from cheap and simple materials. [editor's note]

26 Alexandra Renewal Project (ARP), *Overall Proposals,* April 2002, p. 4

27 ARP (2002), p. 4

housing units during the lifespan of the project. However, by 2004 very little progress had been made in meeting these targets. As a consequence, various sections of the community, often led by new social movements, began to mobilise to demand the provision of decent housing. Organisations such as the Vukuzenzele Crisis Committee occupied land to press home their demands. From 2006 the rate of housing delivery accelerated, but it was evident that not everyone would get a house. Inevitably, this generated tensions and struggles over limited resources. It was in this context that the outbreak of xenophobic violence has to be understood. The continuous stream of new arrivals into Alexandra generated considerable anxiety and antipathy amongst older residents who accused the 'newcomers' or 'outsiders' of 'jumping the queue' for housing and jobs. Much of this anger was increasingly directed at African foreigners. Xenophobia is undoubtedly one of the cancers of the new South Africa, and has been present at its birth. The first recorded incident of xenophobia in Alexandra occurred less than a year after the 1994 elections, when the Alexandra Land and Property Owners' Association led a march of about 400 residents to demand the "immediate eviction of foreign residents". Irrational fears about foreign 'outsiders' combined with perceptions about houses and jobs being stolen by such foreigners created a volatile situation that was susceptible to political manipulation. On 11 May 2008 Alexandra exploded into a conflagration of xenophobic violence against foreign Africans living mainly in and around the area known as 'Beirut', where the hostels are located and also the epicentre of the violence of the early 1990s. This has also been one of the main centres in the township that have been experiencing a constant influx of new immigrants since the 1980s.[→ Fig. E] Madala (Men's) hostel, an austere and increasingly dilapidated building, dominates this area. Since at least the 1980s the hostels have experienced a sharp decline in living conditions, with massive overcrowding and decrepit basic

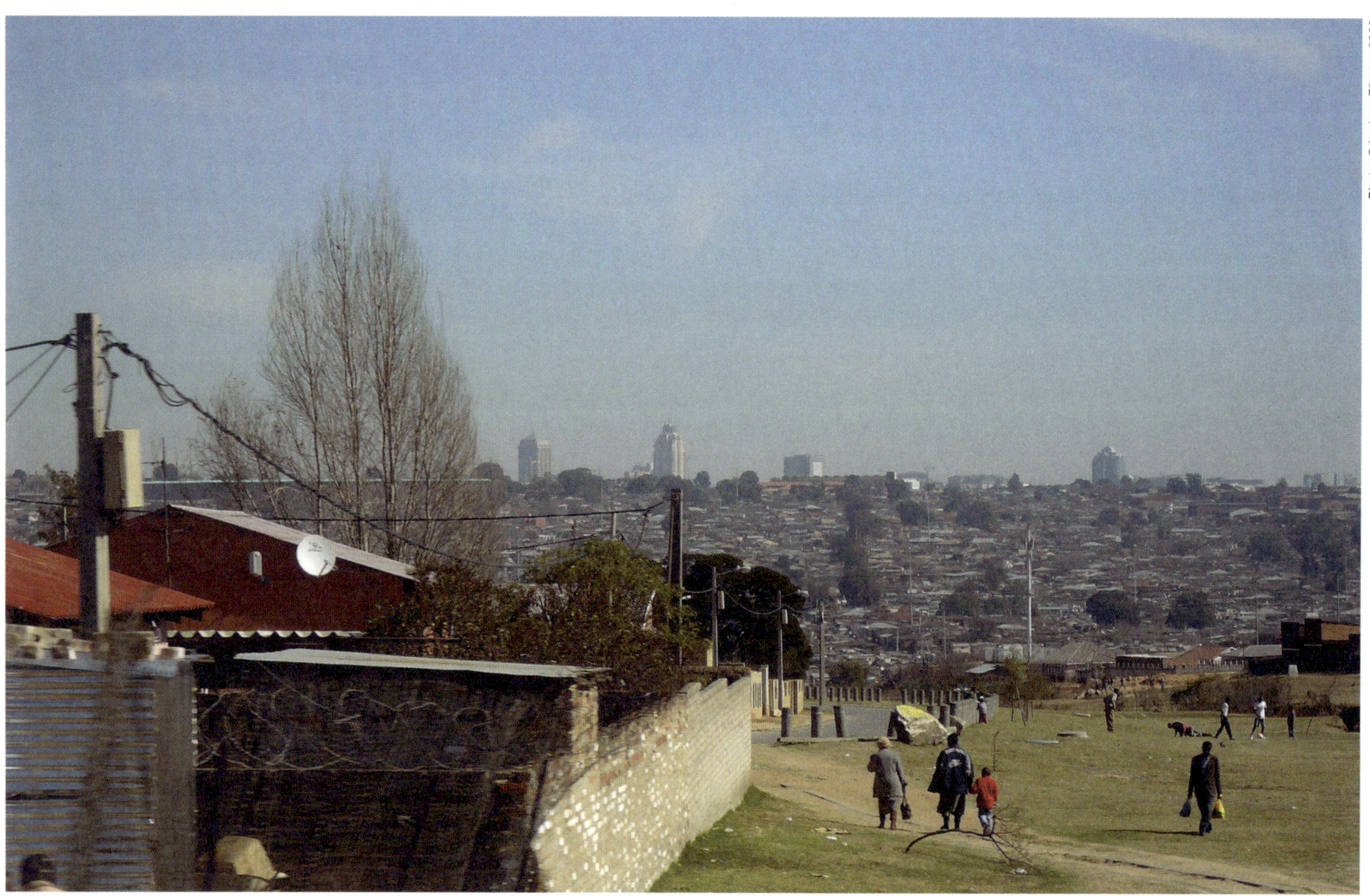

D The towers of Sandton City Shopping Centre, a glamorous shopping mall in the prosperous district of Sandton directly bordering Alexandra, rising above the sea of houses in Alexandra

services. Abutting the hostels is the equally insalubrious and densely concentrated sea of shack settlements, occupied mainly by new arrivals. Immigrants from other parts of Africa have lived in Alexandra, including in the Beirut area, for many years and have generally co-existed with their South African counterparts, struggling with them to eke out an existence under the most trying circumstances. But this sense of communalism is constantly threatened by the divisiveness that emanates from the utter desperation experienced by poor communities. Alexandrans remember how for nearly a week during that event in May 2008 the area resembled a war zone: two people were killed (including one South African), at least sixty were injured and hundreds were forcibly evicted from their homes by gangs of armed young men. This episode of xenophobic violence was mainly about the poor fighting against the poor, even if only for the right to occupy a dilapidated shack. As before, however, a politics of inclusion has prevailed, at least in the short term. A turning point in the violence occurred when residents of the local squatter camp, Setswetla, defended their foreign African neighbours. As had happened countless times in the history of the township, the spirit of community solidarity prevailed. Alexandra has retained its status as a preferred destination for poor black people wanting to find a place in Johannesburg. Over the past few years it has again been the site of major urban development and has regained its role as the incubator of emancipatory politics. As such it is often a place of despair, but also of hope for a genuinely inclusive city.

Editors' notes translated by Andrew Boreham

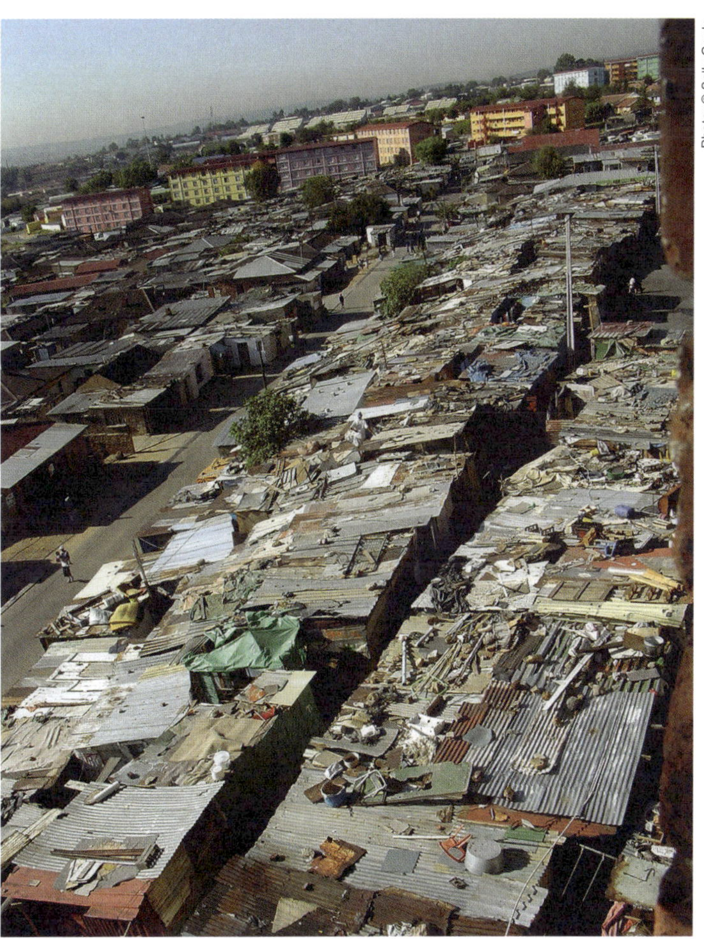

E   In the wake of rapid urbanisation in the 1980s, innumerable shacks sprang up in Alexandra.

The Technicians' Rebellion
Electricity and the Right to the City

THOMAS G. KIRSCH

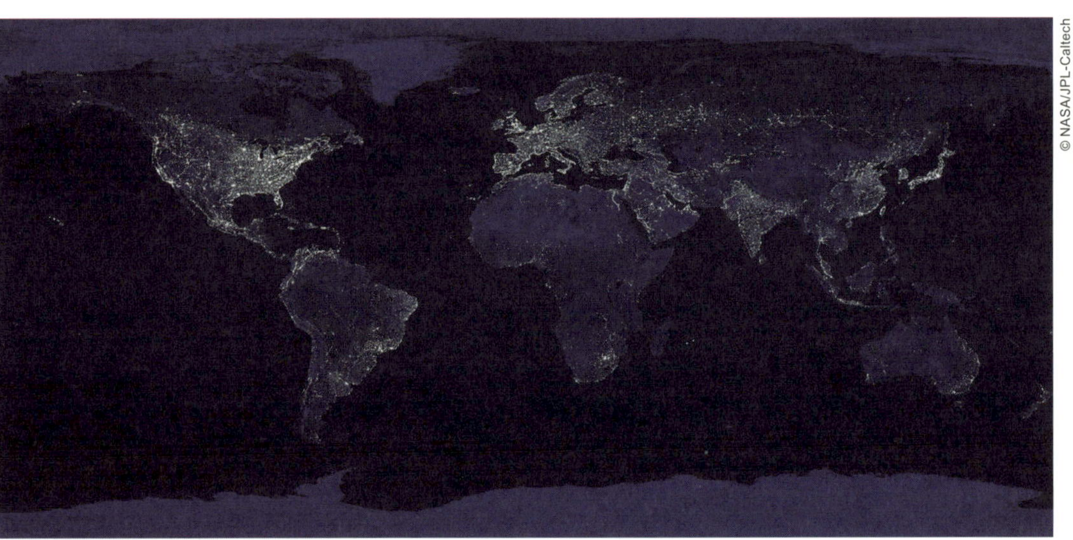

Only at night does the difference emerge. All the continents of the Earth have equal visibility in daylight satellite pictures, but in night-time images it becomes clear what distinguishes Africa from, for example, Europe: whereas these pictures show Europe blanketed with light, a vision of complete electrification, the African continent is literally a 'dark continent' for large parts of its surface. Although the lights of the larger ports along the coasts give a faint indication of the continent's contours, in the African interior the pictures show very few regions with a degree of electric luminosity similar to that of the highly industrialised nations of Europe, America, Asia and Australia.

One notable exception is the city of Johannesburg, in the South African province of Gauteng. Founded in the late 19th century as a makeshift gold-mining settlement, Johannesburg rapidly developed into a regional centre and the transnational linchpin of sub-Saharan Africa's industrialisation, mining and financial markets. The economic dynamism and cosmopolitan importance that this brought the city, today home to well over three million people, has made Johannesburg a metropolis of international status.[1] That status is crucially related to the city's integration into networks that extend across very large areas – networks of communication and of transport, but also the network of electricity supply, which is responsible for Johannesburg's high visibility from the lofty perspective of night-time satellite pictures.

From below, and in terms of the infrastructural detail, the situation looks very different. Since the end of apartheid nearly twenty years ago, the debate on opportunities for socio-political participation has found expression in the conflicted question of the socio-economic rationale that should underlie the connection of private households to the electricity supply network. That question is a problematic one, for when the expansion of the electrical grid was initiated after apartheid in parts of Johannes-

---

1   The development of Johannesburg since the end of apartheid is the object of the following studies: Jo Beall, Owen Crankshaw and Susan Parnell 2002, *Uniting a Divided City*, London; Richard Tomlinson and Robert Beauregard 2003, *Emerging Johannesburg*, New York; Martin Murray 2008, *Taming the Disorderly City*, Ithaca; Sarah Nuttall and Achille Mbembe (eds) 2008, *Johannesburg – The Elusive Metropolis*, Johannesburg.

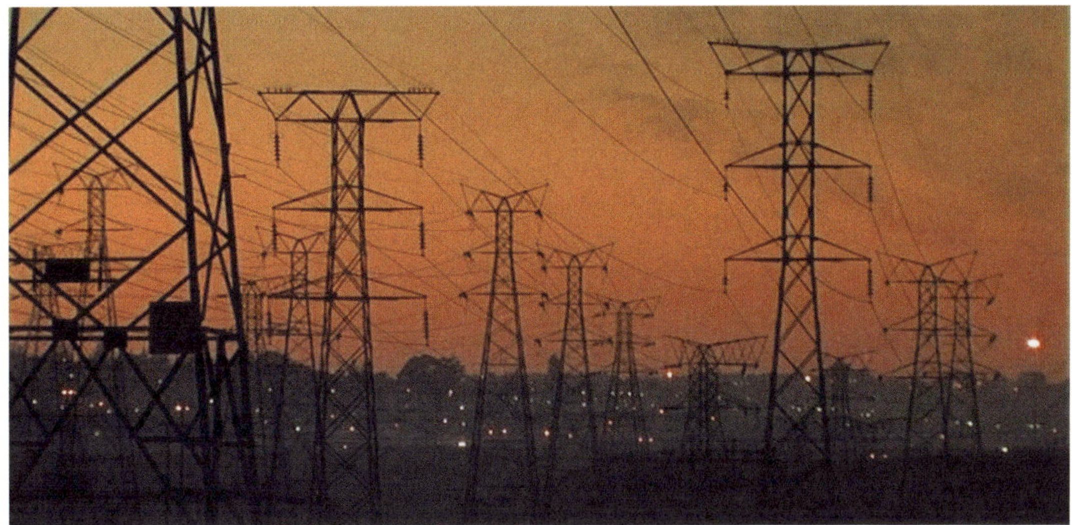

burg that had previously suffered infrastructural neglect, it went hand in hand with the privatisation of the electricity supply industry. This led to a situation where, on one hand, an increasing number of households were connected to the grid but, on the other, those households found it increasingly difficult to pay their electricity bills, so that as the years went by many thousands of people had their power supply cut off. In the context of a neoliberal catch-up modernisation of economically precarious urban spaces, therefore, these households were infrastructurally linked up to the electricity supply, only to be excluded from it again in practice very shortly thereafter.

The cynicism of this situation has not escaped the residents involved. As a result, in 2000 a new social movement formed in Soweto, one of Johannesburg's largest and poorest neighbourhoods: the Soweto Electricity Crisis Committee (SECC). The SECC critically addressed the processes I have just described, and began to reconnect the households cut off by the energy supply industry. They did so informally, with a high degree of technical skill but without official authorisation. This essay looks at this social movement, which works with electricity cables, toolboxes and terminal strips to procure for its members their 'right to the city'.

In focusing on the right to the city, the essay picks up on a theoretical perspective that was developed by the French sociologist Henri Lefebvre in the 1960s and has attained new currency in present-day sociological debates.[2] In this view, social conflicts around the spaces of the city do not only impact upon practical issues such as access to and utilisation of urban spaces, but also raise more far-reaching questions – questions related to the conditions of possibility for legal and political participation in the city, as a sphere of active creativity in which new socio-

political developments and visions are constantly put up for negotiation. In the case investigated here, the commodification of basic urban services in the area of electricity and water supply impedes such participation for many South Africans. It is for this reason that the commodification of energy has become a point of departure for protest movements like the Soweto Electricity Crisis Committee, whose organisational forms and strategies are reminiscent of the civil disobedience campaigns in the struggle against apartheid.

Apartheid: Race, Segregation, Discrimination

Almost two decades after the end of apartheid, Johannesburg's urban space is still marked by the legacy of a system of injustice in which racial classification was the fundamental criterion for processes of differentiation and exclusion within society. In this system, the colour of a person's skin determined not only whether that person was assigned the status of political and legal adulthood or minority, but also his or her opportunities for education and professional or social advancement, as well as the regions of the country – or particular urban areas – in which he or she was to live, which groups of people were allotted to live alongside him or her in a relationship of enforced neighbourhood, and what forms of mobility were open to his or her use.

The greatest number of restrictions was imposed on the population group that was officially classified as 'black', and which today remains the majority within South Africa's population. Thus, the Native (Urban Areas) Act of 1923 and the Group Areas Act of 1950 empowered Johannesburg's administration to segregate the city's inhabitants socially and spatially according to racial criteria and to control the immigration of black individuals. The

2   See Henri Lefebvre 1968, *Le droit à la ville,* Paris; 1973,
    Espace et politique, Paris; 1990, *Du contrat de Citoyenneté,*
    Paris; 2003, *The Urban Revolution;* Minneapolis. See also
    Mark Purcell 2002, Excavating Lefebvre: The Right to the
    City and its Urban Politics of the Inhabitant, *Geo Journal*
    58/2: 99–108; David Mitchell 2003, *The Right to the City:
    Social Justice and the Fight for Public Space,* New York;
    Christian Schmid (ed.) 2005, *Stadt, Raum und Gesellschaft:
    Henri Lefebvre und die Theorie der Produktion des Raumes,*
    Stuttgart; David Harvey 2008, The Right to the City, *New
    Left Review* 58: 23–40; Peter Marcuse 2009, From Critical
    Urban Theory to the Right to the City, *City* 13/2: 185–197.

1951 Prevention of Illegal Squatting Act additionally allowed the city authorities to enforce the resettlement of any unwanted black population group from the central districts into the urban periphery. In combination with the pass laws, which made it obligatory for black persons in 'non-black' spaces to hold specific permission for their presence, these laws unequivocally articulated the apartheid regime's view of the black population as an essentially rural population, whose residence in urban areas must be temporary and serve exclusively the interests of white" citizens.[3]

For many decades, the economically disastrous consequences of linking race to the city space were reflected, among other things, in the fact that the majority of the black population had limited or no access to basic services in the areas of health, waste disposal or water and electricity supply. This applies equally to Soweto, a township in the southwest of Johannesburg founded in 1905 through forced resettlements, where – depending on the estimate – between one and three million people live today.

In South Africa, electricity was introduced towards the end of the 19th century, but until the mid-20th century it was used mainly in the mines and in industry, in transportation and for the domestic supply of households in the white urban population. This history of selective access continued unbroken during the apartheid era, when electricity supply in South Africa followed the logic not of social and political equality, but of political and strategic calculation. The question of which population groups were granted access to electricity and which were not, played a crucial role in controlling opportunities for economic development among the respective groups.[4] In view of the systematic exclusion of the "black" population during apartheid, it is hardly surprising that many Soweto residents were refused connection to the electricity grid until the end of the 20th century.

Post-Apartheid: Class, Modernisation, Neoliberalism

After the end of apartheid and the first fully democratic elections in South Africa, the newly elected African National Congress government undertook strenuous efforts to promote previously marginalised social spaces by means of targeted infrastructural interventions. The goal of connecting all South Africa's private households to the power grid by 2012 was pursued with determination and large investments. As a result, the electrification rate for South African households almost doubled in the period between 1994 and 2002.[5]

In parallel with this catch-up modernisation of many urban spaces in South Africa, however, the neoliberal orientation of the post-apartheid South African government's policies led to a wave of privatisations that also affected the national electricity supplier, Eskom. With this development, electricity must now be supplied on a full-cost-recovery basis whereby individual customers must bear not only the costs of their own specific energy use, but also the infrastructural investment costs for the provision and maintenance of the grid. In some regions, this new corporate policy has led to price rises of more than 400 percent.[6] In many others, prepayment meters have been installed. By requiring customers to pay for their electricity consumption in advance, Eskom aims to prevent low-income South African citizens from falling into arrears due to excessive or uncontrolled electricity consumption.

If bills are not paid, Eskom cuts off the electricity. This practice is in line with the methods of other supply companies worldwide, and would hardly be remarkable were it not for the unusually large scale of disconnections in South Africa over the course of many years. In 2001, Soweto alone saw 20,000 households disconnected each month; only four out of every ten households there remained unaffected by the problem.[7] In the following year, thirteen per cent of the South African population – more than three million people – had their electricity cut off, at least temporarily.[8] As Trevor Ngwane, a leading figure in the Soweto Electricity Crisis Committee, remarked critically in a 2002 interview: "The post-apartheid society was supposed to be a society of connections, connecting all those black working-class people who had been deprived under apartheid. Instead, the new South Africa is a society of disconnections."[9] This double-edged critique draws attention to the fact that a person's access or lack of access to electricity is not simply a matter of everyday or pragmatic values, such as reducing workloads through the use of electrical domestic appliances – symbolic values are also of crucial significance. Just as in the early days of Europe and Africa's electrification, in present-day Soweto, connection to the power supply emblematises the aspiration to participate in the project of modernity. As an infrastructural symbol it stands for the successful achievement of desegregation and political participation by previously excluded population groups. From this point of view, it is unsurprising that, over the past few years, many Soweto residents have repeatedly offered resistance to what they see as a renewed exclusion and a questionable, profit-based reorientation in the provision of basic services.

Illegal Connections

Disconnecting a Soweto household's electricity on behalf of Eskom entails real risk for the Eskom employees who carry it out; physical confrontations are not infrequent, and in some cases are even fatal. For example, in 2001 an exchange of fire with four people injured was reported after several Soweto residents

3   For a survey of developments in the urban space during apartheid, see Paul Maylam 1990, The Rise and Decline of Urban Apartheid in South Africa, *African Affairs* 89/354: 57–84.

4   See also Renfrew Christie 1984, *Electricity, Industry and Class in South Africa,* London; Barbara Praetorius 2000, *Power for the People: Die unvollendete Reform der Stromwirtschaft in Südafrika nach der Apartheid,* Münster.

5   Electrification Plan "Will Need Huge Subsidies", *Business Day,* 7 March 2002

6   Maj Fiil-Flynn 2001, *The Electricity Crisis in Soweto,* Johannesburg, p. 6

7   Fiil-Flynn (2001), p. 16

8   David McDonald 2002, The Bell Tolls for Thee: Cost Recovery, Cutoffs, and the Affordability of Municipal Services in South Africa, in David McDonald (ed.), *The Crisis of Service Delivery in South Africa,* Johannesburg, p. 1–16, here p. 12

9   Is it a Crime to Fight for Services? *Socialist Worker,* 17 August 2002

confronted the Eskom technicians who were cutting off their electricity.[10] In another case, an Eskom employee was forced under threat of violence to reverse the disconnections he had just carried out. He said: "A machete-wielding man threatened to cut me into pieces and set me alight if I did not reconnect. With the machete at my back, I had to reconnect ten homes, although I had only disconnected three."[11]

Aside from violent confrontations of this kind, however, the residents of Soweto also make use of technical stratagems to connect private homes to the grid in an informal, unauthorised and ultimately illegal manner. Manipulating the electricity meter is one of the most common methods. Others consist of tying a partially stripped cable to a brick and throwing it across the overhead power lines so as to siphon off electricity, or else hooking a cable into the power line using a sharp piece of bamboo, which is done at night so that it can be removed in the daytime, leaving the theft of electricity undiscovered.[12]

In some cases, the creation of illegal electricity connections serves not to supply energy for a single household, but to carry out a business by selling on the tapped electricity to others. In 2003, for example, the South African media reported on a woman who had supplied electricity from her own household to more than fifteen other homes: "The cables were carefully buried in trenches dug in the ground around the house and extended across the street to the nearby informal settlement. In places the tarred road had been dug up and the wires buried and then covered up again. David Chauke, a hawker and a resident, said that at the end of the month there were long queues outside the woman's house as people waited to pay their accounts, while others waited to be connected."[13]

But even with such a high degree of professionalism, many of Soweto's residents are sceptical of do-it-yourself connections to the grid. Far too frequently, the cables used for such connections are not buried deep enough and leave live segments visible, so that passers-by or playing children can tread on them, with fatal consequences. Furthermore, the provisional nature of these connections means that short-circuits are common and often result in catastrophic fires, especially in informal settlements.[14] As a result, it is not only the police and Eskom staff who try to prevent illegal connections, but in some places also vigilante groups, taking the law into their own hands to prevent such activities in their neighbourhoods.

The Soweto Electricity Crisis Committee

However, not all illegal connections to the power supply are carried out by technically knowledgeable private individuals. Some are the work of representatives of the Soweto Electricity Crisis Committee (SECC), which was founded in 2000 as an affiliate of the Anti-Privatisation Forum (APF). With its slogan "Electricity is a right not a privilege", the SECC began a high-profile campaign of reconnecting households whose power supply had been cut off by Eskom, working without authorisation from the energy supplier.[15] *Operation Khanyisa* – whose name portrays its technicians as bringers of light (*khanyisa*) – is carried out by volunteer SECC technicians using guerrilla tactics. But the SECC flanks *Operation Khanyisa* with a great diversity of political activities, in the course of which it has several times come into physical conflict with the authorities of the state. In April 2002, for example, an SECC member was shot by a security guard as he protested in front of the home of the then Mayor of Johannesburg, Amos Masondo.[16] During the previous year, SECC activists had been arrested when they cut off the water and power supply to the mayor's private household in order to give him "a taste of his own medicine".[17]

Thanks to spectacular actions of this kind and their consequences, the activists today sometimes refer to their campaign as "a struggle that already has heroes, legends and martyrs".[18] In SECC press statements, parallels are frequently drawn between the Committee's own activities and the historical resistance struggle against the apartheid regime. For instance, the SECC describes *Operation Khanyisa* as being "done in the spirit of the defiance campaigns of the '50s and '60s where the working people of South Africa refused to obey unjust, oppressive and exploitative laws."[19] The SECC thus regards itself as part of a social movement in South Africa that, although it is new and addresses new problems, draws on "the traditions, the fire, the experience of the old days" of South Africa's history of political resistance.[20] But the SECC also goes beyond this national historical framework, emphasising that its political orientation gives continued life to a powerful international tradition of civil disobedience: "Underlying this great tradition and weapon of struggle, used by heroes such as Mahatma Gandhi, Martin Luther King and our own Nelson Mandela, is the basic philosophy that the power and command of those on top is based on the cooperation and consent of those at the bottom. We, the residents of Soweto, are withdrawing our cooperation with Eskom and by so doing we are helping each other to discover that Eskom is not so powerful after all, that Eskom's power is premised on our consent, that, in fact, the power lies with us the people."[21]

In 2003, the SECC had around 7,000 members and twenty-two branches. From the very beginning it has been led by directly elected representatives, with Trevor Ngwane, mentioned earlier, taking up a central and almost charismatic leadership role. After studying sociology, Ngwane first taught as a university lecturer, then worked for the Transport Workers Union. In 1990 he joined the African National Congress (ANC), and four years later he was elected councillor for the Pimville ward in Soweto. In 1999

10 Soweto Power Cuts Turn Violent, *South African Broadcasting Corporation,* 5 June 2001

11 Soweto Power Cuts Turn Violent, *South African Broadcasting Corporation,* 5 June 2001

12 Electricity Suppliers Liaison Committee 2001, *Report,* p. 4 ff.

13 Informal Power, *Sunday Times,* 23 March 2003

14 Fire Eats up Family Homes, *Sunday Times,* 8 September 2002

15 For further analysis of the SECC, see Helen Meintjes and Caroline White 1997, *"Robbers and Freeloaders": Relations between Communities and Eskom in Gauteng Townships,* Johannesburg; Anthony Egan and Alex Wafer 2004, *The Soweto Electricity Crisis Committee,* Durban; Prishani Naidoo and Veriava Ahmed 2009, From Local to Global (and Back Again?): Anti-Commodification Struggles of the Soweto Electricity Crisis Committee, in David McDonald (ed.), *Electric Capitalism,* Cape Town, p. 321–337.

16 Electricity Protesters to Stay in Jail for a Week, *The Star,* 9 April 2002

17 People's Power in Soweto!, *SECC Press Release,* 18 October 2001

18 Neoliberalism and Resistance in South Africa, *Monthly Review,* January 2003: 276–277

19 The Electricity Crisis in Soweto, *SECC Press Release,* 6 June 2001

20 Sparks in the Township (interview with Trevor Ngwane), *New Left Review,* August 2003

21 The Electricity Crisis in Soweto, *SECC Press Release,* 6 June 2001

Ngwane was removed from office in the course of internal ANC conflicts over the comprehensive plans for privatisation in Johannesburg.[22]

Since then, Trevor Ngwane has been working primarily to criticise unregulated globalisation processes and to address head-on the social consequences of neoliberal political agendas. Over the years, he and his fellow campaigners have succeeded in building up a global institutional network and extensive international publicity for the SECC. Today Ngwane can be called a global player of the political left. In a 2004 collection edited by the historian Tom Mertes, *A Movement of Movements*[23], Trevor Ngwane's biography stands alongside an interview with the key protagonist of left-wing movements in Mexico, *Subcomandante Marcos,* and an article on the anti-globalisation organisation ATTAC. As this shows, the activities of the SECC now have more than merely local significance in the urban space of Johannesburg; they have achieved global visibility.

At its heart, the object of the SECC's social and political critique is the free-market logic that drives electricity supply in today's South Africa – a logic that, as one SECC press release put it, "contradicts the spirit of the country's constitution, which seeks to guarantee access to basic services".[24] The SECC contests this rationale of free enterprise by advocating a "decommodification" strategy for electricity and demanding that the power supply be returned to the hands of state authorities in a process of renationalisation.[25] Specifically, the organisation's protests have, in the course of the years, been directed at issues such as the mass cut-offs of households among South Africa's low-income population groups, inconsistencies in the reading of electricity meters (which are often defective), cases of corruption among Eskom personnel, and tariff structures that it accuses of being unfair and discriminatory to the core.[26] The SECC also criticises the fact that Eskom hires private contractors to cut off household electricity, awarding them a bonus for each disconnection carried out. Some of these subcontractor companies belong to the very politicians who pushed for the privatisation of Eskom. All these issues are cited as reasons for the continuation of *Operation Khanyisa.* In 2001 and 2002 alone, the campaign reconnected almost 150,000 households to the power supply. Partly as a result of this, in late 2009 only half of all Soweto households paid an electricity bill.[27]

The Right to the City

What does it mean for Soweto residents, marginalised for so long and often caught up in economically precarious situations, to have fought for and won themselves a place in their city – a right to their city? Members of the Soweto Electricity Crisis Committee recount the gratitude of residents whose power supply has been restored by the SECC, and observe that connection to the grid is more than just a practical matter for them: it has great symbolic value. At stake for these residents is human dignity and participation in a modern lifestyle which their labour made possible for other – white – South Africans during the apartheid era, but of which they themselves have been deprived. Yet the right to the city that the SECC demands is not guided by demarcations and exclusions, but by the desire to participate in something that symbolises a networked form of South African urban life – a network that crosses frontiers, extends its capillaries into other districts of Johannesburg, and indeed reaches beyond the boundaries of the specific urban space. The rebellion of the technicians, thus, pursues far more than purely technical goals.

Translation from German by Kate Sturge

Unless otherwise noted, the illustrations are taken from Florian Opitz's documentary *The Big Sellout* (2007). The film addresses privatisation processes in South Africa, the Philippines, the UK and Bolivia, and shows the Soweto Electricity Crisis Committee at work. © Florian Opitz / Majestic Filmverleih GmbH

22 Sparks in the Township (interview with Trevor Ngwane), *New Left Review,* August 2003

23 Tom Mertes (ed.) 2004, *A Movement of Movements: Is Another World Really Possible?* London

24 The Electricity Crisis in Soweto, *SECC Press Release,* 6 June 2001

25 Power to the People in South Africa: Operation Khanyisa! and the Fight against Electricity Privatization, *Multinational Monitor,* February 2002

26 The Electricity Crisis in Soweto, *SECC Press Release,* 6 June 2001

27 South Africa Crisis Creates Crusading Electricians, *BBC,* 24 November 2009

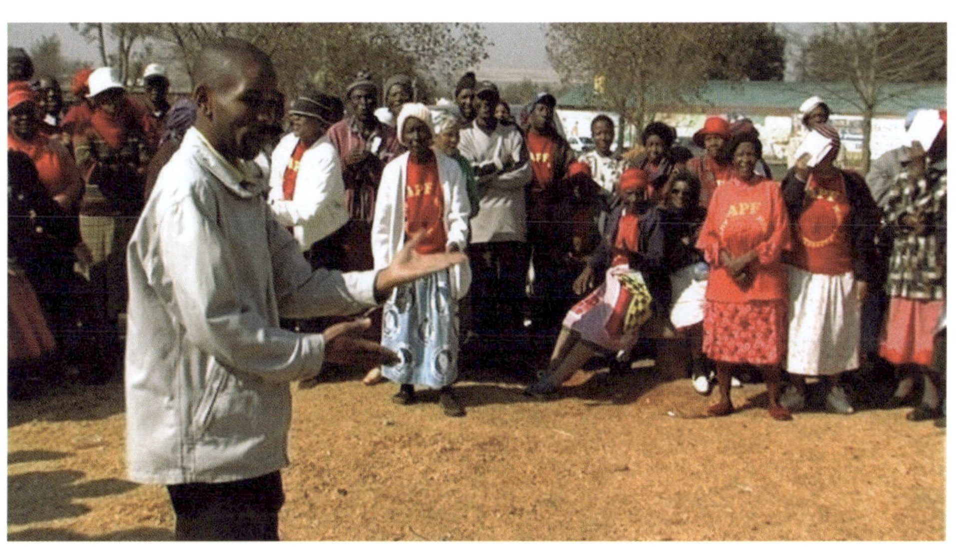

← Activist Bongani Lubisi at a Soweto Electricity Crisis Committee event campaigning for the electrification and re-electrification of Soweto households.

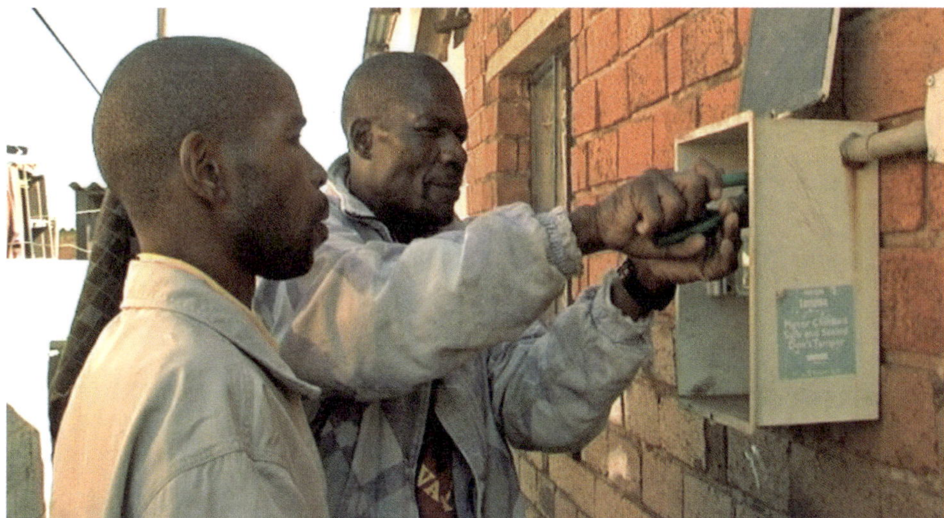

← Members of the Soweto Electricity Crisis Committee reconnecting a household to the Eskom power supply.

Stylizing the Self [1]

SARAH NUTTALL

Johannesburg is a city wrought from its surfaces and depths, from that which is apparent, on display, there to be seen, ambitious, brash, innovative – and that which lies underneath, hidden in part, heaving at times to the surface, whether as earth once bearing gold, ready for extraction and manned by a labor system long based on a racial division of labor, or as a memory of the past which persists beneath, erupts, and works to shape the surfaces of the present. Several authors in this book explore the idea of Johannesburg as a city of surfaces and depths. In the introduction, Achille Mbembe and I argue that the entanglement between surface and underneath constitutes one of the defining metaphors by which to understand this city, both historically and in its contemporary forms.

One of the ways in which Johannesburg projects its surface is through its representations: in many ways, it is a city studded with texts. Billboards, newsprint, magazine covers, road signs, even the entire surfaces of buildings constitute a stream of local and global city signs, of Johannesburg representation. These texts are really a part of visual culture, and most of the time, they have sartorial and aural accompaniments. As surfaces, they are sometimes just that, but they also on occasion suggest a deeper diagnostic, a layering in which, for example, the apparent fixity of race so often privileged in accounts of the city is underwritten by the potential unfixing of the commodity form, or in which the past resurfaces in the present. Taken together, these city texts reveal something of the force and power of attempts by young black people in particular to conquer the right to be urban in the present: to occupy the center of the city, its subjective core, to produce forms of city style at tremendous velocity – in direct response, perhaps, to an apartheid past in which black people were required to work in the city but not live in it, to perform its labor, and then retreat from its center.

In this essay I want to discuss several forms of Johannesburg representation, of self-making in the city, forms that are quite different from before, even as they cite or acknowledge a past, a deeper history, which is, they assert, gone but not entirely to be discarded. Indeed, what makes these representations and forms of self-stylization they produce local in their resonances and their reach while undoubtedly spliced with the global is their remixing of a past that is South African and specific: the past of apartheid. The forms I discuss are moments in Johannesburg's history, ones that will metamorphose before long, but which nevertheless operate as important signals, even in their transience, of the remaking of the racial city toward its metropolitan form. They reveal versatile approaches to the media and information technology and produce imaginaries that are flexible, at times contradictory and eminently contingent. [2] They constitute one part of Johannesburg's distinctively modern aura, an aura, as Michael Watts [3] has written, which derives as much from its zine culture and its metropolitan imaginings as from its memorializations, its psychic wounds, and its fugitive underground worlds.

The essay stays in part with the surface as an analytic location. It tries to capture something of the immense coincidence, so tangible in Johannesburg at present, between the end of apartheid and the rise of new media culture and cultures of consumption. It aims to show how we might take the surface more seriously in our analyses of contemporary cultural form but equally how contemporary youth media cultural forms in Johannesburg still signal to and cite the underneath of an apartheid past. As such they are firmly focused on the making of the future, while retaining a memory of the past, increasingly remade in the present. They act as screens across which emergent selves flicker, revealing traces of certain kinds of urban, bodily lives and certain sorts of investments in being in the city.

In the first part of the essay below, I explore the rise of a youth cultural form widely known as Y Culture. Y Culture, also known as *loxion kulcha* for reasons I explain below, is an emergent youth culture in Johannesburg that moves across various media forms and which generates a "compositional remixing" that signals the supercession of an earlier era's resistance politics by an alternative politics of style and accessorization, while simultaneously gesturing, in various ways, toward the past. It is a culture of the hip bucolic that works across a series of surfaces, requiring what Paul Gilroy [4] calls "technological analogies," in order to produce enigmatic and divergent styles of self-making. While drawing on black American style formations, it is an explicitly local reworking of the American sign – a reworking that simultaneously results in and underscores significant fractures in Gilroy's paradigm of the black Atlantic. [5]

In my analysis, I find it useful to draw on Foucault's concept of "stylizing the self". Foucault invokes practices of self-stylization or self-fashioning through which individuals create "a certain number of operations on their own bodies and souls, thoughts, conduct and ways of being so as to transform themselves" [6].

---

1   This text is a reprint of the primary publication Sarah Nuttall and Achille Mbembe (eds) 2008, *Johannesburg – The Elusive Metropolis, A Public Culture Book,* Johannesburg, p. 91–118. Therefore, the spelling of the American English was maintained.

2   I draw here on the work of Dominique Malaquais, especially her introductory remarks to a special issue of *Politique Africaine* (N° 100, 2005), which she guest-edited.

3   Michael Watts 2005, Baudelaire over Berea, Simmel over Sandton?, *Public Culture,* 17/1: 181–192

4   Paul Gilroy 2000, *Between Camps. Nations, Cultures and the Allure of Race,* London

5   In his book *The Black Atlantic: Modernity and Double Consciousness* (1993), Gilroy introduces the idea of a transatlantic black culture – which he terms the "black Atlantic" – whose practices and ideas transcend both ethnicity and nationality. Black people, he argues, shaped a shared, transnational, diasporic culture, that in turn shaped the history of modernity. He explores this transatlanticism in black music and writing and reveals the shared contours of black and Jewish concepts of diaspora. Although he does not write about them in his book, both Brazil and South Africa partook of, and in turn helped to shape, this "black Atlantic culture".

6   Michel Foucault 2003, *Society must be Defended: Lectures at the Collège de France, 1975–1976,* New York, p. 225

Such processes of self-stylization draw on technologies of the self to ensure that what emerges from the moment of political liberation are indeed practices of freedom.

I find, too, that in attempting to understand Y Culture forms, cultural analysis that relies on ideas of translation or translatability, embedded in a model of reading, is useful only up to a point, and that what is required instead – or at least equally – is an understanding of how cultural forms move. While translation relies on an idea of a gap – a gap between one meaning or text and another – I find that what is needed in order to properly understand this cultural form is something closer to an interface in which meaning morphs continuously into something else, rather than losing its initial sense. While the idea of the gap in meaning inhabits our theorizing about culture generally, it deserves elaboration and adjustment when it comes to reading the innovations of contemporary urban cultural forms. In the second part of the essay, I consider a recent set of advertisements that have appeared on billboards and in magazines in the wake of Y Culture. I show how they simultaneously engage with and push in unexpected directions one of the most striking aspects of Y/loxion culture, an attempt at rereading race in the city. In analyzing the ads, I consider ways in which commodity images, and the market itself, come to produce some of the most powerful reimaginings of race South Africa has known in some time. At the same time, the idea of the gap (here between what you have and what you want) is continually reconstituted at the heart of the commodity in order to propel new desires.

Y Culture, Johannesburg Circa 2006

Y Culture was first launched by a radio station called YFM, today South Africa's largest regional station, beamed over the airwaves from Johannesburg to nearly two million listeners. The station was set up in 1996. Its primary audience was young, mostly black people, who tuned in to hear a mix of popular, mostly local music. When democracy came to South Africa in 1994, there was no airspace, on the AM or PM dials, dedicated to the country's young black people. The South African Broadcasting Corporation (SABC) had a spare frequency, which it handed over to the team that would eventually found YFM. Stringent conditions were attached: the station would be granted a license only if eighty per cent of its capital was black-owned, fifty per cent of its staff was female and, within three years, at least half its playlist was made up of South African music. The station was to be a multilingual urban entity that informed, educated, and entertained a young audience. All of this was well in line with the founding team's goals. YFM, says general manager Greg Maloka, was to be a "phenomenon … for us and by us. We saw [its creation] as another June 16, 1976," he adds, alluding

to the spontaneous uprising of tens of thousands of children and adolescents in Soweto, a massive call-to-action against the apartheid state that marked the beginning of the end of the white regime. Twenty-two years had passed. Apartheid was officially dead. Suddenly, the youth market was what everyone was talking about.[7]

YFM launched *kwaito,* South Africa's first globally recognized local music form, a potent blend of city and township sound that emerged after the democratic transition in 1994, mixing the protest dancing and chanting known as *toyi-toyi* with slow-motion house, local pop (known as "bubblegum"), and a dash of hip-hop. In 1998, the station spawned a print spin-off, *Y Magazine* (or *YMag*). Making use of state of the art branding techniques, the magazine associated itself closely with both YFM and *kwaito*. Its tagline, prominently displayed on the spine of each issue, is an anthem to the art of being in the know – hip, cool, plugged in: "Y – Because You Want to Know". The same is true of the name chosen by the company that owns the publication, YIRED, a play on notions of being young and "wired" – up to date and connected in all the right places. In 2002, the YFM stable launched a fashion label called *Loxion Kulcha* (LK).[8] "Loxion" is a text-message contraction of the word "location", a synonym of "township"; "Kulcha" is an ironic deformation of the word "culture". The brand name invokes a remixing: an infusion of black township culture, long kept at a violent remove from the urban centre, into the heart of the (once white) city itself. In *YMag,* Loxion Kulcha is described as a "pride-driven line," a "brand born of the YFM era", one that remixes African-American styles to its own purposes and in ways that speak to its own, particular cultural precursors.[9] Its designers, Wandi Nzimande and Sechaba "Chabi" Mogale, are "typical generation Yers, children of the 1980s who are old enough to understand what the political fuss [of the apartheid era] was about, yet young enough to keep an open mind [to the present and future]".[10]

Y Culture is located most visibly in an area called the Zone, in Rosebank, a residential neighborhood-cum-business district that has been attracting a young, hip workforce since the 1980s, thanks to a concentration of information technology, travel and tourism enterprises, retail and fashion outlets, cinemas, and restaurants. Increasingly, to serve this young workforce, a process of infill has occurred, in which shopping complexes expand by incorporating spaces and structures that predate them. The Zone – home to the YFM studios and to shops showcasing Loxion Kulcha and related fashion labels such as the popular Stoned Cherrie brand – is one of these infills.[11] Here, enclosed shopping venues and open areas are linked by indoor and outdoor "roads," in an approach to architecture that, as one critic observes, turns the notion of public space inside out.[12]

---

7   Liz McGregor 2005, *Khabzela,* Johannesburg
8   Loxion Kulcha began with a collection of hand-knitted beanies (hats) that then grew into urban streetwear, mainly denims, printed T-shirts, and sports shoes. Recent designs include branded overalls and men's suits.
9   Bulelwa Mstali 2000, Street Couture, *YMagazine* May: 61–62
10 Mstali (2000)

11 The name "Stoned Cherrie" plays on a series of puns and local references. "Stoned" refers in part to the violence of the 1980s in the townships but also to being high on marijuana. It may also refer to the pit (stone) of the cherry. "Cherrie" recalls the fruit of the same name but this particular spelling also refers to a slang term, originally from Afrikaans, meaning girl or woman or girlfriend. In 1965, for example, Casey Motsisi, writing in *Drum* magazine, wrote: "I had to invite that most fascinating cherie in this man's town, Sis Sharon with goo goo eyes." Thus the term Stoned Cherrie contains many resonances, including the retro term for young township girls of the 1950s and 1960s. It places the girl or woman at the centre of its frame of reference but also stands for a general sense of having a good time.
12 Tanya Farber 2002, *Loaded with Labels. The Meanings of Clothing amongst Urban Black Youth in Rosebank, Johannesburg,* Master Thesis, University of the Witwatersrand, p. 73

In the Zone, yellow and blue neon tubes, glitter tiles, columns clad in reflective aluminum, and exposed steel trusses give it an industrial look that combines elements of the factory and the club. [→ Fig. A] As one makes one's way through its spaces, one is struck by their fluidity. Distinctions – thresholds – between public and private, pavement and mall, inside and out, seem to fall away. The Zone's indoor roads sometimes feel like catwalks – and at others like a state-of-the-art gym (television screens hang over the walkways). Throughout, surfaces (shiny, mirrorlike) and colors (an energetic metallic gray flecked with primary colors) differentiate the space from the neutral beige found in the city's other shopping centers.[13] Wherever possible, the Zone's architecture maximizes the intersection of gazes: people on the escalators produce a spectacle for diners seated at strategically located restaurants; the main indoor roads function simultaneously as means of access and vantage points; signifiers one would usually rely on to orient oneself outside (street signs, for instance) are reappropriated to define interior spaces.[14]

As a locus of social interaction, the Zone is complex. On the one hand, as a privatized public space, it speaks of exclusion: though it is possible for poorer citizens to come to the Zone, they are not welcome there.[15] At the same time, it is one of Johannesburg's relatively few upmarket open spaces where some manner of the unexpected is possible: theatre, mime, and dance groups perform here, parades are organized, and people come from all over the continent to trade in a large African craft market located near its entrance. The Zone is by no means a place of extensive social mixing. Heavily regulated and subjected to close

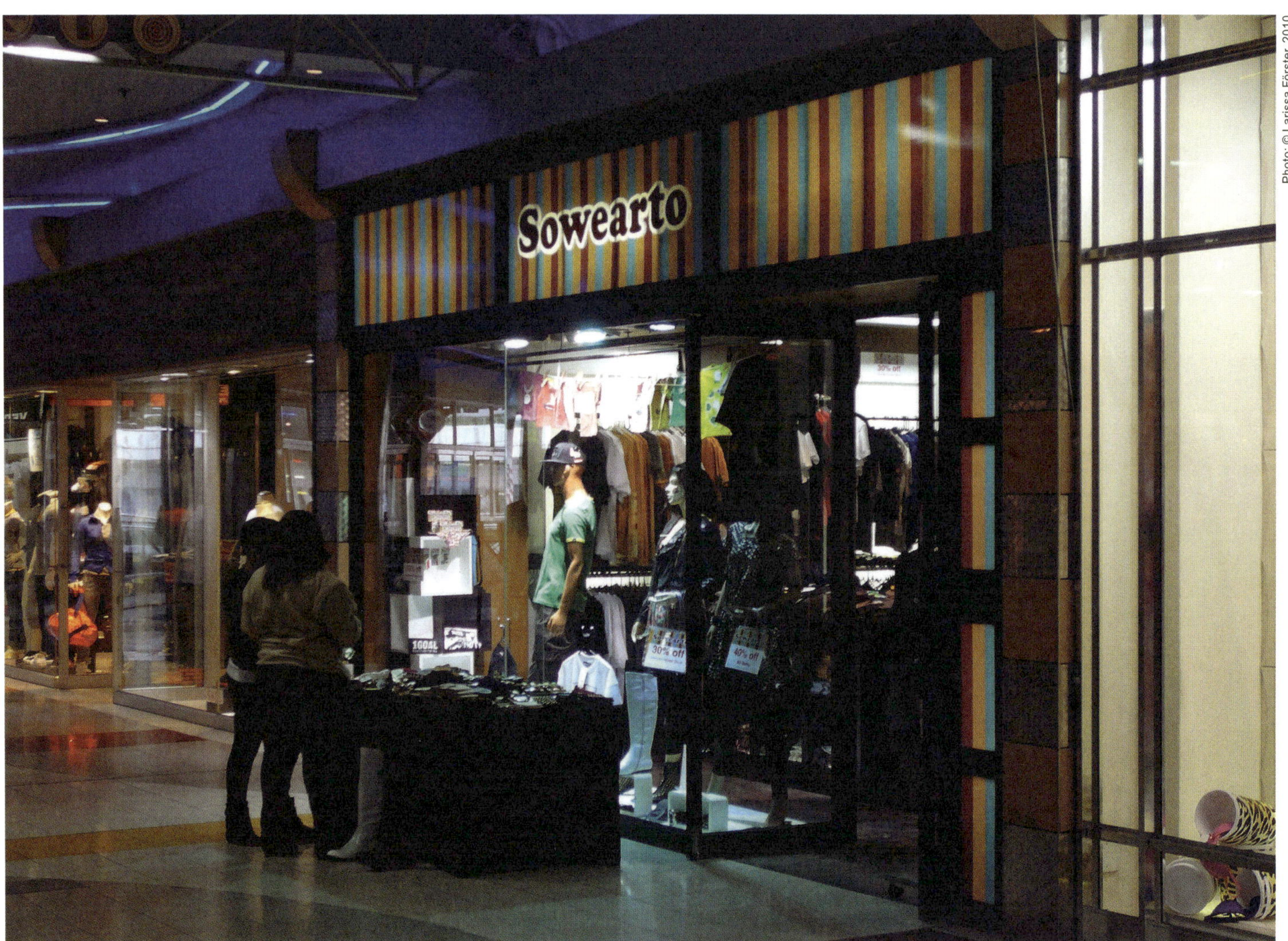

Photo: © Larissa Förster, 2010

A The Zone shopping mall in Rosebank, a center of Y culture. The Sowearto label references the township of almost the same name.

13 I am grateful to Lindsay Bremner for her discussions with me on these points.

14 Farber (2002), p. 87

15 Private security at the Zone is less apparent than in regular malls around the city. CCTV cameras can sometimes be seen, but in general there are few security guards and the outdoor precincts are not secured as such.

scrutiny by expedient mall governors, the craft market at its door underscores this. Still, as a result of its presence, there is a sense here of broader horizons: a young person (or anyone else) walking around the Zone circulates within an imagined Africa much larger than Johannesburg alone.

Thus, despite the influence on it of American models of mall design and commerce, the Zone does not yet display the nihilism that characterizes consumer culture in the United States – an approach to selling style and individuality in which each customer is pegged to a specifically managed and increasingly reified identity. This in part is due to the still recent emergence of the black body from its history of invisibility under apartheid – an erasure from the city which Y Culture, in certain respects, seeks to recall, but that it is largely bent on transforming – and to the relative fluidity with which black middle-class culture locates itself in the urban matrix after a long period of exclusion. Elaborating on this point, we could perhaps also argue that under apartheid, black people faced the oppressive binaries of either being made entirely invisible – or being made hypervisible. It is this hypervisibility that Y Culture, but especially the advertisements I discuss in the second part of this essay, works with and parodies.[16]

The Zone, as well as housing smaller fashion outlets like the Stoned Cherrie brand store and Young Designers Emporium, is home to the ubiquitous mall chain stores. Among these are Exclusive Books and CD Warehouse. Both are found at shopping arcades throughout the city and in urban centers across the country. At this particular branch of Exclusive Books, the bestsellers are not what they are elsewhere. The books that sell the best in most Exclusive Books locations are by US pulp authors like John Grisham and Dan Brown. In the Zone, they take second billing. The top sellers are Niq Mhlongo's *Dog Eat Dog* (2004) and Phaswane's Mpe's *Welcome to our Hillbrow* (2000). The first is the story of a young Sowetan trying to hustle his way through Wits University, long a bastion of white education; the second is a tale of xenophobia and Aids in inner-city Johannesburg. The Zone branch of CD Warehouse also differs from its sister stores elsewhere in the city. It carries a prominent and exhaustive range of *kwaito* CDs as well as some of the best sounds from the continent and black America. Next to CD Warehouse is the YFM Internet café and the Y-Shoppe, where local designers showcase their work and whose designs generally invoke the city by name or image, draw on puns or pastiches of the past and play with the "Y" logo.[17] The shop leads to the heart of the radio station, the Y Studios, a slick, black-lined maze of soundproof booths. Through large windows, one can see DJs at work creating the Y sound at banks of sophisticated equipment. The DJs themselves are young, glamorous, mostly black skinned and black-clad.[18]

Remix

Y is a hybrid phenomenon that appeals to young people across borders of class, education, and taste. Key to its success in this regard is a dual remixing it effects – of the township and the city and the township in the city. The young designers who launched the Loxion Kulcha label are incarnations of this intraculture. Wandi styles himself a *kasi,* or "township boy", Chabi a *Bana ba di Model C* (a "Model C kid"). As such, they represent the remix at work in the making of Y. A *kasi* is typically someone who grew up in a black township, a world often associated with poverty, crime, overcrowding and lack of resources. At the same time, while this is indeed the environment in which Wandi was raised and which he references in speaking of himself as a *kasi,* the word today has acquired so many connotations that it can now stand alone, quite apart from location, to imply a certain way of life (see Mbembe's interview of Dlamini and Khunou in this volume). Chabi's take on himself tells of a different world. When the South African education system was first integrated after 1994, privileged schools in formerly white, bourgeois neighborhoods opened their doors to black students. These schools were classified as "Model C" establishments. Though the term is no longer used as a formal education category, over time it has acquired a meaning of its own. It refers to black high-school students who have taken on a cross-racial style and social set.

Loxion Kulcha's intracultural success is less a matter of appearance than a matter of branding. The point may be to bring the township into the city, and cultural knowledge of where "township culture" is heading is certainly at the heart of what makes Wandi and Chabi hip, but Loxion Kulcha is not about spreading a "township look". The label – the brand, explicitly set forth and marketed with brio – is the thing here, as Mpolokeng Bogatsu quite accurately points out.[19] This privileging of brand over look simultaneously reflects and shapes structures of class and race within the city's emergent youth culture.

Although Loxion Kulcha's market is intraclass (to the extent that it encompasses both city youth and those living in generally lower-middle-class township homes), sartorial markings are often seen to reveal sharp distinctions between Zone kids (well-to-do young people who make a habit of coming to Rosebank) and township kids, who do frequent the Zone but to a lesser extent and are not particularly welcome there. Rocking the brand is good, essential even, but it doesn't occult where you come from. Young people interviewed in the Zone make this quite clear: "Township girls", says one, "wear Rocabarroco [brand] shoes that are square-shaped with laces … They will wear bright-[colored] jeans with a collar-type shirt. A Zone kid will wear [blue] jeans and a nice [read hip, collarless] top." Another glosses this as: "They dress similarly, but you can tell them apart. Model C girls

---

16 I am grateful to Isabel Hofmeyr for our discussions on this point.

17 For example, one set of T-shirts is emblazoned with the word "SHARPEVILLE!" This is a reference to the notorious events of 21 March 1960, when thousands of Africans demonstrated against the Pass laws instituted by apartheid. It was a nonviolent demonstration but police killed sixty-nine people and wounded hundreds of others. Many view it as a turning point in the mounting struggle for liberation. The phrase also plays on the colloquialism "sharp", which means "cool". It suggests that Jozi is a city with a past (a political struggle) but is also a cool place to be.

18 McGregor (2005)

19 Mpolokeng Bogatsu 2003, *Loxion Kulcha. Cultural Hybridism and Appropriation in Contemporary Black Youth Culture Popular Culture*, Honors Research Essay, University of the Witwatersrand, Johannesburg

have an air of sophistication, whereas township girls could snap anytime." Some interviewees focus less on sartorial differences than on skin color. This they do, however, in ways that stand at a distinct remove from earlier, pre-1994 discourses of race and, by extension, class. Notes one young Zoner: "In our generation, we all kind of dress the same. Some blacks dress outrageously wrong and some whites do too, but we all wear the same things. If you check around, you can't notice a difference between whites and blacks here, apart from the color of their skin."[20] Difference is still located on the skin, as color, even as skin color becomes less determined within this sartorially inflected set of practices and signs.

The foregoing underscores the fact that racial identities emerging from Y/loxion culture are new in relation to the apartheid era legal classification of people as "White", "Black", "Indian", or "Colored". These categories operated on an everyday basis through processes of urbanization, policing, and the manipulation of cultural difference to political ends. Since 1994, when this system was officially abolished, young people have occupied these categories in changing ways, using them to elaborate shifting identities for themselves in the new, "postracist" dispensation. Nadine Dolby argues that "taste" at times comes to displace orthodox constructs of race and culture as the carrier of social distinctions among urban students – this as popular culture comes to increasingly contest the church, family, and neighborhood as the primary site where racial identities are forged. The criteria that define bodies, clothing, and culture as "White", "Colored", or "Black" are not stable, as fashion and music tastes undergo one metamorphosis after another. Class dynamics work into the constitution of racialized taste patterns, at times taking on charged connotations despite constant style fluctuations. What is clear is that new youth cultures are superseding the resistance politics of an earlier generation, while still jamming, remixing, and remaking cultural codes and signifiers from the apartheid past.

How these codes are reappropriated and transformed makes for fascinating cultural (and business) practice. Stoned Cherrie, one of the most popular fashion labels at the Zone, puts signs of the past to striking use. Notably, it recycles images of boxing champions, beauty queens and musicians from *Drum,* a politically engaged magazine for black readers popular during the 1950s, integrating them into contemporary fashion styles. *Drum* was associated with places like Sophiatown, the heart of Johannesburg's counterculture in the 1950s. It courted and actively constructed an expressly cosmopolitan target audience, "the new African cut adrift from the tribal reserve – urbanized, eager, fast talking and brash"[21]. Stoned Cherrie's designs speak in several registers. In part they play on the taste for "retro" (a current global trend in styling), by drawing on 1950s imagery – imagery for

which *Drum,* a showcase for some of the best urban photography in South Africa, is a particularly fruitful source. At the same time, they make extensive use of parody, as they brand unquestionably dated *vieux jeu* images onto mass-produced T-shirts. Retro and parody, in turn, combine to invoke nostalgia for "the location". Emblematic figures of Johannesburg's mid-20th century past – *pantsulas*[22], the "bad boys" of the 1950s; migrant and blue-collar workers; black cover girls whose very existence and whose sophistication stood on its head white culture's claim to superiority – are recreated, brought to life anew and remixed, in Loxion Kulcha. This past, recalled and reworked, is in turn cross-pollinated with references to African-American culture(s) and styles. In an analysis of how Loxion Kulcha remakes township culture and, more specifically, blends pantsula and African-American street culture styles, Nthabiseng Motsemme shows how *isishoeshoe* and *iduku* (shoes and headcloths worn by black married township and rural migrant women employed as domestic workers in the city during the apartheid era) have been recaptured, reinterpreted, and transformed into iconic fashion items on display in Rosebank.[23] The point, here, is not a political one – not, in any event, in the sense that resistance movements to apartheid understood the term. There is no real (or intended) engagement here with the horrors of the pre-1994 past. This is underscored by another Loxion Kulcha product: a recent line of low-cut, tight-fitting T-shirts on which liberation theorist and apartheid martyr Steve Biko's image and name appear in a brilliant, stylized red.[24] It is not so much the Black Consciousness message spread by Biko that is being commemorated here, although "BC" still has a broad resonance for young people only vaguely aware of its message. Rather, something different is being introduced: a sartorial style is being marked as an in-your-face contemporary phenomenon through the remixing and recoding of an icon.

While township culture and identity have existed as long as the townships themselves, it is the *performance* of township culture that has emerged with new vigor in the contemporary context. "Like *kwaito* music", writes Bogatsu, "Loxion Kulcha claims the streets of South Africa's townships as its cultural womb but occupies the centre of the city with its new forms."[25] Township culture is translated from a socioeconomically stagnant into a high-urban experience. The latter gives rise to what is increasingly known as "Afro-chic." A case in point: in the 2000/2002 Loxion Kulcha collections, overalls were big. [→ Fig. **B**] Mostly, they were single-color outfits, inspired by the work clothes of migrant laborers and miners. Their design was similar to that of *mdantsane,* two-piece coveralls consisting of pants and a zip-up jacket generally worn by workers on a factory assembly line or by miners in a shaft. Unlike the protective garments on which they were modeled, however, the LK pieces emphasized bright, eye-catching

20 Farber (2002), p. 11–16

21 Lewis Nkosi 1983, *Home and Exile and Other Selections,* London, p. 34

22 A *pantsula* is a young urban person (usually a black man) whose attitudes and behavior, especially his speech and dress, are of the most popular current fashion. The term is sometimes applied retrospectively to *tsotsis* (gangsters) of the 1950s who dressed in expensive clothing, particularly cuffed trousers, one shoes, and a felt hat. More recently, a diversity of urban slang and sartorial styles has emerged.

23 Nthabiseng Motsemme 2002, YFreedom – Nthabiseng on Blackness in Post-Apartheid South Africa, *WISER In Brief* 1/2: 6

24 Steve Biko was born in 1946 in King Williamstown, went to medical school in Natal, and was co-founder and first president of the all-black South African Students Organisation (SASO). Until then, the struggle against apartheid had been nonracial, but Biko asserted that black people had been psychologically affected by white racism and had internalized a sense of racial inferiority, and therefore that they needed to organize politically as a separate black group. Biko's aim was to raise "black consciousness" in South Africa. He was banned in 1973 and assassinated in detention by apartheid police in 1977. His political and personal legacy lives on, despite South Africa's negotiated transition to democracy in 1994.

25 Bogatsu (2003), p. 14

primary colors. The utility-oriented, mass-produced overall was made chic, appropriated with great success to new cultural ends. Here too, class and race, rethought Y-style, emerge as key concerns. In LK's designs, the township is referenced – gestured to explicitly – yet, in the same breath, cast aside. To sport LK gear is to say one wants out of (or to brag that one has definitely left behind) the location. An insistence on staying in the township, Bogatsu notes[26], is increasingly marked within Y Culture as a self-defeating show of "negritude" wearing LK 's flash-in-your-face overalls makes it clear: this is emphatically not how you plan to live your life. You have no intention of toiling the way your parents did. The economic violence done them is not forgotten, but neither is it openly critiqued. Instead a largely uncritical celebratory focus is placed on the city's burgeoning service economy. LK's overall becomes the signifier, worn with pleasure and pride, of a young workforce whose members labor as waiters and shop attendants in the Zone, becoming both providers for wide family networks and, when off duty, consumers who buy clothes and music in the area and hang out in Rosebank's many clubs.

A Stylistics of Sensation

Turning to a series of images from *YMag,* we can see how Y Culture signals to, but increasingly breaks with, the past in its adoption of an elaborated stylistics of sensation and singularization. A cover image from August 2002 reveals a striking example of the foregrounding of the capacity for sensation, of the new investment in the body's special presence and powers, and of the ascendancy of the sign of blackness. Here, selfhood and subjectivity can no longer be interpreted as merely inscriptions of broader institutional and political forces; instead, the images project an increased self-consciousness of the fashioning of human identity as a manipulable, artful process. [→ Fig. **C**]

Representations of the self as an expressive subject have for some time been seen by scholars to signal a subject that is fractured, multiple, shifting, and produced through performativity.[27] What loxion kulcha's image-texts emphasize, by contrast, are practices based on specific aesthetic values and stylistic criteria and enabled by various emerging techniques of the self.[28] The *YMag* "Kwaito Nation" cover image (April/May 1998) bears this out, as do others published of late by the magazine. It shows sixteen *kwaito* artists. All are black men, and all are dressed in black, with one or two white shirts showing underneath. The emphasis is on the glamour and style of blackness, reflected metonymically in the color of the clothes themselves. In a fashion sequence called "Angel Delight" (October/November 2002), the theme is the color white, and the shoot is dominated this time by women but also by a cross-racial group: white and Colored women are foregrounded, and cross-racial and cross-

gendered sexual desire is clearly being played with in the images. Here, then, is a quite different version of *Y Magazine*'s projected reader, and this difference is part of a broader remixing of identity, including racial identity, in a shifting signifying chain.

The identities and forms of selfhood projected here are compositional. The self in this instance is above all a work of art. So too are the stylizations of the self projected in the magazine's images based on a delicate balance between actual emerging lifestyles of middle-class black youth and the politics of aspiration. An exchange in the letters-to-the-editor column in the June/July 2002 issue underscores this: "After reading *YMag* for a while now I've concluded that it would appeal more to the 'miss thangs' and 'brother mans' living or trying to live the so-called hip life in Jozi. Some of us live in different areas in the country and you only portray a certain kind of youth. The rest of us then

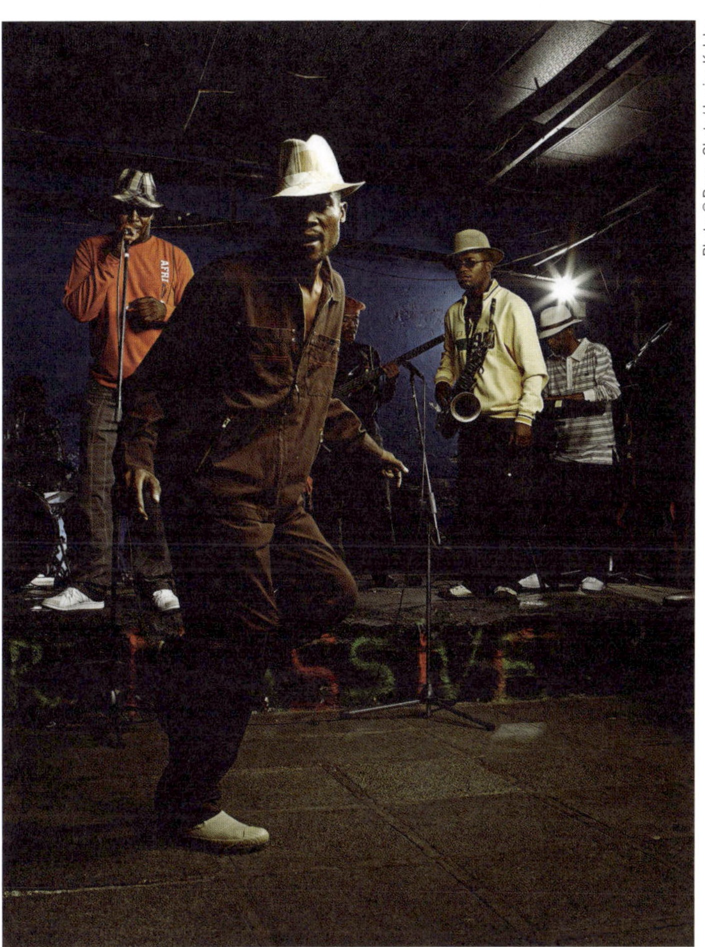

B Part of the Loxion Kulcha fashion label collection, 2000–2002. The two-piece outfit (in the foreground) is designed around the working clothes worn in the mines and industry.

26 Bogatsu (2003), p. 21
27 See Judith Butler 1993; *Bodies that Matter: On the Discursive Limits of "Sex",* New York; Judith Butler 1999, *Gender Trouble: Feminism and the Subversion of Identity,* New York.
28 Michel Foucault 2001, *Herméneutique du Sujet,* Paris

feel like the odd ones out, making us feel like aliens or something. Please broaden your scope so that most people can find it appealing, not just those who live in Jozi."29 The editors' reply follows: "We are all aliens if you think about it, depending where you come from. But seriously, though, *YMag is for you. YMag doesn't necessarily portray reality as each of us would see it, that is, we're aspiring as well.* We obviously can't reflect every kind of person under the good sun but every young person can and will find at least one thing they like inside *YMag*."30
In acknowledging that their product is made for those who aspire to (but cannot necessarily claim) hip, cutting-edge, largely middle-class lifestyles in the city, the editors signal a potential gap – a gap of potential – between what is and what could be. The present and the possible interlace to form a stylistics of the future. We could also draw out this idea of a gap from the words of one young South African whom Tanya Farber interviewed in the Zone: "We understand where we come from, but I am not interested in politics and about what happened in the '80s because I wasn't there. And even if I was, I live for the future."31 Since this interviewee is in his early twenties, he was in fact "there" in the 1980s, during the worst of the apartheid struggle and the height of the resistance to it. Indirectly acknowledging this by his phrase "and even if I was", he nevertheless insists on the fact that his project and investment lie in a search for the future. His words,

we could say, mark him as a public representative of "the now" in South Africa, as he signals the remainders of the past but also speaks the future-oriented language of Y-Gen aspiration.
Y Magazine, in naming a subject who aspires, also draws consumers into a competitive system in which not everyone can have what he or she aspires to. In *Lifebuoy Men, Lux Women,* Tim Burke, one of the few theorists of African consumer culture, points to pitfalls inherent in such processes.32 As the pleasures of consumption in the twentieth (and twenty-first) century have become increasingly and explicitly tied to satisfaction of the flesh and its needs, he asks, have we not perhaps made too much of the body as a unique site for the elaboration of forms of self-stylization? In so doing, do we not "risk separating individuals from their bodies, seeing, for example, the bodies of women as separate from the selves of women?" This, of course, is not a specifically African phenomenon. Dipesh Chakrabarty is similarly concerned with the gap between body and self that a culture of commodification would seem to imply: the commodification of culture as lifestyle, he argues, can never completely encompass the life-worlds upon which it draws.33 On the one hand, it requires a suppression of embodied idiosyncrasies and local conjunctures, but on the other it needs the tangibility of objects and people, a "corporeal index", as Beth Povinelli34 puts it, to lend credibility and desirability to its abstract claims. Thus Chakrabarty draws attention to the gap at the heart of the commodity form, caught as it is between embodiment and abstraction.
Yet the making of the contemporary self is not so easily readable in the self-representations and subjective practices, the powerful parodic languages, the in processes of self-styling in which the body plays such an important part – in the seductive "surface forms" of youth culture. Critics generally disavow the "surfaces" of youth culture as an insufficient analytic space.35 Yet, arguably it is here, on the surfaces of youth culture, that we come most powerfully to encounter the enigmatic and divergent ways of knowing and self-making that mark its forms. Pursuing the surfaces of cultural form implies a reading, however, that positions itself at the limit of the by now ubiquitous cultural analytic notion of translatability36: it demands that we push beyond the dual notions of reading and translating to understand.

Mind the Gap

A conventional reading of Y Culture would rely on tropes of translatability – and indeed the latter can take us quite far into the analysis of this cultural form. The cover stories of *YMag* signal a transnational, multilingual hybridity that a focus on translation goes a long way toward explicating. The title "Skwatta Kamp: Hard to the Core Hip Hop" (August/September 2002), for example, suggests the influence of American hip hop on the local

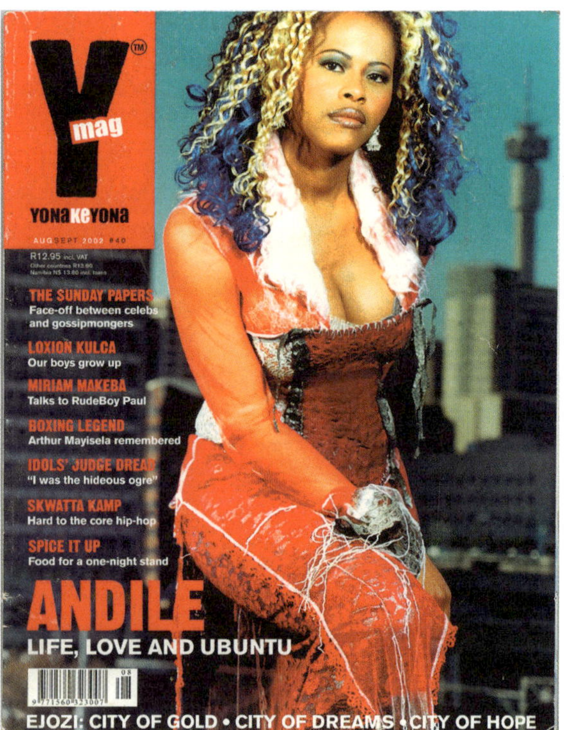

Photo: © Y Magazine

C   *Y Magazine,* August 2002

29 The website www.urbandictionary.com defines *miss thang* as "a person who thinks they are, are, like so totally, like better than, like, you know everyone else, like." In other words, a woman who thinks she's way too cool. *Brother man* would seem to speak for itself. *Jozi* is an increasingly popular term used by young residents of Johannesburg, referring not only to the city itself but to its surrounding townships, including Soweto and Alexandra.

30 *YMag* 2002 June/July: 12 (emphasis by the author)

31 Farber (2003), p. 28

32 Timothy Burke 1996, *Lifebuoy Men, Lux Women. Commodification, Consumption, and Cleanliness in Modern Zimbabwe,* Durham, N.C.

33 Dipesh Chakrabarty, n.d. *Historical Difference and the Logic of Capital: Towards a Different Marxism,* manuscript, quoted in William Mazarella 2003, *Shoveling Smoke. Advertising and Globalization in Contemporary India.* Durham, N.C., p. 20

34 Elizabeth A. Povinelli 2001, Consuming Geist. Popontology and the Spirit of Capital in Indigenous Australia, in: John Comaroff et al. (ed) 2001, *Millennial Capitalism and the Culture of Neo-liberalism,* Durham, N.C., p. 241–270

35 John L. Comaroff, Jean Comaroff, Robert P. Weller (eds) 2001, *Millennial Capitalism and the Culture of Neo-liberalism,* Durham

36 Translatability emerges from the rise in the last decade or so of translation studies. The latter focuses on such issues as how the translation is connected to the "foreign text"; the relative autonomy of the translated text – and thus the impossibility of translation, since it is really a new text which is created; how the effects of translation are social, and have been harnessed to cultural, economic, and political agendas including colonial projects and the production of national literatures. Translation studies is beset by arguments between those who see language as hermeneutic and inter-

scene (Skwatta Kamp is a local rap group), even as it invokes the local topography of the squatter camp – the ubiquitous sign of homelessness and poverty in urban South Africa. "Vat en Sit: Shacking Up in Y2K" (June/July 2002) explores how young black South African couples flout older orthodoxies of sex and marriage; it draws simultaneously on the Afrikaans expression *vat en sit* ("take and live with", a colloquialism used by black migrant workers who would meet and live with women in the city despite having a wife in the rural area or town they came from – a practice of which both women were often aware) and on the English word "shack" (used to denote the makeshift quarters of the poorest in South Africa's townships and squatter camps). "The Colour of Music: Whiteys and Kwaito" (February 2000) signals an interest in and a projection of crossover cultural and racial cultural codes in post-apartheid South Africa, as does "Darkies and Ecstasy: Is It the New Zol?"[37]

Translatability and multilingualism are built into the text of *Y Magazine.* This is less visible in the body of the text, as the main articles are written in English, than in the interstices. It is in the in-between spaces – the sound bites, the gossip pages, the reviews – that language emerges most forcefully as a locus for practices of translation. Acronyms, wordplay, colloquialisms, and "deep" meanings are some of the devices drawn on within the culture of translatability at work here. A review of a new CD release by local *kwaito* act Bongo Maffin reads, in Zulu, "Aahyh, Ngi yai bon'indlela en'ibalwe BM" (Ah, I see the road and it says BM [Bongo Maffin][38]). The phrasing plays on the widely admired style and road performance of BMWS, and also recalls a classic of South African music, Dorothy Masuka's classic "Imphi indlela" (Where's the road/the way).[39] The same review then shifts from Zulu to Tswana: "Kego tsaela 99, Bongo Maffin ihlile" (I'm telling you straight up, Bongo Maffin has arrived).

These shifts in language and frame of reference question standard notions of location and publics. They show us that the "world" appears increasingly as a set of fragments, bits and pieces with which young people grapple. Sutured onto these bits and pieces are the histories of isolation from, and connection to, the world that South Africans carry.[40] These fragments come to be refracted in ways that produce resemblances across different signs and languages between signs – what Mbembe has referred to as "the powers of the false"[41] – revealing the ability of Africans to inhabit several worlds simultaneously. As these fragments and their multiple meanings travel, they also encounter resistant edges, and in Y Culture one of these edges is the sign of black America. As Y youth come to inhabit a culture of selfhood shaped in part by African American hip-hop culture, they also rebel against it, resulting in a form of pastiche. A cut-and-paste appropriation of American music, language, and cultural practices is simultaneously deployed and refuted. An example of this can be found in the self-styling of Trompies, a kwaito group that epitomizes the contemporary version of *mapantsula*. The group is now sponsored by FUBU (For Us by Us), an African American clothing label often worn by U.S. rap artists. In the June/July 2000 issue of *YMag,* Trompies is accused of making a "fashion faux pas", since they call themselves pantsulas yet adopt a hip-hop style.[42] At the same time, it is also acknowledged that the 1950s pantsula culture emanated from America. Although the black American is embraced as a "brother", the Y reader does not want to be assimilated into his culture.[43]

Tropes of translatability can reveal much, then, about the workings of Y Culture – but they can take us only so far. The idea of (cultural) translation relies, like the theorizations of Burke and Chakrabarty discussed above, on an idea of "the gap". Increasingly, however, scholarly work on the technologies of public forms, including popular cultural forms, has tended to move toward a focus on circulation and transfiguration, replacing or at least complicating earlier preoccupations with meaning and translation. As analytic vectors of the social, the latter rely on methods of reading derived from the tradition of the book, a tradition that stipulates that a cultural text be meaningful – in the words of Dilip Gaonkar and Beth Povinelli, "that it be a text and confront us as a text whose primary function is to produce meaning and difference and to captivate us in the dialectic play between these two poles"[44]. Such a tradition, moreover, implies a theory of translation grounded in the question of how to translate *well* from one language to another, as meaning is borne across the chasm of two language codes. Once we set foot in a "terrain of chasms and gaps", as Gaonkar and Povinelli note, "we are swept up in the maelstrom of debates about incommensurability, indeterminacy, and undecidability in translation": translation is seen as a productive failure.[45] Rather than, or in addition to, asking what happens to meaning as it is borne across languages, genres, or semiotic modes (to "read for meaning"), we might ask what movements of cultural form and techniques for mapping them appear in worlds structured increasingly by cultures of circulation. In other words, as Gaonkar and Povinelli so usefully put it, we need "to foreground the social life *of* the form in question rather than reading social life *off* it"[46].

pretative, opening up the gaps of meaning, and those who see it as communicative and instrumental, which seek equivalence with the original text. In sum, an analytics of the gap is at the heart of this work. See Lawrence Venuti (ed.) 2000, *The Translation Studies Reader,* London.

37 *Zol* refers to a hand-rolled marijuana cigarette.

38 Nappy Head 1998, Into Yam, Bongo Maffin, *YMag* October/November: 46

39 Dorothy Masuka (*1935) is a famous singer in southern Africa who sang with the African Ink Spots and later with Miriam Makeba. She sang songs of political resistance that were banned in apartheid South Africa. She still sometimes performs in different parts of the world.

40 The way post-apartheid youth engage with the world has been shaped by often violent histories of international connection (through migration from elsewhere in Africa and the diffusion of British and American culture) and by the fact of apartheid South Africa's international isolation (as the figure of the grotesque in the colonial historical narrative and the international sanctions and boycotts that cut it off from the rest of the African continent).

41 Achille Mbembe 2002, On the Power of the False, *Public Culture* 14/3: 629–641, here p. 636

42 Bulelwa Mstali, T. Masemola, T. Gule 2000, Manga-Manga, *YMag* June/July: 19

43 Thami Masemola 2000, Dlala Mapantsula, *YMag* June/July: 47. In the April/May issue, the editors write: "Our relationship with black Americans is only by virtue of us all being African descendants. The reality is that their true ancestors, the slaves that crossed the ocean in the dungeons of those ships, were taken from the West Coast of the continent. We aren't preaching any anti-African-American theories. As much as we appreciate the music, there really is no need to patronize us." (April/May 2000, p.52) Other instances in the magazine reveal that black South Africans turn to the apartheid struggle and explicitly not to slavery in the making of black identity. For a longer discussion of this, see Sarah Nuttall 2004, Stylizing the Self. The Y Generation in Rosebank, Johannesburg, *Public Culture* 16/3: 430–452.

44 Dilip Gaonkar, Elizabeth Povinelli 2003, Technologies of Public Forms. Circulation, Transfiguration, Recognition, *Public Culture* 15/3: 385–397, here p. 388

45 Gaonkar and Povinelli (2003), p. 388

46 Gaonkar and Povinelli (2003), p. 394

Such an approach proves particularly productive in understanding Y/loxion culture. It is a cultural form that cuts across sound, sartorial, visual, and textual cultures to reveal a process of "compositional remixing". In this setting, processes of circulation, parallels and slippages between genres, play a fundamental role. In the reviews pages of *YMag,* crossover styles are elaborated so that a sound might be used to describe an image, or an image a word, or a clothing line a taste. "His writing is reminiscent of Tracy Chapman's singing," writes one book reviewer[47]. Another describes a book by way of allusion to a television chat show[48]. A review of a CD by Thievery Corporation in *Y's* sister magazine, *SL,* references fashion to describe sound: "Picture some cool geezer in a black Armani shirt, grey slacks, and DKNY sandals, smoking a doobie like a zeppelin. That pretty accurately describes the sound of Thievery Corporation."[49] Thus the processes of self-stylization that emerge from *YMag* further accessorize a range of cultural texts that, reframed within crossover media forms, become elements in the aestheticization of the self.[50] Race, especially blackness, as it plays out across these surfaces of form, itself becomes more of a mutating formation than before, less a finished and stable identity than something open to transformation, even proliferation – a phenomenon that actively resists attempts at reading or translation.

Revisiting the Analytics of the Gap

I turn, now, to a second set of cultural texts, a series of advertisements that have appeared since 2005 both in *YMag* and on billboards around Johannesburg. The ads elaborate on the cultural opening that Y Culture has provided, particularly in relation to the prominence given to "style" in the making of contemporary identity in the city. They take up notions of self-making and stylization in order to deconstruct South Africa's racial past – and they do so through an attempt at beginning to define notions of the "post-racial"[51]. Drawing on the enormous popularity of Y Culture itself among young South Africans, they use irony and parody to work even more specifically and provocatively than *YMag* and its related brands have in the past with questions of race. A mix of image and text (a point I will return to), the ads emerge as important sites for reading the South African "now", for they just begin to make explicit ideas and passions that are "out there" in society, and therefore have an articulatory function – a function that palpably affects life worlds. Each of the advertisements can be thought of in terms of the commodity image. The latter, as William Mazarella reminds us[52], can be theorized as a compelling point of mediation between culture and capital and as an index of wider transformations within the field of public culture. The commodity image is

at once a flashpoint for the key ideological issues of the day, a rendering of national community as aesthetic community, and, conventionally at least, a vector of cultural difference offered up for consumption.

The first two advertisements are for a brand of sports shoes called K-Swiss, an American make recently introduced in the South African market. The first is filmed against the backdrop of what was formerly a lower-middle-class section of Johannesburg and is now a mixed-income neighborhood. [→ Fig. **D**] Though the neighborhood is not identified, it is in all likelihood Brixton, a part of the city popular among a certain set for its "retro" look. The ad shows a person in the process of being arrested by the police while others look on. The people on the street stand beneath a sign that says "WHITES ONLY". The scene is an explicit allusion to a widely known genre of image: an urban scene typical of 1970s South Africa, depicting a black man being arrested on grounds that he is not carrying a pass to legitimize his presence in the city. The image relies on both irony and parody to achieve its effect: it is not quite what it seems. The crime that the man being arrested has committed, it turns out, is not a pass but a style crime: he is not dressed properly. Specifically, he is not dressed in the color white; most egregiously, he is not wearing the white sports shoes that are being advertised. The image works on many levels: it suggests that the greatest crime is now a style crime; that whiteness (and therefore blackness) is a matter less of race than of style; and that style is itself a crossover phenomenon, working across race. It also comments on the style pecking order in contemporary urban South Africa: in the style stakes marked out on the street, the average white guy languishes at the back; next comes the black woman; coolest of all is the black man, shown here sporting a 1970s (now retro-cool) Afro hairdo and a body language that suggests cultural confidence and hipness as well as street credibility. In general, the ad plays with the notion that the way you look – the way you dress – defines you as in or out, legal or illegal, official or unofficial: it insists on self-styling as a critical mode of self-making. The second ad in this series [→ Fig. **E**] works on the same principle: the past is acknowledged but ironically recast in the post-apartheid present. Here, the scene is a men's urinal. One man is cleaning the floor while others make use of the urinal. We might recall that under apartheid the spaces of segregation included macrospaces such as schools, churches and cemeteries, but also, importantly, microspaces, which functioned as key loci for the staging of humiliation. One such locus was the "whites only" urinal, which a black man could enter under one condition only: to clean it. The image with which we are concerned gestures to that past and its legacy in South Africa's collective memory, but with a twist. The men using the urinal are both black and white. What differentiates the users from the man cleaning the floor is

47 Andy Davis 2000, review of "Magnum Chic" by Harper Engler, *YMag* November: 30

48 Phindi Gule 2000, review of "Yesterday I Cried" by Iyanla Vazant, *YMag* October: 89

49 Ross Campbell 1999, review of "Thievery Corporation", *SL* February: 105. *YMag* was conceived by the YIRED publishers as a counterpart to *SL* magazine (*SL* stands for Student Life), which targets largely white but also crossover youth audiences. The intention was to overcome the dominant industry model, in which youth magazines targeted limited "readership ghettoes" in order to attract specialized advertising. The relationship between the two titles was initially conceived as a move toward establishing the first multiracial youth-oriented product to succeed in South Africa. *Y* and *SL* share irony and parody as dominant rhetorical modes as well as crossover reviewing styles and the accessorization of media forms within a broader process of self-stylization.

For a discussion of this, see Nuttall (2004).

50 Cultural texts – books, for example – become forms of quotation: book reviews attest to the constant dismembering of the book, harnessed to specific textual genres as readers, reviewers, and magazine publics exercise the capacity to choose and discard: the book loses its supposed autonomy, its power as a self-contained artifact: there is no book in and of itself but only a textual fragment in the technological constitution of the self. For a more detailed analysis, see Nuttall (2004).

51 This is a term one has to use with caution. I do so here to signal that while South Africa in general is not a postracial society, aspects of its culture are experimenting with spaces one could tentatively refer to in this way, in that the imperative, driven increasingly by what is patently a cross-racial market for goods, is that race no longer signifies as it did before, and that class, based on money, increasingly struc-

not skin color but the color of their respective clothes. The users are dressed in the sign of whiteness, white clothes, and more specifically white shoes; the man cleaning the floor is *not* wearing the right shoes – he is badly dressed, the ad suggests, out of style, unwilling or incapable of playing the market to project a particular (life)style.[53]

The adverts were launched in 2004. South Africa was celebrating its first ten years of democracy, and the company wanted to run a campaign that spoke to this particular context. The target market K-Swiss was aiming at was fourteen- to twenty-six-year-olds: young people whom market research showed were increasingly thinking and acting in a cross-racial manner. The ads had been a success with this group; surveys showed that young people found the ads clever and "funny" (the only group who were not amused, he added, were fifty- to sixty-five-year-old white Afrikaner men).[54] They were based on market research showing that whereas South Africa was once the ultimate signifier of race difference, the situation is now much more striated and complex. A recent survey released by the Human Sciences Research Council shows that, in 1997, forty-seven percent of respondents described themselves in terms of racial categories. By 2000, the figure had fallen to only twelve percent (in the same period, references to gender- and class-related identities declined, while allusions to religious identity increased). What had been a fairly limited and predictable set of self-descriptions had given way to what the authors of the survey termed "a whole range of individual, personalized descriptions"[55]. Another survey, "TrendYouth", which focused on black and white youth from emerging and affluent households in major metropolitan areas (and which included 2,400 face-to-face interviews and thirty focus groups), shows clothing brands to be the main ingredients in the development of a "new and clearer South African identity" and notes that the country's seven- to twenty-four-year-olds "are the most racially integrated [group] in the country, with friendships now based more on shared interests like music and fashion than on skin colour."[56]

The K-Swiss ads underscore, on the one hand, that the cross-racial life-styles of urban youth today, while strikingly different from those one might have encountered twenty years ago, still cite (or quote) a racially segregated past that remains in the collective memory; on the other hand, they reveal that, increasingly, "desegregation" takes place under the sign of a reinscribed "whiteness", this time elaborated around social class rather than race. Formerly, the ads state in no uncertain terms, you had to be white to adopt a particular lifestyle; now you have to know how to be stylish – stylish, that is, by K-Swiss's standards. What

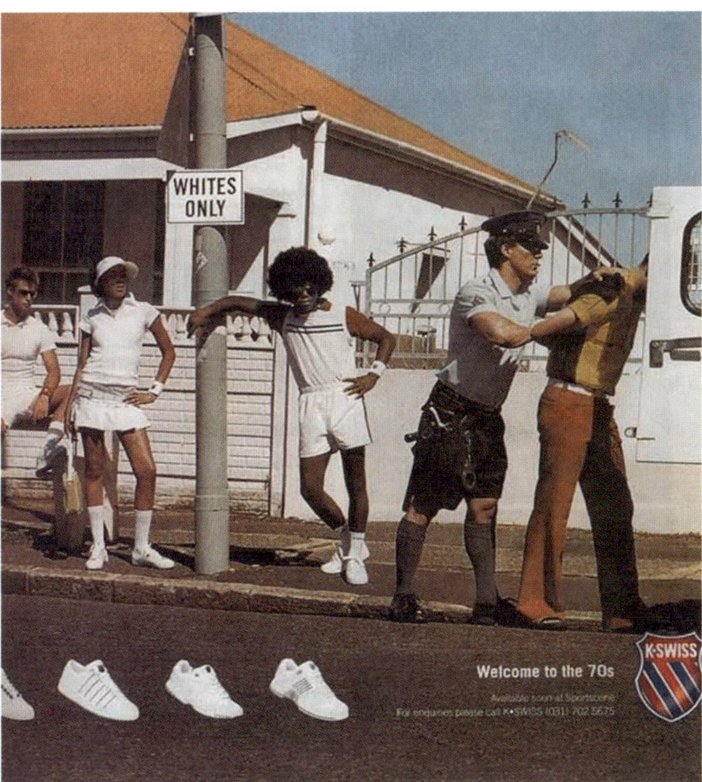

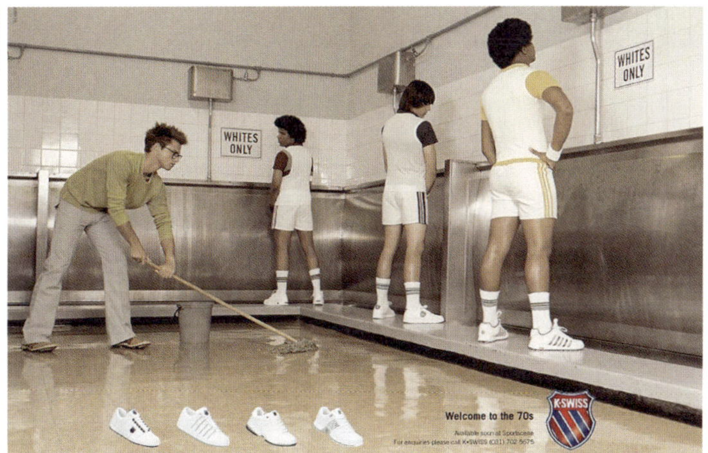

D/E Advertising for K-Swiss sports shoes

tures certain kinds of social relations. This is not to say that race doesn't – and won't in future – reassert itself in unexpected ways.

52 William Mazarella (2003)

53 It is fascinating to compare these ads with those discussed by Eve Bertelsen, which appeared in the years of the mid-1990s, immediately after political transition, as a measure of how much has changed in the public discourse of nation building and identity. An ad for shoes is accompanied by the text: "When a new nation stands on its feet …," while an ad for milk contains the text, "Why cry over spilt milk, when we can build a healthy nation." For a detailed analysis, see Bertelsen 1998, Ads and Amnesia. Black Advertising in the New South Africa, in Sarah Nutall, Carli Coetzee (eds), *Negotiating the Past. The Making of Memory in South Africa*, Cape Town, p. 221–241.

54 Telephone interview with K-Swiss manager, Jeremy Nel, April 2005

55 Bert Klandermans, Marlene Roefs, Johan Olivier 2001, *The State of the People. Citizens, Civil Society and Governance in South Africa*, 1994–2000, Pretoria

56 Trend Youth 2005, under the leadership of the University of Cape Town Unilever Institute of Strategic Marketing in cooperation with the marketing-consulting firms Youth Dynamix and Instant Grass.

they don't say but of course imply is that you no longer have to be white, but you do have to be middle class, or at least you must find the money to buy products such as those celebrated in the ads. Increasingly, in fact, young people who are not middle class are buying *fong kong:* fake products available especially in the inner city that are cheaper versions of Y or Ioxion cultural style, thus enabling them to circumvent some of the restrictions of class and economic status.

Two further images, forming a paired advertisement, play on similar notions. Both are close-ups of men's faces, one black and one white. Together, they suggest a message that is at once subjective and "in your face". The visuals in the ads depend for their effect on the verbal text that accompanies each image, making the meaning of the paired images explicit and, again, distinctly in your face. The text in the first ad reads: "I HATE BE-ING BLACK. If it means some people think that they know my criminal record. My rhythm. My level of education. Or the role affirmative action has played in my career. I'm not someone else's black. I'm my own. And I LOVE BEING BLACK." [→ Fig. F] The second text reads: "I HATE BEING WHITE. If it means some people think that I'm not a real South African. That I'm racist. Privileged. Paranoid. Or Baas. I'm not someone else's white. I'm my own. And I LOVE BEING WHITE." [→ Fig. G] Taken together, these ads suggest an imperative that is both antiracist ("I hate being black"; "I hate being white") and prorace ("I love being black"; "I love being white"). The message they project is that the fact of being white or black becomes banal, that older mean-ings can be erased or evacuated in order to be able to inscribe onto the words black and white whatever meanings one wishes. Yet in the ads themselves, the racial habitus remains – at the same time as, socially, culturally and politically speaking, there are more possibilities for entering new racial spaces. While these ads appear to rely on the texts for their impact (as I first suggested above) – to domesticate the visual, as it were – one could also note that a visual medium itself is being used here to critique conventional notions of the image, to show the extent to which we rely on the verbal to narrate and explicate the visual.[57] Thus the ads stage a fascinating engagement with the nature of contemporary visuality.

As I remarked above, all of the ads aim to work toward what one could tentatively term "post-racial" configurations, while also re-vealing the complexity of this task. The difficulty of it all is under-scored by a striking feature of the adverts: they can simultane-ously be seen to move beyond and to reconfirm the power of race in the contemporary public sphere of the city. A one line is involved. The ads attempt to "soften" race and class difference by invoking the powerful notion of style, and in particular self-stylization. Working with the idea that "everyone" wants to be stylish – to wear good shoes, for example – the ads undercut a

more "antagonistic" reading of race and class difference. As we have seen, they rely for their effect on citation or quotation of historical, political context. Simultaneously, they tap into deeper issues at stake relating to the psychic life of things. That is, they tap into the place things occupy in a given historical moment, what desires they organize, what fantasies they provoke, via what epistemologies they are as signed meaning – or, as Bill Brown puts it, how they represent us, comfort us, help us, change us.[58] The psychic life of things activates deep impulses of desire that are commonly shared beyond race: it is these that the ads seek to draw out, rather than relying on less sophisticated technolo-gies of race and class. The shift is made from a form of crude governmentality so characteristic of the apartheid period to a different sort of social potency, which displaces the terms of recognition. Earlier in this essay I considered some of the limits of a theory of "the gap". These ads return us not only to the gap of the social, which middle-class commodity cultures rely on in the very moment of aiming to bridge the gap of race, but also to how the gap (of desire) is continuously reconstituted at the heart of the commodity. For while the commodity seems to eliminate the gap, it must constantly reopen it in order to propel new de-sires – to sell itself.

Finally, it is worth considering the ads I have discussed above in relation to the history of consumerism and the production of the modern subject. In relation to the first, we might reflect on a long history of denial of Africans as consumers – either through their portrayal as eternally rural or as being objects of charity – that is, as receiving commodities rather than as purchasing them as modern subjects. Nick Green and Reg Lascaris show that early advertising in South Africa was aimed at the white settler. [59] In the interwar years, there was a growing American presence in the South African economy rather than growing black partici-pation in the market. In the 1930s, ads were aimed not at the black consumer but at the "black specifier" (the person who de-cides what is to be bought for his white employer). Also in the 1930s, black job seekers began to advertise themselves ("capa-ble, clean houseboy, very quick and obliging, honest", read one ad in 1937). The latter implied an acceptance of race classifica-tion but also revealed new references to education. By 1957, a personal ad in the *Star* read: "Situation wanted: African under-graduate seeks position as clerk, general office work". By the late 1950s, the affordable transistor radio came to South Africa – and more and more black people made it a priority purchase. At this time, too, print media emerged aimed specifically at black readers (*Drum* 1951, *Bona* 1956). Until the 1970s, Green and Lascaris observe[60], a "schizophrenic" marketing scene was in place in relation to black viewers, based on uncertainty whether (a) the black consumer would respond best to ads in black me-dia, featuring black faces and black situations, with a message

57 I am grateful to Dilip Gaonkar and Ackbar Abbas for their comments along these lines at a summer institute, *Media Cultures, Everyday Life and Cultures of Consumption,* held at Hong Kong University in June 2005.

58 Bill Brown 2003, *A Sense of Things: The Object Matter of American Literature,* Chicago, p. 12

59 Nick Green, Reg Lascaris 1988, *Third World Destiny. Reco-gnizing and Seizing the Opportunities Offered by a Changing South Africa,* Cape Town

60 Green and Lascaris (1988), p. 41

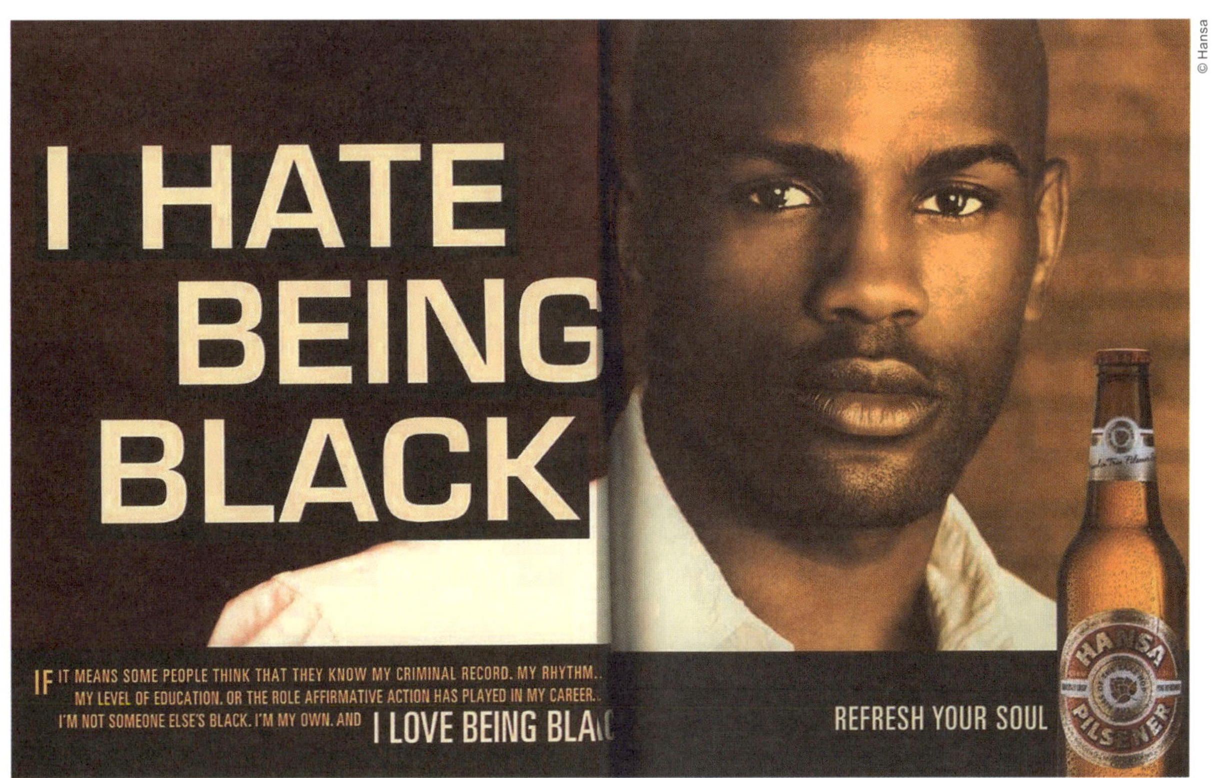

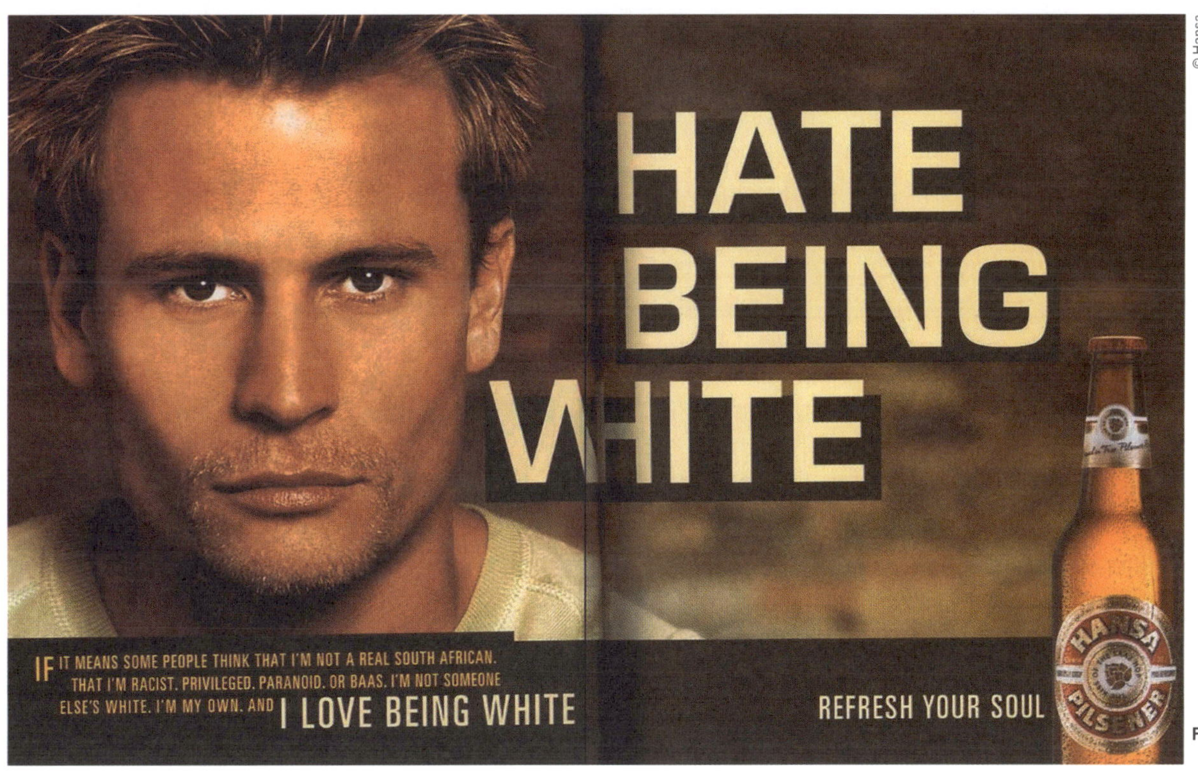

F / G Advertising for Hansa beer

that had particular relevance for a black consumer (the assumption until then), or (b) would an ad aimed at an ostensibly white audience have such "aspirational pull" that black consumers would be irresistibly draw into the target market? It was only in the late 1970s and early 1980s that marketers started to look at similarities between race groups rather than concentrating on the characteristics that divided them – with Brazil rather than the United States and Europe as their case study and reference point. It was then that the crossover market emerged with a vengeance, creating a system for marketing brands no longer based on race (though still revealing, in Green and Lascaris's terms, the realities of being black, white, and brown in South Africa today).

Consumerism is frequently equated with the production of the modern subject – an equal and modular citizen brought into being through the possession of mass-produced goods. What seems distinctive about post-apartheid South African consumerism (though its current crossover appeal could be seen to have taken root by the late 1980s) is that it seeks to recoup the modernist moment described above but to do so through prevailing postmodern technologies – and within an active cultural project of desegregation. Advertising, such as examples I have looked at above, emerges, then, as an attempt to give content to modernist subjectivity and to engage with ideas about citizenship – and South Africa's future.[61]

Conclusion

In the first part of this chapter, I showed that a study of Y Culture reveals the preoccupations of increasingly middle-class young black people in Johannesburg and the intricacy of their modes of self-making. The city itself be comes the engine for this self-stylizing. I have argued that the emergence of new stylizations of the self, embedded in cultures of the body, represents one of the most decisive shifts of the post-apartheid era. Integral to this shift, I have sought to show as well, is the use of a range of cultural texts, which, reframed within crossover media forms, become elements – accessories – in an aestheticization of the self. Foucault took self-stylization to be a process through which the "subject constitutes himself in an active fashion, by the practices of the self". For Foucault, self-styling implies an increased sense of singularity, performing a certain practice of freedom. I have used the notion in a similar fashion in this essay, in an effort to take youth cultures, and Y Culture in particular, beyond the problematic unidimensional types of readings to which they are typically subjected.

I argued that a notion of the gap remains central in cultural theory, while also testing its limits and the notion of translatability on which it relies, and vice versa. Increasingly, I suggested, what is needed is a theory of the circulation of forms, one that necessarily draws on technological analogies. I observed how consumer cultures (which draw on youth cultures such as *Y/loxion kulcha*) work to reopen the gap of desire. Thus we need a cultural theory of contemporary forms that takes the surfaces of form more seriously as an analytic construct, registers the limits of the gap, but that is simultaneously alert to the continual reopening of the gap as cultural forms and consumerism draw closer and closer together.

In the second half of the chapter, I considered ways in which a series of advertisements take up aspects of Y Culture's increasing remixing of race and attempt more explicitly to reconfigure race along the lines of the market. The market, here, comes to the fore as a powerful vector for calming racial passions in a setting characterized by the emergence of a politically empowered black middle class and the presence of a substantial white minority that holds considerable economic power and cultural clout. The market becomes an important place for projecting racial conviviality and therefore a sphere in which the idea of living together is experimented with. As an earlier discourse of nonracialism has increasingly shown its limits, the market begins to project ideas of race that rework that earlier discourse.[62]

The market and cultures addressed in this essay, I have made clear, are largely middle-class entities. Although it has not been my subject here, new work now needs to be done on the intersection of cultures of consumption and poverty in South Africa. There, no doubt, the question of the gap and its limits will prove more complex, more treacherous and, potentially, more productive still.

---

61 I am very grateful to Isabel Hofmeyr for her discussion of these ideas with me.

62 *Nonracialism*, a term used widely during the anti-apartheid struggle and in tended to signify the idea of a society freed from the credo of race, has faded from public political discourse in the 1990s and after, as the politics of black empowerment have moved center stage and have played an important role in shifting inherited institutional power structures. This has occurred at the same time as many more choices have become available to people in terms of racial identification, especially in metropolitan centers and in the sphere of culture.

The Underground, the Surface and the Edges
A Hauntology of Johannesburg

LEORA FARBER
AND ANTHEA BUYS

Haunted places are the only ones people can live in[1]

A former mining camp whose acquisition of the aesthetic markers of a metropolis was almost instantaneous, Johannesburg has always represented, economically and philosophically, a dual geography. In the words of Sarah Nuttall and Achille Mbembe, from whose book *Johannesburg – The Elusive Metropolis[2]* we borrow the title of our video programme[3] – *The Underground, the Surface and the Edges* – the dialectic between the surface and the underground, and the concomitant activation of a third space or "the edges", characterises "the African modern of which Johannesburg is the epitome"[4]. The rapid development of Johannesburg out of the Highveld dust was not only justified, but also caused, by the discovery in the late 1800s of a reef of subterranean gold close to the surface of the ground. This discovery literally furnished early mining magnates with means and a reason to build a modern city above ground. As Nuttall and Mbembe write: "The entire history of Johannesburg's built structures testifies not only to its inscription into the canons of modern Western urban aesthetics, but also to the originary tension virtually built into its morphology and geological structure between the life below the surface, what is above, and the edges."[5] Johannesburg's underground and surface are linked causally and economically, but this connection plays out politically and metaphorically as well. The mining industry, with its traversal of the subterranean and the economy that plays out on the surface, saw the inception of the politics of racial inequality and segregation that were institutionally upheld in the city under apartheid. At the most obvious level, white South African and European mining magnates benefited financially from the subterranean toil of predominantly African, but also Chinese, Indian, Malay and mixed-race labourers. This class and wealth disparity along racial lines played out in a further spatial dimension: labourers were typically forced to live in peripheral, invisible, temporary or threatening spatial environments, such as miners' barracks, hostels, informal 'squatter camps', and, sometimes, within the mines themselves for limited periods of time. Meanwhile, white middle-to-upper-class citizens occupied legitimate and permanent living quarters in the central and northern suburbs, and enjoyed a comparatively unrestricted urban lifestyle. This forced inhabitation of peripheral spaces relegated labourers classified as 'non-white' to "the edges" of mainstream cultural, social and political life in Johannesburg. However, a counter-culture emerged from this peripheral spatiality that ultimately challenged the hegemony of white culture. In this sense, life along Johannesburg's edges is, historically, essential to the contemporary city.

This essay and the selection of video works that we have arranged under the title *The Underground, the Surface and the Edges* acknowledges Nuttall's and Mbembe's important steps towards a theoretical historiography of Johannesburg. At the same time, however, this project departs from the foundation that they have laid, pursuing its allusive strands. These strands begin with the implication in Nuttall and Mbembe's text of a certain porousness between the different spatialities identified, an analogy between the space of the underground and the tomb, and a passing introduction referring to the notion of spectrality in the opening pages of the book.[6] We propose that the underground, the surface and the edges are at once identifiable modalities which emerge coherently in the works we have selected and that are interconnected inflections of a singular urban phenomenon. They are folds in the same fabric of the city. Building on this, we observe that dialectic between the underground and the surface in the context of Johannesburg contains an echo of the literary and artistic trope of 'burial' and 'resurrection', or 'exhumation', and the related trope of the spectral or ghostly. In his reading of the legacies of Marxism and dialectical materialism, *Specters of Marx,* Jacques Derrida writes of the spectral as that which "happens" only between two apparently exclusive terms, such as "life and death".[7] "What happens between two, and between all the 'two's' one likes, such as between life and death, can only *maintain itself* with some ghost, can only *talk with or about* some ghost."[8]

The ghost is neither living nor properly dead. It haunts life with the prospect of death, while ultimately withholding the finality of that prospect. In some sense, when we, as curators of the video

---

1   Michel de Certeau 1988, *The Practice of Everyday Life,* Berkeley, p. 108

2   Sarah Nuttall and Achille Mbembe 2008, Introduction: Afropolis, in: idem (eds), *Johannesburg – The Elusive Metropolis,* Johannesburg, p. 1–33, here p. 15

3   This initial programme was shown as part of the *Johannesburg and Megacities Phenomena* conference, hosted by the Research Centre, *Visual Identities in Art and Design,* University of Johannesburg on 11 April 2008, at the Lister Building, Johannesburg. The programme, titled *Too Close to Comfort,* was thereafter screened as part of the *Performing South Africa* festival, held in Berlin from 18 to 27 September 2008. The screening took place on the 20 September at the Hebbel Theatre in Berlin. Thereafter it was shown at the Goethe Institute, Johannesburg, on 28 November 2008. Further screenings under the new title *Collaborations/Articulations* took place at FADA Gallery, University of Johannes-

burg; University of Cape Town, and Michaelis Art Gallery.

4   Nuttall and Mbembe (2008), p. 17

5   Nuttall and Mbembe (2008), p. 18

6   Nuttall and Mbembe (2008), p. 6–7

7   Jacques Derrida 1994, *Specters of Marx the State of the Debt, the Work of Mourning, and the New International,* translated by Peggy Kamuf, New York, p. 17

8   Derrida (1994), p. 17 [italics in original]

programme, think and speak of Johannesburg as a metropolitan phenomenon, we think and speak of a spectral, interstitial realm that exists in between the strata of surface (the stratum of life, goodness, health and visibility) and underground (a catacomb where the dead, the corrupt and the ailed are hidden).

The Edges

This condition of inhabiting a spatiality between two terms (underground – surface, surface – edges, edges – underground and so on) problematises the possibility of a clearly articulated boundary separating these terms. In terms of the geographic spatialities of Johannesburg itself, and in terms of our discussion of selected video works in this essay, we see this relationship between these terms as porous – as a fluid interchange, wherein constant mediation takes place. This resonates with Fredrick Jameson's description of "mediation", as the "classical dialectical term for the establishment of […] symbolic identities between the various levels, as a process whereby each level is folded into the next, thereby losing its constitutive autonomy".[9]
The limit-border or edge, less the instant of traversal from one state to another, is in fact a third term, a hiatus between now and then, and an indeterminate spatiality between here and there, below and above, death and life. Stephen Greenblatt describes this state of in-betweenness in terms of liminality, noting that "the limen, [is] the threshold or margin, the place that is no-place, in which the subject is rendered invisible".[10] "The edges", the third spatial term in the title of this curatorial project, share the qualities of Greenblatt's notion of the limen. The geographic and social peripheries or "edges" are in fact liminal spatialities, rather than being simply, absolutely, excluded ones. In the context of a city such as Johannesburg, the subjects who inhabit the edges are vital to the economic life of the city despite their symbolic geographic and aesthetic exclusion from mainstream city life.
Whilst this essay is primarily concerned with concepts of liminality in relation to marginalised communities and as a state of transition, with particular reference to how these play out in relation to Johannesburg, we include a discussion of Berni Searle's video work, *Vapour* (2004), which was filmed in Athlone, a lower-class suburb of Cape Town located on the eastern margins of the city centre known as the Cape Flats. We do so because this work exemplifies the kind of in-betweenness we associate with a reading of "the edges". Through her use of the video medium, and through her evocation of the Athlone space and its inhabitants as located on the geographic and social "edges" of South African society, Searle's work has much in common with that interstitial, spectral realm which we associate with our reading of Johannesburg as a metropolitan phenomenon.

Tracey Murinik notes that the visual impetus for Vapour was a newspaper photograph of a feeding project in Cape Town in celebration of the Muslim festival of *Eid*[11]. Here, 107 large pots of food, intended to feed 42,000 people, were prepared outdoors on open fires. For the video, Searle recreated a scaled-down version of the event, using fifty pots laid out over burning fires in an Athlone landscape.[12] Yet, as Murinik proposes, despite the recognisability of imagery such as close ups of burning wood, the heavy bulkiness of the cast-iron pots and the misty veils of steam, "what we are presented with in her recreation is unclear. The nature of the event taking place, or coming to an end as it would seem, is not defined […] Filmed and photographed at dusk […] *Vapour* reveals a procession of sorts: rows of massive cooking pots and a number of figures that snake methodically, barefoot, between them, occasionally lifting lids, vulnerable in their exposure, but seemingly impervious to the unpredictable elements around them."[13]

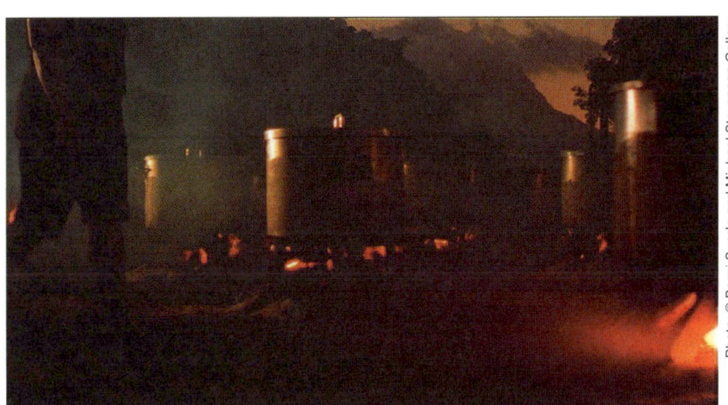

BERNI SEARLE, **VAPOUR**, VIDEO STILL (1-CHANNEL-VIDEO, 4 MIN.), 2004

In her recreation, Searle strategically replaces cooking food with boiling water. This substitution of food for water, Murinik argues, alters the potential of the scene, changing it from generous abundance and goodwill, to "an ambiguous situation to decipher. It appears poised on the edge of possibility and disillusionment: while the general details of the original event are recalled, the overriding sense is of lack and a type of desolation."[14]
The title *Vapour* itself suggests a state of liminality; the steam rising from the pots is elusive, intangible, and impossible to capture or pin down; it is translucent, transient, ephemeral and ethereal; "that which exists and builds, accumulates quietly, creating pressure until it is allowed to escape, or bursts, or alternatively dissipates."[15] The ambiguity of the scene is heightened by its being filmed at dusk, that liminal time when it is not yet night and no longer day. The combination of the ambiguous elements of fading light and the billows of boundary-less steam, which exists in the in-between state of being neither a liquid nor a gas,

9   Frederick Jameson 1981, *Postmodernism, or the Cultural Logic of Late Captialism,* Durham, N.C., p. 39
10 Stephen Greenblatt 1995, Liminal States and Transformations, in: Stuart Morgan and Frances Morris (eds), *Rites of Passage. Art for the End of the Century,* London, p. 28

11 Tracey Murinik 2004, Berni Searle, *Art South Africa,* 2/4: 80
12 Adele Adendorff 2005, *Nomadic Figurations of Identity in the Work of Berni Searle,* University of Pretoria, MA-dissertation, p. 111
13 Murinik (2004), p. 80
14 Murinik (2004), p. 80
15 Murinik (2004), p. 80

from the pots are visually suggestive of the folkloric and popular representation of ghosts as spirit entities, neither fully visible nor fully invisible. This metaphor echoes the limited social visibility experienced by the inhabitants of the peripheral location in which the work is set.

While Searle associates geographic and social marginality, or life on "the edges", with the more provisional, existential condition of liminality, Steven Cohen, in his performance video *Chandelier* (2001/02), approaches an informal settlement in Johannesburg in such a way that he recasts this ordinarily peripheral site as hegemonic.

In an extreme drag costume, the most striking feature of which is a heavy crystal chandelier worn as a dress, Cohen performs a character that is both physically precarious and socially unwelcome in this site. Dressed in a carefully wrought chandelier fashioned into a tutu-like skirt, corset and stockings with suspenders, head shaven, his face whitened and with his buttocks exposed, Cohen walks (or, to use David Bunn's phrase, "tinkle[s] [...] like an angel"[16]) through an informal settlement of illegal squatters in Newtown, which is being demolished by municipal workers. Of this performance, Cohen writes: "A white man in high heels wearing an illuminated chandelier tutu and improvising movement amidst a community of black squatters whose shacks are being destroyed by city council workers in their own ballet of violence [...] is very South African [...] I felt displaced (hectic in heels and a strange place to be near-naked)."[17] The video piece shows excerpts of responses to Cohen's presence from the residents of the settlement about to be bulldozed. Some ridicule him, others threaten violence, and still others deify him or sympathise with and try to protect him. Cohen's performance of his 'queerness' and deliberate (dis)placement of himself as a marginalised queer in another marginalised community is provocative. He is at the mercy of a community whose own immediate vulnerability is heightened through their displays of power in relation to him. The community of squatters are being literally displaced through removal of their homes, yet the kind of displacement Cohen speaks of is social, cultural, and political. Intertwined with displacement is its corollary – belonging – which raises questions such as: Who has a right to public space? What signifies a claim to space? What signifies cultural 'belonging'? In larger trajectories, this work highlights the complex problem of dwelling and being 'at home' in Johannesburg.

Referring to the contradictory views of citizenship raised by urban squatters and illegal land occupation which are being fought out in regenerated inner-city spaces such as Newtown, Bunn notes that "Cohen brings the spectacle of the perverse into spaces and situations associated with the limits of the new democracy",[18] because the forced removals instituted by the neoliberal agenda of the Mbeki government "[…] are fuelled by a wider public paranoia about illegal work seekers. Quite literally, these are haunted civic programmes, in that they both evoke and are fearful of the return of the ghosts of forced removals from the apartheid past."[19] The appropriation of space by the city's homeless and immigrant populations contrasts markedly with the security enclaves of Johannesburg's northern suburbs. Squatter camps and sprawling informal settlements around the city's periphery speak of changing ways in which homes are being made, under conditions framed by insecurity, fear, migration and an increasing sense of 'not-at-homeness'.

Cohen's performance emphasises the contested nature of home, or homely, spaces in Johannesburg's liminal zones, and his own aberrance in relation to the community he encounters positions him as the embodiment of the foreign, or the 'unhomely'. This may be related to Sigmund Freud's concept of 'the uncanny', a concept best expressed in Freud's original German, *Das Unheimliche,* literally, "the unhomelike" – the opposite of *heimlich* (homely) and/or *heimisch* (native).[20] Seemingly paradoxically, Freud writes of the uncanny as a phenomenon which appears aberrant, but only because of its closeness or resemblance to, or origins in, that which is familiar. In a sense, *Das Unheimliche* 'comes out' of *Das Heimliche*. The uncanny, Freud writes, is "… nothing new or alien, but something which is familiar and old-established in the mind and which has become alienated from it … through the process of repression."[21]

Das Unheimliche symbolically enables an encounter with a part of the self which has been split off, repressed. It marks a return of the unfamiliar – that which has become disturbing, frighteningly foreign or strange – in the psychic economy. It reveals that

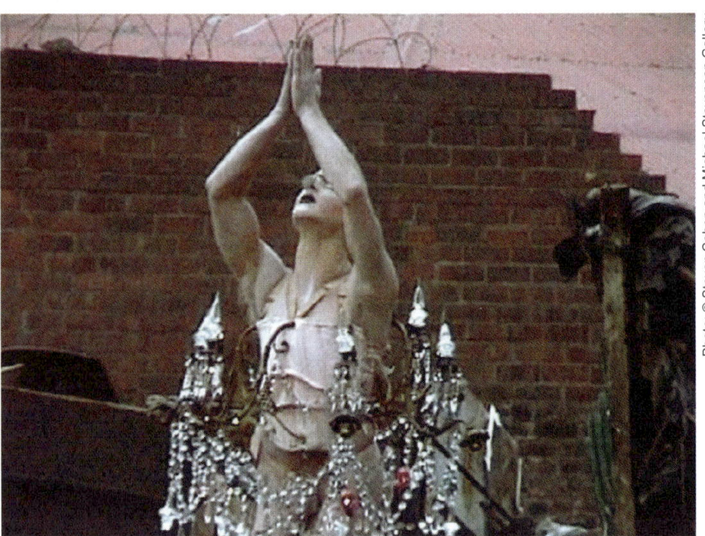

STEVEN COHEN, **CHANDELIER**, VIDEO STILL (1-CHANNEL-VIDEO, 16 MIN.), 2001/2002

16 David Bunn 2008, Art Johannesburg and Its Objects, in: Sarah Nuttall and Achille Mbembe (eds) 2008, *Johannesburg – The Elusive Metropolis*, p. 165

17 Steven Cohen cited in Shaun De Waal and Robyn Sassen 2003, Surgery without Anaesthetic. The Art of Steven Cohen, in: Jillian Carman, *Steven Cohen,* Johannesburg, p. 71

18 Bunn (2008), p. 164

19 This contemporary paranoia is strongly echoed in South Africa's apartheid past, wherein the framing of race in social/ geographic terms was engineered to create Johannesburg as a white suburban city. Particularly from the years 1900 –1940, Johannesburg became a city of boundaries determined by class and race. As Nuttall and Mbembe point out, in these years, the discourse of race was translated into a discourse of health and urban sanitisation. Cleansing the city of the poor and those deemed 'undesirable' – whilst simultaneously subjecting them to the reality of exploitation – required ridding of the inner city area its slums. This entailed forced removals of working-class and lower middle-class white families (which included impoverished Afrikaners), to peripheral townships in the western areas of Johannesburg such as Vrededorp, Burgersdorp and Brickfields. See Nuttall and Mbembe (2008), p. 20.

20 Sigmund Freud 1955 [1919], The uncanny, in: *The Standard Edition of the Complete Psychological Works of Sigmund Freud,* London, p. 226

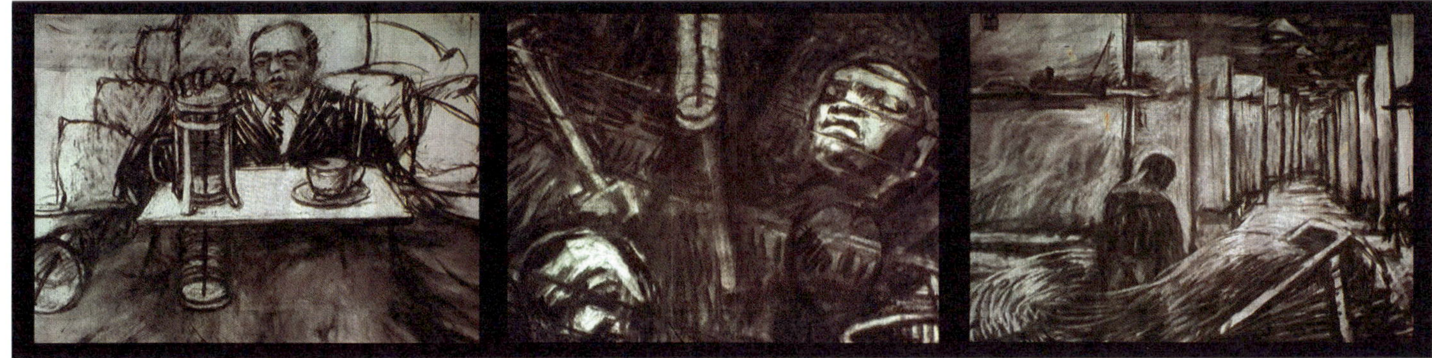

WILLIAM KENTRIDGE, **MINE**, VIDEO STILL (1-CHANNEL-VIDEO, 6 MIN.), 1991

which is private, concealed, hidden – not only from others, but also from the self. As Friedrich Wilhelm Joseph Schelling states: "*Unheimlich* is the name for everything that ought to remain secret and hidden but has come to light."[22] An encounter with the uncanny is thus an encounter with that which lies beneath the surface of consciousness, and in the context of Cohen's work, it is partially the spectre of apartheid that cannot be ignored or repressed. For, exactly as Couze Venn observes, the effect of the uncanny can "[bring] to mind the out-of-jointness that Jacques Derrida [...] related to an 'hauntology' – an ontology haunted by disjunct, invisible-yet-present traces of a traumatic or troubled past, and the disquieting figure of the other. In the context of displacement, one can relate it to the process of the reinvention or refiguring of oneself which is shadowed by a recalcitrant and disorientating memory of place and space that must be worked through for newness to emerge."[23]

Seen in this light, Cohen's performance is an imaginative refiguring of the self that brings in tow the memory of apartheid-induced spatial and social traumas. The shared experience of threat that plays out in Cohen's exchange with the inhabitants of the informal settlement catalyses a certain 'working through', and bringing to the surface, of this 'troubled past'.

The Underground

As Nuttall and Mbembe note, "the underground" is not to be understood simply in terms of an infrastructure and subterranean spaces, but includes "the underworld" of the "lower classes, the trash heap of the world above, and subterranean utopias".[24] We suggest that, in addition to the latter, the underground can function as a metaphor for that which is repressed, or lies beneath the surface of consciousness and therefore for the disquieting strangeness of the uncanny. Bunn eloquently summarises this in his comment that "what distinguishes Johannesburg from the metropolitan norm [...] is that the rhetoric of the sur-

face has been implicated in an act of historical repression: in an inability to come to terms with the real origins of surplus value, in apartheid labour practices, and especially in the buried life of the black body, instrumentalised and bent into contact with the coal face, or ore seam, in the stopes far below."[25]

Two works that are deeply evocative of Bunn's words are William Kentridge's *Mine* (1991) and Johan Thom's *Challenging Mud – After Kazuo Shiraga* (2008). *Mine* is the second of the *Nine Soho Eckstein Films* which Kentridge produced from 1989 to 2003, forming part of a series titled *Drawings for Projection*. These films feature three of Kentridge's stock characters, namely, Soho Eckstein, the randlord who embodies greed, avarice and world-weary pessimism; the anxious and guilt-ridden Felix Teitlebaum (Eckstein's alter ego), and Mrs Eckstein, who cuckolds Soho with her liaisons with Felix.

In *Mine,* the dialectic relationship between surface and depth is metaphorically articulated by the image of the coffee plunger, through which Soho Eckstein, propped up in a quilted bed with pillows under his head, "initiates a violent descent, as it becomes an elevator cage, passing through an older stratigra-

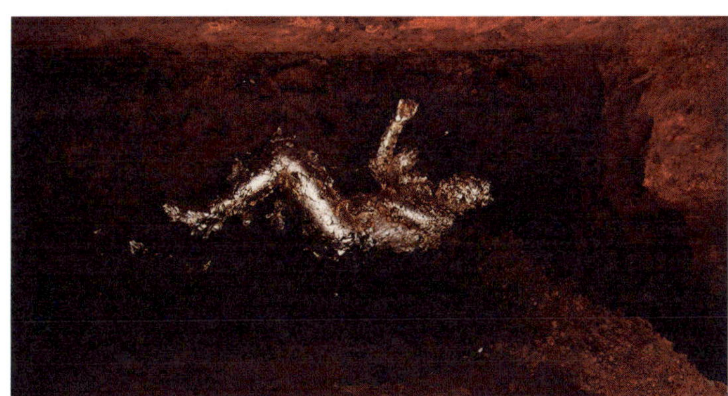

JOHAN THOM, **CHALLENGING MUD – AFTER KAZUO SHIRAGA**, VIDEO STILL (1-CHANNEL-VIDEO, 10 MIN., PROJECTED ON FLUOR), 2008

21 Freud (1955), p. 226. Freud puts forward a semantic study of the German adjective *heimlich* and its antonym *unheimlich* which suggests that a negative meaning close to that of the antonym is already embedded within the positive term *heimlich*. *Heimlich* can denote that which is 'friendly', 'homelike' or 'comfortable', yet can also signify that which is 'concealed' or 'kept from sight'. 'Canny' in English means 'deceitful' and 'malicious', 'to go behind someone's back'. Thus, as Kristeva observes, "in the very word *heimlich*, the familiar and intimate are reversed into their opposites, brought together with the contrary meaning of 'uncanny strangeness' harboured in *unheimlich*". Julia Kristeva 1991, *Strangers to Ourselves,* New York, p. 182

22 Friedrich Wilhelm Joseph Schelling, cited in: Freud (1955), p. 119

23 Couze Venn 2010, Aesthetics, Politics, Identity: Diasporic Problematisations, *Critical Art* 24/3, [s.p.]

24 Nuttall and Mbembe (2008), p. 22

25 Bunn (2008), p. 135

phy".[26] As Bunn observes, this gesture binds "different areas of merchant capitalism, colonialism, and imperialism, base to super-structure, post-object to whole machine"[27] as the cage, rather like a pneumatic drill, descends to the underground levels of the mines, and thereafter ascends back to the surface. Along the plunger's subterranean journey, it conjures up images of the heads of the miners sleeping in their bare barracks, while Eckstein languishes in his plush bed. However, its metaphorical path through the earth also suggests that the heads are buried deep underground, that beneath Eckstein's capitalist dream, a trove of oppression and exploitation is submerged. "The buried life of the black body" (to return to Bunn's phrase) is clearly depicted as the foundation of white capital gain.[28] This work slips between personal and public histories in the years of transition leading up to the official demise of apartheid. Kentridge notes: "I have never tried to make illustrations of apartheid, but the drawings and films are certainly spawned by, and feed off, the brutalised society left in its wake."[29]

Performance artists Johan Thom and Anthea Moys also adopt the motif of burial in representations of contemporary Johannesburg. Thom, like Kentridge, traces the history of the city to deep-cast mining. However, in *Challenging Mud – After Kazuo Shigara,* Thom enacts the burial of gold rather than its extraction. Thom himself, clad in a gold sheath, lies in a grave-like hole, as what initially appears to be soft brown earth but later becomes apparent as gold-dust, is shovelled over him until he is almost entirely buried. In placing his own body under threat in this performance, Thom highlights the inseparability of Johannesburg's gold economy from human vulnerability. This act of burial also alludes to a common fear, identified by Freud in his study *The Uncanny* and explored time and again in Gothic literature – the fear of being buried alive. Freud writes that "to some people, being buried alive by mistake is the most uncanny thing of all."[30] In *Challenging Mud,* Thom's voluntary burial, and the visible reflex to resist it, which becomes apparent as his face is gradually covered, enacts this particular manifestation of the uncanny.

Anthea Moys' videos *Gautrain Series: Ophelia* (2008) and *Gautrain Series: Tunnel Shout* (2008) also stage interactions of vulnerability, in which Moys is at the mercy of giant construction machines being used to create a tunnel for the Gautrain (a high-speed underground train in Johannesburg). Both performances are filmed on building sites – transitional sites that point to the 'in-betweenness' of being in construction and in the process of becoming. *Gautrain Series: Ophelia* obliquely references John Everett Millais' painting, *Ophelia* (1851/52). Moys lies in a self-dug 'grave' of sand on the construction site, appearing almost doll-like in relation to the scale of the heavy-duty graders around her. In an artist's statement[31] Moys speaks poignantly of the futility of digging a hole to lie in while being surrounded by heavy-duty graders, and the sense of powerlessness that this evoked for her. Her powerlessness and vulnerability are conveyed to viewers watching the mechanical shifting of earth taking place at close proximity to her body. The smallness of her doll-like scale enhances this sense of helplessness and draws attention to her femininity, referencing the incongruity of her female body in a conventionally masculine environment.

Moys likens this sense of powerlessness which she evokes in the work to a broader sense of powerlessness which she believes "a lot of South Africans are feeling at the moment"[32]. She wears a hard hat and safety clothing for protection, which she sees as a metaphor for the need for protection when walking in the streets of Johannesburg. Yet, within this seemingly hopeless, or even suicidal act (taking the reference to John Millais' painting *Ophelia* more literally) of 'burying' herself, lies what she acknowledges to be quiet acceptance of her own powerlessness.

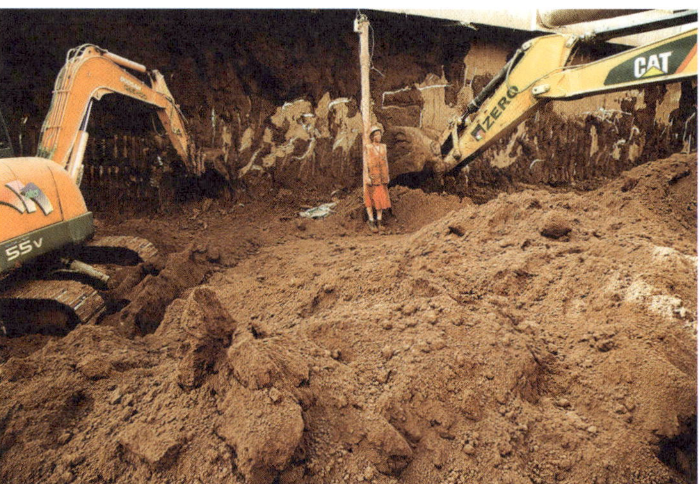

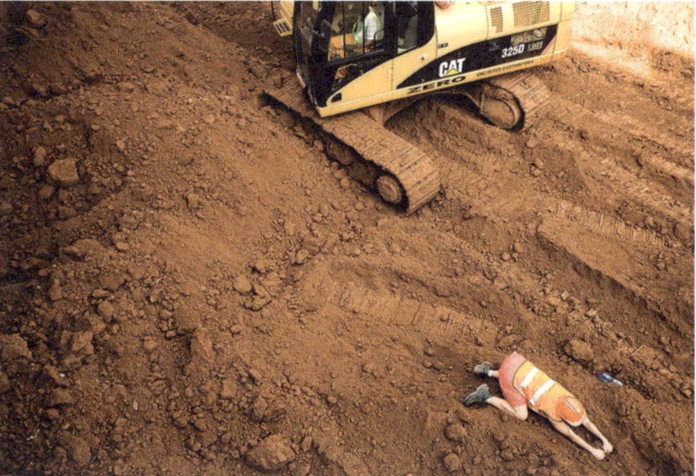

ANTHEA MOYS, **GAUTRAIN SERIES: STANDING WITH GRADERS** AND **DIGGING**, STILL PHOTOS OF A THREE-HOUR PERFORMANCE, 2008

26 Bunn (2008), p. 141
27 Bunn (2008), p. 141
28 Kentridge's technique of erasure of charcoal images from the paper surface leaves traces that suggest temporal shifts between event and memory. These temporal shifts are enhanced by the non-linearity of the scene sequences. The constant erasure of an image as it is formed on a page, and its transmutation into something else, speaks of the partiality and fragility of memory, as well as of the fluidity between political and personal expressions of struggle.
29 Kentridge cited in: Carolyn Christov-Bakargiev 1998, *William Kentridge.* Brussels
30 Freud (1955), p. 12
31 Anthea Moys 2008, Artist's statement, in: *Too Close for Comfort: Belonging and Displacement in the Work of South African Video Artists* (Catalogue), Johannesburg [s.p.]

32 Moys (2008) [s.p.]

For her, it is through "acceptance of uncertainty and change that we manage the world we live in. In this acceptance … is also a quiet celebration of the potential, of what is to come."[33]

The Surface

The medium of video shares with film and other lens-based media an undeniable ocular centrism. The lens of the camera, which acts as a prosthetic monocular eye, directs "how *we see, how we are able, allowed, or made to see*"[34]. The transmutation of raw video material into an artwork, as a shift in perceptual and philosophical context, in turn frames "how *we see* this seeing and the unseeing therein"[35]. Video automatically calls us to engage in and reflect upon the processes of vision and the lexicon of the visual, and in this sense it is bound up in the surface world of the visible, with revelation and with spectacle. Attempts to undermine this natural or default ocular centrism are well established in the genre of video art, but the point holds that in video, one must always grapple with a surface of visibility.

Marcus Neustetter and Stephen Hobbs' *Entracte* (2010) exemplifies not only an instance in which video is thematically concerned with surface, but also how the medium can be implicated in the construction of surface. *Entracte* is a stop-frame animation that documents a photographic intervention on the surface of a building in Dakar, Senegal, in which multiple visual hypotheses for the future of the building were projected onto its external walls. Describing the process by which the work was created, Hobbs and Neustetter write the following: "Located in Zone A, Sicap (Dakar) *Maison 46* is a building which has been standing for ten years and now destined for demolition to make way for a new development. In collaboration with students from the *Ècole de Beaux Arts* in Dakar, a series of projection and performance scenes were developed as a reflection on the pathetic state of this building and the expectations of a new architecture to come."[36]

The performance scenes that took place, many of them inside the building, as part of this original presentation are lost in the video documentation of *Entracte*. The viewer is left with a time-lapsed stitching together of images of the skin of the building as it carries different optical projections, which in turn represent thought projections concerning the future of the building. As the building is reduced to its skin in *Entracte,* this particular surface of visibility becomes the stage for the imagining of a *milieu* to come, which is not necessarily bound to conditions in the present. Although the work might appear disconnected from Johannesburg, and therefore the broader thematics of this curatorial project, its treatment of architectural surface in fact speaks very directly to a phenomenon of imagining urban futures that is at play in contemporary Johannesburg. The inner city of Johannesburg, which in the 1990s was cast off as a hopeless slum, is now host to a new kind of prospector, the urban property developer. With increasing rapidity, several buildings and zones within the inner city of Johannesburg are undergoing refurbishment with a view to the gentrification of the city. Both metaphorically and literally (as architects construct hypothetical visual representations of the refurbishments they aim to conduct), Johannesburg is pre-inscribed with a plenitude of visions for its future, some of which are contradictory. Moreover, *Entracte* came about as the eventuality of a mapping intervention originating in Johannesburg, titled the *UrbanNET – Hillbrow/Dakar/Hillbrow* (2006/07). In this project, the artists interviewed Senegalese residents of Johannesburg, asking them to draw maps of Dakar. From these maps, Hobbs and Neustetter navigated Dakar and discovered *Maison 46* as one of several partially completed buildings.

In Minnette Vári's *Quake* (2007), the integrity of the city's visible surfaces is under threat through the introduction of a veil of fluidity that intervenes between the raw visual data of the city and the surface of presentation witnessed by the viewer. Elements such as the solidity of earth, the stillness of cityscapes, unified subjective identities and the eventuality inherent in an understanding of linear time are visually and analogously destabilised as ordinarily solid entities melt and disintegrate into each other. In *Quake* we are presented with the "restless, autophagic architecture of the city"[37] in which the creaking and grinding cityscape mutates, momentarily solidifying only to disintegrate as new buildings manifest themselves, exist briefly and then turn to shadow and fade away. At times this city is identifiable as Johannesburg through certain iconic buildings that appear in the fleeting skyline. As the silhouettes and edges of the buildings and the figures flicker, their boundaries blur and are, thus, metaphorically transgressed. The familiar is hinted at, and then irrevocably disturbed, evoking the disquieting strangeness of the uncanny. In this "uncertain, slightly hallucinatory landscape"[38] cloaked and silhouetted figures travel across a vast, desert-like space. Vári performs the role of these travellers, providing "the template figure" on which images of "female bodies and faces from every possible human predicament [...] age, culture or location" are projected.[39]

This desert-like landscape does not appear to be solid because the sand is in constant writhing motion, appearing to reference "highly charged electrical particles" or the "white noise" of a signal-less television screen.[40] Vári plays on the pun of 'static', as she observes, "[t]here is an ambiguity to the sand field, a 'static' field that is never static."[41] The figures travel from the edges of the metropolis towards the viewer and then out of the frame, thus appearing to always occupy the marginal, 'empty' places between cities. The soundtrack, which comprises what Vári describes as "disembodied voices, carried away by the wind whipping through

33 Moys (2008) [s.p.]

34 Hal Foster 1988, *Vision and Visuality (Discussions in Contemporary Culture 2)*, New York, p. IX, [Italics in Original]

35 Foster (1988), p. IX, [italics in original]

36 Marcus Neustetter in an e-mail to the author on 14 August 2010.

37 Vári cited in: James Sey 2007, *Quake*. An Interview with Minnette Vári [retrieved on 7 March 2012 from http://www.minnettevari.com/M_Vari_Quake_2007.pdf]

38 Christy Rennie 2010, *Privileging Corporeal Identity. An Embodied Approach to Artmaking Practice,* University of Johannesburg, Mtech dissertation, p. 151

39 Vári cited in: Sey (2007) [s.p.]

40 Vári cited in: Sey (2007) [s.p.]

41 Vári cited in: Sey (2007) [s.p.]

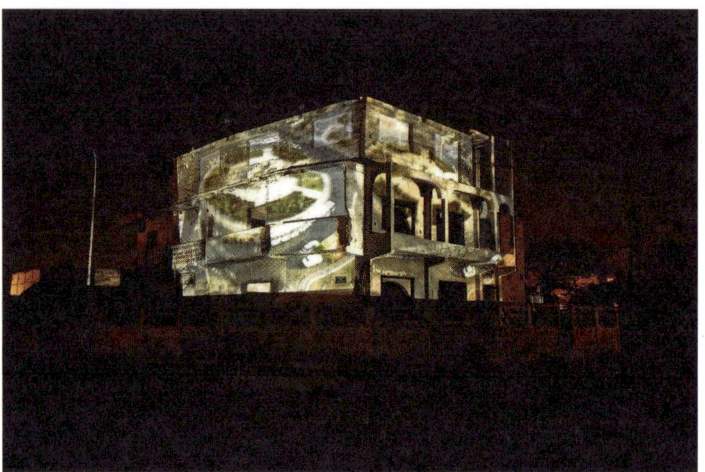

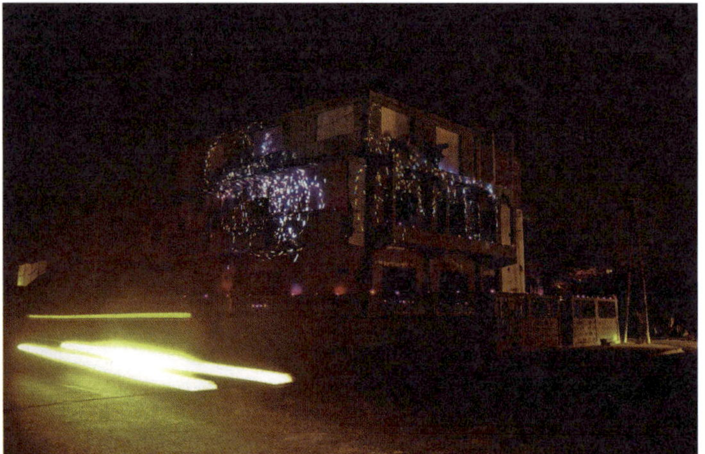

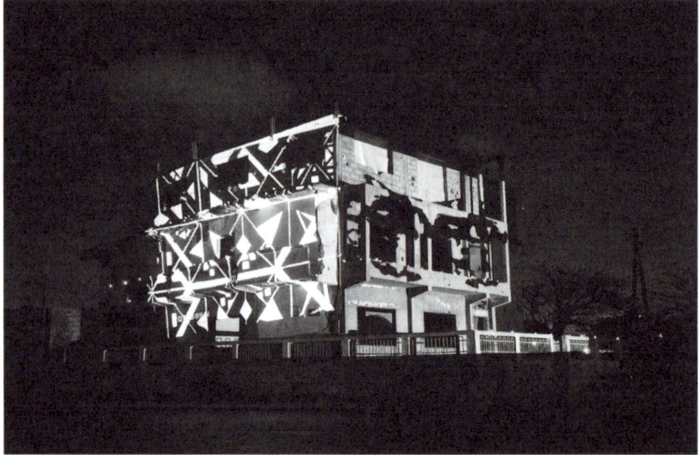

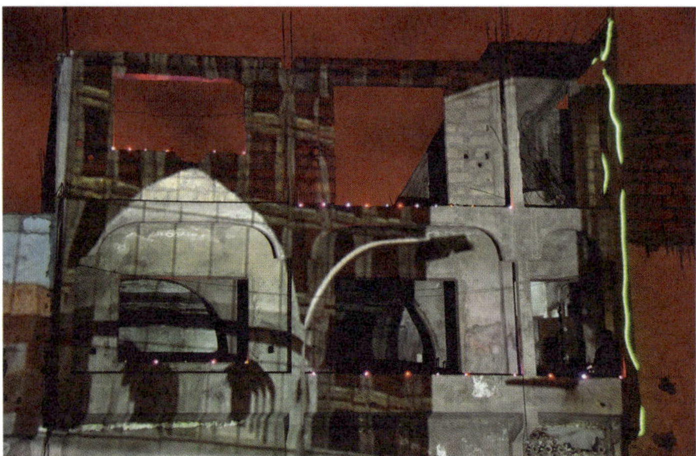

MARCUS NEUSTETTER AND STEPHEN HOBBS, **ENTRACTE**, VIDEO STILLS (1-CHANNEL-VIDEO), 2010

the desert, like sonic semiotic ghosts who dwell on the far limits of some great, semiotic metropolis"[42] serves to further emphasise the uncanny ambiguity of the landscape.

Writing about urban regenerationists' perceptions of the lives and "loose citizenship" of migrants in marginal areas such as Joubert Park in Johannesburg, Bunn describes these existences as "horizontal affiliations", upon whose rapid expansion Johannesburg's future seems to exist.[43] These views of the migratory 'citizenship' – as we have discussed in relation to *Chandelier* – contrast with more conventional understandings of what citizenship means, given that "their lives are not directed toward the making of phenomenologically lived spaces"[44]. Bunn describes this lifestyle as "flickering", a mode of living "lightly on [the] surface" in his description of how urban regenerationists might view these migrants. And, as Christy Rennie observes, perhaps, the flickering, migratory figures of *Quake* could be seen as analogous to that marginalised part of the city which Bunn describes as being "like a screen, across which flickering desires track"[45], wherein representation becomes "[…] a kind of frottage: a rubbing of a new layer of meaning against an indirectly perceived texture below, without direct sight of it. Amnesiac in nature, the present acts of being encounter the older urban footprint very indirectly; the ash of the present is bedded down on the recent past, showing vague outlines."[46] Rennie proposes that these flickering, mutating anonymous figures of *Quake* traversing a constantly shifting "wasteland of static" are evocative of Bunn's imagery.[47] As they move towards the viewer, the background constantly creates and recreates itself as restless cityscape.

Mocke Jansen van Veuren and Theresa Collins' *Minutes 2010* treats the visible urban environment with a similar veil of motility and flux to that which Vári applies to the city in *Quake,* albeit through a markedly different approach to the medium of video. *Minutes 2010* is a triptych depicting diverse public areas of Johannesburg photography observed in real time, and then presented as a time-lapse animation that highlights the tides of activity in specific urban locales. Taxi ranks, parks, libraries, cemeteries, swimming pools and other spaces of leisure, function and contemplation all appear as dynamic, ever-changing scenes. Through the use of time-lapse photography and experimental sound recordings, the city is shown as being in constant states of motion and transformation; its workings and dynamics captured on video as transient and random temporal moments. The compression of time reveals rhythms of everyday life that are ordinarily invisible, 'buried', as it were, in the slowness and clutter of lived real-time. This 'invisible' data is brought to the surface in the traces of flux – meeting points and human interactions – with each other and the city space. In this sense, viewers may be prompted to re-evaluate their daily experiences and

42 Vári cited in: Sey (2007) [s.p.]
43 Bunn (2008), p. 156
44 Bunn (2008), p. 156
45 Rennie (2010), p. 156
46 Bunn (2008), p. 156
47 Rennie (2010), p. 156

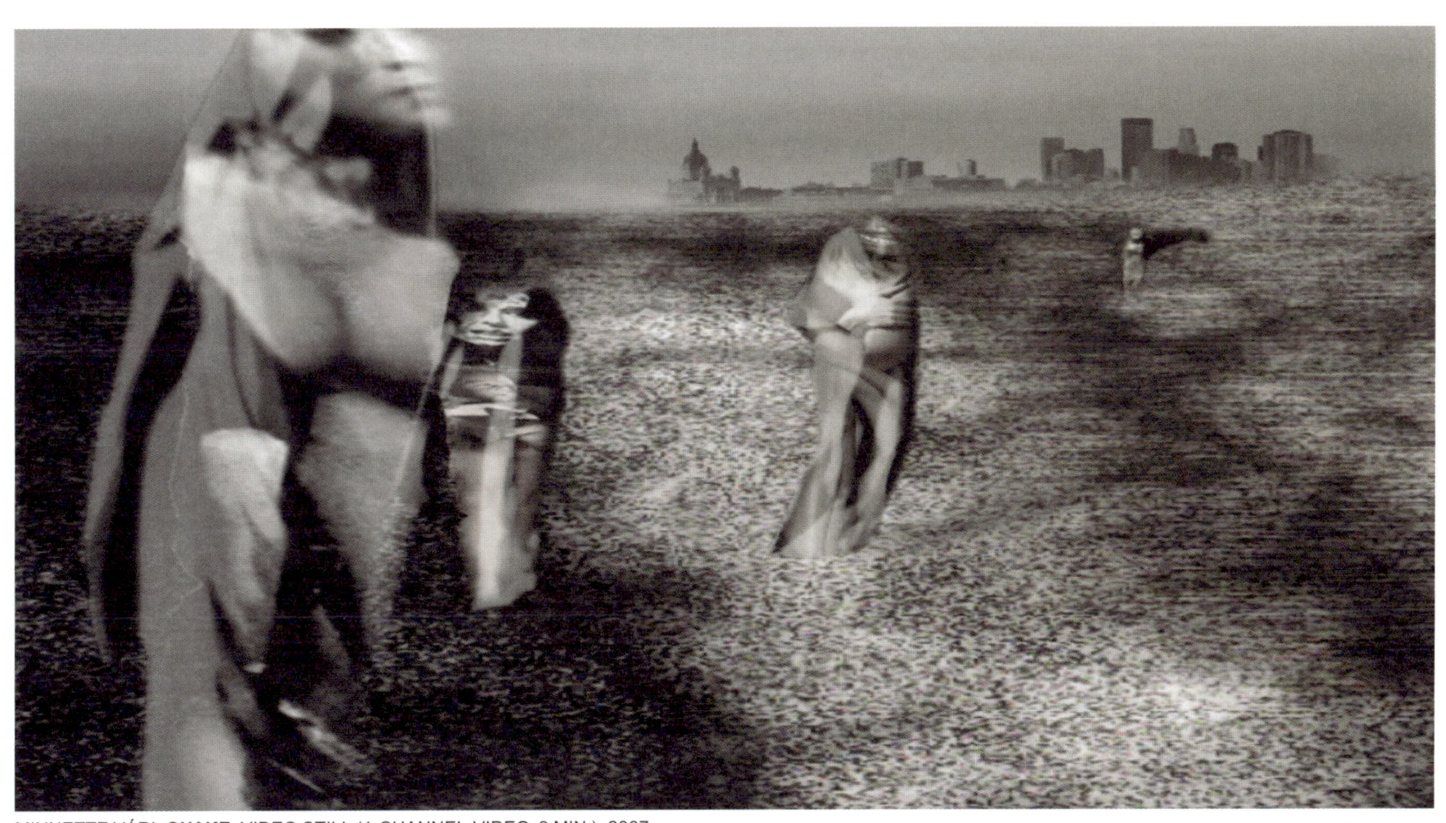

MINNETTE VÁRI, **QUAKE**, VIDEO STILL (1-CHANNEL-VIDEO, 3 MIN.), 2007

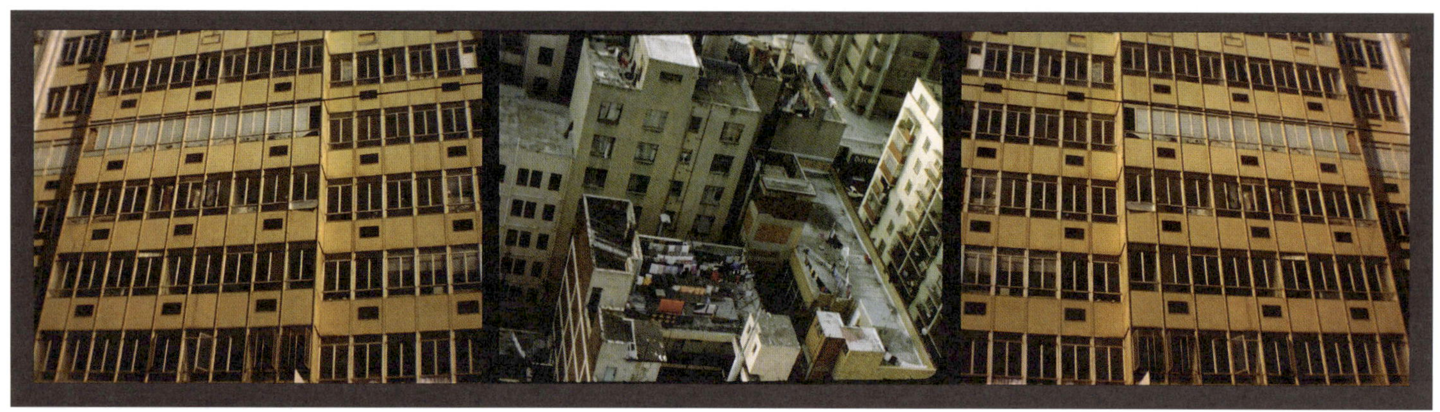

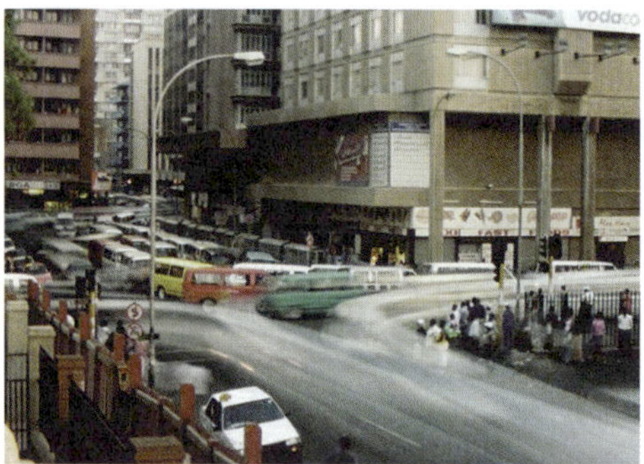

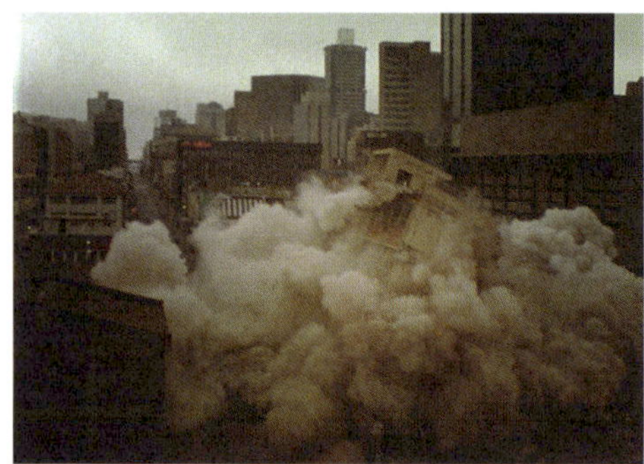

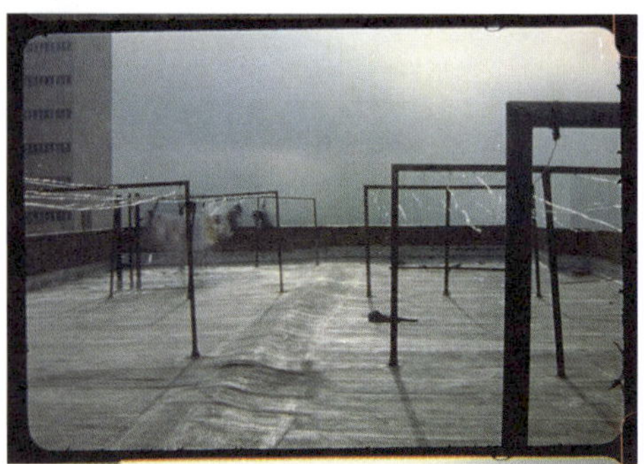

THERESA COLLINS AND MOCKE JANSEN VAN VEUREN, **MINUTES 2005** UND
MINUTES 2008, INSTALLATION STILL AND SINGLE STILLS (VIDEO, 17 MIN.)

Minutes 2010 is based on *Minutes 2005* and *Minutes 2008*.

assumptions around patterns of spatial usage, as these hidden moments and spaces are brought into our spatial field. The camera becomes an observant, analytical tool, albeit that the artists do exercise subjective choices in terms of selecting the site, viewpoint, time of day and duration of frames.

In their recording of the city's rhythms, Van Veuren and Collins take up what appears to be a voyeuristic position, as they capture activities within potentially hostile urban spaces, transitory spaces, spontaneous or orchestrated occupation of spaces, and the mingling of lives in public recreational areas. This kind of voyeuristic viewing might be likened to surveillance; the visual recording of users of the space who are unaware that they are being videoed and will later be viewed. Van Veuren comments: "Although many of the places we film are familiar to me […] the relationship changes when the camera separates […] the object in front of the lens from the real or implied, current or future viewing subject; images are literally 'captured' for a later gaze with undisclosed intentions […] once the camera is engaged and running, it has become in some ways an instrument of surveillance, covert and alien, operating outside the awareness, consent or comprehension of its subject."[48]

Yet, as Van Veuren points out, the settings they choose on the camera tend to obscure or "smudge" the identities of people in the shot; moreover, the subject, "is not an individual or group of people" but rather the interaction of "space, time, movement, rhythm, generated by human presences, bodies and minds engaged in the task of passing the day, governed by habit, culture, law, commerce, desires, roads, architecture [and the] cyclical transitions between day and night".[49]

Van Veuren and Collins' approach to videoscopic sight subjects what are apparently opposite terms – visibility and invisibility, hiddenness and revelation – to a paradox. Through *Minutes 2010,* city life is rendered both more and less visible. While the camera reveals the hidden rhythm of the city, it also obscures the material of this rhythm, the faces, lives, actions and intentions of individual people. Through an act of mechanical engagement with and translation of a perceptual surface, this work, just as automatically, uncovers the subtext of the city. In this regard, *Minutes 2010* underscores the collusive, mutually porous relationship between the surface and the underground – and the resultant activation of the strange liminal spatiality, which we have called "the edges", that is at play throughout the selection of works that comprises *The Underground, the Surface and the Edges.*

Rather than an attempt to represent the essence of a city as spatially and socially complex as contemporary Johannesburg.

(if this were even possible), *The Underground, the Surface and the Edges* highlights a set of spatial relations, or rather, a mode of spatial relating, that gives rise to this state of complexity. Perhaps this tripartite spatiality is characteristic of the city, that, according to our reading, picks out the recurrence of this spatial motif of constant oscillation between that which lies beneath the visible landscape, the surface of the metropolis and that which is concealed or embedded in other orders of visibility. Thus, this project aims merely to open up this reading of Johannesburg; a reading which, almost paradoxically, demonstrates the insufficiency of any unitary view of the city.

48 Mocke van Veuren, 17 September 2008, notes from unpublished article in an e-mail to the author.
49 Mocke van Veuren, 17 September 2008

Itchy City

KGAFELA OA MAGOGODI AND JYOTI MISTRY

Itchy City is a poem by author and spoken-word artist Kgafela oa Magogodi. The poem is part of *I mike what I like,* a play which Magogodi turned into a film with filmmaker Jyoti Mistry. *Itchy City* (2006) is a five-minute sequence where elements of Magogodi's live performance are superimposed with real and painted city views of Johannesburg to create a powerful commentary on everyday life and absurdities in a city with an "itching soul".

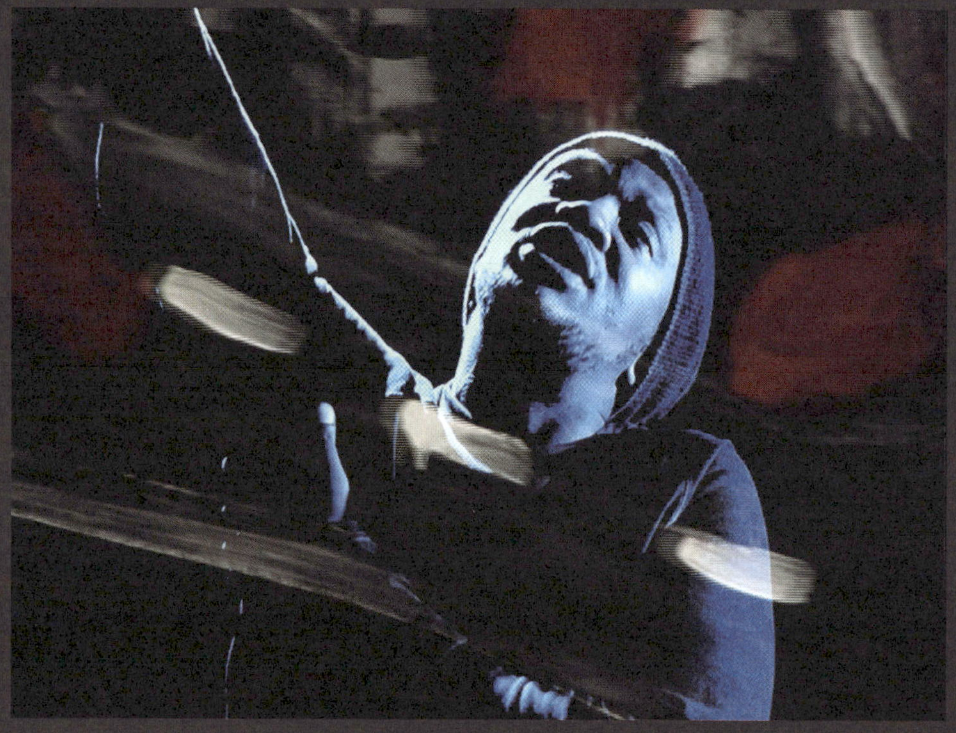

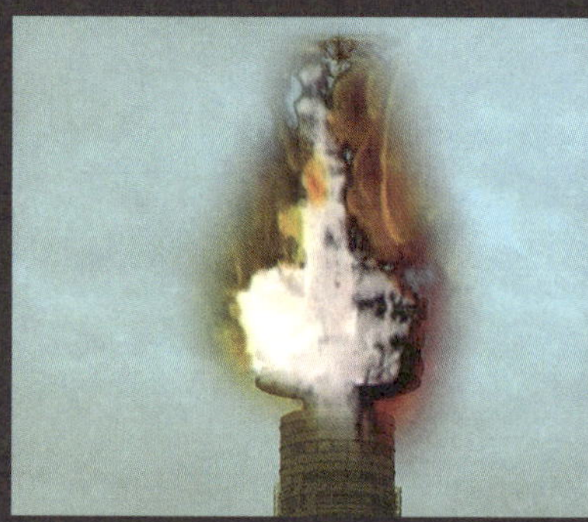

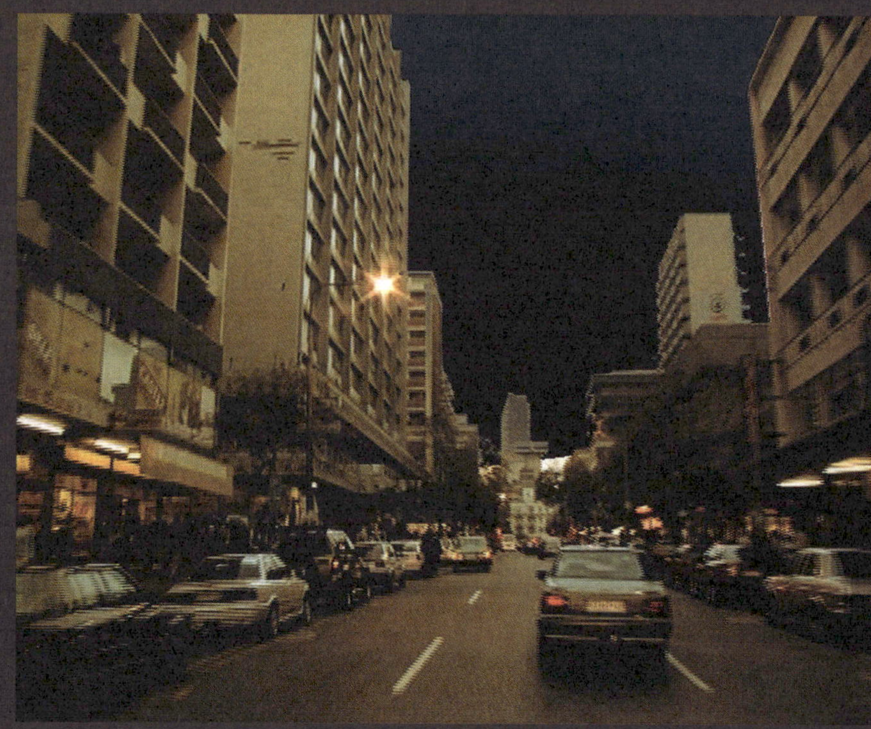

babyjakes come in small packages they pack dynamites in their trumpet blows break down the walls of jericho's temples biblical brimstone and fire in the city of cold blood flows cheaply like pavement tomatoes the streets are red rivers dead bodies and gold-platted teeth five-star smile in the face of a corpse heh banna who stole the red bandana from the head of ponte city now we know who's been hiding the blues itchy city blues deep as the froth of cappuccino made in nino's kitchen hot as spicy chicken wings fry them before the fly fry them before they fly scramble their eggs and feed on fowl foetus spew out vegetarian views at lunch meatings munch and run to pay the gym to make you slim

in small street you soak in the sounds of hustlers and hawkers selling secret socks starter packs and ama-empty empty empty cassette two for five rand ama-empty cassette

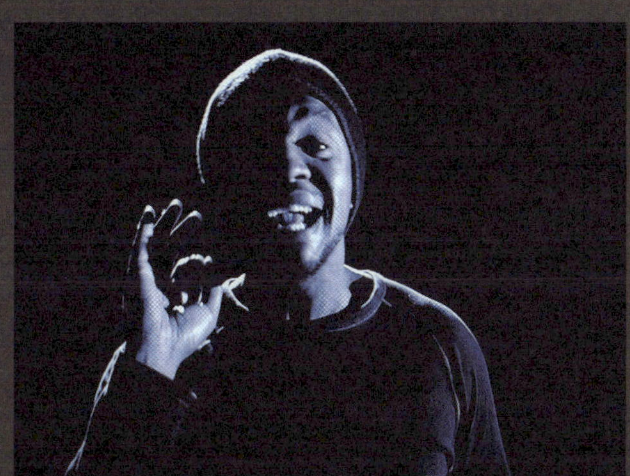

itchy city people sweet as a pimple in the heart of a dimple but not as simple as sorting apples and oranges choice-assorted like a peacock parade of sex workers do a quick job before you get home to wife and family every tom dick and pipi with cash gets their kuku in the city of golden wishes beggars ride horses of small change

"uncle please small change asseblief"

itchy city lights kill the night not even god is bored riding the back of a hijack short left short right cut a corner

it's a chase scene down delvers street the screeching soundtrack draws tapes of hungry circles around us hungry circles surround us but we can't be swallowed not even the mouth of a gun will bury us in the belly of time we live eternally in the scratch of a dj's needle on the skin of a turntable we write ourselves in soundscapes of the wind in strobe lights of the sun we run cables of lyrics in the veins of the underground but after sips of black label some show off their secret socks

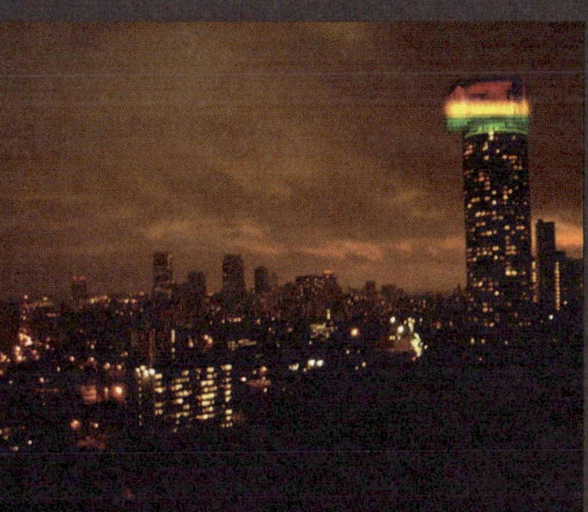

every dog has its day of chewing the sweet bone of a cellular telephone god is running out of airtime in the city god is running out of airtime in the city loan sharks are jesus save us from landlords of rotten buildings and busted water pipes stink like killers of saddam's sons they cut your power cables unpaid electricity bills and riots in san jose faceless fires and curtains of flames flagging and roaring through dark caves in the jungle trees of skyscrapers their monstrous shadows are blinding we can't even see the second coming of babylon running towards us

garvey's kids in house of hemp robes catch a fire of holy herbs the smoke is red gold and green red gold and green rings of smoke to cure the sufferers from babylonchitis sobukwe's flock grow cabbages and sweet potatoes on street pavements to feed clothe and school the children school the children teach them to walk on fire who says the fire is fictitious it's a furious figment of the city's madness we point fingers at nigerians but who is shooting poison needles in the arms of wingless angels heaven help us lead us not to babylon by putco bus at least let us climb to the top of pyramid schemes

before police tear down these dreams. will we escape these ulcers of fires inside us ulcers of fires eating up the bowels of our poor yet television fables say that "we are one" but we are the ones who know the itching soul of the city

Very Ugly / The Funeral

SAM NHLENGETHWA

Sam Nhlengethwa started working as an artist in the 1970s. Since then, his art has always traced and reflected the changes of the city in which he lives. In the 1980s and 1990s, he created a series of collages exploring Johannesburg's streets and, in this way, focused on a key location in the city's public, social and political life. In these works, violence, death and loss become visible as one element in the urban experience of the South Africa of apartheid.

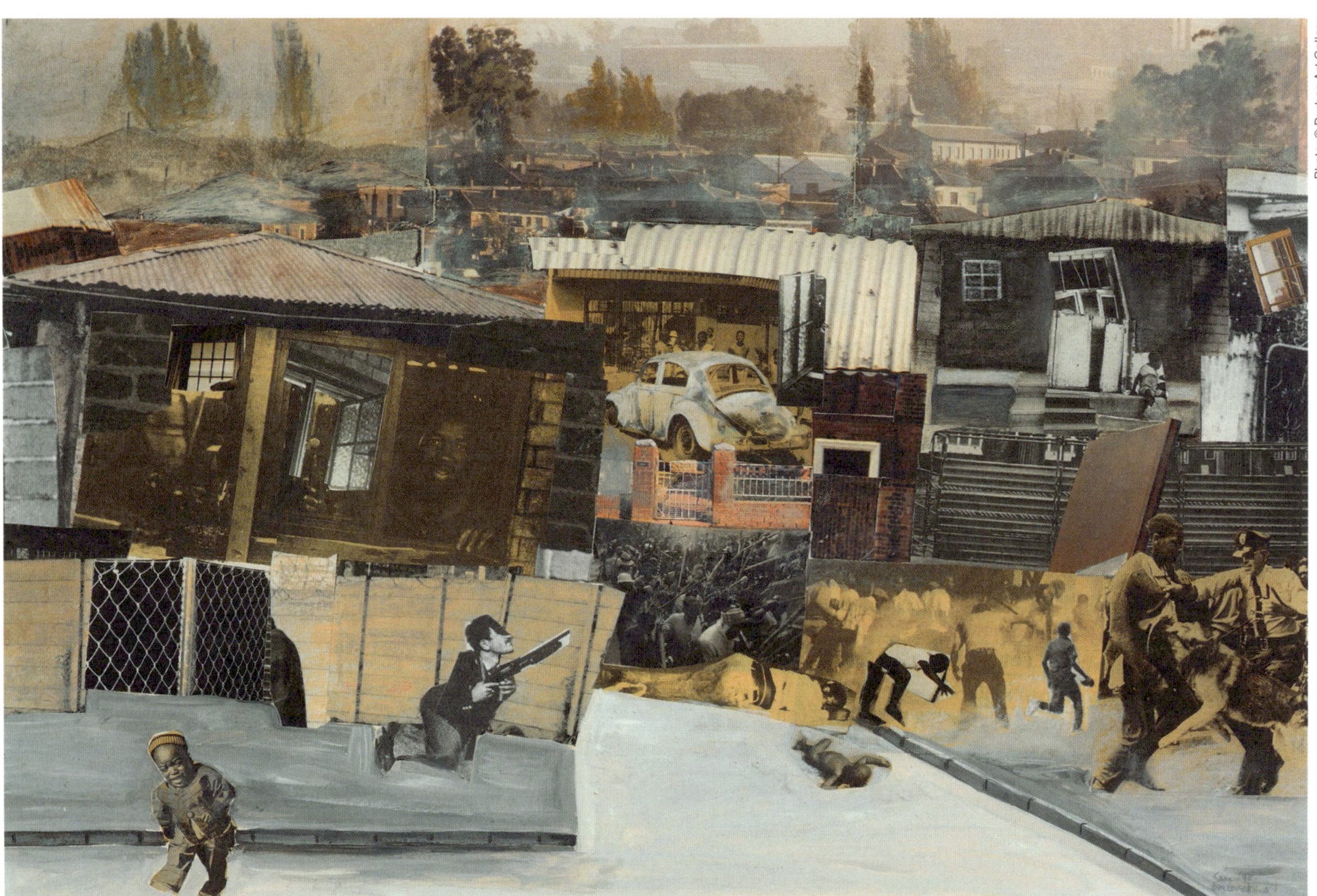

VERY UGLY, 1992, COLLAGE AND WATERCOLOUR ON PAPER, 42,5 × 62 CM

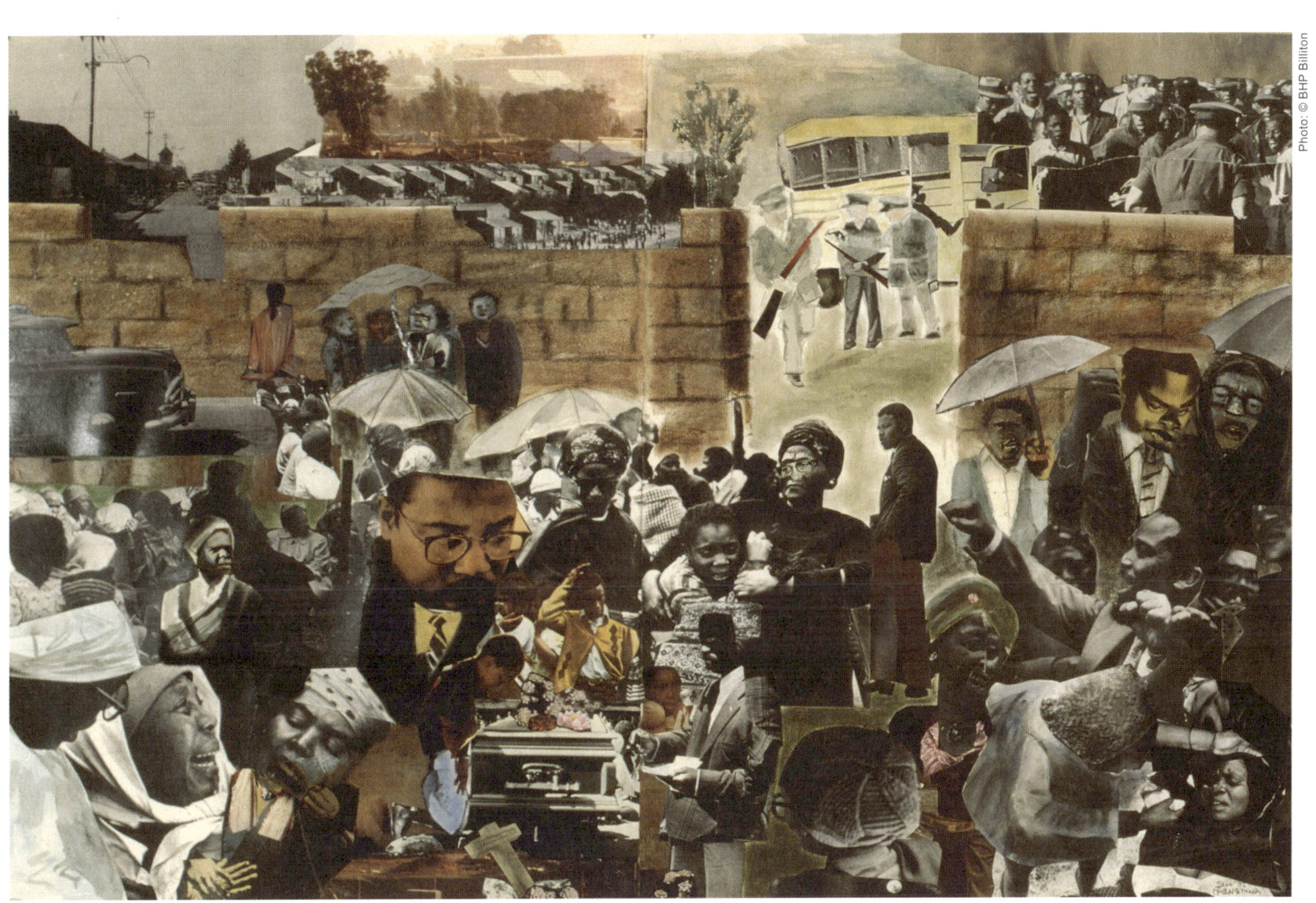

LALA NGXOLO (REST IN PEACE) AKA **THE FUNERAL**, 1992, COLLAGE, 112 × 75 CM

Oswenka—The Jeppe Hostel Swankers

TJ LEMON

TJ Lemon has worked for over fifteen years as a photojournalist in Johannesburg. His *Oswenka* (2000) series records an *Oswenka* competition one evening in the Jeppe Hostel in downtown Johannesburg. The *Oswenka* event is a type of fashion show where elegantly dressed men present themselves to a lay jury which ranks them by the style and taste of their clothes. Just like *Isicathamiya* singing competitions, *Oswenka* events are part of the history and culture of labour migrants in Johannesburg. Since the city was founded, the mines and, later, the secondary industries have attracted tens of thousands of migrants from the rural areas. The lodgers at the Jeppe Hostel primarily come from KwaZulu-Natal.

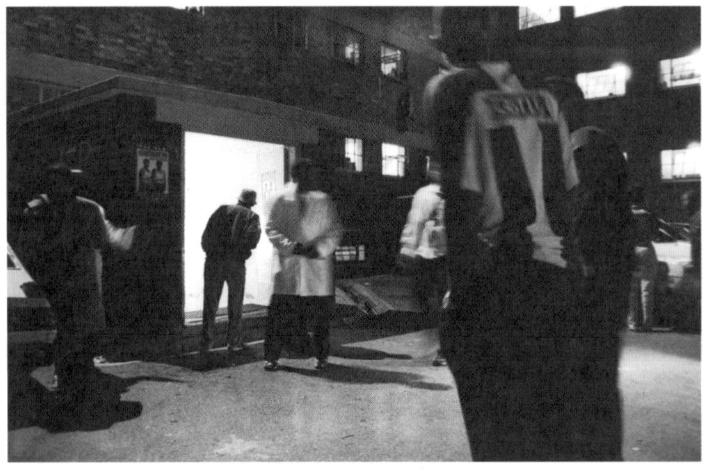

← The *Oswenka* gather in front of the Jeppe Hostel. They are wearing white coats to protect their suits from dust and dirt.

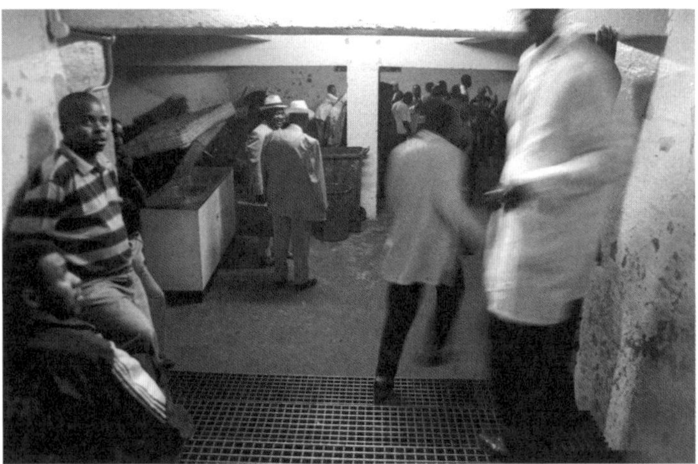

← The low admission price entitles the audience to a seat on a wooden bench for the nightly *Oswenka* fashion show and *Isicathamiya* performances.

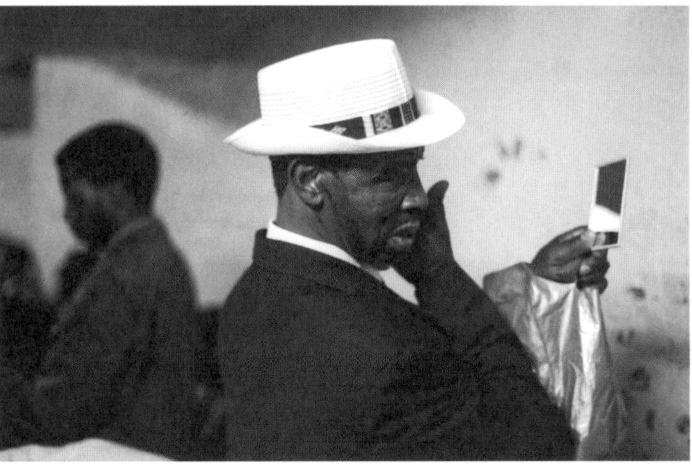

← To ensure they are perfectly prepared for the competition, the contestants bring a mirror, shoes, comb and *muti,* a substance from traditional medicine said to bring them luck.

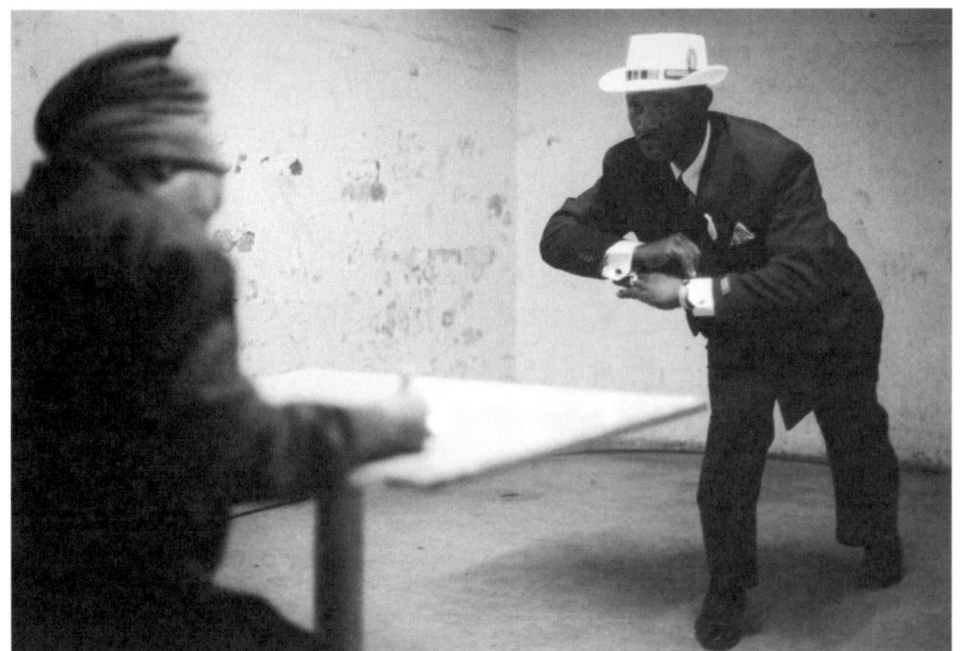

← Since his youth, Dingani Zulu has worked with a jackhammer on urban demolition projects. The judges are much impressed by his distinctive style and winning smile.

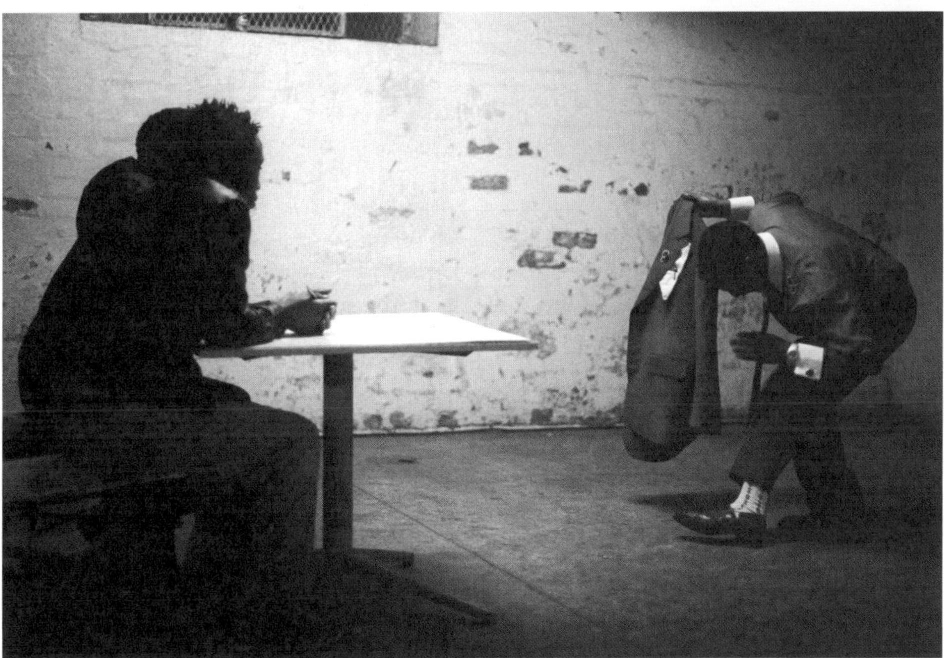

← Each contestant has his own personal style of clothing, and his own individual approach to presenting his clothes. Some highlight their masculinity, while others emphasise grace and suppleness. The evening's winner is Dalton Manqele.

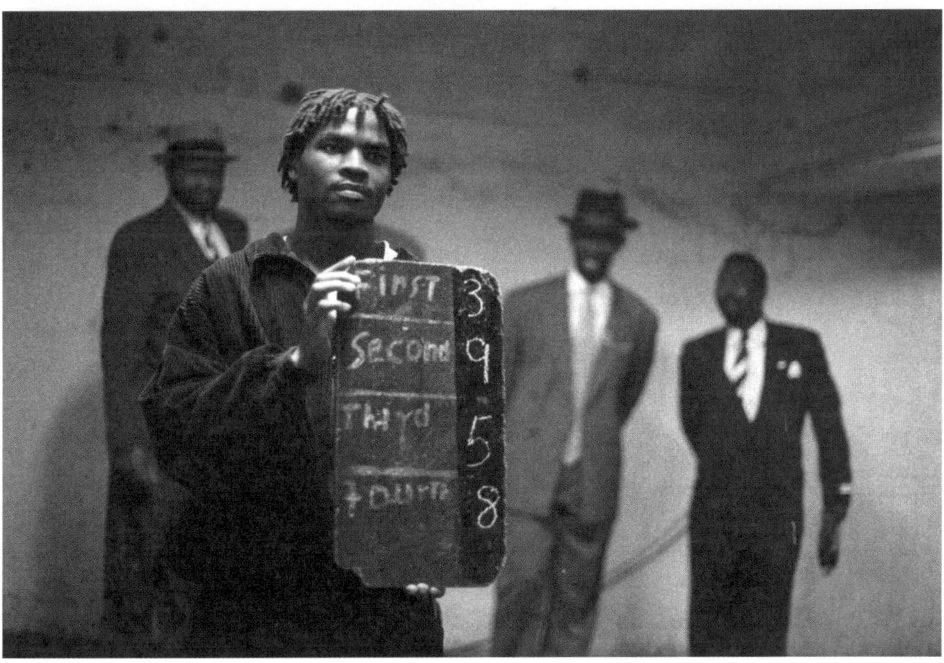

← The independent judge announces the evening's winner.

Trolley Project

ISMAIL FAROUK

Urban geographer Ismail Farouk from Johannesburg researches the city's social networks, taking them as a basis to develop participative artistic projects. His *Trolley Project* (2009) grew out of a cooperation with the trolley pushers who use shopping carts to transport heavy luggage in downtown Johannesburg. The project's aim was to legalise the trolley pushers by providing them with newly designed and manufactured trolleys. In his project, Farouk highlights the social, political and economic implications of the different uses of urban space.

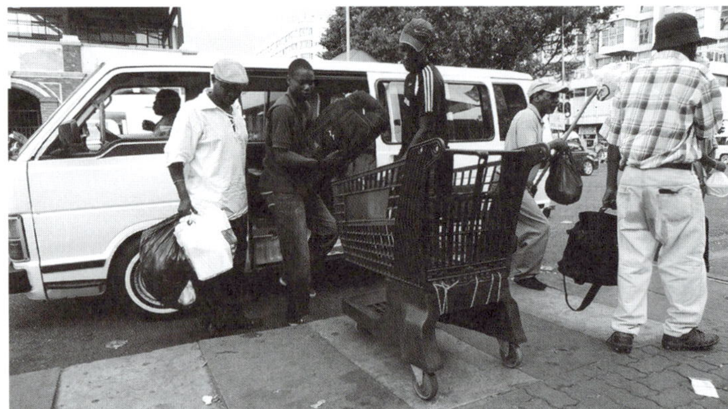

← A Mozambican trolley pusher helps a customer requiring baggage-carrying assistance (January 2009).

Trolleys for sale (March 2008). Theft of supermarket trolleys is a highly organised business. The trolleys are supplied by Zimbabwean youth, who utilise hired trucks and vans to transport stolen trolleys from shopping centres to the downtown area, where they are sold on the streets. ↓

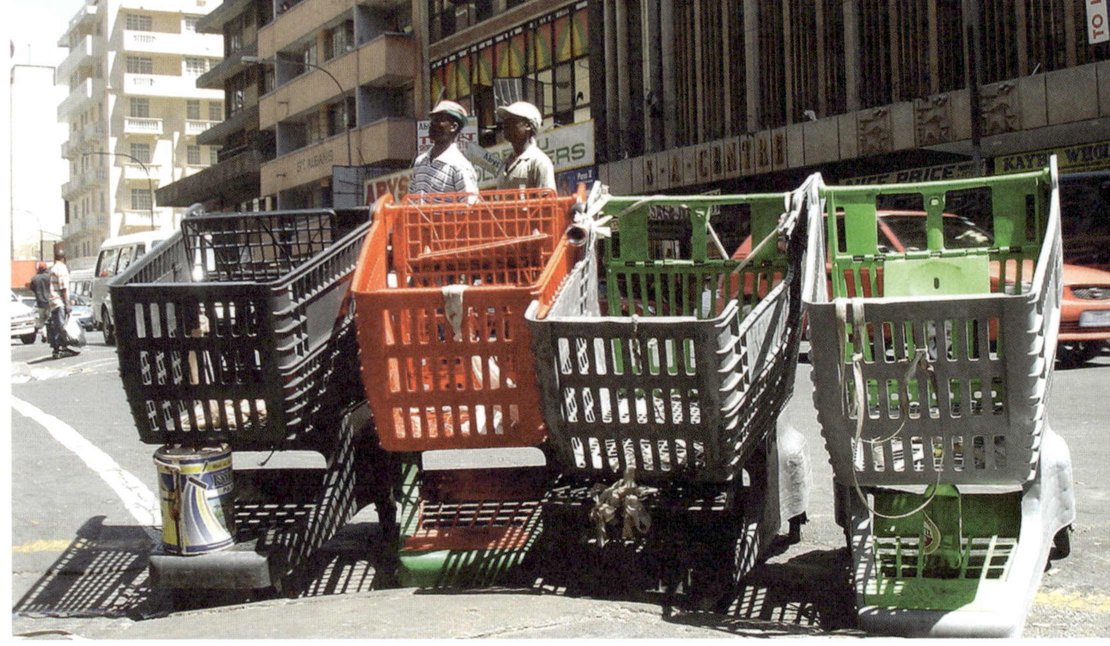

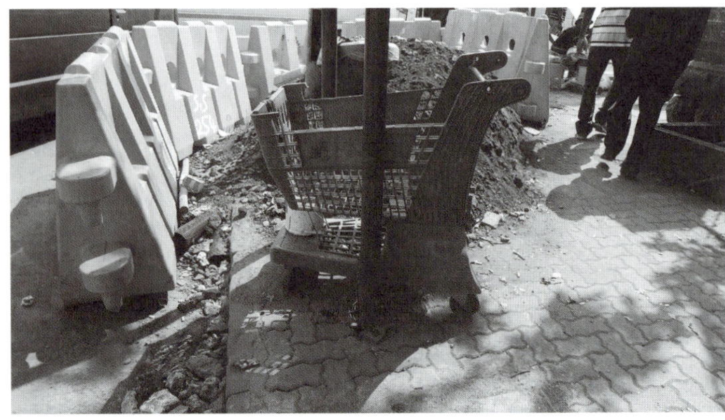

← Secured plastic trolley (April 2009). In the period from 21 March to 5 April 2009, 877 trolleys were confiscated in Joubert Park in downtown Johannesburg.

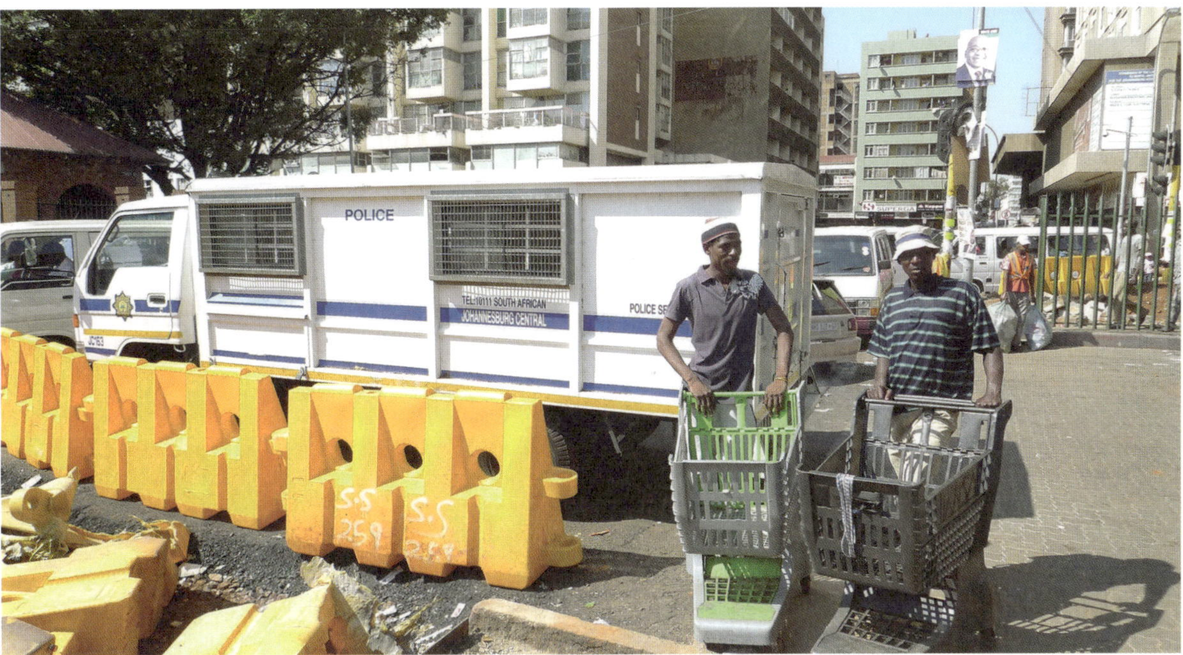

↑ Criminal trolley pushers (April 2009). A major problem associated with trolley-pushing activity has been victimisation by the police. Every time a raid occurs, trolley pushers are fined 300 Rand and trolleys are confiscated.

Keith and the protestors (May 2008). A recent protest action against the criminalisation of trolley pushing in Joubert Park demonstrated that the trolley pushers are united against police harassment. During the protest, trolley pushers addressed members of the police force and highlighted the fact that they were creating jobs and were not mere criminals. →

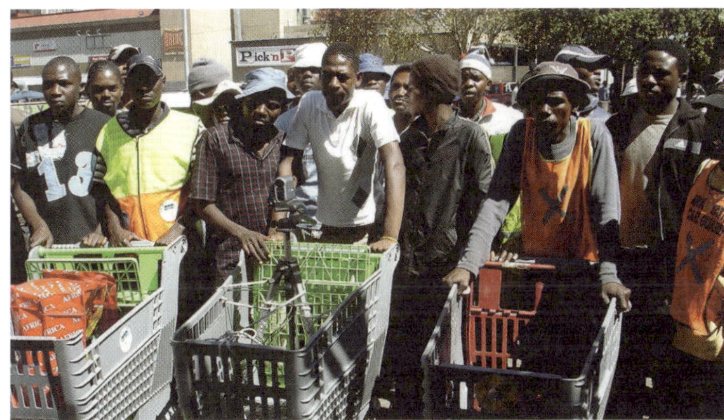

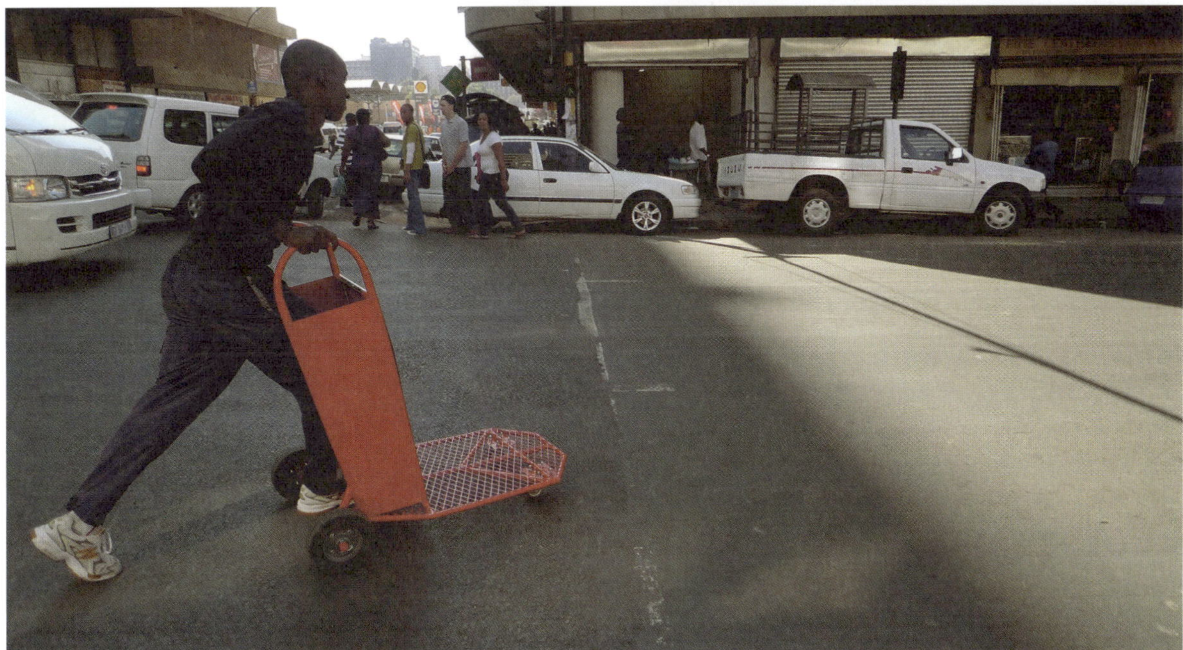

↑ Hansa Monsaka tries out the new trolleys on Bree Street (May 2009).

The Calling

MINNETTE VÁRI

Minnette Vári's video works focus on reflections about her role as a (white) artist in the new South Africa. In a metaphorical, almost mythological investigation into a "broken metropolis", her video installation *The Calling* (2003) explores Johannesburg, the city where she lives and works. Accompanied by the music and writings of the 12th-century Benedictine visionary and mystic Hildegard von Bingen, Minnette Vári changes and transforms herself against a cityscape panorama of Johannesburg, Brussels and New York.

O Ierusalem, aurea civitas, ornata Regis purpura. O aedificatio summae bonitatis, quae rutilas in aurora, et o laudabilis adolescentia, quae ardes in sole. ... O Ierusalem, fundan perditae oves erant, sed per Filium Dei inventae ad te cucurrerunt et in te positi sunt. Dein volaverunt. Et ita turres tuae, o Ierusalem, rutilant et candent per ruborem et per candorer coronati, qui habitatis in Ierusalem, et o tu, Ruperte, qui es socius eorum in hac habitatio

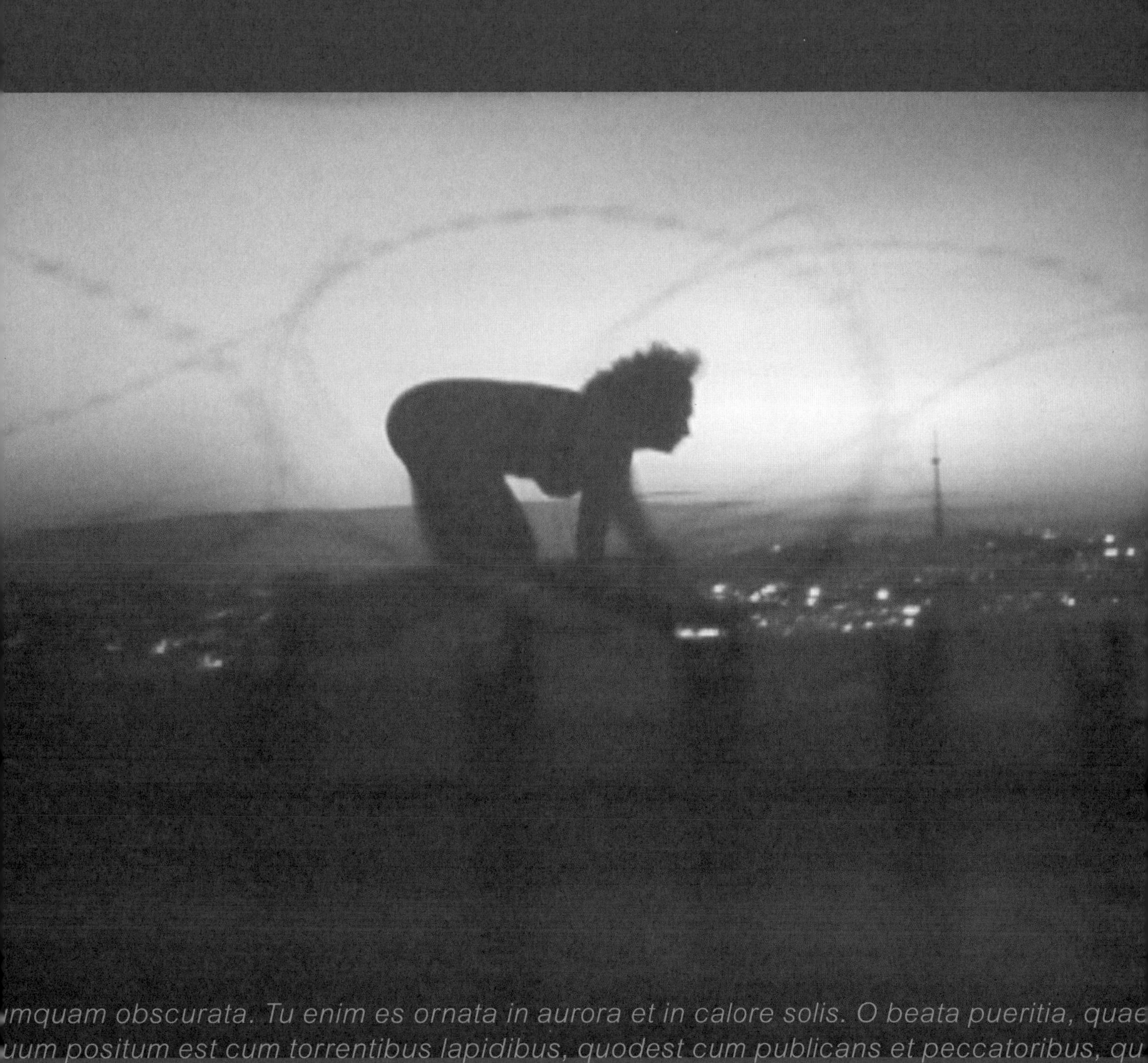

De Sancto Ruperto. O Ierusalem. Hildegard von Bingen (1098 – 1179)

THE CALLING, 2003, VIDEO STILL (2-CHANNEL-VIDEO, 3 MIN.)

Majesty Wholesale
The Biography of a Building

NAOMI ROUX AND HANNAH LE ROUX

Naomi Roux and Hannah le Roux are researchers at the University of the Witwatersrand in Johannesburg. In their work, they research and describe the city from theoretical perspectives in (architectural) history, urban studies and design. For *Afropolis,* they have sketched the social biography of a building and a district in downtown Johannesburg. The Medical Arts Building (today Majesty Wholesale) represents in an exemplary way the metamorphosis that Johannesburg's inner city has undergone since the 1970s. Through historical and current photos, oral history interviews and an exploration of the space in the former Medical Arts Building, they reveal contemporary forms of appropriating modernist architecture. *Majesty Wholesale* is a project exploring the same building as *Passage* by the artist duo Deadheat.

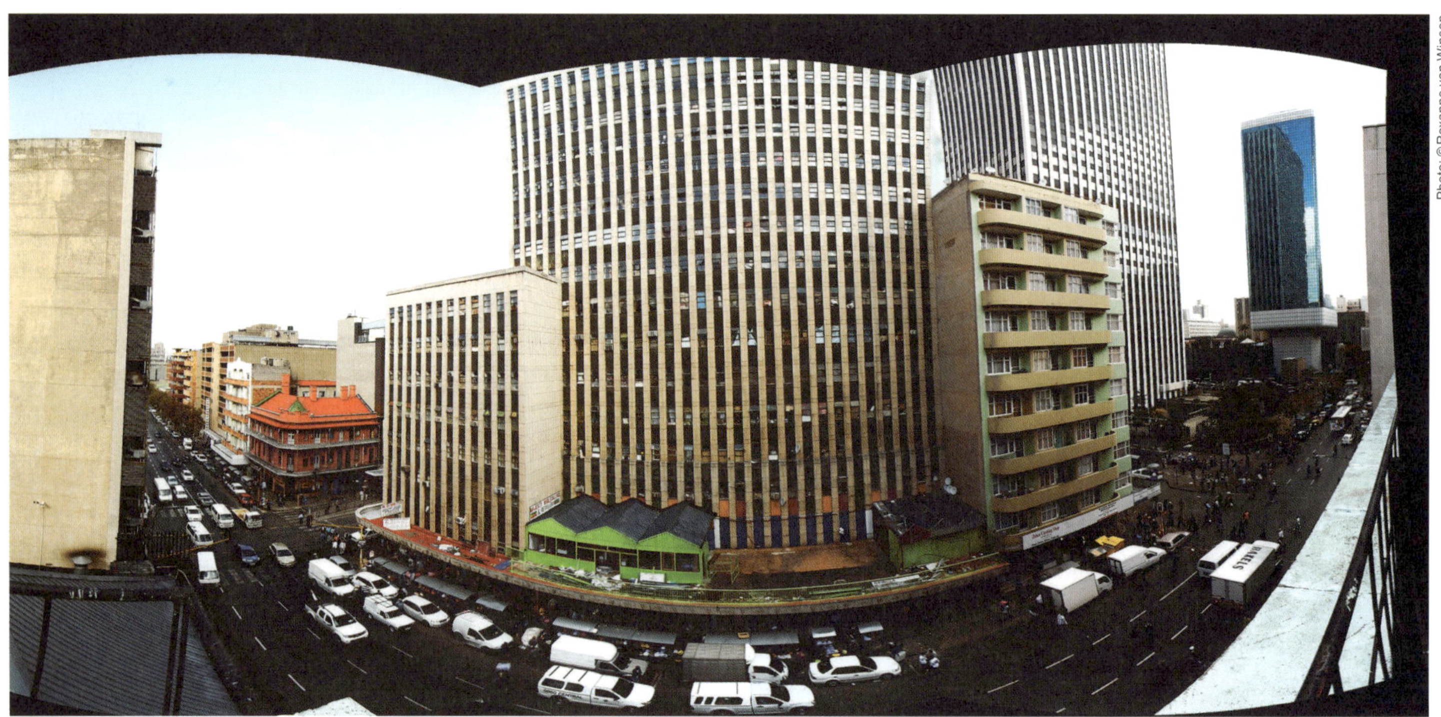

↑ A panoramic view of the Medical Arts Building in downtown Johannesburg (Jeppe Street). The former medical centre building is today called "Majesty Wholesale" and primarily houses retail outlets. Taken from the roof of a building across the road, this image includes architectural examples from a range of eras – the 1950s Medical Arts Building in the centre, 1970s Sanlam Centre/Marble Towers across Delvers Street to the right of Medical Arts, and on the far right the blue glass of the Johannesburg Sun Hotel built in the 1980s.

Corner Jeppe and Troye streets, 1989. The edge of the Medical Arts Building is visible on the far right – the blank wall on the edge of the photograph is the eastern side of Medical Arts, which faces onto Troye Street. By the late 1980s the face of the city was changing rapidly, as the apartheid state was forced to relax or ignore the influx control laws that had previously kept black South Africans out of the city centre. In the late 1980s and early '90s, many of the white occupants of office blocks and businesses in this area began to leave for the northern suburbs, and for a period many of the buildings here – including Medical Arts – stood empty and dilapidated. Empty buildings were often illegally occupied by people desperate for accommodation in the city. The area developed a reputation as a dangerous, semi-deserted space, which it has begun to shed in the last decade as these blocks have been revived by immigrant traders and businesspeople. →

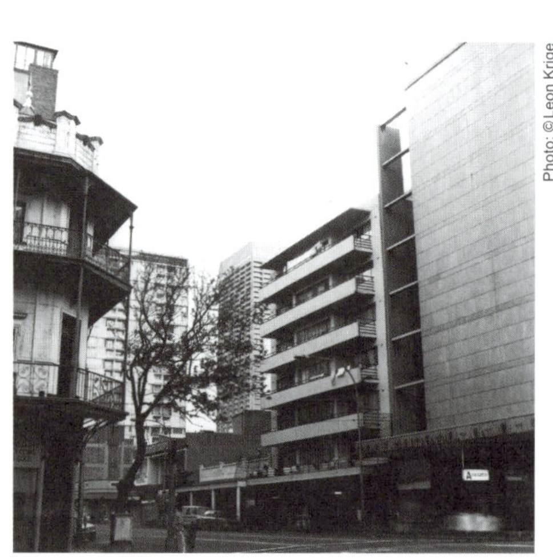

"Johannesburg was not my goal. I heard about Johannesburg when I was in Kenya, from other refugees, that there were many opportunities here … No, I was not scared when I came here, because I had nothing: I had left so many things behind. When I first came to this building and saw our people, wow! You can't imagine how I felt. I never expected this, to find so many people from home here: doing business, growing, growing."

Business owner, Majesty Wholesale
(Extracts from interview with Naomi Roux, May 2010)

The so-called Ethiopian area of Johannesburg's inner city is a temporary and compromised space that nonetheless represents a highly contemporary "cityness". Developing outwards and upwards from where an Ethiopian diaspora trader turned a vacant pavement space into a stall, sometime around 1995, it is now a dynamic network of spaces, goods and services that link Ethiopian, Eritrean, Asian, Malawian and South African businesses across four city blocks. The spaces they occupy have a history in the previous era of dynamic urban growth between 1945 and 1975, when developers built the city up in modernist tower blocks. The Medical Arts/Majesty Wholesale building frames two overlapping processes: constructed, occupied and abandoned by white professionals between 1954 and the 1980s, it was bought, occupied and redecorated by Asian and African tenants from the 1990s onwards. In between these two eras, it reverted to pure structure, a concrete imminence. It vividly illustrates the ambivalent role of modernism in the global city, as a frame for the organisation of its new ways of life that in turn capacitate flux. The movement of people, goods and above all finance is the reverse to any illusion of built stability.

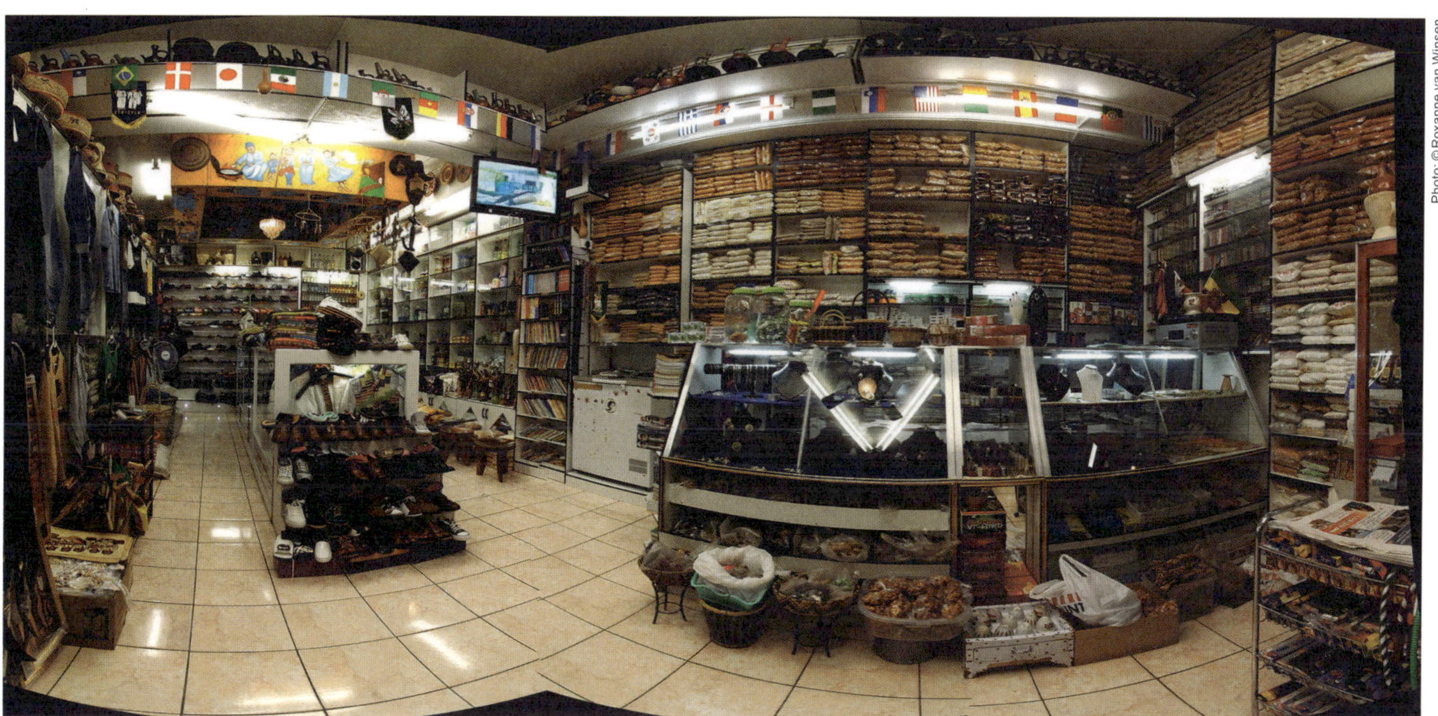

↑ Interior, "Netsi Ethio Traditional Shop". First floor, Medical Arts Building/Majesty Wholesale. In its previous incarnation, this was the reception and waiting area for the doctors' offices on this floor, partly closed off with a large glass window. Today, the large and busy shop sells clothing, T-shirts, artwork, coffee-making equipment, posters, Amharic newspapers, incense, toiletries and accessories, mostly imported directly from Addis Ababa by the shop owner.

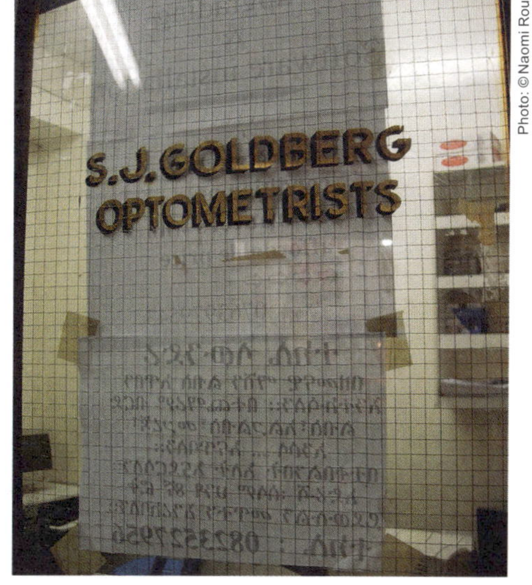

This door marks the entrance to what was once the practice of Dr Stephen J. Goldberg, an optometrist who worked in the Medical Arts Building from the early 1980s until the mid-1990s. Today, the space houses a small Internet café. Dr Goldberg's practice has moved to the northern Johannesburg suburb of Highlands North. →

313

Passage

DEADHEAT

Deadheat is the Johannesburg artist duo of Dorothee Kreutzfeldt and Bettina Malcomess. Their work approaches urban space through public interventions and subjective reflection, usually in a textual form. *Passage* (2010) is a narrative of fragments about the history and users of downtown Johannesburg's Medical Arts Building, now an economic hub for Ethiopian migrant networks in the city. In their one-day intervention on the building's balcony, Deadheat question access to informal migrant spaces and networks, and how such access can be negotiated. *Passage,* an installation created especially for *Afropolis,* explores the same downtown Johannesburg building and quarter as Naomi Roux' and Hannah le Roux's *Majesty Wholesale* research project.

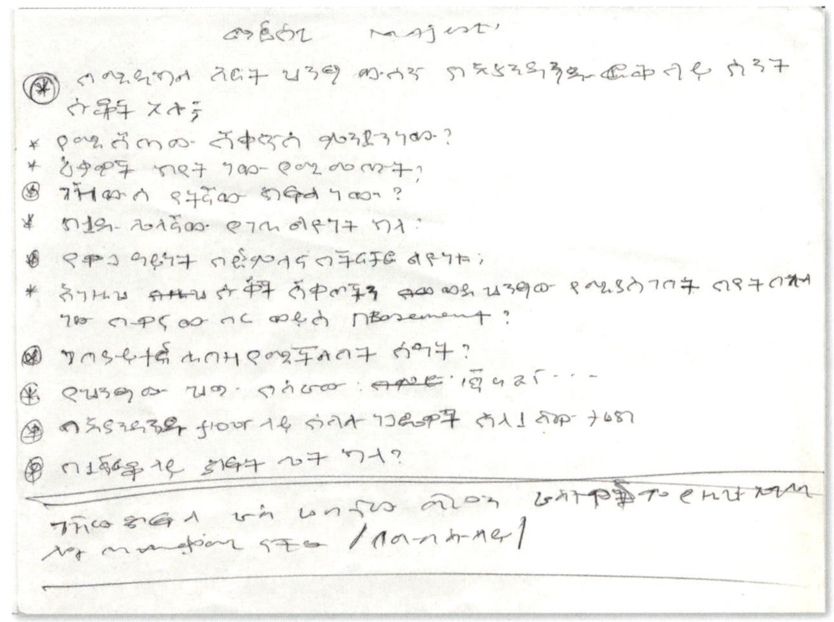

← Notes by N.M., taken during conversations about the Medical Arts Building and trading community[1]

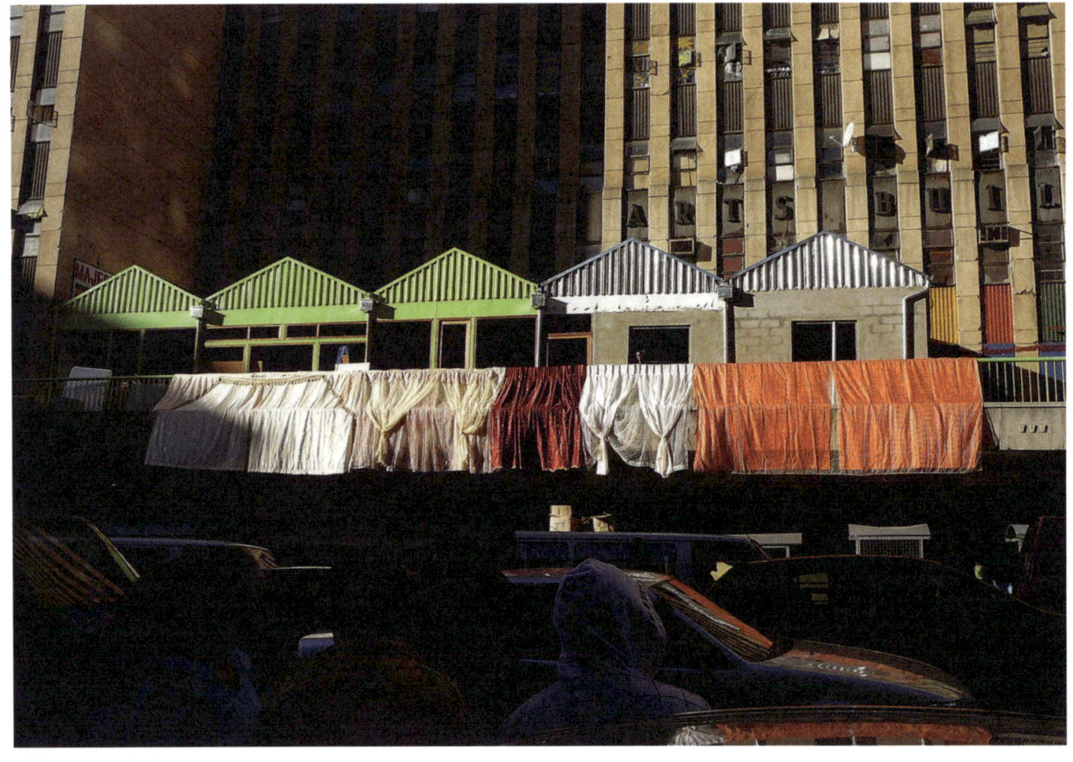

← Façade of the Medical Arts Building, 220 Jeppe Street (13 May 2010)

1.   *"Inside: there are five shops, selling jeans, shoes, fashion bags (all China). There are two souvenir shops. On the first floor there are seven shops, two souvenirs, one clothing. There are six Ethiopian shops, one Eritrean-run shop. The stock for the souvenir shops arrives from Addis Ababa to Johannesburg by plane, once or twice a week, a middleman is met at the airport, the goods are exchanged and he returns. It is mainly South Africans who buy the curtains, to resell. There are also customers from Malawi, Mozambique and Zimbabwe. All the embroidery work comes from Ethiopia. The rent of the shops varies according to size and display space, and from floor to floor. Two Ethiopians 'own' the building, from the ground to the fifth floor; they have signed a lease of two to three years with the landlord. From the fifth floor to the top is storage space for the shops here and the other buildings, as well as the hawker stalls along the pavements. All the traders make individual deals with the owners."*[2]

2.   *"I knew I would not come back the same the direction I had come. I had one small backpack; all that was in it was a bible (a gift), my diary, one jeans, one shirt. All my money was in my pocket. It was very dark; you crossed a small river and caught a bus on the other side. I reached the village on the other side and eventually the bus came. I took a seat, paid and gave them my passport. The driver threatened to call the police. Two brothers from Uganda overheard the whole story. They lied to the driver that they were going to Maputo and paid him 400 kwacha. They were also going to South Africa, and warned me not to give away where I was going. It was a long journey… I came to Jo'burg. I meet many people from my place here. I went to the Home Affairs. From there I became like any other foreigner."*

3.   We meet at regular intervals over the course of two months. It becomes clearer how precarious and carefully organised existence here is, that the condition for survival and self-preservation is often invisibility: people operate according to a set of codes between the legal, the demands and pressures of the quotidian and the limits of what is permissible.[3] We attempt to suspend a series of curtains from the newly built structures on the balcony of the first floor of the Medical Arts, acting to both cover and reveal them. The curtains propose an inversion, making the exterior of street, the channel between the buildings, into a passage, a reflection of the passage of goods, bodies and information. The work proves almost impossible to do, a process of delays, returns, evasions, renegotiations with the owners of the future restaurant. People are friendly, polite but cautious. The passage becomes a metaphor for our navigation of the labyrinthine corridors of the building itself, the rows of shops, the staircase and elevator shaft to the higher floors, where goods are stored behind locked doors. It is a passage with no point of entry, a movement through, revealing only a series of transactions.[4]

4.   *Arrive at 9, to call the owner who had promised to be there. Says to call his brother (partner) because he's presently not in the building. His brother will open up. The brother refuses on the grounds of 'problems', which have to do with the interrupted building process of the future restaurant. An obstruction. Walking up to the seventh floor, each person who we come across asks what we are looking for. I cannot hang anything inside, in a building as busy as this one. Here, there are no forgotten spaces, every corner is being used.*

5.   The Medical Arts is not unique, like the other buildings within these four blocks of the city, it is a mixture of restaurants, tradi-tional coffee shops, souvenir shops, hair salons and Internet cafés, and retail shops selling goods mass produced in China. In every restaurant there are flat screens displaying CNN, BBC, Al Jazeera, music television, sport, American talk shows, never local programming. Next to this, an image of Addis Ababa, with a superimposed highway intersection. An elsewhere is always present. Most people who trade here do not live in the inner city; they seek the apparent safety and quiet of the suburbs. Chinese stock is bought from massive warehouses, with names like Dragon City, situated outside of the city in an area called Crown Mines. In another shop, montage images are sold. They present fictional landscapes, made in Egypt, with no actual coordinates. They are piled in stacks amongst a stock of clocks, lights, T-shirts and bags with fashion house labels, and flags for the 2010 World Cup.

6.   *I forgot to mention that they hung proper curtains the day after I hung the ones over the balcony.*

---

1   We work with N.M., a trader originally from Ethiopia, asking him a set of questions about the economies, both visible and invisible, that define the Ethiopian and Eritrean community trading in this building and area. We are not only interested in the constant movement of goods, but also of people, of bodies between buildings, cities, countries across the continent, from Johannesburg to Addis Ababa from China to Africa.

2   Notes (by N.M.) in response to questions regarding the quantity, type and location of shops in the Medical Arts Building, as well as origin and movement of shop owners. The Medical Arts or Majesty Wholesale forms one of several adjacent buildings occupied by Ethiopian and Eritrean traders: Jo'burg and Africa Mall, Nadiba, Panama, Delvers Square, Johannesburg Wholesale Centre 1 (former Medical Centre) and Johannesburg Wholesale Centre 2.

3   While South African immigration law grants asylum to refugees from the continent, the process for receiving formal refugee status, which allows for trade, employment and permanent residence is notoriously corrupt and inconsistent. The interminable waiting period for interviews for refugee status coupled with the requirement that asylum seeker status be continually renewed (every two to three months), puts most immigrants' legality under continual threat, at the mercy of officials demanding bribes and police authorities patrolling the streets, asking at random for identity documents.

4   There is an economy of information, it is brokered and traded, in the same invisible networks that ensure the movement of goods, people. This includes our own passage.

Untitled – The Year 2010

SABELO MLANGENI

Sabelo Mlangeni discovered the medium of photography when he was working as a street photographer. In his work, Mlangeni shows the city and its inhabitants in unobserved moments in their everyday life – at night, in private rooms, in their ordinary routines. His series builds on the intimacy of the encounter between the subject and photographer. In *Untitled – The Year 2010,* created in June/July 2010 for *Afropolis,* Mlangeni captures quiet moments away from and after the turmoil and excitement of the World Cup.

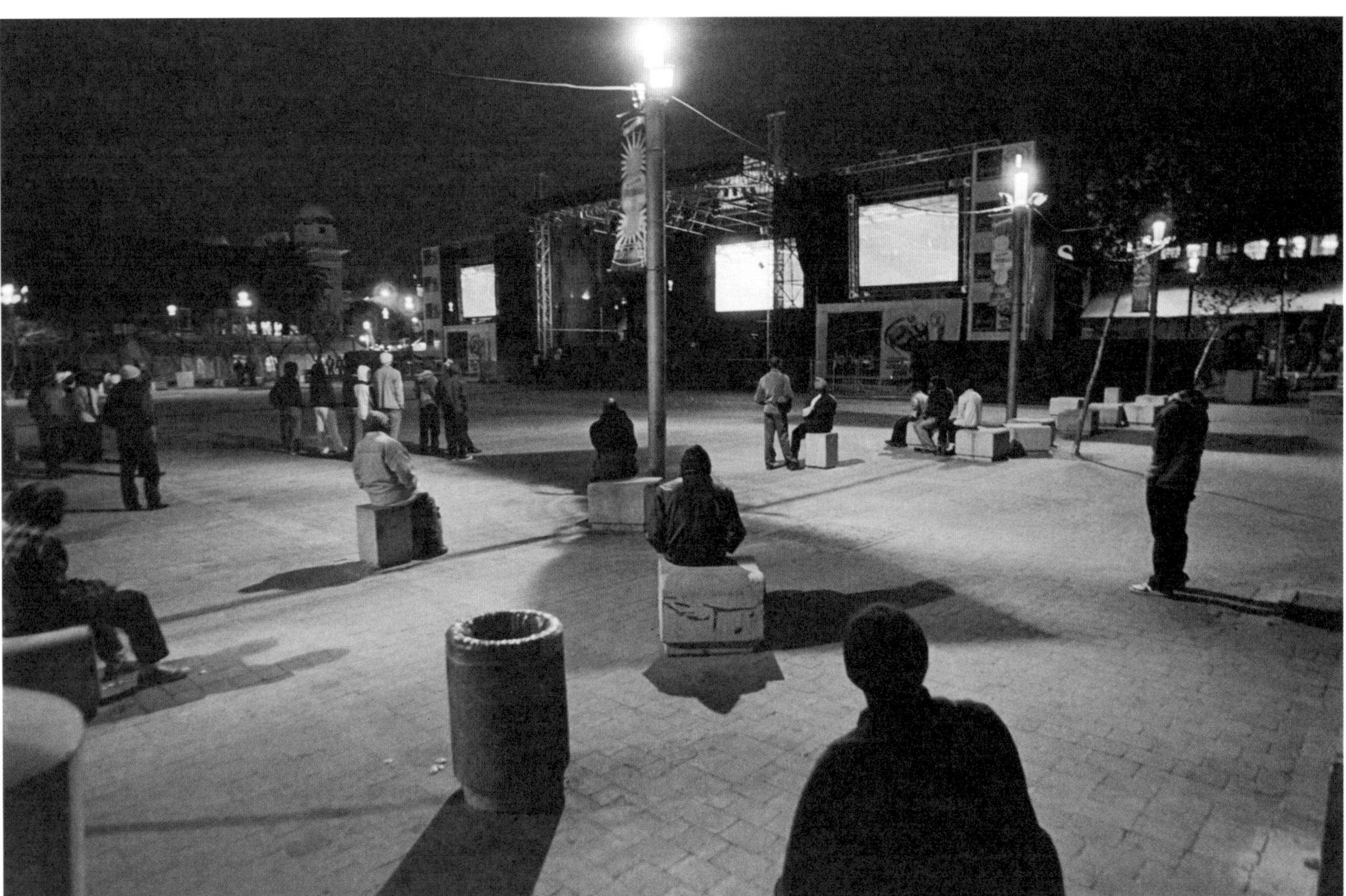

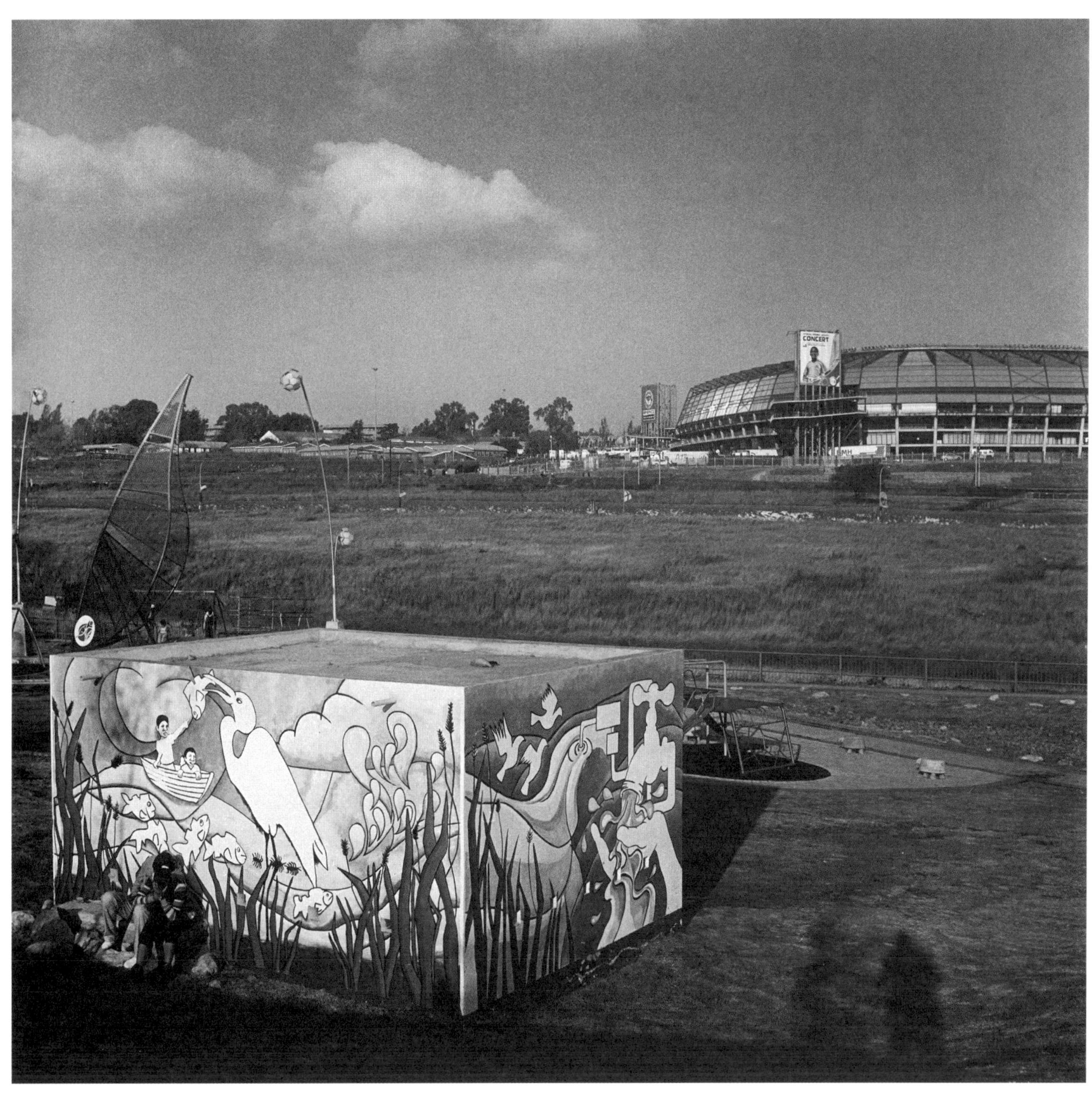

Authors

David Adjaye, born in Dar es Salaam in 1966, studied architecture at the Royal College of Art in London and opened his own architectural practice in 1994. In 2002, he founded Adjaye Associates, with offices in Berlin and New York. Adjaye Associates has won a wide range of commissions, including such prestigious projects as *Electra House* (2000, London) and the *Idea Store Whitechapel* (2005, London). Informed by his own biography and in search of alternative concepts and patterns of urbanity, David Adjaye has photographed and documented key cities in Africa, primarily focusing on the informal structures of the built environment.

Anthea Buys is a freelance curator and author based in Johannesburg. Her articles regularly appear in South African newspapers and journals such as the *Mail & Guardian* and *Art South Africa,* and include a quarterly column on contemporary art. As a research fellow in the Research Centre Visual Identities in Art and Design, University of Johannesburg, her work addresses and explores curatorial practice in South Africa.

Hany Darwish, born in Cairo in 1974, is a journalist and literary critic. He regularly contributes to the arts pages of *Al-mus-taqbal,* a Lebanese weekly, and the daily Pan-Arab newspaper *Al-Hayat* published in London.

Filip De Boeck is the coordinator of the Institute for Anthropological Research in Africa (IARA), University of Leuven, and is actively involved in teaching, promoting, coordinating and supervising research in and on Africa. For over twenty years, he has been conducting extensive field research in the Democratic Republic of the Congo. His research fields over the recent years have focused on youth and the politics of culture, as well as the cultural transformation of urban landscapes in central Africa. He has published extensively in works including: *Kinshasa. Tales of the Invisible City* (2004), a joint project with photographer Marie-Françoise Plissart, and *Makers and Breakers. Children and Youth in Postcolonial Africa* (2005), edited by Alcinda Honwana. Together with architect and critic Koen Van Synghel, Filip De Boeck has also curated numerous exhibitions. In 2009, he directed *Cemetery State,* a documentary on the politics of death in a graveyard in Kinshasa.

Denis Ekpo is the coordinator of the Comparative Literature Programme, University of Port Harcourt, Nigeria. He has published widely on postcolonial thought, literature and art. He is a member of *Third Text's* Advisory Council and was guest editor of the special issue *Beyond Négritude* (2010). His most important publications include *Neither Anti-imperialist Anger nor the Tears of the Good White Man* and *La philosophie et la littérature Africaine.*

Leora Farber is an artist and director of the Research Centre Visual Identities in Art and Design, University of Johannesburg. She has published widely in such scholarly journals as *Critical Arts, Cultural Politics, N. Paradoxa* and *De Arte,* and is the recipient of numerous funding awards from organisations including the National Research Foundation of South Africa. At present, she is registered for a practice-based Ph.D. in Visual Art at the University of Pretoria. Leora Farber has shown her art works nationally and internationally since 1993, and they are part of various private and public South African collections.

Larissa Förster is a research associate at the Morphomata International Center for Advanced Studies / Genesis, Dynamics and Mediality of Cultural Figurations, University of Cologne. Her doctoral thesis was published in 2010 as *Postkoloniale Erinnerungslandschaften. Wie Deutsche und Herero in Namibia des Kriegs von 1904 gedenken* (Postcolonial landscapes of memory. How Germans and Hereros in Namibia commemorate the war of 1904). She has spent long periods in Namibia and South Africa for her research, which focuses primarily on museum studies, visual and material culture, and the history and cultures of remembrance in southern Africa. She also co-curated the exhibition *Namibia – Deutschland: eine geteilte Geschichte: Widerstand, Gewalt, Erinnerung* shown in the Rautenstrauch-Joest-Museum in Cologne and the Deutsches Historisches Museum in Berlin (2004/2005).

Regina Göckede studied art history, modern history, political science and archaeology in Münster and Bochum, and holds a doctorate in Art History. From 2003 to autumn 2005, she was an intern at the Jewish Museum Berlin and museum assistant at the Staatliche Museen zu Berlin. In October 2005, she was appointed assistant professor in the Art History Department at the Brandenburg University of Technology in Cottbus. Since 2008, she has been leading the project *Neues Bauen in der Fremde* at the university funded by the German Research Foundation (DFG). Her research interests include the late-colonial globalisation of architectural modernity, which she is researching for her postdoctoral thesis.

Charles Didier Gondola is a professor of African History and Africana Studies at Indiana University-Purdue University, Indianapolis. He has published numerous articles on popular cultures (music, fashion, gambling and memory), gender and postcolonial issues in Central Africa, and the African diaspora in France. His latest book *Africanisme: La Crise d'une Illusion* (2007) examines links between African studies in France and French policies in Africa. Charles Didier Gondola is also the co-editor (with Charles Tshimanga and Peter Bloom) of *Frenchness and the African Diaspora: Identity and Uprising in Contemporary France* (2009).

Marie-Hélène Gutberlet grew up in West Germany, Benin and Switzerland, and studied art history, philosophy and theatre, film and TV studies in Frankfurt/Main and Basel. She is currently a member of the academic staff at the Institute for Theatre, Film and Media Studies, Goethe-Universität Frankfurt/Main. Her doctoral thesis appeared in 2004 entitled *Auf Reisen – Afrikanisches Kino* (African Cinema on the Road). She has published widely in her field, and curated film series and programmes on such topics as African cinema and diaspora, cities and everyday culture, experimental and avant-garde films (including the *Reel to Real* experimental film series at Künstlerhaus Mousonturm Frankfurt/Main from 2003 to 2009) and exhibitions (Bamako 2011; Johannesburg/Capetown 2011).

Christian Hanussek, born in Frankfurt/Main in 1953, is an artist, author and curator currently based in Berlin. He studied art and art theory at the Städelschule in Frankfurt and at ateliers 63 in Haarlem (NL). His art often combines three-dimensional painting with film and video, and his works include a number of permanent installations. Since 2001, he has published a series of articles on art from Africa. In 2005/2006, he curated the project *Gleichzeitig in Africa …* with exhibitions, seminars and discussions in several German cities.

Manuel Herz is an architect with offices in Basel and Cologne whose completed projects include the recently constructed Jewish Community Center in Mainz. After studying at RWTH Aachen and the Architectural Association in London, and teaching at the Bartlett School of Architecture, London, the Berlage Institute, Rotterdam and the Harvard Graduate School of Design, he currently heads teaching and research at ETH Studio Basel–Institute of the Contemporary City, together with Jacques Herzog and Pierre de Meuron. Manuel Herz's research and writings focus on the themes of diaspora, migration and architecture.

Thomas G. Kirsch received his doctorate in Anthropology from the European University Viadrina in Frankfurt / Oder. After teaching at the Institute of Anthropology and Philosophy in Halle / Saale, he was appointed to the Department of Anthropology at Goldsmiths College, University of London. Since September 2009, Thomas G. Kirsch has held the new professorial chair of Social and Cultural Anthropology at the University of Konstanz. His research focuses on criminality and crime prevention in urban South Africa.

Matthias Krings is a professor of Anthropology and Popular Culture in Africa at Mainz University. Before his appointment, he was a research fellow at the universities of Cologne and Frankfurt / Main, and conducted field research in Nigeria and Tanzania. His publications primarily focus on film and video in Africa, as well as on religion and media. He currently heads a DFG-funded project on the process of negotiating culture in music and video in Tanzania, and is preparing a book on the appropriation of foreign media formats in Africa.

Dominique Malaquais is a researcher, author and publisher (*Politique Africaine, Chimurenga Magazine*) whose work concentrates on urban cultures, political and economic violence, and creative involvement in African cities. She is a senior researcher at the *Centre d'Etudes des Mondes Africains*, C.N.R.S. in Paris, and director, together with artist / activist Kadiatou Diallo, of SPARCK (Space for Pan-African Research, Creation and Knowledge – The Africa Centre, Cape Town, South Africa). Dominique Malaquais is currently Sheila Biddle Ford Foundation Fellow at the W.E.B. Du Bois Institute for African and African American Research, Harvard University, and preparing a book on the 1974 'Rumble in the Jungle' in Kinshasa.

Noor Nieftagodien is a senior lecturer in the History Department, University of the Witwatersrand, Johannesburg. He serves as deputy chair of the History Workshop, heads the *Local Histories – Present Realities* research programme, and is on the board of the South African History Archives. His research interests are specifically directed to township histories, civil rights movements and local authorities. Noor Nieftagodien has co-authored *Kathorus – A History* (2001) and *Alexandra – A History* (2008), and published popular histories on the Johannesburg Townships of Orlando West and Ekurhuleni. He is currently researching into the Vaal Triangle, and the Chemical, Electricity, Paper, Plastic and Allied Workers' Union.

Sarah Nuttall is a professor of Literature and Cultural Studies at the Wits Institute for Social and Economic Research (WISER) in Johannesburg. She is the author of *Entanglement: Literary and Cultural Reflections on Post-Apartheid* (2009), editor of *Beautiful/Ugly: African and Diasporic Aesthetics* (2004) and has co-edited *Johannesburg – The Elusive Metropolis* (2008) as well as *Load Shedding: Writing On and Over the Edge of South Africa* (2007).

Tom Odhiambo is a lecturer in the Department of Literature, University of Nairobi. He completed his doctorate in Cultural Studies and Literature at the University of the Witwatersrand, Johannesburg, and taught there between 2003 and 2007. His research interests focus on literature, popular culture and the media.

Edgar Pieterse holds the South African Chair in Urban Policy, and is director of the African Centre for Cities, University of Cape Town. His current publications include *Counter-Currents: Experiments in Sustainability in the Cape Town Region* (2010), *The African Cities Reader* (2010) and *City Futures: Confronting the Crisis of Urban Development* (2008) (see www.africancentreforcities.net). Edgar Pieterse also serves on the advisory board of the prestigious international exhibition project *Critical Mass: Design and Urbanization* (Smithsonian Cooper Hewitt, National Design Museum).

Kerstin Pinther is a professor for African Art at the Department of Art History, Freie Universität Berlin. Until early 2010, she was a research associate at Goethe University Frankfurt / Main. Within her general research fields of photography and visual cultures in West Africa, she is presently focusing on architecture and urbanity in Africa, and on specific issues related to Africa's contemporary art and cultural production in a global context. Her most recent publication is *Wege durch Accra. Stadtbilder, Praxen und Diskurse* (2010). Kerstin Pinther curated the exhibition *Black Paris. Kunst und Geschichte einer schwarzen Diaspora* (2006). She has spent periods of research in Accra, Paris, Lagos and Cairo.

Peter Probst is a professor of African Art and Visual Culture and fellow at the Center for the Humanities, Tufts University, Boston. He has published widely in his research fields, addressing issues of mediality, identity and collective memory in the arts in western and southern Africa. His latest book *Osogbo and the Art of Heritage. Monuments, Deities, and Money* (2011) is based on extensive field research into the politics of art and the art of heritage in Nigeria.

Deyssi Rodriguez-Torres is a political scientist and professor at the Catholic University of Mons, Belgium. She has published widely in her research fields focusing specifically on Kenya and generally on East Africa, and addressing the issues of adolescent violence and delinquency, socio-political dislocations and styles of survival in the urban milieus in Africa.

Naomi Roux was born in and is based in Johannesburg. After completing an M.A. in Fine Arts and Heritage Studies at the Wits School of the Arts, Johannesburg, she is presently a researcher at the Centre for Urbanism and Built Environment Studies, University of the Witwatersrand. Her research interests focus on public history, urban transformation and the policies of memory.

Hannah le Roux is an architect and senior lecturer at the University of the Witwatersrand, Johannesburg. She teaches, practises, curates and writes on architecture. At present, she is completing her doctoral thesis *Lived Modernism* to be presented at the Institute for Practice-Based Research in the Arts in Belgium. In her thesis, she addresses the changes in modernist spaces, and drafts and maps design practices capable of being catalysts for the social appropriation of space. Hannah le Roux's works have focused on Johannesburg's downtown area, West Africa and migrant spaces in Europe.

Viola Shafik is a freelance filmmaker, curator and film scholar. After completing her doctorate in Islamic Studies at Hamburg University, she has published numerous books and articles, primarily on Arab cinema and culture, as well as on transnational filmmakers. Apart from lecturing at the American University of Cairo, Viola Shafik has worked for national and international festivals, and is a member of several film commissions, including the Berlinale World Cinema Fund. She has also directed experimental and documentary films, including *Shajarat al-laymun/The Lemon Tree* (1993). Viola Shafik lives in Cairo and Berlin.

Bisi Silva is a freelance curator and founding director of the Centre for Contemporary Art (CCA) Lagos, an arts venue set up in 2007. As CCA Director, she has curated, for example, *Fela, Ghariokwu Lemi and The Art of the Album Cover* (2007), *Ndidi Dike, Waka-into-bondage: The Last ¾ Mile* (2008) and *George Osodi, Paradise Lost: Revisiting the Niger Delta* (2008). Bisi Silva has also co-curated *Dak'Art Biennale de l'Art Africain Contemporain* (2006), *Contact Zone: Contemporary Art from West and North Africa* (National Museum of Mali, 2007) and the *2nd Thessaloniki Biennale of Contemporary Art* (Greece, 2008).

AbdouMaliq Simone is currently a professor of Sociology at Goldsmiths College, University of London, and an urbanist in a very broad sense of the word. His work addresses the constitution of power relations, cultural forms of expression, governance and urban planning discourses, and space and time in the world's cities. Aside from teaching at a number of universities, he has worked for various NGOs in Africa as well as municipal and regional institutions, including the Council for the Development of Social Science Research in Africa and the United Nations Centre for Human Settlements. His major publications include *For the City Yet to Come: Changing Urban Life in Four African Cities* (2004) and *City Life from Jakarta to Dakar: Movements at the Crossroads* (2009).

Gary Stewart is the author of two books on African music: *Rumba on the River: A History of the Popular Music of the Two Congos* (2000) and *Breakout: Profiles in African Rhythm* (1992). Together with John Amman, he has also published *Black Man's Grave* (2007), a chronicle of Sierra Leone's civil war. Aside from his many articles and book contributions, he has written numerous entries for the *The New Grove Dictionary of Music and Musicians* as well as many liner notes for LPs and CDs. He lives near Washington D.C. in the USA.

Mbugua wa Mungai teaches in the Department of Literature, Kenyatta University, Nairobi. In 2005, he presented his doctoral thesis on folklore at the Hebrew University in Jerusalem, Israel. His research interests include Kenyan popular culture, urban folklore, disability in culture, and contemporary theatre, and he has published a range of articles in these areas.

Akram Zaatari is an artist living and working in Beirut. As co-founder of the Arab Image Foundation, he has investigated photographic practices in the Middle East, examining in particular how far photography has been used to influence aesthetic, moral and social ideas. He interviewed Van Leo in Cairo in 1998, and took their discussion as the basis for his 2001 video *Her + Him Van Leo*. Since 1999, his research has focused on the archive of the Studio Shehrazade in Saida, Lebanon. In this project, Zaatari analyses, indexes and presents the work of the photographer Hashem el Madani to create a catalogue of social relations and photographic practices.

Artists

Akinbode Akinbiyi was born in Oxford in 1946 of Nigerian parents, and attended school and university in Nigeria, England and Germany. He has been a freelance photographer since 1977. Akinbiyi is co-founder of the UMZANZSI cultural centre in Clermont Township, Durban, South Africa. For some years his publications have explored and documented the four largest cities in Africa: Lagos, Nairobi, Kinshasa and Johannesburg. Aside from his work as a photographer, Akinbode Akinbiyi has also curated numerous exhibitions. He lives and works in Berlin.

Lara Baladi, born in 1969 of Lebanese-Egyptian origin, is a multidisciplinary artist working in a range of media and formats. The diversity of her artistic repertory reflects her attempt to break down the borders of traditional photography. Lara Baladi's œuvre embraces prints, montage, installations, architectural constructions, embroideries and carpets, videos and even perfumes. At the Cairo Biennale in 2008/09, she was awarded the Grand Nile Prize. Lara Baladi is represented by the Townhouse Gallery of Contemporary Art, Cairo and Gallery Isabelle van den Eynde, Dubai.

Pume Bylex, born in the Democratic Republic of the Congo in 1968, lives and works in Kinshasa. In his art, he combines drawings, costumes, models and furniture to create his own universe where he is simultaneously researcher, inventor of ideas and artist, conducting an almost scientific investigation into the intangible rules and processes of the world. Bylex is not interested in the everyday realities of Kinshasa, but focuses on what lies beyond the horizon of the visible.

Deadheat is the artist duo of **Dorothee Kreutzfeldt** and **Bettina Malcomess**. Dorothee Kreutzfeldt lives and works in Johannesburg. Her work comprises painting and collaborative projects, often set in particular urban spaces, addressing their specific socio-political context. Bettina Malcomess lives and works in Cape Town. She is a writer, teacher and curator as well as, under the name of Anne Historical, a performance and installation artist. The cooperation between Kreutzfeld and Malcomess resonates with their interests in spatial practices, whether in public, urban or gallery space. At present, they are writing a book on Johannesburg entitled *Not No Place.*

Members of the **Department of Architecture and Urban Planning UGent**:
Luce Beeckmans is a doctoral candidate at Groningen University, preparing her thesis on the urban planning history of the three African cities of Kinshasa, Dar es Salaam and Dakar from a comparative perspective. She has published articles in such scholarly journals as *Afrika Focus, Stadsgeschiedenis, Hagar* and *OASE.*
Guy Châtel is a practising architect (general planner) and associate professor in Architectural Sciences and Design at Ghent University. He has published widely on architecture and the visual arts in books and magazines, and designed the exhibition display for *Piranesi. The Collection of Drawings of Ghent University* (Museum of Fine Arts, Ghent, Autumn 2008).
Johan Lagae is associate professor in Architectural History at Ghent University. His research focuses on colonial/postcolonial architecture and planning in central Africa, as well as buildings as a colonial legacy. His most recent publications are *Kinshasa. Architecture et Paysage Urbains* (2010, together with Bernard Toulier and Marc Gemoets) and the catalogue *Congo belge en images* (with Carl De Keyzer, 2010).

Hala Elkoussy, born in 1974, studied at the American University of Cairo and Goldsmiths College, University of London. From 2002 to 2003, she lectured on photography at the American University of Cairo. Together with other artists, she co-founded the Contemporary Image Collective in Cairo in 2004. From 2004 to 2006, she was resident artist at the Royal Academy of Visual Arts in Amsterdam. Most recently, her works have been exhibited at the Stedelijk Museum in Amsterdam, Göteborg Konsthall in Göteborg, the 9th Sharjah Biennale in the United Arab Emirates, Kunsternes Hus in Oslo, the Istanbul Biennale and the Townhouse Gallery of Contemporary Art, Cairo.

Hawa Essuman, born in Hamburg, discovered a love of telling stories early in her life – but only pursued it much later. She performed on stage in various plays before she found her way into the world of production. After working on TV commercials and documentary films, she was finally able to direct a Kenyan TV drama series. Her debut as a film actor was in *Project Daddy* (2004) and the Italian film *Piano Solo* (2007). In 2009, she directed two one-hour films: *Selfish* and *The Lift.* Her latest film *Soul Boy* was premiered at the Göteborg Film Festival. At present, she is working on a new screenplay for a feature film.

Ismail Farouk is an artist and urban geographer. His work explores creative responses to issues in social, racial, political and economic justice. Ismail Farouk is presently employed as a research officer at the African Centre for Cities, University of Cape Town, where he coordinates the Central Citylab.

Constanze Fischbeck, born in Berlin in 1968, works as a freelance set designer and video artist. In her video works, she explores the intersection between documentary and staged moments in the context of an urban environment. Since 2001, she has developed a series of video works and installations investigating the function of society in such diverse cities as Magdeburg, Berlin, São Paulo, Sarajevo, Lagos and Tehran. Her work *Benzin. A Reconstruction of Exchange Systems in Lagos* (2008–2009) has been shown in the Goethe-Institut in Lagos and at the Haus der Kulturen der Welt in Berlin.

Ganzeer started to work as a professional graphic designer in 2003. Since 2005, he has been running the *Ganzeer. Experimental Arts Unit* graphic studio and compiling his *Ganzeer* Internet blog. With the launch of *Shakloh,* a monthly electronic magazine, he established a platform for Arab artists working in the fields of painting, graphic design and photography; however, the project had to cease publication after only eight issues. Ganzeer himself experiments with contemporary Arabic fonts and a mix of Arab and Latin typefaces.

Mandy Gehrt, born in Gera in 1977, graduated in Art Education and German from the University of Leipzig before moving to Oslo to study Printmaking. Since 2009, she has been studying Media Art at the Leipzig Academy of Visual Arts (HGB). She has received numerous funding awards for her work from, for example, the International Studio Programme of the ACC Galerie Weimar and the City of Weimar (2005), the Institut für Auslandsbeziehungen in Stuttgart, and the Townhouse Gallery for Contemporary Art in Cairo (2007). Mandy Gehrt has shown her works in a range of exhibitions including *Die Kultur der Angst* (2006, Leipzig/Weimar), *Czech-point* (2006, Prague), *Absent Without Leave* (2006, International Biennial of Young Artists, Bucharest), *Erbstücke* (2007, Ahrenshoop) and *PhotoCairo4* (2008, Cairo).

Sam Hopkins initially studied History and Spanish before taking a postgraduate degree in Contemporary Art. His work responds to the social and political context around him by investigating places of memory, experimenting with models of participatory practice, and analysing how public space is produced. After living, working and studying in Europe, he is currently based in Nairobi where he coordinates Slum-TV, a grassroots media initiative which he founded in 2006 together with Alexander Nikolic and Lukas Pusch.

Laura Horelli, born in Helsinki in 1976, lives and works in Berlin. Her works explore the intersection and overlapping of the private and public spheres. Over the last years, she has been working with a range of documentary video forms, often together with other filmmakers. Since 2000, her works have been shown in numerous international exhibitions, including the Venice Biennale (2001 and 2009), Manifesta 5, Donostia, San Sebastian, Spain (2004). She has also held solo shows in, for example, the Galerie im Taxispalais, Innsbruck (2004) and Galerie Barbara Weiss, Berlin (2003, 2007).

Chris King is a filmmaker, born in Australia and raised in Africa.

Daniel Kötter is a director and video artist with a special interest in multi-channel video installations and alternative concert formats. He has been living and working in Berlin since 1996. His works explore and oscillate between different media and institutional contexts, combining techniques of structuralist experimental film with documentary and spatial elements. His video installations have been shown at festivals and venues including the CCA Ujazdowski Castle in Warsaw, Haus der Kulturen der Welt in Berlin, atelier Frankfurt, Kunstfilmbiennale Cologne, Kunstfilmtag Düsseldorf, Rencontres Internationales Paris/Madrid/Berlin, the Museo de la Ciudad Queretaro, alterna y corriente Mexico DF, and St Marks Church, New York. Together with Constanze Fischbeck, he developed and realised the project *state-theatre # 1 LAGOS*.

TJ Lemon's career began when Nelson Mandela was released in 1990. As a press photographer, his work documented how South Africans joyously embraced the new democracy, yet simultaneously struggled to reorganise society after the end of apartheid. For fifteen years, he was chief photographer of the *Sunday Independent Newspaper* in Johannesburg, and taught photojournalism at the Market Theatre Photography Workshop. TJ Lemon's works have been shown in the USA, France, Spain and South Africa, and he has received numerous awards for his photographic essays and text coverage. Since June 2010, he has been working as a freelance photographer and teaching young photojournalists.

Salifou Lindou was born in Foumban, Cameroon, in 1965 and now lives in Douala. He works primarily in the media of painting, sculpture, installation and video. Aside from his works on canvas, he uses sheets of iron to convey his vision of an urban machine. Some of his installations feature cars or motorbikes with the surfaces ground down to give them a metallic shine. He is a member of the Cercle Kapsiki Collective, founded in 1998 in Douala, which has organised such public space artistic interventions as *Hors les Murs* (Douala 1998) and *Scénographies Urbaines* (Strasbourg 2000, Douala 2002/2003 and Alexandria 2004).

Kgafela oa Magogodi is known for his work as a stand-up poet and spoken-word theatre director. He is a prolific producer of poems, short stories, essays, audio recordings and live shows. Kgafela oa Magogodi has taught at the African Literature Department and at the Wits School of Arts in Johannesburg, and is currently teaching Literature at the English Department of the North West University in Mafikeng.

Charles Njoroge Matathia is an author and social scientist living in Nairobi (http://theblackcampaign.org).

Masai Mbili Artists' Collective:
Otieno Gomba was born in Nairobi in 1974 and grew up there. He left school in 1994 hoping to study Graphic Design, but could not afford the fees. After getting to know a signwriter and learning the basics, he then set himself up as a largely self-taught signwriter in Kibera. Together with Otieno Kota, he founded the Masai Mbili (Two Masai) Artists' Collective in 2001. In the meantime, the collective has gained an

international reputation. Otieno Gomba's art primarily focuses on the medium of painting and sculpture, and the workshops he gives in this area include social work projects in Kibera. He has also participated in international art projects, usually on art in public spaces, in, for example, Austria and Sweden.

George "Ashif" Malamba, born in Nairobi in 1972, works in acrylic on canvas and with murals. He joined the Masai Mbili Collective in 2003 and has participated in numerous local and international workshops. Most recently, his works have been shown in Nairobi at venues including the International School of Kenya, Godown Arts Centre, Ramoma Gallery and the Kuona Trust, and internationally at exhibitions in Austria, Norway, Sweden and Italy. George "Ashif" Malamba has also been involved in social work projects, primarily with children in Kibera. After the unrest and violence in Kenya after the elections in 2007/2008, he launched a peace project as a therapeutic process of reconciliation.

Mbuthia Maina, aka "Mbumai", has been part of Nairobi's art scene for more than fifteen years, working in a wide range of materials from painting, sculpture and print to video, digital photography, installation and murals. From 1997 to 2003, he studied at the Kuona Trust's Art Studios at the National Museums of Kenya, where he also trained as a curator. Mbumai has participated in art workshops and held residencies in Kenya, UK and Uganda, and his works have been exhibited both in Kenya and internationally in, for instance, the UK, Sweden, Austria, the USA, Australia, and Uganda. In 2002, he was chosen to represent East Africa at the Liverpool Biennial. At present, he is involved in the arts programme for children in Kibera.

Otieno Rabala was born in the Homa Bay District, Nyanza Province, Kenya, in 1969 and grew up in the home of the artist Samson Raballa. Later, he worked as a security guard at Gallery Watatu, Nairobi's best known gallery, before intensively developing his own paintings. He is presently working in Kibera together with ten other artists in the Masai Mbili Collective. The Collective not only provides an opportunity for the artists to develop their own work, but is also active in teaching art to children and young people in the district.

Kevin Irungu was born in Kibera in 1987, and grew up there. He started painting in late 2004 at the Masai Mbili studio. Since then, he has participated in workshops with local and international artists including Bili Bidjocka, Simon Njami and Andrew

Tshabangu, and has exhibited widely, both in Kenya and abroad.

Méga Mingiedi, born in 1976 in Zaire, in the present-day Democratic Republic of the Congo, lives and works in Kinshasa. After studying sculpture at the Academy of Fine Arts (Académie des Beaux-arts) in Kinshasa, he received a scholarship to attend the École Supérieure des Arts décoratifs in Strasbourg. His *Kinshasa Wenze Wenze* installation launched his approach to artistic research, which he often conducts as part of the Eza Possibles Collective. Since 1997, Méga Mingiedi has been working with visual urban cartographies, creating imaginary cities that address real problems of geographic and social space. He has participated in numerous local and international projects.

Jyoti Mistry is a filmmaker, lecturer, and Head of Television at the Wits School of Arts, University of the Witwatersrand, Johannesburg. She has taught at New York University, the University of Vienna, and Arcada University in Helsinki. Her filmography includes short films, documentaries and installations. Her research interests focus on cultural policy, questions of identity and multiculturalism. Jyoti Mistry is also active as a photographer and film curator. Her most recent film *Le Bœuf sur le Toit* was premiered at the Durban International Film Festival and is part of a new installation project.

Sabelo Mlangeni was born in Driefontein, Mpumalanga in 1980. In 2001 he moved to Johannesburg and joined the Market Photo Workshop, graduating in 2004. He was the recipient of the Edward Ruiz Mentorship Award in 2006 and the Tollman Award for the Visual Arts in 2009. *Invisible Women,* his first solo show, was held in 2007 at the Warren Siebrits Gallery in Johannesburg. His *Men Only, At Home* and *Country Girls* series were shown in the Michael Stevenson Gallery in Cape Town (2009/2010) and the Brodie/Stevenson Gallery, Johannesburg (2010). His works have been shown in group exhibitions in Johannesburg, Graz and Berlin.

Mowoso is a multidisciplinary collective founded in 2006 centred in and around Kinshasa. The collective comprises artists and scholars whose projects explore the collision of physical and virtual worlds.
Dikoko Boketshu is President of the Mowoso Collective. After spending his early childhood in the Equateur province, he grew up in Ngbaka, a vibrant neighbourhood in the heart of Kinshasa. He developed his work in the contemporary media of video, music and dance as present or emerging in the *cités* and 'ghettos' of the Democratic Republic of the Congo, at places where art and life necessarily meet and merge.
Eléonore Hellio, co-founder of the Mowoso Collective, is a pioneer in France in the art of developing open systems employing network technologies. She utilises her experience with subcultures and countercultures and her involvement in the Urban Games project to question the impact of digital globalisation and the processes of assimilation and resistance pervading complex postcolonial realties.
Bienvenue Nanga is a visual artist who lives and works in Kinshasa. In his sculptures, he creates spaceships, robots and extraterrestrial villages from materials which he finds on the city streets. His worlds reflect the tensions and distances lying between modern machines and the socio-economic realities of the Democratic Republic of the Congo.

Rana El Nemr, born in 1974, studied photojournalism, advertising and art at the American University of Cairo. Her works have been exhibited in Egypt, Beirut, Switzerland, Germany, Japan, Finland and the USA, and include *Metro* shown at the Townhouse Gallery of Contemporary Art in Cairo, *Coastline* at Gallery Image in Arhaus (Denmark), *Telekinesis,* shown as part of Lumo/International Photography Triennial in Jyväskylä (Finland) and *The Olympic Garden* in 2008. Rana El Nemr has won numerous awards for her work including a prize at the Nile Salon Photographic Exhibition in Egypt (2003) and the Grand Prix at the Bamako Biennial (2005). She has also been nominated twice for the Paul Huf Young Photographer of the Year Award (2007 and 2009).

Sam Nhlengethwa was born in 1955 in Payneville, Springs, a mining community east of Johannesburg, and grew up in a family of jazz lovers. From 1977 to 1978, he studied at the Rorke's Drift Art Centre in Natal, and in 1994 won the Standard Bank Young Artist Award. He has taught at the Fuba School of Dramatic and Visual Arts in Johannesburg and the College of DuPage in Chicago, and conducted workshops for the Gerard Sekoto Foundation, MTN Art Institute and Vaal Technikon. His works have been bought by South African and international collections. At present, Sam Nhlengethwa is focusing on collage.

Cédrick Nzolo, born in Kinshasa in 1985, graduated in 2008 from the École Supérieure des Arts décoratifs in Strasbourg. In his work as a photographer, he primarily explores scenes of everyday life on Kinshasa's night-time streets. As a designer, he has created various street furniture projects, regarding himself as a social actor at the service of those living under difficult conditions. He develops simple and pragmatic solutions for lamps and seats in public space that encourage encounters, exchanges and communal use.

Emeka Ogboh, born in 1977, is a Nigerian media artist. In his work, he applies a range of approaches to investigate the aural infrastructure of cities, in particular in his hometown of Lagos. He seeks to initiate a constructive dialogue between, on the one hand, the materiality of a city and, on the other, the imagined and imaginary city. In his view, the architecture of the megacity Lagos opens up questions about cultural narcissism, 'third world' mobility and globalisation processes. Emeka Ogboh is the co-founder of the Video Art Network Lagos, and a member of the African Centre for Cities project on African Urbanism and the Locus Sonus International streaming project. He has participated in media workshops and exhibits both in Nigeria and internationally including, for example, at the Venice Biennial as part of the *One Minutes Train* series.

Uche Okpa-Iroha was born in Enugu, Enugu State, Nigeria in 1972, and now lives in Lagos. He started working with photography in 2004, seeking to heighten the awareness among politicians and the broad general public for those topics which impact the local population and the environment. Uche Okpa-Iroha is a founder member of the Blackbox Photography Collective. His works have been shown in numerous exhibitions in Nigeria and internationally. Most recently, he has contributed to the book *Lagos – A City at Work*. He also regularly works as a kidney health campaigner. He was awarded the Seydou Keita Prize at the 8th Biennial for Photography in Bamako, Mali.

Kainebi Osahenye was born in Agbor, Delta State, Nigeria in 1964. He studied at the Auchi Polytechnic and Yaba College of Technology, majoring in painting in 1989. He has held several solo exhibitions and participated in numerous group exhibitions both within Nigeria and internationally. In 2004 and 2008, he was awarded residencies at the Vermont Studio

Center and the School of Visual Arts in New York. He lives and works in Lagos, and has a studio in Auchi, Edo State.

The artist duo of **Wouter Osterholt** and **Elke Uitentuis** (born in the Netherlands in 1979 and 1977) have held solo exhibitions in the Townhouse Gallery in Cairo (2009) and in the Schunck, Museum of Contemporary Art in Heerlen (2010). They participated in group exhibitions in the Mak Center in Los Angeles (2009) and at the YYZ in Toronto (2008). Most recently, Wouter Osterholt and Elke Uitentuis have been working on projects for Capacete in Rio de Janeiro and IASKA in Perth.

SADI – Solidarité des Artistes pour le Développement Intégral is an artists' collective founded in 2007 by students at the Academy of Fine Arts, Kinshasa. SADI has realised projects in different districts of the city, always in a dialogue with the local residents.

Trésor Mukonkole, born in Kinshasa in 1982, is a performance artist, sculptor and painter. He became interested in painting through Simanbote, an artist in his neighbourhood. He studied at the Academy of Fine Arts (Académie des Beaux-arts) in Kinshasa and participated in the city's *Scénographies Urbaines* project in 2006. In his current works, he creates amorphous sculptures from the old plastic bags littering Kinshasa's streets which, using his *kotumba* technique, he then fuses into a solid shape.

Alain Polo Nzuzi, born in Kinshasa in 1985, has been interested in drawing, architecture and fashion since his childhood. After graduating, he worked with different forms of installation and performance before deciding to concentrate on design and fashion, creating his own *b rela* style, a composite of "being relaxed through elegance". In his art works, he sets out to promote human dignity independent of a person's social status.

Yves Sambu is a photographer, video artist and performer. Born in Lukula in 1980, he spent some of his childhood in Brussels. He initially trained as a sculptor. In 2001, he was a founder member of the Mboka Moko theatre group in Boma. He later studied at the Academy of Fine Arts (Académie des Beaux-arts) in Kinshasa, and is currently working together with sapeurs and prostitutes in the Kintambo cemetery on *La Beauté de la Peur* (*The Beauty of Fear*), a photo and video project exploring the themes of beauty, fear and death.

Fransix Tenda, born in Kinshasa in 1984, studied painting at Kinshasa's Academy of Fine Arts (Académie des Beaux-arts). In his current project *Boule na Biso,* he uses painting and photography to explore the question of happiness in one of the city's 'hot' districts: Is happiness expensive clothes? Or owning a house? There can be no definitive answer.

Karola Schlegelmilch, born in Berlin in 1964, studied art and visual communication at the Berlin University of the Arts and Braunschweig University of Art (HBK). She completed her studies as a master-class student in 1993. Karola Schlegelmilch works as a freelance photographer, video artist and filmmaker, and her works have been shown in diverse solo and group exhibitions, and at numerous festivals. She realised projects in Iceland (1993–1996) and West Africa (2000–2006), where she made her film *Formen der Fremdheit* and developed her photo project on popular newly constructed buildings.

Magdy El Shafee was born in Libya in 1961. He first published a comic series for children in the weekly *Alaa Eddin* in 2003, and has published his comics in the liberal *El Dostoor* newspaper since 2005. In the same year, he also launched the first comics website in Arabic (www.magdy-comics.com). He has published many underground and independent works in Egypt, and was awarded the UNESCO Best African Comics Prize in 2006. His graphic novel *Metro* was his first comic for an adult audience. Released in 2008, it was banned on publication for "offending public morals" and is no longer available. Together with writer Ahmed Alaidy, he has recently completed a new comic entitled *The Parkour War.*

Slum–TV is a grassroots collective of video activists based in Mathare, Nairobi. Founded in 2007, it regularly produces a local news magazine performed on an open square in Mathare. The Slum-TV members come from Mathare and have no formal media training, but learn recording and editing techniques on the job during production. Slum-TV documents stories from Mathare and other slums, collecting them as material for an archive on the history of informal settlements.

Olakunle Tejuoso and **Weyinmi Atigbi (Watigbi)** are cultural producers from Lagos. Olakunle Tejuoso is also a publisher and music critic. He is the founder and publisher of the arts journal *Glendora Review,* owner of the Glendora bookstore and the Jazzhole music store, and produces music on the Jazzhole Records label. He originally studied Mathematics and Applied Science at the University of Wisconsin, and completed an M.Sc. in electrical engineering at New York University. Weyinmi Atigbi is a creative director, designer and photographer. He studied fine arts at the University of Ife, Ile Ife, Nigeria, and regards himself as an experimental graphic artist. Weyinmi Atigbi is the Director of the M2DC design office, and together with Tejuoso, produced the book *Lagos. A City at Work* (2005).

Emeka Udemba, born in 1968, is a visual artist, and curator for artistic interventions in public space. In 2007, his *Lagos Open* project received a special mention in the Best Art Practices awards for young curators given by the Italian Culture Department of Bolzano, South Tyrol. Emeka Udemba lives and works in Germany and Nigeria.

Minnette Vári is a video artist, and lives and works in Johannesburg. In her art, she radically de- and re-contextualises a range of text and image media. Her works employ both historical film material and performances, often integrated with a digital metamorphosis of her body, fusing it with natural landscapes or the architecture of modern cities. She has lectured extensively on such topics as identity politics, dystopic histories and the evolutions of myths. Minnette Vári took part in the 10th Biennale of Havana (2009), the Venice Biennale (2001 and 2007), and the 1997 Johannesburg Biennale. The Lucerne Museum of Art, Switzerland has dedicated a solo exhibition to her works.

Thanks to

A Abdilatif Abdalla
Mohamed Abla
Jide Adeniyi-Jones
Guy Adam Ailion
Akinbode Akinbiyi
Hesbon Alphayo
Doa Aly
Salim Amin
Olu Amoda
Peter Anders
Federica Angelucci
Jude Anogwih
David Aradeon
Christa Aretz
Zeina Arida
Weyinmi Atigbi
Jelili Atiku
Sherif El Azma
B Omar Badsha
Lara Baladi
Adé Bantu
Andrew Bell
Larissa Bender
Wolfgang Bender
Nikki Berriman
Frank Beune
Naeem Biviji
Andreas Bolten
Eckhard Breitinger
David Brodie
Antawan I. Byrd
C Boyzie Cekwana
Tom Chapman
Daron Chatz
James Chege
Linda Chernis
Clive Chipkin
Kudzanai Chiurai
Sana Chkeibane
Lisa Cloete
D Constantinos Doxiadis Archives
Sabine Cornelis
Gary Cox
Friedrich Dahlhaus
Thorsten Deckler
Mamadou Diawara
Fernandez Diaz
Ndidi Dike
Karel Dombrecht
Hauke Dorsch
Durban Art Gallery
Shiraz Durrani
E Heidi Erdmann
F Leora Farber
Marwan Fayed
Katharina Fink

John Fleetwood
G Ganzeer
Françoise Gardies
Sally Gaule
Graham Goddard
Goethe-Institut Nairobi
George Gona
Goodman Gallery
Anne Graupner
Brenden Gray
Günter Gretz
Katharina Greven
Henrike Grohs
H Khaled Hafez
Hans Peter Hahn
Marianne Halter
Grant Harris
Kay Hassan
Peter van Heerden
Stephen Hobbs
Barbara Honrath
Lindsay Hooper
Viola Hörbst
Johannes Hossfeld
Akbar Hussein
I Uche James Iroha
Shahira Issa
J Sabakinu Kivilu Jacob
Doung Jahangeer
Danda Jaroljmek
Thomas Jeffery
Davina Jogi
Janie Johnson
Hilton Judin
K Billy Kahora
Peterson Kamwathi
Junior Diatezua Kannah
Amal Kenawy
Marietta Kesting
Hassan Khan
Karl-Heinz Kohl
Dorothee Kreutzfeldt
Cynthia Kros
Terry Kurgan
L Kiprop Lagat
Jean Christophe Lanquetin
Emma Laurence
Christina Linortner
Faustin Linyekula
Kareem Lotfy
Lisa Lounis
Huda Lutfi
M Maha Maamoun
Majestic Filmverleih
Idah Makukule
Dominique Malaquais

Mario Marchisella
Zen Marie
David Marks
Christoph Marx
Jaqui Masiza
Debora Matthews
Athena Mazerakis
Louise Meintjes
Ronja Metzger
Kerstin Meyer
Yolanda Meyer
Philip Miller
MOFIS
Edith Molnar
M. Mpela
Paul Mpungu
Anna Mülter
James Muriuki
Raphael Mwangi
N Omar Nagati
Sabah Naim
Moataz Nasr
Abdulqadir A. Nassir
Nicolette Naumann
Ndjabulo S. Ndebele
Greet De Neef
Rana El Nemr
Marcus Neustetter
Anja Kervanto Nevanlinna
Shady El Noshokaty
Wandi Nzimande
O Lucia Obi
Sandra Mbanefo Obiago
Anja Oed
Emeka Ogboh
Iria Ojeikere
J.D. Okhai Ojeikere
Joseph Okeyo
Uche Okpa-Iroha
Alfred Omenya
Robyn Orlin
Kainebi Osahenye
P Jay Pather
Jennifer-Akosua Peters
Sophie Pinther
Rodney Place
Editha Platte †
Rita Potenza
R Khamis Ramadhan
Hany Rashed
Ciraj Rassool
Bethan Rayner
Coco Reher
Barbara Reich
Ute Röschenthaler
Karl Rössel

Maximilian Rose
Sabine Rostock
Hannah le Roux
Athi-Patra Ruga
S Doris Sachmann
Jürgen Salm
Sammlung Perthes Gotha
University and Research
Librabry Erfurt/Gotha
Vera Sander
Claudia
and Jürgen Schadeberg
Gerlind Scheckenbach
Enid Schildkrout
Dörte Schlottmann
Usha Seejarim
Ralf Seippel
Magdy El Shafee
Folarin Shasanya
Wael Shawky
Boris Sieverts
Bisi Silva
Gabriele Sistig El-Wati
Dinkies Sithole
Cara Snyman
Brooks Spector
Jenny Stretton
T Olakunle Tejuoso
Johan Thom
Sascha Thoma
Georgina Thomson
V Damien Valette
Ella Verkaik
Luc Vints
Isabel Völker
W Patrick Wangila
Haytham al-Wardani
Steffi Weismann
Gabriele Weisser
William Wells
Anne Welschen
Tobias Wendl
Aljoscha Weskott
Bernd Wiese
Sue Williamson
Stefan Winkler
Dagmar Wittek
Ben Wittner
Yaniv Wolf
Susan Woolf
Y Breeze Yoko

Imprint

This publication accompanies
the exhibition
Afropolis. City, Media, Art.

Rautenstrauch-Joest-Museum
Cultures of the World, Cologne
5 November 2010–13 March 2011
Iwalewa House, University of Bayreuth
21 April 2011–4 September 2011
Preview in Nairobi in cooperation
with the Goethe-Institut Nairobi
22 May–4 June 2010

Exhibition

Idea and Conceptual Design
Kerstin Pinther
Curators
Kerstin Pinther, Larissa Förster,
Christian Hanussek
Co-Curator Nairobi
Sam Hopkins
Co-Curator Lagos
Akinbode Akinbiyi
Curatorial Assistant
Clara Giacalone
Project Manager
Klaus Schneider
Project Assistant
Annabelle Springer
Research Assistant
Ulrike Nestler
Research Assistance
Ahmed Farouk, Günter Gretz
Volunteers
Julia Friedel, Heidrun Mezger,
Judith Rottenburg, Katrin Schaumburg,
Tatjana Wittulski
Public Relations
Annabelle Springer

Exhibition Design and Graphics
Franke | Steinert GbR
Advertising Material
Franke | Steinert GbR
together with Nickel Büro, Katrin Erl
Translations into English
Andrew Boreham
Translations from Arabic
Mahmoud Tawfik

Catalogue

Supervisory Editors, Text and Image
Kerstin Pinther, Larissa Förster,
Christian Hanussek
Editing
Reinhard Kapfer
Project Assistance
Clara Giacalone, Heidrun Mezger,
Ulrike Nestler, Annabelle Springer,
Tatjana Wittulski

For the English edition:
Project Assistant
Hanna Sophie Prenzel
Translations from German
Andrew Boreham, Kate Sturge
Translations from French
Lucy R. McNair
Translations from Arabic
Amy Arif
Editing
Jennifer Gallagher, Megan Southey,
Sean Fraser

Layout and Typesetting
(German and English editions)
Nickel Büro, Katrin Erl
for Franke | Steinert GbR

The German edition published by
Walther König, Köln
Ehrenstraße 4, 50672 Köln
tel   +49 (0) 221 / 20 59 6-53
fax +49 (0) 221 / 20 59 6-60
verlag@buchhandlung-walther-koenig.de

This English edition published by
Jacana Media (Pty) Ltd in 2012
10 Orange Street
Sunnyside, Auckland Park 2092
South Africa
+2711 628 3200
www.jacana.co.za
The English edition produced by
the Goethe-Institut South Africa.

ISBN 978-1-4314-0325-7

Printed by Craft Print, Singapore
See a complete list of Jacana titles at
www.jacana.co.za

The English publication funded by

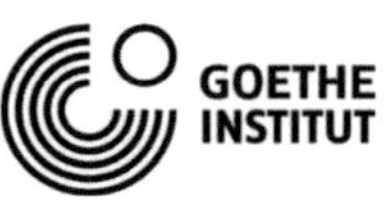

The exhibition and the German
publication funded and
produced by

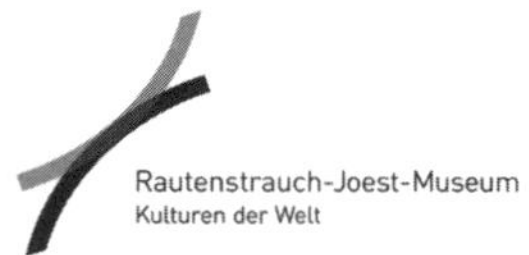

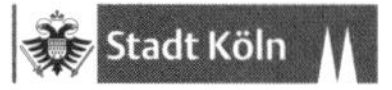

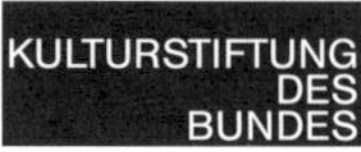

Further funding provided by

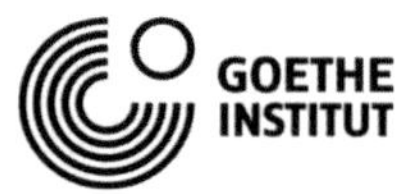

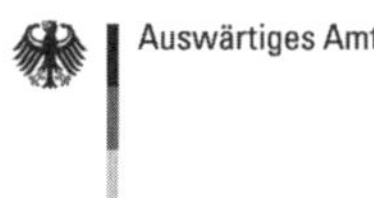

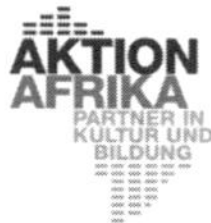

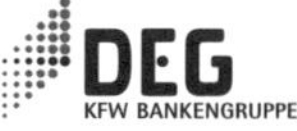

Media partners

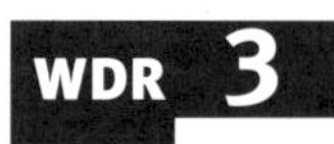

http://museenkoeln.de/ausstellungen/www.afropolis.net/